W9-CJP-247

BIRDS OF NEW JERSEY

BY: *Joan Walsh, Vince Elia, Rich Kane, and Thomas Halliwell*

ILLUSTRATED BY:
David Sibley

PUBLISHED BY:
New Jersey Audubon Society
9 Hardscrabble Road, P.O. Box 126, Bernardsville, NJ 07924
908-204-8998

PRINTED ON RECYCLED PAPER

Printed in the United States of America

ISBN # 0-9624065-2-X

Library of Congress Cataloging-in-Publication Data

First printing - June 1999

Birds of New Jersey / by Joan Walsh ... [et al.] ; illustrated by
David Sibley.
p. cm.
Includes bibliographical references.
ISBN 0-9624065-2-x (alk. paper)
1. Bird populations—New Jersey. 2. Birds—New Jersey-
-Geographical distribution. I. Walsh, Joan M. (Joan Marie), 1959-
II. New Jersey Audubon Society.
QL684.N5856 1999
598'.097949—dc21 99-36727
CIP

NJAS Mission Statement

New Jersey Audubon Society is a privately supported, not-for-profit, statewide membership organization. Founded in 1897 and one of the oldest independent Audubon societies, NJAS has no formal connection with the National Audubon Society.

NJAS fosters environmental awareness and a conservation ethic among New Jersey's citizens, protects New Jersey's birds, mammals, other animals, and plants, especially endangered and threatened species, and promotes preservation of New Jersey's valuable natural habitats.

In order to achieve its purpose, NJAS, through its Board of Directors, professional staff, members, and volunteers, endeavors to:

- Develop, encourage, and support sound conservation practices, programs, and legislation
- Disseminate information on the natural environment through education programs, information services, and publications
- Advance knowledge, through field research, of New Jersey's flora and fauna and their relationship to the habitats on which they depend
- Acquire, establish, and maintain wildlife sanctuaries and educational centers.

The objectives of the Society are implemented by its professional staff under the leadership of its President and supervision of an elected, voluntary Board of Directors.

NJAS Centers

CAPE MAY BIRD OBSERVATORY: CENTER FOR RESEARCH AND EDUCATION
600 Route 47 North
Cape May Court House, NJ 08210
(609) 861-0700

CAPE MAY BIRD OBSERVATORY: NORTHWOOD CENTER
701 E. Lake Drive, P.O. Box 3
Cape May Point, NJ 08212
(609) 884-2736

LORRIMER SANCTUARY
790 Ewing Avenue, P.O. Box 125
Franklin Lakes, NJ 07417
(201) 891-2185

NATURE CENTER OF CAPE MAY
1600 Delaware Avenue
Cape May, NJ 08204
(609) 898-8848

OWL HAVEN NATURE CENTER
250 Route 522, P.O. Box 26
Tennent, NJ 07763
(732) 780-7007

RANCOCAS NATURE CENTER
794 Rancocas Road
Mount Holly, NJ 08060
(609) 261-2495

SCHERMAN-HOFFMAN SANCTUARIES
11 Hardscrabble Road
P.O. Box 693
Bernardsville, NJ 07924
(908) 766-5787

WEIS ECOLOGY CENTER
150 Snake Den Road
Ringwood, NJ 07456
(973) 835-2160

www.njaudubon.org

STAFF

Thomas J. Gilmore, *President*

Karl Anderson, *Sanctuary Director*
Mike Anderson, *Program Director*
Rosanne Asero, *Business Manager*
Pete Bacinski, *Sanctuary Director*
Christine M. Baker, *Sales Manager*
Scott Barnes, *Teacher-Naturalist*
Jane T. Brady, *Director of Major Gifts*
John Carno, *Director of Development*
Denis Cleary, *Store Manager*
Philip De Rea, *Store Manager*
Linda Dill, *Teacher-Naturalist*
Pete Dunne, *Vice President, Natural History Information, and Director, Cape May Bird Observatory*
Vince Elia, *Research Assistant*
Gretchen Ferrante, *Sanctuary Director*
Noelle Gurley, *Teacher-Naturalist*
Patti Hodgetts, *Bookstore Naturalist*
Kathy Iozzo, *Administrative Coordinator*
Patricia Kane, *Vice President, Environmental Education*
Richard Kane, *Vice President, Conservation and Stewardship, and Director, Scherman-Hoffman Sanctuaries*
Walter Koenig, *Membership Coordinator*
John Kolodziej, *Land Steward*
Sheila Lego, *Events Coordinator*
Mindy Lynch, *Development Associate*
John R. Maellaro, *Maint. Supervisor*
Merideth Mueller, *Teacher-Naturalist*
Marleen Murgitroyde, *Admin. Assist.*
William Neil, *Director of Conservation*
Sandra Nelson, *Admin. Assistant*
Rick Radis, *Editor NJAS Magazine*
Wendy Rhoads, *Program Director*
Karla H. Risdon, *Sanctuary Director*
Dale Rosselet, *NJAS Director of Education*
Gordon Schultze, *Sanctuary Director*
Arlene Serell, *Controller*
Sue Ann Slotterback, *Program Director*
Lyda Spear, *Membership Associate*
Patricia Sutton, *Program Director*
Brian Vernachio, *Program Director*
Joan Walsh, *Director of Research*

BOARD OF DIRECTORS

CHAIR
Charles F. West

FIRST VICE CHAIR
Jean Clark

SECOND VICE CHAIR
Wayne D. Greenstone

HONORARY VICE CHAIR
Elmer C. Rowley

SECRETARY
Libbie Johnson

TREASURER
John A. DeMarrais

COUNSEL
Alan H. Bernstein

Rose Blaustein
Barbara Brummer
John E. Courtney
Thomas B. Darlington
Fred L. Ditmars
Jane Morton Galetto
Edward A. Hogan
Robert W. Kean, Jr.
Theodore G. Koven
Sally W. Lee
Milton A. Levy
Randolph S. Little
Linda J. Mack
George J. Mullen, Jr.
Leon M. Rosenson
James A. Shissias
John D. Stewart
Henrietta S. Thomas
Charlotte Todd
A. Richard Turner
Bernard Wallerstein
Henry W. Weis
Leonard W. Weis

Foreword

In your hand is an extraordinary document – a complete accounting of New Jersey's birds as they are found at the end of 20th century. Anyone searching for information relating to the occurrence, distribution, and status of the state's 440+ species will find it housed in these pages. Joan Walsh, Vince Elia, Rich Kane, Tom Halliwell and all whose talents were brought to bear in the writing, editing, and review of this book can be justly proud of the *Birds of New Jersey*.

On my desk is another book with the title the *Birds of New Jersey*. It was published in 1896, more than a century ago, by the Fish and Game Commission of the State of New Jersey. Like this book it offers an historic snapshot of New Jersey's avifauna. Unlike this book, the picture it paints is not so fair.

A century ago, according to that older accounting, the Laughing Gull, a bird whose raucous laugh is as much a part of summer at the "Jersey" shore as the sound of surf and the smell of brine was "rare."

A century ago the familiar Forster's Tern was absent as a nesting bird in the state. Like the Least Tern, like the Gull-billed Tern, Forster's Terns were extirpated to serve the appetite of the millinery trade.

A century ago, the Pileated Woodpecker and the Wild Turkey were unknown in the state. The Wood Duck was heading for extinction. Great and Snowy Egrets were "little more than a remembrance" and the Snow Goose was "very seldom seen in New Jersey."

Owing to the recovery of New Jersey's forests, and/or restoration efforts, Pileated Woodpeckers, turkeys and Wood Ducks are once again widespread and common. Egrets, whose slaughter inspired the Audubon movement and protectionist legislation, are now a familiar sight in coastal wetlands. Snow Geese? New Jersey in 1999 hosts tens of thousands of wintering birds. A person navigating the Delaware Bay shore from December through March would be hard pressed not to see (and hear) hundreds if not thousands.

To be certain, there are species (like Loggerhead Shrike and Henslow's Sparrow) that our ancestors thought common whose populations are diminished or gone and whose decline is also documented here. But in the balance, New Jersey residents a century ago would be envious of the riches we know today. We in turn should be grateful to them. It was their anger and their sense of loss that gave rise to the conservation movement that was the foundation of the New Jersey Audubon Society. The *Birds of New Jersey*, and the success it documents, is in part a tribute to them.

But it also acknowledges our obligation to the future generations of New Jersey residents. If we do not continue the conservation initiative of the last century into the next, the next book written about New Jersey birds will more nearly resemble the 1896 *Birds of New Jersey* than this one.

That would diminish the lesson of the last century and the environmental achievements of this one. And that would be a sad footnote to a book that is the vessel of so much good news, and so much good work.

Thomas J. Gilmore
President, New Jersey Audubon Society

Table of Contents

BREEDING BIRD ATLAS

PRODUCTION NOTES

Authors: Joan Walsh, Vince Elia, Rich Kane, and Tom Halliwell

Contributors: Pete Dunne, Greg Hanisek, Libbie Johnson, and Mike Newlon

Copy Editor: Dorothy Clair

Manuscript Reviewers: Paul Lehman, Wayne Petersen, and Rick Radis

Illustrator: David Sibley

Layout and Design: Joan Snider, Master Design Studio, Inc.

Print Production: Alcom Printing Group, Inc. and Hoster Bindery

Publisher: New Jersey Audubon Society

Breeding Bird Atlas Steering Committee: Pete Bacinski, Bill Boyle, Pete Dunne, Thomas Gilmore, Rich Kane, Paul Kerlinger, and Larry Niles

Breeding Bird Atlas Advisory Committee: Daniel Brauning, Dennis Miranda, Wade Wander, and Kelly Wolcott

PRINTED ON RECYCLED PAPER

Preface

The *Birds of New Jersey* is the New Jersey Audubon Society's most ambitious research project to date. It presents the results of five years of surveys conducted throughout the state to map the ranges of New Jersey's breeding birds, The New Jersey Breeding Bird Atlas. Also included is a synopsis of the changes in breeding bird distribution in the state during the 1900s, a summary of bird migration through the state, a compilation of wintering bird information, and a review of the records of rare birds in the state.

Our understanding of the bird life in New Jersey is constantly changing; and even as this preface is written there are new records of birds for the state that are not included in the body of the book: a Townsend's Solitaire at East Point during the winter of 1998 through April 1999, a Black-headed Grosbeak at a feeder in Goshen, a persistent, yet unconfirmed, report of Sandhill Cranes setting up nesting territories in Cumberland County, a Nashville Warbler that spent the winter of 1998-1999 in West Cape May, and the NJBRC has accepted two new species for the state list – a Red-cockaded Woodpecker specimen from the late 1800s, and a Reddish Egret from Brigantine NWR from the summer of 1998. Indeed, it is the nature of this work that it is destined to be out-of-date before it is printed. Please, take a pencil and fill the margins with new records, report new records to *Records of New Jersey Birds*, follow up on breeding reports of rare species, continue to participate in Christmas Bird Counts, Breeding Bird Surveys, and other monitoring projects, and share the information you gather with those making policy and land-use decisions.

The first stated objective of the New Jersey Audubon Society's constitution, written in 1910, was "To encourage the study of birds... and to use all lawful means for the protection of wild bird and animal life." It was too late to save the Heath Hen from extinction, and the last Passenger Pigeon would soon die, but the society set out on its course of protection for wildlife. It has held to this steady, unwavering course through good times and bad, accomplishments and disappointments. Wallace Stenger wrote in 1990: "The modern environmental movement declares our dependence on the Earth and our responsibility to it." He could have been writing of New Jersey Audubon Society.

The *Birds of New Jersey* shows where we stand at the end of the 20th century in our objective and will serve as a bench mark for our continued efforts in the new millenium. It is our hope this work will inspire those who want to preserve our natural heritage, and it is our mission to present them with some of the information they will need to provide the best stewardship possible for the natural world. The *Birds of New Jersey* provides a reference useful to birders, students, scientists, conservationists, citizens groups, state and federal agencies and regulators, land-use planners, and policy makers. We hope this book will be frequently cited, regularly read, and dog-eared from familiarity!

Red-Winged Blackbird

Acknowledgements

Many people made this book happen, and we apologize for any names omitted from the following list.

We owe a debt of gratitude to the authors who have gone before us and whose work helped shaped our view of bird distribution changes in New Jersey during the 20th century: Charles Shriner, Witmer Stone, Ludlow Griscom, Allan Cruickshank, David Fables, John Bull, Charles F. Leck, William J. Boyle, and David Sibley.

To our fellow breeding bird atlas creators we offer our sincere thanks for blazing the trail so well. Although we used virtually all of the atlases in print, some deserve honorable mention – J.T.R. Sharrock's *The Atlas of Breeding Birds In Britain and Ireland*, Sally Laughlin and Douglas Kibbe's *The Atlas of Breeding Birds of Vermont*, Dan Brauning's *Atlas of Breeding Birds in Pennsylvania*, and Dave Shuford's *The Marin County Breeding Bird Atlas*.

Special acknowledgement must be extended to those organizations that funded the Atlas and the compilation of this book: The Geraldine R. Dodge Foundation, the New Jersey Division of Fish, Game and Wildlife's Non-game and Endangered Species Program (ENSP), The Victoria Foundation, The Fund for New Jersey, The National Fish and Wildlife Foundation, Environmental Systems Research Institute, The U.S. Fish and Wildlife Service, Gibson Tube, Inc., The Montclair Organization for Conservation, and the members of New Jersey Audubon Society (NJAS) and Cape May Bird Observatory (CMBO). Without their generous support and encouragement this project would not have been possible.

Works such as this are brought to fruition by the sheer will of a veritable army of volunteers and the New Jersey Breeding Bird was no exception. The completion of this work is a tribute to the efforts of the volunteers who kept us focussed and made this happen. They are the heart of this work and have helped make this state a better place for everyone who lives here.

The Atlas Regional Coordinators deserve special recognition for their many hours in the field as well as additional hours compiling these data: Scott Angus (1993), Pete Bacinski, Jack and Jessie Connor, Ward Dasey, Don Freiday, Dave Githens, (1993), Tom Halliwell, Dave Harrison, Laurie Larson, Karenne Snow, Don and Jane Sutherland, Clay Sutton, and Louise Zemaitis. Sheryl Forte acted as a Regional Coordinator for the project and, remarkably, did the computer entry of over 40,000 data records for the project. Jim Freeman helped with many technical problems early in the project. The Atlas Steering Committee, including Larry Niles, Dan Brauning, Wade Wander, Bill Boyle, Dennis Miranda, Rich Kane, Pete Dunne, and Paul Kerlinger, helped launch the project. Sharon Paul from ENSP created the original GIS coverages for the Atlas maps.

Records of New Jersey Birds was our primary research reference for information on migratory birds and we are grateful to everyone who reports to the journal and encourage you to continue to report your sightings. We also extend thanks the Regional Editors of RNJB for their careful work over the years. Bill Boyle contributed his Christmas Count database, which was invaluable for charting winter abundance of many species. Geoffrey Le Baron was helpful with questions regarding the Christmas Birds Count information. Data on the hawk migration in Cape May and the seabird migration in Avalon are collected by dedicated watchers. We thank all the counters and interns for their work over the years as well as the USGS, Kowa Optimed, Zeiss Optical, Leica Sports Optics, Swarovski Optik, and Ducks Unlimited for their support of these projects.

We owe special thanks to the past and present New Jersey Bird Records Committee (NJBRC), and Louis Bevier, Paul Lehman, and Paul Buckley for verifying specimen identification in museum collections.

This manuscript was helped immeasurably by the careful review of Rick Radis, Paul Lehman, and Wayne Petersen. It is very possible the best parts of this work are due to their changes and suggestions, and we are indebted to them for sharing their knowledge, and for their patience and time. The artwork fairies smiled upon us and coerced David Sibley to generously allow us the use of his stunning work. Dorothy Clair rescued the manuscript from innumerable crimes against the language when she proofread the entire document (even the tables!). Libby Johnson and Sandy Sherman came through with crucial text editing assists in the eleventh hour. Debbie Shaw also read and improved sections of the final draft of the manuscript, and David Sibley was almost giddy with enthusiasm as he edited the final draft. Fred Sibley located several hard-to-find references for us. Joan Rogers Snider of Master Design Studios, Inc. continued to demonstrate her page-layout magic in designing this book.

We are especially grateful for the support of the NJAS family – the members, the board of directors, and our colleagues. Their enthusiasm and commitment to conservation is humbling and inspiring.

Ms. Walsh respectfully dedicates her portion of this work to Dr. Ron Pulliam, a kind man, an uncommonly clear thinker, a lover of birds – and also a very good teacher. Thank you Ron.

VOLUNTEERS

The data for the New Jersey Breeding Atlas was collected by the following:

Peter Adams, Sandra Amos, Emily Anderson, Karl Anderson, Mike Anderson, Robin Anderson, Gary Anderson Jr., Scott Angus, Christopher Aquila, Fred Armstrong, Margaret Atack, Leo Aus, Pete Bacinski, Tom Bailey, Ryan Bakelaar, Jim Bangma, Scott Barnes, Elaine Barrett, Marjorie Barrett, Elio Bartoli, Louis Beck, Stephanie Belvedere, Chris Bennett, Karen Bennett, Sue Bennett, Ronald Berry, Jean Bickal, Don Birchall, Irving Black, Tiffany Black, Mary Blasko, Bob Blumberg, Rob Blye, Sandy Bonardi, Pete Both, Robert Bowman, Alan Boyd, Doris Boyd, Howard Boyd, Bill Boyle, Maryellen Boyle, Tom Boyle, Alan Brady, Sally Brady, Blais Brancheau, Erica Brendel, Dennis Briede, Dan Brill, Ed Bristow, Patricia Bristow, Joseph Broschart, John Brotherton, Maria Brough, Ann Brown, Richard Brown, Barbara Brozyna, Edgar Bruder, Patricia Brundage, Steven Budnicki, Jane Bullis, Joe Burgiel, Dick Burk, Henry Burk, Jean Burton, Elizabeth Bush, Betty Butler, Steve Byland, Christopher Byrne, George H. Byrne, Geraldine Byrne, Byron Campbell, Claire Campbell, Gail Cannon, John Carey, Mike Carle, Hugh Carola, Mike Carr, George Carty, Virginia Carty, Janice Casper, Michael Casper, Eva Cassel, Robert Cassel, Paul Castelli, David Christ, Judy Cinquina, Christopher Claus, Virginia Cole, Judith Collis, Ruth Comfort, Bob Confer, Janet Confer, R. Conn, Jack Connor, Jesse Connor, Richard Crossley, Joshua Cutler, Muriel Danon, Jay Darling, Ward Dasey, David H. Davis, Vi Debbie, Joseph DeCanio, Linda DeLay, Mike DeLozier, Susan DeLozier, John DeMarrais, Brian Dendler, David Dendler, Robert Dickison, Nicole Dieckmann, Bob Dieterich, Rich Ditch, Bruce Doerr, David Donnelly, Jim Dowdell, Susan Draxler, Richard Dunlap, Linda Dunne, Pete Dunne, Alan Eastwick, Megan Edwards, Scott Edwards, Nancy Eichman, Georgia Eisenhart, Vince Elia, Lee Ellenberg, Bill Elrick, Dick Engsberg, Nancy Eriksen, Jay Estelle, Rose Estelle, John Faber, Dave Fantina, Keith Faust, Joan Ferrante, Stephen Field, Linda Fields, Ed Fingerhood, Benita Fishbein, Bob Flatt, Sheryl Forte, Irene Franz, Mike Franz, Cathy Freiday, Don Freiday, Jeanne Fritz, Mike Fritz, Sharon Fullogar, Jeannine Fuscillo,

Donna Gaffigan, C. Gaitskill, J. Gaitskill, Feliz Gallagher, Anne Galli, Heather Gamper, Steve Gates, Lois Gebhardt, Gary Gentile, Karen Gentile, Ursula Gerhart-Brooks, David Gillen, Thomas Gillen, Christine Githens, Dave Githens, Bill Glaser, Laurie Gneiding, Heather Green, Else Greenstone, Wayne Greenstone, Alan Gregory, Monica Gregory, M. Grosso, Jim Grundy, Chris Gulliksen, Sharon Gurak, Anita Guris, Paul Guris, Robert Guthrie, Jean Gutsmuth, Jerry Haag, Kathryn Hackett-Fields, David Hall, Ward Halligan, Thomas Halliwell, Patrick Hamill, Mike Hannisian, Jennifer Hanson, Brian Hardiman, David Harrison, Jack Harrison, Regina Harrison, Bob Harsett, Kathy Hartman, Eileen Hayes, Jim Hayes, James Herder, Michael Hodanish, Robert Hoek, Deuane Hoffman, Hollace Hoffman, John Holinka, Alfred Howard, Lynn Hunt, Joan Janowitz, Dave Jenkins, Libbie Johnson, Roger Johnson, Betty Jones, Beverly Jones, Donald Jones, Kenn Jones, Robert Jones, Robert Jordan, Sara Ann Joselson, Barbara Jugan, Rich Kane, Eileen Katz, Nerses Kazanjian, Allan Keith, Sandra Keller, Elizabeth Kelley, Charlene Kelly, Linda Kemple, Paul Kerlinger, Steven Kerr, Douglas Kibbe, Hollyce Kirkland, Matthew Klewin, Jonathan Klizas, Carol Knapp, John Knapp, Rosemary Knapp, Dana Knowlton, Arlene Koch, Tom Koelhoffer, Wally Koenig, John Kolodziej, Paul Kosten, Chip Krilowicz, Andy Krivenko, Marie Kuhnen, Peter Kwiatek, Joan Labun, Carolyn LaMountain, Andy Lamy, Daniel Lane, John Lapolla, Laurie Larson, John LaVia, Edmund LeGrand, Robert Leonard, Fred Lesser, Lillian Levine, Milt Levy, Jerry Liguori, Nancy Lilly, Walter Lilly, Joey Little, Len Little, Derek Lovitch, Karl Lukens, Lisa MacCollum, Bob Machover, Linda Mack, Eileen Mahler, Jack Mahun, Al Majewski, Craig Malone, David Mandell, Ann Manger, Joe Mangino, Edward Manners, Joyce Matthews, Charles Mayhood, Bette McCarron, Jack McCarron, Kevin J. McCarthy, Suzanne McCarthy, William McElroy, Doris McGovern, Bruce McNaught, Ron Melcer, Robert Mercer, Diane Merkh, Joe Merlino, Brad Merritt, James Merritt, Jim Mershon, Ronald Midkiff, Clifford Miles, John Miller, Dennis Miranda, Phil Misseldine, John Mitchell, Ralph Mitrano Jr., Bernard Morris, Lois Morris, Pauline Morris, Brian Moscatello, Philip Moylan, Bill Murphy, Naomi Murphy, Barbara Murray, Bruce Murray, John Murray, Leslie Murray, Mike Newlon, Ted Nichols, George Nixon, Valerie Nixon, Sheryl Nowell, Michael O'Brien, Michael R. O'Brien, Joyce O'Keefe, Arlene Oley, Bob Olthoff, Dave Oster, Arthur Panzer, Jackie Parker, Keith Parker, Thomas Parsons, Kathy Pascale, Niroo Patel, Ed Patten, Joyce Payeur,

Linda Peskac, Bert Peterson, Eric Peterson, John Peterson, Kathy Peterson, Matthew Pettigrew, Susan Phelon, Lee Pierson, Linn Pierson, Francis Ponti, Bill Prather, Susan Preiksat, Theodore Proctor, Ken Prytherch, Nick Pulcinella, Elizabeth Radis, Rick Radis, Buster Raff, Martin Rapp, John Reed, Kathi Ricca, Bill Richardson, John Rokita, Dale Rosselet, Michael Rothkopf, George Roussey, Linda Rozowicz, Frank Rush, Richard Ryan, Tom Sabel, Edward Samanns, Ken Samra, Bob Sanders, Starr Saphir, Joseph Sapia, Henry Schaefer, Mike Scheffler, Chris Schmidt, Steve Schnur, Alan Schreck, Gordon Schultze, Dennis Schvejda, Ginny Seabrook, John Seabrook, Keith Seager, Betsy Searight, John Searight, Janet Sedicino, Bill Seng, August Sexauer, Bill Shadel, Mike Shapiro, Roseanne Shapiro, Mary Ellen Shaw, Patricia Shaw, Betty Shemella, Ted Shemella, Sandra Sherman, Barbara Shields, Larry Shields, Dave Sibley, Bob Simansky, Judith Siverson, Nancy Slowik, Cynthia Smith, Don Smith, Mitch Smith, Karenne Snow, Jane Snyder, Steven Sobocinski, Amy Spano, Andrew Spears, Jim Springer, Ray Steelman, Scott Stepanski, Dale Stevens, Phil Stevenson, Susan Stevenson, Joanne Stiefbold, Eric Stiles, Christopher Stitt, Don Sutherland, Jane Sutherland, Hannah Suthers, Clay Sutton, Pat Sutton, Byron Swift, Rich Talian, Paul Taylor, Pam Thier, Stiles Thomas, Karen Thompson, Ken Tischner, Steve Tischner, Alex Tongas, Donald Traylor, Donna Traylor, Max Ugarte, Nilda Ugarte, Rob Unrath, Joe Usewicz, Jon Van De Venter, Marian van Buren, Janet Van Gelder, Lynn Varnum, Sefton Vergiano, Brian Vernachio, Scott Vincent, Fred Virazzi, V. Eugene Vivian, Tim Vogel, Alma Vogels, Earle Vogels, G. Vriens, Joan Walsh, Rosemarie Walsh, Chris Walters, Sharon Wander, Wade Wander, Dave Ward, Fred Ward, Robert Wargo, Ron Warner, Elizabeth Warnke, Philip Warren, Albert Weber, Deborah Wedeking, Paul Wedeking, Leo Weiss, George Wenzelburger, Rosemarie Widmer, Barbara Wilczek, Bill Wilczek, Chris Williams, Dan Williams, Jim Williams, Junius Williams, Karen Williams, Melinda Williams, Paula Williams, John Williamson, Jim Wilson, Tom Wilson, Frank Windfelder, Ken Witkowski, Mark Witmer, Flora Woessner, Karen Wolzanski, Dave Womer, Cynthia Wood, J. Worall, Nancy Wottrich, Kimberly Young, Jim Zamos, Bruce Zatkow, Louise Zemaitis, Joe Zurovchak.

Introduction

In the sweeping mosaic of America, New Jersey is but a small bit. Its superlatives are of dubious interest to the naturalist: a higher population density – 1,029 people per square mile – then either India or Japan, the heaviest road traffic in the nation, endless strip malls, acrid chemical plants, oil refineries. A wayfarer on the New Jersey Turnpike might be forgiven for accelerating as fast, or faster, than the law allows simply to exit the state for more salubrious surroundings. This mythical traveler is forgiven, yes, but pitied as well. For in amongst the nearly eight million people who live in New Jersey is some of the most varied bird life in the nation.

Easily within sight of and almost in the shadow of Manhattan's World Trade Center, Ring-necked Pheasants are hunted by Peregrine Falcons in Jersey City's Liberty State Park. In spring, Red Knots and Sanderlings by the hundreds of thousands blanket the shore of Delaware Bay feasting on Horseshoe Crab eggs – all this as oil tankers gingerly navigate past, going up Delaware Bay into Philadelphia, one of the busiest ports in the nation. Some 50,000 Greater Scaup gather in Raritan Bay prior to a mass migration northward. In summer, suburban gardens echo with melodic arias of nesting song birds. In autumn kettles of migrating raptors spiral into the heavens before rushing off to the south. In September spectacular numbers of Broad-winged Hawks, up to 10,000 in a day in September, may pass the Montclair Hawk Lookout, where a watch has been conducted by the Montclair Bird Club for forty years (Greenstone 1996) – the New York skyline provides the backdrop for the watch. In winter the Brigantine Unit of Forsythe NWR, well in view of the garish towers of Atlantic City, becomes a melting pot of myriad waterbirds finding sanctuary at the refuge.

If New Jersey is packed with people, so it is with birds. The state's bird list is at 443 species and counting. Each year there is an average of 340 species in the state, and about 210 of them are breeders. There are reasons for this abundance, some meteorological, some geographic – but none of the reasons are escapable. New Jersey is ground-zero for migrant birds.

To our mythic turnpike traveler, New Jersey is hard-pressed real estate sandwiched between New York City on the east and Philadelphia on the west – "a keg tapped at both ends," as Benjamin Franklin observed. Like most first impressions, this is misleading.

It is indeed a small state, only 166 miles long from High Point in the northwest to Cape May Point (below the Mason-Dixon Line) in the south. At its widest New Jersey measures only 57 miles. This brings the state to a total of 7,500 square miles. But, surprisingly 42% of that area is still forested. (In 1860 46% of the state was forested.) And 25% of the state, the Pinelands, is barely inhabited by any other humans other than the occasional cranberry farmer. About 19% of the state is wetlands, both freshwater and saltwater. Rimmed on all sides by water except for its relatively short northern boundary, New Jersey with its moderate climate is an essential pit stop on the Atlantic flyway. Its coastline, bogs, swamps, lakes, and forested uplands draw a surprising number of migrant and vagrant species.

Western birds such as Swainson's Hawk, Western Kingbird, and Yellow-headed Blackbird now occur with some regularity. Others, like Violet-Green Swallow, Varied Thrush, Green-tailed Towhee, or Golden-crowned Sparrow, occur only very rarely. Strays from further south occur as overshooting migrants in spring, among them Purple Gallinule, Mississippi and Swallow-tailed Kites, and Swainson's Warbler.

Some winter visitors are normally found in numbers well to the north of the state, such as Northern Shrike and White-winged Crossbill, yet occur in New Jersey annually and sometimes in numbers. In some years, there may be sporadic breeding records following incursions of northern species such as Red Crossbill, Evening Grosbeak, and Pine Siskin. As an ocean state, New Jersey gets pelagic migrants from the south Atlantic, such as South Polar Skua, and from the north, such as Northern Fulmar and Atlantic Puffin. Pelagic rarities, such as the only record of Buller's Shearwater in the Atlantic Ocean, also have occurred in New Jersey's waters. Hurricanes have carried other pelagic rarities to New Jersey's shore, such as Sooty Tern, Bridled Tern, Band-rumped Storm-Petrel, and Black-capped Petrel.

Accidental visitors from the western Palearctic – such as Garganey, White-winged Tern, Mongolian Plover, and Whiskered Tern – have occurred, along with South American species such as Large-billed Tern, Fork-tailed Flycatcher, and Brown-chested Martin.

The loss of farmland in central New Jersey has turned the Garden State into the Garden Apartment State to a considerable extent. But in the north and south some abandoned farmland has reverted to woods to the benefit of avian life. The principal forested regions are in the northern Highlands and the Kittatinny Mountains in the north and the semirural southern counties of Burlington, Ocean, Atlantic, Cumberland, and Cape May – all of which center around the protected Pinelands.

The lowering profile from north to south means New Jersey has a climate variety that belies its small size. Frost comes by the end of September in the Kittatinny Mountains, but not until November or later in Cape May. The reverse, of course, occurs in spring, with the warm weather arriving earlier in the south.

Our Turnpike traveler may be long gone by now. If so, the loss is greater, as there is so much more to see and appreciate. There are spectacular movements of Red-throated Loons in fall visible along the coast from Island Beach to Avalon. Huge concentrations of waterfowl occur throughout the state from the river marshes of Cumberland, Salem, and Gloucester counties in the southwest to the freshwater lakes, bays, and wetlands of northern New Jersey. The rafts of Northern Pintails in late winter on the marshes of Raccoon and Oldman's creeks; the incredible numbers of Snow Geese at Brigantine Refuge in fall and early winter; the thousands of Common Mergansers found on Oradell Reservoir in winter and early spring – all are impressive offerings of the state's riches.

Mountain ridges, running northeast-to-southwest, in northern New Jersey concentrate raptors and other migrants in fall as the birds move south on the west and northwest winds of autumn cold fronts. Large flights of Red-tailed Hawks, with smaller numbers of Golden Eagle and Northern Goshawk pass by the Kittatinny Ridge in October and November.

The river valleys, too, concentrate birds in passage, and host interesting breeding bird communities. Large numbers of gulls, waterfowl, and warblers are often seen in migration along the Delaware River – the same river is the home to recovering breeding populations of Parula Warbler and Common Merganser. Migrant warblers often concentrate in the forests along the Palisades on the Hudson River at State Line Lookout in Alpine.

The centerpiece of the migration phenomenon in New Jersey occurs in Cape May. The Cape May Peninsula seems to act like a funnel constricting autumn flights of passage migrants. With the right weather conditions, many over-land migrants can mass at the tip of the peninsula as they face the formidable obstacle – the water crossing over Delaware Bay. An average of about 56,000 hawks per fall passed over Cape May from 1976 through 1997, hundreds of thousands of passerine passage migrants move through the area each year, an average of 800,000 near-shore migrants passed by the Avalon Sea Watch from 1994 through 1997, and hundreds of owls have been recorded migrating through the Cape May Peninsula each year.

There may be no greater natural history spectacle in our time than the spring shorebird staging that happens on the shores of Delaware Bay in spring. Each spring the Delaware Bay shore in Cape May and Cumberland counties hosts hundreds of thousands of shorebirds. Red Knots, Sanderlings, and Ruddy Turnstones come to the beaches in phenomenal numbers to feed on eggs laid by horseshoe crabs. The shorebirds use the fuel from the horseshoe crab eggs to complete the remaining portion of their northward migration to their breeding grounds in the high Arctic. Virtually the entire hemispheric population of Red Knots and large percentages of the Sanderling and Ruddy Turnstone populations congregate on the bay shore in May. The scale of this event is unlike any other natural history event in the state. The staging of these birds speaks to the recovery of these species during this century, and also to the importance of our understanding our role as stewards of this state's natural history treasures.

Physical Geography

The distribution of breeding birds in the state is determined by the distribution of the habitats they use for breeding. Habitats in turn are the result of the geologic history of an area, a complex mix of elevation, soil type, and bedrock type – the building blocks of the regional classification known as the physiographic provinces. David Fables (1955) was the first author to discuss bird distribution in the state relative to the major physiographic provinces. Beryl Collins and Karl Anderson (1994) provided an excellent discussion of the geologic processes that formed the state's physiographic provinces and the resulting plant communities in the provinces.

For our discussion of the distribution of breeding birds in the state relative to the physiographic provinces, we defined the provincial boundaries by consulting both Fables (1955), and Collins and Anderson (1994). In some cases bird distribution was best addressed by separating some of the classic provinces into smaller physiographic provinces, and those exceptions are noted below.

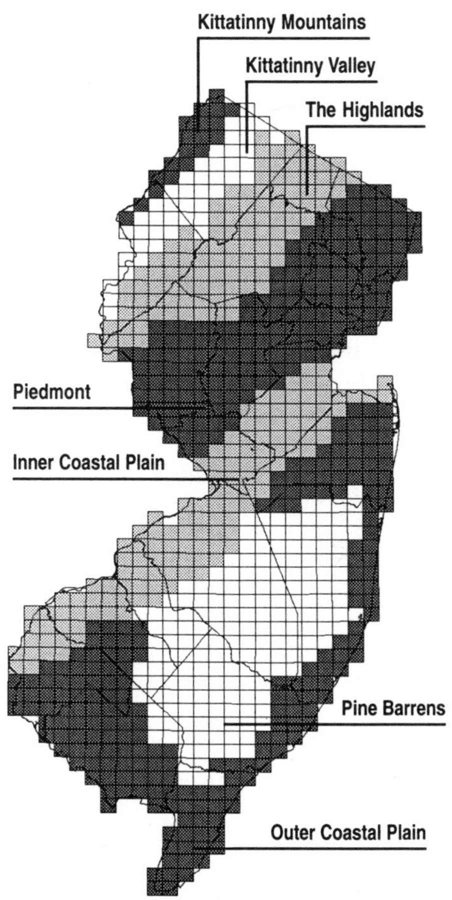

Figure 1. PHYSIOGRAPHIC PROVINCES

NORTHERN NEW JERSEY

The Ridge and Valley Province in northwestern New Jersey encompasses the Delaware River Valley, the Kittatinny Mountain, and the broad, fertile Kittatinny Valley. For the purposes of bird distribution however, these areas are quite different, and we address them as separate provinces – the Kittatinny Mountains (including the Delaware River Valley adjacent to the Kittatinny Mountains) and the Kittatinny Valley.

The Kittatinny Mountains

The Kittatinny Mountains have a distinctive northern and boreal flavor, especially at elevations above 800 feet. The breeding birds include such northern species as Red-breasted Nuthatches, Golden-crowned Kinglets, Blue-headed Vireos, Black-throated Green, Blackburnian, Magnolia, and Nashville Warblers, Purple Finches, Dark-eyed Juncos, and White-throated Sparrows.

The Kittatinny Valley

The Kittatinny Valley is dominated by the Wallkill River in the north and the Paulins Kill to the southwest, and varies from approximately 400 to 1000 feet in elevation. This region has some of the most significant breeding areas for freshwater wetland breeding birds (e.g. the Wallkill River NWR), and, due to the variability in both elevation and habitats, has the highest breeding bird diversity in the state.

The Highlands

Geologically, the Highlands Province in north-central New Jersey is part of the Appalachian Mountains. The Highlands ranges in elevation from 350 to 1,500 feet; the ridges are generally broader, and the valleys are generally steeper than those are in the Kittatinny Valley and Mountains (Collins and Anderson 1994). Although the Highlands are geologically dissimilar to the Kittatinny Mountains, the bird communities are similar.

The Piedmont

East of the Highlands Province lies the Piedmont, now heavily developed, but with some extensive freshwater wetlands remaining. The Piedmont ranges in elevation from approximately 100 to 400 feet, and is generally highest in the northwest. There are several ridges in the Piedmont (e.g., the Watchung Mountains, the

Sourland Mountains, and the Palisades), creating variability in the landscape and the breeding bird communities. There are the remains of several glacial lakes - Glacial Lake Passaic and Lake Hackensack, formed by the Wisconsin Glacier – and the freshwater wetlands legacy that remains from these lakes include Troy Meadows, Great Swamp, and the Hackensack Meadowlands. These large and productive wetlands support notable populations of rails, herons, bitterns, and waterfowl. The Piedmont acts as a boundary between northern and southern New Jersey. There is no finer example of this separation than the distinct line that treads across the Piedmont dividing the range of Black-capped from Carolina Chickadees.

SOUTHERN NEW JERSEY

The southern portion of the state lies in two provinces – the Inner and the Outer Coastal Plain. Although the coastal plain has little variability in altitude, there are strikingly different habitats in the south: barrier beaches, extensive salt marsh and river marsh, pine barrens, oak forest, tidal flats, cedar swamps and hardwood swamps, these habitats can all be found south of the Piedmont. The Pine Barrens, and the hardwood swamps and upland habitats of South Jersey, have a distinctly southern avian flavor, with resident Summer Tanagers, Prothonotary and Yellow-throated Warblers, Blue Grosbeaks, and Chuck-will's-Widows.

The Inner Coastal Plain

The Inner Coastal Plain is separated from the Outer Coastal plain by a series of low hills, called *cuestas* (Collins and Anderson 1994). These hills give the Inner Coastal Plain a higher elevation than the Outer Coastal Plain, although, excluding the *cuestas*, both provinces are generally lower than 100 feet in elevation. The Inner Coastal Plain is characterized by extensive urban, suburban, and agricultural development, which has had a negative effect on the breeding bird communities in the area.

The Outer Coastal Plain

The Outer Coastal Plain includes most of the state's tidal wetlands and barrier islands. These habitats house most of the state's colonial waterbirds (herons, gulls, terns, and skimmers), as well as breeding Ospreys, Willets, Clapper Rails, American Oystercatchers, and Piping Plovers. The Outer Coastal Plain technically includes the Pine

Barrens. However, we analyzed bird distribution by separating the Pine Barrens from the Outer Coastal Plain, due to its unique habitat and very different bird communities.

The Pine Barrens

The Pine Barrens, while having less diverse vegetation than most other forest types, supports extensive populations of Pine and Prairie Warblers, Eastern Towhees, Brown Thrashers, and Field Sparrows. Although this province is often thought of as a homogenous sea of pines, there is some diversity, especially along the stream corridors and in the White Cedar Swamps (Wander 1981).

Conservation of New Jersey's Birds

Conservation is not a discipline that comes naturally to many Americans. It flies in the face of two of our most cherished principles – the notion that America's natural wealth is unlimited and the belief in individual freedom.

These ideals are historically based, anchored in a time when European settlers were shedding the social and political yoke of the Old World and engaging a continent whose environmental wealth seemed limitless. Both have since been modified to fit the mold imposed by a changing world – one in which resources have been proven to be fragile and finite and in which the concept of "the common good" has found common ground in the minds of residents and decision makers alike.

No, the need to protect our state's natural resources is not an ideal quickly or easily accommodated into the decision-making process of this small, densely populated state. But it is nevertheless critical as the failures of the last century prove and successes of this have demonstrated.

The dismal state of New Jersey's environmental inventory at the beginning of the 20th century has been discussed in these pages. Suffice it to say that by 1900, unregulated slaughter, destructive land-use practices and the worst effects of the industrial age had served to reduce New Jersey's birds and other wildlife to a vestige of their former natural abundance.

Steps taken to restore New Jersey's wildlife included: the passage of the New Jersey Wild Bird Bill in 1911; passage of a bill affording protection for most birds of prey (later extended to all raptors) in 1929; legislation limiting development in coastal areas Coastal Zone Management Act (1972) and the Freshwater Wetlands Act (1988).

Beginning in 1961, voters approved several Green Acres bond proposals for the purpose of securing and protecting open space. A voter referendum which called for the purchase of one million additional acres of open space over a ten-year period was passed in 1998.

Pine Barrens Protection...the establishment of the New Jersey Endangered Species Program...Farmland Preservation...all these initiatives were instrumental in, and attest to, the recovery of New Jersey's environmental resources (most particularly its birds).

In addition to these statewide legislative actions, many thousands of acres of land were purchased or procured by federal and state agencies, as well as private land conservation groups like the Nature Conservancy, Natural Lands Trust, and New Jersey Audubon. Late in this century, land-management policies have taken a shift away from single-species management aimed primarily at benefiting game species and now focus more on practices that foster biodiversity.

The environmental partiality manifest in these efforts was anchored in the Audubon Movement of the last century. This crusading spirit was succeeded by the "Environmental Movement" a political force that gained strength in the last half of the 20th century spurred, in part, by the DDT crisis of the 1960s – a biological backfire in which the widespread use of pesticides depleted the populations of many bird species (most notably several birds of prey).

The public outcry against DDT culminated in the establishment of Earth Day in 1970. Its subsequent, annual celebration as well as the environmental education efforts of organizations like New Jersey Audubon have helped fuel the Environmental Movement.

Ironically one element that fostered the Environmental Movement lies at the heart of New Jersey's greatest environmental challenge – the demographic shift from metropolitan to rural areas called "suburbanization." While this move to the suburbs put increasing numbers of people in contact with nature, it has also resulted in the loss of habitat critical to wildlife.

A State Plan exists which directs development away from natural areas and farmland and back into places where supporting infrastructures (such as roads and sewers) already exist. But the State Plan is a guide, not a law, and in this age the municipalities, not the state, dictate land-use policies.

The battle for New Jersey's environment, like many battles, is a battle for land. In the interest of maintaining the natural integrity of New Jersey and not losing the gains of this century, it is incumbent that the following objectives be made policy.

First and foremost, all large, intact, and strategically located tracts of land should be identified, purchased, and protected. As those European settlers discovered three centuries ago, land is wealth. The best way to protect it is to own it.

Second, the State's Master Plan should be enforced, not merely promoted, so that residents and wildlife can live in a state of orchestrated integrity.

Third, landscaping policies that promote natural plants and landscaping schemes that are beneficial to birds and other wildlife should be encouraged through education and local ordinance.

Fourth, environmental education should be made part of the state's school curriculum so that all residents can be made aware of the environmental riches of their state.

Fifth, state and private organizations should remain vigilant for sudden and unforeseen changes in bird populations. This requires a commitment to serious and applied field research. Once identified, problems should be addressed in a manner that gives first priority to righting the imbalance.

Bird conservation is not an objective that is ever truly realized. It is, like nature, an ongoing process, and its scope is global. Most of New Jersey's birds spend only a portion of their lives within our borders. Our best efforts to safeguard birds here may always be undermined by threats thousands of miles away. The sad decline of many neotropical migrants that has characterized the last half of this century seems a case in point.

But this does not excuse us from our obligation to a natural world in which diversity is clearly promoted to ends which no one can claim to understand or perceive. It is incumbent upon us to focus on the conservation objectives we can define, address the threats we can see, and work to protect the habitat that supports the birds of this state for their benefit and the benefit of all who value them.

References

In the 1800s both John James Audubon and Alexander Wilson studied and collected birds in New Jersey, and their books are peppered with references to the bird life in the state. Several important books have been published on the birds in northern New Jersey – notably Ludlow Griscom's *Birds of the New York City Region* (1923) and Allan Cruickshank's *Birds around New York City* (1942). John Bull's *Birds of the New York City Area* (1964) covered nearly the same areas in New Jersey as did Cruickshank and Griscom. Their careful documentation of the status and distribution of birds left a legacy of information that allows comparisons of bird distribution throughout the 20th century – a treasure by any measure.

Early in the 1900s one of the countries most well known regional bird books was published – Witmer Stone's *Bird Studies at Old Cape May* (1937). This book was a landmark in its time and remains a valuable resource for those interested in changes in the bird life of the area. Recent information on the status of the bird life at Cape May was well summarized in David Sibley's *The Birds of Cape May* (1993, 1997). These volumes, like those noted above, give insight into regional changes on the Cape May peninsula during this century.

Four books have been published that cover the status and distribution of birds throughout the entire state: Charles A. Shriner's *The Birds of New Jersey* (1896), Witmer Stone's *The Birds of New Jersey Their Nests and Eggs* (1908), David Fables's *Annotated List of New Jersey Birds* (1955), and Charles F. Leck's *The Status and Distribution of New Jersey's Birds* (1984). William Boyle's *A Guide to Bird Finding in New Jersey* (1986), while primarily a guide to significant areas for bird watching, also has valuable information on the status and distribution of birds in the state.

New Jersey Audubon Society has maintained a regular journal since 1958 for the publication of records of birds seen in the state. These journals, *New Jersey Nature News* (prior to 1975) and *Records of*

New Jersey Birds (from 1975 - present), have provided an ongoing source of information about the distribution and abundance of birds in the state, and often include the results of studies of important bird areas. We relied heavily on the information in RNJB, and any record in this book without a citation is taken from RNJB. The National Audubon Society's publication *American Birds*, including the *Christmas Bird Count* issue, also provided us with information used in the species accounts, particularly in the species maximas and Christmas Bird Count summaries.

Several books served as constant desktop references for summary information while we were writing the species accounts, particularly the *Birds of Massachusetts* (Veit and Petersen 1993), *Lives of North American Birds* (Kaufman 1996), *The Birder's Handbook* (Ehrlich et al. 1988), *The Summer Atlas of North American Birds* (Price et al. 1995), and *The Birds of North America* (Poole and Gill, eds.).

METHODS

The New Jersey Breeding Bird Atlas research was conducted from 1993 through 1997. All blocks within the state were censused during the five years of data collection. During the summer of 1998, one block was re-surveyed due to a data collection error during the official atlas period, and several additional records were added for rare breeding species.

DELINEATION OF BLOCKS

The state of New Jersey is mapped on 168, 7.5 minute, USGS topographic maps. Each USGS map was divided into six nearly equal sections called blocks. First, the maps were divided from north to south along the mid-line, and then the maps were divided in two places from east to west. Each block is roughly 3.75 minutes longitudinally and 2.5 minutes latitudinally. The blocks were then named for their position on the topographic map – from NE, NW, CE, CW, SE, to SW.

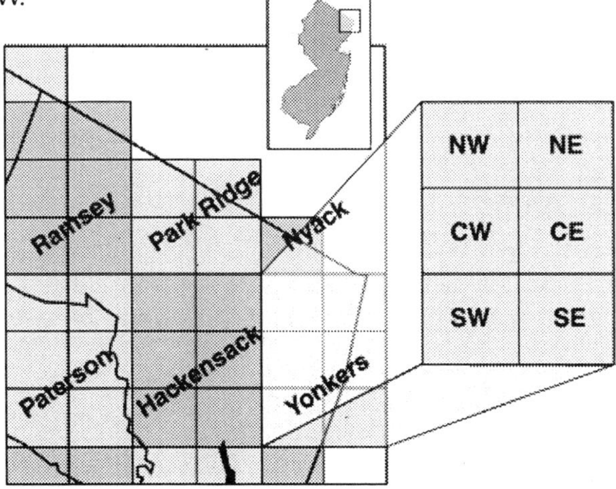

Figure 2. Each USGS map was divided into six nearly equal sections by measuring the map at the margins, and dividing the measurement by two for the north-south line, and by three for the two east-west lines.

Longitude lines converge at the poles, and, therefore, the east to west dimension of an Atlas block was not equal from the southern to northern part of the state. The blocks were widest in the south and thinnest in the north. Lines of latitude are straight, and the north to south dimension of an Atlas block is fixed at 2.87 miles. Since the east-west dimension of a block changed with longitude, the total area within a block also varied. Prior to combining partial blocks, the block areas varied from 8.9 square miles in the north to 9.2 square miles in the south.

If a block was less than one third land, or if less than one third of the block was within the geographic boundary of the state, the block was "lumped" into a neighboring block with similar habitat types. The lumped blocks created some blocks that were larger than a full block, although most partial blocks were lumped into other partial blocks. After partial blocks were lumped, there were 852 blocks in the state (see Appendix A for information on lumped blocks). All blocks in New Jersey were surveyed.

REGIONAL ORGANIZATION

Most Atlas projects depend on a large number of volunteers, and volunteers were managed on a regional basis. The state was divided into 12 regions, based loosely on county borders. Each region fell under the direction of a Regional Coordinator (RC) who assigned blocks to volunteers, received data at the end of the field seasons, evaluated and edited field sightings, and submitted the data to Atlas staff for data entry.

FIELD METHODS

The Atlas of Breeding Birds in Britain and Ireland (Sharrock 1976) first set a standard of field methods and measures of evaluating the status of breeding birds. These methods have been followed by most North American Atlas projects including the New Jersey Breeding Bird Atlas, although there have been some minor changes instituted to suit individual projects. The basic field methods involve surveying roughly equal-sized blocks during the breeding season, recording the breeding behaviors observed, inferring the species' reproductive status from those observations, and repeating those steps until a majority of the breeding species within a block have been located.

Breeding Codes

Observations were made on the behavior of the different species of birds encountered within a block. Some behaviors provide strong evidence of breeding (such as feeding young), whereas other behaviors provide less certain evidence (a single sighting of a species in breeding habitat). This range of behaviors has been categorized into Possible, Probable, and Confirmed categories, with each category providing stronger evidence of breeding.

Timing of the Field Work

Most breeding birds are actively breeding from May through July, and that is the period when most field observation occurred. An obvious challenge was sorting migrants from local breeding birds of the same species. This problem necessitated a table of "safe dates" – dates that defined the period when local breeding birds should be on territory and most migrants have moved on. Observations either before or after the safe dates were excluded from the database unless they resulted in a Confirmation. However, Atlas data that was submitted without a date was included in the database.

Not all species are actively breeding from May through July, and not all species are easiest to find during the day. Observers were encouraged to survey for early-season and late-season breeding birds, as well as for nocturnally actively species.

Atlas Codes

The codes and examples listed below were given to the Atlas volunteers prior to the onset of field work:

OBSERVED

O - Observed. Species seen in block, but not in breeding habitat. Use this code for birds that fly over or feed in your block, but chances are they breed elsewhere. For example, gulls fly over to feed in dump, but there is no nesting habitat in block.

POSSIBLE (must be during safe dates)

X - Seen or heard in breeding habitat and within safe dates, but no other evidence of breeding recorded.

PROBABLE: (must be during safe dates)

- S - Singing male heard in same location, on two occasions at least seven days apart. Also, six or more singing males heard in the block on the same day and within safe dates.
- P - Pair observed in suitable habitat.
- T - Territorial behavior. Many birds defend their home range from intruders of the same species, or competitors. Look for two males chasing one another.
- M - Mist netting of a bird reveals cloacal protuberance or well-developed brood patch. For banders only.
- A - Agitated behavior or anxiety calls. Do not use this code if the bird is responding to "pishing." Look for single bird, or pair hopping around you, chipping, and acting nervous. Move back a bit, and you may see one of the parents coming into the nest with food. Look for birds scolding a snake.
- C - Courtship or copulation. This includes displays and courtship feeding. Often the behaviors are showy, birds fanning their tails or fluttering their wings. For woodcock and nighthawk displays be sure you have heard the birds displaying on two different occasions.
- N - Visiting probable nest site, such as a cavity, but no further evidence (such as food in bill, nest material, fecal sac, sound of begging young) observed. Nesting birds will usually display a higher status code if they are watched for longer.
- B - Nest building by a wren or evacuation of a cavity by a woodpecker with no further evidence of breeding. Wrens build several dummy nests, and woodpeckers will excavate roosting cavities as well as nest holes.

CONFIRMED

- NB - Nest building (by species other than wrens or woodpeckers). You may see birds with grass or other nest building items in bill. Hummingbirds gather spider webs for nest construction: goldfinch frequently gather thistle down.
- DD - Distraction display. Feigning injury, as seen by Killdeer and other ground nesting birds. Bird will flush and fly off awkwardly, or run away dragging a wing. This generally means you are close to a nest and should retreat carefully.
- FE - Mist netted female with egg in oviduct. Banders only.
- UN - Used nest. Most nests are difficult to identify, but some are persistent and diagnostic. Use caution. DO NOT COLLECT NEST!

- FL - Recently fledged young not capable of sustained flight. Use this code with caution as some young will disperse some distance shortly after leaving the nest. Many passerines fledge with downy feathers on their heads and are still dependent upon parents for food. The begging calls of these young are usually loud enough to attract your attention from quite a distance. Do not use this code for gulls, terns, or hawks – all species with long periods of post-fledging care.
- FS - Adult seen with fecal sac. Young passerine birds excrete their waste in a white, membranous sac that the parent removes from the nest and drops a short distance away. The parents frequently drop the fecal sac in the same direction time and time again. Look for whitewash in an inappropriate location and watch the area.
- FY - Adult with food. Watch adults foraging, see if they fly off with food in their bills rather than swallowing the food. Some birds have courtship feeding (terns), or forage far from the nest (most large hawks) so use this code with caution.
- ON- Occupied nest. Cavity nest or nest high in tree where parents are seen exchanging incubation or feeding duties. You'll frequently hear begging young.
- NE - Nest with eggs, or identifiable eggshell found on ground. Adults usually remove eggshells from the nest, and drop the eggshells a short distance from nest. A Brown-headed Cowbird egg in a nest confirms both the cowbird and host species.
- NY - Nest with young, or identifiable young found dead on ground. A Brown-headed Cowbird chick in nest confirms both the cowbird and host species.

Field Protocol

It was not possible to offer field training to the hundreds of Atlas volunteers. In lieu of field training observers were given a field handbook that included field protocol. Observers were asked to census all the different habitats within a block, to visit blocks early in the day when birds were most active, and to visit the block at night. Observers were directed not to use audio tapes, not to enter nesting colonies of any species, not to handle nests, eggs, or young of any species, and not to trespass on posted property.

Coverage

In most cases, the RCs decided if a block was "finished" by the total number of species found, the percent of species in each status category, and the total amount of time spent in the block. The number of species expected in a block was a function of the habitat within the block, and was between 30 species for urbanized blocks to 110 species for some blocks in the northern part of the state. Coverage goals were set at a minimum of 20 hours in each block (although volunteers were encouraged to spend more time if they felt it was necessary) and for 25% of the observations to be in Possible category, 25% Probable, and 50% Confirmed.

Some areas, particularly in the Pine Barrens, were difficult to cover. In those areas, we assigned "blockbusters" to quickly cover several blocks in a few days. In those cases, blocks were generally only covered for one day, and usually for fewer than ten hours.

DATA HANDLING

Observers were given field cards with all regularly occurring species listed and asked to submit the highest code recorded for any species in a block during one year. To avoid the introduction of transcription errors, observers were encouraged not to copy the data from field notes but to enter the data directly onto the field cards. Field cards were sent to the RCs when work was completed each year. The RCs evaluated the data and edited the cards for errors. Next, the cards were forwarded to the Atlas staff, for data entry. Each year the data files were merged, and a computer program selected the highest status code for each species in each block. Only the highest status codes were used to create the maps.

Error Checking

There are several types of errors that can occur with a project of this scale. Over 82,000 records were collected during the course of the project, and 57,400 data points were used to make the maps. Even if the data entry and editing process were 99% accurate, there could still be over 550 errors in the data used to make the maps. As with all field projects there are errors the observer can make in the field that can not be tracked, and these can only be controlled by training.

Data entry errors, however, can be controlled. There were several methods of error checking employed in the database management. First, the RCs evaluated data before it was entered and, in some years, again after data entry. This eliminated many reporting errors prior to data entry, and many data entry errors. Second, after the data were entered into the computer, a series of error checking programs were run to eliminate keystroke errors. Finally, Atlas staff manually checked all data entry against the field cards submitted. All data were compiled using Microsoft Fox-Pro, version 2.5b.

Several rare species required verification of their identification and location. Reports of these species were evaluated by the RCs prior to data submission to the Atlas staff, and the species were verified by additional observers if necessary. For most of these sightings, an exact location was submitted to Atlas staff at the end of the field season.

MAP MAKING

The maps created for the *New Jersey Breeding Bird Atlas* used Environmental Systems Research Institute's (ESRI) Arc-View 3.1. The base map of the state outline, county outlines, and coast outline was created by The New Jersey Division of Fish Game and Wildlife's GIS Department, and the base map of the block overlay was created by Sharon Paul of the New Jersey Endangered and Non-Game Species Program.

SPECIES ACCOUNTS

The order of the species accounts follows The American Ornithologists' Union's *Check-list of North American Birds*, Seventh Edition (1998). There are three types of species accounts – breeding bird accounts, migrant accounts, and rarity accounts. All species (assumed to be wild) found breeding in the state during the Atlas period are included in the breeding bird accounts; all regularly occurring migrants are treated in the migrant accounts; all other species that have been accepted by the NJBRC as of November 1998 are treated in rarities accounts. The NJBRC Review List also includes some subspecies, and those subspecies are included in the species accounts.

Range

The *Range* gives a thumbnail sketch of the species breeding and wintering range. In many cases it is abbreviated to describe the species' range in eastern North America. It is purposefully short, and is not meant to substitute for a full-length range description or range map.

Status

The *Status* line summarizes the species abundance and distribution in the state. It is separated into a breeding status and a migrant status.

BREEDING STATUS

The breeding status categories are based on ideas used in *The Marin County Breeding Bird Atlas* (Shuford 1993). The status describes the number of blocks where the species occurred and gives a qualitative estimate of the probability of encountering the species within a block.

The terms used to describe statewide distribution range from very local to nearly ubiquitous, and have seven categories:

Table A. BREEDING STATUS CATEGORIES.

	# blocks	% of state	# of species
Very Local	1-15	1.8	30
Local	16-154	18.1	76
Somewhat Local	155-293	34.4	24
Fairly Widespread	294-432	50.7	14
Widespread	433-571	67.0	16
Very Widespread	572-710	83.3	21
Nearly Ubiquitous	711-852	100.0	27

We estimated the probability of encountering a species in a block where it breeds, assuming the observer is in appropriate habitat and was afield for four hours. This is based on both the species' density and habits. The estimate is presented in language similar to the abundance classification used in the status line for migrants and ranges from rare to common.

Rare .... Difficult to detect and/or breeds in extremely low numbers.
Scarce .... Infrequently encountered and/or in very limited numbers.
Uncommon .... Not always encountered and/or present in limited numbers.
Fairly common .... Regularly encountered and/or present in moderate numbers.
Common .... Easily encountered and/or numerous.

MIGRATION STATUS

Many factors contribute to the impression of a migrant or wintering bird's status. Weather, habitat, a species' habits, and an observer's experience – all are important ingredients in the perceived status of a given species. While the species' abundance is certainly of primary consideration when discussing status, a species' habits may be just as important.

Some species are frequently encountered, and while not seen in large numbers are still considered common. Red-tailed Hawks are easily seen on most days in winter and would be considered a common winter bird by most observers. However, their numbers never approach those of other common birds, such as European Starling or Herring Gull. Secretive birds, such as rails, owls, and nightjars, are more difficult to estimate. While some of these "shy" species may be present in good numbers, they are just plain hard to see and do not conform especially well to the status descriptions.

Rather than estimate the number of individuals a person may see in a day, we assigned the status classification by balancing the species abundance with its ease in detection. The status assigned to the species distills all of the above characteristics of the species, and assigns a single word to this complex set of variables.

Rare .... Seen only a few times per season.
Scarce .... Not present daily, infrequently encountered, and usually in very limited numbers even in the proper habitat at the proper time of year.
Uncommon .... Present in limited numbers, and not always encountered, or present mainly under favorable weather conditions, in the proper habitat at the proper time of year.

Fairly common....... Usually present, regularly encountered, although usually not numerous, in the proper habitat at the proper time of year.

Common .... Almost always present, easily encountered, and often numerous, in the proper habitat at the proper time of year.

Breeding Accounts

BREEDING SUMMARY TABLES

Two tables are included in the breeding species accounts. One table summarizes the number of blocks the species was found Possible, Probable, or Confirmed, and gives the total number of blocks the species was recorded in. The second table breaks down the species distribution by physiographic provinces as defined above.

The physiographic distribution tables indicate the percentage of a species statewide range within a province, and show how concentrated the species is within each province.

Physiographic Distribution Sample Species	Number of blocks in province	Number of blocks species found breeding in province	Number of blocks species found in state	Percent of province species occupies	Percent of all records for this species found in province	Percent of state area in province
Kittatinny Mountains	19	9	454	47.4	2.0	2.2
Kittatinny Valley	46	27	454	58.7	5.9	5.4
Highlands	110	52	454	47.3	11.5	12.9
Piedmont	165	86	454	52.1	18.9	19.4
Inner Coastal Plain	109	73	454	67.0	16.1	12.8
Outer Coastal Plain	223	133	454	59.6	29.3	26.2
Pine Barrens	180	74	454	41.1	16.3	21.1

Table B. SAMPLE BREEDING DISTRIBUTION TABLE.

Column 1: Physiographic province.
Column 2: The total number of blocks in the province.
Column 3: The number of blocks the species was found in the province.
Column 4: The number of blocks the species was found statewide.
Column 5: The percent of the province the species occupies.
Column 6: The percent of the species statewide range in this province.
Column 7: The percent of the state's area is in the province.

MAP INTERPRETATION AND CONSERVATION NOTES

The **Map Interpretation** section of the species accounts is only used when the methods used for the Atlas tended to over or underestimate the species statewide range. The **Conservation Note** section discusses problems faced by species in decline.

Regularly Occurring Migrants and Wintering Birds

MAXIMA

Maximas are presented for fall, winter, and spring concentrations. If available, two maximas are presented. For species with a tendency to occur in high numbers along the coast, but also to aggregate inland, we present coastal and inland maximas. Unless otherwise noted, all maxima are from RNJB.

MIGRATION MONITORING SITE SUMMARIES

The fall accounts include summaries of two long-term studies conducted by CMBO. Summary statistics are presented for the Cape May Hawk Watch (CMHW) and the Avalon Sea Watch (AŞW). The CMHW data were summarized from 1976 through 1998. These data were collected at Cape May Point State Park, seven days a week, from 15 August through 30 November from 1980-1994, and from 1 September through 30 November from 1976-1979, and from 1995-1998. The ASW data were collected at 7th St. overlooking Townsend's Inlet in Avalon, seven days per week, from 22 September through 22 December from 1993-1997.

CHRISTMAS BIRD COUNT SUMMARIES

The winter accounts include a summary of the National Audubon Society's Christmas Bird Count (CBC) data from 1977 through 1997, and are an indication of the early-winter status for the species in New Jersey. Statistics include the maximum statewide count, the minimum statewide count, the average statewide count, and the high single count for the species. The counts run from mid-December through early January each year, and data are collected in two calendar years. The year of the publication of the count is used in the statistics.

Rarities Accounts

The species included in this book are those that have been accepted by the New Jersey Bird Records Committee (NJBRC) and are included on the Official State List. The processes of accepting a report of a rarity for inclusion on the State List are complex, and understanding the rarities species accounts requires an understanding of these processes. The NJBRC was only intermittently active from 1975 through 1990. In 1991 the committee was revived, and it remains an active body for vetting sightings of rare birds in the state. The NJBRC publishes an annual report of decisions in the fall issue of RNJB. The most recent State List and Review List was published in 1997 (Larson 1997) and will be updated in 1999.

STANDARDS OF ACCEPTANCE

The NJBRC has three levels of acceptance for rarities records: those records accepted by Fables (1955) or Kunkle et al. (1959); those records post-Fables but prior to 1976 – the *historical standard*; and those records post-1976 – the *modern standard*.

Records accepted by the Urner State List Committee for publication in David Fables's *Annotated List of New Jersey Birds* (1955) and for the *First Supplement to the Annotated List of New Jersey Birds* (Kunkle et al.1959) were generally retained by the NJBRC, and these are indicated by a pound sign (#) after the location of the record.

It is difficult to get documentation that meets the *modern standard* for records seen prior to 1976, when few rare birds were photographed and the state was without a records committee. Some historical records were accepted by the NJBRC, although they do not meet the *modern standard*, and these are referred to as *historical standard* records. These *historical standard* records are indicated in the text of this book with an asterisk (*) placed after the location of the record. In addition, there were a few records between 1975 and 1989 that are also given *historical standard* acceptance. For example, when the documentation, photograph, or specimen was lost, or when the record was seen by several observers. The *historical standard* was not used for species that are difficult to identify.

For a species to be added to the Official State List (post-1975) there must be one fully documented *modern standard* record. A *modern standard* would include a detailed and accurate written description, and/or an identifiable photograph/video/or film, and/or a verified specimen, and/or a tape recording.

RECORDS INCLUDED

Reports not accepted by NJBRC are not included in *The Birds of New Jersey*. All the accepted records of a rare species are included in the account if there are fewer than 13 accepted records, although a few species include more records. If there are more than 13 records, the account summarizes the records and may include only photo or specimen records, or out-of-season occurrences. Photographs of rarities, published or in the Rare Bird Photo File (RBPF), are noted in the species account. Specimen locations and numbers are also noted when the museum housing the specimen was known.

METHODS OF DOCUMENTING RARITIES

Written Descriptions

Detailed written descriptions are the mainstay of most rare bird reports. Observers should note all aspects of the bird's plumage, structure, song or call, and habits. Comparisons should be drawn to differences with similar species, and the reasons for eliminating similar species. Even with well-detailed written descriptions, some reports can not be accepted, and further means of documenting a record should always be utilized if possible. Likewise, even if a bird has been photographed, the report should still be accompanied by a detailed written description.

Field Sketches

Field sketches are valuable for documenting records and should be made at the time of observation. Sketches made during or immediately following the sighting, before field guides are consulted, may prove critical in documenting rarities. Even a crude sketch can show enough detail to help identify the species, but a sketch should always be supported by a written description.

Photographs/Video

Photographs have become one of the most important means of documenting the occurrence of species. They are useful for documenting difficult to identify species and birds new to the State List. It is also important to note that photographs, too, need review.

Specimens

Most people do not possess the permits to collect birds, and, thankfully, this method of documenting the occurrence of a rarity is not available to the public at large. Specimens of New Jersey birds are distributed in various museum collections, with good numbers of specimens at the American Museum of Natural History (AMNH), the Philadelphia Academy of Natural Sciences (ANSP), and the U.S. National Museum (USNM).

RECORDS NOT ACCEPTED

Nonacceptance of a record indicates that a report did not contain enough documentation to be included on the Official State List. All reports should be supported by as much evidence as possible. The NJBRC errs on the side of caution, and, undoubtedly, some nonaccepted reports are correct.

PELAGIC RECORDS

One problem plaguing record keeping of seabirds in New Jersey is that the state has no official pelagic boundaries. The records committees in neighboring New York and Delaware have adopted boundaries for their pelagic records. The NJBRC has defined the New Jersey boundaries, and they are presented in the map below. Observers should be careful to record the longitude and latitude of sightings for Review List Species so that the Official State List will be accurate.

Figure 3. *(page 45) Pelagic boundaries for New Jersey out to 200 nautical miles, as adopted by the NJBRC in March 1999. The four latitude-longitude coordinate-pairs shown mark the four corners of the New Jersey pelagic polygon, while the three submarine contours mark the Continental Shelf Break. Note that Hudson Canyon is not in New Jersey's waters, but that Tom's Canyon, Cateret Canyon, and the "tail" of Wilmington Canyon are. Note also that the average position of the main axis of the Gulf Stream transects New Jersey's pelagic waters. Figure and calculations prepared in Arc-View and Arc-Info by P.A. Buckley and M. Nicholson.*

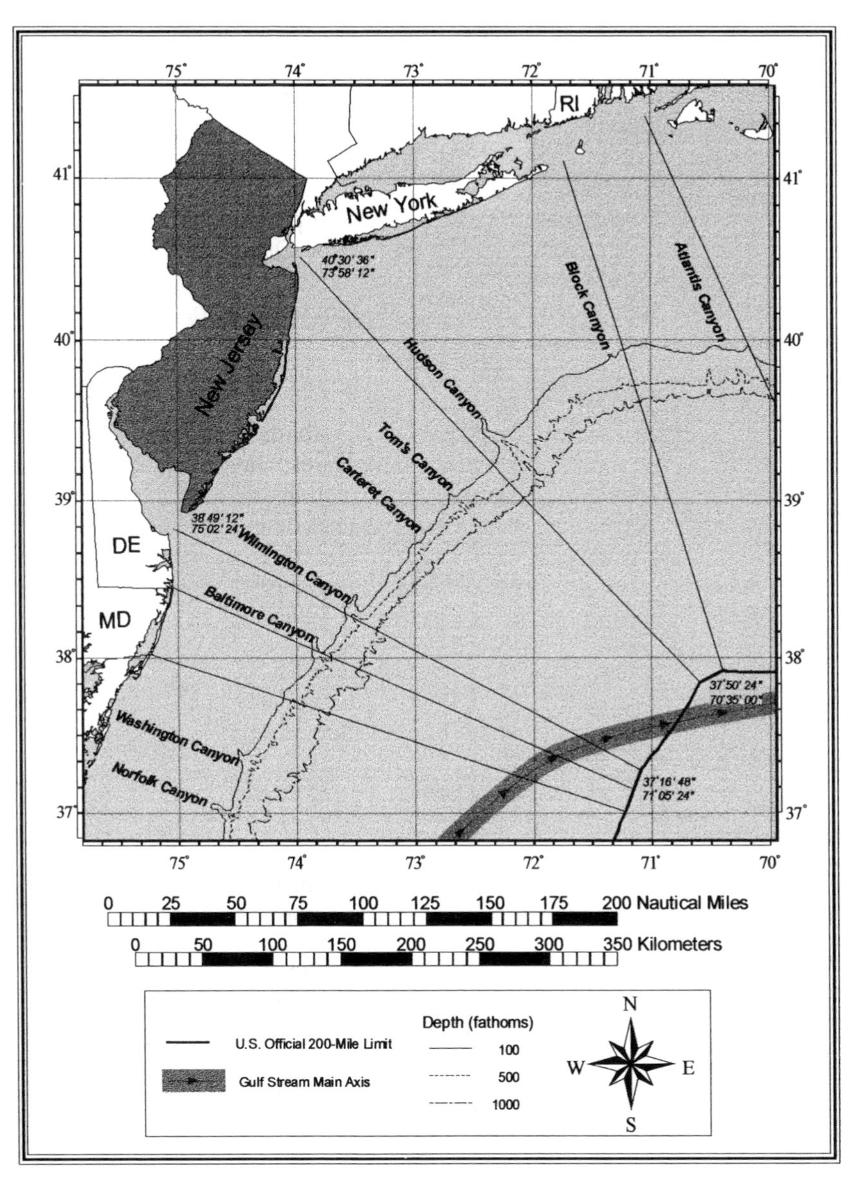

75°
74°
73°
72°
71°
70°
41°
40°
39°
38°
37°
RI
New York
New Jersey
DE
MD
40°30' 36"
73°58' 12"
38°49' 12"
75°02' 24"
37°50' 24"
70°35' 00"
37°16' 48"
71°05' 24"
Hudson Canyon
Block Canyon
Atlantis Canyon
Tom's Canyon
Carteret Canyon
Wilmington Canyon
Baltimore Canyon
Washington Canyon
Norfolk Canyon
0 25 50 75 100 125 150 175 200 Nautical Miles
0 50 100 150 200 250 300 350 Kilometers
U.S. Official 200-Mile Limit
Gulf Stream Main Axis
Depth (fathoms)
100
500
1000
N
W
E
S

Figure 3

ABBREVIATIONS

The following are regularly used abbreviations throughout the text.

AB	American Birds
AFN	Audubon Field Notes
AMNH	American Museum of Natural History (NY)
ANSP	Academy of Natural Sciences of Philadelphia
ASW	Avalon Sea Watch
BBS	Breeding Bird Surveys
CBC	Christmas Bird Count
CMBO	Cape May Bird Observatory
CMHW	Cape May Hawk Watch
Co.	County
coll.	collection
E	East (e.g., E of Barnegat Light), also used in combination with other directions (e.g., ESE, WSW etc.)
EBBA News	Eastern Bird Banding Association News
ENSP	New Jersey Division of Fish, Game and Wildlife Endangered and Non-game Species Program
HMEC	Hackensack Meadowlands Environment Center
KMNH	Kansas Museum of Natural History
m. obs.	many observers
mi.	miles
NAFEC	Atlantic City International Airport an Federal Aviation Administration Technical Center
NJA	New Jersey Audubon Magazine
NJAS	New Jersey Audubon Society
NJBRC	New Jersey Bird Records Committee
NJDEP	New Jersey Department of Environmental Protection
NJDFGW	New Jersey Division of Fish, Game and Wildlife
NJNN	New Jersey Nature News
NJSM	New Jersey State Museum
NRA	National Recreation Area
NWR	National Wildlife Refuge
pers. com.	personal communication
pers. obs.	personal observation
ph	photo
RBPF	Rare Bird Photo File
Res.	Reservoir
RNJB	Records of New Jersey Birds
SF	State Forest
SP	State Park
sp.	species
spec.	specimen
UFO	Urner Field Observer
UMMZ	University of Michigan Museum of Zoology
USGS	United States Geologic Survey
USNM	United States National Museum
Wils. Bull.	Wilson Bulletin
WMA	Wildlife Management Area

Breeding Bird Atlas Results

DATA COLLECTION

The New Jersey Breeding Bird Atlas data was collected from 1 January 1993 through 31 August 1997 and only included sightings of species within the state borders. Due to a recording error during the official Atlas data collection period, one block was resurveyed in 1998. Several records of rare, Threatened, or Endangered Species submitted during 1998 also were added to the data.

Table C. SUMMARY OF RECORDS REPORTED, SPECIES REPORTED, BLOCKS SURVEYED, AND HOURS IN THE FIELDS DURING THE ATLAS PROJECT.

Year	Records	Species Recorded	# of Blocks Surveyed	Field Hours
1993	25,020	198	487	8,813
1994	19,746	196	578	7,987
1995	20,621	197	649	5,949
1996	13,522	192	588	5,843
1997	3,107	180	302	654
1998	52	46	13	N/A

During the surveys all 852 blocks in New Jersey were sampled. Nearly 85% of the fields cards were returned with a summary of the hours spent in the field. However, 15% of the fields cards did not list hours, but many of those represented only incidental visits to a block. Therefore, the total number of hours reported above is a minimum estimate of the total time volunteers spent in the field.

Unlike many other Atlas projects, the New Jersey Atlas project did not start out with a pilot year. The first year of data collection was the most productive, with the most records reported, the highest number of species reported, and the most hours spent in the field. Interest in the project remained high, and by the end of the fourth year 96% of the records that were ultimately collected had been recorded. The fifth year of the project was used to focus on areas that had received little or no coverage during the first four years.

Statewide an average of 67 species were found breeding per block, although there were considerable differences noted in the species totals among the physiographic provinces. Volunteers spent a minimum of 29,246 hours in the field during the five years of surveys, and coverage averaged over 34 hours per block. On average volunteers recorded 17% of their sightings as Possible, 33% as Probable, and 50% as Confirmed. From 1993 through 1997 volunteers submitted 82,116 records on 210 species, two hybrids, and one suspected escaped species. Of the 210 species recorded, eight species did not have a Confirmed sighting and may not have been breeding birds.

Table D. SPECIES WITHOUT CONFIRMED SIGHTINGS

Brown Pelican	Loggerhead Shrike
Common Snipe	Swainson's Warbler
Royal Tern	Mourning Warbler
Short-eared Owl	Red Crossbill

Table E. THE 25 MOST FREQUENTLY RECORDED BREEDING SPECIES IN NEW JERSEY'S BREEDING BIRD ATLAS

Species	Total # of blocks recorded	Species	Total # of blocks recorded
Gray Catbird	839	Tufted Titmouse	791
Mourning Dove	833	Eastern Kingbird	789
American Robin	832	Northern Mockingbird	789
Common Grackle	832	Song Sparrow	783
Common Yellowthroat	813	Downy Woodpecker	779
American Crow	811	House Sparrow	771
European Starling	811	Brown-headed Cowbird	769
Northern Cardinal	809	House Wren	764
Red-winged Blackbird	809	Eastern Towhee	740
Northern Flicker	808	Great Crested Flycatcher	733
House Finch	808	American Goldfinch	731
Blue Jay	793	Wood Thrush	729
Barn Swallow	791		

DIFFERENCES IN SPECIES DISTRIBUTION

Species diversity is usually a function of habitat diversity – areas with a variety of habitats usually have higher species totals than areas with homogeneous habitats. In New Jersey, the physiographic provinces in the northern reaches of the state have more variety in altitude than those in southern New Jersey, and this altitude variation creates a diverse set of habitats for breeding birds to occupy. Consequently, the northern provinces host a high diversity of breeding birds, and, in the case of the Kittatinny Mountain and Valley, the diverse breeding bird communities occur in a geographically small area of the state. This species richness is a significant aspect of the differences in breeding bird distribution in the state.

People put pressure on the landscape. The effects of the sprawl and development in New Jersey can be seen in the distribution of many species of birds in the state, and the breeding bird communities of the Inner Coastal Plain and Piedmont have paid the highest price for our excesses. Many species, the forest obligates in particular, have a gap in their distribution - a "bird-free zone" - separating populations in northwestern New Jersey from central and southeastern New Jersey. This gap in the distribution of some species is unsettling, and is a reminder of the degree to which this state has been altered.

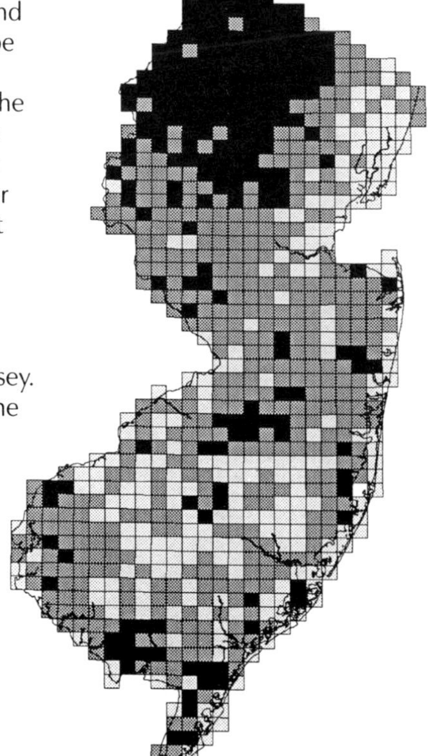

Figure 4. NUMBER OF BREEDING SPECIES PER BLOCK

The physiographic provinces south of the Piedmont have noticeably lower species totals than those in northern New Jersey. The southern provinces have average species totals per block that are similar to one another, but the composition of species within the blocks varies considerably. The differences in the species lists among the Inner and Outer Coastal Plain blocks is probably the result of the unique habitats offered in the coastal marshes and barrier islands of the Outer Coastal Plain, and is also a function of the high degree of agricultural and urban developments in the Inner Coastal Plain.

Table F. AVERAGE NUMBER OF SPECIES PER BLOCK, BY PROVINCE.

Physiographic Province	Average # of species per block
Kittatinny Mountains	94
Kittatinny Valley	99
Highlands	87
Piedmont	62
Inner Coastal Plain	62
Outer Coastal Plain	61
Pine Barrens	60

SPECIALISTS

The most common breeding birds statewide are invariably the most common birds in each province, simply due to their overwhelmingly broad distribution. While understanding the ranges in these common species is important, it is also important to know which species are specialists in each region. It is possible to describe the regional specialists by estimating the percentage of the species' range found within a given province. Small provinces that hold a large percentage of a species range raise red flags for land managers – minor changes in that province may cause dramatic problems for that species' statewide population. Those species with a large percentage of their statewide range in one province are listed below, and those found during the Atlas but not Confirmed breeding, are presented in *italics*.

The Kittatinny Mountain

Although a small province the Kittatinny Mountains provides unique habitats for breeding birds. Many of the species with a large portion of their range in this small province are those normally found well to the north of the state or those found at higher altitudes, although Common Merganser is an indicator that some of the blocks in this region had sections of the Delaware River within their borders. The Kittatinny Mountain specialists (those with more than 20% of their breeding range in a province that occupies 2% of the state's area) are:

Species	Percent of Statewide Range in Province
Common Raven	67
Magnolia Warbler	59
Yellow-bellied Sapsucker	50
Yellow-rumped Warbler	50
Dark-eyed Junco	47
Blackburnian Warbler	38
Nashville Warbler	31
Black-throated Blue Warbler	29
Purple Finch	29
Common Merganser	28
Blue-headed Vireo	24
Black-throated Green Warbler	23
Northern Goshawk	22
Golden-crowned Kinglet	21
Hermit Thrush	21
White-throated Sparrow	20

The Kittatinny Valley

The Kittatinny Valley has a high degree of habitat diversity within its blocks. The provincial specialists include birds of high altitude, those dependent upon freshwater wetlands, and some grassland obligates. There are a high number of species within the Kittatinny Valley that occur in only a small number of blocks statewide, making this province the most species rich province in the state. Those species with 20% or more of their statewide breeding range in the Kittatinny Valley, a province that occupies only 5% of the state's area, are:

Species	Percent of Statewide Range in Province
Short-eared Owl	100
Common Snipe	67
Henslow's Sparrow	50
White-throated Sparrow	50
Common Merganser	45
Vesper Sparrow	44
Hooded Merganser	43
American Coot	39
Sora	37
Cliff Swallow	34
Dark-eyed Junco	33
Green-winged Teal	31
Least Flycatcher	29
Upland Sandpiper	27

The Kittantinny Valley, continued

Species	Percent of Statewide Range in Province	Species	Percent of Statewide Range in Province
Cerulean Warbler	27	Alder Flycatcher	21
King Rail	26	Golden-crowned Kinglet	21
Bobolink	26	American Bittern	20
Common Moorhen	23	Red-headed Woodpecker	20
Common Raven	22	Sedge Wren	20

Highlands

The Highlands is superficially similar to the Kittatinny Mountains province, although it is larger. The two provinces have similar species lists, although by virtue of its larger size the Highlands' has more blocks occupied by the high altitude specialists. Species with a high percentage of their breeding range in the Highlands tend to be birds usually associated with higher latitude forests. Those species with 30% or more of their statewide breeding range in the Highlands (a province that occupies only 13% of the state) are:

Species	Percent of Statewide Range in Province	Species	Percent of Statewide Range in Province
Mourning Warbler	100	Sharp-shinned Hawk	39
Pine Siskin	100	Louisiana Waterthrush	39
Golden-winged Warbler	58	Red-breasted Nuthatch	39
Nashville Warbler	56	Yellow-rumped Warbler	38
Black-throated Blue Warbler	56	Least Flycatcher	37
Blue-headed Vireo	54	Ruffed Grouse	37
Winter Wren	53	Alder Flycatcher	37
Canada Warbler	52	Hermit Thrush	36
Golden-crowned Kinglet	52	Yellow-throated Vireo	35
Yellow-bellied Sapsucker	50	Black-throated Green Warbler	35
Chestnut-sided Warbler	49	Red-shouldered Hawk	34
Northern Goshawk	48	Black-capped Chickadee	34
Northern Waterthrush	47	Northern Saw-whet Owl	33
Pileated Woodpecker	46	Wild Turkey	32
Cerulean Warbler	46	Long-eared Owl	31
Purple Finch	45	Double-crested Cormorant	31
Brown Creeper	43	Rose-breasted Grosbeak	31
Blackburnian Warbler	43	Black Vulture	30
Worm-eating Warbler	42	Veery	30
		Hooded Warbler	30

Piedmont

The Piedmont, densely settled with suburban, urban, and industrial developments, occupies 19% of the state's area. This region is important for three grassland specialists (Dickcissel, Bobolink, and Savannah Sparrow). Those species with 30% or more of their statewide breeding range in the Piedmont are:

Species	Percent of Statewide Range in Province
Dickcissel	50
Black-capped Chickadee	43
Gadwall	39
Bobolink	37
Ring-necked Pheasant	34
Rose-breasted Grosbeak	34
Cliff Swallow	32
Warbling Vireo	32
Common Moorhen	31
Savannah Sparrow	31

Inner Coastal Plain

A small amount of habitat diversity, combined with a large amount of development, has left the Inner Coastal Plain with only one breeding species in the province that occurs at a rate higher than expected – Ruddy Duck. It is the only species with 33% or more of its statewide breeding range the Inner Coastal Plain.

Outer Coastal Plain

The Outer Coastal Plain, a large province, shows the influence of the coastal wetlands on the suite of birds that rely on the province for breeding habitat. Species with 40% or more of their statewide breeding range in a province that occupies only 26% of the state's area are:

Species	Percent of Statewide Range in Province
Brown Pelican	100
Black-necked Stilt	100
Gull-billed Tern	100
Caspian Tern	100
Royal Tern	100
Swainson's Warbler	100
Tricolored Heron	95
Piping Plover	95
Cattle Egret	93
Black Rail	92
Common Tern	92
Boat-tailed Grackle	89
Great Black-backed Gull	89
American Oystercatcher	89
Laughing Gull	88
Forster's Tern	88
Yellow-crowned Night-Heron	87
Clapper Rail	87

Outer Coastal Plain, continued

Species	Percent of Statewide Range in Province
Willet	87
Chuck-wills-widow	87
Black Skimmer	86
Seaside Sparrow	85
Herring Gull	83
Little Blue Heron	82
Saltmarsh Sharp-tailed Sparrow	82
Glossy Ibis	80
Snowy Egret	79
Least Tern	77
Northern Shoveler	75
Great Egret	66
Osprey	62

Species	Percent of Statewide Range in Province
Northern Harrier	60
Marsh Wren	54
Red-breasted Merganser	50
Blue Grosbeak	50
Black-crowned Night-Heron	49
Summer Tanager	47
Blue-winged Teal	47
Yellow-breasted Chat	46
Peregrine Falcon	45
Barn Owl	44
Northern Bobwhite	44
Horned Lark	42
Sedge Wren	40

Pine Barrens

The Pine Barrens, although well known as nearly a "sea of pines," have a few species that occur in the province at a higher than expected rate. Species with 40% or more of their statewide breeding range in a province that occupies only 21% of the state's area are:

Species	Percent of Statewide Range in Province
Loggerhead Shrike	100
Red Crossbill	100
Whip-poor-will	54
Henslow's Sparrow	50
Northern Saw-whet Owl	47
Pine Warbler	45
Common Nighthawk	44
Prothonotary Warbler	43
Summer Tanager	41
Upland Sandpiper	40
Red-headed Woodpecker	40

Red-throated Loon

Gavia stellata

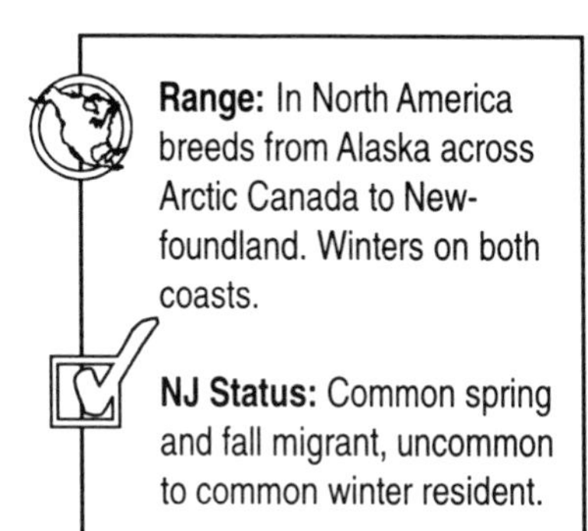

Range: In North America breeds from Alaska across Arctic Canada to Newfoundland. Winters on both coasts.

NJ Status: Common spring and fall migrant, uncommon to common winter resident.

Fall: Red-throated Loons stage spectacular coastal flights that may last for hours. They are not expected before early October, and numbers peak from mid-November to early December. Observations from the Avalon Sea Watch indicated stable numbers of passage migrants from 1993 through 1996, but the season total in 1997 was nearly 15% greater than any other year. There is little documentation of the magnitude of pelagic or overland migrations. They are rare to uncommon inland where they are found on larger bodies of water. **Maxima:** Coastal: 20,000, Avalon, 14 November 1985 (Sibley 1997); 10,978, Avalon Sea Watch, 12 November 1997; Inland: 43, Round Valley Res., 11 November 1985. **ASW Seasonal Stats:** Average: 57,424; Maximum: 65,994 in 1997.

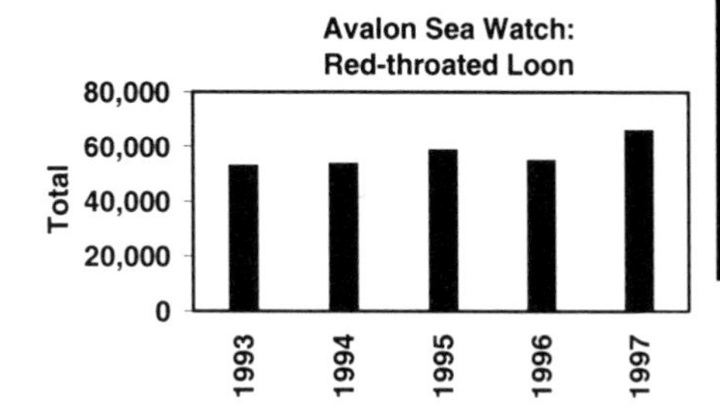

Winter: Red-throated Loons are found on the open ocean and saltwater bays. Numbers are variable from one year to the next, or even from month to month, and this is reflected in CBC totals. They are rare inland. **CBC Statewide Stats:** Average: 316; Maximum: 1,731 in 1985; Minimum: 22 in 1981. **CBC Maximum:** 1,657, Cape May, 1985.

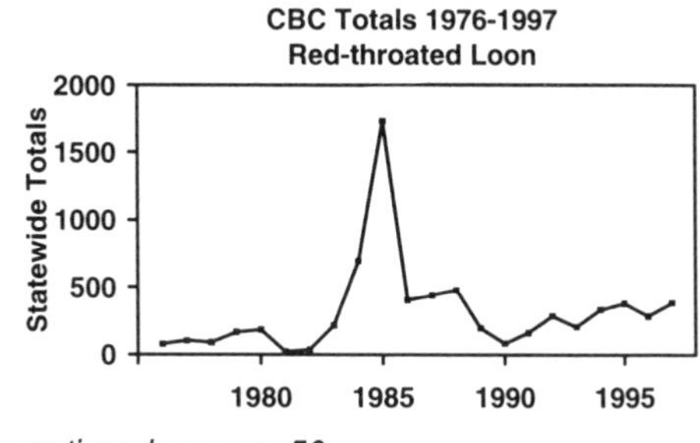

continued on page 56

Red-throated Loon

continued from page 55

Red-throated Loon

Spring: Most of the spring migration of Red-throated Loons is coastal, and they are rare inland. Far fewer birds are seen migrating north along the coast in spring migration compared to fall migration. Staging in Delaware Bay may begin by February, with highest numbers massing from early March through mid-April. The vast concentrations are often visible from shore, and frequently hundreds are seen on any given day. Since the rate of turnover in the flocks is not known, the number visible at any one time may only be a fraction of the total number involved during the entire season (Sibley 1997). The accurate estimation of staging numbers, and geographic delineation of staging areas, should be a research priority. The species is unexpected in New Jersey after mid-May, although one or two stragglers occasionally summer along the coast. **Maxima:** Coastal: 3,000, Cape May Point, 1 April 1977; Inland:18, Swartswood Lake, 19 April 1995. ■

Pacific Loon

Gavia pacifica

Range: In North America breeds from Alaska east to Hudson Bay. Winters primarily on the Pacific Coast.

NJ Status: Accidental. NJBRC Review List.

Occurrence: Pacific Loon was formerly considered conspecific with Arctic Loon. There have been over 30 state reports of Pacific Loons. Many of these are probably correct, but lack sufficient documentation. There are seven records accepted by the NJBRC (five in fall/winter, one in spring, one in summer). The initial record from Round Valley in 1978 was of a bird identified as an Arctic Loon. An examination of photos subsequent to the split revealed it was a Pacific Loon. The seven accepted records are:

Round Valley Res.	*16 November-3 December 1978*	*ph-RNJB 5:4; Hanisek 1979*
Tuckerton	*1-21 August 1986*	*ph-RNJB 12:77*
Merrill Creek Res.	*15-20 November 1988*	
Sandy Hook	*2 December 1989*	
Manasquan Inlet	*1 March-12 April 1992*	*ph-RNJB 18:71*
Manasquan Inlet	*12-18 December 1993*	
Sandy Hook	*23 November 1997*	

Common Loon

Gavia immer

Range: Breeds from Alaska south to Oregon, across Canada south to northern Massachusetts. Winters on both coasts and the Gulf of Mexico, and on large inland lakes and reservoirs in the south.

NJ Status: Common spring and fall migrant, fairly common winter resident.

Fall: Early movements of Common Loons may begin in August, but peak numbers are reached from mid-October through mid-November. They are seen along the coast, and on larger inland lakes and rivers. Common Loons are less numerous than Red-throated Loons along the coast, but they are more numerous than Red-throated Loons inland. **Maxima:** Coastal: 687, Avalon Sea Watch, 31 October 1996; 585, Avalon Sea Watch, 8 November 1995; Inland:180, Culvers Lake, 29 October 1984. **ASW Seasonal Stats:** Average: 4,375; Maximum: 5,026 in 1996.

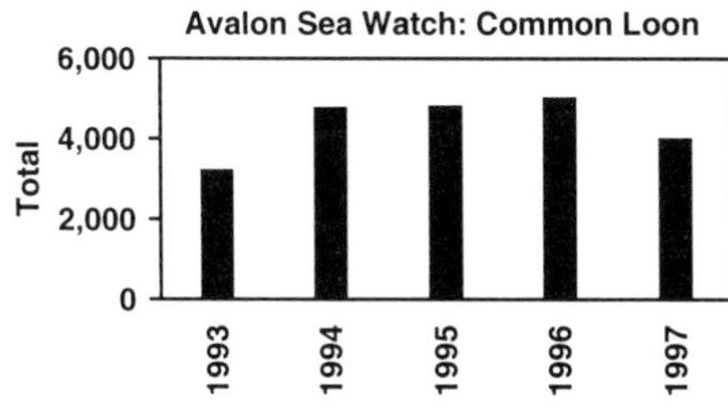

Winter: Common Loons are generally seen on the open ocean and coastal bays, and rarely are seen inland in winter. Numbers vary from year to year, and dramatic fluctuations may occur during a single winter. Although CBC totals are variable, numbers appear higher in the 1990s compared to previous years. Their status offshore is not well known, and they may be more common offshore than along the coast (see Spring occurrence). **CBC Statewide Stats:** Average: 122; Maximum: 427 in 1993; Minimum: 23 in 1990. **CBC Maximum:** 179, Lakehurst, 1993.

Spring: Common Loons are frequently encountered statewide in spring. Maximum counts are attained from early April to mid-May, but a steady, low volume movement can continue to early June (P. Lehman pers. com.). Inland, birds are usually seen flying overhead. Sibley (1997) suggested that large numbers offshore in late winter (e.g., 1000+ at sea off Cape May, 8 March 1987) may be staging for migration and/or feeding while in a flightless phase of molt. This aspect of Common Loon ecology should be investigated, as the near-shore waters of New Jersey may be an area of importance for this species. There are annual reports of a few nonbreeders along the coast, offshore, or on inland lakes through the summer. **Maxima:** Coastal: 150, Avalon, 26 April 1995; Inland: 300, Culvers Lake, 3 April 1985. ■

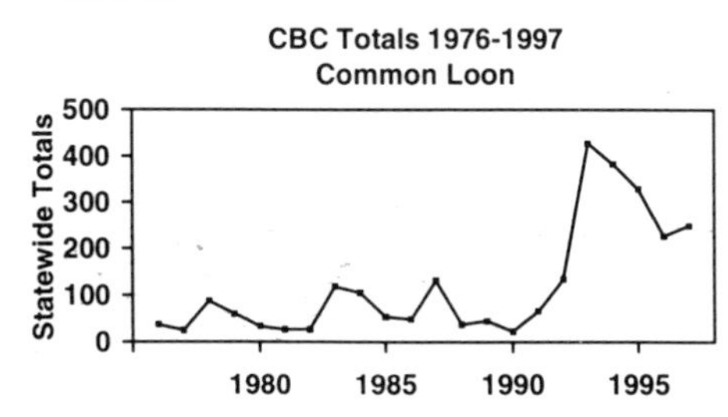

Range: Breeds across the United States and most of southern Canada. Winters mainly in the southern third of the United States, north along the East coast to Massachusetts.

NJ Status: Scarce and local summer resident, uncommon spring and common fall migrant, uncommon winter resident. Endangered Species in New Jersey (breeding only).

Pied-billed Grebe

Podilymbus podiceps

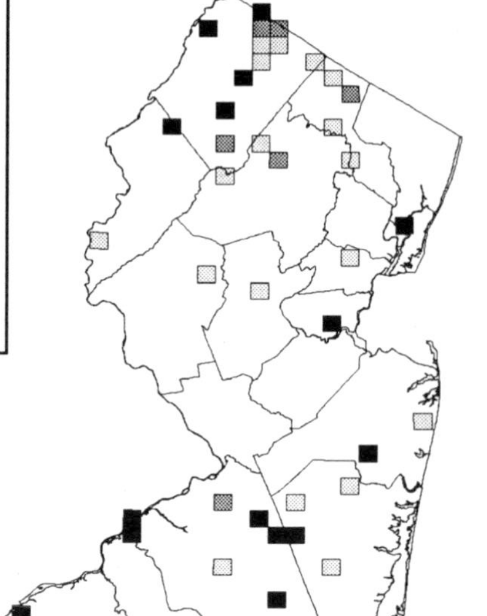

Statewide Summary	
Status	# of Blocks
Possible	26
Probable	10
Confirmed	19
Total	55

Breeding

Habitat: Nests in freshwater marshes with emergent vegetation.

It is likely that Pied-billed Grebes were never widespread or abundant breeding birds in New Jersey due to their specialized habitat requirements. They are secretive during the breeding season, their presence is often noted by loud, cuckoo-like calls. Within appropriate habitat they may become locally common and their density has occasionally been recorded as colonial (Griscom 1923). At the turn of the 20th century, they were unknown from the urbanized sections of northern New Jersey, but were suspected of breeding in the marshes of Hackensack and Newark (Griscom 1923). Stone (1937) reported no breeding records for Cape May County, but knew of one breeding location in Cumberland

Map Interpretation: Pied-billed Grebes can summer in good habitat without mates, leading to an inflated estimate of the number of actual breeding sites. These sites may later be used as breeding sites, and managers should consider these locations important for expanding the range of the species. Also, this species is secretive on the nest and can fledge young late in the season (e.g., 30 July, from Atlas data). Late-season adults should be watched carefully for late season nesting, even if none is suspected.

County. A 1940 survey found 12 nesting localities in northern New Jersey (Bull 1964), and a 1942 compilation listed seven localities in the previous 25 years for southern New Jersey (Miller 1942). Fables (1955) reported the species to be locally common, and Bull (1964) noted that the breeding population had increased.

Recent reports to RNJB indicated the species has some strongholds in the state, but suffered a decline in the 1970s and 1980s, especially in northern New Jersey. The recent declines are suspected to be the result of destruction and degradation of wetland habitats. Kearny Marsh was once an important area for the species, with censuses in 1983 reaching a peak of 150 birds in 30 family groups. Changes in the marsh caused the birds to abandon the area. (They are still active in Kearny East, albeit in smaller numbers.) Areas with a recent history of consistent use by Pied-billed Grebes during the breeding season include Hackensack Meadows, Pedricktown, Assunpink, Mannington Marsh, Whitesbog, and Cape May Point SP. Some sites have a history of successful breeding by Pied-billed Grebe, while others host lone birds summering in what appears to be good habitat.

Atlas surveys found Pied-billed Grebes broadly but thinly distributed throughout the state, with most of the occupied blocks found in the Highlands, Pine Barrens, Outer Coastal Plain, and Kittatinny Valley. The Kittatinny Valley had the highest concentration of breeding Pied-billed Grebes of all the provinces; although the Highlands only occupies 12% of the state, 18% of all occupied blocks statewide were in the Highlands. Similarly, the Kittatinny Valley also hosts a high concentration of occupied blocks. Although the province is small, it held over 16% of the statewide occupied blocks.

Fall: Early movements of Pied-billed Grebes begin by mid-August, reaching a peak from October to November at staging lakes in northwestern New Jersey. In passage they are found on freshwater ponds and brackish backwaters, rarely on the open ocean. **Maxima:** Coastal: 20, Point Pleasant, 23 November 1985; Inland: 122, Lake Musconetcong, 22 October 1995; 107, Lake Musconetcong, 3 November 1997.

continued on page 60

Physiographic Distribution **Pied-billed Grebe**	Number of blocks in province	Number of blocks species found breeding in province	Number of blocks species found in state	Percent of province species occupies	Percent of all records for this species found in province	Percent of state area in province
Kittatinny Mountains	19	1	55	5.3	1.8	2.2
Kittatinny Valley	45	9	55	20.0	16.4	5.3
Highlands	109	9	55	8.3	16.4	12.8
Piedmont	167	5	55	3.0	9.1	19.6
Inner Coastal Plain	128	7	55	5.5	12.7	15.0
Outer Coastal Plain	204	12	55	5.9	21.8	23.9
Pine Barrens	180	12	55	6.7	21.8	21.1

continued from page 59

Pied-billed Grebe

Winter: Pied-billed Grebes are less likely to be found inland and northward. CBC totals are variable, with lower counts when fresh water is frozen during the count period. Large increases in the wintering population have been noted since the early 1900s. Miller (1942) reported a birder might "spend a lifetime afield without a January record," and "the scarcity of reports would indicate that in many years no pied-bills winter at all." **Maximum:** 67, Kearny Marsh, 27 December 1983. **CBC Statewide Stats:** Average: 116; Maximum: 219 in 1976; Minimum: 51 in 1990. **CBC Maximum:** 37, Lower Hudson, 1982.

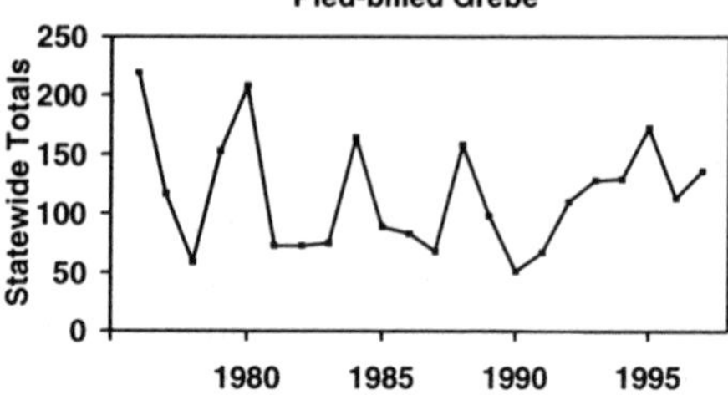

Spring: Pied-billed Grebes are not as conspicuous in spring migration as in fall migration. Peak numbers are reached from late March through mid-April, usually away from the shore. **Maxima:** Coastal: 25, Mannington Marsh, 20 March 1996; Inland: 23, Culvers Lake, 11 April 1977. ■

Horned Grebe

Podiceps auritus

Range: In North America nests from Alaska southeast to Minnesota, also on islands in the Gulf of St. Lawrence. Winters on both coasts.

NJ Status: Fairly common spring and fall migrant, common winter resident.

Fall: Horned Grebes are unexpected before mid-October. Peak flights occur from late October to early December, with coastal migration continuing into early winter. Although mainly a coastal migrant, they are uncommon inland where they may be found on larger lakes. **Maxima:** Coastal: 104, Avalon Sea Watch, 12 November 1997; 60, Avalon Sea Watch, 14 November 1996; Inland: 82, Round Valley Res., 20 October 1975. **ASW Seasonal Stats:** Average: 259; Maximum: 388 in 1997.

Avalon Sea Watch: Horned Grebe

Total: 400, 300, 200, 100, 0

1993, 1994, 1995, 1996, 1997

Winter: Horned Grebes are found mainly along the Atlantic coast in winter, on open ocean as well as

Horned Grebe

continued

protected bays and ponds. They are rare inland. There is considerable fluctuation in wintering numbers; some years the species is uncommon. Higher CBC totals have occurred in the past (e.g., 569, Long Branch CBC, 2 January 1956) suggesting a decline over the past few decades. **Maximum:** Inland: 16, Round Valley Res., 6 January 1990. **CBC Statewide Stats:** Average: 410; Maximum: 917 in 1979; Minimum: 93 in 1981. **CBC Maximum:** 350, Barnegat, 1979.

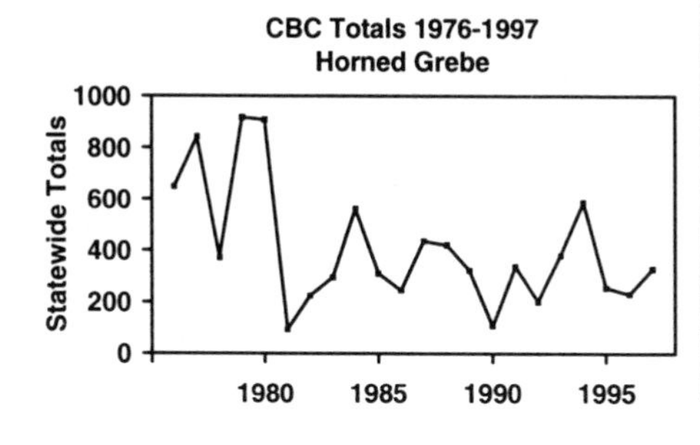

Spring: Peak numbers of Horned Grebes are reached from mid-March to mid-April. They are not expected after mid-May. **Maxima:** Coastal: 225, Pleasantville, 27 March 1977 (AB); Inland: 50, Culvers Lake, 6 April 1990. ■

Red-necked Grebe

Podiceps grisegena

Range: In North America breeds from Alaska southeast through Canada to eastern Ontario and Minnesota. Winters on both coasts.

NJ Status: Rare to scarce spring and fall migrant, rare to scarce winter resident.

Fall: Southbound Red-necked Grebes are most often seen from October through November, and may be found on fresh or salt water. They are encountered regularly, but in small numbers, at the Avalon Sea Watch. **Maximum:** 3, Avalon Sea Watch, 14 December 1995. **ASW Seasonal Stats:** Average: 10; Maximum: 15 in 1996.

Winter: Red-necked Grebes are rare to scarce along the coast, and rare inland. There is evidence of a decline during the 1900s. Stone (1937) found them "present at Cape May in small numbers throughout the winter months," while Sibley (1997) estimated about three records per year in Cape May County. Occasionally, large numbers of Red-necked Grebes can reach the New Jersey coast, possibly in response to freezing of the Great Lakes. During the invasion of February 1994 the coast was inundated by hundreds of Red-necked Grebes (e.g., 178 seen by one observer 21 February 1994 along the New Jersey coast). This was unprecedented in the experience of contemporary observers, but may have been matched by a similar invasion in early 1934. In contrast to the 1934 irruption, few dead or moribund birds were found in 1994. A few are usually found on CBCs. **Maxima:** Coastal: 35, Ocean Drive, 13 February 1994; Inland: 4, Phillipsburg, 10 February 1977.

continued on page 62

continued from page 61

Red-necked Grebe

CBC Statewide Stats: Average: 2; Maximum: 8 in 1993; Minimum: 0 in five years. **CBC Maxima:** 3, Tuckerton, 1980; 3, Lakehurst, 1993; 3, Northwestern Hunterdon, 1997.

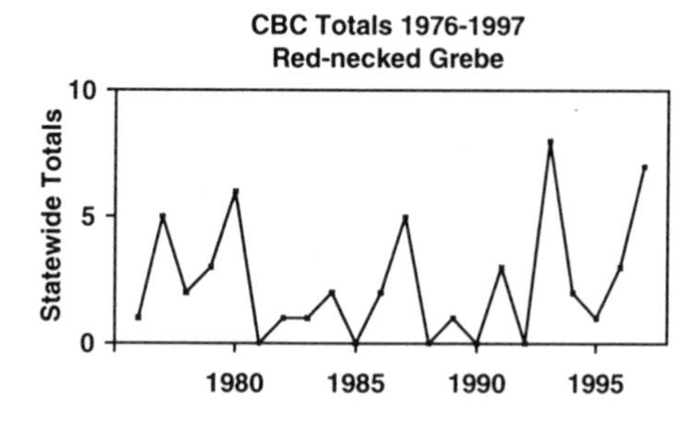

Spring: Most northbound Red-necked Grebes are seen from March through April, with fewer reports into May. They are more likely found on inland northern lakes than along the coast. Very rarely, easterly storms may down large numbers on inland lakes - e.g., 64+, Boonton Res. to Swartswood Lake, 5 April 1959 (Bull 1964). Birds lingering into summer are unusual; there are five summer records all following major winter incursions. **Maxima:** Coastal: 16, Belmar, 4 April 1994; Inland: 18, Culvers Lake, 16 April 1996. ■

Eared Grebe

Podiceps nigricollis

Range: In North America breeds from British Columbia east to Minnesota, south to northern Arizona, northern New Mexico and central Texas. Winters primarily along the west and Gulf coasts.

NJ Status: Very rare. NJBRC Review List.

Occurrence: The first New Jersey record of Eared Grebe occurred on 11 January 1948 at Shark River Inlet. Since that time, there have been about 55 additional reports, and 33 are accepted by the NJBRC. Birds have appeared most frequently between December and March, although the range of occurrence stretches from 1 September through 12 April. All records have been along the coast, with the exception of a report from Malaga Lake, 24 February 1990. It is not clear why Eared Grebes were unreported prior to 1948, but it may have more to do with an increase in observer access to identification information rather than a range expansion of the species. ■

Western Grebe

Aechmophorus occidentalis

Range: Breeds mainly from British Columbia southeast to western Minnesota, south to Colorado. Winters mainly on the West Coast.

NJ Status: Very rare. NJBRC Review List.

Occurrence: There have been 15 state reports of Western Grebes, and 13 have been accepted by the NJBRC (all in fall/winter). All but three of the reports occurred prior to the split of Western and Clark's Grebes. Reports prior to the split are presumed Westerns, but observers should take notes on and photograph any Western-type grebes, as Clark's could occur. The 13 accepted records are:

Beach Haven	*8 January 1939*	*Enyon 1939*
*Sea Bright**	*12 January 1952*	
*Stone Harbor**	*4 February 1954*	
*Barnegat Inlet**	*28 December 1958*	
*Shark River**	*31 December 1966*	
*Centennial Lake**	*3-5 December 1968*	
*Shark River**	*10 January-10 March 1970*	
Barnegat Inlet	*23 January 1971*	
Holgate	*30 December 1973*	
*Sea Girt**	*22 November 1978*	
Shark River	*29 October-9 November 1993*	*ph-RNJB 20:26*
Spring Lake	*30 December 1995*	
Long Beach Island	*1 February 1996*	*partially decomposed*

Black-browed Albatross

Thalassarche melanophris

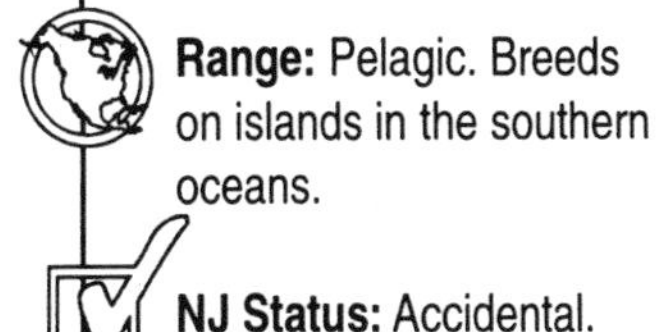

Range: Pelagic. Breeds on islands in the southern oceans.

NJ Status: Accidental. NJBRC Review List.

Occurrence: There have been five state reports of Black-browed Albatross, and one has been accepted by the NJBRC: Manasquan Inlet, 24 October 1989, seen from shore. There is no photograph of this species in North American waters. ■

Northern Fulmar

Fulmarus glacialis

Range: Pelagic. In eastern North America breeds in the high Arctic and in small colonies in Newfoundland and Labrador. Winters south to North Carolina.

NJ Status: Scarce to uncommon visitor far offshore, mainly in cold weather months. Accidental from shore.

Occurrence: There are records for this cold water species from September to June, although it is most regularly seen in cold weather months. Their abundance in New Jersey waters has never been evaluated with systematic observations. Most Northern Fulmar records come from pelagic trips. They are generally seen in small numbers, but occasionally are seen in larger aggregations. There are four records from shore: one exhausted near Ridgewood, early December 1891 (Stone 1937); one captured alive at Beach Haven, 30 January 1949 (Fables 1955); one seen at the Avalon Sea Watch, 22 September 1996; and one off Cape May Point, 12 February 1998. **Maxima:** 150, 60 miles east of Island Beach, 26 May 1979; 105, 40 miles off Brielle, 7 December 1996. ■

Northern Fulmar

Black-capped Petrel

Pterodroma hasitata

Range: Pelagic. Breeds in the West Indies. Disperses to the Caribbean and the Gulf Stream off North America.

NJ Status: Accidental. NJBRC Review List.

Occurrence: There have been five state reports of Black-capped Petrels, and two have been accepted by the NJBRC. The two accepted records are:

	86 mi. E of Barnegat Inlet	*16 September 1991*	*ph-RBPF*
8	*Cape May Point*	*13 July 1996*	*from shore following Hurricane Bertha*

Cory's Shearwater

Calonectris diomedea

Occurrence: Cory's Shearwaters are present offshore from May to early November. Although they are sometimes found relatively close to shore (i.e.,10-15 miles), they are most regularly recorded farther offshore, and numbers are fairly consistent from late May to late October. Cory's Shearwaters are only occasionally seen from shore, but they appeared in abnormally high numbers at the Avalon Sea Watch in July of 1995 and 1996 (e.g., 13, 16 July 1995; 31 total in July 1996; 22 total in July 1997). **Maxima:** 300+, unspecified offshore location, 16 October 1996; 300, pelagic trip to Hudson Canyon, 30 October 1989. ■

Range: Pelagic. Breeds on islands in the eastern Atlantic, and Mediterranean.

NJ Status: Uncommon to fairly common visitor far offshore, mainly from May through October. Very rare from shore.

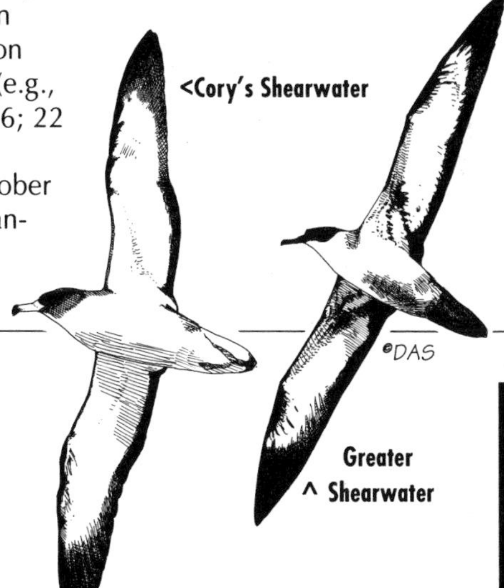

Greater Shearwater

Puffinus gravis

Range: Pelagic. Breeds in the south Atlantic, spending their winter (North American summer) in the north Atlantic.

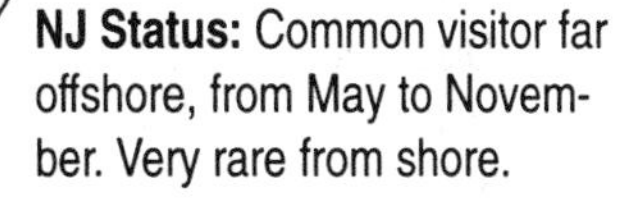

NJ Status: Common visitor far offshore, from May to November. Very rare from shore.

Occurrence: After migrating from nesting grounds in the southern Atlantic, Greater Shearwaters are present offshore from May to November, with the greatest concentrations occurring from late May through late June. Movement is generally toward the eastern Atlantic in summer, resulting in a smaller return flight in the fall, primarily from mid-September to early November (e.g., 150+, 16 October 1996, offshore). Although they are sometimes found relatively close to shore (i.e.,10-15 miles), they are most regularly noted well offshore. Greater Shearwaters are occasionally recorded from shore, but less frequently than the other two large shearwaters, Cory's and Sooty. **Maxima:** 2,500, pelagic trip to Hudson Canyon, 30 May 1981; 2,130, 55 miles E of Barnegat Inlet, 30 May 1987. ■

Buller's Shearwater

Puffinus bulleri

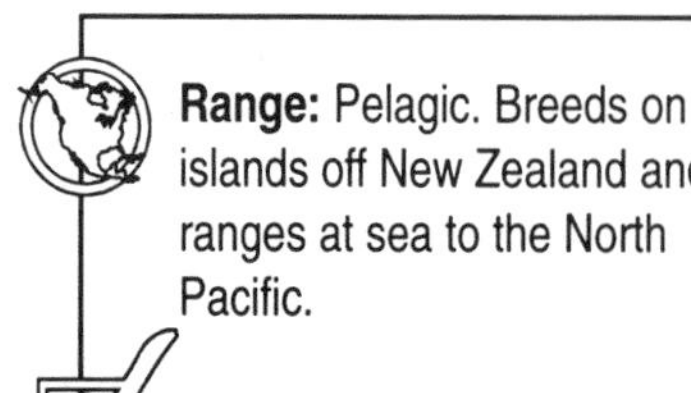

Range: Pelagic. Breeds on islands off New Zealand and ranges at sea to the North Pacific.

NJ Status: Accidental. NJBRC Review List.

Occurrence: There has been only one report and one accepted record of Buller's Shearwater in New Jersey: 31 miles E of Barnegat Inlet, 28 October 1984 (ph-RNJB 11:18). This is the only documented record for this species from the Atlantic Ocean. ■

Sooty Shearwater

Puffinus griseus

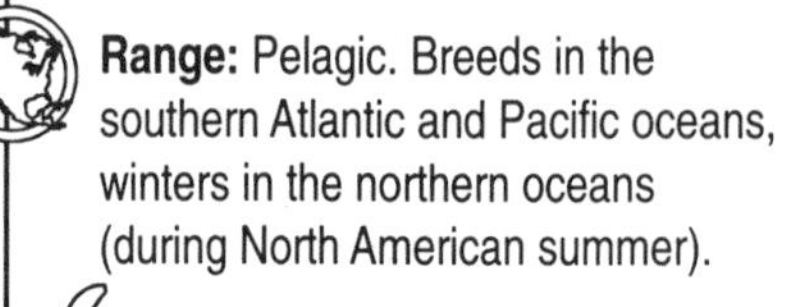

Range: Pelagic. Breeds in the southern Atlantic and Pacific oceans, winters in the northern oceans (during North American summer).

NJ Status: Common spring visitor far offshore, rare at other seasons. Rare from shore.

Occurrence: Sooty Shearwaters, migrating from their southern Atlantic breeding grounds, reach the New Jersey coast in May, and numbers peak in late May and early June. Numbers diminish through the summer as the population shifts north and east to the eastern Atlantic for a return flight south. Harrison (1983) noted that nonbreeders occasionally remain north of the equator, which would account for two seen off Shark River Inlet on 2 December 1986 and one 75 miles off Cape May on 12 February 1990. Although primarily a pelagic species, Sooty is the most likely shearwater to be seen from shore (e.g., 30, Stone Harbor, 28 May 1995; 21, Cape May Point, 20 May 1992). **Maxima:** 2,500, seven miles E of Corson's Inlet, 27 May 1978; 1,023, 55 miles E of Barnegat Inlet, 30 May 1987. ■

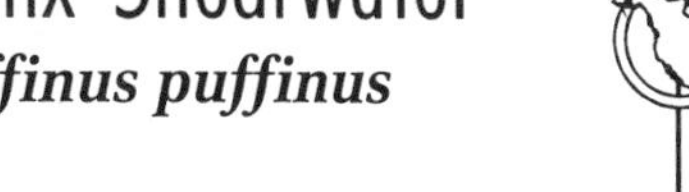

Manx Shearwater

Puffinus puffinus

Range: Pelagic. Breeds primarily in the northeastern Atlantic Ocean. Recently found nesting in North America in Massachusetts (1973) and Newfoundland (1976). Winters off eastern South America.

NJ Status: Scarce to uncommon visitor far offshore, mainly in spring and fall. Accidental from shore.

Occurrence: The first Manx Shearwater in New Jersey was recorded on 31 May 1975 at Hudson Canyon, and there are now records for all months except January and February. The majority of Manx Shearwater sightings are of individual birds, with most occurring during May and again in October to early December. Sightings have increased in recent years, but it is unclear whether this is due to an increase in coverage, or to the recently established presence of a North American breeding populations. Manx Shearwaters are the least likely shearwaters to be seen from shore. **Maxima:** 40-60, 45 mi. E of Barnegat Inlet, 28 October 1984; 8, pelagic trip to Hudson Canyon, 25 September 1987. ■

Audubon's Shearwater

Puffinus lherminieri

Range: Pelagic. Breeds in the Caribbean and western Atlantic Ocean. After breeding disperses at sea from Florida regularly north to New York.

NJ Status: Very rare summer and fall visitor.

Occurrence: There are about 51 reports of Audubon's Shearwaters, nearly all from July through September. Regular offshore visits during the 1990s indicated that they are probably annual in late summer, and occur in fair numbers. Most records come from offshore. Several have been found dead on beaches, including the first state record from Cape May, 2 August 1926 (spec. ANSP; Stone and Palmer 1926). Many reports of Audubon's Shearwaters have been from within 40 miles of shore, although there have been 11 reports of birds 75 or more miles offshore, and the largest concentrations have been reported more than 100 miles from shore. **Maximum:** 225, 100 mi. SE of Barnegat Inlet, 19 September 1976, (Leck 1984). ■

Wilson's Storm-Petrel

Oceanites oceanicus

Occurrence: Northbound Wilson's Storm-Petrels reach the New Jersey coastline by May. They are numerous and widely distributed off the coast in spring and summer and are more likely to be encountered, both inshore and offshore, than any other pelagic species. Wilson's are also the storm-petrels most often seen from shore. They are seen from shore around Cape May Point, and are regularly recorded from the Cape May-Lewes Ferry. They begin to depart the north Atlantic in August and typically become less common by summer's end, although a report of 2,000, 19 September 1987, on a pelagic trip to Hudson Canyon is higher than many spring counts. There are no records from December to March. **Maxima:** 50,000-75,000, pelagic trip to Hudson Canyon, 28 May 1983; 4,000, pelagic trip to Hudson Canyon, 30 May 1981. **Maximum from shore:** 200, Cape May Point, 11 July 1989. ■

Range: Pelagic. Breeds on the Antarctic coastline and on some south Atlantic islands, spending the winter in northern oceans (during North American summer).

NJ Status: Common offshore visitor, spring through fall. Rare to scarce from shore.

White-faced Storm-Petrel

Pelagodroma marina

Range: Pelagic. In the Atlantic breeds on islands off western Africa. Disperses mainly to sea after breeding.

NJ Status: Accidental. NJBRC Review List.

Occurrence: There have been eight state reports of White-faced Storm-Petrels, and two have been accepted by the NJBRC. The two accepted records are:

22.5 mi. SE of Cape May	*26 August 1972*
90 mi. ESE of Barnegat Inlet	*19 September 1979*

The second record was actually in New Jersey waters, although it was also accepted for New York State. ■

Leach's Storm-Petrel

Oceanodroma leucorhoa

Range: Pelagic. In eastern North America breeds on offshore islands from southeastern Labrador to Massachusetts, winters primarily in tropical oceans.

NJ Status: Rare to scarce spring visitor far offshore. Accidental from shore.

Occurrence: Most records of this deep-water species are from May and early June from pelagic trips to Hudson Canyon. Leck (1984) indicated an occurrence of Leach's Storm-Petrels off New Jersey from May to October; however, the return flight in fall is poorly documented. Off Massachusetts, this flight takes place from late September to November (Veit and Petersen 1993), and Bull (1964) noted several specimens found dead onshore in the New York area from September, October, and November. The only recent fall records in New Jersey are of two on a pelagic trip to Hudson Canyon, 28 August 1995: one, Avalon, 25 September 1992, (Sibley 1997): and one on a pelagic trip to Hudson Canyon, 3 December 1994. Stone (1937) considered Leach's Storm-Petrels to be more common than Wilson's Storm-Petrels, an unsubstantiated reversal of current status (Sibley 1997). **Maxima:** 20, pelagic trip to Hudson Canyon, 27 May 1995; 10, pelagic trip to Hudson Canyon, 30 May 1992. ■

Band-rumped Storm-Petrel

Oceanodroma castro

Range: Pelagic. In the Atlantic breeds on islands off western Africa. Disperses at sea to the southern coast of North America.

NJ Status: Accidental. NJBRC Review List.

Occurrence: There have been seven state reports of Band-rumped Storm-Petrels, and one has been accepted by the NJBRC: 11, Cape May Point, 13 July 1996 (and one seen the following day), seen from shore following Hurricane Bertha. ■

White-tailed Tropicbird

Phaethon lepturus

Range: Pelagic. In the Atlantic and Caribbean, breeds on islands throughout the West Indies. Disperses at sea throughout the tropical waters of the western Atlantic.

NJ Status: Accidental. NJBRC Review List.

Occurrence: There have been two state reports of White-tailed Tropicbirds, and one has been accepted by the NJBRC: Barnegat Inlet, 23 November 1985, an adult. Observers should be aware that confusion with juvenile Royal Tern is possible. ■

Red-billed Tropicbird

Phaethon aethereus

Occurrence: There has been only one report and one accepted record of Red-billed Tropicbird in New Jersey: Seaside Heights, 23 May 1983 (ph-RNJB 9:45). The bird was found alive, but oiled, and was photographed while at a rehabilitation center in Surf City. ■

Range: Pelagic. Breeds on islands in the Caribbean, and in the eastern and southern Atlantic. Disperses at sea after breeding to the western Atlantic.

NJ Status: Accidental. NJBRC Review List.

Brown Booby

Sula leucogaster

Range: Breeds on islands in the Caribbean and the tropical Atlantic. Disperses at sea after breeding.

NJ Status: Accidental. NJBRC Review List.

Occurrence: There have been eight state reports of Brown Boobies, and five have been accepted by the NJBRC (three in fall, one in spring, one in winter). Note that only one of the reports followed a hurricane. The five accepted records are:

2	*Island Beach*	*22 October 1979*	
	Cape May Point	*26 May 1980*	*Sibley 1997*
	Cape May Point	*22-23 September 1989*	*ph-RBPF, after Hurricane Hugo*
	Sandy Hook	*26 September 1990*	
	Corson's Inlet	*16 December 1990*	

Northern Gannet

Morus bassanus

Range: In the western North Atlantic breeds from Newfoundland to islands in the Gulf of St. Lawrence. Winters off the Atlantic and Gulf Coasts.

NJ Status: Common spring and fall migrant, fairly common winter resident.

Fall: Northern Gannets are found along the coast and offshore, with only a few birds reaching New Jersey before mid-September. The peak flights, often spectacular, take place from early November to early December. Numbers during all seasons have increased greatly during the 20th century. Stone (1937) knew of no New Jersey daily maximum in excess of 200. The only known inland record is of an immature bird found in a field near Vincentown, late October 1985. **Maxima:** 8,208, Avalon, 14 November 1988; 6,480, Avalon, 6 December 1990. **ASW Single-Day Maximum:** 5,612 on 6 November 1996. **ASW Seasonal Stats:** Average: 48,907; Maximum: 63,498 in 1994.

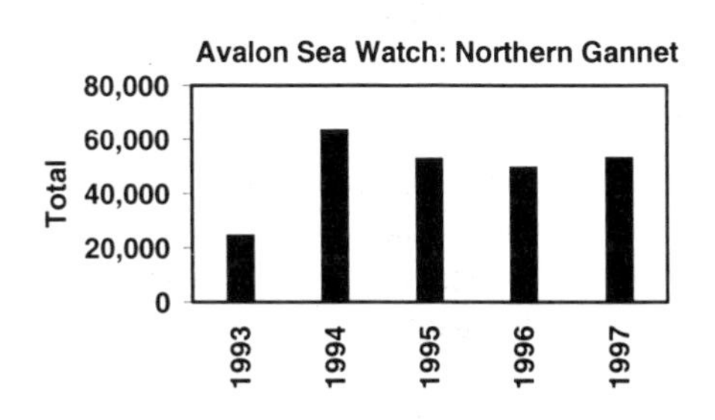

Winter: Numbers of Northern Gannets along the coast and offshore can vary markedly, presumably depending on wind direction and baitfish abundance. They are often commonly seen from shore. CBC numbers are highly variable. **Maximum:** 500, Cape May, 24 January 1976. **CBC Statewide Stats:** Average: 523; Maximum: 1,973 in 1985; Minimum: 17 in 1977. **CBC Maximum:** 1,329, Barnegat, 1985.

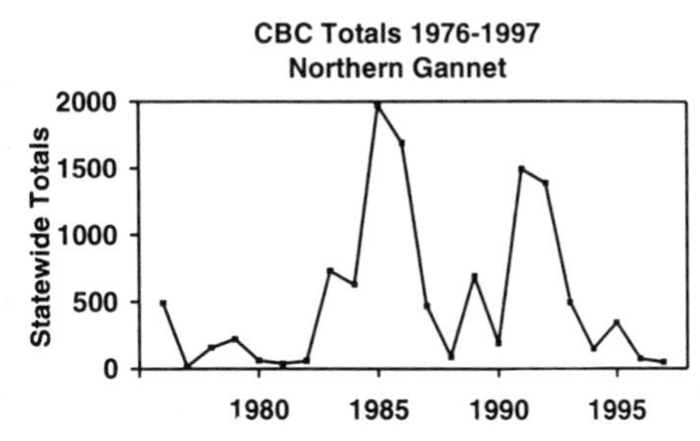

Spring: Peak flights of Northern Gannets occur from late February through early April and again from late April to mid-May; the latter flight is largely of immature birds. Stragglers, occasionally persist through July. Fewer birds are noted migrating north in spring than south in fall. Gannets have been recorded in Delaware Bay as far northern as Salem County. **Maxima:** 2,300, 5 to 15 miles off Cape May, 28 February 1987 (Sibley 1997); 2,000, off South Cape May Meadows, 4 April 1995. ■

American White Pelican

Pelecanus erythrorhynchos

Range: Breeds in scattered colonies across western Canada and the United States east to Minnesota. Winters on the Pacific and Gulf Coasts from the southern United States to Central America.

NJ Status: Very rare visitor, mainly in spring and fall.

Occurrence: More than 60 observations of American White Pelicans have been reported in New Jersey, spanning 11 months. Most records, however, have been in spring or fall, and most have been coastal. It is likely that a number of reports represent multiple sightings of the same highly mobile and obvious individuals. Although a few poorly documented 19th century reports exist, the first modern record was at Beverly, 25 September 1943 (Fables 1955). Sightings have increased markedly since the mid-1970s, and more than 80% of our reports have occurred since then. This situation is probably a reflection of the dramatic eastward breeding range expansion in the eastern Great Plains (Hayes 1984). From 1975 through 1997, the species was seen in all but seven years. **Maximum:** 3, Cape May Point, 7 December 1993. ■

Brown Pelican

Pelecanus occidentalis

Range: In the eastern United States, mainly resident from North Carolina south to Florida and along the Gulf coast to Texas.

NJ Status: Uncommon to fairly common visitor, mainly from May through October.

Occurrence: Brown Pelicans usually arrive in early May and are present throughout October. Numbers vary from year to year, and most birds are seen flying in groups offshore or roosting at concentration points such as Barnegat Bay and Hereford Inlet. Brown Pelicans were recorded only 11 times prior to 1980, but since then they have appeared annually, in variable numbers, peaking in 1992. In May of 1992 they built up to 18 nests on a dredge spoil island in Barnegat Bay. Although no eggs were laid, it is known that pelicans will occupy a new colony for a year or two before nesting successfully (Burger et al. 1993). No nesting attempts were noted during the Atlas survey period, and the number of pelicans around Barnegat Bay has declined. There are two winter records: Lily Lake in Cape May Point, 26-29 January 1977 (presumed to be the same individual found dead, 19 March 1977, North Cape May); Cape May, 12 February 1996. **Maxima:** 340, Barnegat Bay, mid-July 1992; 145-160, Cape May Point, 25 September 1997. ■

Double-crested Cormorant

Phalacrocorax auritus

Range: In eastern North America breeds from southern Manitoba east to Nova Scotia, and south to the Gulf Coast. Winters from New York south to Florida and the Gulf Coast, south to Central America and the West Indies.

NJ Status: Scarce and local summer resident, common spring and fall migrant, scarce to uncommon winter resident.

Breeding

Habitat: Nests in colonies on cliff ledges, on the ground on islands, or in trees or on other structures near or over water.

Double-crested Cormorants were nearly extirpated from the United States by the early 19th century, but the population began to recover in the early 20th century (Hatch 1982). In New Jersey, summering patterns of Double-crested Cormorants throughout the 1970s and 1980s indicated an increasing population. This resulted in continued suspicion that the species was breeding locally and

continued on page 74

continued from page 73

Double-crested Cormorant

Map Interpretation: There was uneven reporting of Double-crested Cormorants among observers (especially in the Possible category), and the mapped range indicates a fraction of the total number of blocks in which the species was seen. Locations scored as Possible indicated appropriate summering habitat and should not be interpreted as potential breeding locations. Only locations scored as Confirmed should be considered as breeding sites.

Possible
Probable
Confirmed

the colonies were overlooked. However, they were not recorded breeding in New Jersey until 1987, when colonies were found in lower Newark Bay (Parsons et al. 1991).

During the Atlas survey, Double-crested Cormorants were Confirmed at five locations. The colonies are in four different physiographic regions, ranging from an inland site in Bergen County to a colony on Delaware Bay in Cumberland County. In each case, they were nest-building on man-made structures.

Statewide Summary	
Status	# of Blocks
Possible	24
Probable	0
Confirmed	5
Total	29

Fall: The main portion of the Double-crested Cormorant migration begins in late August and continues through November, with the peak movement in early to mid-October. They are common along the coast,

Physiographic Distribution: Double-crested Cormorant	Number of blocks in province	Number of blocks species found breeding in province	Number of blocks species found in state	Percent of province species occupies	Percent of all records for this species found in province	Percent of state area in province
Highlands	109	9	29	8.3	31.0	12.8
Piedmont	167	4	29	2.4	13.8	19.6
Inner Coastal Plain	128	4	29	3.1	13.8	15.0
Outer Coastal Plain	204	9	29	4.4	31.0	23.9
Pine Barrens	180	3	29	1.7	10.3	21.1

Double-crested Cormorant

continued

and frequently occur inland as well. At the Avalon Sea Watch, the flight line can range from along back bays to well offshore. **Maxima:** 21,856, Avalon Sea Watch, 17 October 1997; 20,699, Avalon Sea Watch, 11 October 1997. **ASW Seasonal Stats:** Average: 189,768; Maximum: 240,670 in 1996.

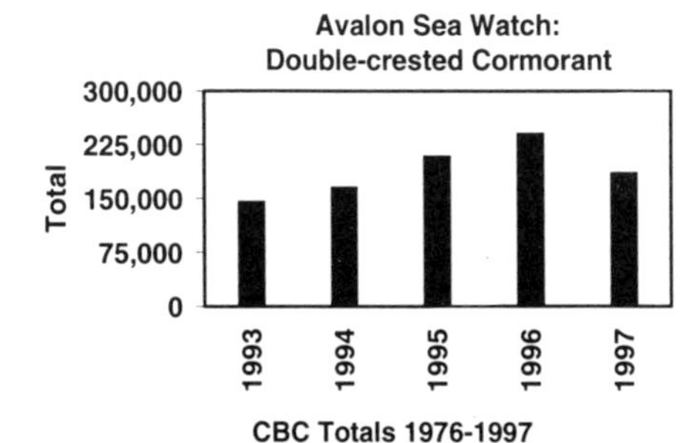

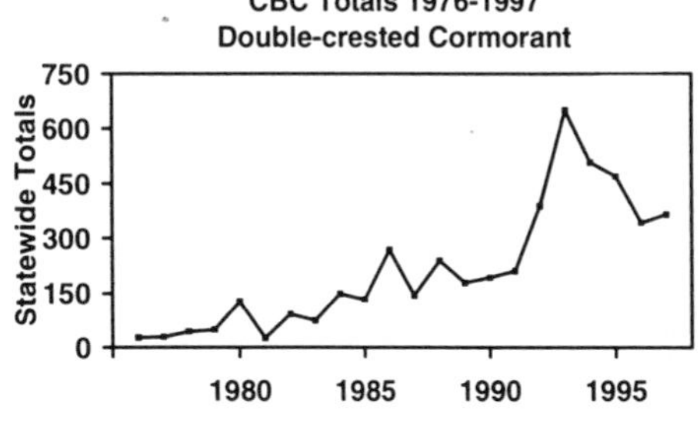

Winter: Double-crested Cormorant counts on CBCs have increased since the early 1980s. Numbers generally diminish throughout January and February. In some years, they can become quite scarce, particularly during harsh winters. **CBC Statewide Stats:** Average: 214; Maximum: 650 in 1993; Minimum: 26 in 1981. **CBC Maximum:** 218, Sandy Hook, 1992.

Spring: The northward migration of Double-crested Cormorants is noticeable by late March or early April, peaking in late April or early May. The spring flight is predominately over land, with many birds crossing from Delaware and dispersing northward up the Cape May Peninsula. Some nonbreeding birds summer in bays and inlets along the coast, and can form fairly large roosting groups. **Maxima:** 3,500, Avalon, 17 April 1981; 3,250, Cape May Point, 18 April 1996. ■

Great Cormorant

Phalacrocorax carbo

Range: In North America breeds around the Gulf of St. Lawrence to Newfoundland, Nova Scotia, and Maine. Winters from the breeding range south to North Carolina.

NJ Status: Scarce spring and uncommon fall migrant, fairly common winter resident.

Fall: Only small numbers of Great Cormorants winter south of New Jersey. However, some southbound migrants are noted by mid-September with movements peaking from late October through early November. Most are noted along the coast. The first inland occurrence in New Jersey was of an immature

continued on page 76

continued from page 75

Great Cormorant

bird at Assunpink WMA, 12 October 1976 (Wander and Brady 1977). **ASW Single-Day Maximum:** 11 on 9 November 1993. **ASW Seasonal Stats:** Average: 87; Maximum: 145 in 1993.

Avalon Sea Watch: Great Cormorant

Total: 150, 100, 50, 0

1993, 1994, 1995, 1996, 1997

Winter: Great Cormorants have increased as winter residents since the mid-1970s. Their wintering population along the New Jersey coast centers around Sandy Hook, with numbers diminishing southward. This is well illustrated by CBC totals, which show maxima on the Sandy Hook count of 227 in 1994 and 214 in 1990, compared to Cape May's maxima of 34 in 1995 and 21 in 1994. The increase in their numbers reflect the overall increase of Great Cormorants in North America (Kaufman 1996). **Maximum:** 104, Long Branch, 15 January 1994. **CBC Statewide Stats:** Average: 184; Maximum: 438 in 1995; Minimum: 17 in 1977. **CBC Maximum:** 227, Sandy Hook, 1995.

CBC Totals 1976-1997
Great Cormorant

Statewide Totals: 500, 400, 300, 200, 100, 0

1980, 1985, 1990, 1995

Spring: Most Great Cormorants depart the state by mid-April, although a few immature birds have summered. **Maximum:** 100+, Sandy Hook, 22 March 1998. ■

Anhinga

Anhinga anhinga

Range: In North America, breeds from North Carolina south to Florida, west to Oklahoma and Texas. Winters from South Carolina southward.

NJ Status: Accidental. NJBRC Review List.

Occurrence: There have been 35 state reports of Anhingas, and eight have been accepted by the NJBRC (five in spring, one in fall, one in winter, and one in summer). Almost all reports are of single birds, and all but two have occurred since 1984 (18 since 1990). Most reports come between May and September.

Anhinga
continued

Anhingas have been reported nearly annually since 1982. Many of those reported are probably correct, but Anhinga reports are frequently coupled with insufficient documentation for addition to the state list. It is possible that the species is over-reported owing to confusion with cormorants. The eight accepted records are:

	*Cape May Point**	*25 September 1971*	
	Cape May Island	*4 May-1 June 1984*	*ph-RBPF*
	Whiting	*16 January 1989*	*ph-RBPF, found dead*
2	*Medford*	*1 May 1992*	
	Allaire SP	*7 May 1994*	
	West Paterson	*24 April 1996*	
	Cape May	*27 June 1996*	
	Sandy Hook	*26 April 1997*	

Frigatebird species

Range: Pelagic. Breeds on islands in the Caribbean and tropical Atlantic. After breeding, disperses at sea throughout the Gulf of Mexico, Caribbean and western Atlantic.

NJ Status: Accidental. NJBRC Review List.

Occurrence: There have been 14 state reports of frigatebirds, and seven have been accepted by the NJBRC (three in summer, three in fall, one in spring). None of these birds were positively identified as *Fregata magnificens*, but are accepted as "frigatebird (sp.)." It is presumed these reports refer to *magnificens*, but both Great and Lesser Frigatebirds have occurred in the continental United States, so caution needs to be exercised. The seven accepted records are:

Cape May#	*3 August 1926*	*after a hurricane*
Brigantine	*15 September 1935*	*Tatum 1936*
Avalon	*8 June 1949*	
*Shark River**	*20-21 June 1969*	
Belmar	*4 November 1976*	
Northvale	*7 April 1982*	
Cape May Point	*8 October 1992*	

Range: In eastern North America breeds from Manitoba to Newfoundland, south to Oklahoma and North Carolina. Winters along the coast from Massachusetts south to Central America and the West Indies.

NJ Status: Scarce and local summer resident, scarce spring and fall migrant, scarce winter resident. Threatened Species in New Jersey (breeding only).

American Bittern

Botaurus lentiginosus

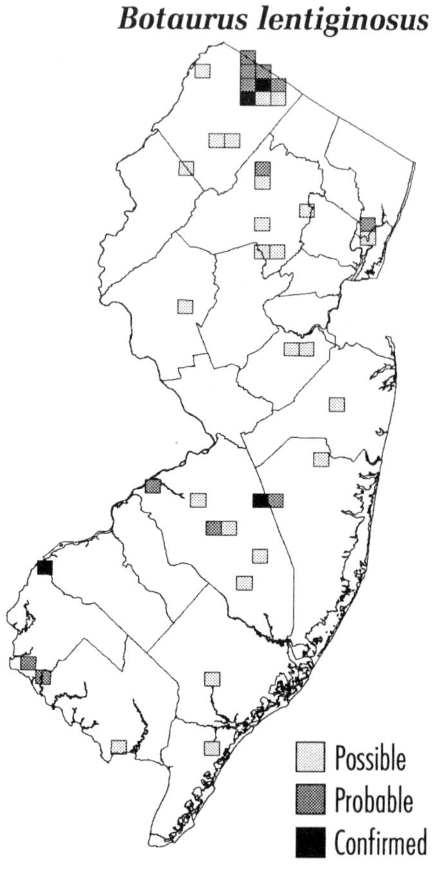

Statewide Summary	
Status	# of Blocks
Possible	24
Probable	12
Confirmed	4
Total	40

Breeding:

Habitat: Nests on the ground in tall, dense vegetation at the edges of fresh or brackish marshes.

Map Interpretation: This species exhibits some of the traits which lead observers to underestimate their distribution; American Bitterns are solitary, secretive, and best detected by nocturnal vocalizations. The current breeding range of American Bittern in New Jersey should include all blocks occupied during safe dates - not just those where the species was Confirmed.

American Bitterns are vanishing breeders from the Lower 48 States, and may have been reduced to relict populations through loss of breeding habitat (Gibbs et al.1992). The pattern of the decline of this species in New Jersey was not well documented, as they remained locally common within appropriate habitat until the late 1940s. Stone (1937) noted that American Bitterns bred on Cape May Island and several other locations in Cape May County, but Atlas research found the species present in only one location in the county. Fables (1955) noted that the species was a disappearing breeder in New Jersey due to habitat degradation, but even as late as 1964, Bull did not express concern over the status of the species.

Physiographic Distribution American Bittern	Number of blocks in province	Number of blocks species found breeding in province	Number of blocks species found in state	Percent of province species occupies	Percent of all records for this species found in province	Percent of state area in province
Kittatinny Mountains	19	1	40	5.3	2.5	2.2
Kittatinny Valley	45	8	40	17.8	20.0	5.3
Highlands	109	7	40	6.4	17.5	12.8
Piedmont	167	6	40	3.6	15.0	19.6
Inner Coastal Plain	128	5	40	3.9	12.5	15.0
Outer Coastal Plain	204	5	40	2.5	12.5	23.9
Pine Barrens	180	8	40	4.4	20.0	21.1

One record indicating the historic density of this species, from an Urner Club survey, found 13 nests in Troy Meadows in June 1947 (Bull 1964). This survey is in stark contrast to a 1984 NJAS survey of the same area that found only one breeding pair (Kane 1985). During five years of Atlas surveys, American Bitterns were Confirmed on only four occasions, and scored as Probable breeders in only 12 other blocks. Patterns of summer occurrence, as reported to RNJB since 1976, indicated few consistently occupied locations for the species (Whitesbog, Celery Farm, and more recently Wallkill NWR are exceptions).

Atlas volunteers found American Bitterns in all physiographic provinces in New Jersey. Their distribution was skewed to the northern part of the state, where 55% of the occupied blocks were located. This species' dependence on the Kittatinny Valley is significant - 20% of the occupied blocks were found in an area that occupies only 5% of the state. In the other physiographic regions American Bitterns occupied less than 7% of the blocks.

Conservation Note: Conservation of the species is dependent upon preservation of freshwater wetlands. Without appropriate measures, it is conceivable the species may be extirpated over the next 25 years.

Fall: American Bitterns are generally scarce at all seasons, becoming somewhat more numerous in fall, particularly along the coast. Nonbreeders or wanderers can be seen as early as late July, and fall migration continues into November, peaking in early October. Bitterns are nocturnal migrants, spending their days secreted in the dense vegetation of a marsh, and usually encountered only as lone individuals. In fall, at coastal concentration points such as Cape May, they can occasionally be seen in small numbers at dusk as they leave a marsh to begin their nocturnal migration. **Maxima:** 23, Cape May Point, 17 October 1997 (heard); 15, Cape May Point, 4 October 1987.

Winter: CBC totals of American Bitterns declined from 1976 to 1997, although the peak year for combined

continued on page 80

continued from page 79

American Bittern

New Jersey counts was in 1996. Like most water birds, numbers in mid-winter are affected by the amount of open water. **CBC Statewide Stats:** Average: 13; Maximum: 37 in 1996; Minimum: 3 in 1995. **CBC Maximum:** 16, Cape May, 1996.

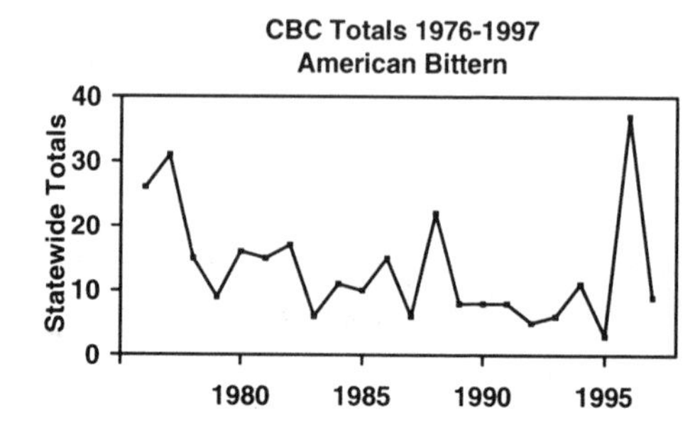

Spring: The return flight of American Bitterns is barely noticeable, and not well documented, but probably peaks in early April. The earliest record for calling American Bittern during the Atlas surveys was 15 May. ■

Least Bittern

Ixobrychus exilis

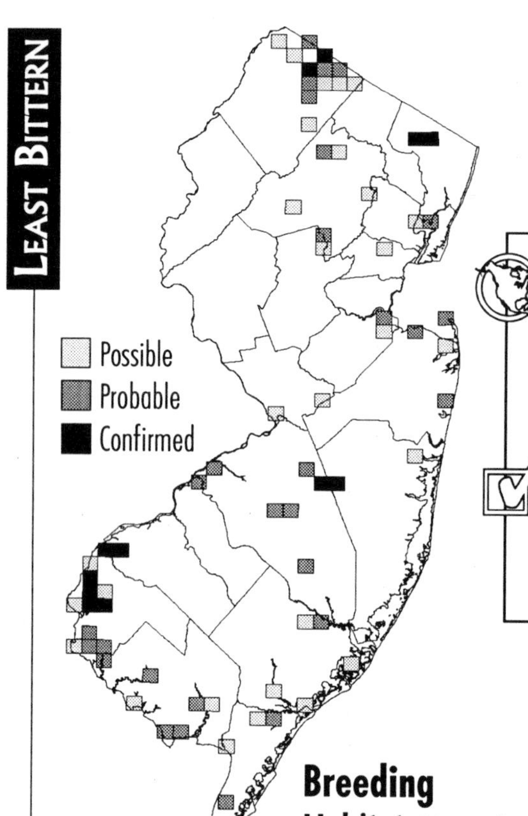

Range: In eastern North America breeds from North Dakota east to New Brunswick, south to Texas and Florida. Winters mainly from Texas and Florida south to Central America and the West Indies.

NJ Status: Uncommon and local summer resident, scarce spring and fall migrant, very rare winter resident.

Breeding

Habitat: Most often found in freshwater marshes, occasionally brackish, with tall, dense vegetation.

Statewide Summary	
Status	# of Blocks
Possible	29
Probable	29
Confirmed	13
Total	71

Least Bittern
continued

Map Interpretation: Least Bitterns are secretive and nest in fairly inaccessible areas. They are difficult birds to see and consequently had a low Confirmation rate. The active breeding range for this species should include all Possible, Probable, and Confirmed locations.

Physiographic Distribution **Least Bittern**	Number of blocks in province	Number of blocks species found breeding in province	Number of blocks species found in state	Percent of province species occupies	Percent of all records for this species found in province	Percent of state area in province
Kittatinny Mountains	19	1	71	5.3	1.4	2.2
Kittatinny Valley	45	7	71	15.6	9.9	5.3
Highlands	109	8	71	7.3	11.3	12.8
Piedmont	167	8	71	4.8	11.3	19.6
Inner Coastal Plain	128	16	71	12.5	22.5	15.0
Outer Coastal Plain	204	19	71	9.3	26.8	23.9
Pine Barrens	180	12	71	6.7	16.9	21.1

The historic status and abundance of Least Bitterns as breeding birds in New Jersey is difficult to assess, although it is likely the species has declined following the loss of freshwater marshes used for breeding. Both Fables (1955) and Leck (1984) indicated Least Bitterns were disappearing from areas of the state as breeding habitat was destroyed. Numbers were also low in remaining wetlands (Kane 1985, Kane et al. 1985). Stone (1937) reported breeding Least Bitterns were less common than American Bitterns in Cape May County, a trend clearly reversed by the 1990s.

Reports to RNJB since 1975 indicated some locations are consistently occupied (e.g., Whitesbog, Salem Marsh, Kearny Marsh, South Cape May Meadows, Cape May Point SP, Wallkill NWR, and Celery Farm), and some breeding locations are noted as having fairly high densities of birds in summer (7 at Kearny Marsh in 1985; 35 at Kearny Marsh in June 1986).

Atlas data indicated Least Bitterns are broadly distributed but local. As with most other freshwater wetland specialists, the Kittatinny Valley is an important province for this species. They are also one of the few species to have a large portion of their statewide population in the Inner Coastal Plain, notably in the marshes of Salem County

Fall: Least Bitterns are infrequently encountered in migration. They are nocturnal migrants and spend their days in dense marsh, both characteristics that make them difficult to detect. In fall, they probably migrate in late August and September; however, it is difficult to
continued on page 82

continued from page 81

Least Bittern

distinguish migrants from local breeding birds. Veit and Petersen (1993) indicated that the Massachusetts birds generally depart in mid-August.

Winter: In some years, Least Bitterns attempt to winter, particularly in the southern part of the state. In 1993, they were heard throughout the winter at Cape May Point until early March when, after a snow storm, three were found dead on 2 March. Other recent winter records include: 1, at Brigantine NWR on 20 February 1994, and several individuals at Cape May on 26 March 1977 (Sibley 1997) and 2 March 1990. Additionally, they were recorded on five CBCs from 1976 to 1997, with a maximum of seven in 1994 on the Cape May count.

Spring: The northward migration of Least Bitterns is barely noticeable and not well documented, but local breeding birds generally arrive in mid-May. ■

Great Blue Heron

Ardea herodias

Range: In eastern North America breeds from southern Manitoba to Nova Scotia, south to Texas and Florida. Winters from Nebraska, and Massachusetts south to Central America.

NJ Status: Uncommon and local summer resident, fairly common spring and common fall migrant, uncommon to fairly common winter resident. Threatened Species in New Jersey (breeding only).

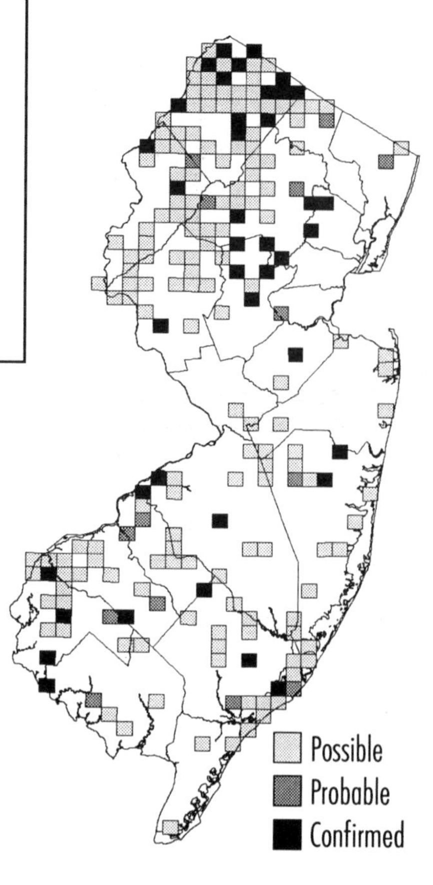

Statewide Summary	
Status	# of Blocks
Possible	154
Probable	14
Confirmed	40
Total	208

Breeding

Habitat: Colonial. Nests in trees, usually over fresh water but may use brackish wetlands.

Great Blue Heron

continued

Details of this species' historic breeding range are scant, but it likely reached into all sections of New Jersey. By the turn of the 1900s, Great Blue Heron numbers were reduced by egg collectors and gunners (Stone 1908). Stone (1908) gave a detailed account of colonies in Salem County, reported there were no colonies in Cape May County or northern New Jersey, and stated there were several colonies along the Atlantic barrier islands that had been abandoned. Great Blue Herons returned to northern New Jersey as a breeding bird in 1940 (Cruickshank 1942), and Bull (1964) reported the species to be increasing, with colonies at Sandy Hook, and at Lafayette in Sussex County. The NJDEP declared the breeding population of Great Blue Heron an Endangered Species in 1975.

The ENSP has conducted several aerial surveys to monitor New Jersey's Great Blue Heron nesting colonies. In 1982 there were five active colonies in New Jersey (Galli 1982). The number of colonies grew, and by 1997 Atlas data indicated Great Blue Herons were Confirmed breeding in 40 blocks. One stronghold for the species is within the bounds of glacial Lake Passaic. Interestingly, although Great Blue Herons were not known to have active colonies in northern New Jersey in the early 1900s, the current distribution of Great Blue Heron is weighted to northern New Jersey (63% of the occupied blocks are located from the Piedmont northward, an area comprising only

continued on page 84

Map Interpretation: Great Blue Herons are difficult to detect at breeding locations due to their relative scarcity, the inaccessibility of the colonies, and the cryptic coloration of the adults. This is in stark contrast to the high visibility of the birds away from the nest. Great Blue Herons were frequently seen away from their nesting sights during the breeding season and can forage up to 30km from the nest site (Butler 1992). This resulted in a high number of Possible sightings, sightings that do not reflect breeding birds on breeding territory. Their true breeding range is represented by the range of Confirmed sightings.

Physiographic Distribution

Great Blue Heron	Number of blocks in province	Number of blocks species found breeding in province	Number of blocks species found in state	Percent of province species occupies	Percent of all records for this species found in province	Percent of state area in province
Kittatinny Mountains	19	15	208	78.9	7.2	2.2
Kittatinny Valley	45	23	208	51.1	11.1	5.3
Highlands	109	52	208	47.7	25.0	12.8
Piedmont	167	22	208	13.2	10.6	19.6
Inner Coastal Plain	128	28	208	21.9	13.5	15.0
Outer Coastal Plain	204	36	208	17.6	17.3	23.9
Pine Barrens	180	32	208	17.8	15.4	21.1

continued from page 83

Great Blue Heron

39% of the state). Although northern New Jersey has a higher concentration of colonies, the species continues to expand into southern New Jersey.

Conservation Note: Conservation of Great Blue Heron breeding sites is important, but conservation of the supporting foraging areas is also needed. The Possible and Probable sightings are important for understanding the size of the area needed for the species during the breeding season. Current conservation should include protection of a wide buffer (>200m) around nest sites during nest initiation (Butler 1992), and continued conservation of freshwater wetlands.

Fall: Migrant or dispersing Great Blue Herons can be seen as early as mid-July, but the bulk of the migration occurs from mid-September to mid-November, peaking in early October. Although not strictly coastal in migration, the highest numbers are usually seen along the southern coast. They are frequently seen coming off the ocean in the early morning at the Avalon Sea Watch. **Maxima:** 3,200, Cape May Point, 2 October 1994; 500, Cape May Point, 3 October 1987. **ASW Single-Day Maximum:** 699 on 2 October 1994. **ASW Seasonal Stats:** Average: 1,097; Maximum: 1,376 in 1996.

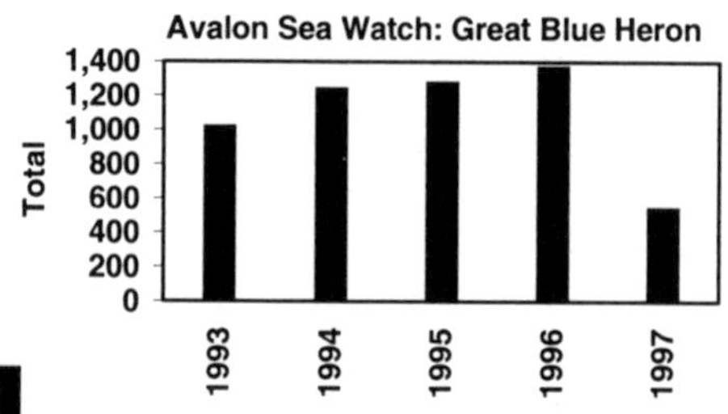

Winter: Numbers of Great Blue Herons vary in winter depending upon the severity of the season. They are more common along the coast in southern New Jersey, particularly in salt marshes where water is more likely to stay open. As with many water-dependent species, deep freezes that last for an extended period can be fatal. Some southward movement continues into January (Sibley 1997), probably in response to weather. A steady rise in CBC totals is likely due both to an increase in observer effort and to the documented increase in colonies. **CBC Statewide Stats:** Average: 597; Maximum: 1,010 in 1993; Minimum: 246 in 1978. **CBC Maximum:** 181, Cape May, 1996.

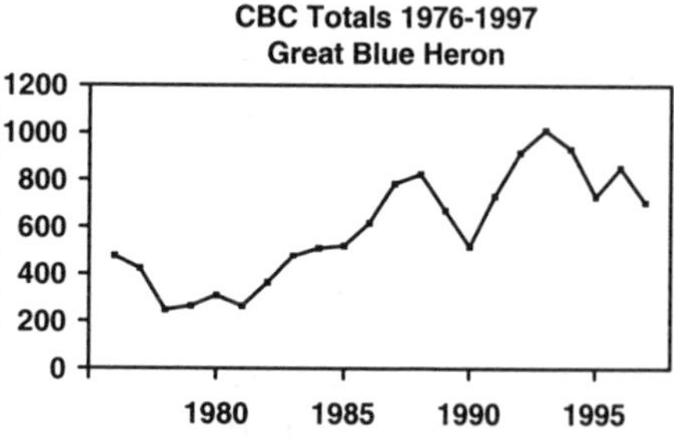

Spring: Northbound Great Blue Herons can be seen by early March. The migration peaks in late March, and most migrants have moved through by the end of April. Away from breeding areas Great Blue Herons are least common in summer, with only small numbers of nonbreeders found at scattered locations. **Maxima:** 200, Sandy Hook, 24 March 1991; 69, Cape May Point, 30 March 1992 (Sibley 1997). ■

Table 1: NJ ENSP Coastal Colonial Waterbird Survey. Comparison of 1978 survey to 1995 survey.

	1978	1995	% change
Great Egret	*601*	*486*	*-19*
Snowy Egret	*3,178*	*1,343*	*-58*
Little Blue Heron	*206*	*223*	*8*
Tricolored Heron	*160*	*197*	*23*
Cattle Egret	*483*	*29*	*-94*
Black-crowned Night-Heron	*1468*	*221*	*-85*
Yellow-crowned Night-Heron	*99*	*82*	*-17*
Glossy Ibis	*3,799*	*1,398*	*-63*

From: RNJB, Vol. 6, number 5, and Vol. 21, number 4.

Great Egret

Ardea alba

Range: In the eastern United States breeds along the coast from Massachusetts south to Florida, across the Gulf Coast and north along the Mississippi River drainage to Minnesota. Winters along the coast from New Jersey to Florida and Texas, and south to the West Indies and northern South America.

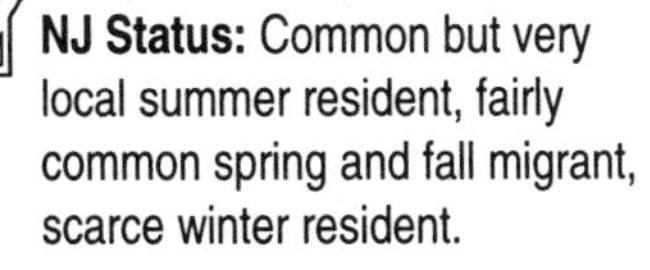

NJ Status: Common but very local summer resident, fairly common spring and fall migrant, scarce winter resident.

Breeding

Habitat: Colonial. Nests along the coast in shrubs or trees near water, usually with other herons and egrets, particularly on uninhabited islands in coastal bays.

After significant depredation for the millinery trade during the late 1800s, Great Egrets were extirpated as breeding birds from the state. For a short time they were rare at any time of year, but sightings increased in New Jersey by the early 1900s (Griscom 1923). Great Egrets were confirmed breeding in New Jersey in 1928, when a nest was found in Marshalltown, Salem County (Stone 1937), and by 1936 the population had increased to three colonies (Stone 1937). There is ample evidence that the nesting record for 1928 was a recolonization rather than a range extension for this species. Although Stone (1937) was skeptical that the species had ever bred in New Jersey, Bent (1926), and Chapman (1939) reported the species as breeding in New Jersey.

Atlas data indicated that the breeding range for Great Egret in New Jersey was entirely coastal, and all colonies were south of the Piedmont. Data from the NJ ENSP Coastal Colonial Waterbird surveys indicated the number of breeding

continued on page 86

continued from page 85

Great Egret

Physiographic Distribution Great Egret	Number of blocks in province	Number of blocks species found breeding in province	Number of blocks species found in state	Percent of province species occupies	Percent of all records for this species found in province	Percent of state area in province
Piedmont	167	1	55	0.6	1.8	19.6
Inner Coastal Plain	128	12	55	9.4	21.8	15.0
Outer Coastal Plain	204	33	55	16.2	60.0	23.9
Pine Barrens	180	9	55	5.0	16.4	21.1

Statewide Summary	
Status	# of Blocks
Possible	38
Probable	2
Confirmed	15
Total	55

Map Interpretation: The breeding range of the species should be interpreted as the range of Confirmed nest locations only. The large number of Possible locations in Salem and Gloucester Counties is presumably the result of foraging birds from the colony on Pea Patch Island, Delaware.

individuals has declined over recent years (Table 1), although the number of colonies remain stable. The reasons for statewide declines are not fully known. For example, during the Atlas surveys one large colony in Stone Harbor was abandoned in 1993 for unknown reasons. Several plausible causes have been suggested (Great Horned Owl predation, cutting of the understory, ditching for mosquito control, and the development of a large American and Fish Crow roost), but the true mechanism was never proven, nor have the birds returned to the rookery as of 1998.

Fall: Away from nesting colonies, the largest concentrations of Great Egrets are seen in late summer during post-breeding dispersal. Post-breeding dispersal can be undertaken in any direction, although much of it is to the north of breeding sites. Not much is known about these movements, and they may vary from year to year. There is a noticeable southbound flight of Great Egrets

Possible
Probable
Confirmed

Great Egret
continued

between late September and early November, normally peaking at the end of October. **Maxima** (away from colonies)**:** 222, Avalon Sea Watch, 29 October 1996; 180, Avalon Sea Watch, 16 October 1995. **ASW Seasonal Stats:** Average: 370; Maximum: 607 in 1995.

Winter: Small numbers of Great Egrets spend the winter in New Jersey, mainly in the southern coastal salt marshes. Periods of sudden freezes of long duration can be fatal to the birds. Numbers of wintering birds vary from year to year, depending on the harshness of the winter. This is sometimes reflected in statewide CBC totals. **CBC Statewide Stats:** Average: 46; Maximum: 163 in 1976; Minimum: 2 in 1990. **CBC Maximum:** 107, Cape May, 1976.

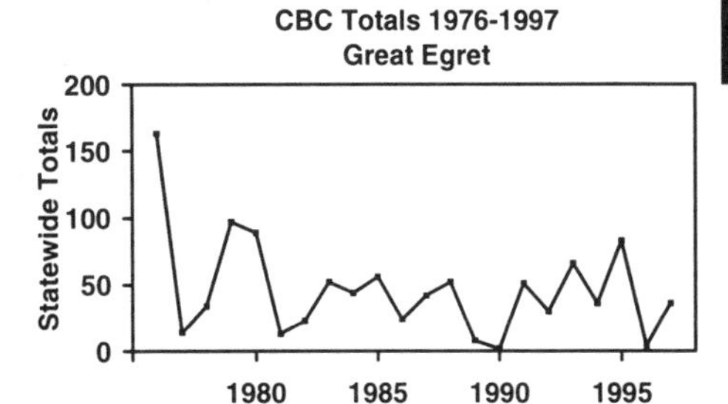

Spring: Northbound Great Egrets can be seen in the southern part of the state as early as late February, but more typically appear in mid-March. Numbers then build through April and May. ■

Snowy Egret
Egretta thula

Range: In the eastern United States, breeds from southern Maine south to Florida, across the Gulf Coast and along the Mississippi River north. Winters along the coast from Virginia south to the West Indies and northern South America.

NJ Status: Common but very local summer resident, common spring and fall migrant, rare to scarce winter resident.

Breeding

Habitat: Colonial. Nests along the coast in shrubs or trees, occasionally in reeds, near water. Often on uninhabited islands in coastal bays, usually with other herons and egrets.

Snowy Egrets were extirpated from New Jersey, and much of the rest of the United States, by the end of the 1800s due to unrestricted hunting by the millinery trade. Stone (1937) reported that they were coastal breeders prior to the 1880s, but the species became so rare that Griscom (1923) refused to accept any sightings from the northeastern United States. After a period with few sightings along the east coast, Snowy Egrets returned to New Jersey in 1928 (Stone 1937). Bull (1964) described the comeback as "phenomenal" and reported that their first post-extirpation nest was discovered in 1939.

The NJ ENSP Coastal Colonial Waterbird Surveys indicated a declin-
continued on page 88

continued from page 87

Map Interpretation: As with the other herons and egrets, the breeding range of the species should be interpreted as the range of Confirmed nest locations. The areas the birds used for foraging during the breeding season are noted in the Possible locations, although this is not an exhaustive inventory of the foraging range. The number of locations scored as Possible in Salem and Gloucester Counties were presumably the result of foraging birds from the colony on Pea Patch Island, Delaware.

ing number of breeding individuals, but a stable number of colonies, in New Jersey (Table 1). From 1978 to 1995 the species declined from 3,178 individuals in 27 colonies to 1,343 individuals in 26 colonies. The cause of the decline is not known, although it parallels a similar decline in the Great Egret population measured by the same study.

Atlas data indicated Snowy Egrets were distributed along the Atlantic shore in mixed rookeries, and revealed the first Probable nesting attempt on the Delaware River, when a pair was observed in a Great Egret rookery in 1997. Further details were not gathered on the success of the pair, but it is possible Snowy Egrets will continue to expand their breeding range along the Delaware Bay shore.

Fall: Away from nesting colonies, the

Statewide Summary	
Status	# of Blocks
Possible	23
Probable	4
Confirmed	11
Total	38

Possible
Probable
Confirmed

Physiographic Distribution Snowy Egret	Number of blocks in province	Number of blocks species found breeding in province	Number of blocks species found in state	Percent of province species occupies	Percent of all records for this species found in province	Percent of state area in province
Inner Coastal Plain	128	6	38	4.7	15.8	15.0
Outer Coastal Plain	204	27	38	13.2	71.1	23.9
Pine Barrens	180	5	38	2.8	13.2	21.1

Snowy Egret
continued

largest concentrations of Snowy Egrets are seen during post-breeding dispersal. As with most herons and egrets, post-breeding dispersal can be undertaken in any direction, mainly to the north of breeding locations. Much is unknown about these movements, but they vary from year to year. A noticeable southbound flight in fall is seen between late September and late October, normally peaking in mid-October. **Maxima:** 525, Kearny Marsh, 7 August 1977; 500, Kearny Marsh, 24 August 1981. **ASW Single-Day Maximum:** 259 on 11 October 1997. **ASW Seasonal Stats:** Average: 333; Maximum: 487 in 1996.

Winter: Snowy Egrets tend to remain in the state only in mild winters, mainly in the extreme south. Unusually high numbers were seen on CBCs in the mid-1970s, but more recent counts have averaged fewer than five birds. **CBC Statewide Stats:** Average: 13; Maximum: 111 in 1976; Minimum: 0 in three years. **CBC Maximum:** 85, Cape May, 1976.

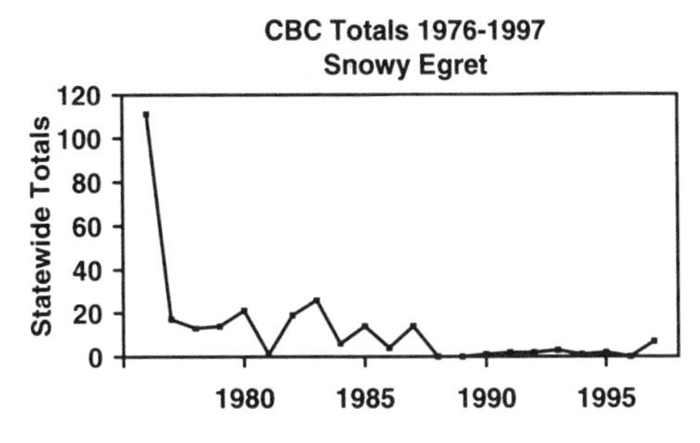

Spring: Snowy Egrets return to southern New Jersey beginning in mid-March, occasionally earlier in mild springs. Numbers build through April and May. ■

Little Blue Heron
Egretta caerulea

Range: Breeds in the eastern United States from southern Maine south to Florida, across the Gulf Coast and north to Oklahoma and Illinois. Winters along the coast mainly from Virginia south to Central America and the West Indies.

NJ Status: Fairly common but very local summer resident, uncommon spring and fairly common fall migrant, very rare winter resident. Threatened Species in New Jersey (breeding only).

Breeding

Habitat: Colonial. Nests along the coast in shrubs or trees near water, usually with other herons and egrets, particularly on uninhabited islands in coastal bays.

Little Blue Herons have a nesting history similar to those of Great and Snowy Egrets. Information on Little Blue Heron's breeding abundance and range prior to 1935 is scant, but the species was

continued on page 90

continued from page 89

Little Blue Heron

described as having a few pairs still breeding in Cape May in 1890 (Stone 1937). A combination of plume hunting and nesting habitat destruction caused the species' retreat from New Jersey. Bent (1926) suggested depredation of Little Blue Herons by the millinery trade was lower than that of the "white" herons. Stone (1937) suggested the species was driven from preferred nesting areas along the Atlantic shore as land was converted to resort homes. There was a period of scarcity early in the 1900s, followed by a return of nesting birds at a rookery south of Camden on the Delaware River in 1935 (Stone 1937).

Atlas data indicated Little Blue Herons had a nesting range similar to that of Snowy Egret, although no Little Blue Heron rookeries were found along the Delaware Bay/River in New Jersey. A comparison of the NJ ENSP Coastal Colonial Waterbird Surveys indicated a stable or slightly increasing population in the state (Table 1), with an increase from 15 to 19 colonies.

Fall: In late summer, away from nesting colonies, Little Blue Herons rarely form large, single-species aggregations. They are often seen feeding with other herons and egrets. As with other wading birds, post-breeding dispersal can be undertaken in any direction. At the Avalon Sea Watch a small flight has been noted in early October. **Maxima:** 92, Avalon Sea Watch, 11 October 1996; 71,

Possible
Probable
Confirmed

Statewide Summary	
Status	# of Blocks
Possible	16
Probable	2
Confirmed	10
Total	28

Physiographic Distribution Little Blue Heron	Number of blocks in province	Number of blocks species found breeding in province	Number of blocks species found in state	Percent of province species occupies	Percent of all records for this species found in province	Percent of state area in province
Inner Coastal Plain	128	3	28	2.3	10.7	15.0
Outer Coastal Plain	204	22	28	10.8	78.6	23.9
Pine Barrens	180	3	28	1.7	10.7	21.1

Little Blue Heron
continued

Avalon Sea Watch, 8 October 1995; 71, Avalon Sea Watch, 3 October 1996. **ASW Seasonal Stats:** Average: 60; Maximum: 201 in 1996.

Winter: Little Blue Herons are rarely encountered after November, and then only in the southernmost part of the state. As of 1992, Sibley indicated no records after 24 January or before 16 March for Cape May County. However, one or two apparently survived the winter in 1993 near Cape May, and several wintered in the southern part of the state in the mild winter of 1997-1998. Since the mid-1980s, statewide CBC counts have been fewer than 15 birds. **CBC Statewide Stats:** Average: 14; Maximum: 96 in 1985; Minimum: 0 in 1997. **CBC Maximum:** 88, Cape May, 1985.

Map Interpretation: As with the other herons and egrets, the breeding range of the species should be interpreted as the range of Confirmed nest locations. The areas the birds require for foraging during the breeding season are noted in the Possible locations, although this is not a complete inventory of areas used. The number of locations scored as Possible in Salem and Gloucester Counties were presumably the result of foraging birds from the colony on Pea Patch Island, Delaware.

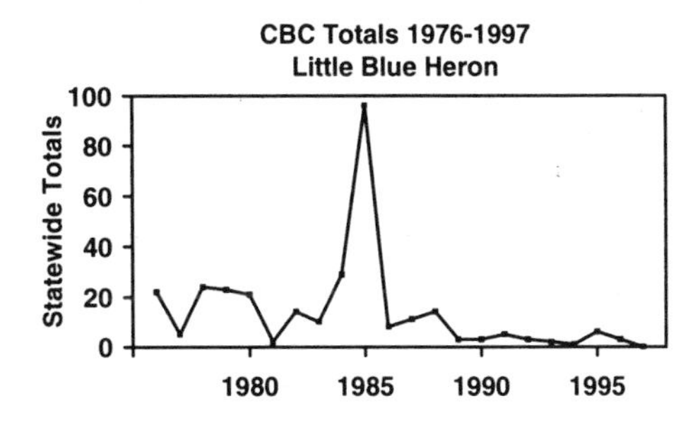

Spring: Little Blue Herons return in late March, occasionally earlier, with numbers building through April and May. ■

Tricolored Heron
Egretta tricolor

Range: Breeds from southern Maine south to Florida, and across the Gulf Coast. Winters mainly from Virginia south to Florida and the Gulf Coast.

NJ Status: Fairly common but very local summer resident, uncommon spring and fall migrant, rare winter resident.

Breeding

Habitat: Colonial. Nests along the coast in shrubs or trees near water, usually with other herons and egrets, particularly on uninhabited islands in coastal bays.

Tricolored Herons are relatively recent breeding birds in New Jersey, with the first reported nest in Stone

continued on page 92

continued from page 91

Tricolored Heron

Harbor in 1948 (Bull 1964). Their colonization of New Jersey was part of general northward range expansion for this species during the 1900s (Kaufman 1996). This species' increase in New Jersey was not well documented until NJAS and ENSP Colonial Waterbird Surveys began in 1977. Comparison of the NJ ENSP Coastal Colonial Waterbird Surveys shows an increasing population in New Jersey (Table 1).

Atlas data indicated all Confirmed nesting locations were on the Atlantic shore, and were in mixed colonies with Great and Snowy Egrets. It is possible Tricolored Heron's breeding population is still augmented by individuals wandering north from their natal breeding range, the same mechanism that brought the species to the state in the early part of this century. This may explain why this species, although very similar in habits and breeding habitat to both Great Egret and Snowy Egret, is showing an increasing rather than a declining population.

Map Interpretation: As with the other herons and egrets, the breeding range of Tricolored Heron should be interpreted as the range of Confirmed nest locations. The areas the birds require for foraging during the breeding season were noted in the Possible locations, although this is not an exhaustive inventory of the foraging range.

Statewide Summary	
Status	# of Blocks
Possible	11
Probable	1
Confirmed	9
Total	21

Possible
Probable
Confirmed

Physiographic Distribution Tricolored Heron	Number of blocks in province	Number of blocks species found breeding in province	Number of blocks species found in state	Percent of province species occupies	Percent of all records for this species found in province	Percent of state area in province
Outer Coastal Plain	204	20	21	9.8	95.2	23.9
Pine Barrens	180	1	21	0.6	4.8	21.1

Tricolored Heron
continued

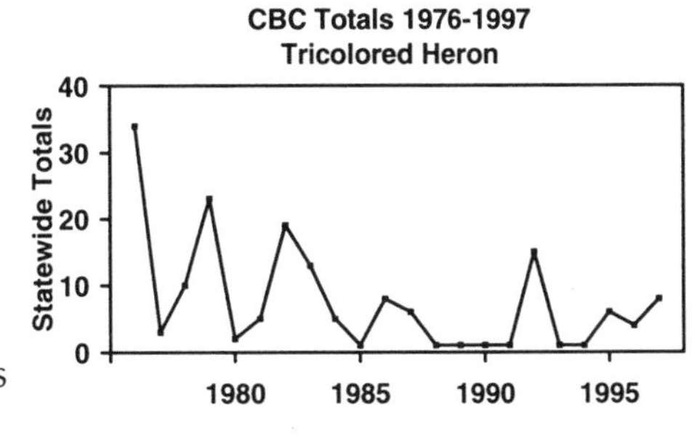

Fall: Away from nesting colonies, Tricolored Herons are most commonly seen in late summer during post-breeding dispersal. As with other herons and egrets, post-breeding dispersal can be undertaken in any direction, with little known about the details of these movements. Their return flight from northward dispersal may go almost undetected in most years. Most individuals are gone by mid-October. **Maxima:** 90, Brigantine NWR, 28 August 1998; 30+, Brigantine NWR, 17 September 1995. **ASW Seasonal Stats:** Average: 10; Maximum: 24 in 1995.

Winter: Tricolored Herons tend to remain in the state only in mild winters, mainly in the extreme south. Although rare at that season, they are encountered more frequently than Little Blue Herons but less so than Great Egrets. CBC totals are variable. **CBC Statewide Stats:** Average: 8; Maximum: 34 in 1976; Minimum: 1 in seven years. **CBC Maximum:** 32, Cape May, 1976.

Spring: Tricolored Herons return in late March, occasionally earlier, and numbers build through April and early May. ■

Cattle Egret
Bubulcus ibis

Range: In eastern North America, breeds from North Dakota east to Maine, south to eastern Texas and Florida. Winters from Texas and Florida south to the West Indies and northern South America.

NJ Status: Scarce and very local summer resident, fairly common spring and fall migrant, accidental in winter.

Breeding

Habitat: Colonial. Nests along the coast in shrubs or trees near water, usually with other herons and egrets, particularly on uninhabited islands in coastal bays.

The first confirmed breeding record for Cattle Egrets in New Jersey was in 1958 in Cape May County. The population quickly expanded to 20 pairs in Stone Harbor by 1960 (Bull 1964). Reports on the breeding distribution of the species in New Jersey are few, but in 1977 there were 70 nesting on Shooter's Island in New York Harbor (Black 1977). Throughout some areas in the United States, there is evidence they are declining (Telfair 1994), and comparisons of the NJ ENSP Coastal Colonial Waterbird Surveys

continued on page 94

continued from page 93

Cattle Egret

indicated a severe decline in New Jersey (Table 1). The 1995 population estimate was about 6% of the 1978 population estimate, although the number of colonies was stable at four.

Only four Cattle Egret colonies were found during the Atlas survey period, and two were located during the first year of field work. This pattern of colonization and decline is similar to that which occurred in Pennsylvania, where the cause for the population decline is unknown (Schutsky 1992a).

Map Interpretation: As with the other herons and egrets, the breeding range of the species should be interpreted as the range of Confirmed nest locations. The number of locations scored as Possible in Salem and Gloucester Counties were presumably the result of foraging birds from the colony on Pea Patch Island, Delaware .

Possible
Probable
Confirmed

Statewide Summary	
Status	# of Blocks
Possible	9
Probable	3
Confirmed	2
Total	14

Fall: Cattle Egrets are most often seen in late summer during post-breeding dispersal. The peak of their abundance is from late August to early September, with numbers diminishing by mid-October. They are rarely seen after mid-November. They are known to wander widely. Unlike other herons and egrets, however, they are usually found in dry upland fields, away from water, often in association with livestock. Maximum numbers have been recorded from farm fields in Salem County. The origin of these large flocks is apparently the heron rookery in the

Physiographic Distribution Cattle Egret	Number of blocks in province	Number of blocks species found breeding in province	Number of blocks species found in state	Percent of province species occupies	Percent of all records for this species found in province	Percent of state area in province
Inner Coastal Plain	128	2	14	1.6	14.3	15.0
Outer Coastal Plain	204	12	14	5.9	85.7	23.9

Cattle Egret
continued

Delaware River on Pea Patch Island, Delaware. There are no comparable concentrations elsewhere in the state. **Maxima:** 2,000, Mannington Marsh, 31 August 1987; 400, near Featherbed Lane, 21 September 1989.

Winter: There is a recent report from Hancock's Bridge, 4 January 1988 on the Middletown, Delaware CBC (which encompasses a portion of Salem Co.).

Spring: Cattle Egrets return in late March or early April, becoming more numerous by mid-April. **Maximum:** 250, Mannington Marsh, 29 April 1984. ■

Green Heron
Butorides virescens

Range: In eastern North America breeds from southeastern North Dakota east to New Brunswick, south to Texas and Florida. Winters mainly from south Florida and the Gulf Coast south to the West Indies and northern South America.

NJ Status: Fairly common and very widespread summer resident, fairly common spring and fall migrant, accidental in winter.

Breeding

Habitat: Nests in woodlands, usually in trees or shrubs, sometimes on the ground. Most often found near water around lakes, ponds, streams, or marshes.

Green Herons are New Jersey's most widely distributed heron. The vernacular name, "Fly-up-the-creek," invokes an accurate picture of this species in breeding habitat. Early observers considered the species to be widespread (Stone 1908, Griscom 1923). A survey in Cumberland County in June 1985 found 69 Green Herons, making them the most common wading bird in the county. (C. Sutton, pers. com.)

Stone (1937) noted a colony of 20 nests at Seven Mile Beach (Avalon), but Atlas observers did not report this species in sufficient density to warrant the term "colony," although it is possible that some sites may have been occupied by several pairs. Green Herons were broadly distributed among the physiographic provinces of New Jersey, but the blocks north of the Piedmont were occupied more frequently than the blocks to the south. Even in the provinces where Green Herons were least numerous (Outer Coastal Plain and Pine Barrens), they were still found in over 50% of the blocks.

continued on page 96

continued from page 95

Green Heron

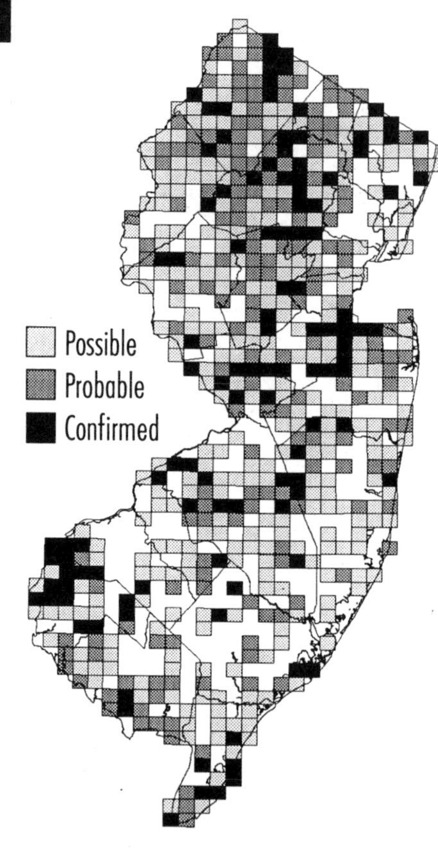

Conservation Note: This species' status in the state may be important to track over time. Atlas data indicated the species is well distributed among the physiographic provinces of New Jersey, and can provide researchers with an opportunity to develop a large sample of study sites.

Fall: Outside the breeding season, Green Herons are usually solitary and secretive. Southbound migrants can be seen by mid-August and most are gone by mid-October. The main part of their movement occurs from late August to mid-September, although they are more numerous earlier in August when local breeding populations disperse to favored feeding areas (e.g., 60,

Statewide Summary	
Status	# of Blocks
Possible	286
Probable	175
Confirmed	114
Total	575

Physiographic Distribution Green Heron	Number of blocks in province	Number of blocks species found breeding in province	Number of blocks species found in state	Percent of province species occupies	Percent of all records for this species found in province	Percent of state area in province
Kittatinny Mountains	19	17	575	89.5	3.0	2.2
Kittatinny Valley	45	42	575	93.3	7.3	5.3
Highlands	109	85	575	78.0	14.8	12.8
Piedmont	167	117	575	70.1	20.3	19.6
Inner Coastal Plain	128	89	575	69.5	15.5	15.0
Outer Coastal Plain	204	126	575	61.8	21.9	23.9
Pine Barrens	180	99	575	55.0	17.2	21.1

Green Heron
continued

Whitesbog, 5 August 1981; 42, Whitesbog, 11 August 1986). They are not as prone to extensive northward dispersal as are other herons and egrets (Davis et al. 1994). **Other maxima:** 35+, South Cape May Meadows, 10 September 1995; 20, South Cape May Meadows, 20 September 1991; 20, South Cape May Meadows, 14 September 1996.

Winter: A few Green Herons may remain into December, and they are seen on CBCs. There are two recent mid-winter records: Cinnaminson, 6 January 1983 and Wildwood Crest, 27 January 1998. **CBC Statewide Stats:** Average: 1; Maximum: 9 in 1980; Minimum: 0 in ten years. **CBC Maximum:** 6, Trenton Marsh, 1980.

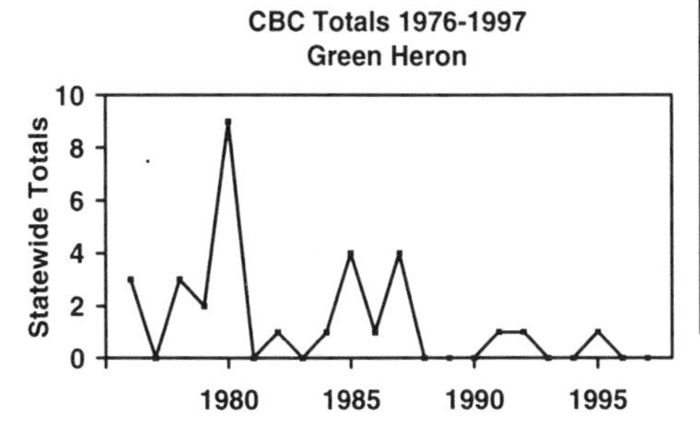

Spring: The first northbound Green Herons are usually seen from early to mid-April, with movement peaking from early to mid-May. **Maximum:** 20, South Cape May Meadows, 22 May 1996. ■

Black-crowned Night-Heron
Nycticorax nycticorax

Range: Breeds along the East Coast from New Brunswick south to Florida. Winters from Massachusetts, south to the southern United States, Central America, and the West Indies.

NJ Status: Fairly common but local summer resident, fairly common spring and common fall migrant, uncommon winter resident.

Breeding

Habitat: Colonial. Nests along the coast, and rarely inland, in shrubs or trees near water, or in reeds on the ground, usually with other herons and egrets.

Black-crowned Night-Heron breeding colonies have a history of persecution throughout their North American range, and New Jersey was no exception. The factors that contributed to this species' decline during the 20th century read like a page from a conservation text: egg taking at the breeding colonies, hunting of adults during the breeding season, breeding habitat loss, and eggshell thinning from DDT are all likely to be factors. In 1908 Stone considered them

continued on page 98

continued from page 97

Black-crowned Night-Heron

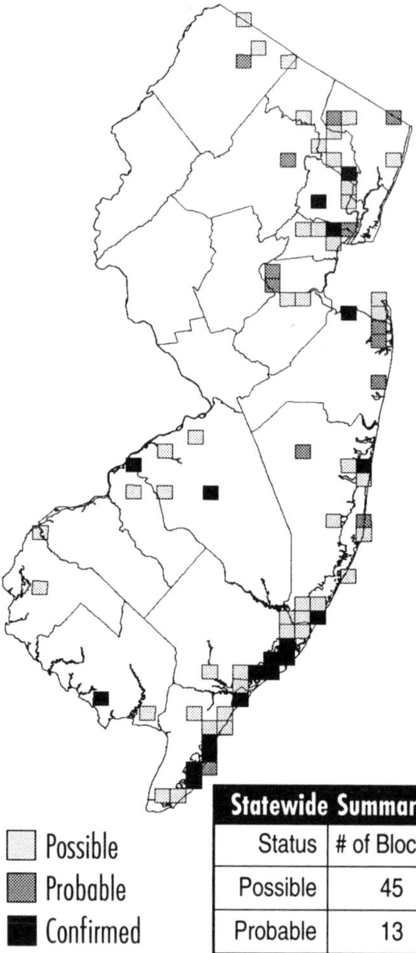

common, especially along the lower Delaware Valley. By 1937 he described substantial habitat destruction and hunting of adults in a colony at Seven Mile Beach (Avalon). At that time some colonies in southern New Jersey were large; one in Cape May

Map Interpretation: Many colonies are easy to locate, as Black-crowned Night-Herons often breed with other herons. Small, single-species rookeries, especially those with ground nests, are easy to overlook by aerial or ground surveys. It is likely that Probable and Possible locations indicate foraging areas used by breeding birds, but in some cases they may indicate small, undiscovered rookeries. They do not breed until their second summer (Ehrlich et al. 1993), and some nonbreeding sub-adults at roost sites can be confused with breeding birds. This may explain the high number of Possible locations that did not yield higher breeding codes.

Possible
Probable
Confirmed

Statewide Summary

Status	# of Blocks
Possible	45
Probable	13
Confirmed	19
Total	77

Physiographic Distribution

Black-crowned Night-Heron	Number of blocks in province	Number of blocks species found breeding in province	Number of blocks species found in state	Percent of province species occupies	Percent of all records for this species found in province	Percent of state area in province
Kittatinny Valley	45	2	77	4.4	2.6	5.3
Highlands	109	3	77	2.8	3.9	12.8
Piedmont	167	19	77	11.4	24.7	19.6
Inner Coastal Plain	128	11	77	8.6	14.3	15.0
Outer Coastal Plain	204	37	77	18.1	48.1	23.9
Pine Barrens	180	5	77	2.8	6.5	21.1

was estimated at over 150 nests. Inland breeding colonies fared worse than colonies along the coast. Griscom (1923) described the species as declining inland in northern New Jersey, and by 1955 Fables indicated the species was rare as a breeding bird in northern New Jersey. A comparison of the NJAS and ENSP Colonial Waterbird Surveys from 1978 to 1995 show a decline of 85% in the number of individuals (Table 1), but the number of colonies declined only by one, from 28 to 27.

The Outer Coastal Plain and Piedmont provinces hold the largest percentages of the statewide population of this species (48% and 25%, respectively). Of the 19 blocks where they were Confirmed, 13 were in the Outer Coastal Plain, underscoring the importance of this region to the species. Conversely, Black-crowned Night-Herons were conspicuous in their absence from the Pine Barrens. The inland record in Burlington County is for a single nest.

Conservation Note: Black-crowned Night-Herons have nearly disappeared as inland breeders, and coastal colonies have been reduced in numbers over the last 20 years. This pattern of decline at inland and coastal colonies has also been observed in Massachusetts (Veit and Petersen 1993) and New York (Levine 1988). Pennsylvania also has had a reduction in the number of Black-crowned Night-Herons breeding in the state (Schutsky1992b). In New Jersey, the Colonial Waterbird Surveys indicated a severe decline for this species since the aerial surveys began in 1977. This species is in need of annual monitoring, and an analysis of the factors which contributed to the population crash.

Fall: After the breeding season, local populations of Black-crowned Night-Herons seek out favored feeding locations, while some disperse to the north. Southbound birds are noted by mid-September, with a peak from early to mid-October. They are primarily nocturnal both when migrating and when foraging. Their passage is often noted just at or after sunset, and they are more often heard than seen. **Maxima:** 250+, Brigantine NWR, 20 July 1991; 200, Cape May Point, 4 October 1987.

Winter: In winter, Black-crowned Night-Herons often assemble in roosts near open water. They are regular on CBCs, and numbers have remained consistent with annual differences probably due to the severity of the weather prior to and during the count period. Although some individuals may spend the entire winter, numbers are reduced during the harshest winters. **CBC Statewide Stats:** Average: 143; Maximum: 284 in 1991; Minimum: 45 in 1980 and 1997. **CBC Maximum:** 187, Oceanville, 1991.

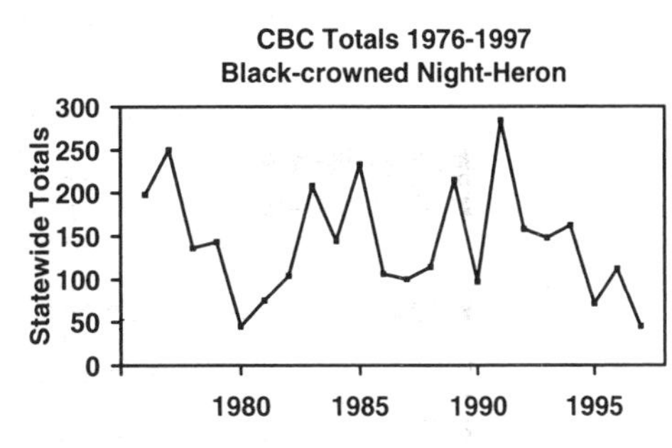

Spring: In spring, Black-crowned Night-Herons are first seen near their breeding colonies, returning in late March, with numbers building through April. ■

Yellow-crowned Night-Heron

Nyctanassa violacea

Range: Breeds from Massachusetts south to Florida, along the Gulf coast and north along the Mississippi River to Wisconsin. Winters mainly from South Carolina to Central America and the West Indies.

NJ Status: Scarce and local summer resident, scarce spring and fall migrant, accidental in winter. Threatened Species in New Jersey.

Possible
Probable
Confirmed

Statewide Summary	
Status	# of Blocks
Possible	7
Probable	4
Confirmed	12
Total	23

Breeding

Habitat: Colonial. Nests along the coast in shrubs or trees near water, usually with other herons and egrets but sometimes alone. May nest in mature pine trees in suburban settings.

Yellow-crowned Night-Herons have expanded their breeding range northward during this century and are a relatively recent addition to the breeding avifauna of New Jersey. The first New

Physiographic Distribution

Yellow-crowned Night-Heron	Number of blocks in province	Number of blocks species found breeding in province	Number of blocks species found in state	Percent of province species occupies	Percent of all records for this species found in province	Percent of state area in province
Piedmont	167	1	23	0.6	4.3	19.6
Inner Coastal Plain	128	1	23	0.8	4.3	15.0
Outer Coastal Plain	204	20	23	9.8	87.0	23.9
Pine Barrens	180	1	23	0.6	4.3	21.1

Map Interpretation: Many colonies are easy to locate, as Yellow-crowned Night-Herons often breed in mixed heron colonies. Small single-species rookeries, however, are easy to overlook by aerial or ground surveys. It is likely that Probable and Possible locations within one block of a Confirmed breeding site indicate foraging areas used by local breeding birds. However, studies on foraging flight distance during the breeding season indicate short foraging distances (Custer and Osborn 1978). Therefore, areas with Probable and Possible locations without central Confirmation sites are likely to indicate undiscovered rookeries.

Jersey nest was discovered in 1927 at Seven Mile Beach (Avalon), and by 1935 there were three nests in the same rookery (Stone 1937). The range expansion was widespread for this species, and there is suspicion that the species may have been recolonizing rather than moving into new areas (Bull 1964, Watts 1995). Despite their 50-year presence as a breeding bird in New Jersey, and a small increase in the number of colonies (from 15 to 17 colonies between 1978 and 1995), the species remains one of New Jersey's least numerous breeding herons or egrets (Table 1).

Yellow-crowned Night-Herons have remained coastal in their breeding-site selection in New Jersey. Atlas data indicated this species was Confirmed only in Cape May and Atlantic Counties. There was one colony located in a residential area where the birds were nesting in pine trees.

Conservation Note: Colonial Waterbird Surveys have indicated the number of breeding individuals in New Jersey declined by 17% from 1978 to 1995 (Table 1). Given the small population size, and the difficulty in locating small colonies, this decline may be over- or underestimated.

Fall: Yellow-crowned Night-Herons are not often seen away from colonies or feeding areas. They show a strong preference for crustaceans, particularly crabs (Watts 1995), and can often be found in salt marsh creeks near nesting colonies, foraging for fiddler crabs. The timing of their migration is difficult to ascertain as they occur in small numbers north of New Jersey, and their migration is almost entirely nocturnal. Most have left the state before the end of October, and it is likely that they begin moving south fairly early in fall.

Winter: From 1976 to 1997, Yellow-crowned Night-Herons were recorded on four CBCs (i.e., 1977, 1979, 1981, and 1991) and there are four other December reports. The only recent mid-winter report is of one at Linwood on 10 February 1979. These sightings are exceptional, and the species should not be expected in winter.

Spring: The first returning Yellow-crowned Night-Herons generally arrive at nesting colonies by late March. The only recorded maxima are at nesting colonies (e.g., 26, Stone Harbor, 20 April 1989). Interestingly, this count matches exactly one noted in Stone Harbor in 1966 (Leck 1984). ■

White Ibis

Eudocimus albus

Occurrence: There have been more than 75 reports of White Ibis in New Jersey, representing over 150 birds. The majority of the reports have been of immature birds during post-breeding dispersal between July and September, although dates span 18 April to 16 October. One hardy bird remained in Cape May through 10 February 1978. By far the largest influx occurred in 1977, when about 50 birds were reported around the state. Adults are rare in New Jersey, with approximately ten known reports. Although most reports are coastal, there have been at least 13 inland reports, in both northern and southern New Jersey. Historically White Ibis was an accidental visitor, and over 85% of the records have come since 1975. The species was not reported in only four years from 1975 to 1998. This increase probably reflects the consolidation of breeding range in North Carolina and extension into southern Virginia in the mid-1970s. **Maxima:** Coastal: 21, Moore's Beach, summer 1977; Inland: 3, Hawthorne, 16 July 1985. ■

Range: In eastern North America breeds from the Gulf and Atlantic coast states sparingly north to southern Virginia. Winters in same range.

NJ Status: Very rare. NJBRC Review List.

Glossy Ibis

Plegadis falcinellus

Range: In North America, breeds from Maine south to Florida and west along the Gulf coast to Louisiana. Winters mainly from Florida and the Gulf Coast south to the West Indies.

NJ Status: Fairly common but very local summer resident, common spring and fall migrant, very rare in winter.

Breeding

Habitat: Colonial. Nests along the coast in shrubs or trees near water, sometimes on the ground in reeds, usually with other herons and egrets, particularly on uninhabited islands in coastal bays.

Glossy Ibis have only recently become breeding birds in New Jersey. The first nest was found in 1955 in Cape May. By 1958 the species had increased in range and numbers with three rookeries reported in Atlantic County and a large rookery in Stone Harbor (Kunkle et al.1959). Glossy Ibis began to breed in New York at about the same time, with the first breeding record for New York from Jamaica Bay in 1961 (Bull 1964).

Glossy Ibis

continued

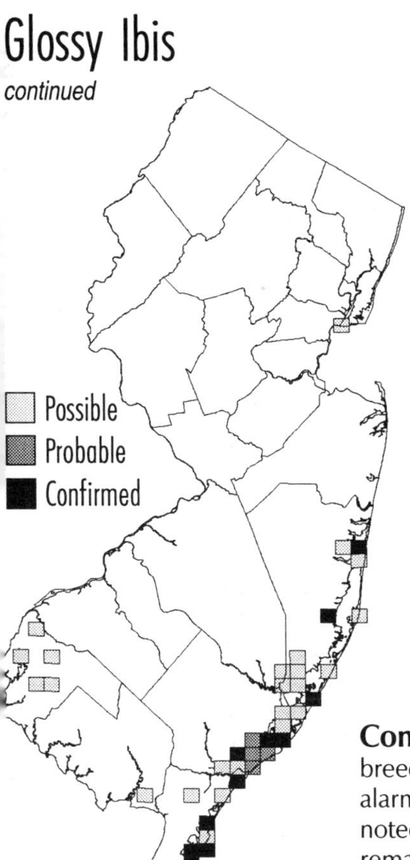

Map Interpretation: The large number of Possible locations in Salem County is suspected to be due to the colony on Pea Patch Island, Delaware.

Atlas surveys Confirmed Glossy Ibis only in Ocean, Atlantic, and Cape May counties, and all colonies were coastal. Comparison of two Colonial Waterbird Surveys indicated a severe decline for the species in the state. Glossy Ibis were the most numerous wading bird on both the 1978 and 1995 ENSP Coastal Colonial Waterbird Surveys, but their numbers were reduced by 63% during that time (Table 1). During the same period, however, the number of colonies declined only 20%, from 25 in 1978 to 20 in 1995.

Conservation Note: The decline in breeding wading birds is cause for serious alarm in New Jersey. These declines were noted for most species of wading birds and remain unexplained.

Fall: Glossy Ibis are most numerous in summer after local breeders disperse. Southward movements begin relatively early, in mid-July, and most individuals have migrated south by mid-September. **Maxima:** 400+, Brigantine NWR, 23 July 1995; 250+, Brigantine NWR, mid-July 1998.

continued on page 104

Statewide Summary	
Status	# of Blocks
Possible	24
Probable	4
Confirmed	11
Total	39

Physiographic Distribution Glossy Ibis	Number of blocks in province	Number of blocks species found breeding in province	Number of blocks species found in state	Percent of province species occupies	Percent of all records for this species found in province	Percent of state area in province
Piedmont	167	1	39	0.6	2.6	19.6
Inner Coastal Plain	128	3	39	2.3	7.7	15.0
Outer Coastal Plain	204	31	39	15.2	79.5	23.9
Pine Barrens	180	4	39	2.2	10.3	21.1

continued from page 103

Glossy Ibis

Winter: Individual Glossy Ibis may linger into early January, and they are occasionally recorded on CBCs. Five seen at Heislerville on 21 February 1976, and two near Voorhees, 21 February 1983, may represent very early spring migrants rather than wintering birds. **CBC Statewide Stats:** Average: 2; Maximum: 17 in 1976; Minimum: 0 in 12 years. **CBC Maximum:** 15, Cape May, 1976.

CBC Totals 1976-1997
Glossy Ibis

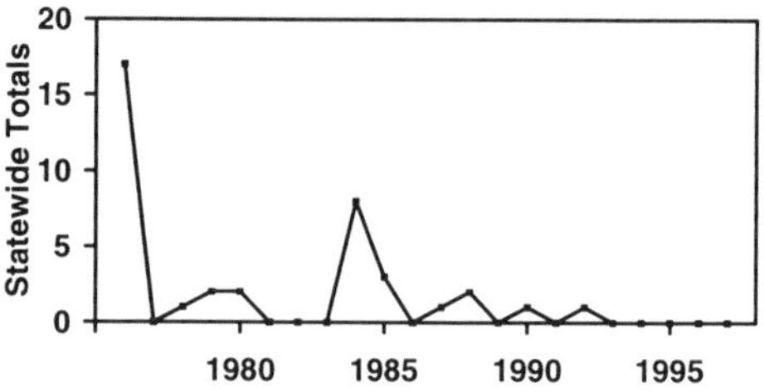

(Chart: Statewide Totals, y-axis 0, 5, 10, 15, 20; x-axis 1980, 1985, 1990, 1995)

Spring: Northbound Glossy Ibis are first seen in late March, with numbers peaking in mid-April. In spring they often can be found foraging in wet or damp grassy areas, such as flooded farm fields. **Maximum:** 275, Goshen, 17 April 1996. ■

White-faced Ibis

Plegadis chihi

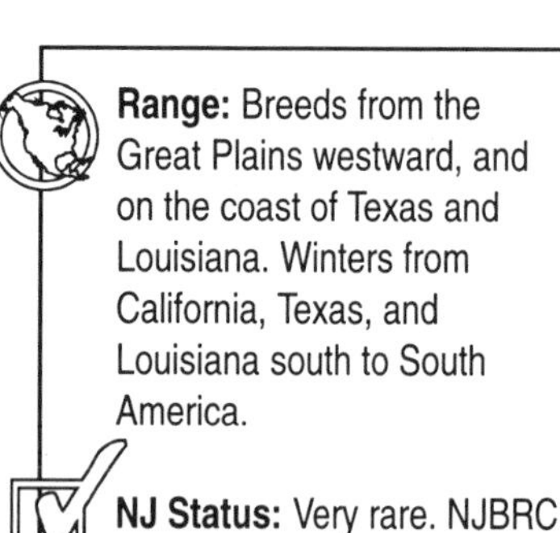

Range: Breeds from the Great Plains westward, and on the coast of Texas and Louisiana. Winters from California, Texas, and Louisiana south to South America.

NJ Status: Very rare. NJBRC Review List.

Occurrence: There have been 17 state reports of White-faced Ibis, and 12 have been accepted by the NJBRC (six in spring, six in summer). The two 1977 sightings were accepted as one record. The 12 accepted records are:

Brigantine NWR	*7 April 1977*	
Tuckerton	*21 April 1977*	*Galli and Penkala 1978*
Brigantine NWR	*19 June 1981*	
Cape May Point	*25 April 1982*	
Brigantine NWR	*24 July-mid-August 1983*	
Brigantine NWR	*2-3 August 1986*	*ph-RBPF*
Brigantine NWR	*22-25 July 1990*	
So. Cape May Meadows	*17-18 May 1991*	
Brigantine NWR	*25 May 1991*	
Brigantine NWR	*31 August-early September 1992*	
Brigantine NWR	*17-25 July 1993*	*ph-RBPF*
Cape May	*19 April 1994*	
Cape May	*10-12 May 1998*	

Roseate Spoonbill

Ajaia ajaja

Range: In North America breeds from Florida west to Texas.

NJ Status: Accidental. NJBRC Review List.

Occurrence: There has been only one report and one accepted record of Roseate Spoonbill in New Jersey: Linden, 24 August 1992. ■

Wood Stork

Mycteria americana

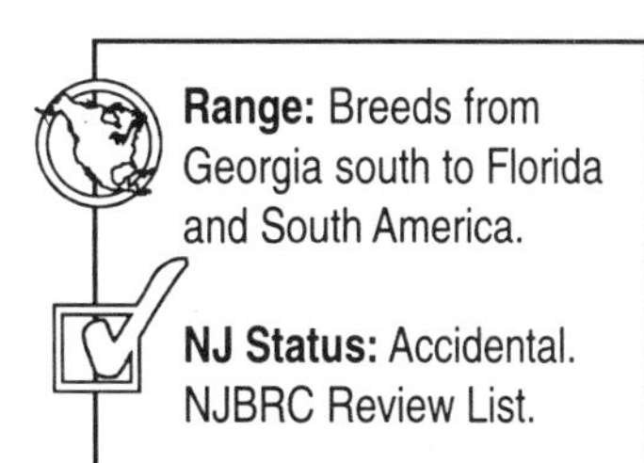

Range: Breeds from Georgia south to Florida and South America.

NJ Status: Accidental. NJBRC Review List.

Occurrence: There have been nine state reports of Wood Storks, and seven have been accepted by the NJBRC (four in summer, three in fall). The seven accepted records are:

	Cape May Point,	*10 August 1922*	
4	*Cape May Point*	*7 July-18 August 1923*	*ph-Stone 1937*
	Stone Harbor#	*23 September 1951*	
	Cape May Point	*13 November-24 December 1977*	*ph-NJA/RNJB 4:38; Dunne 1978*
	*Cape May Point**	*19-20 August 1979*	
2	*Cape May Point*	*15 August-23 September, 15 October 1983*	*phs-RNJB 9:69, 9:86*
	Cape May Point SP	*11 and 18-19 November 1994*	*ph-RNJB 22:81*

Black Vulture

Coragyps atratus

Possible
Probable
Confirmed

Statewide Summary	
Status	# of Blocks
Possible	140
Probable	30
Confirmed	11
Total	181

Range: Resident from southwestern Ohio, and western Connecticut south to Texas and Florida.

NJ Status: Uncommon and somewhat local summer resident, uncommon spring and fall migrant, uncommon winter resident, locally common at roost sites.

Breeding

Habitat: Nests in open country; on ground in thickets, stumps or hollow logs, caves, or abandoned buildings.

Black Vultures are a recent addition to the list of the breeding birds of New Jersey, and the timing of this species' colonization is well documented in RNJB. The first nest was recorded in 1981 at Tewksbury Township in Hunterdon County (Hanisek 1981b), and from that point on, the rate of colonization was rapid. Reports to RNJB indicated that Black Vultures were suspected

Physiographic Distribution

Black Vulture	Number of blocks in province	Number of blocks species found breeding in province	Number of blocks species found in state	Percent of province species occupies	Percent of all records for this species found in province	Percent of state area in province
Kittatinny Mountains	19	4	181	21.1	2.2	2.2
Kittatinny Valley	45	31	181	68.9	17.1	5.3
Highlands	109	56	181	51.4	30.9	12.8
Piedmont	167	24	181	14.4	13.3	19.6
Inner Coastal Plain	128	13	181	10.2	7.2	15.0
Outer Coastal Plain	204	44	181	21.6	24.3	23.9
Pine Barrens	180	9	181	5.0	5.0	21.1

of breeding near Hope, Warren County in 1984; by 1986 they were reported as probable breeders near Princeton; in 1990 they were suspected to be breeding near Mannington in Salem County; and by 1991 they were confirmed breeding at Gandy's Beach in Cumberland County.

Black Vultures were recorded in 21% of the blocks in New Jersey, although they were Confirmed in only 11 blocks. They were conspicuously absent from the Pine Barrens, and the urbanized areas in the eastern Piedmont. If only Confirmed nest sites are evaluated, the species' range is heavily weighted to the areas north of the Piedmont.

Map Interpretation: Because of the combined effects of the solitary nature of these birds near their nest sites, the widespread availability of nest sites, and their conspicuousness while on foraging flights, Atlas codes are not well suited to defining this species' actual breeding range. The Probable and Possible codes are likely to overestimate the range of the species, while the range of Confirmed sites is likely to underestimate the species range.

Historic Changes: Black Vultures have greatly expanded their range and are now a familiar sight in New Jersey at all seasons. As of 1955, Fables was aware of only eight records of Black Vultures in New Jersey. By the early 1980s, they had become regular, and numbers have increased dramatically since that time.

Fall: The pattern of abundance of Black Vultures as migrants in New Jersey is difficult to discern. Peak numbers have occurred throughout the fall – in mid-September, mid-October, and mid-November – although they appear to be most numerous in November amid the large movements of Turkey Vultures. Seasonal totals from the Cape May Hawk Watch may be misleading as some of the same individuals recur on successive days of northwest winds. **Maximum:** 112, Lambertville, 19 October 1996 (roost). **CMHW Daily Maximum:** 32 on 10 October 1998. **CMHW Seasonal Stats:** Average: 48; Maximum: 369 in 1997.

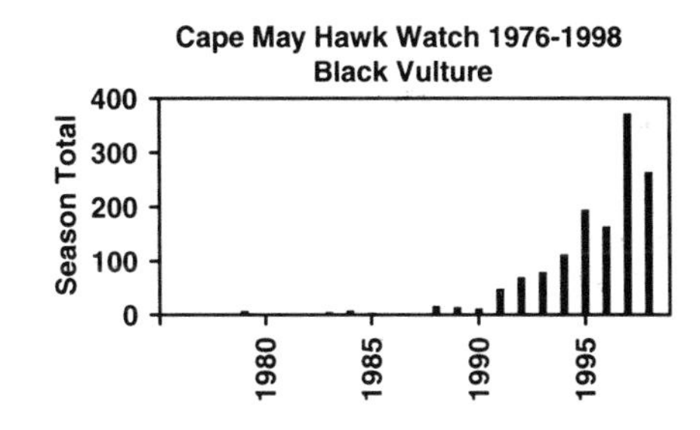

Winter: In winter, Black Vultures are most frequently encountered at or near roost sites. Statewide CBC totals have shown a marked increase since the first two were seen in 1981. **Maxima:** 200+, Compromise Road, 25 March 1996; 150, Lummis Mill Pond, 26 January 1998. **CBC Statewide Stats:** Average: 125; Maximum: 411 in 1995; Minimum: 0 in five years. **CBC Maximum:** 102, Princeton, 1995.

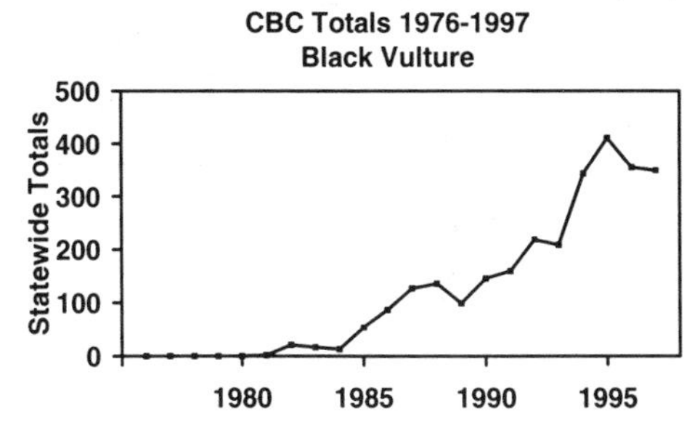

Spring: Black Vultures are present year-round in most of New Jersey making it difficult to distinguish a northbound migration for this species. ■

Turkey Vulture

Cathartes aura

Range: In eastern North America breeds from southern Manitoba to central Maine, south to Texas and Florida. Winters along the Atlantic coast to South America.

NJ Status: Fairly common and widespread summer resident, common spring and fall migrant, common winter resident.

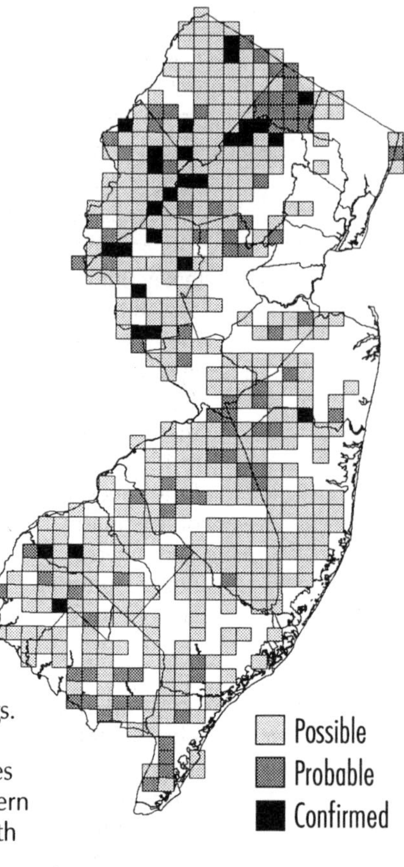

Statewide Summary	
Status	# of Blocks
Possible	400
Probable	85
Confirmed	28
Total	513

Breeding

Habitat: Nests on the ground in thickets, in stumps or hollow logs, rock crevices or caves, or abandoned buildings.

During the early 1900s, Turkey Vultures were considered common birds in southern New Jersey, but rare stragglers to the north (Stone 1908). Evidently, their numbers increased in the north, as Griscom (1923) reported they were common nesting birds

Physiographic Distribution Turkey Vulture	Number of blocks in province	Number of blocks species found breeding in province	Number of blocks species found in state	Percent of province species occupies	Percent of all records for this species found in province	Percent of state area in province
Kittatinny Mountains	19	13	513	68.4	2.5	2.2
Kittatinny Valley	45	41	513	91.1	8.0	5.3
Highlands	109	104	513	95.4	20.3	12.8
Piedmont	167	58	513	34.7	11.3	19.6
Inner Coastal Plain	128	78	513	60.9	15.2	15.0
Outer Coastal Plain	204	95	513	46.6	18.5	23.9
Pine Barrens	180	124	513	68.9	24.2	21.1

Map Interpretation: Atlas methods, coupled with Turkey Vulture's wide-ranging foraging habits, secretive nature around nest locations, and the presence of large numbers of nonbreeding immature birds, are likely to overestimate the breeding range with an excess of Probable and Possible blocks, yet to underestimate the range if only Confirmed sightings are evaluated.

in northern New Jersey but were absent as breeders from the eastern part of the state. They were recorded as common nesting birds in the "swampy thickets" of Salem County and nested along the dunes in Cape May County (Stone 1937). There is telling evidence of the species abundance in Salem County; in the 1920s Turner McMullen examined 71 Turkey Vulture nests in Salem County - an astounding number of nests to locate (Stone 1937).

Atlas data indicated Turkey Vultures are fairly common breeding birds throughout most of New Jersey in the summer. The only province with few reports is the highly urbanized eastern Piedmont. Observers found Turkey Vultures present in over 60% of the blocks surveyed, but the vultures were Confirmed in only 3% of the blocks statewide. The distribution of Confirmed nests is clearly weighted to the provinces north of the Coastal Plain. Unlike Black Vultures, Turkey Vultures are commonly reported from the Pine Barrens, although no nests were Confirmed in that province.

Fall: Although present year-round in the southern United States, northern populations of Turkey Vultures are migratory. In fall, peak movements at the Cape May Hawk Watch occur from early to mid-November. As with many raptors, the highest concentrations are seen at Cape May, however, they are also common along inland ridges. **Maxima:** 784, Cape May Hawk Watch, 3 November 1996; 602, Cape May Hawk Watch, 29 October 1996. **CMHW Seasonal Stats:** Average: 1,348; Maximum: 6,425 in 1996.

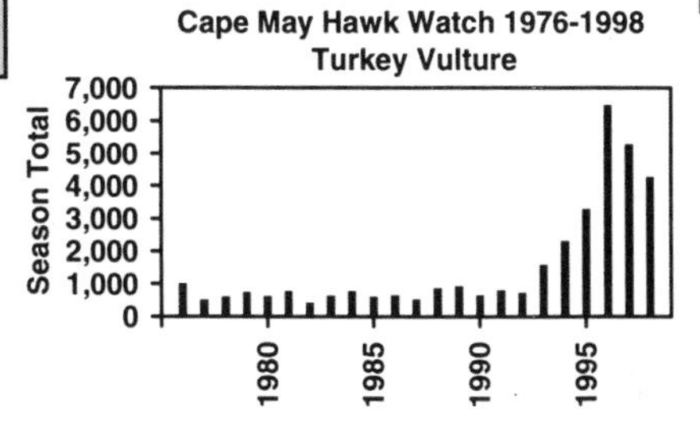

Winter: The increase in the winter population of Turkey Vultures in New Jersey since 1976 is notable. CBC totals rose dramatically from fewer than 200 birds in the mid-1970s to more than 2,000 birds in the mid-1990s. The reasons for this dramatic increase are unclear, but may be related to an overall increase in the population, rather than simply changes in the wintering patterns for this species. **Maxima:** 1,000, Lambertville, 19 December 1994; 471, Princeton, 9 February 1985. **CBC Statewide Stats:** Average: 1,333; Maximum: 2,469 in 1992; Minimum: 151 in 1981. **CBC Maximum:** 634, Elmer, 1989.

continued on page 110

continued from page 109

Turkey Vulture

Spring: The northward movements of Turkey Vultures are less obvious than the southward movements during fall. Migration is seen in early March, generally peaking from late March through early April. These movements are more noticeable over inland ridges than along the coast. **Maxima:** 164, Montclair, 28 March 1989; 122, Montclair, 26 March 1991. ■

Fulvous Whistling-Duck

Dendrocygna bicolor

Range: In the eastern United States breeds mainly in coastal Texas, Louisiana, and Florida, south to South America. Winters throughout breeding range.

NJ Status: Very rare. Added to the NJBRC Review List in 1996.

Occurrence: There have been 25 state reports of Fulvous Whistling-Ducks, and 20 have been accepted by the NJBRC. Although added to the review list in 1996, these reports represent a complete review of historic sightings. The first state record was of six, Brigantine NWR, 28 October-early December 1961. They were more frequently encountered in the 1960s and 1970s, and there has been no accepted record since 1985.The most recent records accepted are:

	North Arlington	*26 April-31 August 1974*	
17	*Tuckahoe*	*early May-19 May 1974*	
17	*Brigantine NWR*	*19 May-August 1974*	*probably the same individuals as previous record*
2	*Cape May Point*	*16 August-late October 1974*	*ph-RNJB 1:3*
	*Brigantine NWR**	*10 May 1975*	
	*North Arlington**	*25 June-20 July 1975*	
	*Brigantine NWR**	*19 July-1 September 1975*	
	Brigantine NWR	*13 August 1982*	*ph-RBPF*
	South Cape May Meadows	*17 November-12 December 1985*	*ph-RNJB 12:1*

Greater White-fronted Goose

Anser albifrons

Range: In North America breeds from Alaska to the Northwest Territories. In the United States winters from California to Louisiana.

NJ Status: Very rare spring and fall migrant, very rare winter visitor.

Historic Changes: The first state record of Greater White-fronted Goose in New Jersey was a bird on Barnegat Bay, 28 November 1926 (Griscom 1923). Since that time there have more than 60 state reports. Only 14 of the reports came prior to 1975, but by the 1980s Greater White-fronted Geese had become annual in migration.

Fall: Southbound Greater White-fronted Geese are usually seen in October and November. Although they are recorded more often in fall than spring, they remain a very rare migrant even during this season. There is a historic maximum of five, Beach Haven Inlet, 16 November 1945 (Fables 1955).

Winter: Greater White-fronted Geese were recorded on seven CBCs from 1976 to 1997. The CBC records are mostly of singles, but occasionally of pairs. There are a few other winter records outside of the CBC period .

Spring: There are fewer spring migrant Greater White-fronted Geese than fall migrants. Northbound birds are seen most often in March and April.

Subspecies: Some of the reports of Greater White-fronted Geese were believed to be birds of the Greenland race, *A. a. flavirostris*, however, identification is difficult (Kaufman 1994). A bird at Brigantine NWR, 17 December 1957-early January 1958, was shot and identified as *A. a. flavirostris* (Kunkle et al. 1959). One from Salem, 11 November 1958, was shot and identified as *A. a. frontalis* (Kunkle et al. 1959). ■

Snow Goose

Chen caerulescens

Range: Breeds in Arctic Canada from Ellesmere Island south to northern Ontario. On the East Coast, winters from New York to North Carolina.

NJ Status: Common spring and fall migrant, common winter resident.

Fall: The first Snow Geese arrive in late September, and they become more numerous as October progresses. Although they are seen in fair numbers inland, particularly flying along

continued on page 112

continued from page 111

the ridges, they are more often seen along the coast. Most have arrived at preferred locations by early November. Tens of thousands congregate at Brigantine NWR by mid-October, with some later moving to the Delaware Bay shore in Cumberland and Salem counties. **Maxima:** Coastal: 50,000, Brigantine NWR, late October 1976; 30,000, Brigantine NWR, 28 October 1994; Inland: 5,000+, over Chimney Rock, 1 November 1992. **ASW Single-Day Maximum:** 5,933 on 11 December 1995. **ASW Seasonal Stats:** Average: 8,069; Maximum: 17,146 in 1995.

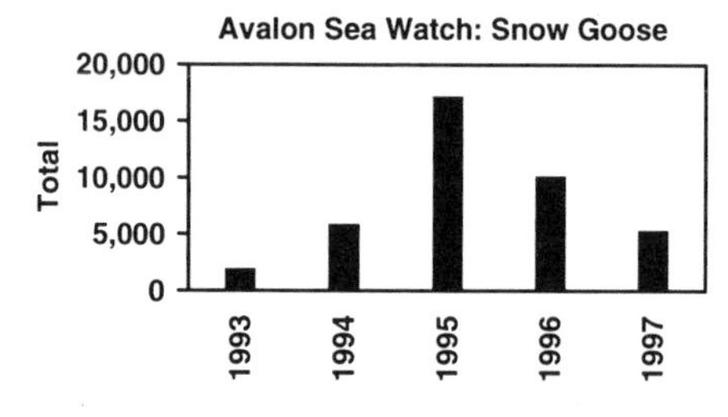

Winter: Flights of Snow Geese, either northward or southward, can occur all winter in response to freezes and thaws. For instance, at Cape May Point, on 11 February 1996, 7,500 were seen heading north, while on 6-8 February 1995, 1,550 passed heading south. CBC totals vary considerably. **CBC Statewide Stats:** Average: 32,438; Maximum: 88,710 in 1997; Minimum: 1,580 in 1981. **CBC Maximum:** 50,100, Cumberland County, 1996.

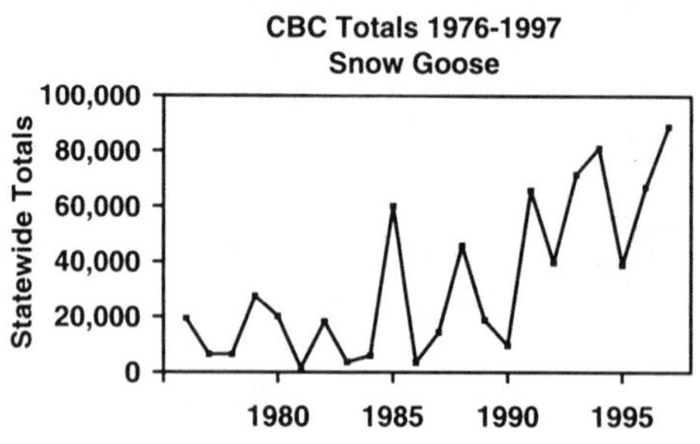

Spring: The northward migration of Snow Geese is difficult to distinguish from the local movement of wintering birds. Highest numbers are usually reached between late February and early March when local wintering birds are joined by migrants from the south. They rarely linger beyond mid-May. **Maxima:** Coastal: 20,000, Featherbed Lane, 20 March 1991; 13,000, Heislerville, 20 March 1977; Inland: 1,500, over Culvers Lake, 29 March 1987.

Subspecies: Early authors (Stone 1937, Fables 1955) considered *C. c. hyperborea*, "Lesser Snow Goose," to be a vagrant from the west. Griscom (1923) referred to that race as accidental. Sibley (1997) indicated that although "Greater Snow Goose," *C.c. atlantica*, is the predominant migrant in New Jersey, *C.c. hyperborea* occurs in small numbers. He also indicated that the dark-morph "Blue Goose," although relatively rare in number when compared to white-morph geese, constitutes a higher percentage of Lesser than Greater Snow Geese in southern New Jersey. "Blue Geese" are often seen in mixed flocks with white-morph geese: however sizable flocks of the dark-morphs are sometimes seen, e.g., 120 over Cape May Point on 27 February 1994 (Sibley 1997). ■

Ross's Goose
Chen rossii

Range: Breeds in Arctic Canada east to Hudson Bay. Winters mainly in California, with smaller numbers east to Louisiana.

NJ Status: Rare fall migrant and winter resident. NJBRC Review List.

Occurrence: There have been over 40 state reports of Ross's Geese, but only 13 records are accepted by the NJBRC (ten in fall, two in spring, one in winter). Many of the reports are probably correct, but they were insufficiently documented for addition to the state list. Most reports are of single birds, and all but six have been at Brigantine NWR in fall. Identification of this species is difficult, and observers need to carefully rule out hybrids. The thirteen accepted records are:

	Location	Dates	Documentation
	*Brigantine NWR**	*30 January-23 April 1972*	
	Brigantine NWR	*late October-4 December 1982*	*ph-RNJB 9:1*
	Brigantine NWR	*November 1983*	*ph-RNJB 9:18*
	*Brigantine NWR**	*22 October-3 November 1984*	
	*Brigantine NWR**	*5-11 October 1986*	
	*Brigantine NWR**	*24-31 October 1987*	
	*Brigantine NWR**	*8 October-19 November 1988*	
	*Brigantine NWR**	*28-29 October 1989*	
	Brigantine NWR	*17 October-10 November 1993*	*ph-RBPF*
2	*Sharptown*	*25 February-2 April 1995*	*ph-RNJB 21:57*
	Amwell	*24 March 1996*	
	Brigantine NWR	*13 October-21 December 1996*	
	Brigantine NWR	*1 October-9 November 1997*	

Canada Goose
Branta canadensis

Range: *B. c. canadensis*, the primary transient, breeds mainly in eastern Quebec, Labrador, and Newfoundland and winters along the East Coast. Feral Canada Geese breed throughout the East.

NJ Status: Common and very widespread summer resident, fairly common spring and common fall migrant, common winter resident.

Breeding

Habitat: Local populations nest on or near lakes, ponds, marshes, parks, and golf courses.

The history of Canada Geese as breeding birds in New Jersey is poorly documented. There is no

continued on page 114

continued from page 113

Canada Goose

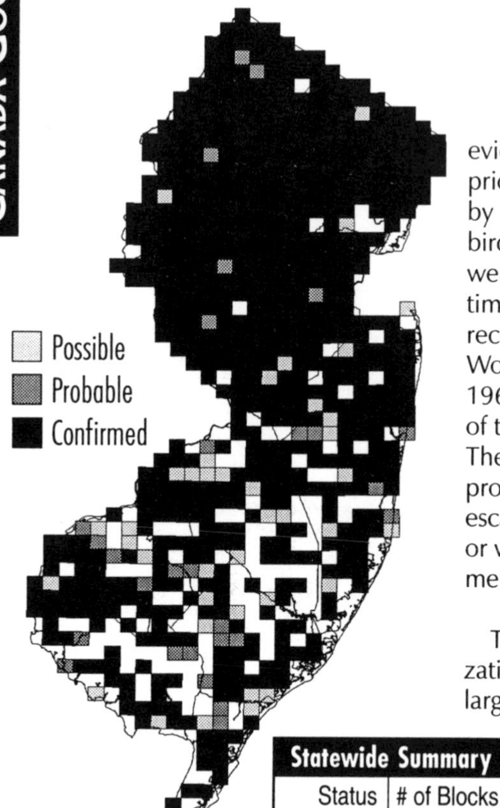

evidence that they bred in the state prior to the 1930s (Stone1937), but by 1955, Fables reported that some birds summered, suggesting birds were breeding in the state by that time. Although there are breeding records for Oradell Reservoir and Woodcliff Lake in 1962 (Komorowski 1962), tracking the range expansion of the species in the state is difficult. The breeding population was probably established from birds that escaped from waterfowl collections or were released at wildlife management areas.

The scale of Canda Goose colonization in New Jersey is impressively large. Atlas work showed that they are breeding in over 80% of the blocks statewide, with a slight preference for northern over southern New Jersey. They were found in more than 85% of the blocks in all provinces except the Pine Barrens and Outer Coastal Plain.

Statewide Summary

Status	# of Blocks
Possible	39
Probable	28
Confirmed	619
Total	686

Physiographic Distribution

Canada Goose	Number of blocks in province	Number of blocks species found breeding in province	Number of blocks species found in state	Percent of province species occupies	Percent of all records for this species found in province	Percent of state area in province
Kittatinny Mountains	19	19	686	100.0	2.8	2.2
Kittatinny Valley	45	45	686	100.0	6.6	5.3
Highlands	109	107	686	98.2	15.6	12.8
Piedmont	167	156	686	93.4	22.7	19.6
Inner Coastal Plain	128	111	686	86.7	16.2	15.0
Outer Coastal Plain	204	128	686	62.7	18.7	23.9
Pine Barrens	180	120	686	66.7	17.5	21.1

Historic Changes: As local breeding populations have exploded, the numbers of migrant Canada Geese have declined. Maximum counts of 50,000, Island Beach, 20 October 1967 (Leck 1984) and 30,000, Cape May Point, 1 October 1974 (Sibley 1997) are indicative of numbers that continued into the 1980s. However, the highest count recorded since 1990 was of 5,013 over Chimney Rock, 11 October 1996. The high count at the Avalon Sea Watch, a location with a designated counter from dawn to dusk during the peak of their migration, is 4,053 on 30 September 1994.

Fall: Migrant Canada Geese begin to arrive in mid-September, with numbers generally peaking from early to mid-October. Flocks can often be heard while flying overhead at night. Although their typical chevron flight formations were once an obvious daytime signal of the change of seasons, their numbers are sadly diminished. **Maxima:** See above. **ASW Seasonal Stats:** Average: 6,705; Maximum: 12,206 in 1994.

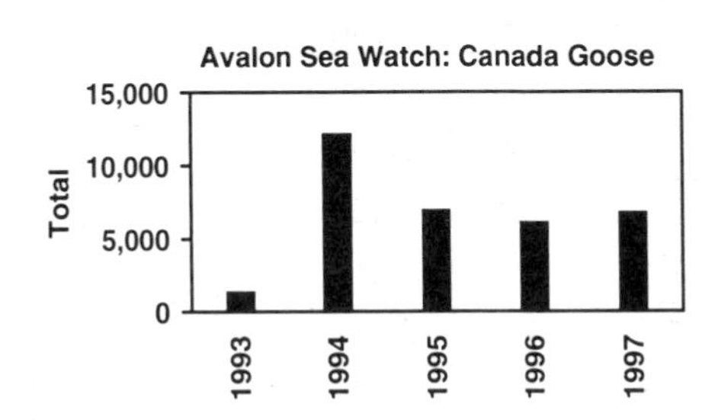

Winter: Although migrant Canada Geese have declined, CBC totals indicate a tremendous increase overall, with the increase apparently coming from nonmigratory populations. Statewide CBC totals rose dramatically from the late 1970s to the mid-1990s. **CBC Statewide Stats:** Average: 68,131; Maximum: 129,286 in 1996; Minimum: 14,377 in 1977. **CBC Maximum:** 28,313, Princeton, 1996.

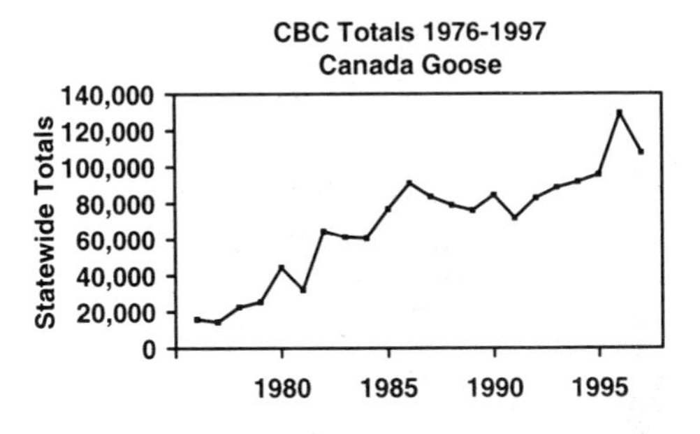

Spring: The northbound migration of Canada Geese takes place from mid-March to mid-April, but the migration of true migrant Canada Geese is difficult to distinguish from the movements of year-round residents.

Subspecies: Most of the migrant Canada Geese seen in New Jersey are the large subspecies, *B. c. canadensis*. Rarely, small Canada Geese are seen, presumably of the subspecies *B. c. hutchinsii* or possibly *B. c. parvipes*. Sibley (1997) indicated three records of apparent *B. c. hutchinsii* at Cape May and one possible record of *B. c. parvipes*, with several other small geese unidentified to subspecies. Stone (1937) considered small Canada Geese to be occasional strays and "very rare" on the East Coast. This status appears to be unchanged. ■

Brant

Branta bernicla

Range: In North America breeds in Alaska and high Arctic Canada. In the east winters from southern New England to North Carolina.

NJ Status: Common spring and fall migrant, common winter resident.

Historic Change: Stone (1937) considered Brant scarce in the Cape May area, and indicated the main concentrations were centered around Barnegat Bay. At that time the main food source for Brant was eelgrass, which was then suffering from a blight. The loss of this food source was considered the major factor in a serious decline in their numbers. Since then, Brant have switched to other food sources and eelgrass has made a partial recovery (Kaufman 1996).

Fall: A few Brant arrive in late September and numbers slowly increase to the peak in early to mid-November. Some are seen migrating over inland ridges, but they are most commonly encountered along the coast. **Maxima:** Coastal: 20,000, Brigantine NWR, 18 November 1990; 15,000, Brigantine NWR, 21 November 1992; 15,000, Brigantine NWR, 18 November 1989; Inland: 3,500, Raccoon Ridge, 26 October 1976. **ASW Single-Day Maximum:** 3,915 on 30 October 1995. **ASW Seasonal Stats:** Average: 13,056; Maximum: 16,558 in 1997.

Winter: Tens of thousands of Brant spend the winter in New Jersey's saltwater bays and estuaries. CBC totals have been fairly consistent from year to year, as Brant seem to remain in the area more readily in severe weather than do other waterfowl. **CBC Statewide Stats:** Average: 44,690; Maximum: 70,212 in 1992; Minimum: 16,341 in 1977. **CBC Maximum:** 32,000, Oceanville, 1979.

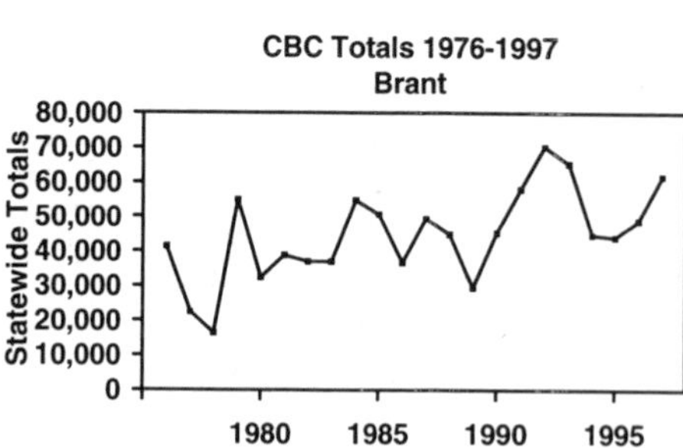

Avalon Sea Watch: Brant

Total

20,000
15,000
10,000
5,000
0

1993
1994
1995
1996
1997

Spring: Brant are fairly common into early May, but most have departed from New Jersey by the end of May. Occasionally, large groups have been seen inland during migration in late May (e. g., 200, over Trenton,

Brant

continued

25 May 1980; 100, over Lyons, 23 May 1990; and 100, over Stokes State Forest, 27 May 1995). Occasionally, a few Brant remain in the state through the summer.

Subspecies: Nearly all Brant in New Jersey are the eastern, light-bellied, *B. b. hrota*. "Black" Brant, *B. b. nigricans*, are reported occasionally, and *nigricans* X *hrota* intergrades are possible. Not all dark-bellied individuals are *nigricans*, as there is another dark-bellied population nesting in northwestern Canada that could occur in the state (Sibley 1997). The *nigricans* subspecies was added to the Review List in 1996. ■

Mute Swan

Cygnus olor

Range: Introduced to North America. Resident from New Hampshire to Virginia and locally around the Great Lakes.

NJ Status: Fairly common but somewhat local resident.

Breeding

Habitat: Nests in a variety of wetland areas including park ponds, marshes, lakes, etc.

Mute Swans were first introduced to the United States in 1910 (Bull 1964), and they had spread to New Jersey by 1916 (Stone 1937). Unfortunately, the pattern of the expanding breeding range in the state was poorly documented. In 1975 the species was noted to be expanding rapidly in RNJB Region 2 (Black 1975), and had reached the Pequannock watershed in 1980 (Hanisek 1981a).

Atlas surveys found Mute Swans nesting in all the provinces of New Jersey, with provinces from the Piedmont northward hosting the highest concentration of occupied blocks. They were well distributed in the Outer Coastal Plain, but scarce in the Pine Barrens, Inner Coastal Plain, and in Mercer, Middlesex, and Hunterdon counties.

Fall: After the breeding season, Mute Swans remain near their natal territories. Although usually described as nonmigratory, freezing temperatures can force them to travel far enough to find open water with available food.

Winter: Mute Swans can gather in large, loose flocks at favored sites, with family groups remaining intact through the winter. They are occasionally seen on the ocean after sudden, hard freezes. After a decline in CBC totals from 1981 to 1983, counts in the mid-1990s have

continued on page 118

continued from page 117

Mute Swan

steadily risen. **CBC Statewide Stats:** Average: 683; Maximum: 1,343 in 1995; Minimum: 159 in 1982. **CBC Maximum:** 741, Lakehurst, 1977.

Spring: There is little, if any, noticeable movement of Mute Swans in spring. ■

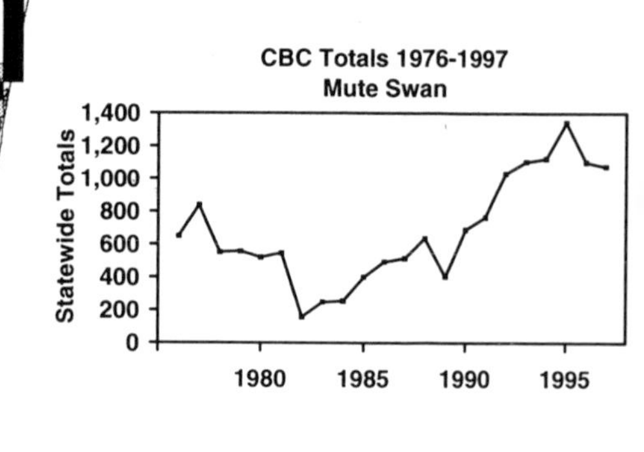

Possible
Probable
Confirmed

Statewide Summary	
Status	# of Blocks
Possible	24
Probable	32
Confirmed	108
Total	164

Physiographic Distribution **Mute Swan**	Number of blocks in province	Number of blocks species found breeding in province	Number of blocks species found in state	Percent of province species occupies	Percent of all records for this species found in province	Percent of state area in province
Kittatinny Mountains	19	2	164	10.5	1.2	2.2
Kittatinny Valley	45	29	164	64.4	17.7	5.3
Highlands	109	44	164	40.4	26.8	12.8
Piedmont	167	28	164	16.8	17.1	19.6
Inner Coastal Plain	128	7	164	5.5	4.3	15.0
Outer Coastal Plain	204	38	164	18.6	23.2	23.9
Pine Barrens	180	16	164	8.9	9.8	21.1

Tundra Swan
Cygnus columbianus

Range: Breeds on the Arctic tundra from Alaska east to northwestern Quebec. On the East Coast, winters from New Jersey to northern South Carolina.

NJ Status: Fairly common fall and uncommon spring migrant, uncommon winter resident.

Historic Changes: Tundra Swans have become more common in New Jersey during the latter half of the 20th century. Fables (1955) considered this species "a rare transient," and Leck (1984) referred to them as "uncommon or rare transients" that had increased since 1960. He also indicated that statewide counts for all CBCs typically numbered under 200 birds. Statewide totals for all CBCs from 1976 to 1997 have averaged much higher (see below).

Fall: Tundra Swans are often seen migrating along the coast as they move south to wintering grounds on the Chesapeake Bay or eastern North Carolina. The earliest groups can be seen in late October, and peak numbers pass from mid- to late November. At that time large numbers can also be seen staging at locations such as Brigantine NWR, where they often remain through December. **Maxima:** 1,150, Wading River, 27 December 1985; 1,000, Brigantine NWR, 15 November 1986. **ASW Single-Day Maximum:** 151 on 31 October 1996. **ASW Seasonal Stats:** Average: 192; Maximum: 257 in 1997.

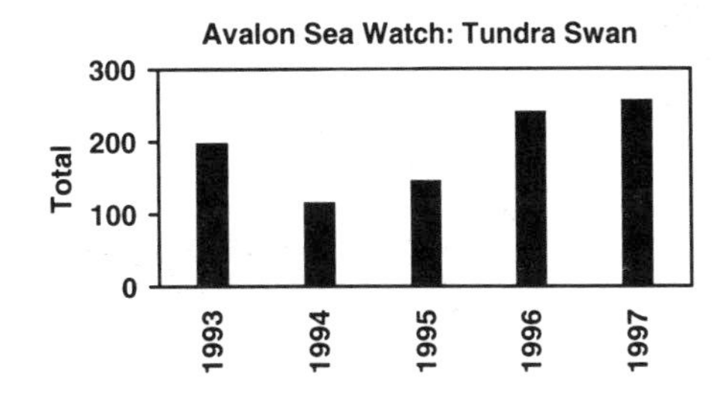

Winter: CBC totals of Tundra Swans peaked in the mid-1980s, but have declined into the mid-1990s. The number of Tundra Swans diminishes in mid-winter, particularly during hard

continued on page 120

Tundra Swan

continued from page 119

Tundra Swan

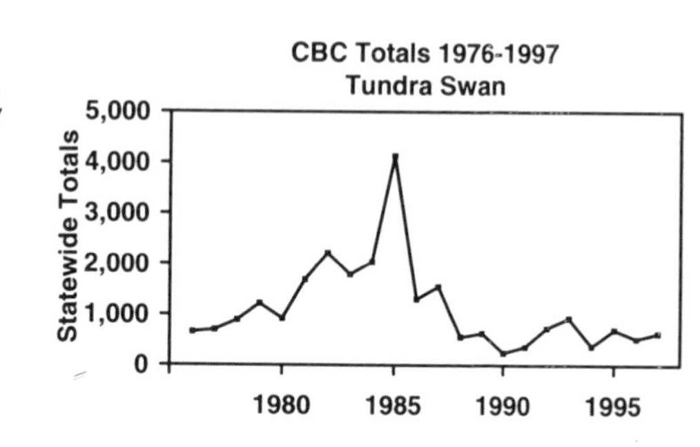

freezes. **Maxima:** 1,400, Elmer, 5 February 1984; 800, Mannington Marsh, 15 March 1977. **CBC Statewide Stats:** Average: 1,127; Maximum: 4,131 in 1985; Minimum: 250 in 1990. **CBC Maximum:** 2,333, Elmer, 1985.

Spring: The spring flight of Tundra Swans, which is considerably smaller than that of fall, begins in mid-February and is usually over by early April. ■

Wood Duck

Aix sponsa

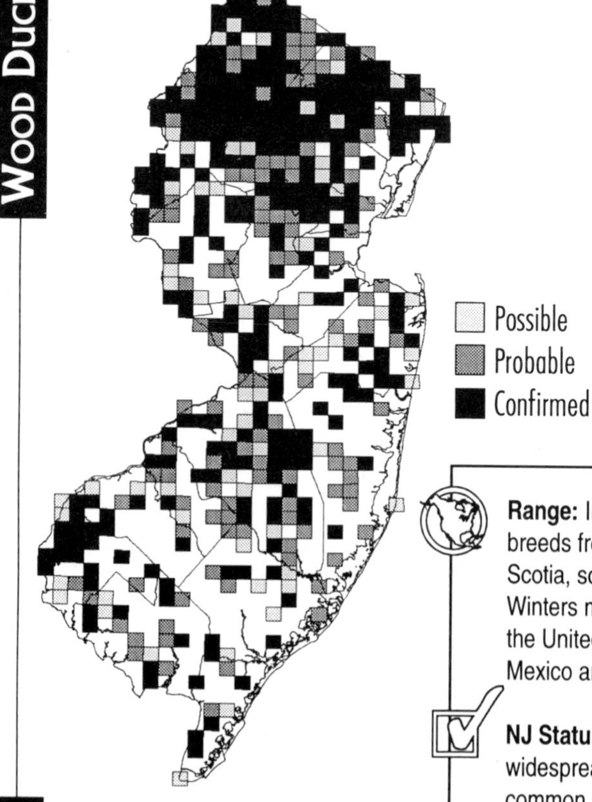

Statewide Summary	
Status	# of Blocks
Possible	64
Probable	119
Confirmed	276
Total	459

Range: In eastern North America breeds from Manitoba east to Nova Scotia, south to east Texas and Florida. Winters mainly in the southern half of the United States, and south to northern Mexico and the West Indies.

NJ Status: Fairly common and widespread summer resident, fairly common spring and fall migrant, rare to scarce winter resident.

Wood Duck

continued

Breeding

Habitat: Nests in cavities, including man-made boxes, in forested wetlands and ponds.

Stone (1908) described Wood Ducks as "formerly a common species, but rapidly reduced in numbers." In 1923 Griscom listed Wood Ducks as "extirpated, rare or local." The recovery of this species was remarkable, and, by 1937, Stone reported the population was increasing in Cape May. Their rapid recovery was probably due to the reproduction of isolated pockets of Wood Ducks that had somehow survived the massive market hunting of the 1800s and early 1900s (Hepp and Bellrose 1995). In the 1970s Great Swamp NWR was a stronghold for the species, with late summer surveys reporting high numbers of young (1,000 young in 1977; 1,238 young in 1978; 1,500-2,000 young in 1979, 5,000 young in 1980).

Atlas data indicated Wood Ducks are one of our most widely distributed breeding ducks, nesting in all provinces of New Jersey. They are, however, most concentrated north of the Piedmont. River courses through the Pine Barrens (e.g., the Mullica and Wading rivers) provide often-used breeding habitat in the south. Wood Ducks require mature forests with trees large enough to provide appropriately sized nesting cavities. They are wetland breeders, and are dependent upon a complex vegetation structure with a mixture of water tolerant trees and shrubs and open water (Hepp and Bellrose 1995). Nest boxes are often used in areas where nest trees are missing.

Fall: Aggregations of post-breeding Wood Ducks are noted in late summer. In certain areas those numbers can reach into the hundreds or thousands (see above). At the Avalon Sea Watch, the first migrants are noted in mid-September. The peak movement occurs from mid- to late October, with most having passed by mid-November. Although they are frequently seen as near-shore migrants, they are rarely seen using any type of

continued on page 122

Physiographic Distribution

Wood Duck	Number of blocks in province	Number of blocks species found breeding in province	Number of blocks species found in state	Percent of province species occupies	Percent of all records for this species found in province	Percent of state area in province
Kittatinny Mountains	19	18	459	94.7	3.9	2.2
Kittatinny Valley	45	41	459	91.1	8.9	5.3
Highlands	109	93	459	85.3	20.3	12.8
Piedmont	167	96	459	57.5	20.9	19.6
Inner Coastal Plain	128	71	459	55.5	15.5	15.0
Outer Coastal Plain	204	62	459	30.4	13.5	23.9
Pine Barrens	180	78	459	43.3	17.0	21.1

continued from page 121

Wood Duck

saltwater wetland. **ASW Single-Day Maximum:** 257 on 17 October 1995. **ASW Seasonal Stats:** Average: 896; Maximum: 1,303 in 1995.

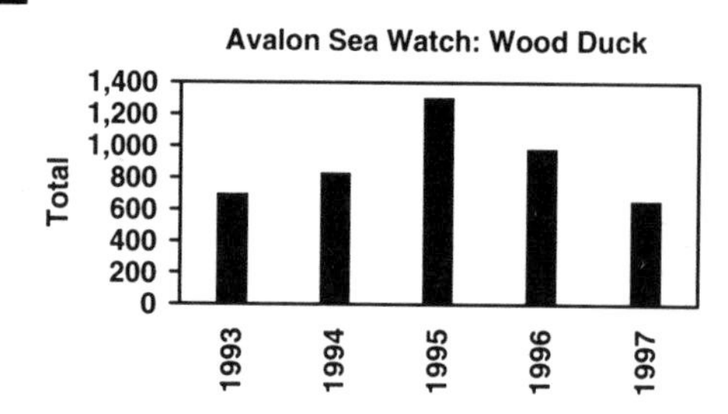

Spring: The northward movement of Wood Ducks is poorly documented. They can return early in March in some years, with the main movement probably occurring from late March through early April. **Maximum:** 30, Mannington Marsh, 3 April 1991. ■

Winter: CBC totals for Wood Ducks vary with the availability of open water. They become hard to find in mid-winter, particularly during hard freezes, and are very rare in the harshest winters. **CBC Statewide Stats:** Average: 68; Maximum: 187 in 1991; Minimum: 26 in 1981. **CBC Maximum:** 99, Great Swamp, 1991.

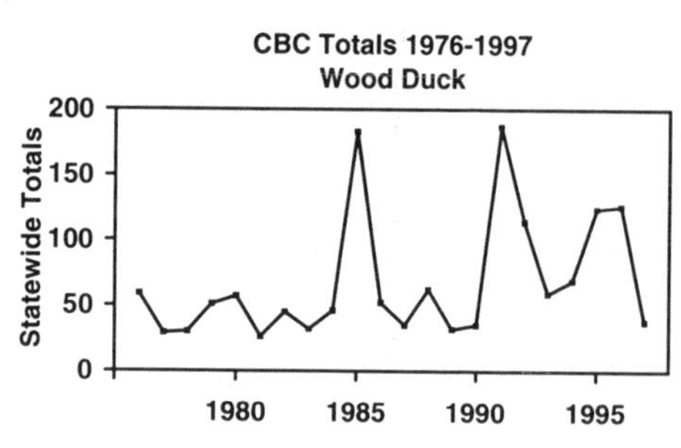

Gadwall

Anas strepera

Range: Breeds primarily in western and north-central North America. In the East, breeds sporadically across southern Canada east to Nova Scotia south to North Carolina. In the East, winters from Massachusetts south to Florida, along the Gulf coast and in Mexico and Cuba.

NJ Status: Uncommon and local summer resident, common spring and fall migrant, uncommon to fairly common winter resident.

Breeding

Habitat: Breeds in fresh and brackish marshes.

The first breeding record of Gadwalls in New Jersey was at Egg Island, near Fortescue, in 1949. By 1952 there were reports of seven broods in the same area (Fables

Gadwall

continued

1955). Since that time this species has expanded in New Jersey, especially along the southern coast, and along the Hackensack River. Prior to the Atlas surveys, Gadwalls were confirmed at North Arlington (1975), Manahawkin (1977), Kearny Marsh (1975-1978), and Great Swamp (1980).

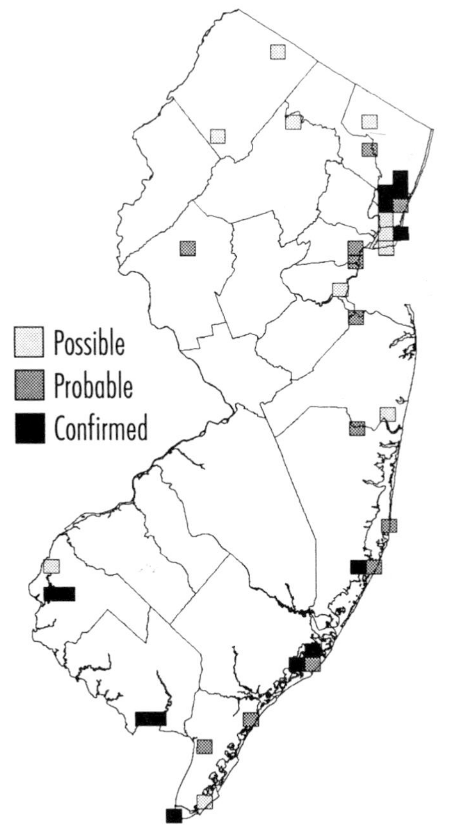

During the Atlas the total number of known active breeding locations for Gadwall increased notably. They were found breeding in six provinces, but they were only found in 4% of the blocks statewide. In northern New Jersey, the Hackensack River marshes host many breeding pairs (20 broods at HMEC in 1993, 80 individuals at Kearny Marsh in July 1995, 200 at Kearny Marsh in 1996, 140 at HMEC in 1996). The stronghold for the species in southern New Jersey is the Atlantic coast and Delaware Bay marshes.

continued on page 124

Statewide Summary

Status	# of Blocks
Possible	11
Probable	12
Confirmed	13
Total	36

Physiographic Distribution

Gadwall	Number of blocks in province	Number of blocks species found breeding in province	Number of blocks species found in state	Percent of province species occupies	Percent of all records for this species found in province	Percent of state area in province
Kittatinny Valley	45	1	36	2.2	2.8	5.3
Highlands	109	2	36	1.8	5.6	12.8
Piedmont	167	14	36	8.4	38.9	19.6
Inner Coastal Plain	128	4	36	3.1	11.1	15.0
Outer Coastal Plain	204	14	36	6.9	38.9	23.9
Pine Barrens	180	1	36	0.6	2.8	21.1

continued from page 123

Gadwall

Fall: A few migrant Gadwalls can be seen by late summer, but most arrive from late October to early November and remain throughout the winter. They are recorded in very small numbers at the Avalon Sea Watch. **Maxima:** 500+, Mannington Marsh, 25 October 1993; 350, Mannington Marsh, 8 November 1990. **ASW Single-Day Maximum:** 21 on 16 November 1997. **ASW Seasonal Stats:** Average: 22; Maximum: 53 in 1995.

Winter: CBC totals of Gadwalls have increased from 1976 to 1997, mirroring their general increase in the East. Wintering numbers will drop in mid-winter if conditions turn harsh for an extended period. **CBC Statewide Stats:** Average: 738; Maximum: 1,416 in 1997; Minimum: 190 in 1981. **CBC Maximum:** 600, Oceanville, 1984.

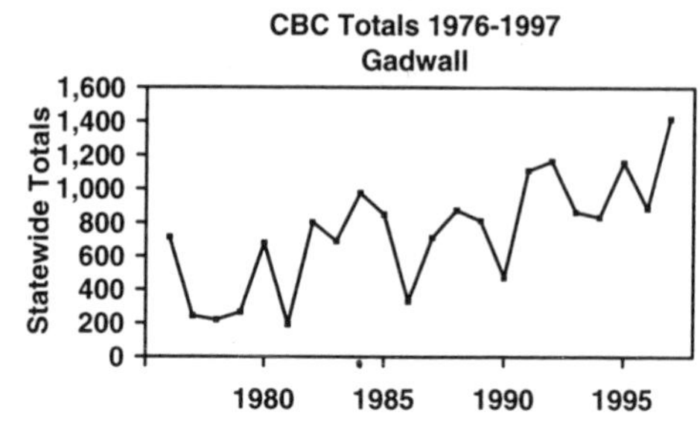

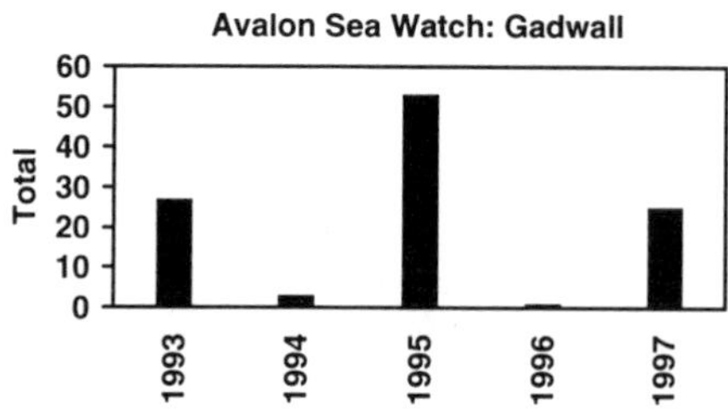

Spring: An influx of northbound migrant Gadwalls in March combines with local wintering birds to form a peak that diminishes through April. **Maxima:** 600, Mannington Marsh, 8 March 1992; 400+, Kearny Marsh, 11 March 1995. ■

Eurasian Wigeon

Anas penelope

Range: Breeds across northern Europe and Asia. Winters on both coasts of North America, and more rarely inland.

NJ Status: Rare spring and fall migrant, rare winter visitor.

Fall: Eurasian Wigeon may arrive as early as late August, and some sites are used year after year. They are usually found with flocks of American Wigeons in late fall and winter, typically along the coast. Sightings of males far outnumber those of females, although this disproportion is probably due to the difficulty in distinguishing female American Wigeon from female Eurasian Wigeon.

Eurasian Wigeon

continued

Winter: Stone (1937) was aware that a few Eurasian Wigeon wintered in the state each year, although he included no records from Cape May County. Their status remained unchanged into the late 1980s, when, in 1986 and 1987, there were three or four birds present in the state. However, since that time sightings have increased with up to ten birds present in the state each year. Kaufman (1996) has suggested the possibility of breeding on the North American continent, which could account for the increase. A few are usually found on CBCs. **Maximum:** 3, Cape May Point, 22 December 1996. **CBC Statewide Stats:** Average: 3; Maximum: 6 in 1993; Minimum: 0 in four years. **CBC Maximum:** 3, Long Branch, 1991; 3, Oceanville, 1991; 3, Cape May, 1997.

Spring: Eurasian Wigeons will sometimes linger into spring but they are usually gone by early April, only occasionally staying into early May. ■

American Wigeon

Anas americana

Range: In the East, breeds locally from Manitoba east to Nova Scotia, south to northern New York. In the East winters from Massachusetts to Illinois, and south to Central America and the West Indies.

NJ Status: Common spring and fall migrant, fairly common winter resident.

Fall: The first southbound American Wigeons arrive in New Jersey by late August. Peak numbers pass from mid- to late October, and most have passed by mid-November. They are uncommon at the Avalon Sea Watch, suggesting that some of their migration may take place either at night or inland. Kaufman (1996), however, suggests that they may travel mostly by day. **Maxima:** 2,000+, Mannington Marsh, 31 October 1993; 1,700, Mannington Marsh, 14 October 1990. **ASW Single-Day Maximum:** 250 on 30 October 1995. **ASW Seasonal Stats:** Average: 473; Maximum: 1,037 in 1995.

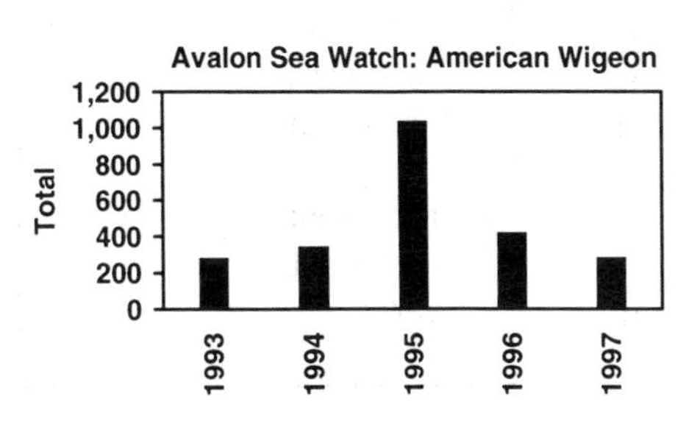

Winter: From 1976 to 1997, CBC totals for American Wigeons were variable. Numbers are apt to be lowest in mid-winter, particularly in harsh winters when open water is

continued on page 126

continued from page 125

American Wigeon

scarce. **CBC Statewide Stats:** Average: 1,827; Maximum: 3,178 in 1976; Minimum: 897 in 1989. **CBC Maximum:** 1,941, Long Branch, 1982.

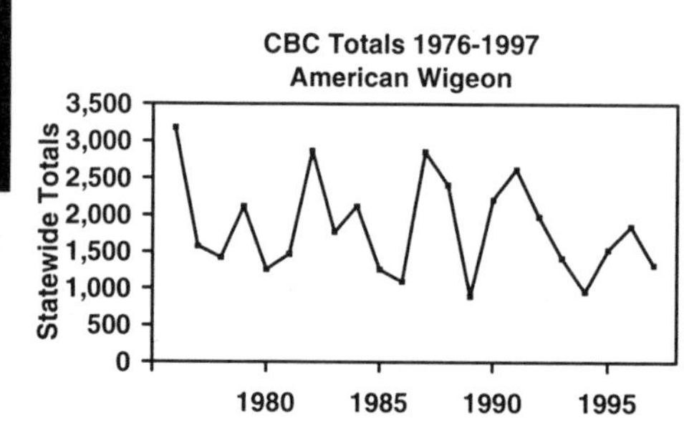

Spring: Northbound American Wigeons arrive and augment the wintering population in early March. The peak passes quickly and numbers dwindle throughout April, with most gone from New Jersey by the end of that month. **Maxima:** 2,500, Mannington Marsh, 8 March 1992; 1,000+, Mannington Marsh, 6 March 1991. ■

American Black Duck

Anas rubripes

Range: Breeds from Saskatchewan east to Labrador, south to North Dakota and North Carolina. Winters throughout much of the eastern United States, south to northeast Texas and northern Georgia.

NJ Status: Fairly common but somewhat local summer resident, common spring and fall migrant, common winter resident.

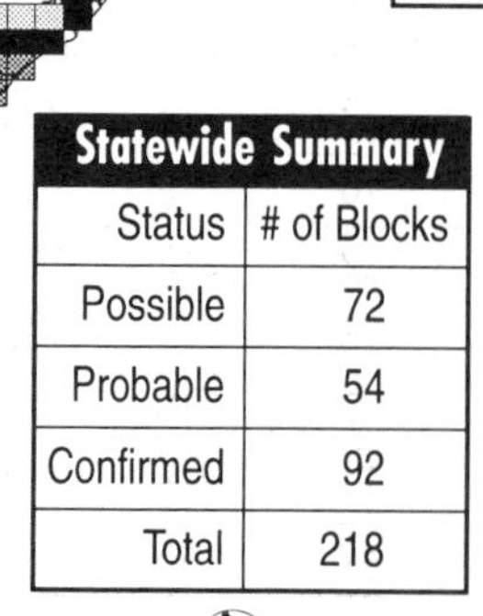

Possible
Probable
Confirmed

Statewide Summary	
Status	# of Blocks
Possible	72
Probable	54
Confirmed	92
Total	218

Breeding

Habitat: Variable, from marsh edges to woodlands, usually near water but some nests are in forest interior.

American Black Duck

continued

American Black Ducks have undergone at least two periods of decline during the 1900s. Bent (1923) considered them the dominant species of waterfowl in the eastern United States. Stone (1937) reported market gunning nearly extirpated the species at the turn of the century, but the species was quick to rebound once given adequate protection. During the 1970s and early 1980s, they had a second period of decline. The causes for that decline were thought to be loss of breeding habitat, hybridization with Mallards, and over-harvesting. In the early 1980s, there was a marked decline in breeding reports for this species in northern New Jersey. In 1981 they were reported as being displaced by Mallards in RNJB Region 1 (Hanisek 1981), and by 1984 only three black ducks were reported in both RNJB Region 1 and Region 2 (Hanisek 1984, Black 1984). In 1985 there were no breeding reports for this species in Region 1 (Hanisek 1985). By the late 1980s, black ducks were either recovering in northern New Jersey or were searched for more effectively.

Atlas observers found American Black Ducks breeding in all provinces, although the birds were more concentrated in areas south of the Piedmont. Many of the provinces had more than 20% of their blocks occupied by black ducks, indicating the variety of nesting habitats suitable for this species. The Outer Coastal Plain and Pine Barrens had impressively large contiguous areas of occupied blocks.

continued on page 128

Map Interpretation: American Black Duck's habit of nesting in woodlands, occasionally far from water and sometimes off the ground, makes it difficult to find nests, especially in the interior of New Jersey. It is likely there are more nests in the interior part of the state than the Atlas data indicated.

Physiographic Distribution

American Black Duck	Number of blocks in province	Number of blocks species found breeding in province	Number of blocks species found in state	Percent of province species occupies	Percent of all records for this species found in province	Percent of state area in province
Kittatinny Mountains	19	2	218	10.5	0.9	2.2
Kittatinny Valley	45	16	218	35.6	7.3	5.3
Highlands	109	22	218	20.2	10.1	12.8
Piedmont	167	23	218	13.8	10.6	19.6
Inner Coastal Plain	128	37	218	28.9	17.0	15.0
Outer Coastal Plain	204	71	218	34.8	32.6	23.9
Pine Barrens	180	47	218	26.1	21.6	21.1

continued from page 127

American Black Duck

Fall: The first migrant American Black Ducks are typically seen in mid-September. Migration is protracted, continuing well into December, with the peak movement occurring in early to mid-November. At the Avalon Sea Watch, totals for the season are surprisingly low, indicating that many may migrate at night. Large numbers congregate at Brigantine NWR and throughout coastal salt marshes of the state. **Maxima:** 647, Avalon Sea Watch, 30 October 1995 (with an additional 585 the following day); 488, Avalon Sea Watch, 14 November 1996. **ASW Seasonal Stats:** Average: 2,962; Maximum: 4,422 in 1995.

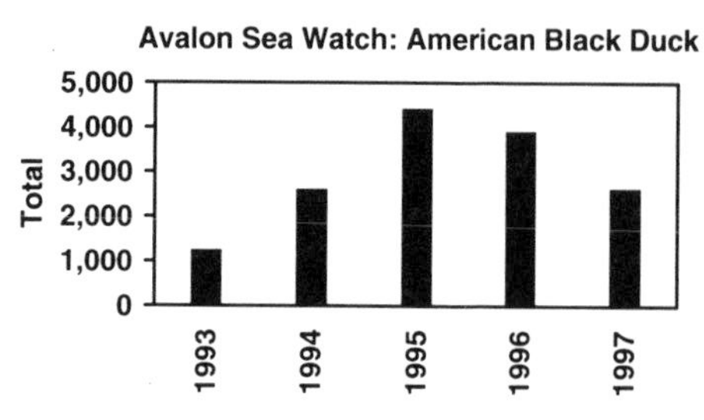

Winter: Although breeding populations from interior parts of their overall range have declined dramatically (Kaufman 1996), statewide CBC totals of black ducks in New Jersey were variable from 1976 to 1997. **Maxima:** 50,000, Brigantine NWR, 30 January 1983; 20,000-25,000, Pedricktown, 19 January 1991. **CBC Statewide Stats:** Average: 18,986; Maximum: 27,685 in 1988; Minimum: 11,437 in 1976. **CBC Maximum:** 11,080, Oceanville, 1994.

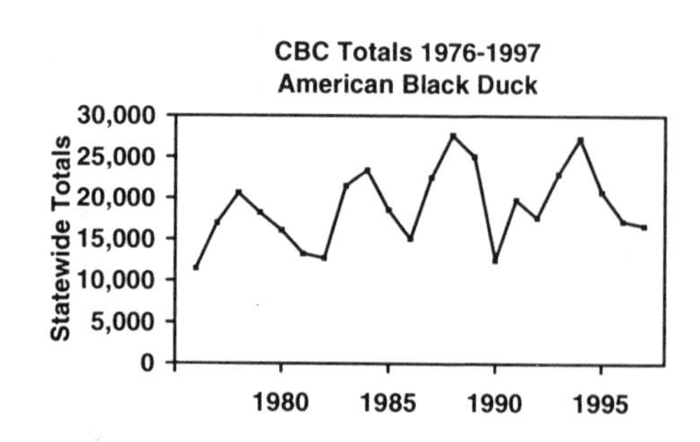

Spring: Spring migration is difficult to detect, and is noted mainly by reduced numbers of wintering birds. By May, most American Black Ducks that remain are local breeders. ■

American Black Duck x Mallard Hybrid

Breeding

Hybridization of American Black Ducks with Mallards is frequently cited as one of the possible reasons for recent declines in black duck populations. Stone (1908) reported an American Black Duck X Mallard hybrid as a rarity, but Bent (1923) indicated many hybrid specimens had been collected. There is little information on the frequency of this hybrid in New Jersey, as it was noted for the first time in RNJB 1993.

Atlas observers found American Black Duck X Mallard hybrids breeding in 47 blocks. The incidence of hybridization is probably more common than these data indicated, because many observers were unable to detect hybrid plumages. A regional pattern of occurrence for the hybrids is difficult to discern. The Piedmont and Pine Barrens had the highest concentration of hybrids, with nearly 30% of the blocks occupied by the hybrids in each province. The areas in southern New Jersey with the highest densities of American Black Ducks (coastal Salem, Cumberland, Cape May, and Atlantic counties) only had two blocks with reports of hybrids. ■

Possible
Probable
Confirmed

Statewide Summary	
Status	# of Blocks
Possible	7
Probable	11
Confirmed	29
Total	47

Physiographic Distribution

American Black Duck x Mallard Hybrid	Number of blocks in province	Number of blocks species found breeding in province	Number of blocks species found in state	Percent of province species occupies	Percent of all records for this species found in province	Percent of state area in province
Kittatinny Valley	45	1	47	2.2	2.1	5.3
Highlands	109	6	47	5.5	12.8	12.8
Piedmont	167	14	47	8.4	29.8	19.6
Inner Coastal Plain	128	9	47	7.0	19.1	15.0
Outer Coastal Plain	204	4	47	2.0	8.5	23.9
Pine Barrens	180	13	47	7.2	27.7	21.1

Mallard

Anas platyrhynchos

Range: In eastern North America, breeds from Manitoba southeast to Nova Scotia, south to northern Texas and South Carolina. Winters throughout most of the United States.

NJ Status: Common and very widespread summer resident, uncommon spring and fall migrant, common winter resident.

Statewide Summary

Status	# of Blocks
Possible	65
Probable	124
Confirmed	471
Total	660

Physiographic Distribution

Mallard	Number of blocks in province	Number of blocks species found breeding in province	Number of blocks species found in state	Percent of province species occupies	Percent of all records for this species found in province	Percent of state area in province
Kittatinny Mountains	19	18	660	94.7	2.7	2.2
Kittatinny Valley	45	45	660	100.0	6.8	5.3
Highlands	109	104	660	95.4	15.8	12.8
Piedmont	167	155	660	92.8	23.5	19.6
Inner Coastal Plain	128	102	660	79.7	15.5	15.0
Outer Coastal Plain	204	135	660	66.2	20.5	23.9
Pine Barrens	180	101	660	56.1	15.3	21.1

Breeding

Habitat: Widespread in most freshwater habitats; marshes, swamps, ponds, lakes, and city parks.

Historically Mallards were much less common than their current abundance suggests. Bent (1923) listed Mallards as breeding in New Jersey only as far north as Burlington and Passaic counties. In 1937 Stone considered Mallards rare breeders and questioned the origin of breeding records, suspecting they may have been escapes. Fables (1955) described the New Jersey nesting population as descendents of escaped or semi-feral birds. Mallard populations have benefited from stocking programs, although these same programs may have contributed to declines in American Black Ducks. Mallards are adaptable to suburban environments and, unlike American Black Duck, will use degraded or developed wetlands.

Atlas data indicated that Mallards have become New Jersey's most widespread breeding duck, occurring in 77% of the blocks statewide. Regionally, they are most common from the Piedmont northward, recorded in over 90% of the blocks in the Piedmont, Kittatinny Mountains, Kittatinny Valley, and Highlands. They were recorded less frequently in the provinces south of the Piedmont.

Fall: Discerning the migration patterns of wild Mallards from semi-tame and feral populations is difficult. Relatively few birds are seen at the Avalon Sea Watch flying south over the ocean. However, if those seen are true migrants, the timing of their movements matches that of American Black Ducks. Information from the Sea Watch indicated a protracted movement peaking from early to mid-November. **ASW Single-Day Maximum:** 140 on 2 November 1993. **ASW Seasonal Stats:** Average: 357; Maximum: 494 in 1995.

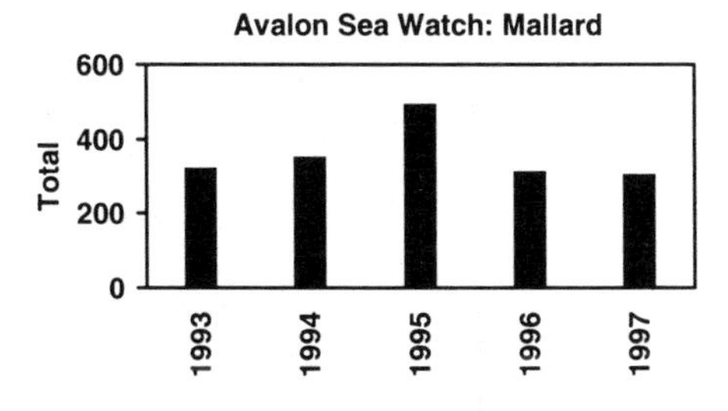

Winter: CBC totals of Mallards have increased from 1976 to 1997, with an average statewide total similar to that of American Black Duck. **CBC Statewide Stats:** Average: 19,304; Maximum: 27,311 in 1994; Minimum: 15,017 in 1987. **CBC Maximum:** 4,100 Great Swamp, 1994.

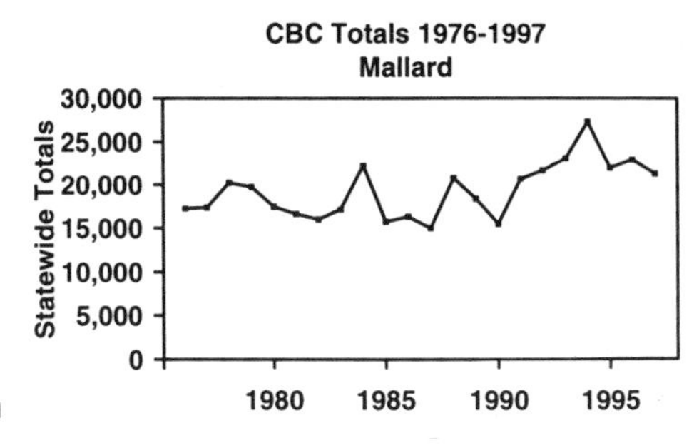

Spring: Spring movements of true wild Mallards are even more difficult to discern than those of fall. Numbers along the Maurice River, where most of the birds are assumed to be wild, begin to dwindle in early March (pers. com. C. Sutton). ■

Blue-winged Teal

Anas discors

Range: In eastern North America breeds from northern Manitoba east to Nova Scotia and south to Texas and North Carolina. Winters from North Carolina and Texas south to South America.

NJ Status: Scarce and very local summer resident, fairly common spring and common fall migrant, rare winter resident.

Statewide Summary	
Status	# of Blocks
Possible	6
Probable	3
Confirmed	6
Total	15

Breeding

Habitat: Nests on freshwater ponds and marshes, occasionally brackish marshes.

Stone (1937) reported evidence of several Blue-winged Teal nests in southern New Jersey. Bent (1923) reported that blue-wingeds had declined over much of their North American range from the late 1800s to the early 1900s and nested in only a few locations in the East. Fables (1955) stated that they were breeding in six New Jersey counties, but that they remained rare breeders. Bull (1964) noted them as scarce breeders with six known breeding locations in northern New Jersey. However, Kane (1974) reported

Physiographic Distribution Blue-winged Teal	Number of blocks in province	Number of blocks species found breeding in province	Number of blocks species found in state	Percent of province species occupies	Percent of all records for this species found in province	Percent of state area in province
Kittatinny Valley	45	1	15	2.2	6.7	5.3
Piedmont	167	4	15	2.4	26.7	19.6
Inner Coastal Plain	128	3	15	2.3	20.0	15.0
Outer Coastal Plain	204	6	15	2.9	40.0	23.9
Pine Barrens	180	1	15	0.6	6.7	21.1

Blue-winged Teal were the most abundant breeding ducks in the Hackensack Meadows. He indicated that "more than 100 birds could be seen in a single day along the dikes in July of 1971 and 1972. The maximum number of broods seen in a single day was seven."

Blue-winged Teal probably breed annually in New Jersey. The current statewide population is small and broadly distributed, and no locations have supported breeding teal for many years. Kearny Marsh is the notable exception, with confirmed nesting by this species from 1975-1978 (Kane 1978). Mercer County Park also has had the modest history of hosting nesting Blue-winged Teal in 1976 and 1980.

Atlas data indicated the species was a very local breeding bird in New Jersey. They were reported from all provinces except the Highlands and Kittatinny Mountains, and were noted as Confirmed along the Hackensack River, at Mannington Marsh, Dividing Creek, and in the South Cape May Meadows.

Map Interpretation: Most of the mapped Probable locations were dated after 15 May, which suggests these are sightings of breeding birds (Hartman 1992a). This species occurs in low numbers over much of the state, but is easy to overlook. The Atlas data are likely to under-represent the breeding range of this species.

Fall: The first southbound Blue-winged Teal can be seen in mid-August, with peak numbers usually occurring in September. As with many dabbling ducks, the largest concentrations are generally encountered at Brigantine NWR. They are infrequently recorded at the Avalon Sea Watch, with most seen there in late September and early October. **Maxima:** 2,000+, Brigantine NWR, 5 September 1994; 1,000+, Brigantine NWR, 1 October 1995. **ASW Single-Day Maximum:** 37 on 15 October 1995. **ASW Seasonal Stats:** Average: 37; Maximum: 84 in 1995.

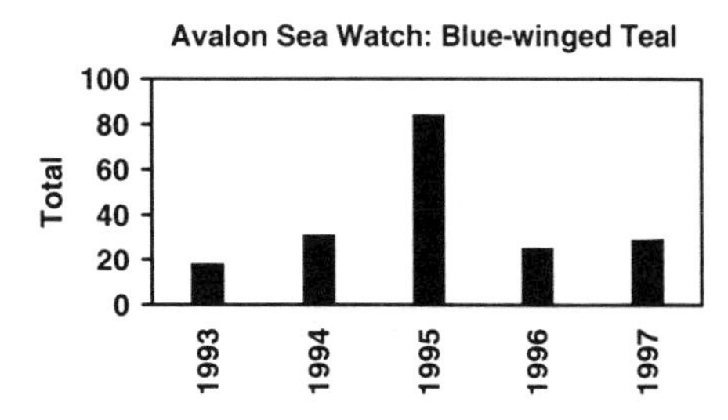

Winter: Unlike other dabbling ducks, Blue-winged Teal become scarce by December and are the least likely dabbler to be seen in mid-winter. A few are seen on CBCs each year, particularly in years when the weather is mild. **CBC Statewide Stats:** Average: 10; Maximum: 35 in 1985; Minimum: 0 in 1996 and 1997. **CBC Maximum:** 33, Marmora, 1985.

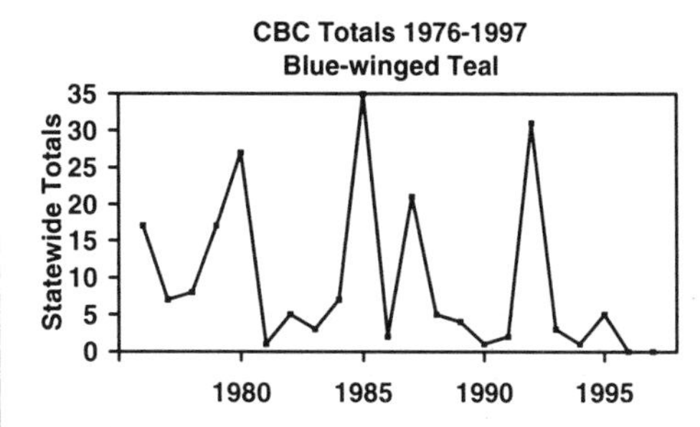

Spring: Returning Blue-winged Teal are first seen from mid- to late March, and movements continue into May. Typically, numbers diminish after early May, although the maximum spring count of 250 was recorded at Great Swamp in May 1976. **Other maxima:** 31, Fishing Creek Marsh, 4 April 1996; 30, Corbin City, 28 March 1992 (Sibley 1997). ■

Cinnamon Teal

Anas cyanoptera

Range: Breeds in southwestern Canada and throughout the western states east to Montana and western Texas. Winters from California east to Texas, south to northern South America.

NJ Status: Accidental. NJBRC Review List.

Occurrence: There have been ten state reports of Cinnamon Teal, and two have been accepted by the NJBRC. The two accepted records are:

Brigantine NWR	*9 June-1 July 1974*	
Manahawkin	*18 April-8 May 1976*	*ph-RBPF*

Northern Shoveler

Anas clypeata

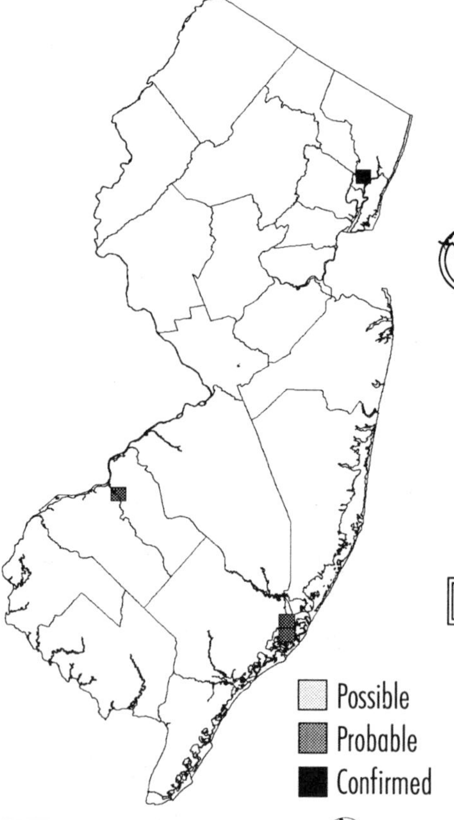

Range: Breeds mainly in western North America. In the East, breeds locally from the Great Lakes east, and sporadically south to Delaware. Winters on the East Coast from Massachusetts south to Florida, in the Mississippi Valley, and from the Gulf Coast south.

NJ Status: Scarce and very local summer resident, fairly common spring and fall migrant, uncommon to fairly common winter resident.

Northern Shoveler
continued

Physiographic Distribution Northern Shoveler	Number of blocks in province	Number of blocks species found breeding in province	Number of blocks species found in state	Percent of province species occupies	Percent of all records for this species found in province	Percent of state area in province
Piedmont	167	1	4	0.6	25.0	19.6
Inner Coastal Plain	128	1	4	0.8	25.0	15.0
Outer Coastal Plain	204	2	4	1.0	50.0	23.9

Statewide Summary	
Status	# of Blocks
Possible	0
Probable	3
Confirmed	1
Total	4

Breeding

Habitat: Nests on the edges of freshwater ponds and marshes.

Fables (1955) listed only two breeding reports for Northern Shoveler in New Jersey; one report from southwestern New Jersey in 1950 and a second report from Fortescue in 1952. A male summered in Kearny Marsh in 1978, but no further evidence of breeding was observed (Kane 1978). The Atlas survey provided one Confirmed breeding record for this species in New Jersey, when a brood was observed 26 June 1994 at the Hackensack Meadowlands. The other three records from the Atlas project were all sightings of pairs, but none of the reports included dates, and none yielded higher breeding codes.

Historic Changes: Stone (1937) considered these western ducks to be rare visitors to Cape May. Northern Shovelers increased in the state during the following decades, but numbers have stabilized since the late 1960s. Although they are fairly common from October to April, the largest concentrations rarely exceed 200 in any location.

Fall: Northern Shovelers can arrive as early as late August but become more common later in the fall, particularly amid the dabbling duck concentrations at Brigantine NWR and at Mannington Marsh. They are notably scarce as coastal migrants at the Avalon Sea Watch. **Maximum:** 200+, Brigantine NWR, 28 October 1995. **ASW Single-Day Maximum:** 14 on 13 November 1997. **ASW Seasonal Stats:** Average: 25; Maximum: 31 in 1993.

continued on page 136

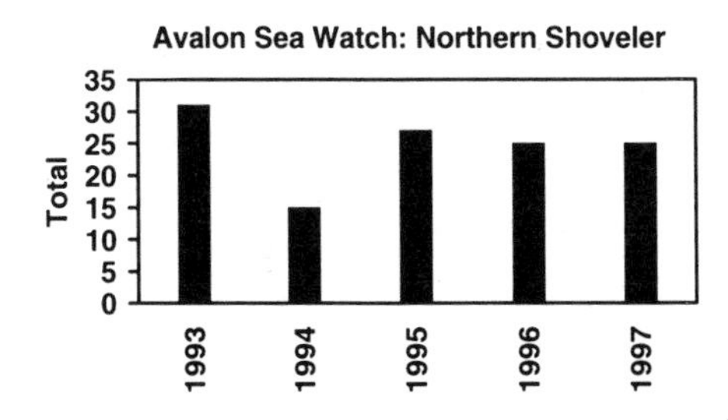

continued from page 135

Northern Shoveler

Winter: Harsh mid-winter conditions can force Northern Shovelers to migrate. From 1976 to 1997, statewide CBC totals were somewhat variable, although the numbers appear to indicate a slight decline since the mid-1980s. **Maximum:** 200, Brigantine NWR, 15 January 1995.

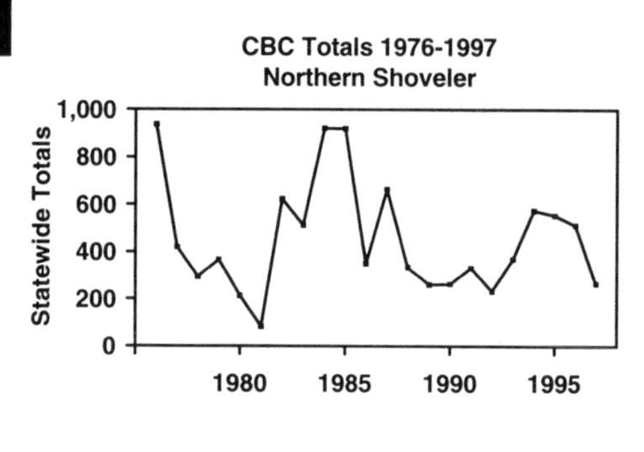

CBC Statewide Stats: Average: 455; Maximum: 938 in 1976; Minimum: 83 in 1981. **CBC Maximum:** 775, Oceanville, 1976.

Spring: Overall, Northern Shovelers are most numerous in late March and early April when the numbers of wintering birds are augmented by northbound migrants. Most have departed the state by early May. **Maxima:** 225, Brigantine NWR, 23 March 1997; 200, Mannington Marsh, 16 March 1991. ■

Northern Pintail

Anas acuta

Range: In eastern North America breeds from Manitoba east to Newfoundland, south to northern Texas and the Great Lakes. Winters from Nebraska to Massachusetts, south to Central America, and the West Indies.

NJ Status: Common spring and fall migrant, fairly common winter resident.

Historic Changes: There is only one historic breeding record of Northern Pintail for New Jersey; an adult female with a brood of downy young was observed on a freshwater pond of the New Jersey Turnpike, 5 July 1985 (Wander 1986). None were suspected of breeding during the Atlas period.

Fall: The first Northern Pintails can be seen in late August, and migration is well under way by mid- to late September. Most pintail are thought to migrate at night (Austin and Miller 1995), although they are regularly seen at the Avalon Sea Watch during the day. Migration is protracted, tapering off after early November. Large groups congregate at Brigantine

Northern Pintail

continued

NWR in late fall, remaining as long as there is open water. **Maxima:** 6,000+, Brigantine NWR, 22 October 1995; 4,000, Brigantine NWR, 29 September 1991. **ASW Single-Day Maximum:** 677 on 30 October 1995. **ASW Seasonal Stats:** Average: 986; Maximum: 2,238 in 1995.

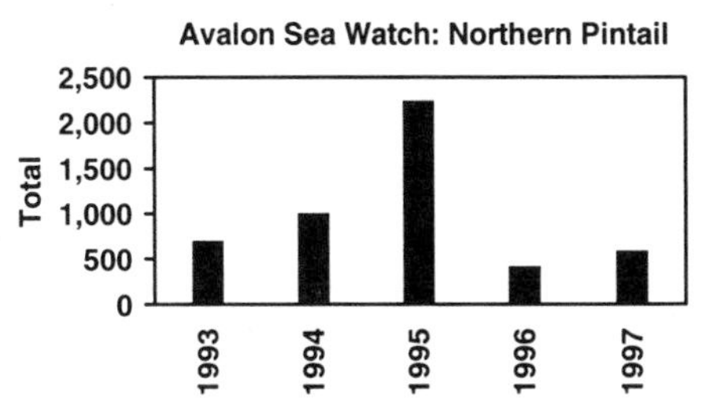

Spring: Northern Pintails are one of the earliest nesting ducks in North America (Austin and Miller 1995), and staging concentrations form early, from late February through early March in New Jersey. Numbers slowly diminish through March and most are gone by mid- to late April. **Maxima:** 50,000, Oldman's/Raccoon creeks, 24 February 1990; 40,000, Oldman's/Raccoon creeks, late February 1991. ■

Winter: As with most waterfowl, pintail abundance in midwinter depends upon open water, and hard freezes can force birds out of any given area. **CBC Statewide Stats:** Average: 1,001; Maximum: 2,109 in 1976; Minimum: 179 in 1981. **CBC Maximum:** 1,447, Lower Hudson, 1976.

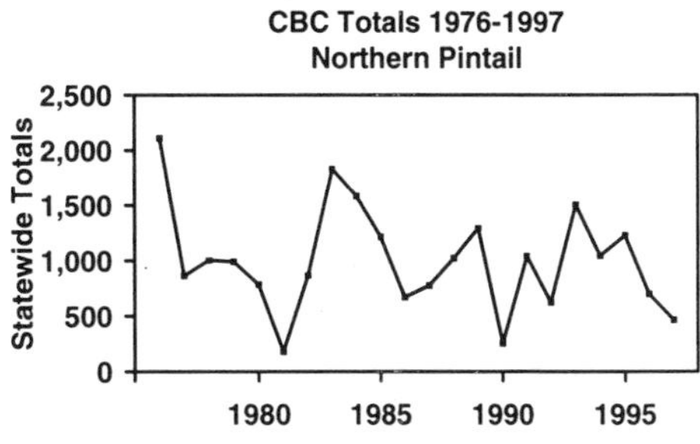

■

Garganey

Anas querquedula

Occurrence: There has been only one report and one accepted record of Garganey in New Jersey: Brigantine NWR, 9-15 June 1997, a drake. ■

Range: Breeds from Europe to Siberia. Winters south through Africa, Asia, and Australia.

NJ Status: Accidental. NJBRC Review List.

Green-winged Teal

Anas crecca

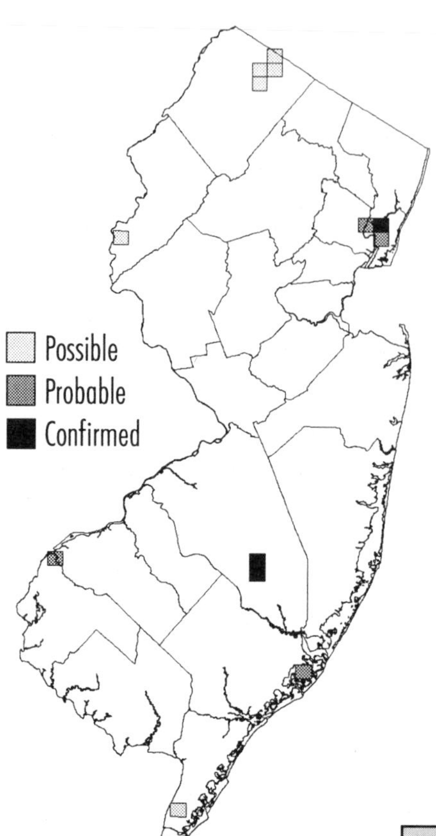

Range: In eastern North America breeds from the Northwest Territories east to Labrador, south to western Nebraska and the Great Lakes. Winters along the coast from Massachusetts to the southern United States and Central America.

NJ Status: Scarce and very local summer resident, common spring and fall migrant, fairly common winter resident.

Map Interpretation: It was estimated that a high percentage of breeding Green-winged Teal are overlooked, even when systematic nest search techniques are used to find nests (Hartman 1992b). It is therefore possible that the Atlas data yielded a low-end estimate of the breeding range of the species in New Jersey.

Statewide Summary

Status	# of Blocks
Possible	6
Probable	4
Confirmed	3
Total	13

Physiographic Distribution

Green-winged Teal	Number of blocks in province	Number of blocks species found breeding in province	Number of blocks species found in state	Percent of province species occupies	Percent of all records for this species found in province	Percent of state area in province
Kittatinny Valley	45	4	13	8.9	30.8	5.3
Highlands	109	1	13	0.9	7.7	12.8
Piedmont	167	3	13	1.8	23.1	19.6
Inner Coastal Plain	128	1	13	0.8	7.7	15.0
Outer Coastal Plain	204	2	13	1.0	15.4	23.9
Pine Barrens	180	2	13	1.1	15.4	21.1

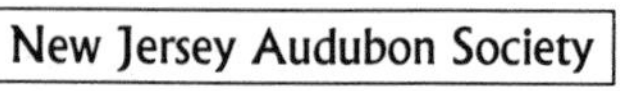

Breeding

Habitat: Nests near wooded ponds or freshwater marshes.

Green-winged Teal expanded their North American breeding range southward and eastward during the 1950s and 1960s. The first New Jersey breeding record was at Brigantine NWR in 1960 (Bull 1964). They were present at the Hackensack Meadowlands during May of 1962, but probably first bred at that site in 1963. Green-winged Teal nested annually at Kearny Marsh from 1975 through 1978 (Kane 1978), and again in 1979 and 1985. In 1980 and 1995 they were recorded breeding at Whitesbog.

Green-winged Teal remain one of New Jersey's rarest breeding birds. Atlas data indicated the only breeding sites during the Atlas survey period were at Wallkill NWR, Kearny Marsh, the Delaware River in Hunterdon County, Wharton State Forest, Raccoon Creek in Gloucester County, Brigantine NWR, and Fishing Creek Marsh in Cape May County. Their scarcity as breeders confounds interpretation of their distribution.

Fall: The earliest southbound Green-winged Teal can be seen by mid-August, but the fall peak occurs from mid- to late October, and movements continue into November. Although many individuals migrate at night (Johnson 1995), they can also be seen migrating during the day along the coast, frequently mixing with flocks of scoters. Large groups congregate at Brigantine NWR in late fall where they remain as long as there is open water. **Maxima:** 25,000+, Brigantine NWR, 22 October 1995; 15,000, Brigantine NWR, 3 October 1996; 15,000, Brigantine NWR, 10 October 1997. **ASW Single-Day Maximum:** 3,197 on 27 October 1996. **ASW Seasonal Stats:** Average: 6,456; Maximum: 8,423 in 1996.

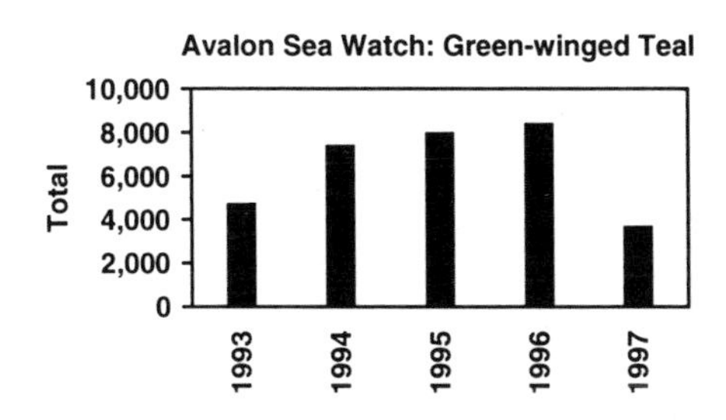

Winter: Green-winged Teal can be common in winter and will often use tidal marshes and coastal estuaries. CBC totals vary considerably depending upon the severity of the weather preceding or during the counts. **CBC Statewide Stats:** Average: 957; Maximum: 2,699 in 1979; Minimum: 36 in 1981. **CBC Maximum:** 2,500, Oceanville, 1979.

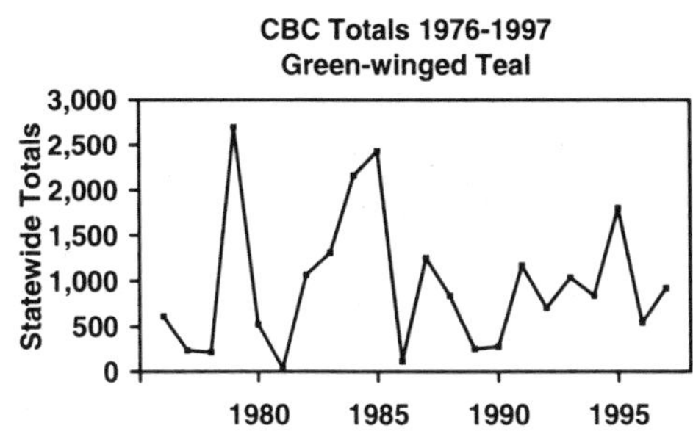

Spring: An increase in the numbers of Green-winged Teal is noted in late February, and those numbers continue to build to a peak in late March. At that time, they are frequently found in the salt

continued on page 140

continued from page 139

Green-winged Teal

marshes on the Delaware Bay shore, where they can be seen feeding on open mudflats by the hundreds and even thousands. Numbers slowly diminish through April, and they become scarce by early May. **Maxima:** 3,500, Goshen Landing, 11 March 1991; 2,000, Mannington Marsh, 28 March 1992.

Subspecies: "Eurasian" Green-winged Teal, *A. c. crecca,* breed throughout much of Europe and Asia. They are very rarely encountered as vagrants in New Jersey, mainly from late February to early April. Current identification information only allows males to be identified in the field. **Maximum:** 3, Tuckahoe WMA, 2 April 1982 (Sibley, 1997). ■

Canvasback

Aythya valisineria

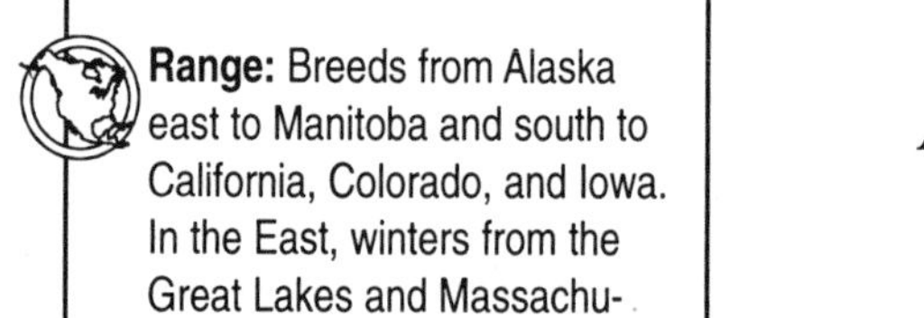

Range: Breeds from Alaska east to Manitoba and south to California, Colorado, and Iowa. In the East, winters from the Great Lakes and Massachusetts south to Central America and Florida.

NJ Status: Uncommon spring and fall migrant, fairly common winter resident.

Fall: The first southbound Canvasbacks typically arrive in early November with movements continuing into mid-December. They are seen infrequently at the Avalon Sea Watch. Southbound birds are seen on inland lakes and reservoirs, generally in small numbers. **Maxima:** Coastal: 6,000, Bayonne, 16 December 1979; 5,000, Newark Bay, 17 December 1978; Inland: 150, Lake Musconetcong, 9 November 1984. **ASW Single-Day Maximum:** 12 on 12 December 1995. **ASW Seasonal Stats:** Average: 12; Maximum: 31 in 1995.

Winter: Canvasbacks are found on salt water in winter, often using bays, and estuaries. Historically, numbers wintering in New Jersey have been variable. During the first third of the 20th century numbers declined, but rebounded to a peak in the late 1970s. Since the late 1980s, however, CBC totals have declined considerably.

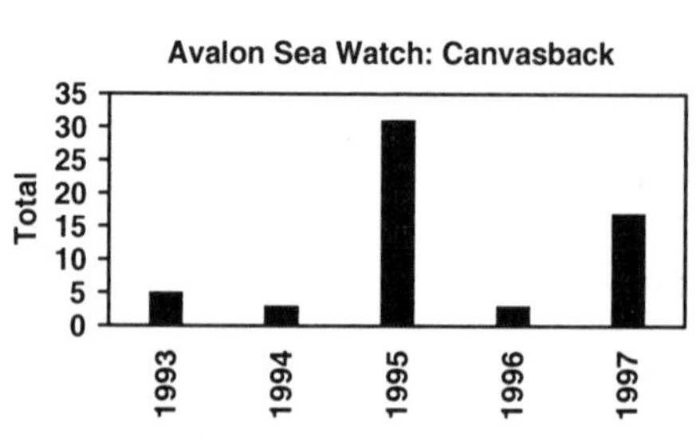

Canvasback

continued

CBC Statewide Stats: Average: 8,583; Maximum: 30,229 in 1976; Minimum: 1,247 in 1994. **CBC Maximum:** 11,535, Lakehurst, 1976.

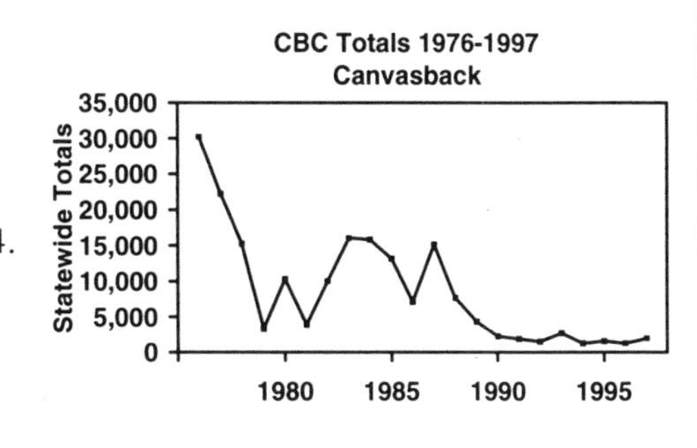

Spring: Canvasbacks depart the state early in spring, and most have left New Jersey by late March or early April. Northbound migrants are occasionally seen in small numbers inland. **Maxima:** Coastal: 300, HMEC, 7 March 1998; 150, Brigantine NWR, 12 March 1994; Inland: 70, Assunpink, 7 March 1976. ■

Redhead

Aythya americana

Range: Breeds mainly in the West from Alberta south to California and New Mexico, sporadically in the East, mostly around the Great Lakes. In the East, winters from the Great Lakes and Massachusetts south to Mexico, Florida, and Cuba.

NJ Status: Scarce spring and fall migrant, uncommon winter resident.

Historic Changes:

Redheads were probably never common birds in New Jersey during the 1900s. Griscom (1923) reported Redheads were rare anywhere in northern New Jersey. Stone (1937) noted that Redheads were "of irregular and rather infrequent occurrence about Cape May." He also lamented a decline for the species around Barnegat Bay in the late 1920s. In the 1980s the hunting season for Redheads was closed, a management strategy that may have helped restore the Redhead population.

Fall: Redheads arrive late in fall, and the first birds are usually seen during early November. They are scarce at the Avalon Sea Watch. **Maxima:** Coastal: 24, Avalon Sea Watch, 27 November 1995; Inland: 105, Round Valley Res., 25 November 1976. **ASW Seasonal Stats:** Average: 14; Maximum: 50 in 1995.

continued on page 142

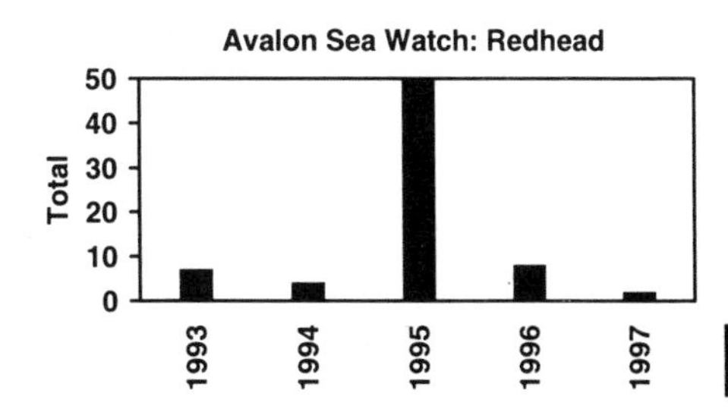

continued from page 141

Redhead

Winter: Redheads will use both salt and fresh water habitats during winter. As with other ducks, they may all move to the coast in harsh winters when fresh water is frozen. CBC totals show a peak in the mid- to late 1970s, but numbers have declined considerably since. The maximum statewide CBC total occurred in 1978 (see below), but the total has been under 100 since that time. The decline is severe, and during the 1990s the highest count was 22 in 1994-1995. The three listed maxima (Winter, Statewide CBC, and CBC) all occurred in the coldest winter on record, when many coastal wetlands in the Northeast were frozen. **Maximum:** 500, Barnegat Inlet, 1 January 1978. **CBC Statewide Stats:** Average: 94; Maximum: 943 in 1978; Minimum: 5 in 1992. **CBC Maximum:** 902, Lakehurst, 1978.

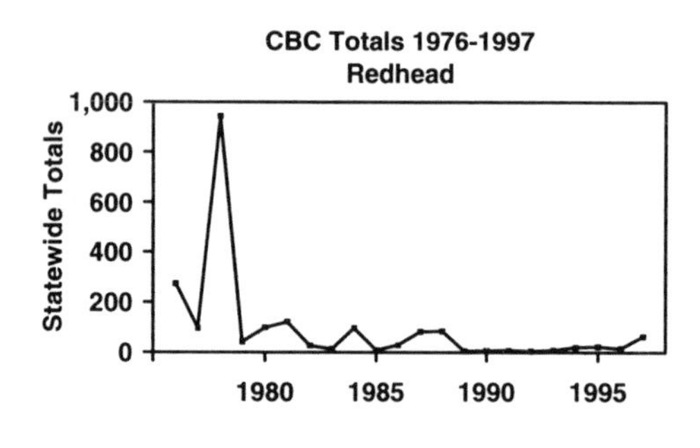

Spring: Redheads depart very early in spring, with northbound birds found at large lakes and reservoirs in early March. Most have left New Jersey by early April. **Maxima:** Coastal: 300, Manahawkin, 7 March 1976. Inland: 120, Spruce Run Res., 6 March 1976. ■

Ring-necked Duck

Aythya collaris

Range: In eastern North America, breeds from Manitoba east to Newfoundland, south to Minnesota, the Great Lakes, and Maine. In the East winters from southern Illinois and Massachusetts, south to Central America and Florida.

NJ Status: Common spring and fairly common fall migrant, fairly common winter resident.

Historic Changes: Ring-necked Duck have become more common in New Jersey during the 1900s. Stone (1937) first reported Ring-necked Duck at Cape May in 1935, although they were reported from Barnegat Bay at that time. Fables (1955) called them rare winter transients, but noted that their numbers were increasing. Leck (1984) considered them "formerly scarce," but increasing and uncommon.

Fall: Ring-necked Ducks begin to arrive in mid-October, peak from early to mid-November, and migration tapers off by

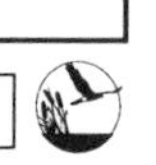

Ring-necked Duck

continued

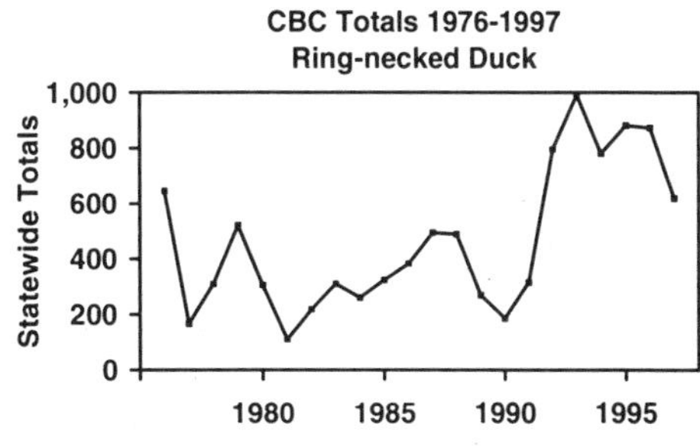

early December. This freshwater species is far more common on inland lakes and reservoirs than along the coast. Ring-neckeds are seen only in small numbers at the Avalon Sea Watch. **Maxima:** Coastal: 201, Avalon Sea Watch, 4 November 1994; Inland: 700, Wolf Lake, 15 November 1997; 371, Wolf Lake, 3 November 1993. **ASW Seasonal Stats:** Average: 151; Maximum: 350 in 1994.

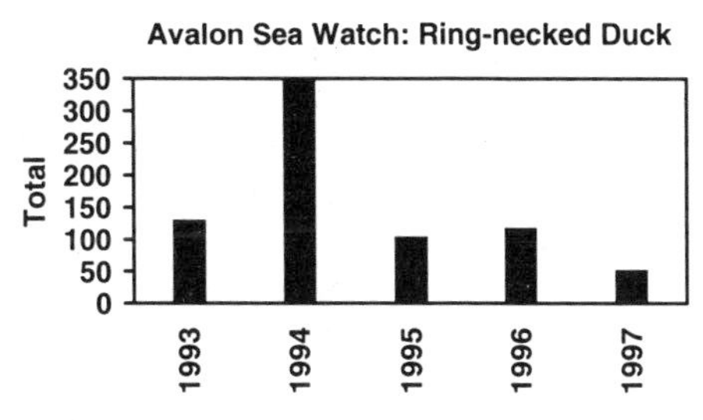

Winter: Their preference for wooded freshwater ponds can affect Ring-necked Duck numbers in harsh winters, when prolonged hard freezes can force them to migrate. Statewide CBC totals were fairly consistent from the mid-1970s through the 1980s, but were higher in the 1990s. **Maxima:** 500, Wells Mills, early January 1988; 350, NAFEC, 20 December 1975. **CBC Statewide Stats:** Average: 466; Maximum: 992 in 1993; Minimum: 110 in 1981. **CBC Maximum:** 600, Boonton, 1993.

Spring: The highest numbers of Ring-necked Ducks occur inland in March, as birds begin to move north. Only a few are seen after mid-April. **Maxima:** Coastal: 100+, Thompson Park, 23 March 1994 and 10 March 1997; Inland: 750, 21 March 1987, Spruce Run Res.; 500, 23 March 1996, Spruce Run Res. ■

Tufted Duck

Aythya fuligula

Range: Breeds from Iceland east across Europe to Siberia. Winters in Europe, North Africa, and southern Asia.

NJ Status: Accidental. NJBRC Review List.

Occurrence: There have been 15 state reports of Tufted Ducks, and ten have been accepted by the NJBRC (all wintering birds).
continued on page 144

continued from page 143

Tufted Duck

The ten records may involve multiple sightings of the same individuals returning in successive years. The ten accepted records are:

	*Edgewater**	*18 February-1 April 1966*	
	Edgewater	*30 November 1966-16 January 1967*	
	*Edgewater**	*mid-fall-30 December 1967*	
	*Pt. Pleasant**	*26 January 1969*	
	*Bay Head**	*early February 1971*	
	Bay Head	*26 December 1971-21 February 1972*	
	Weehawken	*early February 1989*	*ph-RBPF*
3	*Monmouth Beach*	*27 November 1994-early March 1995*	*ph-RBPF*
	Sandy Hook	*26 December-12 January 1997*	
	Sandy Hook	*27 December-10 January 1998*	

Greater Scaup
Aythya marila

Fall: Southbound Greater Scaup can be seen in early October, and peak numbers are seen from early to mid-November. The fall movement is mainly along the coast, with only a few seen inland (e.g., 5, Yards Creek, 9 November 1979). The flight can continue well into December. **Maximum:** 8,000, Conasconk Point, 26 October 1982. **ASW Single-Day Maximum:** 213 on 1 November 1996. **ASW Seasonal Stats:** Average: 594; Maximum: 872 in 1995.

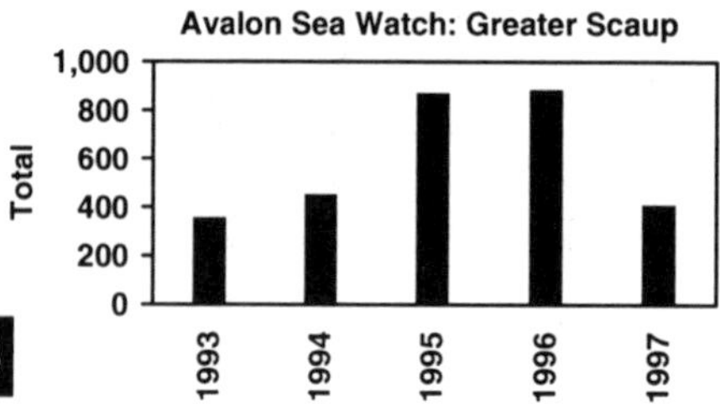

Range: In North America, breeds from Alaska east across northern Canada to Newfoundland. Winters from the Great Lakes and Newfoundland, south along the east coast to northern Florida, and along the Gulf coast to Texas, and locally in the interior.

NJ Status: Common spring and fall migrant, common winter resident.

Winter: Greater Scaup can be one of the most abundant ducks in the state in winter, and huge rafts may gather in coastal estuaries such as Raritan Bay. Although Greater Scaup prefer salt water, and Lesser Scaup show

Greater Scaup
continued

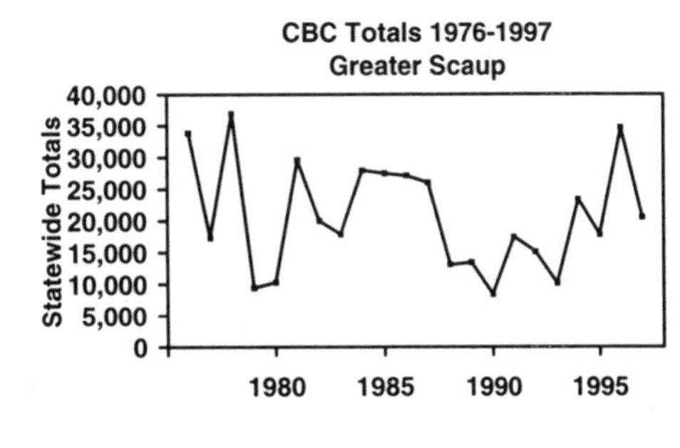

a preference for fresh water, there is complete overlap in the habitats used by both species. Greater Scaup, however, outnumber Lesser Scaup by about 10:1 on CBCs. Deep freezes in the northern United States can send birds south at any time during the winter (e.g., 1,000, Avalon, 19 February 1995, southbound). **Maxima:** 50,000, Sandy Hook, 10 February 1991; 50,000, Raritan Bay, winter 1994-1995. **CBC Statewide Stats:** Average: 20,798; Maximum: 36,966 in 1978; Minimum: 8,375 in 1990. **CBC Maximum:** 34,053, Sandy Hook, 1996.

Spring: Along the coast, numbers of Greater Scaup gradually decrease during March. Most are gone from New Jersey by mid-April. They are more common inland in spring than in fall, with small numbers seen in March and early April (e.g., 30, Lake Musconetcong, 9 April 1994). ■

Lesser Scaup
Aythya affinis

Range: Breeds from Alaska east to Ontario, and south to Oregon and Colorado. In the East winters from southern Great Lakes and Massachusetts south to Central America.

NJ Status: Fairly common spring and fall migrant, uncommon winter resident.

Fall: The first Lesser Scaup arrive in early October, numbers peak in early to mid-November, and migration continues into December. Overall, they are less numerous than Greater Scaup, although they can outnumber Greater Scaup at freshwater sites. The timing of fall migration is similar to that of Greater Scaup, although Lesser Scaup arrive slightly earlier, and are more likely to appear inland. **Maxima:** Coastal: 193, Avalon Sea Watch, 10 November 1995; 173, Avalon Sea Watch, 20 November

continued on page 146

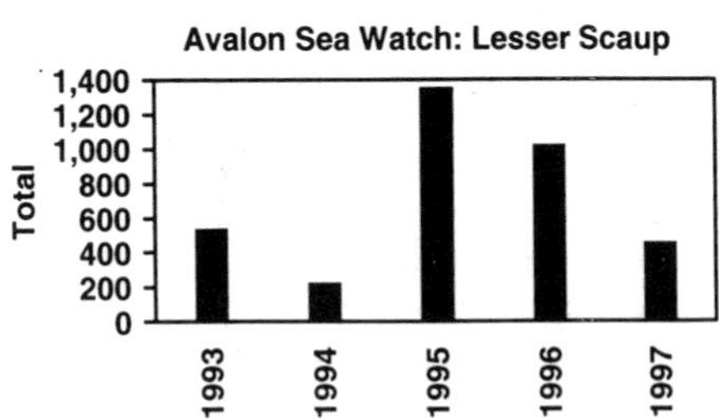

continued from page 145

Lesser Scaup

1997; Inland: 150+, Yard's Creek Res., 25 November 1981. **ASW Seasonal Stats:** Average: 719; Maximum: 1,355 in 1995.

Winter: Statewide CBC totals of Lesser Scaup are quite variable. Numbers have been consistently lower since the late 1980s, although there was a jump in the count in 1997. Statewide CBC averages fell from an average of 4,117 from 1976 through 1987, to an average of 1,292 from 1988 through 1997. **Maximum:** 500, Delaware River, Camden, winter 1984-1985. **CBC Statewide Stats:** Average: 2,213; Maximum: 7,275 in 1978; Minimum: 83 in 1979. **CBC Maximum:** 5,576, Lakehurst, 1978.

Spring: Since many Lesser Scaup spend the winter south of New Jersey, there is a noticeable return flight in spring that occurs from late March to early April. This migration is more often noted inland than along the coast (e.g., 200, Assunpink, 10 April 1982, and 100, Lake Musconetcong, 3 April 1982). ■

King Eider

Somateria spectabilis

Range: In North America breeds in Arctic Alaska and Canada south to western Hudson Bay. Small numbers winter along the East Coast from Labrador to North Carolina but is most numerous north of New Jersey.

NJ Status: Rare spring and rare to scarce fall migrant and winter resident.

Fall: At the Avalon Sea Watch only a handful of King Eiders are noted in migration. The few that are seen generally occur in October and November, although the maximum count occurred in early December (see below). **Maximum:** 17, Barnegat Inlet, 29 November 1997. **ASW Single-Day Maximum:** 7 on 9 December 1997. **ASW Seasonal Stats:** Average: 9; Maximum: 21 in 1997.

Winter: The most consistent location to see King Eiders in New Jersey is at Barnegat Inlet. They can occasionally outnumber Common Eiders in mid-winter, but in most years they are less numerous than Common

King Eider

continued

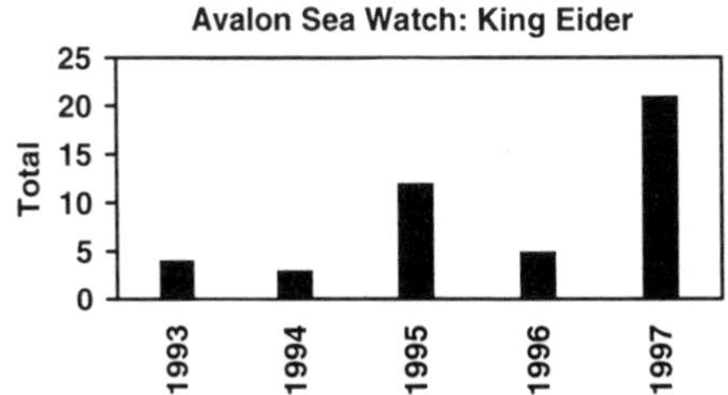

Eiders. The historic maximum was a concentration of 20-30 King Eiders at Longport through February 1971, the highest number south of Montauk Point, New York (UFO). When encountered in New Jersey, they are usually found as lone individuals or in small groups foraging around jetties and breakwaters.

Other maxima: 8, Barnegat Inlet, winter 1985-1986; 6-8, Barnegat Inlet, 14 February 1993. **CBC Statewide Stats:** Average: 5; Maximum: 15 in 1978; Minimum: 0 in 1989. **CBC Maximum:** 12, Lakehurst, 1978.

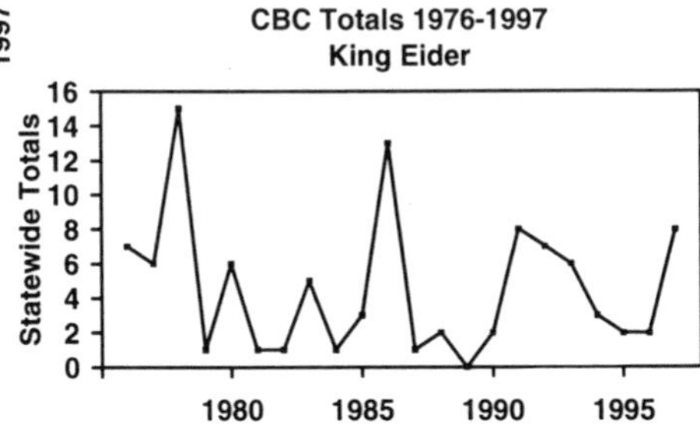

Spring: King Eiders typically leave by late April, although there are three recent June records: 9 June 1986, Island Beach; 9 June 1990, Cape May; and 10 June 1991, Cape May. ■

Common Eider

Somateria mollissima

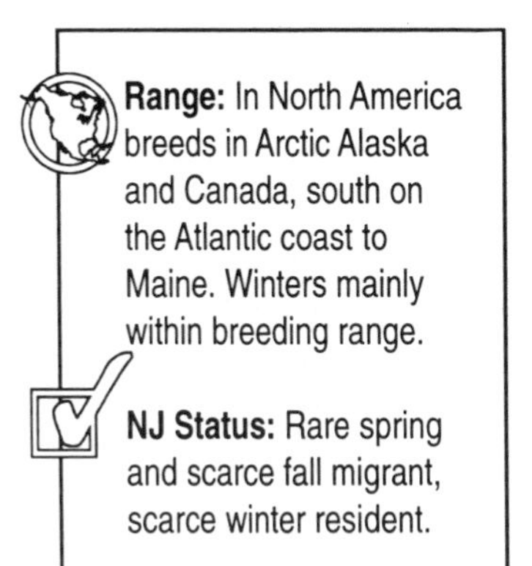

Range: In North America breeds in Arctic Alaska and Canada, south on the Atlantic coast to Maine. Winters mainly within breeding range.

NJ Status: Rare spring and scarce fall migrant, scarce winter resident.

Fall: The first southbound Common Eiders can be seen by mid-September, but the peak at the Avalon Sea Watch occurs from late November to early December. Common Eiders are encountered more frequently than King Eiders in migration. **Maxima:** 26, Avalon Sea Watch, 14 November 1996; 22, Cape May, 1-30 November 1987. **ASW Seasonal Stats:** Average: 51; Maximum: 106 in 1996.

continued on page 148

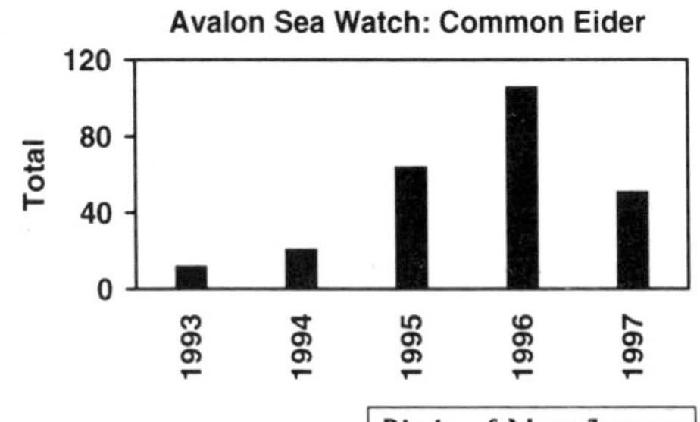

continued from page 147

Common Eider

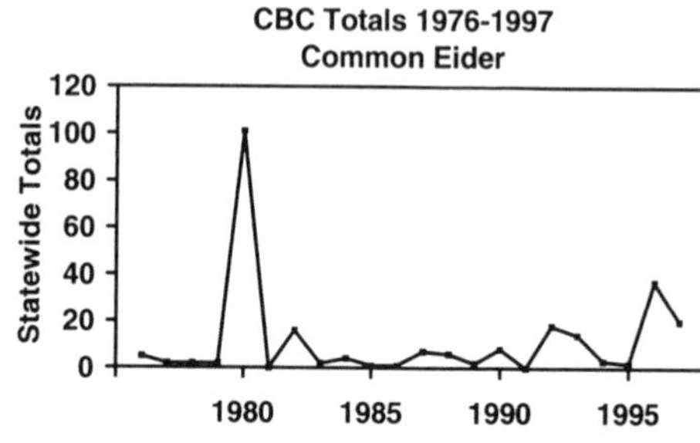

Winter: Statewide CBC totals of Common Eiders are highly variable, and in most years fewer than ten birds are recorded. One notable exception was the maximum count at Island Beach in 1980 (see below). Although they are never numerous, they are regularly seen at Barnegat Inlet. **CBC Statewide Stats:** Average: 12; Maximum: 101 in 1980; Minimum: 0 in 1981 and 1991. **CBC Maximum:** 100, Island Beach, 1980.

Spring: Although there are spring and early-summer records for Common Eiders, there are also records of birds lingering throughout the summer. One bird spent the entire summer at Cape May Point in 1988, and three spent the summer there in 1997. ■

Harlequin Duck

Histrionicus histrionicus

Range: In eastern North America breeds from Baffin Island to the Gulf of St. Lawrence. Winters south to Virginia.

NJ Status: Rare spring and fall migrant, scarce winter resident.

Historic Changes: Prior to 1950, Harlequin Ducks were even less common in New Jersey than they are today, with the first recorded for Cape May County 28-30 January 1954 (Sibley 1997). Stone (1937) was aware of only a few records for the Jersey shore, and Fables (1955) listed only eight records for the state as of 1955.

Fall: Typically, the first Harlequin Ducks are seen in mid-October. Very few are recorded at the Avalon Sea Watch. **Maximum:** 6, Avalon Sea Watch, 24 October 1993. **ASW Seasonal Stats:** Average: 4; Maximum: 9 in 1993.

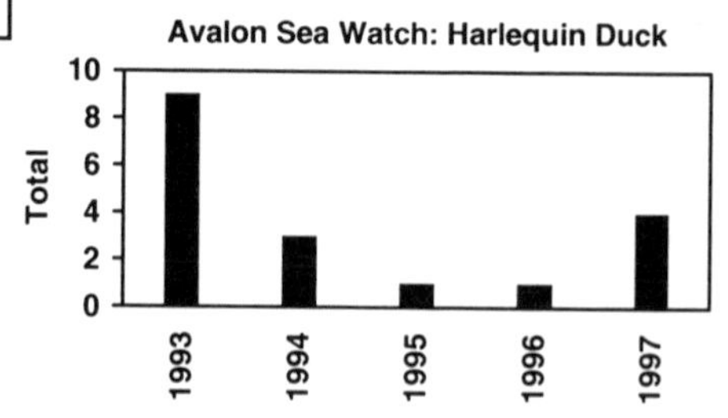

Winter: The location to see Harlequin Ducks most consistently in New Jersey is at Barnegat Inlet, where small flocks spend the winter each year. CBC totals have shown a modest

Harlequin Duck

continued

increase in recent years, due mainly to the increase in the size of the wintering flock at Barnegat. **Maxima:** 23, Barnegat Inlet, 16 February 1997; 19, Barnegat Inlet, 20 February 1995. **CBC Statewide Stats:** Average: 8; Maximum: 20 in 1997; Minimum: one in 1984 and 1987. **CBC Maximum:** 20, Barnegat, 1997.

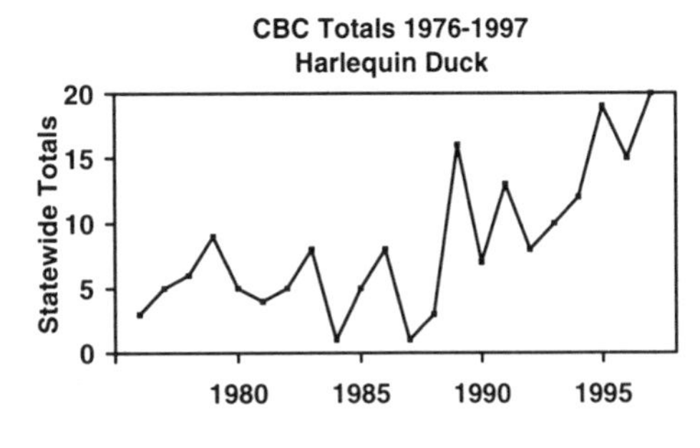

Spring: Although few Harlequin Ducks winter south of New Jersey, northbound migrants are occasionally seen from April through mid-May. ■

Labrador Duck

Camptorhynchus labradorius

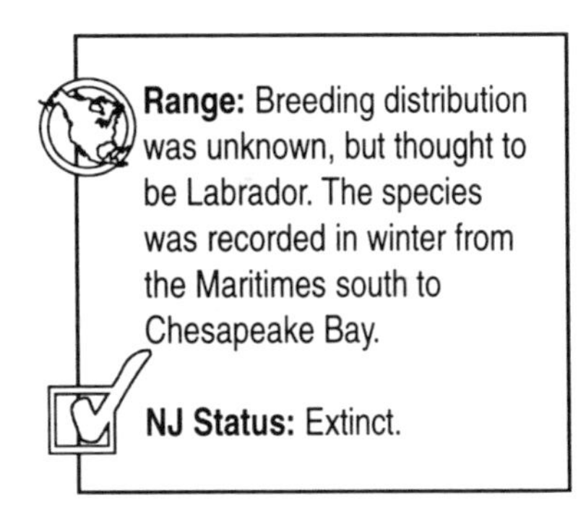

Occurrence: The historic status of Labrador Duck in New Jersey must be reconstructed from published accounts, as there are no extant specimens taken from New Jersey. Giraud (1844) noted that "in New Jersey it is called Sand-shoal Duck." Phillips (1926) reported that from the 1840s to the 1860s birds were sold in the New York market and that specimens (without dates or locales) were "...nearly all from New England, New York, or New Jersey waters." He noted the last specimen in museum collections with data was taken in autumn 1875 on Long Island waters by J.G. Bell (spec. USNM #77126).

Stone (1937) and Fables (1955) regarded Labrador Ducks as hypothetical in New Jersey and cited unlabelled specimens in Philadelphia (ANSP) supposed to have been taken in the 1850s from Great Egg Harbor or Cape May, where Philadelphia gunners hunted. Leck (1984) also included Labrador Duck as a hypothetical. Based on anecdotal evidence and proven patterns of occurrence in nearby waters, the NJBRC reviewed their status and accepted this species on the state list. ■

Surf Scoter

Melanitta perspicillata

Range: Breeds from Alaska east across northern Canada to Labrador. In eastern North America winters primarily on the coast from Newfoundland to Georgia.

NJ Status: Common spring and fall migrant, fairly common winter resident.

Fall: Surf Scoter flights along the coast are spectacular. Southbound Surf Scoters arrive in mid-September, and numbers slowly build until they outnumber Black Scoters by early October. Surf Scoter numbers peak from mid- to late October, with migration continuing into early December. They are the least likely scoters to be seen inland, with only a few seen each year. **Maxima:** 33,255, Avalon Sea Watch, 31 October 1995; 32,559, Avalon Sea Watch, 18 October 1996. **ASW Seasonal Stats:** Average: 124,545; Maximum: 191,804 in 1995.

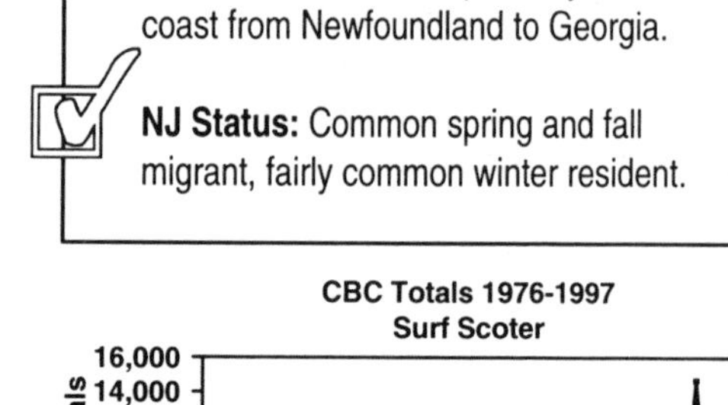

Avalon Sea Watch: Surf Scoter

Total: 200,000; 150,000; 100,000; 50,000; 0

1993 1994 1995 1996 1997

Winter: In most years Surf Scoters are outnumbered by Black Scoters by a small margin in winter. Statewide CBC totals vary considerably, and in most years fewer than 300 are counted. Unfortunately, there are no pelagic CBCs in New Jersey, so the total for scoters is probably lower than the actual number in New Jersey's waters. **CBC Statewide Stats:** Average: 1,215; Maximum: 14,692 in 1996; Minimum: 44 in 1985. **CBC Maximum:** 14,501, Cape May, 1996.

Spring: Spring scoter migration in New Jersey is puzzling. In some years, Surf Scoters congregate in large numbers in Delaware Bay in March and early April (e.g., 10,000, mostly Surf Scoters off South Cape May, 28 March 1995), but details regarding their exodus are lacking. In April at Cape May, high, late evening flights of several hundred scoters have been noted cutting across the peninsula moving east. A few sub-adults may spend the summer along the coast each year. ■

White-winged Scoter

Melanitta fusca

Range: Breeds primarily in Alaska and western Canada. In the East, winters along the coast from Newfoundland to North Carolina.

NJ Status: Uncommon spring and fairly common fall migrant, uncommon winter resident.

Fall: White-winged Scoters are much less common in migration than either Black or Surf Scoters. A few white-wingeds arrive in late September or early October, but most are seen between mid-October and mid-December. Peak movements are generally in mid- to late November. White-winged Scoters are scarce but fairly regular inland during fall migration. **Maxima:** Coastal: 4,500, Brigantine Island, 17 November 1980; 4,000, 38 miles off Cape May, 6 March 1994; Inland: 10, Culvers Lake, early October 1975. **ASW Single-Day Maximum:** 961 on 23 November 1995. **ASW Seasonal Stats:** Average: 4,101; Maximum: 6,126 in 1995.

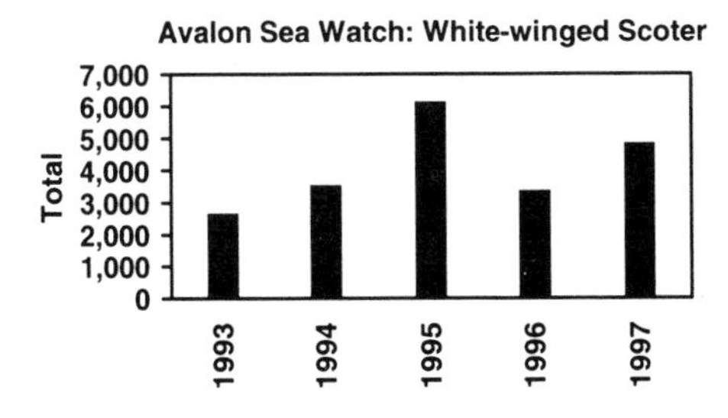

Winter: White-winged Scoters are most common in winter. In some years, statewide CBC totals of white-wingeds exceed the other scoters. While White-winged Scoter totals do vary, they seem to be without the massive swings in abundance that both Surf and Black Scoters' numbers show, and only occasionally number over 1,000. **CBC Statewide Stats:** Average: 437; Maximum: 1,213 in 1981; Minimum: 60 in 1990. **CBC Maximum:** 1,142, Barnegat, 1981.

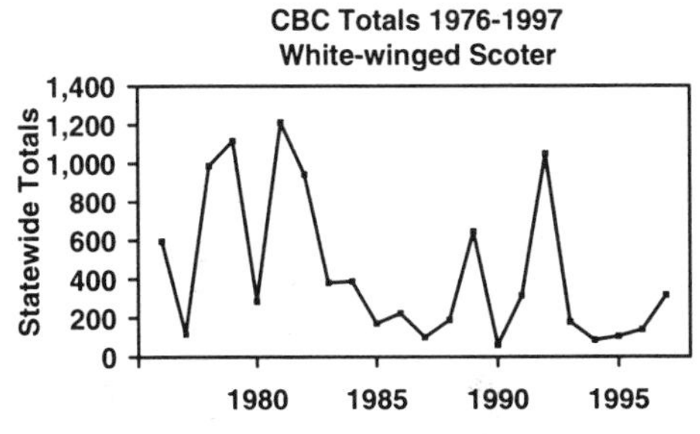

Spring: As with the other two scoter species, details of spring movements are lacking. Along the coast they probably depart earlier than either Surf or Black Scoters and are the least likely to be encountered in summer. Interestingly, White-winged Scoters are the most common scoters inland in spring, and the highest counts are in early to mid-May (e.g., 90, Culvers Lake, 19 May 1994, and 58, Culvers Lake, 6 May 1978). **Maxima:** 4,000, up to 38 miles off Cape May, 6 March 1994; 1,000+, off Brigantine Island, 16 April 1981. ■

Black Scoter

Melanitta nigra

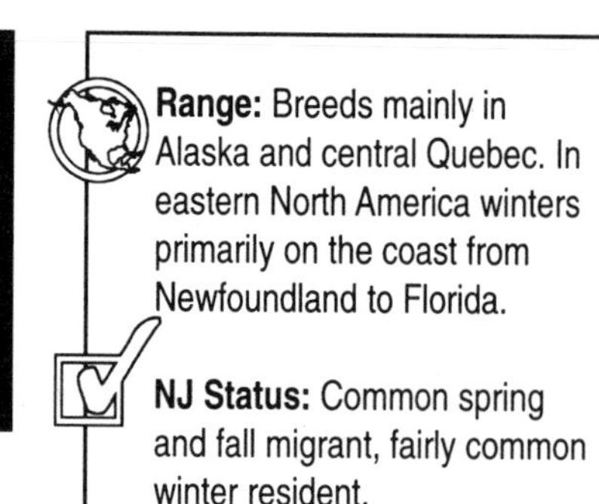

Range: Breeds mainly in Alaska and central Quebec. In eastern North America winters primarily on the coast from Newfoundland to Florida.

NJ Status: Common spring and fall migrant, fairly common winter resident.

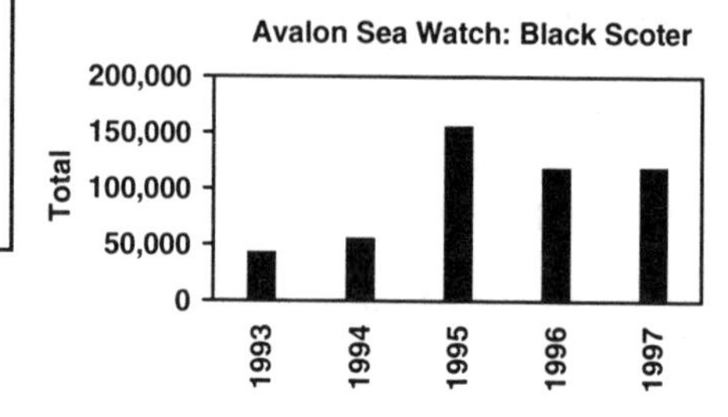

Fall: Southbound Black Scoters begin to arrive in mid-September and numbers build to a peak from mid- to late October. The coastal flights are spectacular; flights can continue all day, and are often close to shore. Migration continues in diminishing numbers into early December. Black Scoters are also regularly seen in small numbers inland, particularly on large bodies of water. **Maxima:** Coastal: 37,340, Avalon Sea Watch, 12 October 1997; 36,816, Avalon Sea Watch, 31 October 1995; Inland: 250, Culvers Lake, 23 October 1980. **ASW Seasonal Stats:** Average: 98,693; Maximum: 156,005 in 1995.

Winter: Overall, Black Scoters appear to be the most common scoter in winter. Statewide CBC totals vary from year to year, with most years under 500. **CBC Statewide Stats:** Average: 1,286; Maximum: 8,952 in 1976; Minimum: 115 in 1991. **CBC Maximum:** 8,500, Cape May, 1976.

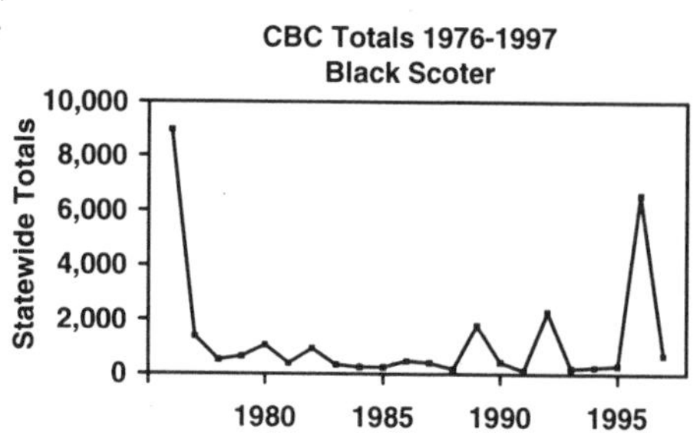

Black Scoter

Black Scoter

continued

Spring: Although tens of thousands of scoters migrate south past New Jersey in fall, relatively few are noted on a return flight in spring. Some are noted staging at the mouth of the Delaware Bay from mid-March through April (e.g., 2,000 Black and Surf Scoters off Cape May Point on 2 April 1993). Staging offshore has also been recorded (e.g., 2,000, up to 38 miles off Cape May, 6 March 1994). However, how scoters complete their northbound movement through or past New Jersey in spring is a mystery. Occasionally at Cape May in April, high flights of several hundred scoters have been noted at dusk flying over the peninsula moving east. They are rare to scarce inland in spring, with records generally occurring from late March through early April. A few young birds spend the summer along the coast each year. ■

Oldsquaw

Clangula hyemalis

Range: In North America breeds in the Arctic of Alaska and Canada south to northern Manitoba and Labrador. Winters on the Great Lakes and on the East Coast south of the breeding range to Georgia.

NJ Status: Common spring and fall migrant, common winter resident.

Fall: The first southbound Oldsquaws are generally seen in mid-October. Migration is protracted, with a peak typically occurring in early December. Although primarily a coastal migrant, Oldsquaws also occur inland on large lakes and reservoirs in small numbers. **Maxima:** Coastal: 1,603, Avalon Sea Watch, 8 December 1993; 753, Avalon Sea Watch, 3 December 1997; Inland: 50, Culvers Lake, 13 November 1990. **ASW Seasonal Stats:** Average: 3,347; Maximum: 4,159 in 1996.

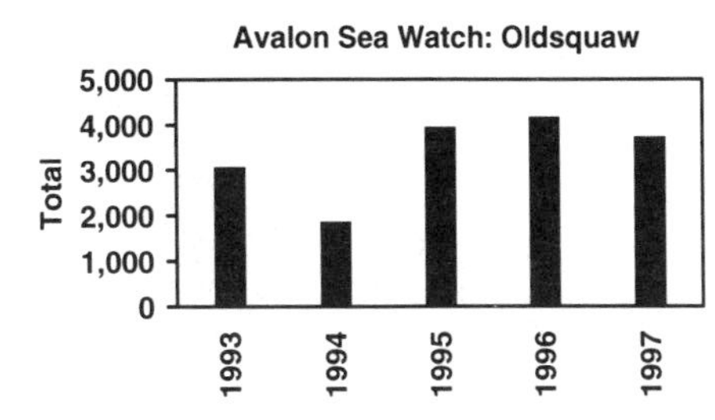

Winter: Southbound migration of Oldsquaws can continue well into the winter (e.g., 1,007, Avalon, 16 February

continued on page 154

continued from page 153

Oldsquaw

1995) in response to hard freezes. The variation in CBC totals may be due to influxes of northern birds frozen out of their wintering locations. The statewide high count (see below) occurred in 1981, the same year that Nantucket Sound, a major wintering area, became frozen (Veit and Petersen 1993). **Maxima:** 3,000, Barnegat Inlet, 15 February 1997; 2,500, 30 miles off Cape May, 11 March 1995. **CBC Statewide Stats:** Average: 3,907; Maximum: 11,332 in 1981; Minimum: 1,045 in 1997. **CBC Maximum:** 8,937, Barnegat, 1981.

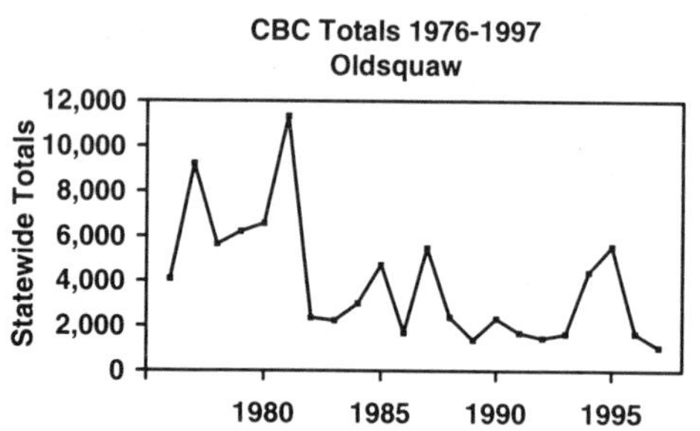

Spring: Oldsquaws are regularly seen inland in late March and April on large lakes and reservoirs (e.g., 75, Lake Parsippany and 32, Culvers Lake, both 20 March 1990). Sibley (1997) noted that large concentrations of Oldsquaws can occur offshore in the late winter, which may indicate staging for northward migration (e.g., 1,200, up to 38 miles off Cape May, 6 March 1994; also, see Winter Maxima). Overall, numbers diminish through April with few birds remaining by the end of the month. ■

Bufflehead

Bucephala albeola

Range: In North America breeds from Alaska east across Canada to central Quebec. On the East Coast winters from Nova Scotia to Florida.

NJ Status: Common spring and fall migrant, common winter resident.

Historic Changes: Stone (1937) considered Buffleheads to be rare ducks at Cape May, blaming the dwindling numbers on poor breeding success and hunting pressure. However, Fables (1955) considered them a regular winter visitor in increasing numbers.

Fall: At the Avalon Sea Watch the first southbound Buffleheads are seen in late October with numbers quickly peaking in early November. Migration continues into early December, but numbers diminish. Buffleheads are the most widespread migrant diving ducks in both spring and fall,

Bufflehead

continued

occurring in numbers both inland and along the coast. **Maxima:** Coastal: 1,000s, Shark River Inlet, 19 November 1994; Inland: 98, Lake Mohawk, 1 November 1994. **ASW Single-Day Maximum:** 729 on 2 November 1996 (with 596 the following day). **ASW Seasonal Stats:** Average: 1,377; Maximum: 2,428 in 1996.

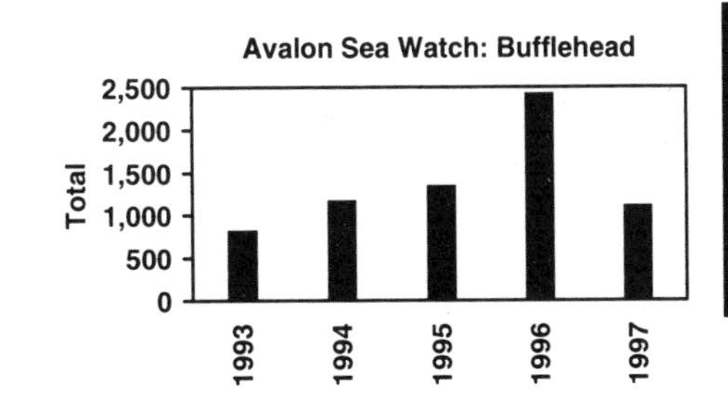

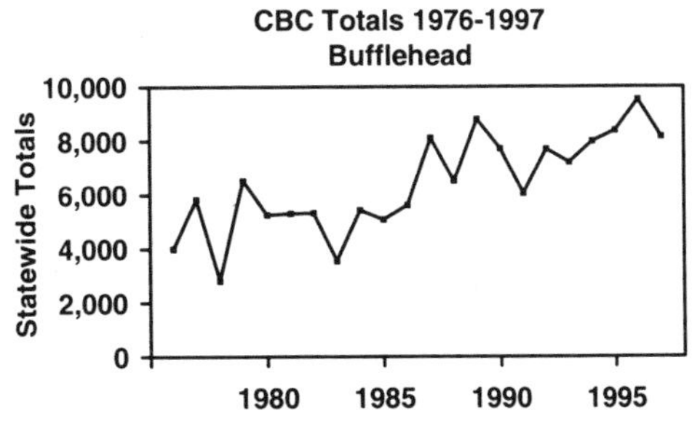

Winter: From 1976 to 1997, statewide CBC totals of Buffleheads showed a steady increase. They are a common sight on open water throughout the state, but are most numerous on the back bays of the coast. **Maximum:** 900, East Point, 24 January 1994. **CBC Statewide Stats:** Average: 6,401; Maximum: 9,512 in 1996; Minimum: 2,814 in 1978. **CBC Maximum:** 3,751, Barnegat, 1997.

Spring: Along the coast, migration of Buffleheads is not often noted as migrants join the large wintering population. However, migrants are noted inland in March and early April (e.g., 130, Culvers Lake, 13 April 1996). Most Buffleheads are gone from New Jersey by late April, with a few remaining into May. They are rarely seen after early June. ■

Bufflehead

Common Goldeneye

Bucephala clangula

Range: In eastern North America breeds from Manitoba east to Newfoundland, south to northern Minnesota and northern New Hampshire. Winters in the East from the Great Lakes and Newfoundland south to Texas and Florida.

NJ Status: Fairly common spring and common fall migrant, common winter resident.

Fall: Common Goldeneyes are late migrants, and are unexpected before early November. At the Avalon Sea Watch a noticeable peak in numbers occurs in early December. Many migrate overland, and they are fairly common on inland lakes and reservoirs. **Maxima:** Coastal: 266, Avalon, 18 November 1988; Inland: 52, Culvers Lake, 18 November 1983. **ASW Single-Day Maximum:** 52 on 13 December 1995. **ASW Seasonal Stats:** Average: 215; Maximum: 290 in 1995.

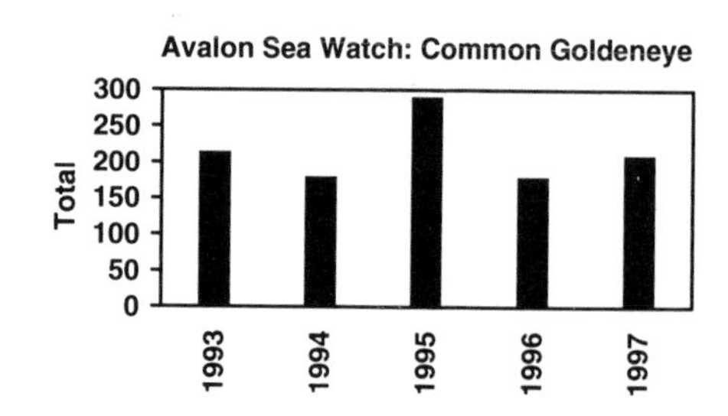

Winter: Common Goldeneyes are most numerous along the coast in winter. Statewide CBC totals are variable. **Maxima:** 1,200+, Fortescue, winter 1991-1992; 600+, Reed's Beach, 14 January 1990. **CBC Statewide Stats:** Average: 1,329; Maximum: 2,584 in 1992; Minimum: 748 in 1995. **CBC Maximum:** 1,370, Cumberland, 1992.

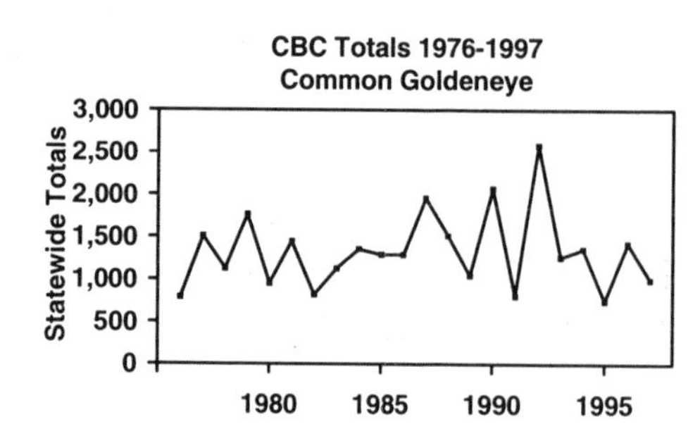

Spring: Although there is little noticeable spring movement of Common Goldeneyes along the coast, numbers on inland lakes and reservoirs increase in early March. Most have departed the state by early to mid-April. **Maxima:** Inland: 400, Culvers Lake, 11 March 1983; Coastal: 225, Sandy Hook, 3 April 1997. ■

Barrow's Goldeneye

Bucephala islandica

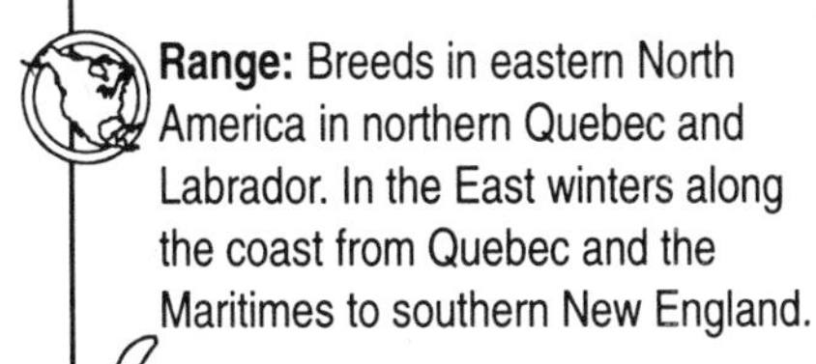

Range: Breeds in eastern North America in northern Quebec and Labrador. In the East winters along the coast from Quebec and the Maritimes to southern New England.

NJ Status: Very rare. NJBRC Review List.

Occurrence: There have been 22 state reports of Barrow's Goldeneye, and 12 have been accepted by the NJBRC (11 in winter, one in fall). The 12 records include one (which is believed to involve only one male) that visited 14 consecutive winters, at Shark River, from 1970 to 1983 (ph-RNJB 6:45). Some of the other records may involve the same individuals returning to the same area. The other accepted records are:

Keansburg#	*5 January 1936*
Leonardo	*5 February 1939*
*Sandy Hook**	*9 March 1968*
Barnegat Inlet	*2 January 1977*
Sandy Hook	*27 November 1994-4 March 1995*
Cinnaminson	*26 December 1994-12 March 1995*
Leonardo	*February-16 March 1995*
Leonardo	*16-17 March 1996*
Cinnaminson	*25 November-27 December 1996*
Sandy Hook	*21 December 1996-8 March 1997*
Sandy Hook	*20 December 1997-10 January 1998*

Hooded Merganser

Lophodytes cucullatus

Range: In eastern North America breeds from Manitoba east to Nova Scotia, south to Illinois and northern New Jersey. Winters mainly in the southeastern United States from Oklahoma and southern Illinois east to Massachusetts and Florida.

NJ Status: Scarce and local summer resident, common spring and fall migrant, fairly common winter resident.

Breeding

Habitat: Nests in cavities near fresh water, typically in wooded swamps.

There is no evidence Hooded Mergansers bred in New Jersey prior to the 1900s. Cruickshank suggested that Hooded Mergansers would

continued on page 158

continued from page 157

Hooded Merganser

extend their breeding range into New Jersey, as they had recently extended their breeding range into Pennsylvania and Connecticut (1942). The first nest in New Jersey was from Tuckahoe in 1949, when a Hooded Merganser's nest was parasitised by a Wood Duck. Both Hooded Merganser and Wood Duck young hatched (Fables 1955). Bull (1964) adds an additional breeding record for Warren County in 1962, and Leck (1984) lists seven breeding records for New Jersey. A general review of reports to RNJB from 1980 through 1993 showed that Hooded Mergansers were found breeding less frequently than once per year.

Possible
Probable
Confirmed

Statewide Summary

Status	# of Blocks
Possible	9
Probable	5
Confirmed	7
Total	21

Map Interpretation: Hooded Mergansers nest in wooded swamps early in the spring, and they are scarce in New Jersey. It is likely that the combination of these characteristics causes Atlas methods to underestimate their breeding range in the state.

Physiographic Distribution

Hooded Merganser	Number of blocks in province	Number of blocks species found breeding in province	Number of blocks species found in state	Percent of province species occupies	Percent of all records for this species found in province	Percent of state area in province
Kittatinny Mountains	19	3	21	15.8	14.3	2.2
Kittatinny Valley	45	9	21	20.0	42.9	5.3
Highlands	109	6	21	5.5	28.6	12.8
Piedmont	167	3	21	1.8	14.3	19.6

The Atlas surveys greatly increased the number of known breeding sites for Hooded Mergansers. During the Atlas survey period Hooded Mergansers were Confirmed eight times in seven blocks, and they were Confirmed in each of the five years of data collection. All Atlas Confirmations were north of the Coastal Plain and were in Sussex, Morris, or Passaic counties. The Kittatinny Valley hosted a large percentage of the state's Hooded Merganser breeding records.

Fall: Hooded Mergansers are late fall migrants, usually arriving in late October, with a peak in late November. Migration continues into December. Migration through New Jersey is distributed both inland and along the coast, although they are uncommon at the Avalon Sea Watch. In addition, Hooded Mergansers apparently often migrate at night (Dugger et al. 1994). **Maxima:** Coastal: 1,000, Brigantine NWR, 11 December 1982; 405, NAFEC, 18 December 1976; Inland: 100, Swartswood Lake, 23 October 1984. **ASW Single-Day Maximum:** 113 on 13 November 1997. **ASW Seasonal Stats:** Average: 225; Maximum: 371 in 1995.

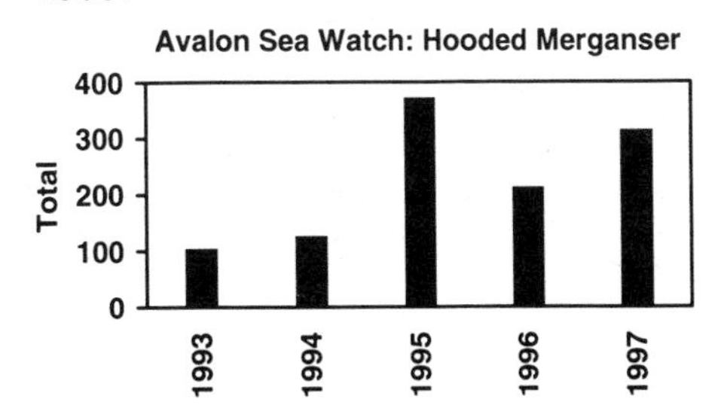

Winter: Statewide CBC totals of Hooded Mergansers from 1976 to 1989 averaged just over 500 birds, but from 1990 to 1997 that average rose to over 1,300 - a notable increase. Along the coast they are found in salt marsh creeks and sloughs and are only outnumbered there by American Black Ducks. **CBC Statewide Stats:** Average: 770; Maximum: 1,799 in 1995; Minimum: 88 in 1981. **CBC Maximum:** 694, Oceanville, 1983.

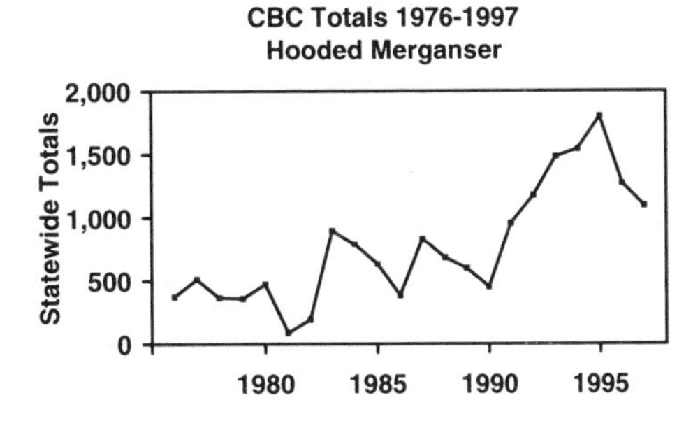

Spring: Hooded Mergansers are early spring migrants, with concentrations noted in early March. **Maxima:** Coastal: 100, Corbin City, 12 March 1994; Inland: 70, Culvers Lake, 19 March 1996. ■

Common Merganser

Mergus merganser

Range: In eastern North America breeds from Manitoba east to Labrador, south to New Jersey. In eastern North America winters south to northern Texas and northern North Carolina.

NJ Status: Scarce and local summer resident, common spring and fall migrant, common winter resident.

Breeding

Habitat: Nests in cavities along wooded streams and around forested lakes.

Common Mergansers are a recent addition to New Jersey as breeding birds. The first confirmed breeding record for Common Mergansers in New Jersey was along the Delaware River in Sandyston Township in 1973 (Wolfarth, 1973). There is no strong evidence that Common Mergansers bred in New Jersey prior to this record, but there was an unconfirmed report of nesting activity in 1969 (Wolfarth, 1969).

In New Jersey, Common Mergansers have continued to expand their range south along the Delaware River and into the Wallkill River. Atlas volunteers Confirmed Common Mergansers in 22 blocks, with most in the Kittatinny Ridge and Valley provinces. Notably, the Pennsylvania Atlas found Common Mergansers to be more widely distributed than previously suspected, and a concurrent increase of sightings on Breeding Bird Surveys in Pennsylvania supported their Atlas findings (Reid 1992a). The reason for the range expansion in Pennsylvania may be related to improvements in water quality (Reid 1992a), which may also be the case in New Jersey.

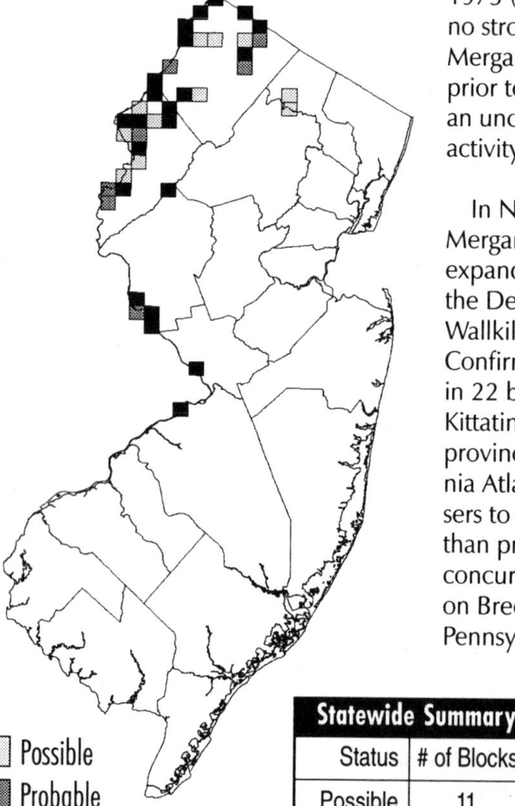

Possible
Probable
Confirmed

Statewide Summary	
Status	# of Blocks
Possible	11
Probable	7
Confirmed	22
Total	40

Physiographic Distribution Common Merganser	Number of blocks in province	Number of blocks species found breeding in province	Number of blocks species found in state	Percent of province species occupies	Percent of all records for this species found in province	Percent of state area in province
Kittatinny Mountains	19	11	40	57.9	27.5	2.2
Kittatinny Valley	45	18	40	40.0	45.0	5.3
Highlands	109	5	40	4.6	12.5	12.8
Piedmont	167	4	40	2.4	10.0	19.6
Inner Coastal Plain	128	2	40	1.6	5.0	15.0

Fall: Large aggregations of southbound Common Mergansers can be found in late November through December on large lakes and reservoirs in the northern part of the state, especially Oradell and Old Tappan reservoirs. They are more common inland and along the Delaware River than along the coast, and are notably scarce at the Avalon Sea Watch. In the southern part of the state they frequent the Delaware Bay shore marshes. **Maximum:** 4,000, Old Tappan Reservoir, 10 December 1986. **ASW Single-Day Maximum:** 5 on 13 December 1995. **ASW Seasonal Stats:** Average: 6; Maximum: 12 in 1995.

Winter: In winter, freeze-ups force many Common Mergansers out of some areas, particularly in the north. Statewide CBC totals are quite variable, with large numbers in years when open water is available. **CBC Statewide Stats:** Average: 3,054; Maximum: 7,458 in 1992; Minimum: 351 in 1981. **CBC Maximum:** 5,245, Hackensack-Ridgewood, 1995.

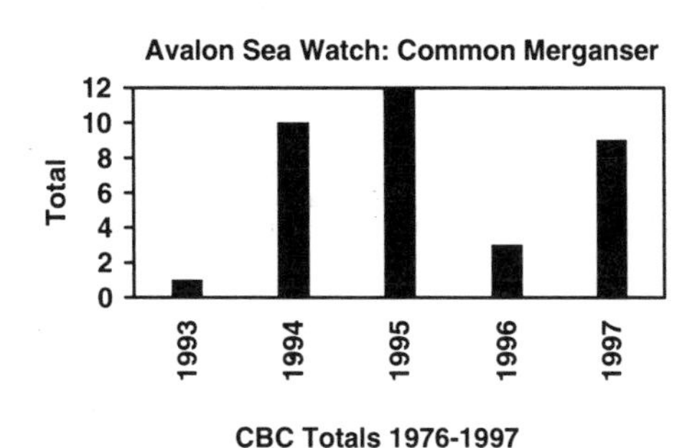

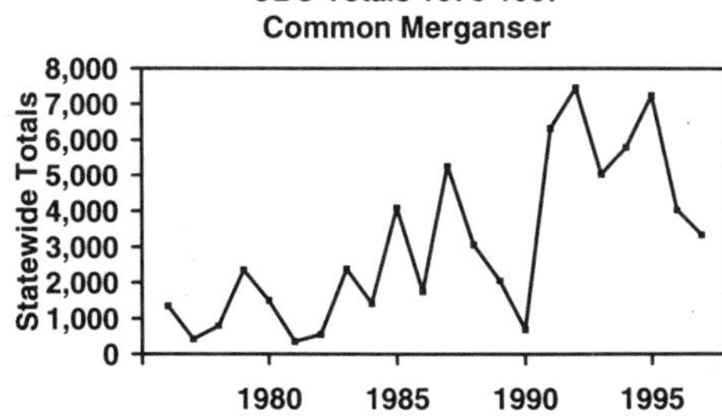

Spring: Common Mergansers return to large lakes and reservoirs in the northern part of the state as soon as open water permits, with peak numbers noted in late February and March. **Maximum:** 5,100, Oradell Res., 28 February 1995. ■

Red-breasted Merganser

Mergus serrator

Range: In North America breeds from Alaska east to Labrador, and regularly south to the Great Lakes and Maine. Winters on the Great Lakes, and from Newfoundland to Florida and Texas.

NJ Status: Rare and very local summer resident, common spring and fall migrant, common winter resident.

Breeding

Habitat: Near freshwater or saltwater wetlands, nest placed on the ground close to water.

Red-breasted Mergansers breed only inconsistently in New Jersey. This species was first recorded breeding in New Jersey on Barnegat Bay in 1937, but the next breeding record was found many years later, in 1950 (Leck 1984). There was again a lapse of many years before the next nesting records were reported in 1982 and 1983.

Possible
Probable
Confirmed

Statewide Summary	
Status	# of Blocks
Possible	3
Probable	0
Confirmed	1
Total	4

Physiographic Distribution — Red-breasted Merganser	Number of blocks in province	Number of blocks species found breeding in province	Number of blocks species found in state	Percent of province species occupies	Percent of all records for this species found in province	Percent of state area in province
Piedmont	167	1	4	0.6	25.0	19.6
Inner Coastal Plain	128	1	4	0.8	25.0	15.0
Outer Coastal Plain	204	2	4	1.0	50.0	23.9

During the Atlas surveys, Red-breasted Mergansers were Confirmed breeding in only one block when a female with downy young was seen along Seven-Bridges Road in Tuckerton in 1996. It is unlikely that the locations scored as Possible were breeding birds, although, all summering individuals should be watched for signs of confirmed breeding.

Fall: Red-breasted Mergansers generally arrive in mid-October and migration continues well into December. Peak flights occur in mid-November. They are seen most commonly along the coast, although small numbers are also found inland during migration. **Maxima:** Coastal: 819, Avalon Sea Watch, 7 November 1996; 680, Avalon Sea Watch, 19 November 1993; Inland: 15, Round Valley Res., 1 November 1976. **ASW Seasonal Stats:** Average: 4,574; Maximum: 5,577 in 1995.

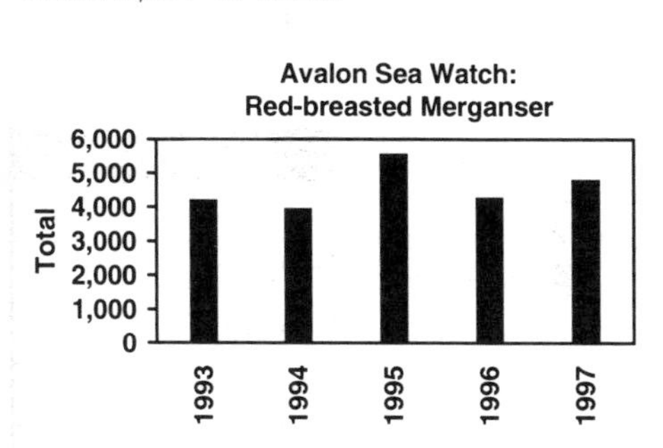

Winter: Red-breasted Mergansers are most abundant in winter when they congregate in large numbers in bays and estuaries along the Atlantic coast. Statewide CBC totals increased dramatically in the late1980s, and counts since then have been double or triple counts from the 1970s and the early 1980s. **Maxima:** 4,000, Sandy Hook, 14 January 1991; 500+, Sandy Hook, 19 January 1985. **CBC Statewide Stats:** Average: 2,310; Maximum: 5,054 in 1988; Minimum: 627 in 1980. **CBC Maximum:** 3,500, Sandy Hook, 1988.

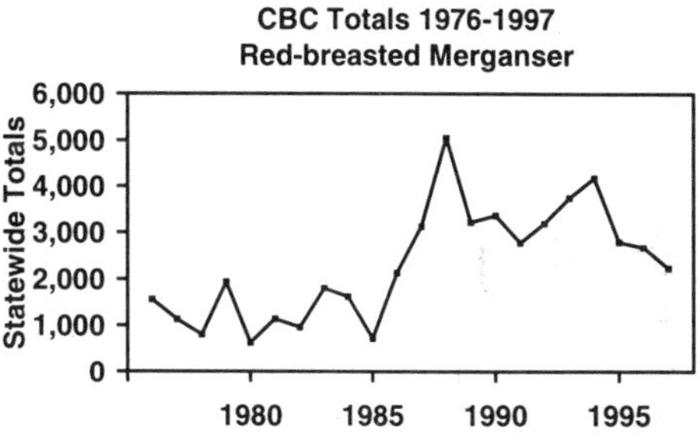

Spring: The northward movement of Red-breasted Mergansers occurs from late March through April, when small numbers of birds appear on inland lakes and reservoirs. The movement is more difficult to detect along the coast, given the large wintering population. A few are noted lingering throughout May, and more rarely, throughout the summer. **Maxima:** Coastal: 400-500, Delaware Bay shore, 25 March 1988; 350, Sandy Hook, 28 March 1986; Inland: 28, Spruce Run Res., 1 May 1976. ■

Ruddy Duck

Oxyura jamaicensis

Range: Breeds mainly in western North America east to southeastern Manitoba and northern Iowa, and sporadically farther east. Along the east coast winters from Massachusetts to Florida.

NJ Status: Rare and very local summer resident, fairly common spring and fall migrant, fairly common winter resident.

Possible
Probable
Confirmed

Statewide Summary	
Status	# of Blocks
Possible	6
Probable	1
Confirmed	2
Total	9

Breeding

Habitat: Nests on the edges of freshwater marshes in thick reeds or vegetation.

The first confirmed breeding record for Ruddy Ducks in New Jersey was at the Hackensack Meadowlands in 1958 (Bull 1964). They continued to expand their range in the state and were confirmed at Brigantine NWR in 1960 (Leck 1984). They nested annually at Kearny Marsh from 1975 through 1978, reaching a peak of 14 pairs in 1978. The population declined at that

Physiographic Distribution — Ruddy Duck	Number of blocks in province	Number of blocks species found breeding in province	Number of blocks species found in state	Percent of province species occupies	Percent of all records for this species found in province	Percent of state area in province
Kittatinny Valley	45	1	9	2.2	11.1	5.3
Piedmont	167	1	9	0.6	11.1	19.6
Inner Coastal Plain	128	4	9	3.1	44.4	15.0
Outer Coastal Plain	204	3	9	1.5	33.3	23.9

site, and they were reduced to three pairs at Kearny Marsh by 1981.

During the Atlas surveys, Ruddy Ducks were Confirmed at only two locations - Mannington Marsh and Petty's Island. They were not found breeding at their previous stronghold, Kearny Marsh. The mapped Possible locations are likely to refer to lingering migrants, rather than potential breeding birds. However, Ruddy Ducks breed late in the summer, and occasionally can have downy young as late as September (R. Kane pers. obs.), suggesting lingering birds should be watched for signs of late-season nesting.

Historic Changes: Ruddy Ducks have an erratic history in New Jersey. Numbers were substantially depleted in the mid-1930s, rebounded in the 1950s, but seem to have declined somewhat since the mid-1970s.

Fall: Ruddy Ducks generally arrive from mid- to late October, with peak numbers present in mid-November. They are recorded in small numbers at the Avalon Sea Watch and are only occasionally seen migrating. They are fairly common on inland lakes and reservoirs and are most common at sites along the Delaware River. **Maxima:** Coastal: 17,280, Floodgates; 16 November 1975; 5,000, Floodgates, 20 November 1978; Inland: 1,200+, Mehrhoff Pond, 23 November 1986. **ASW Single-Day Maximum:**19 on 31 October 1995. **ASW Seasonal Stats:** Average: 37; Maximum: 67 in 1996.

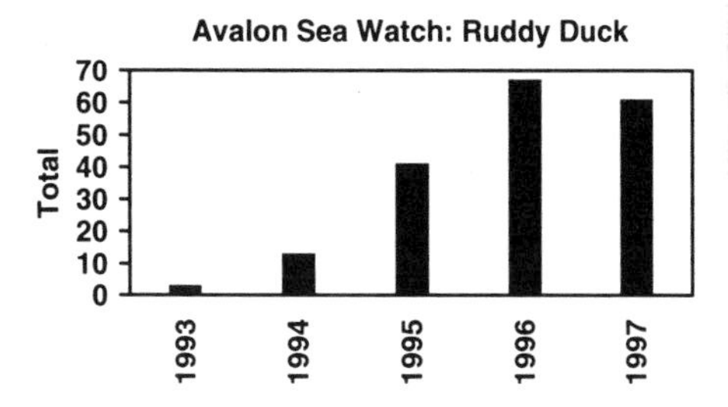

Winter: Ruddy Ducks seem to prefer fresh water but will use estuaries and bays in winter, especially if fresh water is frozen. In the late 1970s statewide CBC totals of Ruddy Ducks averaged over 3,700 birds, mostly in Gloucester County. Since that time most counts have been closer to 1,000. **Maximum:** 5,800, Reed's Beach, 12 January 1993. **CBC Statewide Stats:** Average: 1,722; Maximum: 5,509 in 1980; Minimum: 131 in 1981. **CBC Maximum:** 4,120, Northwest Gloucester, 1976.

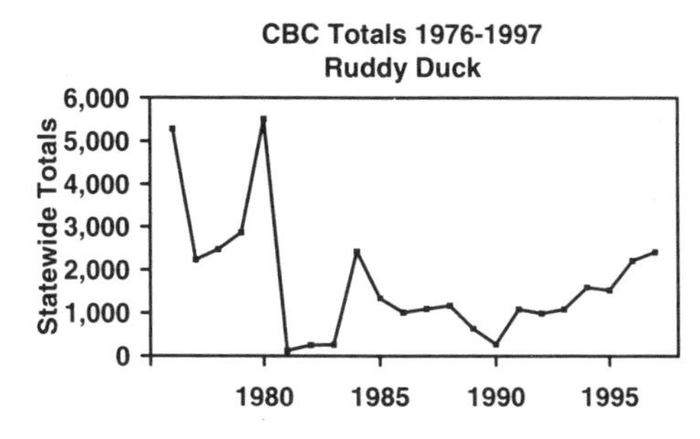

Spring: Northward movement of Ruddy Ducks is noted from mid-March to early April. As with many other diving ducks their migration is more apparent inland when birds reappear after being absent during the winter. **Maxima:** 5,000, Pennsauken, 12 March 1977; 600+, Mehrhoff Pond, 14 April 1997. ■

Osprey
Pandion haliaetus

Range: In eastern North America breeds from Manitoba east to Newfoundland, south to east Texas and along the coast from Nova Scotia to Florida. Winters from Texas and Florida south to South America.

NJ Status: Fairly common but local summer resident, fairly common spring and common fall migrant, very rare winter visitor. Threatened Species in New Jersey.

Breeding

Habitat: Breeds mainly on man-made platforms or structures, primarily in coastal salt marshes.

The return of Ospreys as breeding birds is one of the great success stories of the conservation movement of the late 1900s. Stone (1937) reported Ospreys as common breeding birds of the salt marshes, a status echoed as late as 1955 by Fables. By 1964, Ospreys had declined dramatically (Bull 1964). Frier (1982) recounted the decline in New Jersey from approximately 500 nests prior to 1950 to 50 pairs in 1974. The decline was caused by poor reproduction due to chemical contamination, including contamination from the pesticide DDT, which was widely-used at the time. After DDT was removed from sale in the United States in 1968, the ENSP began hacking programs designed to restore Ospreys to their former breeding range. By 1979 the population had increased to 87 active nests and by 1993 the population had grown to 200 active nests.

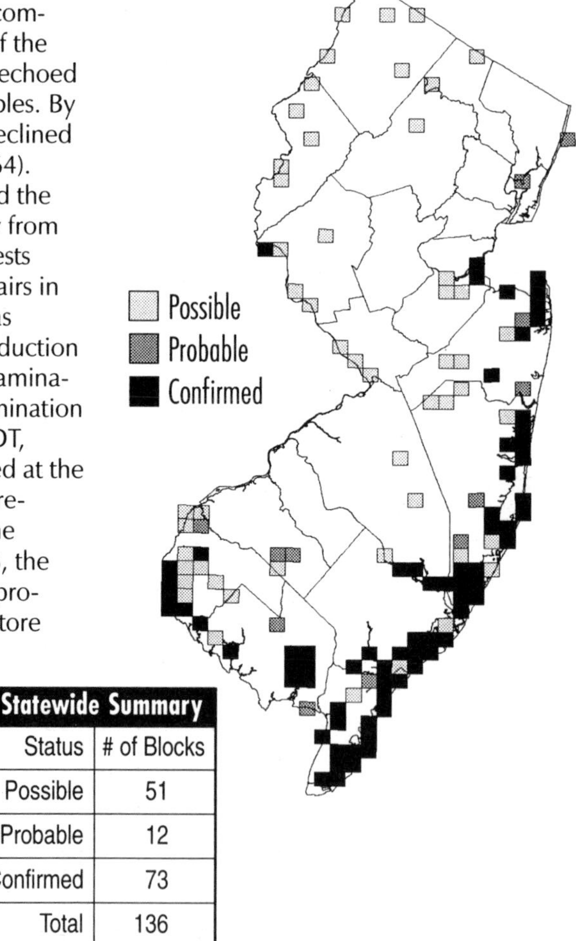

Statewide Summary	
Status	# of Blocks
Possible	51
Probable	12
Confirmed	73
Total	136

Atlas surveys indicated Osprey's breeding range occupied much of the available habitat on the Atlantic Coast. With the exception of the larger river courses in the state (e.g., the Maurice and Mullica Rivers), they were rarely Confirmed nesting away from the coast. Some of the inland locations scored as Possible may indicate birds prospecting for future nest sites. It is likely that, absent any new assaults, Ospreys will continue to expand their range to nest farther north along the Delaware River, and near some of the larger inland reservoirs and lakes.

Osprey

Conservation Note: There continues to be concern regarding the reproductive success of this species. During 1997 and 1998 Ospreys along the Atlantic coast suffered widespread failure for unknown reasons. This current problem seems to be affecting only the birds on the Atlantic Coast, as nests monitored along Delaware Bay and its estuaries had higher levels of reproduction during the same two years (K. Clark, ENSP, pers. com.).

continued on page 168

Physiographic Distribution Osprey	Number of blocks in province	Number of blocks species found breeding in province	Number of blocks species found in state	Percent of province species occupies	Percent of all records for this species found in province	Percent of state area in province
Kittatinny Mountains	19	3	136	15.8	2.2	2.2
Kittatinny Valley	45	6	136	13.3	4.4	5.3
Highlands	109	5	136	4.6	3.7	12.8
Piedmont	167	7	136	4.2	5.1	19.6
Inner Coastal Plain	128	18	136	14.1	13.2	15.0
Outer Coastal Plain	204	82	136	40.2	60.3	23.9
Pine Barrens	180	15	136	8.3	11.0	21.1

continued from page 167

Osprey

Fall: A cold front in mid- to late August can bring the first migrant Ospreys. Numbers build during September, peak from late September to early October, and they become scarce by early November. Regionally, Ospreys are most abundant along the coast, but are also seen in good numbers along inland ridges. **Maxima:** 1,023, Cape May Hawk Watch, 3 October 1989; 800, Cape May Hawk Watch, 2 October 1986. **CMHW Seasonal Stats:** Average: 2,577; Maximum: 6,734 in 1996.

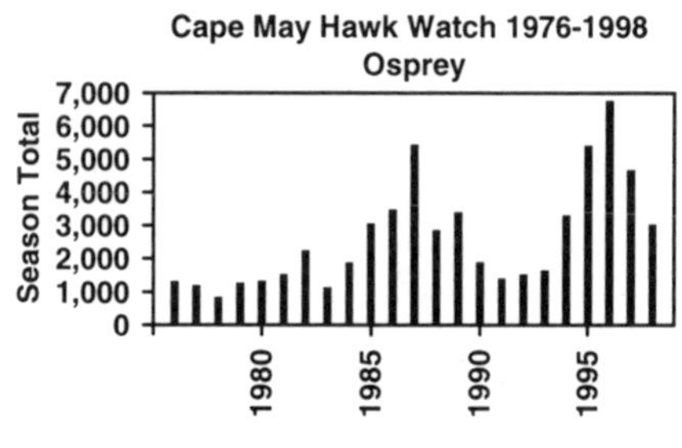

Winter: A few Ospreys linger into December, and they were recorded on nine CBCs from 1976 to 1997. They become very rare after late December, with only three or four midwinter records from 1976 to 1997.

Spring: Fewer Ospreys are noted moving north in spring than are seen moving south in fall. The first Ospreys return in mid-March with peak movements generally occurring in mid-April. **Maxima:** 270, Cape May, 17 April 1988; 76, Sandy Hook Hawk Watch, 12 April 1983; 76, Phillipsburg, 29 April 1984. ■

Swallow-tailed Kite

Elanoides forficatus

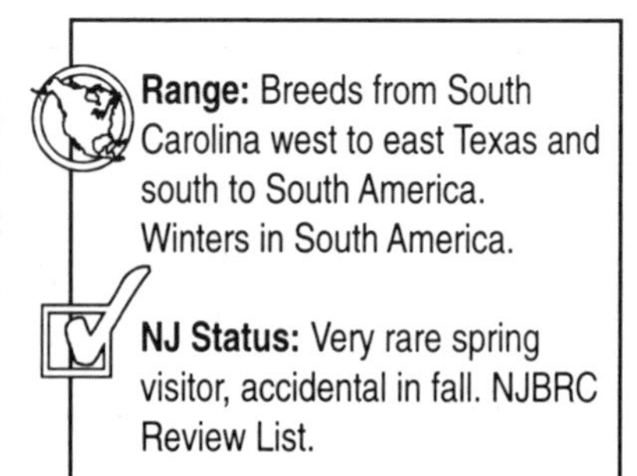

Range: Breeds from South Carolina west to east Texas and south to South America. Winters in South America.

NJ Status: Very rare spring visitor, accidental in fall. NJBRC Review List.

Occurrence: There have been over 60 state reports of Swallow-tailed Kites, and 44 have been accepted by the NJBRC. The first state record was in 1857 (Stone 1908). Nearly all reports have been from April to June, with more than half recorded in May. There are, however, four September reports. Most records are from the coast, and most are of one-day-only flybys. Occasionally birds will linger, notably one from 26 May-8 June 1982 at Greenbrook Sanctuary, (ph-RNJB 8:78). **Maximum:** 2, Morristown, 18 September 1887 (Stone 1937). ■

White-tailed Kite

Elanus leucurus

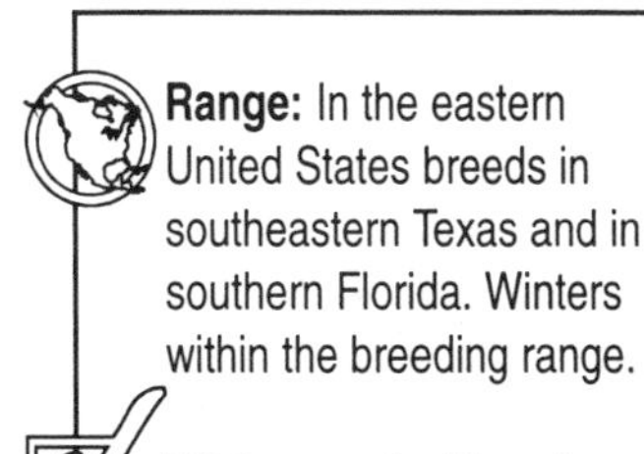

Range: In the eastern United States breeds in southeastern Texas and in southern Florida. Winters within the breeding range.

NJ Status: Accidental. NJBRC Review List.

Occurrence: There have been five state reports of White-tailed Kites, and one has been accepted by the NJBRC: Hidden Valley Ranch, 4 June 1998 (ph-RNJB 24:93, 24:109). ■

Mississippi Kite

Ictinia mississippiensis

Range: Breeds from southeastern Colorado and northwestern Texas east to North Carolina and northern Florida. Winters in South America.

NJ Status: Scarce spring and early summer visitor, very rare fall migrant.

Fall: In the 1980s there was a pattern of Mississippi Kite records in August and September. In more recent years they have been more rare in fall, with three records from 1991-1998.

Spring: Mississippi Kites wander north of their southern United States breeding range in spring, and can arrive as early as late April and are occasionally seen into mid-July. Most records come from Cape May, although they have been recorded throughout the state. Estimating the number passing through Cape May is difficult because some birds remain in the area for several days, and some individuals may even return after leaving for a period of time.

Sibley (1997) estimated that, on average, about nine individuals pass through Cape May in a season. Most sightings are of first-year birds, and there are very few documented records of adults. **Maxima:** 7, Cape Island, 25 May 1986; 7, Cape Island, 19 June 1998. ■

Bald Eagle

Haliaeetus leucocephalus

Range: In eastern North America breeds from Manitoba east to Newfoundland and south to the Gulf Coast and Florida. In the East, winters mainly along or near the coast from the Maritimes south.

NJ Status: Scarce and local summer resident, scarce spring migrant and uncommon fall migrant, uncommon winter resident. Endangered Species in New Jersey.

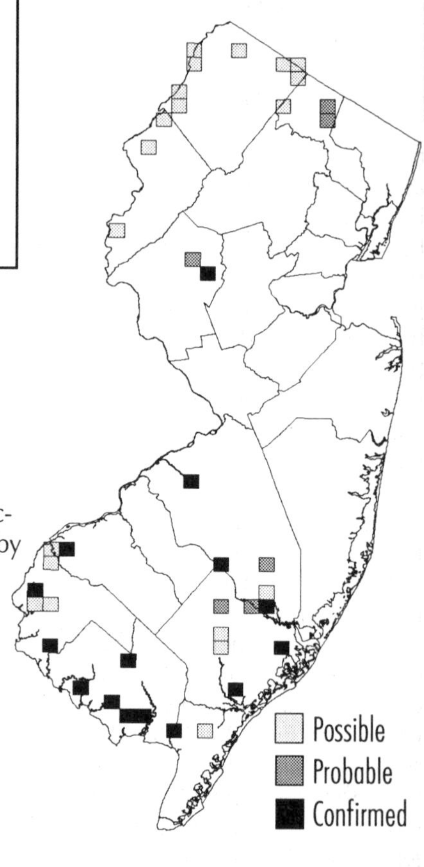

Breeding

Habitat: In New Jersey, nests in tall trees, usually near water.

Although Bald Eagles have been persecuted by illegal shooting, destruction of nest trees, and contamination by pesticides, they have made a remarkable recovery in New Jersey. Historically, Bald Eagles ranged into

Statewide Summary	
Status	# of Blocks
Possible	20
Probable	6
Confirmed	15
Total	41

Physiographic Distribution — Bald Eagle	Number of blocks in province	Number of blocks species found breeding in province	Number of blocks species found in state	Percent of province species occupies	Percent of all records for this species found in province	Percent of state area in province
Kittatinny Mountains	19	5	41	26.3	12.2	2.2
Kittatinny Valley	45	4	41	8.9	9.8	5.3
Highlands	109	5	41	4.6	12.2	12.8
Piedmont	167	2	41	1.2	4.9	19.6
Inner Coastal Plain	128	6	41	4.7	14.6	15.0
Outer Coastal Plain	204	10	41	4.9	24.4	23.9
Pine Barrens	180	9	41	5.0	22.0	21.1

Map Interpretation: Some of the Possible and Probable locations on the map likely involve sightings of known breeding birds from other blocks, or sightings of post-breeding adults. These clusters of sightings give an inflated estimate of the number of breeding individuals.

northern New Jersey and nested as far north as Greenwood Lake in Passaic County (Fables 1955), but they have always been most numerous in southern New Jersey. Stone (1908) noted that the species was declining at the turn of the 20th century, but he reported that they were still fairly common in the late 1930s (Stone 1937).

Fables (1955) described Bald Eagles as declining birds in the state. By 1957 there were 15 nests in southern New Jersey, and that was further reduced to only seven nests by 1961, and only one of the seven nests produced young (Bull 1964). The situation became even more dire when the nesting population was reduced to one pair in New Jersey (Leck 1984). In 1983, the ENSP began hacking programs designed to restore the breeding population of Bald Eagles. These projects, coupled with natural recolonization, were successful and as of 1997 there were 14 nests in the state, but only one nest was north of the Coastal Plain (E. Stiles, ENSP, pers. com.).

Atlas data found Bald Eagles were Confirmed nesting south of the Piedmont, with only one exception - a nest in eastern Hunterdon County. Their pattern of colonization has been from south to north, and it is likely that, given adequate protection, the Possible and Probable locations in northern New Jersey will host some Confirmed nest sites within a few years.

Fall: Bald Eagles have shown a marked increase during the 1990s, both as migrants along the coast and along inland ridges. The number of migrant Bald Eagles at the Cape May Hawk Watch has increased dramatically since the first count in 1976. The seasonal total averaged just over 10 birds per year in the first four years of the count, over 20 birds per year from 1980-1985, and about 45 birds per year through 1990. After leveling off somewhat in the early 1990s, the counts jumped to 144 in 1994, 135 in 1995, and to an incredible 284 in 1996. The 70 Bald Eagles that passed through Cape May from 18-21 September 1996 bested the total Bald Eagle count of most seasons prior to that year. Although the Bald Eagle flight is smaller along the ridges, the counts at the Montclair Hawk Watch mirror the same pattern of increase (E. Greenstone, pers. com.)

Bald Eagle patterns of movement are complex. With the increased breeding population in the state, sightings of Bald Eagles at any time of year could be from the resident population, or could be wandering or migrant individuals. **Maxima:** 30, Chimney Rock, 20 September 1996;24, Cape May Hawk Watch,19 September 1996. **CMHW Seasonal Stats:** Average: 62; Maximum: 284 in 1996.

continued on page 172

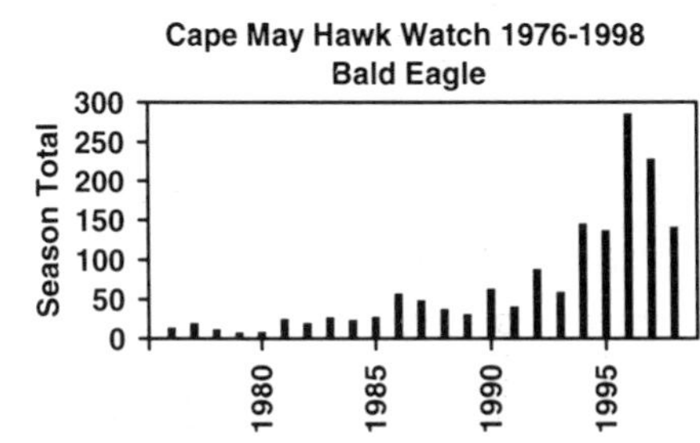

continued from page 171

Winter: In addition to the increased abundance of fall migrants, the number of Bald Eagles wintering in the state has also increased. A winter eagle survey has been conducted in New Jersey since 1978 by ENSP, and a dramatic increase in numbers is evident in those data. Statewide the number of wintering Bald Eagles rose from six in 1978, to 70 in 1990, and to 176 in 1997 (E. Stiles, ENSP, pers. com.). Statewide CBC totals have also increased markedly since the mid-1970s. **CBC Statewide Stats:** Average: 23; Maximum: 64 in 1996; Minimum: 3 in 1976. **CBC Maximum:** 18, Cumberland, 1994; 18, Belleplain, 1996.

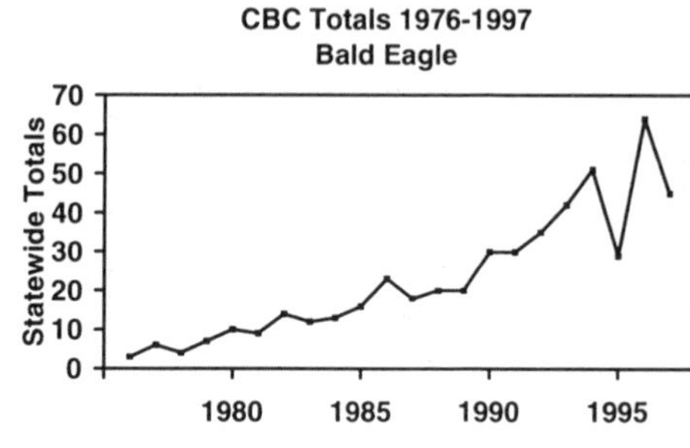

Spring: Movements of Bald Eagles are complex. Those seen in March and early April may be migrants returning north. However, immature birds seen in late spring and summer may be local birds or nonbreeding juveniles wandering from breeding sites elsewhere. **Maxima:** 5, Cape May Point,17 April 1989; 5, Cape May Point, 22 May 1989. ■

Bald Eagle

Northern Harrier

Circus cyaneus

Range: In eastern North America breeds from Manitoba east to Quebec, south to Oklahoma and Virginia. Winters locally throughout much of the United States.

NJ Status: Scarce and local summer resident, fairly common spring and common fall migrant, fairly common winter resident. Endangered Species in New Jersey (breeding only).

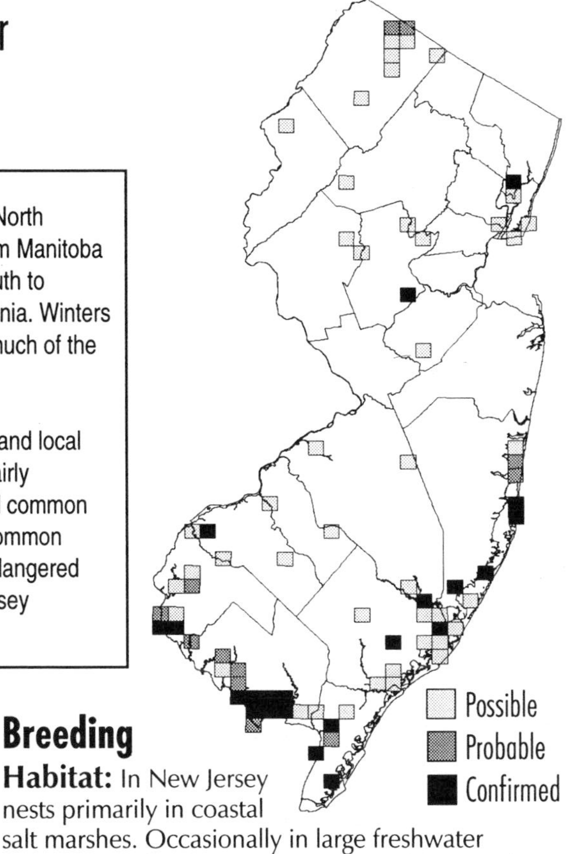

Breeding

Habitat: In New Jersey nests primarily in coastal salt marshes. Occasionally in large freshwater marshes or inland pastures. Nests on the ground.

Statewide Summary	
Status	# of Blocks
Possible	44
Probable	12
Confirmed	22
Total	78

Northern Harriers are one of New Jersey's most imperiled breeding birds. The species is declining nationwide, but the rate of decline is slow and there are areas that are maintaining stable populations (MacWhirther and Bildstein 1996). Historic informa-

continued on page 174

Physiographic Distribution

Northern Harrier	Number of blocks in province	Number of blocks species found breeding in province	Number of blocks species found in state	Percent of province species occupies	Percent of all records for this species found in province	Percent of state area in province
Kittatinny Valley	45	7	78	15.6	9.0	5.3
Highlands	109	3	78	2.8	3.8	12.8
Piedmont	167	10	78	6.0	12.8	19.6
Inner Coastal Plain	128	8	78	6.3	10.3	15.0
Outer Coastal Plain	204	44	78	21.6	56.4	23.9
Pine Barrens	180	6	78	3.3	7.7	21.1

continued from page 173

tion on the size of the New Jersey population in the early 1900s is anecdotal, but Stone (1937) recounted a population of breeding Northern Harriers in Cape May County larger than occurs today. Fables (1955) indicated that the species was declining in the interior of New Jersey, and Bull (1964) reported the species was "greatly reduced." Surveys in New Jersey in 1979 found 19 pairs; in 1980, 24 pairs; and in 1983, 43 nests along the coast of New Jersey (Dunne 1984). Differences among these counts, however, reflect a change in survey methods and not an increase in the population.

Atlas volunteers Confirmed Northern Harriers in only 22 blocks during five years of surveys. Their stronghold in the state is in Cumberland County along the Delaware Bay shore, and into Salem County. They are thinly distributed along the Atlantic shore, with what amounts to a remnant population surviving. They have become nearly absent away from the coastal marshes.

Conservation Note: Northern Harriers are disappearing as breeding birds both along the Atlantic coast of New Jersey and inland. The reasons for the declines in the coastal population are unknown and need to be discovered if this species is to persist in the state. Management and conservation of inland grasslands and fallow farmland should be a priority for increasing the inland breeding population.

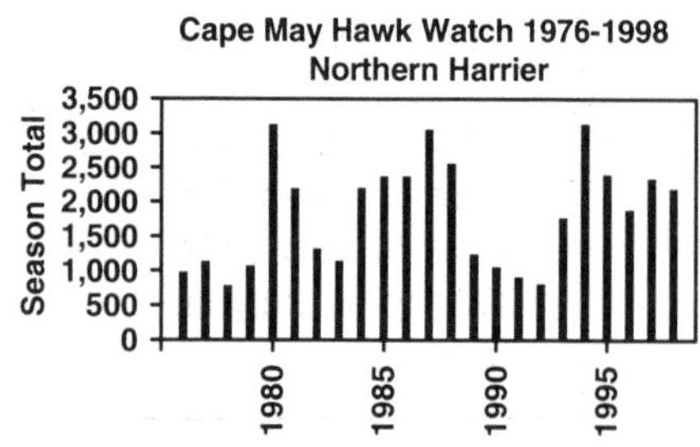

Map Interpretation: Due to the Northern Harrier's secretive habits, Confirmations are extremely difficult. In most cases Probable sightings likely denote breeding birds. Along the coast, single records of birds scored Possible may refer to foraging birds from breeding locations in adjacent blocks. All Northern Harriers seen inland during the breeding season should be watched closely for the possibility of locating new inland breeding sites.

Fall: Northern Harrier migration is protracted, with the first birds seen in July and movement continuing into early December. There are generally two periods of peak flights, one in early October and the other in early November. The early flight consists mainly of immature birds; the second constitutes the main movement of adults. Harriers are most abundant along the coast, but they also occur in good numbers along inland ridges. They are known to fly in foul weather, and they readily cross the Delaware Bay under most conditions. As evidence of their water-crossing abilities, the Avalon Sea Watch averaged 68 birds per year from 1994 through 1997. **Maxima:** 278, Cape May Hawk Watch, 12 November 1980; 266, Cape May Hawk Watch, 2 October 1986. **CMHW Seasonal Stats:** Average: 1,789; Maximum: 3,115 in 1994.

Northern Harrier

continued

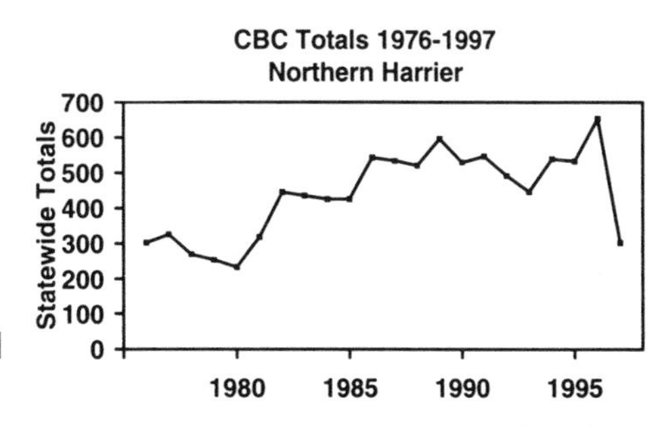

Winter: New Jersey's coastal salt marshes are prime wintering areas for Northern Harriers, as are the grasslands in northwestern New Jersey. Although the harrier's status as a breeding bird is Endangered, statewide totals of CBCs increased steadily throughout the early 1980s and have since remained stable. The protection of winter roost sites, such as the Alpha Grasslands, may be an important component to recovery of the inland breeding population. **Maxima:** 50, Alpha, 28 January 1990; 35, Point Breeze, winter 1991. **CBC Statewide Stats:** Average: 440; Maximum: 653 in 1996; Minimum: 234 in 1980. **CBC Maximum:** 146, Cumberland, 1996.

Spring: As with most raptors, spring migration of Northern Harriers is much less noticeable than fall migration. Northward migration can be detected as early as late February, and these early movements are usually of adult males. The peak movement generally occurs in mid-April, with some migration continuing into May. **Maxima:** 90, Sandy Hook Hawk Watch, 12 April 1983; 68, Sandy Hook Hawk Watch, 12 April 1993. ■

Sharp-shinned Hawk

Accipiter striatus

Range: In eastern North America breeds from Manitoba east to Newfoundland, south to Minnesota and New Jersey, and along the Appalachians to northern Georgia and Alabama. Winters throughout much of the eastern United States

NJ Status: Scarce and local summer resident, fairly common spring and common fall migrant, uncommon winter resident.

Breeding

Habitat: Nests in large forested tracts, usually conifers, occasionally in deciduous trees.

The historic range of Sharp-shinned Hawks in New Jersey is difficult to determine, although it is likely the species was always rare as a breeder. Reports of their distribution are confounded by the difficulty in separating this species from the more common Cooper's Hawk. Stone (1908) lists Sharp-shinned Hawks as rare breeding

continued on page 176

continued from page 175

Sharp-shinned Hawk

birds in New Jersey. In 1934 he indicated there was a record of a nest in Cape May County, although this was south of the species' known range. Fables (1955) stated that Sharp-shinned Hawks nested mainly in the northern part of the state. Both Bull (1964) and Leck (1984) reported that Sharp-shinned Hawks were rare and declining breeding birds. Their history includes reports of persecution by humans, and they were described as "one of the few hawks that are not entitled to protection" (Stone 1908). More recently, Sharp-shinned Hawk populations appeared to decline in the mid-1900s, possibly in response to poor reproductive success due to contamination by pesticides (Kaufman 1996).

Hanisek (1990) referred to Sharp-shinned Hawks as "either the rarest or most stealthy breeding accipiter" in northwestern New Jersey. Their possible presence as a breeding bird on the Coastal Plain of southern New Jersey was suggested by Wander who found

Possible
Probable
Confirmed

Statewide Summary	
Status	# of Blocks
Possible	55
Probable	11
Confirmed	18
Total	84

Physiographic Distribution **Sharp-shinned Hawk**	Number of blocks in province	Number of blocks species found breeding in province	Number of blocks species found in state	Percent of province species occupies	Percent of all records for this species found in province	Percent of state area in province
Kittatinny Mountains	19	11	84	57.9	13.1	2.2
Kittatinny Valley	45	12	84	26.7	14.3	5.3
Highlands	109	33	84	30.3	39.3	12.8
Piedmont	167	11	84	6.6	13.1	19.6
Inner Coastal Plain	128	7	84	5.5	8.3	15.0
Outer Coastal Plain	204	4	84	2.0	4.8	23.9
Pine Barrens	180	6	84	3.3	7.1	21.1

Map Interpretation: Many observers, even those with years of experience, have difficulty separating Sharp-shinned from Cooper's Hawks - especially if the bird is only observed for a short period of time. For that reason, it is prudent to accept only Confirmed sightings as a low-end estimate of the species' breeding range.

two individuals in June in a cedar swamp (Wander 1981). He stated that the finds "suggest that this species may breed, although probably rarely, in southern New Jersey."

Atlas volunteers found few Confirmed breeding sites for Sharp-Shinned Hawks, despite five years of surveys. Their stronghold remains in northern New Jersey, with only one Confirmed nest south of the Piedmont. Over 50% of the blocks occupied by Sharp-shinned Hawk were in the Kittatinny Mountains and Highlands.

Fall: The first southbound Sharp-shinned Hawks can be seen in early September and peak numbers occur from late September through early October. Migration can continue into early December. Sharp-shinned Hawks have accounted for over 50% of all hawks counted at Cape May from 1976 through 1998, and over 85% of the Sharp-shinned Hawks passing through Cape May are hatching year birds (Sibley 1997). Sharp-shinned Hawks are common along inland ridges and the percentage of adults is much higher along the ridges. There is some evidence that the apparent downward trend in the counts of Sharp-shinned Hawks at fall hawk watch locations throughout the eastern United States indicates a real decline in the population. **Maxima:** 11,096, Cape May Hawk Watch, 4 October 1977; 7,000, Cape May Hawk Watch, 4 October 1984. **CMHW Seasonal Stats:** Average: 31,089; Maximum: 61,167 in 1984.

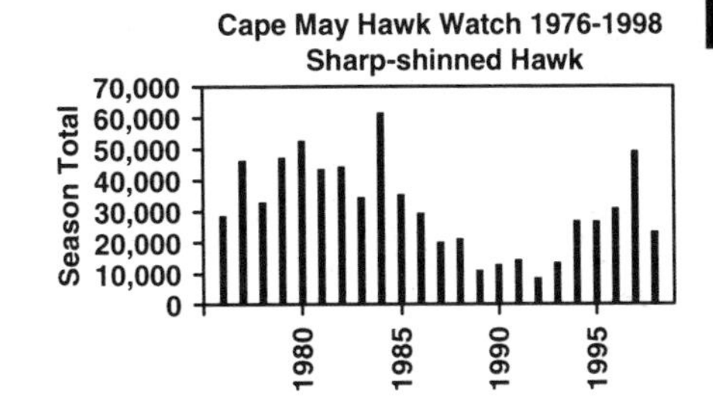

Winter: Although totals of migrant Sharp-shinned Hawks have generally declined throughout the eastern United States, CBC totals have increased markedly from 1976 to 1997. Statewide totals from the mid-1970s are now matched by the Cumberland County count alone. **CBC Statewide Stats:** Average: 165; Maximum: 364 in 1996; Minimum: 41 in 1976. **CBC Maximum:** 46, Cumberland, 1990.

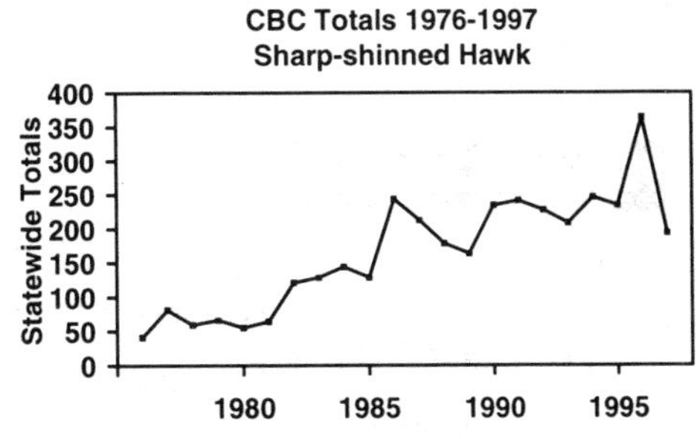

Spring: Sharp-shinned Hawks are less numerous in spring migration than fall, and they appear to be evenly dispersed over the state. Migrants appear in mid-March and peak in late April to early May. **Maxima:** 2,297, Sandy Hook Hawk Watch, 5 May 1986; 1,514, Sandy Hook Hawk Watch, 5 May 1980. ■

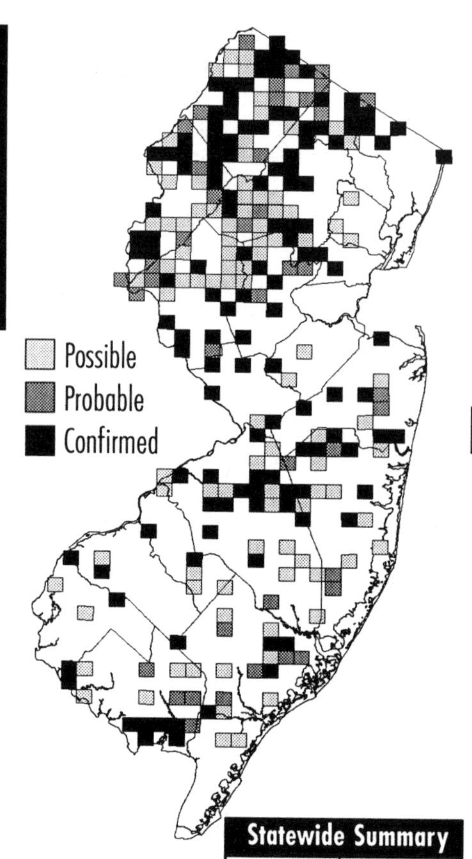

Cooper's Hawk

Accipiter cooperii

Range: Breeds across southern Canada and throughout much of the United States. Winters throughout much of the United States.

NJ Status: Uncommon and somewhat local summer resident, fairly common spring and common fall migrant, uncommon winter resident. Threatened species in New Jersey.

Statewide Summary	
Status	# of Blocks
Possible	97
Probable	41
Confirmed	127
Total	265

Breeding

Habitat: Breeds in coniferous or mixed coniferous/deciduous woodlands. Frequently found in wet woods or near water.

Historically, Cooper's Hawks have been the most numerous accipiter nesting in New Jersey, outnumbering both Sharp-shinned Hawks and Northern

Physiographic Distribution

Cooper's Hawk	Number of blocks in province	Number of blocks species found breeding in province	Number of blocks species found in state	Percent of province species occupies	Percent of all records for this species found in province	Percent of state area in province
Kittatinny Mountains	19	11	265	57.9	4.2	2.2
Kittatinny Valley	45	32	265	71.1	12.1	5.3
Highlands	109	71	265	65.1	26.8	12.8
Piedmont	167	40	265	24.0	15.1	19.6
Inner Coastal Plain	128	27	265	21.1	10.2	15.0
Outer Coastal Plain	204	31	265	15.2	11.7	23.9
Pine Barrens	180	53	265	29.4	20.0	21.1

Goshawks (Stone 1908). Griscom (1923) described Cooper's Hawks as relatively common breeding birds in northern New Jersey, but as absent near New York City. Stone (1937) knew of no breeding records in Cape May County, but recounted several nests from Salem County. Fables (1955) indicated the species was distributed evenly throughout New Jersey, but described the species as declining.

In 1976 Cooper's Hawks were described as "sadly diminished" in northern New Jersey when only one nest was reported to RNJB (Hanisek 1976). By 1985 Leck noted that the species was possibly increasing in New Jersey, and that the population was centered in Sussex, Warren, and Hunterdon counties. In 1990 Cooper's Hawks were reported on a "decade long upswing" in northern New Jersey (Hanisek 1990), a pattern reported to continue throughout the state in the 1990s. Like many other raptors, Cooper's Hawks were shot as pests and suffered from environmental contamination and loss of breeding habitat (Rosenfield and Bielefeldt 1993). They have shown a remarkable ability to rebound from their decline and are now the third most common breeding raptor in New Jersey.

Atlas data indicated Cooper's Hawks are distributed throughout the state, with the exception of the highly urbanized sections of the eastern Piedmont, the barrier islands, and Cape May County. They are also widely distributed in the northern provinces, occurring in over 50% of the blocks in the Kittatinny Mountains, Kittatinny Valley, and Highlands. The relative success of this species in contrast to Sharp-shinned Hawk may be due, in part, to Cooper's Hawk's less restrictive nesting habitat requirements. Unlike Sharp-shinned Hawks, Cooper's Hawks will use areas near human development and will nest in the Coastal Plain and Pine Barrens.

Fall: Southbound Cooper's Hawks can be seen as early as late August, with numbers peaking slightly later than Sharp-shinned Hawks, typically from early through mid-October. Migrants are seen into early December. Although they occur in highest numbers at Cape May, they are also fairly common along inland ridges. Immature birds are more common than adults along the coast, and, like Sharp-shinned Hawks, a much higher percentage of adults occurs inland. **Maxima:** 456, Cape May Hawk Watch, 3 October 1994; 421, Cape May Hawk Watch, 11 October 1985. **CMHW Seasonal Stats:** Average: 2,224; Maximum: 5,009 in 1995.

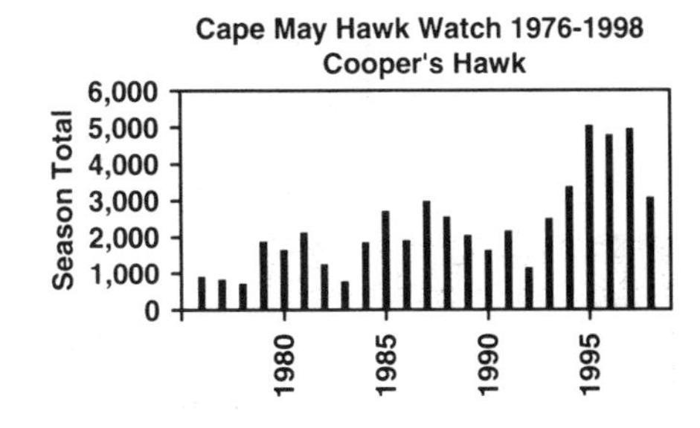

Winter: The increase in the population of wintering Cooper's Hawks mirrors that of Sharp-shinned Hawks. A distinct rise was recorded in statewide CBC totals from 1976 to 1997. **CBC Statewide Stats:** Average: 58; Maximum: 212 in 1996; Minimum: 11 in 1976 and 1978. **CBC Maximum**: 22, Cumberland, 1996.

continued on page 180

continued from page 179

Cooper's Hawk

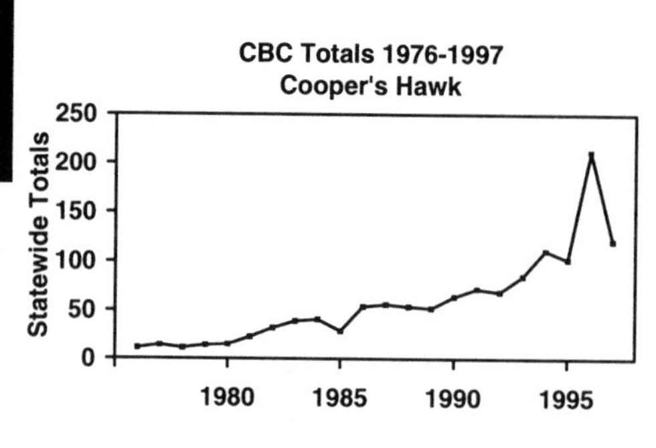

Spring: Northbound Cooper's Hawks are less numerous than those headed south in fall. A few migrants can be seen from mid- to late March, but the peak movement generally occurs in late April and continues, in decreasing numbers, into May. **Maxima:** 50, Sandy Hook Hawk Watch, 29 April 1987; 46, Sandy Hook Hawk Watch, 20 April 1984. ■

Northern Goshawk

Accipiter gentilis

Range: In eastern North America, breeds from Manitoba east to Labrador, south to Minnesota, and northern New Jersey. Winters from the southern edge of the breeding range south to Nebraska and Virginia.

NJ Status: Scarce and local summer resident, rare spring and scarce to uncommon fall migrant, rare winter resident. Endangered Species in New Jersey.

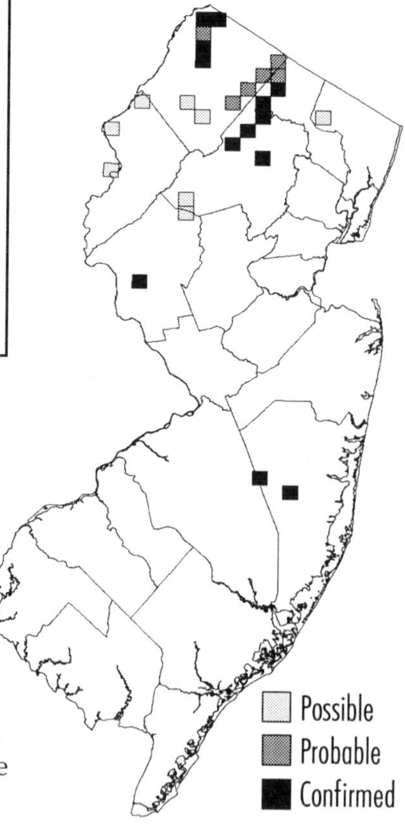

Breeding

Habitat: Typically nests in large, mature tracts of mixed coniferous/ deciduous woods.

Northern Goshawks are relatively recent additions to the list of breeding birds in New Jersey. Fables (1955) recounted a bird with prey seen in June 1945 in Sussex County for what may be the first breeding record in the state. The first nest found in New Jersey was at

Northern Goshawk

continued

Greenwood Lake in 1964 (Speiser and Bosakowski 1984). This was followed by the observation of courtship flights at the Pequannock Watershed in April 1969, and a subsequent sighting at the Pequannock Watershed in 1971 (Black 1972). Several nests were located in northern New Jersey during the 1970s (Speiser and Bosakowski 1984), and they have expanded their breeding range slowly since then.

Atlas data indicated most breeding Northern Goshawks were concentrated in a small area in Sussex, Passaic, and Morris counties in the Kittatinny Mountains and Highlands provinces. Their range has expanded however, and, unexpectedly, two nests were found in the Pine Barrens.

Fall: Although migrant Northern Goshawk numbers vary considerably from year to year, their timing is usually fairly consistent. Their numbers usually peak from late October through early November. They are more likely to be encountered along inland ridges than along the coast. At the hawk watch at Cape May, seasonal totals vary from a low of nine in 1989 to a high of 89 in 1997. **Maxima:** 14, Skyline Ridge, 20 October 1977; 13, Cape May Hawk Watch, 29 October 1985; 13, Cape May Hawk Watch, 15 November 1997. **CMHW Seasonal Stats:** Average: 36; Maximum: 89 in 1997.

continued on page 182

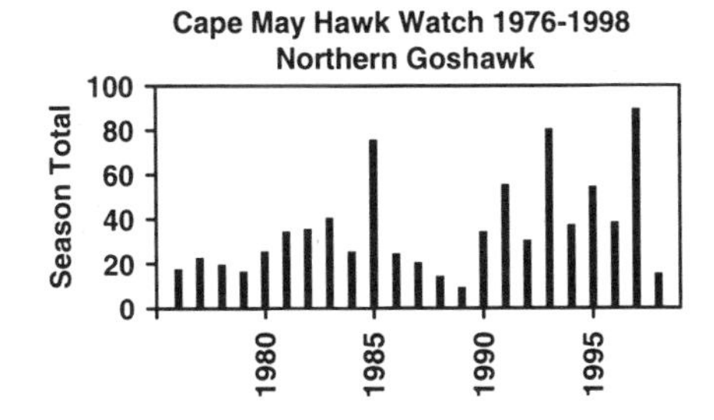

Statewide Summary	
Status	# of Blocks
Possible	8
Probable	6
Confirmed	13
Total	27

Map Interpretation: Speiser and Bosakowski (1984) found the Northern Goshawk population in New Jersey contained a large number of floaters (nonbreeding adults or sub-adults). It is therefore prudent to consider only Confirmed nests when estimating the breeding range.

Physiographic Distribution Northern Goshawk	Number of blocks in province	Number of blocks species found breeding in province	Number of blocks species found in state	Percent of province species occupies	Percent of all records for this species found in province	Percent of state area in province
Kittatinny Mountains	19	6	27	31.6	22.2	2.2
Kittatinny Valley	45	3	27	6.7	11.1	5.3
Highlands	109	14	27	12.8	51.9	12.8
Piedmont	167	2	27	1.2	7.4	19.6
Pine Barrens	180	2	27	1.1	7.4	21.1

continued from page 181

Northern Goshawk

Winter: Northern Goshawks are rarely encountered in winter, even in years when fall totals have been relatively high. Statewide CBC totals are generally fewer than ten birds. **CBC Statewide Stats:** Average: 7; Maximum: 18 in 1983; Minimum: 2 in three years. **CBC Maximum:** 4, Boonton, 1983; 4, Lower Hudson, 1989.

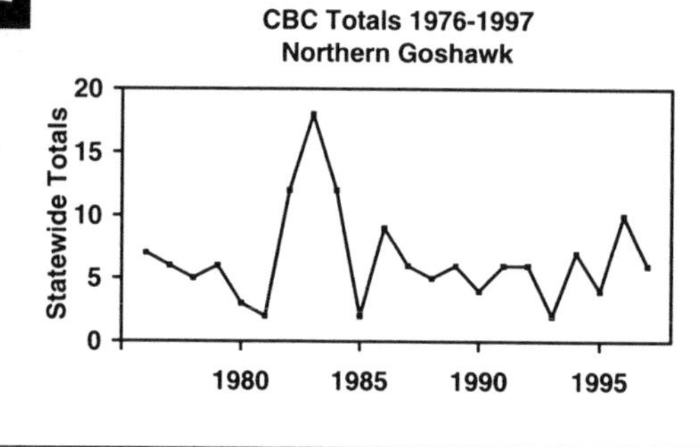

Spring: Few northbound Northern Goshawks are encountered in spring, and many follow the interior ridges. The Sandy Hook Hawk Watch averaged fewer than one bird per spring between 1979 and 1994. **Maximum:** 4, Raccoon Ridge, 6 March 1976. ■

Red-shouldered Hawk

Buteo lineatus

Possible
Probable
Confirmed

Range: In eastern North America breeds from eastern Minnesota to New Brunswick south to eastern Texas and Florida. Winters throughout much of the eastern United States.

NJ Status: Uncommon and local summer resident, uncommon spring and fairly common fall migrant, scarce to uncommon winter resident. Endangered Species in New Jersey (breeding), Threatened Species in New Jersey (nonbreeding).

Red-shouldered Hawk

continued

Breeding

Habitat: Typically nests in fairly extensive hardwood swamps.

It is likely that Red-shouldered Hawks were always fairly local breeders in New Jersey during the 1800s and 1900s. Stone (1908) and Griscom (1923) reported that they were common breeding birds, but regionally restricted and more common in northern New Jersey. Stone (1937) knew of nesting records from Salem County and suspected the species nested in Cape May County. Leck (1984) contended they had declined as breeding birds and were mostly restricted to northern New Jersey wetlands. As a measure of the decline, a survey in southern New Jersey from 1991 through 1992 found only nine pairs nesting in the region (Dowdell and Sutton 1993).

Atlas data showed the stronghold for the species remains northern New Jersey, but there are nests scattered throughout the Coastal Plain and Piedmont. They are notably rare in the Inner Coastal Plain and western Piedmont. Interestingly, although Fables (1955) noted this species was rarely reported from the Pine Barrens, Atlas volunteers found over 14% of their statewide range was in the Pine Barrens. Their Confirmation rate in the Pine Barrens was low, however. Habitat loss is considered to be a major reason for the decline in this species (Ehrlich et al. 1993), although other factors (pesticide accumulation and human disturbance) may also be contributing to the population decline (Crocoll 1994).

continued on page 184

Statewide Summary

Status	# of Blocks
Possible	45
Probable	34
Confirmed	32
Total	111

Physiographic Distribution

Red-shouldered Hawk	Number of blocks in province	Number of blocks species found breeding in province	Number of blocks species found in state	Percent of province species occupies	Percent of all records for this species found in province	Percent of state area in province
Kittatinny Mountains	19	6	111	31.6	5.4	2.2
Kittatinny Valley	45	19	111	42.2	17.1	5.3
Highlands	109	39	111	35.8	35.1	12.8
Piedmont	167	17	111	10.2	15.3	19.6
Inner Coastal Plain	128	6	111	4.7	5.4	15.0
Outer Coastal Plain	204	8	111	3.9	7.2	23.9
Pine Barrens	180	16	111	8.9	14.4	21.1

continued from page 183

Red-shouldered Hawk

Red-shouldered Hawk

Conservation Note: Red-shouldered Hawks return to the same nest site year after year (Crocoll 1994). Conservation of known breeding locations would be the minimum action required to maintain the breeding population in New Jersey. Without further protection of freshwater wetland nesting sites, the New Jersey population will continue to decline. The New Jersey Freshwater Wetlands Protection Act is critical to the stability of the Red-shouldered Hawk population.

Fall: A few migrant Red-shouldered Hawks are seen by mid-September, but the peak southbound movement occurs in November and can continue into early December. They are seen inland along ridges but are typically more concentrated at Cape May. **Maxima:** 165, Cape May Hawk Watch, 10 November 1994; 162, Cape May Hawk Watch, 13 November 1980. **CMHW Seasonal Stats:** Average: 437; Maximum: 872 in 1994.

Cape May Hawk Watch 1976-1998
Red-shouldered Hawk

Season Total: 1,000 / 800 / 600 / 400 / 200 / 0 — 1980, 1985, 1990, 1995

Winter: Red-shouldered Hawks tend to be difficult to find in winter, adding to the impression of their scarcity. Statewide CBC totals indicate a fairly small, winter population. **CBC Statewide Stats:** Average: 32; Maximum: 60 in 1996; Minimum: 17 in 1985. **CBC Maximum:** 15, Cape May, 1979.

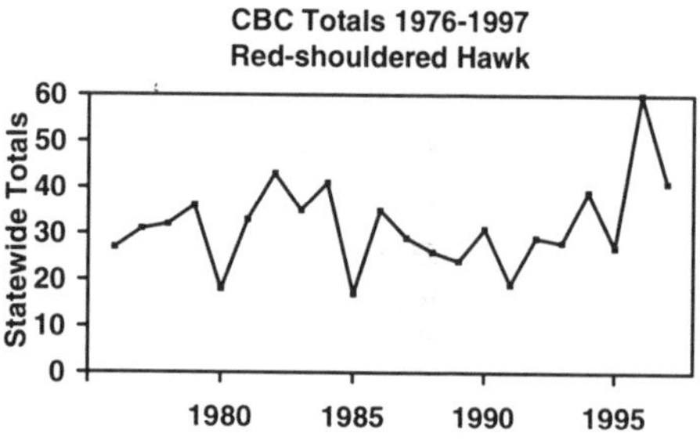

Spring: Red-shouldered Hawks are considerably less common as migrants in spring than in fall. They head north very early, with movements beginning in late February and peaking in mid-March. Few migrants are seen after mid-April. **Maxima:** 58, Sandy Hook Hawk Watch, 15 March 1981; 55, Sandy Hook Hawk Watch, 14 March 1985. ■

Broad-winged Hawk

Buteo platypterus

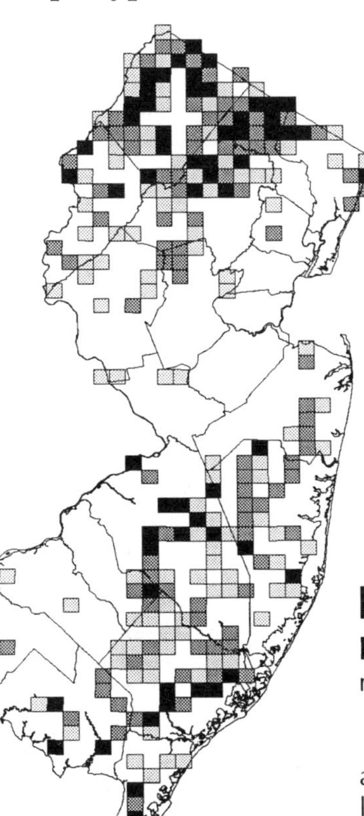

Range: Breeds from central Alberta east to Nova Scotia, south to eastern Texas and northwestern Florida. Winters mainly in Central and South America.

NJ Status: Uncommon and somewhat local summer resident, fairly common spring and common fall migrant, accidental in winter.

Possible
Probable
Confirmed

Statewide Summary	
Status	# of Blocks
Possible	106
Probable	94
Confirmed	59
Total	259

Breeding

Habitat: Breeds in dense deciduous or mixed woodlands, frequently near water.

Historic information on the range and abundance of Broad-winged Hawks is likely to be confounded by misidentification of this species prior to the 1930s (Griscom 1923). Stone (1908) described Broad-winged Hawks as less common breeders than Red-shouldered

continued on page 186

Physiographic Distribution Broad-winged Hawk	Number of blocks in province	Number of blocks species found breeding in province	Number of blocks species found in state	Percent of province species occupies	Percent of all records for this species found in province	Percent of state area in province
Kittatinny Mountains	19	17	259	89.5	6.6	2.2
Kittatinny Valley	45	25	259	55.6	9.7	5.3
Highlands	109	66	259	60.6	25.5	12.8
Piedmont	167	27	259	16.2	10.4	19.6
Inner Coastal Plain	128	7	259	5.5	2.7	15.0
Outer Coastal Plain	204	34	259	16.7	13.1	23.9
Pine Barrens	180	83	259	46.1	32.0	21.1

continued from page 185

Hawks, which is contrary to modern patterns of abundance and may be an artifact of identification problems. Fables (1955) and Leck (1984) described a breeding range similar to that defined by Atlas data. In 1992 reports of nesting broad-wingeds to RNJB Region 4 had declined enough to consider it a cause for alarm (Dasey 1992).

In New Jersey, Broad-winged Hawks are found in the provinces with the greatest forest cover (i.e., Kittatinny Valley, Kittatinny Mountains, Highlands, and Pine Barrens). Conversely, the Inner Coastal Plain, a province with little forest cover, had Broad-winged Hawks reported in less than 6% of the blocks in that province. If this species has declined in New Jersey, it is most likely that the decline is in the Inner Coastal Plain and Piedmont.

Fall: Broad-winged Hawks are early migrants, typically arriving in late August and departing by mid-October. They migrate through New Jersey in a very short season, with most of the ridge-flight occurring in mid-September. They are more common along inland ridges than along the coast, especially the Watchung ridges. They peak at Cape May later in the season than inland, and can be seen along the coast in small numbers into early November. **Maxima:** 18,500, Scott's Mt., 14 September 1983; 17,491, Chimney Rock, 20 September 1996.

CMHW Daily Maximum: 9,400 on 4 October 1977. **CMHW Seasonal Stats:** Average: 3,179; Maximum: 13,918 in 1981.

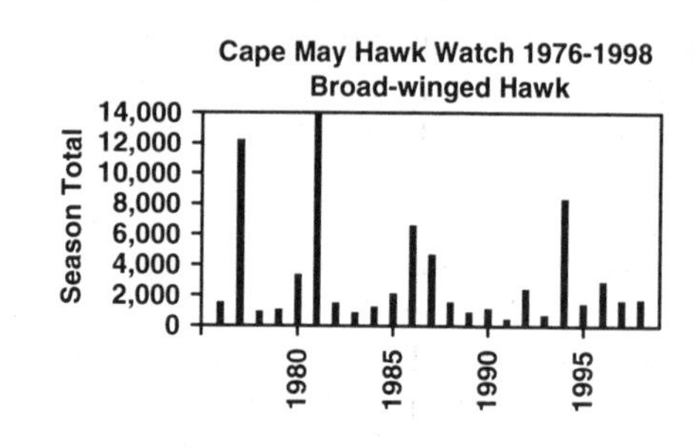

Winter: Stone (1937) considered winter reports of Broad-winged Hawks to be misidentified Red-shouldered Hawks, as did Fables (1955). Bull (1964) was also skeptical of sight reports and considered most to be inaccurate; Leck (1984) made no reference to winter reports at all. However, in 1993 an adult spent the winter near Medford, the only documented mid-winter record. Broad-winged Hawks will only rarely linger into early December and one was reported on the Cape May CBC in 1992.

Spring: Broad-winged Hawks are fairly late migrants in spring and are usually first encountered in early to mid-April. The peak generally occurs in late April, with movements continuing throughout May. At Cape May, kettles of nonbreeding sub-adults can be seen into early June. **Maxima:** 1,329, Montclair, 25 April 1988; 1,000+, Phillipsburg, 22 April 1987; 1,000, Warren Township, 26 April 1997. ■

Swainson's Hawk

Buteo swainsoni

Range: Breeds in western Canadian provinces and western states east to Illinois. Winters in South America.

NJ Status: Rare fall migrant, accidental at other seasons. NJBRC Review List.

Occurrence: The NJBRC has not undertaken a complete review of all historic reports of Swainson's Hawk, but there have been at least 95 reports in the state. There have been at least 88 reports from September through November, and at least 69 of the reports come from the Cape May area.

The first state record for Swainson's Hawk was at Oradell on 22 October 1947 (Bull 1964). There were no further reports until 1971, and they were irregularly reported throughout the 1970s. Since 1980 the species has been reported annually. There is one winter report from the Tuckerton CBC, 23 December 1971, and there are a few spring reports. From 1996 through 1997, there have been four reports of Swainson's Hawk, and two have been accepted by the NJBRC. They are:

Cape May Point	*12 November 1997*
Cape May Point	*24 November 1997*

Maximum: 3, Cape May Hawk Watch, 25 September 1981. **CMHW**
Seasonal Stats: Average: 3; Maximum: 10 in 1998. ■

Red-tailed Hawk

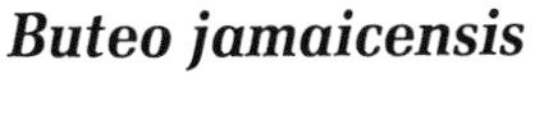

Buteo jamaicensis

Range: Widespread throughout much of Canada and all of the United States. Winters throughout most of the United States.

NJ Status: Fairly common and very widespread summer resident, fairly common spring and common fall migrant, common winter resident.

Breeding

Habitat: Nests in almost any wooded area near open country.

Land-use changes, and declines in persecution by humans, have encouraged a range expansion of Red-tailed Hawks. Historic accounts of the range and abundance of Red-tailed Hawks in New Jersey detail a population that was a shadow of their present day abundance. Stone (1937) knew of only one nest in southern New Jersey, in Salem County. Fables (1955) described the population

continued on page 188

continued from page 187

Red-tailed Hawk

Statewide Summary	
Status	# of Blocks
Possible	179
Probable	212
Confirmed	284
Total	675

as declining from 1925 to 1950. Even as recently as 1984, Leck described Red-tailed Hawks as scarce breeding birds. Red-tailed Hawks have expanded their range and abundance in the eastern United States during the late 1900s, and New Jersey is no exception. This range expansion is considered to be a result of an increase in breeding and foraging habitats created by forest fragmentation. The increase in Red-tailed Hawks has been suspected to have resulted in a decrease of Red-shouldered Hawks in eastern North America (Preston and Beane 1993).

Atlas data indicated the astounding recovery of this species in New Jersey. Red-tailed Hawks were found to be New Jersey's most widely distributed diurnal raptor, and occupied more than 67% of each physiographic province. Their

Physiographic Distribution Red-tailed Hawk	Number of blocks in province	Number of blocks species found breeding in province	Number of blocks species found in state	Percent of province species occupies	Percent of all records for this species found in province	Percent of state area in province
Kittatinny Mountains	19	18	675	94.7	2.7	2.2
Kittatinny Valley	45	45	675	100.0	6.7	5.3
Highlands	109	107	675	98.2	15.9	12.8
Piedmont	167	126	675	75.4	18.7	19.6
Inner Coastal Plain	128	106	675	82.8	15.7	15.0
Outer Coastal Plain	204	137	675	67.2	20.3	23.9
Pine Barrens	180	136	675	75.6	20.1	21.1

distribution is most notable for the areas from which they were absent: the highly urbanized northeastern corridor, the barrier islands, and some isolated patches in the Pine Barrens.

Fall: The bulk of the Red-tailed Hawk migration occurs between late September and early December, and numbers peak from early to mid-November. They can be equally common along inland ridges and at Cape May. **Maxima:** 1,022, Cape May Hawk Watch, 11 November 1994; 720, Cape May Hawk Watch, 3 November 1996. **CMHW Seasonal Stats:** Average: 2,000; Maximum: 5,135 in 1996.

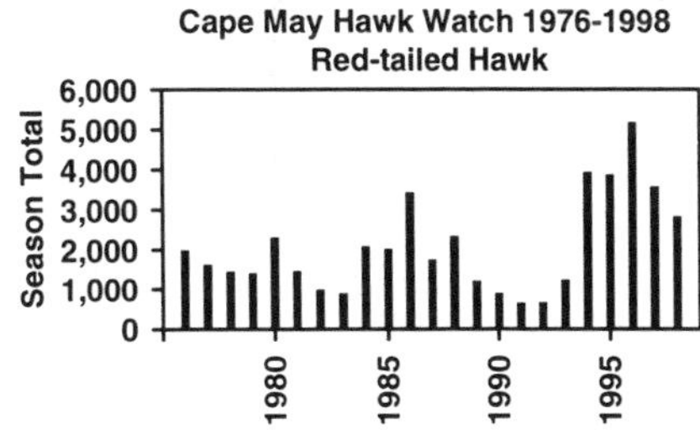

Winter: Statewide CBC totals of Red-tailed Hawks have increased since 1976. In the late 1970s, statewide CBC totals averaged just under 600 birds. That total rose to just over 1,000 during the 1980s and to nearly 1,300 in the early 1990s. Apparently, New Jersey's breeding population is resident and is augmented by migrant red-taileds from the north. It is unknown if the increase on CBCs is due to a more numerous breeding population, a larger wintering population, or a combination of the two. **CBC Statewide Stats:** Average: 1,014; Maximum: 2,036 in 1996; Minimum: 476 in 1976. **CBC Maximum:** 182, Salem, 1996.

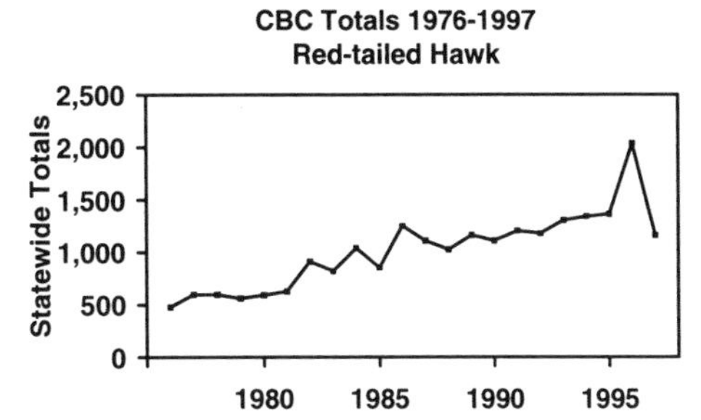

Spring: Red-tailed Hawks are early spring migrants, moving north from early March through early May. Spring numbers are relatively low compared to fall, and the peak of migration is evenly spread from mid-March to mid-April. **Maxima:** 225, Montclair, 20 April 1986; 92, Phillipsburg, 18 March 1984.

Subspecies: Two subspecies of Red-tailed Hawks occur regularly in New Jersey. *B. j. jamaicensis*, which breeds in the eastern United States including New Jersey, and *B. j. abeiticola*, which breeds in eastern Canada (Sibley 1997). The pale western subspecies, *B. j. krideri*, has been reported on four occasions at Cape May Point (Sibley 1997). A few dark-morph Red-tailed Hawks have also been reported at Cape May. Sibley (1997) attributed two records to the western subspecies *B. j. calurus*. A handful of other dark-morph reports may refer to *B. j. calurus*, *B. j. harlani*, intergrades between subspecies, or melanism. ■

Rough-legged Hawk

Buteo lagopus

Range: Breeds throughout much of the Arctic of Alaska and Canada. In the eastern United States winters from southern Minnesota east to Nova Scotia, south to northern Texas and Virginia.

NJ Status: Scarce fall migrant, uncommon winter resident, rare spring migrant.

Fall: Migrant Rough-legged Hawks are seen late in the fall, usually in late October and November. They are relatively more common along inland ridges than along the coast, but only small numbers are seen in either region. At Cape May, seasonal totals usually number from one to four birds. Their southward movements can be protracted and may occur into January (Sibley 1997), after hawk watch locations have closed down. **CMHW Daily Maximum:** 4 on 13 November 1983. **CMHW Seasonal Stats:** Avg. 4; Maximum: 10 in 1980.

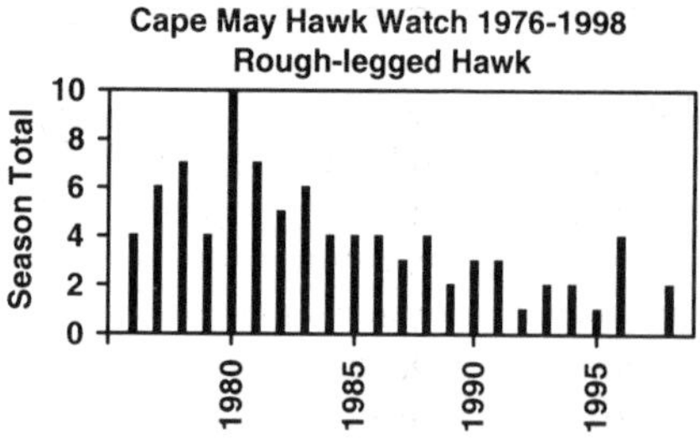

Winter: Rough-legged Hawks are more frequently encountered in winter than in other seasons, and they are primarily seen in coastal marshes. There is a considerable amount of annual variation in wintering numbers throughout their range, possibly the result of varying prey availability to the north. In some years very few are seen in the state. CBC numbers were consistently lower during the 1990s than in previous decades. **Maxima:** 30, Manahawkin, 12 December 1980; 16, Lyndhurst, 30 January 1982. **CBC Statewide Stats:** Average: 70; Maximum: 137 in 1982; Minimum: 11 in 1997. **CBC Maximum:** 24; Barnegat, 1995.

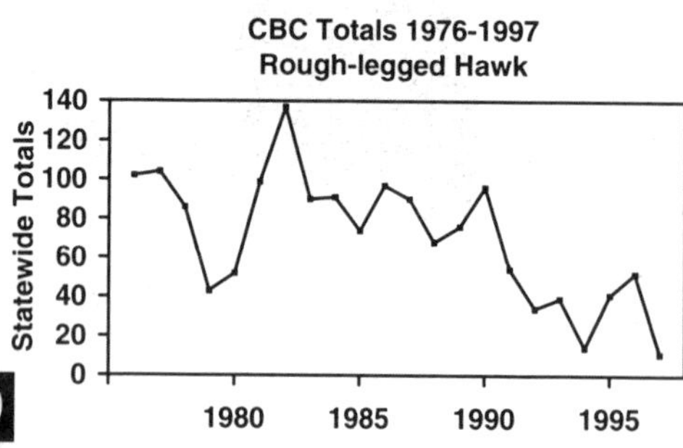

Spring: There is little noticeable spring migration, with a few northbound birds seen mainly in March and April. Only 11 Rough-legged Hawks were counted during the 16 years of the Sandy Hook Hawk Watch. ■

Golden Eagle

Aquila chrysaetos

Range: Widespread west of the Rocky Mountains, but in the East breeds mainly in Canada. In the East, winters locally from Massachusetts south.

NJ Status: Very rare spring and scarce fall migrant, scarce winter resident.

Fall: Golden Eagles are late fall migrants, generally seen beginning in mid-October. The peak of the flight occurs from early to mid-November, and movements continue into December. Golden Eagles are generally more common along inland ridges than along the coast. In Cape May they are usually seen only on days of strong northwest winds. **Maxima:** 17, Raccoon Ridge, 12 November 1987; 12, Raccoon Ridge, 10 November 1994. **CMHW Daily Maximum:** 8 on 3 November 1996. **CMHW Seasonal Stats:** Average: 12; Maximum: 38 in 1996.

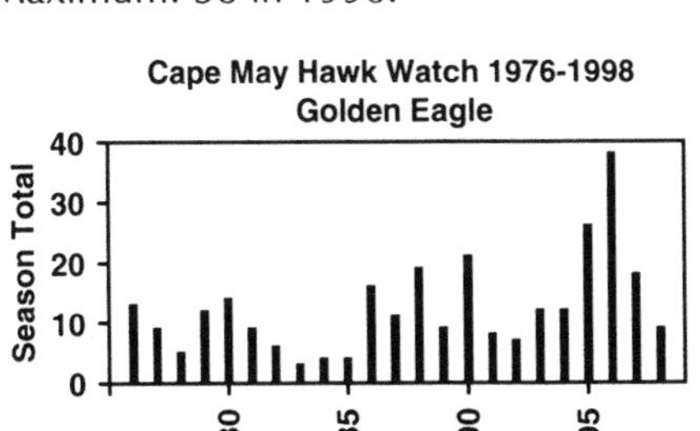

Winter: The few Golden Eagles that winter in New Jersey are typically found on large undisturbed salt marshes (e.g., the Mullica River and estuary), or along the Delaware River where they are often seen with Bald Eagles. CBC totals are low and variable. **Maximum:** 4, Brigantine NWR, 12 January 1997. **CBC Statewide Stats:** Average: 2; Maximum: 4 in 1980 and 1981; Minimum: 0 in four years. **CBC Maximum:** 3, Walnut Valley, 1979.

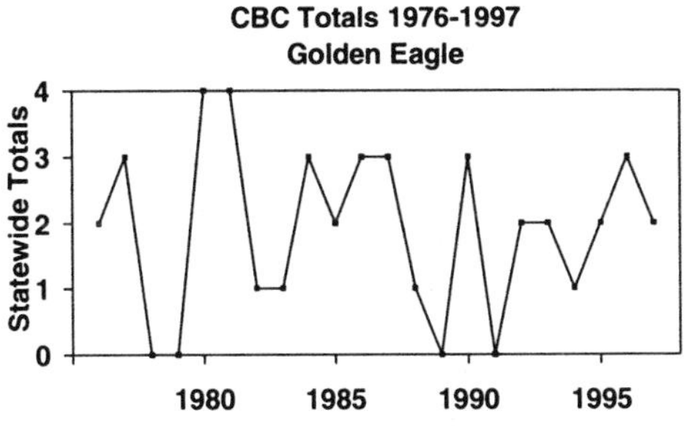

Spring: Golden Eagles are rarely encountered in spring, with only one recorded in 16 years at the Sandy Hook Hawk Watch. ■

Golden Eagle

Eurasian Kestrel

Falco tinnunculus

Occurrence: There have been six state reports of Eurasian Kestrels, and one has been accepted by the NJBRC: Cape May Point, 23 September 1972 (ph-RBPF), banded. ■

Range: Breeds throughout Europe and Asia. Winters south to Africa and Southeast Asia.

NJ Status: Accidental. NJBRC Review List.

American Kestrel

Falco sparverius

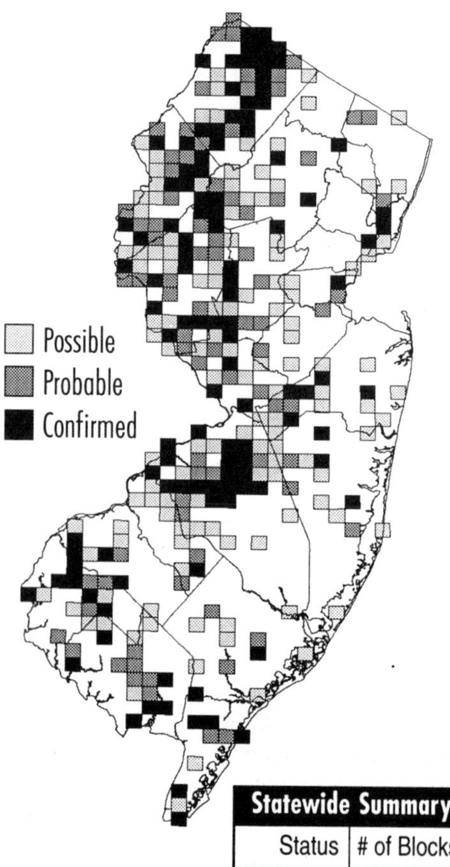

Statewide Summary	
Status	# of Blocks
Possible	126
Probable	81
Confirmed	113
Total	320

Range: Breeds throughout most of temperate North America. Winters throughout most of the United States.

NJ Status: Uncommon but fairly widespread summer resident, fairly common spring and common fall migrant, fairly common winter resident.

Breeding

Habitat: Nests in cavities near open country, frequently in old buildings and barns.

American Kestrels have been reduced over the eastern portion of their breeding range in New Jersey. Because of their widespread abundance,

American Kestrel

continued

Griscom (1923) noted that it was "useless to cite its status in greater detail" and "in all sections it cannot be overlooked throughout most of the year." Stone (1908) listed American Kestrels as common residents and enumerated several nests in the Cape May area in the 1930s (Stone 1937). Leck (1984) considered American Kestrels to be present throughout the state. Beginning in 1990, RNJB Regional Editors in northern and central New Jersey began to express concern regarding the status of American Kestrels as breeding birds (Hanisek 1990, Larson 1990). Concern for this species continues to grow.

American Kestrels are found in several different habitats, from agricultural areas to urban settings, and nest in holes in trees or cavities in buildings. Atlas data indicated 51% of their occupied blocks were from the Piedmont northward, an area representing only 40% of the state. They were most thinly distributed in the Pine Barrens and Outer Coastal Plain, where they occupied less than 27% of each province.

Conservation Note: American Kestrels are still fairly widespread breeding birds in New Jersey, but they have certainly declined in the state during the 20th Century. There is evidence that breeding birds, migrants, and wintering bird numbers have all declined. Research should be done to evaluate aspects of their breeding biology (i.e., reproductive rates, nest-site availability, contaminant loads, prey availability, etc.), and applied conservation projects undertaken to restore the population.

Fall: Hawk watch data indicates American Kestrels have declined as migrants in New Jersey since the late 1980s. They are one of the earliest migrant raptors, found as early as late July and seen in good numbers by mid-August. The flight peaks from late September through early October and diminishes by early November. Although American Kestrels occur inland in good numbers, the bulk of the fall flight takes place along the coast. They are considerably more abundant at Cape May than along the ridges, although their numbers are also declining

continued on page 194

Physiographic Distribution

American Kestrel	Number of blocks in province	Number of blocks species found breeding in province	Number of blocks species found in state	Percent of province species occupies	Percent of all records for this species found in province	Percent of state area in province
Kittatinny Mountains	19	10	320	52.6	3.1	2.2
Kittatinny Valley	45	34	320	75.6	10.6	5.3
Highlands	109	54	320	49.5	16.9	12.8
Piedmont	167	65	320	38.9	20.3	19.6
Inner Coastal Plain	128	62	320	48.4	19.4	15.0
Outer Coastal Plain	204	53	320	26.0	16.6	23.9
Pine Barrens	180	42	320	23.3	13.1	21.1

continued from page 193

American Kestrel

along the ridges (E. Greenstone, pers. com.). An estimate of 24,875 kestrels on 15 October 1970 at Cape May (Leck 1984) is more than six times higher than any recent daily count. **Other maxima:** 3,694, Cape May Hawk Watch, 1 October 1987; 3,538, Cape May Hawk Watch, 24September 81. **CMHW Seasonal Stats:** Average: 10,683; Maximum: 21,821 in 1981.

Cape May Hawk Watch 1976-1998
American Kestrel

Season Total: 0; 5,000; 10,000; 15,000; 20,000; 25,000
1980; 1985; 1990; 1995

Winter: In addition to a decrease in the numbers of migrants in New Jersey, the winter population of American Kestrels also appears to be declining. Statewide CBC totals have dropped steadily from the mid-1980s to the mid-1990s. Given their reliance on open areas for hunting, it may be that the disappearance of this habitat, through succession or loss of

farmland to development, is at least partly responsible. **CBC Statewide Stats:** Average: 556; Maximum: 812 in 1983; Minimum: 164 in 1997. **CBC maximum:** 124, Long Branch, 1979.

Spring: Most of the northward movement of American Kestrels occurs between late March and early May, with a peak in early April. Although the return flight is smaller than that of fall, and somewhat more dispersed, they still show a preference for the coast. **Maxima:** 851, Sandy Hook Hawk Watch, 8 April 1986; 783, Sandy Hook Hawk Watch, 4 April 1983. ■

American Kestrel

Merlin

Falco columbarius

Range: Breeds from Alaska east to Newfoundland and south to Minnesota and Maine. In the East winters mainly south of New Jersey to the West Indies and South America.

NJ Status: Uncommon spring and common fall migrant, scarce winter resident.

Fall: The first Merlins generally arrive from early to mid-September, peaking from late September through early October. Numbers of migrants diminish by early November. They are mainly coastal migrants, and are less commonly encountered along inland ridges. Although most raptor flights usually peak by early afternoon, Merlin flights often continue into the late afternoon or early evening hours. **Maxima:** 558, Cape May Hawk Watch, 29 September 1994; 309, Cape May Hawk Watch, 18 September 1994. **CMHW Seasonal Stats:** Average: 1,617; Maximum: 2,875 in 1985.

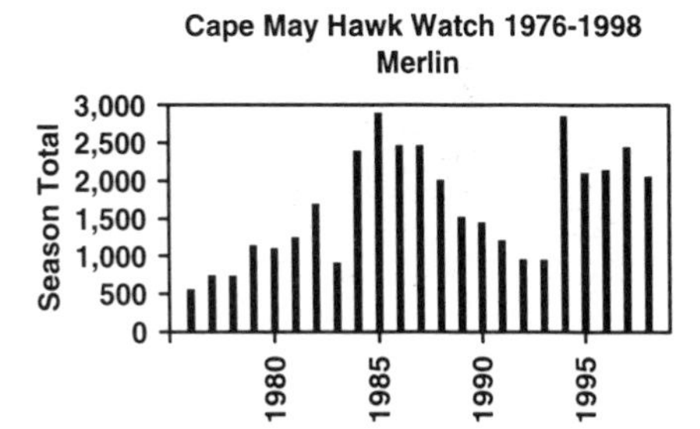

Winter: In New Jersey, winter sightings of Merlins have increased in the last 15 years, but statewide CBC totals are usually fewer than 25 birds. **CBC Statewide Stats:** Average: 16; Maximum: 27 in 1994; Minimum: 3 in 1976. **CBC Maximum:** 7, Barnegat, 1985.

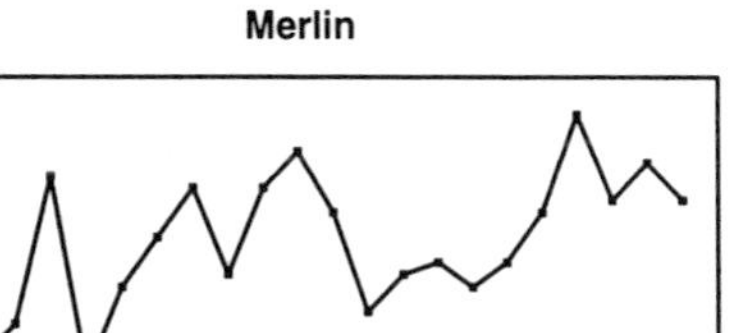

Spring: Most Merlins move north in April and early May, peaking from mid- to late April. As in the fall, they show a strong preference for the coast. **Maxima:** 101, Sandy Hook Hawk Watch, 26 April 1985; 60, Sandy Hook Hawk Watch, 15 April 1993.■

Gyrfalcon
Falco rusticolus

Range: In North America breeds from Alaska to northern Labrador. Winters south to the northern United States, occasionally farther south.

NJ Status: Very rare. NJBRC Review List.

Occurrence: There have been 44 state reports of Gyrfalcons, and 14 have been accepted by the NJBRC. About half of the sightings have occurred from December through February. A number of reports of Gyrfalcon are from hawk lookouts, mostly from October through November. The 14 accepted records are:

*New Jersey**	*before 1869*	*spec. ANSP #1209*
Brigantine NWR#	*9 February 1941*	
Raccoon Ridge#	*21 October 1945*	
Raccoon Ridge#	*19 November 1946*	
Branchville#	*12 March 1950*	
East Rutherford#	*4 January 1953*	
Brigantine NWR	*18 December 1971-18 April 1972*	*ph-AB 26:553*
*Brigantine NWR**	*February-April 1972*	
Brigantine NWR	*15 March-late March 1975*	
Stokes State Forest	*8 November 1982*	*ph-RNJB 9:3*
Linwood	*November 1982-April 1983*	*ph-RNJB 9:21*
Cape May	*28 February 1987*	
Raccoon Ridge	*19 November 1988*	
Sandy Hook	*November 1989-January 1990*	*ph-RNJB 16:31*

Peregrine Falcon
Falco peregrinus

Range: Breeds mainly in the Canadian Arctic and Greenland, although released birds breed at scattered locations. Winters mainly from the southern United States south to South America, in smaller numbers north to New England.

NJ Status: Scarce and local summer resident, scarce spring and common fall migrant, scarce winter resident. Endangered Species in New Jersey.

Breeding

Habitat: In the Arctic, nests on cliffs. In New Jersey typically nests on bridges, towers, and other man-made structures.

Historically Peregrine Falcons bred in New Jersey, but they were extirpated in the late 1950s or early 1960s. The story of their

Peregrine Falcon

continued

Possible
Probable
Confirmed

recovery has become one of the great success stories for the Endangered Species Act, but also shows the importance of understanding natural history when reintroducing extirpated species. Peregrine Falcons typically breed on cliffs or, more recently, on tall structures in urban environments. Stone (1908) listed nest sites on the Palisades of the Hudson River, and elsewhere in northern New Jersey. Griscom (1923) indicated the nests on the Palisades were still active. Fables (1955) wrote that Peregrine Falcons were still seen in urbanized northern New Jersey and had attempted to nest on ledges of tall buildings. At some point in the late 1950s Peregrine Falcons were probably extirpated from the state, although Bull (1964) suggested a remnant population remained in northern New Jersey. Leck (1984) chronicled the pace and location of the New Jersey reintroductions and lists the first modern breeding record as 1980.

continued on page 198

Map Interpretation: True to their name, Peregrine Falcons wander widely during the breeding season. This probably resulted in the species being over-reported. Only Confirmed locations should be considered part of their active breeding range.

Statewide Summary	
Status	# of Blocks
Possible	7
Probable	5
Confirmed	8
Total	20

Physiographic Distribution Peregrine Falcon	Number of blocks in province	Number of blocks species found breeding in province	Number of blocks species found in state	Percent of province species occupies	Percent of all records for this species found in province	Percent of state area in province
Highlands	109	2	20	1.8	10.0	12.8
Piedmont	167	4	20	2.4	20.0	19.6
Inner Coastal Plain	128	4	20	3.1	20.0	15.0
Outer Coastal Plain	204	9	20	4.4	45.0	23.9
Pine Barrens	180	1	20	0.6	5.0	21.1

continued from page 197

The reintroduction programs introduced breeding peregrines into the salt marshes, a habitat they often used during migration, but did not use for breeding. These programs were successful, and have helped establish eight Peregrine Falcon nests in New Jersey. However, their current breeding range in New Jersey is unlike their pre-extirpation range. Ironically, the introduction of the species to the barrier islands has given rise to unanticipated problems such as Peregrine Falcon's predation on other Endangered Species, such as Least Terns.

Subspecies: The current breeding population of Peregrine Falcons is a different subspecies from the historic peregrines of the eastern United States. The subspecies *F. p. anatum* was the historic breeder in New Jersey. Hacking programs to reintroduce the species used a hybrid subspecies.

Fall: Migrant Peregrine Falcons can be seen as early as late August, but peak numbers occur from late September through early October. Movements diminish by late October. Their breeding population recovery is reflected in Cape May's fall hawk watch totals. Numbers have risen dramatically from a low count of 60 in 1977 to a high of 1,791 in 1997. Most peregrines migrate along the coast with few seen along inland ridges, although many birds migrate well offshore. The Avalon Sea Watch averaged 85 peregrines per year from 1994 through 1997. **Maxima:** 291, Cape May Hawk Watch, 7 October 1997; 206, Cape May Hawk Watch, 1 October 1996 (with 176 the following day). **CMHW Seasonal Stats:** Average: 561; Maximum: 1,791 in 1997.

Cape May Hawk Watch 1976-1998
Peregrine Falcon

Winter: Statewide CBC totals for Peregrine Falcons have steadily increased since the late 1970s. This increase is probably related to the increase in New Jersey's breeding population, which is probably nonmigratory, and to the general recovery of the population in the eastern United States. **CBC Statewide Stats:** Average: 14; Maximum: 33 in 1995; Minimum: 0 in 1977. **CBC maximum:** 12, Oceanville, 1995.

CBC Totals 1976-1997
Peregrine Falcon

Spring: Few Peregrine Falcons are noted in spring migration, which suggests that they return to the breeding grounds over a broad front. Most migrants are seen in April and early May. The seasonal high at the Sandy Hook Hawk Watch was five in 1992. ■

Ring-necked Pheasant

Phasianus colchicus

Range: Introduced. Resident in eastern North America from Minnesota east to Nova Scotia and south.

NJ Status: Uncommon and somewhat local resident, augmented by population restocking.

Possible
Probable
Confirmed

Breeding

Habitat: Nests on the ground in open country such as farms, fields, and marsh edges.

Ring-necked Pheasants, native to Asia, were introduced to North America. The New Jersey population is sustained by releases for sport

continued on page 200

Statewide Summary	
Status	# of Blocks
Possible	95
Probable	83
Confirmed	29
Total	207

Map Interpretation: The distribution of this species among provinces may reflect release sites locations rather than a natural, preferred distribution for Ring-necked Pheasants.

Physiographic Distribution

Ring-necked Pheasant	Number of blocks in province	Number of blocks species found breeding in province	Number of blocks species found in state	Percent of province species occupies	Percent of all records for this species found in province	Percent of state area in province
Kittatinny Mountains	19	5	207	26.3	2.4	2.2
Kittatinny Valley	45	26	207	57.8	12.6	5.3
Highlands	109	41	207	37.6	19.8	12.8
Piedmont	167	70	207	41.9	33.8	19.6
Inner Coastal Plain	128	28	207	21.9	13.5	15.0
Outer Coastal Plain	204	28	207	13.7	13.5	23.9
Pine Barrens	180	9	207	5.0	4.3	21.1

continued from page 199

Ring-necked Pheasant

hunting. The first large-scale introductions in New Jersey were in 1897 (Stone 1908), and they were present as uncommon breeding birds in Cumberland and Salem counties in the 1920s and 1930s (Stone 1937). Hunting pressure, land-use changes, and a low rate of reproduction keeps the population in check.

Atlas data showed that Ring-necked Pheasants were found in all provinces in the state, but were most thinly distributed in the Pine Barrens and the Outer Coastal Plain. Brauning (1992a) suggested the Pennsylvania population was declining, but that their fairly high Confirmation rate (32%) was evidence they were successfully reproducing. The Confirmation rate in New Jersey was only 14%, and many of the Possible or Probable observations may have been nonbreeding birds from recent release programs. The cluster of Confirmed reports from Bergen and Hudson counties represents an actively reproducing population that inhabits the Hackensack Meadowlands and adjacent landfills.

Fall: There is no published information on the occurrence of fall migration of Ring-necked Pheasants in New Jersey.

Winter: The number of Ring-necked Pheasants on CBCs varies from year to year as the population is unstable. Totals were consistently higher in the late 1970s and early 1980s than at present. **CBC Statewide Stats:** Average: 137; Maximum: 239 in 1982; Minimum: 65 in 1990. **CBC Maximum:** 94, Northwest Hunterdon, 1977.

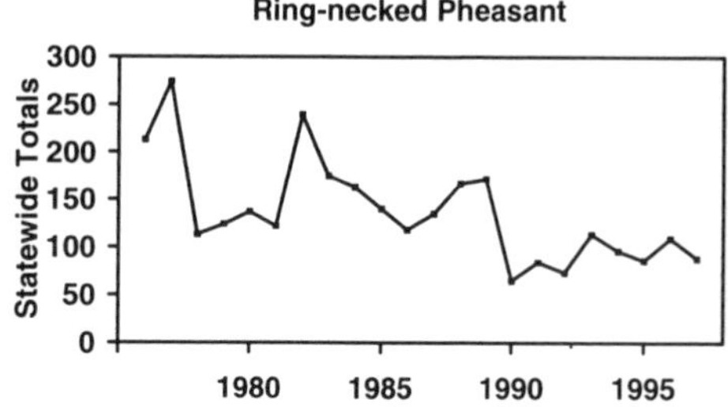

Spring: There is no published information of spring migration for Ring-necked Pheasants, although birds will occasionally show up in odd places, as was the case with one perched on the Concrete Ship at Cape May Point on 27 March 1992 (Sibley 1997). ■

Ruffed Grouse

Bonasa umbellus

Range: In eastern North America, resident from Manitoba east to Newfoundland, south to Iowa and New Jersey, and along the Appalachians to northern Georgia.

NJ Status: Uncommon and somewhat local resident.

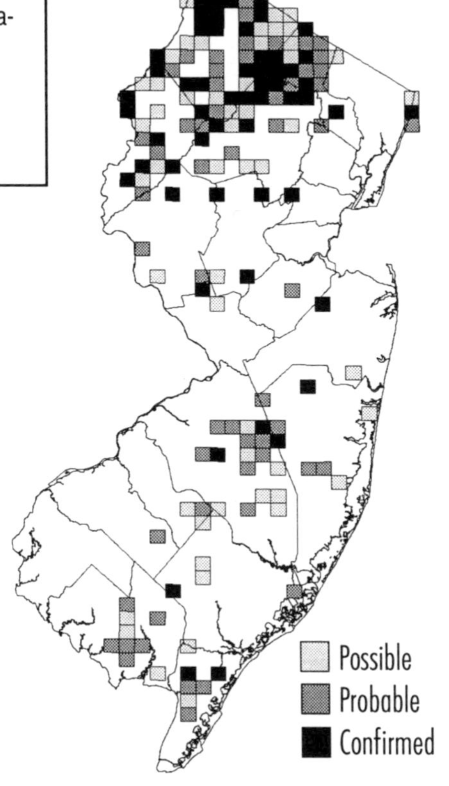

Breeding

Habitat: Nests on the ground in dense cover in the understory of wet deciduous or mixed woods, often in wet woods.

continued on page 202

Statewide Summary	
Status	# of Blocks
Possible	52
Probable	57
Confirmed	59
Total	168

Physiographic Distribution — Ruffed Grouse	Number of blocks in province	Number of blocks species found breeding in province	Number of blocks species found in state	Percent of province species occupies	Percent of all records for this species found in province	Percent of state area in province
Kittatinny Mountains	19	15	168	78.9	8.9	2.2
Kittatinny Valley	45	24	168	53.3	14.3	5.3
Highlands	109	62	168	56.9	36.9	12.8
Piedmont	167	15	168	9.0	8.9	19.6
Inner Coastal Plain	128	5	168	3.9	3.0	15.0
Outer Coastal Plain	204	16	168	7.8	9.5	23.9
Pine Barrens	180	31	168	17.2	18.5	21.1

continued from page 201

Ruffed Grouse are the rarest upland game bird in New Jersey, and the only upland game bird that is not stocked for sport hunting. As early as 1908, Stone wrote that the population of Ruffed Grouse in New Jersey was declining. Griscom (1923), however, enumerated several breeding sites in northern New Jersey, and declared Ruffed Grouse to be "positively abundant" in the Kittatinny Mountains. Historic breeding records in southern New Jersey are few, with Stone (1937) reporting no Cape May County breeding birds, and listing two records in Cumberland County. Fables (1955) and Leck (1984) described a distribution similar to that found by Atlas volunteers: heaviest in the mountains and ridges, scarce in the Coastal Plain, and a few in the Pine Barrens. Recent reports to RNJB indicated periods of recovery (Wolfarth 1975a), and periods of good numbers (Hanisek 1980). Unfortunately, the 1990s have produced a period of sustained low numbers (W. Dasey, D. Harrison, pers. com.).

Atlas data indicated the stronghold for this species is north of the Piedmont. Ruffed Grouse are widely distributed within each northern province, occurring in 53-79% of the blocks in the Kittatinny Mountains, Kittatinny Valley, and Highlands. The current range of Ruffed Grouse in New Jersey is heavily skewed to the area that provides the best deciduous forest cover in the state. There are, however, many areas in the state where Ruffed Grouse are reduced to remnant populations. Ruffed Grouse numbers are known to be cyclic, and it is possible that the Atlas surveys were conducted at a low point in their cycle.

Fall: Ruffed Grouse are nonmigratory, permanent residents. There is no published information on the occurrence of fall migration of Ruffed Grouse in New Jersey.

Winter: Populations of Ruffed Grouse are known to be cyclical and apparently a downward cycle that began in the mid-1980s has continued through the 1990s. CBC totals for the state reached lows in the mid-1990s. **CBC Statewide Stats:** Average: 35; Maximum: 72 in 1983; Minimum: 10 in 1994. **CBC Maximum:** 19, Boonton, 1981.

CBC Totals 1976-1997
Ruffed Grouse

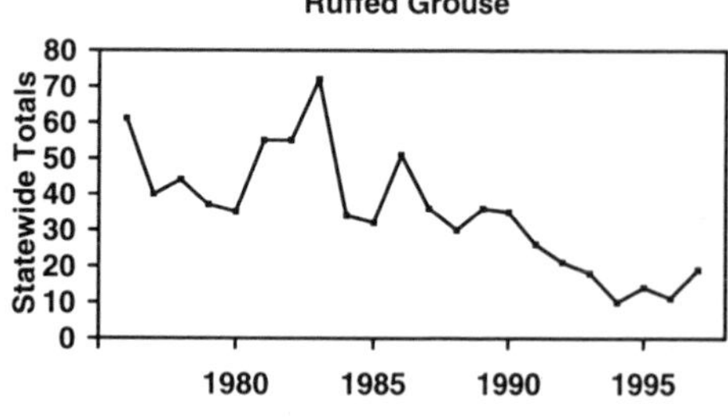

Spring: Ruffed Grouse are nonmigratory, permanent residents. There is no published information on the occurrence of spring migration of Ruffed Grouse in New Jersey. ■

Greater Prairie-Chicken

Tympanuchus cupido

Range: Formerly resident in the East from Massachusetts south to Maryland.

NJ Status: Extinct former resident.

Occurrence: In New Jersey, Greater Prairie-Chicken (then known as Heath Hen) was reportedly common in the Pine Barrens in Ocean and Burlington counties (Fables 1955, Leck 1984). They were also reported as far north as Schooley's Mountain, Morris County, but were extirpated from New Jersey by 1870 by excessive shooting (Bull 1964). Two specimens are extant from the original population, both from Burlington County: Ong's Hat, 1850, and New Hanover, "prior to 1892" (both at ANSP, L. Bevier, pers. com.). The last Greater Prairie-Chicken in the East was recorded on Martha's Vineyard in 1932. ■

Wild Turkey

Meleagris gallopavo

Range: In eastern North America, resident from central New England and northern New York south to the Gulf Coast states.

NJ Status: Fairly common and fairly widespread resident.

Breeding

Habitat: Typically nests in oak-dominated woods with nearby clearings.

The history of Wild Turkey in New Jersey is a study of highs and lows. Stone (1937) reviewed accounts from the 1700s and 1800s, and suggested Wild Turkeys were abundant throughout New Jersey. Despite their former abundance, they were extirpated from New Jersey (and many other states) at some point in the 1800s. Fables (1955) reported they disappeared by 1840, but the exact timing of their extirpation is unknown. Pennsylvania was the only state in the northeastern United States to maintain a native population of Wild Turkeys, a population that was augmented by releases in the early 1900s (Wunz and Brauning 1992).

Bull (1964) stated that Wild Turkeys repopulated New Jersey from semi-wild Pennsylvania stock beginning in 1954, but it is unlikely the birds used in the

continued on page 204

continued from page 203

Wild Turkey

Pennsylvania stocking program (naïve, farm-raised birds) were able to establish a population in New Jersey. In 1977 NJDFGW began a transplanting program designed to re-establish this species with wild stock of the subspecies native to New Jersey (*M. g. sylvestris*). Beginning in 1977, there was a steady increase in the number of reports of breeding turkeys to RNJB, creating a fairly complete picture of the pace and scope of this species' recolonization of New Jersey. The New Jersey population was further enhanced by transplanting wild birds to areas around the state during the 1980s and 1990s.

Regionally, Atlas data showed Wild Turkeys were best established in the Kittatinny Mountains, Kittatinny Valley, and Highlands where they occurred in over 90% of the blocks. They are also well established in the western Piedmont, and they are becoming established in the Pine Barrens, and in Salem and Cumberland counties. They are

Possible
Probable
Confirmed

Statewide Summary	
Status	# of Blocks
Possible	66
Probable	65
Confirmed	199
Total	330

Physiographic Distribution Wild Turkey	Number of blocks in province	Number of blocks species found breeding in province	Number of blocks species found in state	Percent of province species occupies	Percent of all records for this species found in province	Percent of state area in province
Kittatinny Mountains	19	18	330	94.7	5.5	2.2
Kittatinny Valley	45	44	330	97.8	13.3	5.3
Highlands	109	104	330	95.4	31.5	12.8
Piedmont	167	77	330	46.1	23.3	19.6
Inner Coastal Plain	128	11	330	8.6	3.3	15.0
Outer Coastal Plain	204	48	330	23.5	14.5	23.9
Pine Barrens	180	28	330	15.6	8.5	21.1

Wild Turkey

continued

only weakly colonizing the Inner Coastal Plain and Cape May, Atlantic and Ocean counties. Over 60% of the Atlas records are Confirmations, suggesting many of the birds found in New Jersey during the summer are successfully breeding.

Fall: Wild Turkeys are nonmigratory, permanent residents. There is no published information on the occurrence of fall migration of Wild Turkeys in New Jersey.

Winter: Statewide CBC totals of Wild Turkeys from the late 1970s and early 1980s were fewer than 50 birds. As recently as 1990 the statewide count broke 100 for the first time, and have skyrocketed through the 1990s. **CBC Statewide Stats:** Average: 160; Maximum: 902 in 1997; Minimum: 1 in 1979. **CBC Maximum:** 252, Sussex County, 1996.

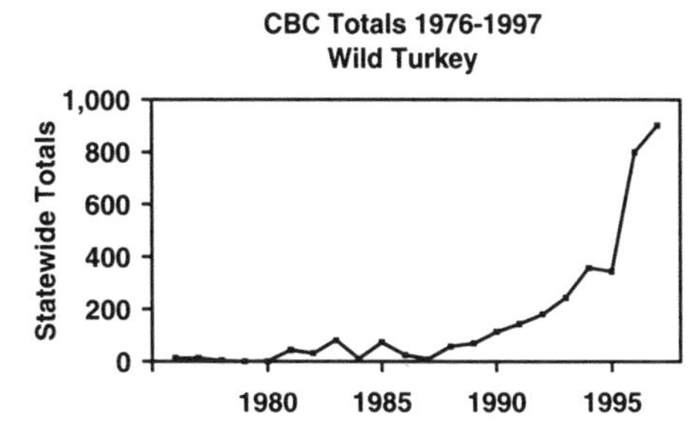

Spring: Wild Turkeys are nonmigratory, permanent residents. There is no published information on the occurrence of spring migration of Wild Turkeys in New Jersey. ■

Northern Bobwhite

Colinus virginianus

Range: Resident from southern South Dakota east to southern Massachusetts, south to Texas and Florida.

NJ Status: Uncommon but fairly widespread resident.

Breeding

Habitat: Nests on the ground in semi-open country such as farms, brushy fields, and marsh or woods edges.

The history of Northern Bobwhites in New Jersey is well recorded. Their populations fluctuate widely between years, probably because of hunting pressure, the number of releases, and the severity of winters. The population has probably declined due to changes in land-use practices and destruction of habitat. Stone (1937) lamented the introduction of non-native bobwhite stock to the eastern United States (similar to other game introductions, i.e., Wild Turkey), and which may have compromised the subspecies resident in New Jersey. As Sibley (1997) related, the subspecific composition of the current New Jersey population is unknown.

continued on page 206

continued from page 205

Northern Bobwhite

Atlas data found Northern Bobwhites in 41% of the blocks in the state, but over 90% of their range was south of the Piedmont. The birds were absent from the highest elevations, the barrier islands, and from the center of the Pine Barrens.

Conservation Note: BBS data indicated that the population of Northern Bobwhites has been declining over their range (Price et. al. 1995).

Fall: Northern Bobwhites are nonmigratory, permanent residents. Sibley (1997) referred to an account of migrating quail in the fall of 1902 at Cape May as "inexplicable, as this species is not known to be migratory." There is no other published information of migratory concentrations in fall.

Winter: Statewide CBC totals of Northern Bobwhites have declined dramatically since the mid-1970s, with a brief recovery in the early 1980s. Like most game species, restocking and hunting

Possible
Probable
Confirmed

Statewide Summary	
Status	# of Blocks
Possible	87
Probable	219
Confirmed	43
Total	349

Physiographic Distribution Northern Bobwhite	Number of blocks in province	Number of blocks species found breeding in province	Number of blocks species found in state	Percent of province species occupies	Percent of all records for this species found in province	Percent of state area in province
Kittatinny Valley	45	3	349	6.7	0.9	5.3
Highlands	109	10	349	9.2	2.9	12.8
Piedmont	167	20	349	12.0	5.7	19.6
Inner Coastal Plain	128	87	349	68.0	24.9	15.0
Outer Coastal Plain	204	137	349	67.2	39.3	23.9
Pine Barrens	180	92	349	51.1	26.4	21.1

Northern Bobwhite

continued

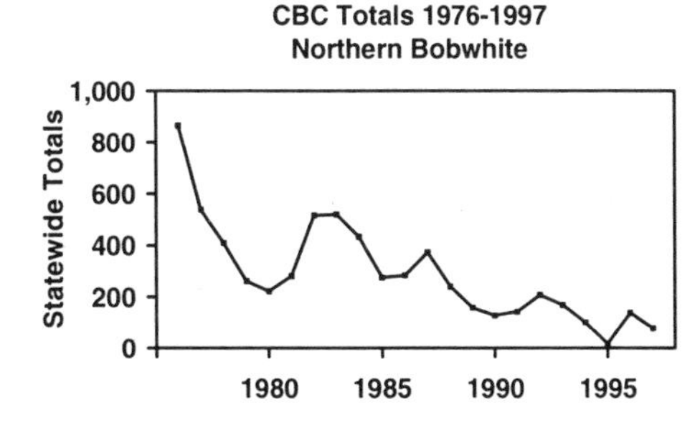

pressure play a major role in the fluctuations of population numbers. However, the steady decline in numbers, particularly since 1983, would indicate additional problems (i.e., the loss of breeding habitat). **CBC Statewide Stats:** Average: 289; Maximum: 866 in 1976; Minimum: 16 in 1995. **CBC Maximum:** 174, Northwest Gloucester, 1976.

Spring: Northern Bobwhites are nonmigratory, permanent residents. There is no published information on the occurrence of spring migration of Northern Bobwhites in New Jersey. ■

Yellow Rail

Coturnicops noveboracensis

Range: Breeds from Alberta to New Brunswick, south to Michigan and Maine. Winters along the coast from North Carolina to Texas.

NJ Status: Very rare. NJBRC Review List.

Occurrence: There have been about 50 state reports of Yellow Rails, and 30 have been accepted by the NJBRC. Yellow Rails are probably regular migrants through New Jersey, but they are extremely secretive. Many of the accepted records are documented with specimens; there are 14 extant specimens, and seven more that were lost. The majority of the records are from late September through October. There is only one winter record, and just three from spring. Some reports of heard-only birds from the 1930s and 1940s at Troy Meadows preceded the discovery of the Virginia Rail's "kicker" song, and may or may not have referred to Yellow Rail (for song identification problems, see Stone 1937). ■

Yellow Rail

Black Rail

Laterallus jamaicensis

Range: On the East Coast of the United States, breeds from Long Island to northern Florida. Winters from Florida to the Gulf Coast of Texas and Louisiana.

NJ Status: Rare and very local summer resident. Migrant and winter status poorly known. Threatened Species in New Jersey.

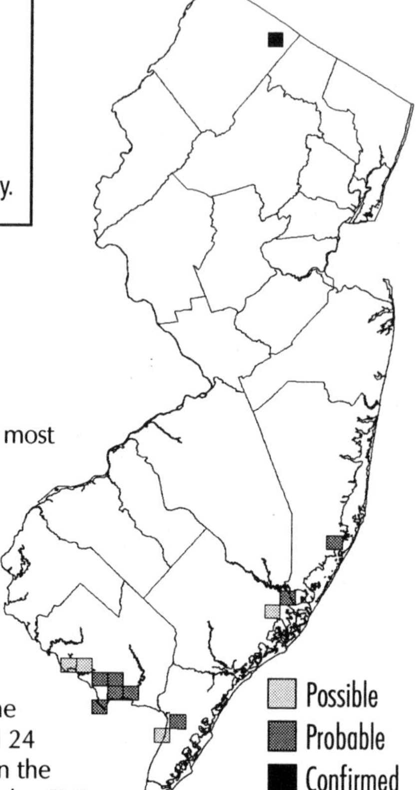

Breeding

Habitat: Nests mainly in brackish or saltwater marshes

Black Rails are one of the rarest and most enigmatic breeding birds in New Jersey. Their rarity, coupled with their secretive habits, makes them difficult to find even in areas where they are known to breed. Comparisons of the Atlas data with accounts of their historic distribution indicated that Black Rails have declined, especially in southern New Jersey. Stone (1937) related that one observer found 24 Black Rail nests in coastal New Jersey in the early 1900s, and Fables (1955) related that T. E. McMullen found 80 nests in New Jersey. Both of these reports are staggering numbers by today's standards. Five years of Atlas effort (including extra-effort censusing night birds in Cape May and Cumberland counties) found Black Rails in only 13 blocks statewide.

Atlas volunteers did discover New Jersey's first Confirmed inland breeding Black Rails, when chicks

Statewide Summary	
Status	# of Blocks
Possible	4
Probable	8
Confirmed	1
Total	13

Physiographic Distribution Black Rail	Number of blocks in province	Number of blocks species found breeding in province	Number of blocks species found in state	Percent of province species occupies	Percent of all records for this species found in province	Percent of state area in province
Highlands	109	1	13	0.9	7.7	12.8
Outer Coastal Plain	204	12	13	5.9	92.3	23.9

Black Rail

continued

were observed at Wallkill NWR in 1993. The Atlas map of Black Rails distribution in the state is similar to that reported by Kerlinger and Sutton (1989). There were some differences noted between the two studies, however. Unlike Kerlinger and Sutton, Atlas observers found birds present at the Mullica River basin, although the Atlas observers did not locate Black Rails in the Great Egg River basin. Importantly, both studies found that the stronghold for the population is along the Delaware Bay in Cumberland County

Conservation Note: This species presents significant conservation and research challenges. Given Black Rail's legendary shyness, small population size, nomadic behavior (Kerlinger and Wiedner 1991), and a drop in the population during this century, focused work should be done to map all breeding locations and to attempt to track the species statewide. Given the small number of blocks that Black Rails were found in, it is reasonable to question whether they are able to maintain their population by reproduction or whether their New Jersey population is maintained by nomadic, colonizing birds.

Fall: Very little is known about the migratory habits of Black Rails. Eddelman et al. (1994) suggested that most individuals of the East Coast population probably migrate, mainly from mid-September to mid-October.

Winter: There are only one or two reports of Black Rails in winter, and their status in New Jersey at this season is poorly known.

Spring: Although evidence on their movements is scant, it is suspected that Black Rails move north between mid-March and early May (Eddelman et al. 1994). ■

Corn Crake

Crex crex

Range: Breeds throughout much of Europe and into central Asia. Winters from the Mediterranean south through Africa.

NJ Status: Accidental NJBRC Review List.

Occurrence: There have been four state reports of Corn Crake, and three have been accepted by the NJBRC (two in fall, one in winter). The three accepted records are:

Salem	*fall 1854*	*spec. ANSP*
Bridgeton	*January 1856*	*spec. ANSP*
Dennisville	*11 November 1905*	*spec. ANSP*

Clapper Rail

Rallus longirostris

Range: Breeds along the Atlantic coast from Massachusetts to Florida, and along the Gulf coast to Texas. Winters in most of breeding range, withdraws from the north.

NJ Status: Common but local summer resident, scarce spring and fall migrant, uncommon winter resident.

Statewide Summary	
Status	# of Blocks
Possible	12
Probable	42
Confirmed	29
Total	83

Breeding

Habitat: Breeds in coastal salt and brackish marshes.

Clapper Rails are New Jersey's most numerous rail. Wilson (1812) described large "egging" parties collecting Clapper Rail eggs and recounted "100 dozen of eggs have been collected by one man in one day." Egg-collecting and large-scale shooting reduced the population during the 1800s, and the draining of wetlands further diminished the population in the 1900s (Stone 1908, Griscom 1923, Stone 1937). It is unknown if the population has fully recovered from these declines, but

Physiographic Distribution Clapper Rail	Number of blocks in province	Number of blocks species found breeding in province	Number of blocks species found in state	Percent of province species occupies	Percent of all records for this species found in province	Percent of state area in province
Piedmont	167	1	83	0.6	1.2	19.6
Inner Coastal Plain	128	7	83	5.5	8.4	15.0
Outer Coastal Plain	204	73	83	35.8	88.0	23.9
Pine Barrens	180	2	83	1.1	2.4	21.1

today they are generally regarded as locally common breeding birds (Sibley 1997). Even in areas with high human populations and fragmented marshes (i.e., Wildwood salt marshes), Clapper Rails can become quite numerous.

Clapper Rails are primarily salt marsh breeders, and their distribution is heavily skewed to the Outer Coastal Plain. Eighty-eight percent of the blocks occupied by Clapper Rail were in the Outer Coastal Plain, with only a few blocks in other provinces. They were conspicuously absent from the upland side of Barnegat Bay.

Fall: The status of Clapper Rails outside of the breeding season is poorly known. It is possible that some of the breeders are resident, although some may move farther south in severe winters. It is also likely that birds from the more northern parts of their range pass through or winter in New Jersey. As nocturnal migrants, they are rarely seen on migration, although Sibley (1997) cited a pattern of groundings in bad weather in late August and September. One exceptional grounding took place on 28 August 1998 at Cape May Point, when 24 were seen after the passage of Hurricane Bonnie.

Winter: CBC totals for Clapper Rails are variable, which lends support to the idea that their presence in the state in winter is tied to the severity of the weather. **CBC Statewide Stats:** Average: 51; Maximum: 234 in 1997; Minimum: 9 in 1986. **CBC Maximum:** 111, Belleplain, 1997.

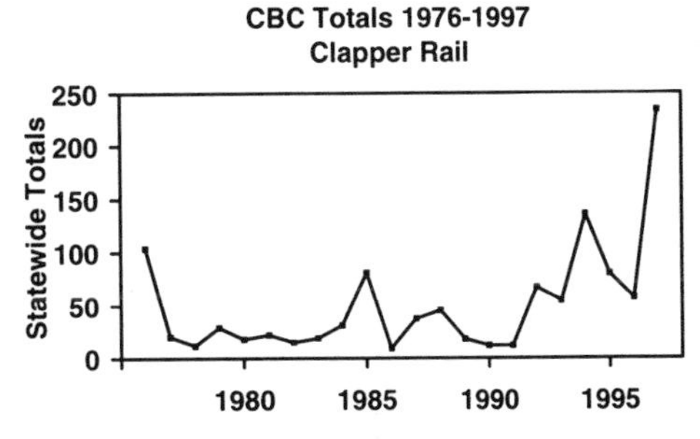

Spring: Spring: The return of Clapper Rails in spring is masked by the presence of the winter population. High numbers present at local breeding areas by mid-April suggests an early return. ■

Clapper Rail

King x Clapper Rail Hybrids

Breeding

King and Clapper Rails, although often separated into freshwater and saltwater marshes, can show complete overlap in nesting habitat use (Meanley 1957). When they occur in the same habitat, they can hybridize. In one brackish marsh on Delaware Bay, a male King and a female Clapper were found with five eggs (Meanley and Wetherbee 1962). Only one instance of King X Clapper Rail hybridization was reported during the Atlas surveys. In Cheesequake SP, Middlesex County, a male King Rail and a female Clapper Rail were seen with downy young (R. Kane, pers. obs.). ■

Physiographic Distribution: King x Clapper Rail Hybrids	Number of blocks in province	Number of blocks species found breeding in province	Number of blocks species found in state	Percent of province species occupies	Percent of all records for this species found in province	Percent of state area in province
Inner Coastal Plain	128	1	1	0.8	100.0	15.0

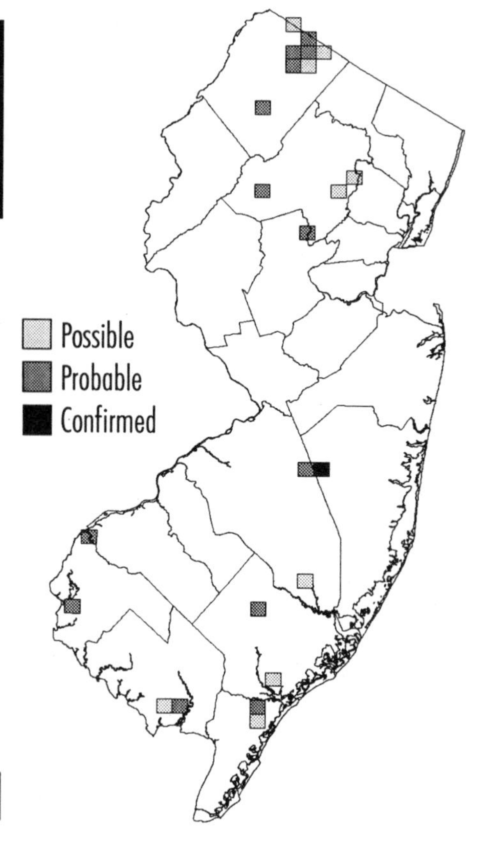

King Rail

Rallus elegans

Range: Breeds locally from North Dakota east to Massachusetts, south to Texas and Florida. Winter range poorly known, but probably south to Central America.

NJ Status: Scarce and local summer resident, rare at other seasons.

Statewide Summary	
Status	# of Blocks
Possible	9
Probable	13
Confirmed	1
Total	23

King Rail

continued

Breeding

Habitat: Nests in fresh and, occasionally, brackish marshes.

One of New Jersey's rarest breeding birds, King Rails were only Confirmed in one block during the Atlas period. The accuracy of some historic and current information on their range and abundance is confounded by the vocal similarity of King and Clapper Rails. Even today, most field ornithologists can be hard-pressed to identify a calling bird in marginal habitat. Griscom (1923) noted that the range of the species was poorly described, but still considered the species to be rare. Stone (1908, 1937) described the species as more abundant than current information indicates and enumerated several nests in Cape May County. Bull (1964) knew of only one northern New Jersey breeding record from 1942 through 1964 (Fair Haven in 1956) and suggested that the species was over-reported on the basis of "heard only" reports. Great Swamp Refuge staff estimated 40 there in June 1973 and found one nest the same year (Black 1973).

Atlas data indicated King Rails breed in isolated pockets in New Jersey. Some of these locations are historic and indicated the possibility that some areas may have self-sustaining populations (i.e., the Great Swamp mosaic). Their presence at other locations is ephemeral, and King Rails may be present in one year and absent the next (e.g., the mapped Cumberland County sites). As with many of the other freshwater marsh nesting birds, the Wallkill River basin stands out as an important area for this species.

Conservation Note: The loss of freshwater wetlands during this century is likely to have reduced King Rail's abundance and range statewide. There is little information on the factors that encourage colonization, or keep a site occupied for years. The rarity of this species begs the question, " How is this species able to persist in the state – by immigration or by reproduction?"

Fall: Encounters with King Rails are infrequent, making it difficult to draw conclusions about their patterns of

continued on page 214

Physiographic Distribution King Rail	Number of blocks in province	Number of blocks species found breeding in province	Number of blocks species found in state	Percent of province species occupies	Percent of all records for this species found in province	Percent of state area in province
Kittatinny Valley	45	6	23	13.3	26.1	5.3
Highlands	109	3	23	2.8	13.0	12.8
Piedmont	167	3	23	1.8	13.0	19.6
Inner Coastal Plain	128	1	23	0.8	4.3	15.0
Outer Coastal Plain	204	4	23	2.0	17.4	23.9
Pine Barrens	180	6	23	3.3	26.1	21.1

continued from page 213

King Rail

migration. Scattered records at sites without breeding populations indicate that fall movement peaks from mid-September through early October.

Winter: King Rail's abundance in winter is also difficult to ascertain. From 1976 to 1997 the statewide CBC average was less than one per year, and only a handful of other winter reports have occurred outside the counts. Stone (1937) referred to a few winter records, and Bull (1964) knew of 21 records outside the breeding season, including 15 records in winter.

Spring: The return of King Rails in spring is not well documented, but probably occurs in April and May. ■

Virginia Rail

Rallus limicola

Range: In eastern North America breeds from southern Manitoba east to Nova Scotia, south to Kansas and North Carolina. Winters along the East coast from Long Island south to Central America.

NJ Status: Fairly common but local summer resident, scarce spring and fall migrant, scarce to uncommon winter resident.

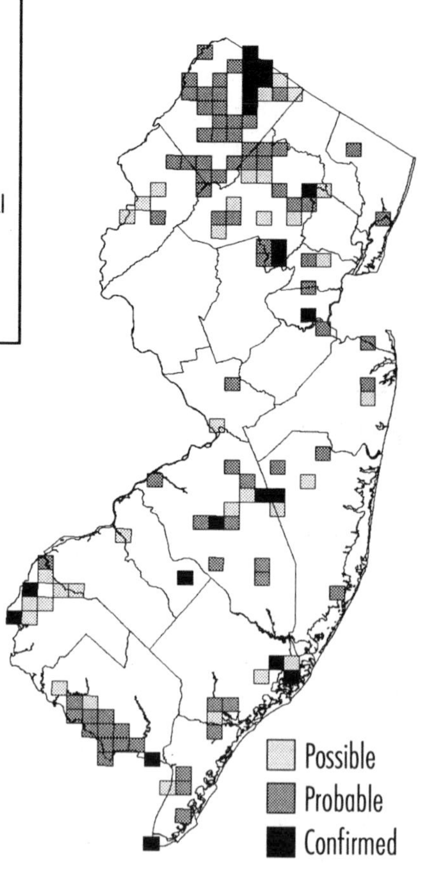

Breeding

Habitat: Nests in grassy or reedy fresh or brackish marshes.

There is evidence Virginia Rails have declined over their entire North American range (Conway 1995), and their history in New Jersey is similar. Stone (1908) reported they were very common along the Delaware River marshes from Cape May to Trenton, an assertion contrary to the Atlas data. His more focused account of

Virginia Rail

continued

their distribution and abundance near Cape May suggests the species was declining there due to destruction of habitat (Stone 1937), a sentiment echoed for northern New Jersey by Bull (1964).

The decline for this species is exemplified by several reports to NJNN and RNJB: one report indicated a decline at Troy Meadows from 25 pairs in 1947 to three pairs in 1984 (Kane 1985). Also, refuge staff reported 230 at Great Swamp, 30 June 1973 (Black 1973), but only nine were found there in June 1983 (Kane et al. 1985).

Statewide Summary	
Status	# of Blocks
Possible	33
Probable	73
Confirmed	21
Total	127

Almost simultaneously, Hanisek (1987) reported Virginia Rails occurred in "virtually every suitable piece of habitat in Sussex County." These three reports support the idea that the species is using what remains of suitable habitat, but is probably less abundant.

The Atlas data provided the first statewide search for Virginia Rails in New Jersey, and they were found in only 15% of the blocks statewide. Clearly, the Outer Coastal Plain, Kittatinny Valley, and Highlands are important breeding areas for this species, although they were found in each province in the state.

Conservation Note: This species occurs in smaller, less densely packed colonies than do Clapper Rails. Although Virginia Rails are found in more blocks than Clapper Rails, there are probably many fewer individuals statewide. There is strong evidence that this species has had a large-scale decline in both range and abundance in the state, and Virginia Rails should be monitored closely for signs of further decline. Enforcement of the New Jersey Freshwater Wetlands Protection Act is critical to the survival of this species.

continued on page 216

Physiographic Distribution

Virginia Rail	Number of blocks in province	Number of blocks species found breeding in province	Number of blocks species found in state	Percent of province species occupies	Percent of all records for this species found in province	Percent of state area in province
Kittatinny Mountains	19	5	127	26.3	3.9	2.2
Kittatinny Valley	45	23	127	51.1	18.1	5.3
Highlands	109	22	127	20.2	17.3	12.8
Piedmont	167	14	127	8.4	11.0	19.6
Inner Coastal Plain	128	18	127	14.1	14.2	15.0
Outer Coastal Plain	204	26	127	12.7	20.5	23.9
Pine Barrens	180	19	127	10.6	15.0	21.1

continued from page 215

Virginia Rail

Fall: Most sightings of Virginia Rails come from known haunts, but a few reports from locations where they do not breed suggest fall migration from mid-September through early November.

Winter: Virginia Rails are found year-round in New Jersey. Individuals that are found in winter may be migrants, but it is possible that some local breeders may spend the winter in New Jersey. Statewide CBC totals are low and considerably variable. **CBC Statewide Stats:** Average: 20; Maximum: 38 in 1980; Minimum: 6 in 1989. **CBC Maximum:** 22, Cape May, 1995.

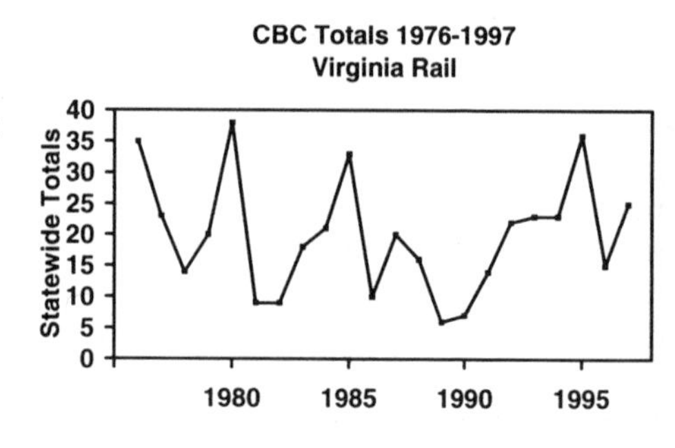

Spring: There is little documentation on spring migration for Virginia Rails. Breeding birds probably arrive back on territory by early to mid-April. The earliest recorded calling during the Atlas was on 7 April. ■

Sora

Porzana carolina

Range: In eastern North America, breeds from Manitoba east to Nova Scotia south to Kansas and Maryland. Winters from the southeastern United States south to northern South America.

NJ Status: Scarce and local summer resident, uncommon spring and fall migrant, accidental in winter.

Soras may be the most numerous and widespread rails in the United States, but they are increasingly rare as breeding birds in New Jersey. Historic data suggests there were small nesting populations in northern New Jersey in previous decades. Stone (1937) knew of only one nesting record in southern New Jersey at his time. Cruickshank (1942) considered Troy Meadows to be the stronghold for this species in New Jersey, and Fables (1955) and Leck (1984) also describe the breeding range as northern New Jersey.

Atlas data indicated that the Wallkill River basin in the Kittatinny Valley and the Highlands are the strongholds for this species in New Jersey. Soras are con-

Breeding

Habitat: Nests in freshwater marshes and wet meadows.

Sora

continued

spicuous in their absence from much of the rest of the state. Their decline appears to have gone nearly undetected, as many field observers are expressing new-found concern for this species after reviewing Atlas data.

Conservation Note: Soras near absence from much of New Jersey is cause for alarm. Known nest locations should be monitored annually, and locating new nest areas should be a high priority for management of this species. It is likely that the decrease in freshwater marshes during this century has caused the species to decline, as is suspected in Pennsylvania (Reid 1992b).

Fall: Southbound migration of Soras is protracted, with the first birds seen as early as late July. Numbers peak from late August through early September, and *continued on page 218*

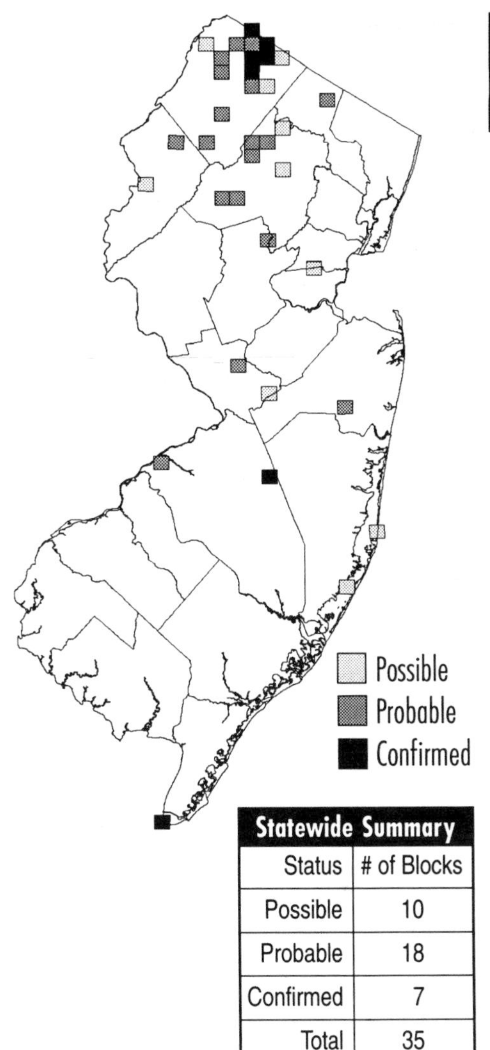

Statewide Summary	
Status	# of Blocks
Possible	10
Probable	18
Confirmed	7
Total	35

Physiographic Distribution Sora	Number of blocks in province	Number of blocks species found breeding in province	Number of blocks species found in state	Percent of province species occupies	Percent of all records for this species found in province	Percent of state area in province
Kittatinny Mountains	19	2	35	10.5	5.7	2.2
Kittatinny Valley	45	13	35	28.9	37.1	5.3
Highlands	109	10	35	9.2	28.6	12.8
Piedmont	167	2	35	1.2	5.7	19.6
Inner Coastal Plain	128	3	35	2.3	8.6	15.0
Outer Coastal Plain	204	4	35	2.0	11.4	23.9
Pine Barrens	180	1	35	0.6	2.9	21.1

continued from page 217

Sora

migration can continue into October. Soras were much more abundant in migration in the early part of the 20th century. Stone (1937) noted that there must "be a very heavy" migration given the number of dead Soras found along roads. He also considered Soras "*the* rail of the Delaware," with thousands shot from Philadelphia to the Cape May County border. **Maximum:** 7, Brigantine NWR, 19 August 1975.

Winter: In most years one or two Soras are reported statewide on CBCs, and there are a few December records outside the CBC period. There is one January record from the South Cape May Meadows in 1999 (A. Robinson, pers. obs.).

Spring: The first Soras returning are usually seen in early April, and the peak occurs from late April to early May, with numbers tapering off toward the end of May. They are quite vocal during spring, making detection easier than in fall. **Maximum:** 20, Pond Creek Marsh, 7 May 1989 (Sibley 1997). ■

Purple Gallinule

Porphyrula martinica

Range: In North America breeds from Texas to Florida, north along the Atlantic coast to South Carolina. Winters from Florida to South America.

NJ Status: Very rare. NJBRC Review List.

Occurrence: There have been over 60 reports of Purple Gallinule, and 47 haven been accepted by the NJBRC. Prior to 1985 most reports occurred in spring, especially in May. Since 1985, however, reports from autumn have predominated. There have been several records of Purple Gallinules summering in dense freshwater marsh habitat (e.g., Paulinskill Marsh, 1975; Cape May Point, 1979, 1981 and 1982; and Brigantine NWR, 1985), although no evidence of breeding was obtained. The species has bred at Dragon Run, Delaware, so nesting in New Jersey is possible.

Purple Gallinules have a well-known penchant for appearing in unlikely places at unlikely times. Several of New Jersey's records are of exhausted and disoriented birds grounded near homes or on roads well away from typical habitat. Three times birds have been found 14-25 miles offshore. There are even two mid-winter records of individuals found dead: Cape May, 24 January 1987; Cape May Point, 5 January 1992. Most records have been along the southern coast, but birds have wandered north and inland as far as Sussex, Morris, and Passaic counties. ■

Common Moorhen

Gallinula chloropus

Range: In North America, breeds from southeastern Minnesota to Maine, south to eastern Texas and Florida. Winters along the coast from New Jersey south to Central America.

NJ Status: Uncommon and local summer resident, uncommon spring and fall migrant, very rare winter resident.

Possible
Probable
Confirmed

Breeding

Habitat: Nests in freshwater and brackish marshes, and reedy ponds.

Common Moorhens are relatively new breeding birds in the state. The first New Jersey nests were discovered in Trenton in 1904, and in 1906 they were discovered nesting in the Newark marshes (Stone 1908). Griscom (1923) described the

continued on page 220

Statewide Summary	
Status	# of Blocks
Possible	13
Probable	14
Confirmed	21
Total	48

Physiographic Distribution

Common Moorhen	Number of blocks in province	Number of blocks species found breeding in province	Number of blocks species found in state	Percent of province species occupies	Percent of all records for this species found in province	Percent of state area in province
Kittatinny Mountains	19	1	48	5.3	2.1	2.2
Kittatinny Valley	45	11	48	24.4	22.9	5.3
Highlands	109	4	48	3.7	8.3	12.8
Piedmont	167	15	48	9.0	31.3	19.6
Inner Coastal Plain	128	8	48	6.3	16.7	15.0
Outer Coastal Plain	204	8	48	3.9	16.7	23.9
Pine Barrens	180	1	48	0.6	2.1	21.1

continued from page 219

Map Interpretation: Due to Common Moorhen's secretive nature most Probable and Possible locations are likely to be breeding birds. If this species occurs in small numbers, it can be easily overlooked, especially in areas that received limited coverage. The Atlas map likely represents a low-end estimate of the statewide population.

species as "exceedingly local," and listed several nesting locations that were destroyed as marshes were filled. Cruickshank (1942) suggested that Troy Meadows was the best locale in northern New Jersey to find this species, but knew of "a half a dozen" other breeding locations in northern New Jersey. Interestingly, Bull (1964) reported two observers estimated 200 pairs of breeding Common Moorhens – a staggeringly high density – in the Hackensack Meadows during 1962 after portions of the marsh were cut off from tidal flow. In the summer of 1973 there were estimated to be 140 individuals in the Great Swamp (Black 1973).

RNJB reports since 1977 indicated this species is prone to dramatic population swings (see Region 2 reports from 1978-1987, Region 3 reports 1977-1983). The population changes may reflect changes in marsh structure, indicating Common Moorhen's ability to colonize a marsh and capitalize on an ephemeral situation.

Common Moorhens require a complex marsh structure for successful breeding. This makes their distribution map a directory to some of the state's most important wetland sites – the Wallkill River system, the Hackensack Meadowlands, Great Swamp, and Mannington Marsh.

The New Jersey population has increased during this century – a tren similar to that observed in Pennsylvania (Leberman 1992a), but contrary to that observed in New York (Sibley 1988a) and Massachusetts (Veit and Petersen 1993).

Fall: Like many other marsh bird Common Moorhens are nocturnal migrants and are rarely seen away from their marsh habitats. Typically, the largest concentrations are seen in September at large marshes whe local populations are augmented by southbound migrants. A few will linger into the late fall. **Maxima:** 200+, Great Swamp, 30 Septembe 1976; 200, Mannington Marsh, 27 September 1994.

Winter: In mild years a few Common Moorhens will successfully winter. One or two are usuall seen in the state on CBCs, but numbers are much lower than those in the mid- to late 1970s. **CBC Statewide Stats:** Average: 5; Maximum: 29 in 1977; Minimum: 0 in five years. **CBC Maximum:** 14, Lower Hudson, 1977.

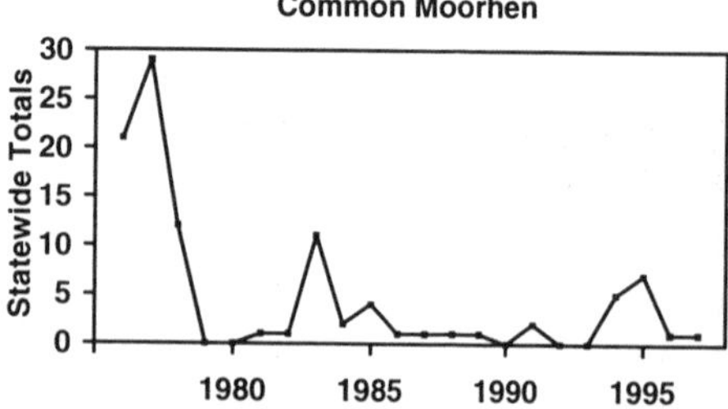

Spring: Returning Common Moorhens arrive in late April, with no documented concentrations of migrants. ■

American Coot

Fulica americana

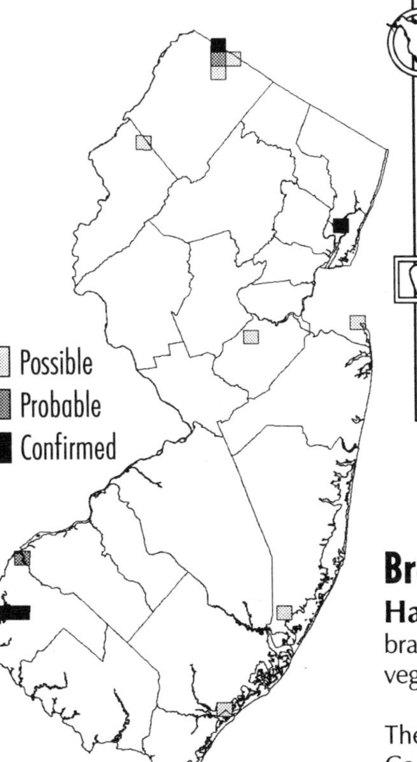

Range: In eastern North America breeds from Manitoba east to Quebec, south to Texas and New Jersey. Winters in the southern United States to northern Illinois and north along the coast to Massachusetts.

NJ Status: Scarce and very local summer resident, common spring and fall migrant, fairly common winter resident.

Statewide Summary	
Status	# of Blocks
Possible	7
Probable	2
Confirmed	4
Total	13

Breeding

Habitat: Nests in freshwater or brackish marshes and ponds with dense vegetation.

The first breeding record for American Coots in New Jersey may have been in 1887 (Stone 1908), although this record was not well documented. Stone (1908) and Griscom (1923) listed the next breeding record as 1907 in the Newark marshes. Stone (1937) reported several late spring records in Cape May County,

continued on page 222

Physiographic Distribution American Coot	Number of blocks in province	Number of blocks species found breeding in province	Number of blocks species found in state	Percent of province species occupies	Percent of all records for this species found in province	Percent of state area in province
Kittatinny Valley	45	5	13	11.1	38.5	5.3
Piedmont	167	1	13	0.6	7.7	19.6
Inner Coastal Plain	128	4	13	3.1	30.8	15.0
Outer Coastal Plain	204	3	13	1.5	23.1	23.9

continued from page 221

but no breeding records for southern New Jersey. Fables (1955) listed the species as locally common from Trenton Marsh northward, and Bull (1964) discussed a virtual population explosion in the late 1950s and early 1960s. In 1958 observers noted 100 nesting pairs in Hackensack Meadows, and, in 1962, 300 pairs were reported (Bull 1964). An astonishing total of 800 were reported in the summer of 1980 at Kearny Marsh (Leck 1984). This colony declined owing to a change in marsh structure.

Atlas data indicated American Coot is a very local breeding bird, with only four Confirmations in the state during the project. This species' pattern of colonization, expansion, and contraction in New Jersey is similar to that of Common Moorhen. Like the moorhen's range, the coot's range is an indication of some of New Jersey's most important, large-scale wetlands: the Wallkill River system, the Hackensack Meadowlands, and Mannington Marsh.

Conservation Note: American Coots have a tenuous position in New Jersey. This species deserves focussed research, as it has had a considerable decline in the state.

Fall: A few coots arrive as early as late August or early September. The largest concentrations are generally seen from late October through November. **Maxima:** 4,000, Mannington Marsh, 30 November 1995; 3,000, Mannington Marsh, late October 1994.

Winter: Throughout the winter months, American Coot numbers vary from year to year, and with the harshness of the winter. This is reflected in statewide CBC totals. **CBC Statewide Stats:** Average: 1,203; Maximum: 4,988 in 1976; Minimum: 298 in 1991. **CBC Maximum:** 1,900, Salem, 1995.

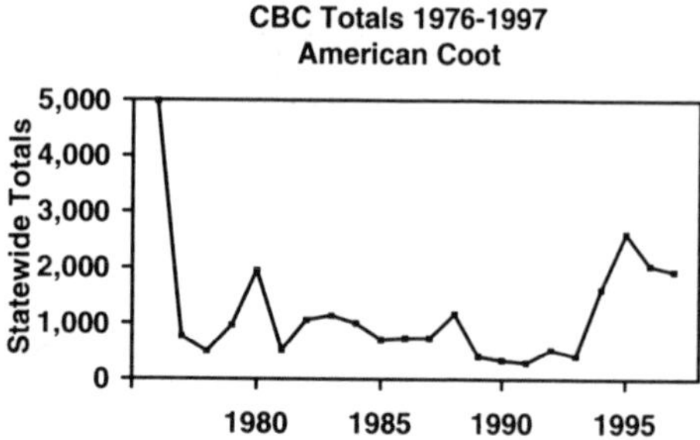

Spring: American Coot numbers peak again in March as birds return as soon as open water is available. **Maximum:** 4,000, Mannington Marsh, March 1995. ■

Sandhill Crane

Grus canadensis

Range: In North America breeds in Alaska, throughout western Canada, southeast to Michigan, and sporadically farther south and east to Florida. Winters in the southern United States and Mexico.

NJ Status: Rare spring and fall migrant, very rare winter visitor.

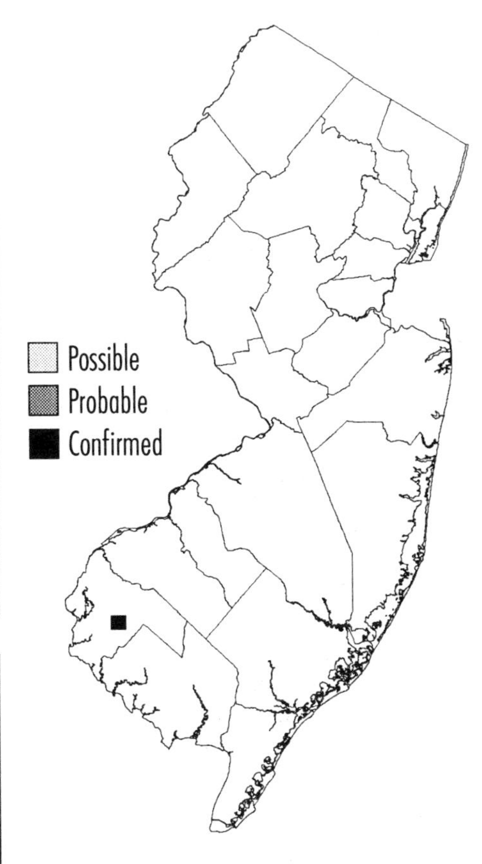

Statewide Summary	
Status	# of Blocks
Possible	0
Probable	0
Confirmed	1
Total	1

Physiographic Distribution Sandhill Crane	Number of blocks in province	Number of blocks species found breeding in province	Number of blocks species found in state	Percent of province species occupies	Percent of all records for this species found in province	Percent of state area in province
Outer Coastal Plain	204	1	1	100.0	0.5	23.9

Breeding

Habitat: Nests near large freshwater wetlands.

It is unlikely that Sandhill Cranes had ever bred in New Jersey prior to an unusual report during the Atlas research period. In 1995, a mixed pair of Sandhill and Common Cranes (*Grus grus*) bred successfully in Salem County. It was likely that the Common Crane was an escaped bird (and may have been the Common Crane that wintered near Mannington Marsh in 1994). The origin of the Sandhill Crane, however, was never determined.

continued on page 224

continued from page 223

Sandhill Crane

The Sandhill Crane was not banded and showed no other attributes suggesting it was an escaped bird. The mixed pair of cranes raised hybrid young for two successive years, and young from the 1995 nest returned in 1996 to join the parents and young from the 1996 nest. The birds eventually abandoned the breeding site in 1996.

Historic Changes: It is likely that an adult Sandhill Crane found at Tuckerton on 12 May 1957 was the first in the state in over a century. The second modern sighting was of 30 birds flying past Chimney Rock Hawk Lookout on 14 October 1962 (Conn 1996). While their numbers never approached the 1962 maximum, Sandhill Cranes occurred with increasing frequency over the next two decades. They have been reported regularly since 1991, and the reports have come from all sections of the state.

Fall: Sandhill Cranes are now rare passage migrants through New Jersey, occurring from October through December. Although Sandhill Cranes have been documented throughout New Jersey, they are far more likely along the coast.

Winter: Sandhill Cranes have been reported six times on CBCs from 1976 to 1997, all on the southernmost counts (i.e., Cape May, Cumberland, and Salem). Other winter reports are also from the southern half of the state.

Spring: Northbound Sandhill Cranes are recorded from March to May. Many of the spring observations have occurred in northern New Jersey. There are at least three records of birds remaining to summer in the state. **Maximum:** 18, over Newark, 27 March 1997. ■

Northern Lapwing

Vanellus vanellus

Range: Breeds across much of Europe and central Asia. Winters in southern Europe and Asia, south to northern Africa.

NJ Status: Accidental. NJBRC Review List.

Occurrence: There have been two state reports of Northern Lapwing, and both have been accepted by the NJBRC. The two accepted records are:

20-30 miles N of Fortescue	*8 March 1953*	
Goshen	*1-4 January 1997*	*ph-RBPF*

Black-bellied Plover

Pluvialis squatarola

Range: In North America breeds in the high Arctic from Alaska to Baffin Island. On the East Coast, winters from southern New England south to South America.

NJ Status: Common spring and fall migrant, fairly common winter resident.

Fall: Typically, adult Black-bellied Plovers begin to return from their high Arctic nesting grounds in mid-July, although the earliest birds are occasionally noted by late June. Juveniles begin arriving in late August. The peak flight is protracted and varies from mid-August to early November. Black-bellied Plovers are much more common along the coast than inland. **Maxima:** Coastal: 1,500+, Avalon, 21 August 1981; 1,000+, Brigantine NWR, 29 August 1996; Inland: 56, Wallkill sod farms, 17 August 1992.

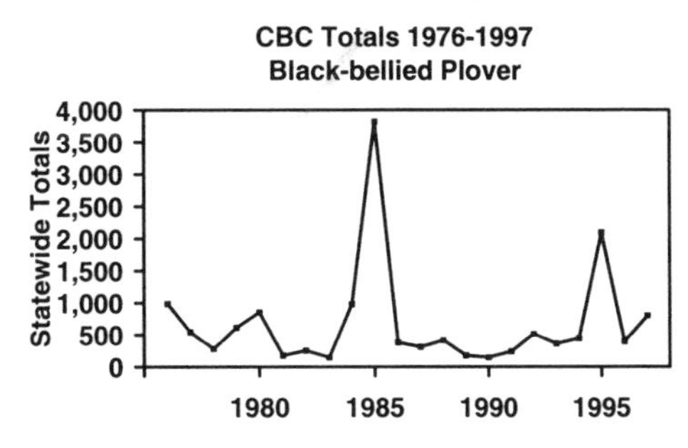

Winter: Black-bellied Plovers are fairly common along the outer beach, although CBC totals are considerably variable. The listed statewide maximum (see below) was exceptional and was many times higher than an average year. Their winter status has changed during the 20th century. In 1908 they were unknown as wintering birds (Stone 1908). Wintering was first documented by Charles Urner in 1932 (Stone 1937), and by the mid-1950s the species was regarded as regular in winter (Fables 1955). **CBC Statewide Stats:** Average: 678; Maximum: 3,821 in 1985; Minimum: 146 in 1983. **CBC Maximum:** 2,760, Cape May, 1985.

Spring: The spring flight of Black-bellied Plovers occurs between late April and early June. Highest numbers are recorded from mid- to late May. They are rare to scarce inland. As with other shorebirds, nonbreeders occasionally may linger through June. **Maxima:** Coastal: 1,800, Week's Landing, 23 May 1982; 1,500-2,000 (overhead), Mannington Marsh, 26 May 1996; Inland: 16, Freehold, 19-20 May 1990. ■

American Golden-Plover

Pluvialis dominica

Range: Breeds from Alaska across the tundra of Canada south to northern Manitoba. Winters in central South America.

NJ Status: Scarce spring and uncommon fall migrant.

Fall: Adult American Golden-Plovers normally arrive in mid-August; juveniles follow about a month later, with numbers peaking from mid-September to early October. Movement continues through mid-November with very infrequent reports into December. They are recorded most frequently, and in the largest numbers, inland, where they use short-grass habitats. **Maxima:** Inland: 433, Great Meadows, 7 September 1986; 400, Plainsboro, 7 September 1975 (AB). Coastal: 225, North Arlington, 28 September 1975;

Spring: Northbound American Golden-Plovers begin to appear during early April, and peak from mid-April to early May. Most have left by late May, and only a few birds have been reported after early June. Formerly a rare spring transient in New Jersey, reports have increased markedly in the past two decades. **Maximum:** 50, Hainesport, 14 April 1982. ■

Mongolian Plover

Charadrius mongolus

Range: Breeds in central and northeastern Asia and has bred in North America in northern and western Alaska; winters in southern Asia and southern Africa.

NJ Status: Accidental. NJBRC Review List.

Occurrence: There has only been one reported and accepted record of Mongolian Plover in New Jersey: North Wildwood, 13 July 1990 (ph-RBPF), an adult. This is one of only a handful of records for this species in eastern North America. ■

Wilson's Plover

Charadrius wilsonia

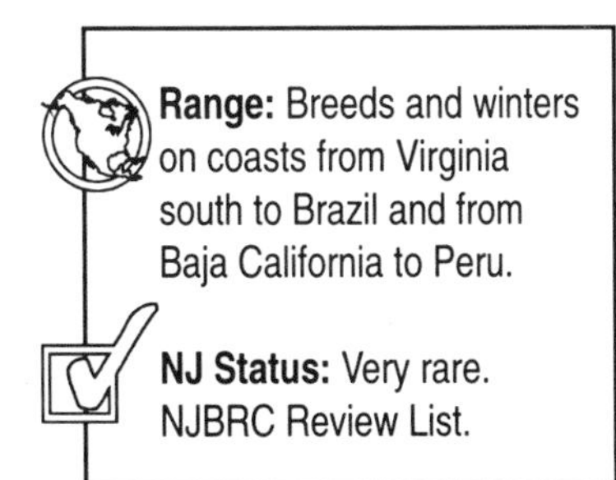

Range: Breeds and winters on coasts from Virginia south to Brazil and from Baja California to Peru.

NJ Status: Very rare. NJBRC Review List.

Occurrence: Wilson's Plovers were extirpated as breeding birds in New Jersey during the early to mid-1800s (Stone 1937). They reappeared circa 1940 as uncommon breeders on the outer coast in Atlantic and Ocean counties (Cant 1941), and the last known breeding attempt was at Holgate in 1963. Since then, there have been 16 state reports of Wilson's Plover, and six have been accepted by the NJBRC (all in spring). All records are from the vicinity of the outer coast from Tuckerton south to Cape May. The six accepted records are:

3	*Stone Harbor**	*19 May 1970*	
	Brigantine NWR	*26 May 1979*	
	South Cape May Meadows	*16-21 March 1983*	*ph-RNJB 9:65*
	Longport	*23-24 April 1983*	*ph-RNJB 9:64*
	Longport	*13-14 May 1986*	*ph-RNJB 12:67*
	Cape May	*4-5 May 1996*	*ph-RNJB 22:57*

Semipalmated Plover

Charadrius semipalmatus

Range: Breeds from Alaska across northern Canada to Nova Scotia. On the East Coast, winters mainly from North Carolina south to South America.

NJ Status: Common spring and fall migrant, very rare winter resident.

Fall: Adult Semipalmated Plovers can return by late June, although initial arrival from early to mid-July is more typical; juveniles begin to arrive by mid-August. The period of maximum abundance is reached from late August through mid-September, although movement continues through November, gradually

continued on page 228

continued from page 227

Semipalmated Plover

diminishing in magnitude. They are scarce to uncommon inland on pond shores, flooded fields, etc. **Maxima:** Coastal: 10,000+, Brigantine NWR, 15 August 1998; 5,000-6,000, Brigantine NWR, 28 August 1992; Inland: 32, Spruce Run Res., 14 August 1998.

Winter: In most years a small number of Semipalmated Plovers remain into December along the southern coast, and they are sometimes recorded on CBCs. They have successfully wintered on a few occasions. **CBC Statewide Stats:** Average: 5; Maximum: 16 in 1984; Minimum: 0 in eight years. **CBC Maximum:** 16, Cape May, 1984.

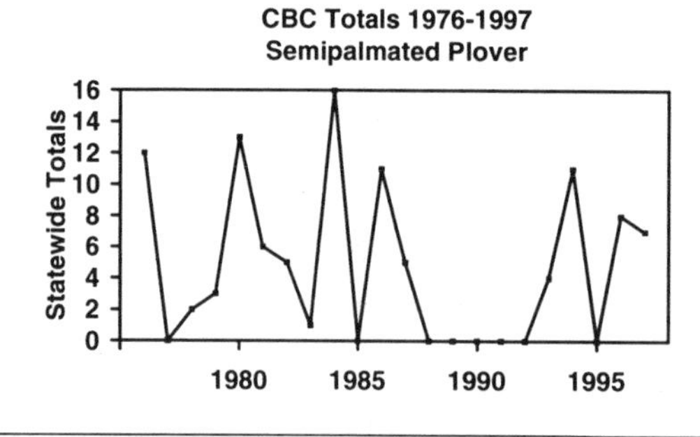

Spring: The earliest northbound Semipalmated Plovers are usually noted by late April. In contrast to the protracted autumn passage, the spring flight quickly builds to a mid-May peak and declines to an early June conclusion. Nonbreeding birds occasionally remain through June, straddling the northbound and southbound flights. They are uncommon inland. **Maxima:** Coastal: 2,940, Avalon-Stone Harbor, 16 May 1989; 600, Nummy Island, 13 May 1984; Inland: 20, Sharptown, spring 1993. ■

Piping Plover

Charadrius melodus

Range: Breeds along the coast from Newfoundland to North Carolina, and locally from the Great Lakes west to Alberta. Winters on the coast in the southeastern United States south to the Caribbean.

NJ Status: Uncommon and local summer resident, scarce to uncommon spring and fall migrant, accidental in winter. Endangered Species in New Jersey.

Breeding

Habitat: Nests on open sandy beaches.

Piping Plovers have been struggling as breeding birds since the late 1800s when development of the barrier islands destroyed or degraded

Piping Plover
continued

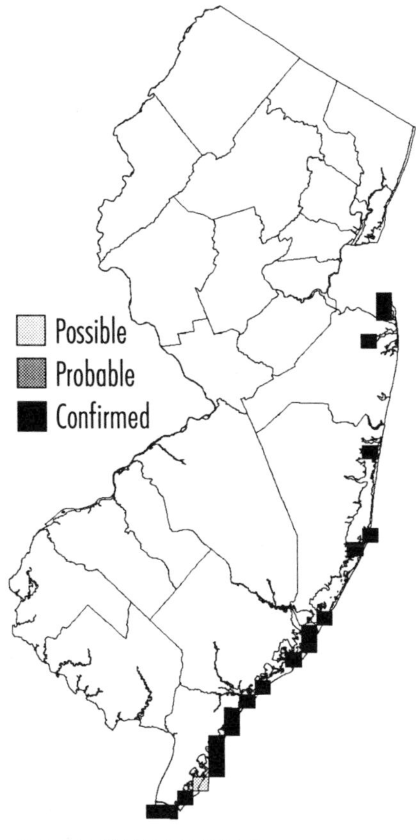

Statewide Summary	
Status	# of Blocks
Possible	1
Probable	0
Confirmed	20
Total	21

suitable breeding habitat, and large-scale, unregulated hunting reduced populations of nearly all shorebirds. Historically Piping Plovers were recorded as locally common along suitable beaches in New Jersey, and Wilson (1812) described them as abundant at Sommer's Beach at the mouth of Great Egg Harbor River. By 1908, Stone was doubtful that they occurred in New Jersey at all. The first nesting attempts in the 1900s were in 1921 at Brigantine Beach and Barnegat (Leck 1984). By 1942, Cruickshank reported that Piping Plovers had responded well to protection and were repopulating eastern New York.

Atlas data indicated Piping Plovers were breeding in 21 blocks statewide. There are only a small number of sites in the state with more than a few pairs, and the statewide population continues to decline at an alarming rate.

Conservation Note: Piping Plovers may be the most intensively managed breeding birds in New Jersey. The plovers require barrier beaches with little human traffic and few ground-based predators. This, coupled with their low local population, is a challenging mixture of elements for managers. Unfortunately, even with the intense management scheme in place today (fences around most nests to exclude predators, intense education programs for off-

continued on page 230

Physiographic Distribution Piping Plover	Number of blocks in province	Number of blocks species found breeding in province	Number of blocks species found in state	Percent of province species occupies	Percent of all records for this species found in province	Percent of state area in province
Inner Coastal Plain	128	2	21	1.6	9.5	15.0
Outer Coastal Plain	204	19	21	9.3	90.5	23.9

continued from page 229

road vehicle users, and near daily nest monitoring) the population is declining. Sandy Hook, a section of Gateway NRA, holds the most breeding pairs and fledges the most young in New Jersey.

Fall: The highest concentrations of Piping Plovers occur at breeding sites in late summer, when local adults and young are probably joined by some southbound migrants. It is difficult to distinguish migrants from local populations, and the passage of southbound birds is usually unrecorded. A few will sometimes linger late into fall. **Maximum:** 60, Brigantine Island, 30 August 1977.

Winter: Piping Plovers are recorded only rarely on CBCs, most recently in 1976, 1977, and 1978. They very rarely attempt to winter.

Spring: In spring, Piping Plovers return to breeding locations very early, often by early March. Inland sightings are rare. A recent inland record occurred at Spruce Run Res. on 18 May 1978, and the first Salem County record was recorded at Artificial Island on 15 March 1997. **Maximum:** 50, Longport, 14 March 1976. ■

Killdeer

Charadrius vociferus

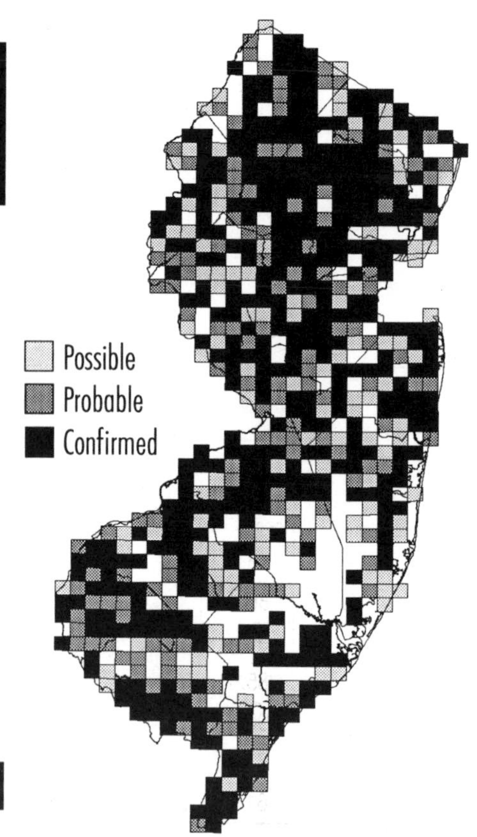

Range: Breeds throughout temperate North America. On the East Coast winters from southern New England south to northern South America.

NJ Status: Common and very widespread summer resident, common spring and fall migrant, fairly common winter resident.

Killdeer

continued

Breeding

Habitat: Nests in open grassy areas, pastures, farmland, gravel roads, and even highly developed areas such as parking lots or driveways.

In the 1800s Killdeer were widely hunted, and their numbers declined. However, even at their lowest levels, they were considered common breeding birds. Comparisons of Stone's 1908 description of their abundance and range indicated Killdeer increased markedly in this century, especially in northern New Jersey. He listed breeding locations which, when compared to their current range, suggest the species was absent or reduced to small numbers in 1908. Griscom (1923) asserted Killdeer were scarce in the urbanized regions of northern New Jersey, within 20 miles of the Hudson River. Fables (1955) considered the species somewhat restricted to agricultural areas in northern New Jersey.

Atlas data indicated Killdeer have successfully colonized or re-colonized most of the state. Their affinity for almost any type of open habitat – from agricultural fields to parking lots – creates nearly limitless breeding habitat for this species. Analyses of their distribution by physiographic province indicated they were least common in the Kittatinny Mountains and Pine Barrens, but occurred in more than 78% of the blocks in all other physiographic provinces.

Statewide Summary	
Status	# of Blocks
Possible	113
Probable	147
Confirmed	417
Total	677

Fall: Southward migration of Killdeer is very protracted in fall. Post-breeding dispersal begins in late June, and movements continue into November or December when early-season snowfalls may drive birds southward. Their migration is widely distributed throughout the state. Peak movements usually

continued on page 232

Physiographic Distribution Killdeer	Number of blocks in province	Number of blocks species found breeding in province	Number of blocks species found in state	Percent of province species occupies	Percent of all records for this species found in province	Percent of state area in province
Kittatinny Mountains	19	12	677	63.2	1.8	2.2
Kittatinny Valley	45	39	677	86.7	5.8	5.3
Highlands	109	99	677	90.8	14.6	12.8
Piedmont	167	142	677	85.0	21.0	19.6
Inner Coastal Plain	128	116	677	90.6	17.1	15.0
Outer Coastal Plain	204	159	677	77.9	23.5	23.9
Pine Barrens	180	110	677	61.1	16.2	21.1

continued from page 231

Killdeer

occur in mid- to late October. **Maxima:** Coastal: 1,400, Cape May Point, 26 October 1996; 1,049, Cape May Point, 17 October 1997; Inland: 1,000, Mount Holly, 15-17 October 1979.

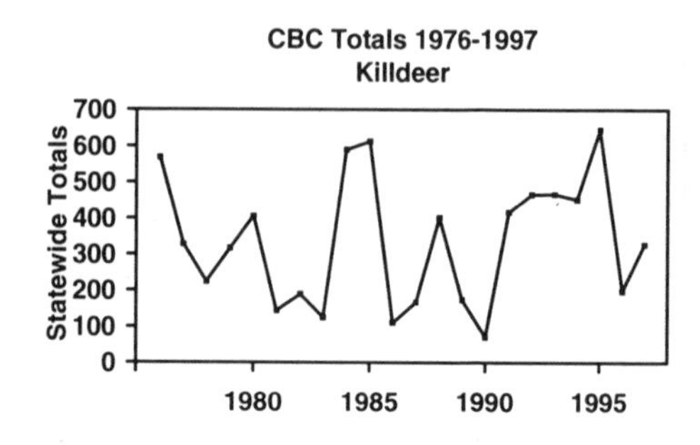

Winter: The numbers of Killdeer recorded in winter are variable and are probably dependent on the amount of snow cover, particularly in the northern portion of the state. CBC totals reflect the variability in numbers. **CBC Statewide Stats:** Average: 336; Maximum: 645 in 1995; Minimum: 70 in 1990. **CBC Maximum:** 251, Cape May, 1984.

Spring: Killdeer often return in late winter when the snow cover melts, only to be driven south again by a late season storm. Peak spring numbers usually occur in late March. **Maxima:** 300+, Cape May Island, 1 April 1997; 110+, Dorbrook Park, 22 March 1998. ■

American Oystercatcher

Haematopus palliatus

Breeding

Habitat: Nests along the coast on isolated sandy beaches or marsh islands

Range: Breeds along the Atlantic coast from Massachusetts to Florida and along the Gulf coast to Texas. Winters from New Jersey to Florida and the Gulf Coast.

NJ Status: Fairly common but local summer resident, fairly common spring and fall migrant, fairly common winter resident.

American Oystercatchers nested in southern New Jersey during the early 1800s (Stone 1937), but their numbers subsequently declined until they were extirpated by 1896 (Griscom 1923). There is no single cause for the decline, but, as with many other shorebirds, the influx of humans onto the barrier beaches, hunting, and egg collecting are likely causes (Nol and Humphrey 1994). There first modern breeding record in New Jersey was in

American Oystercatcher

continued

1947, when a nest was located at Little Beach Island in Ocean County (Bull 1964). In 1954 the Delaware Valley Ornithological Club located 11 American Oystercatcher nests in a survey of southern New Jersey (Fables 1955). Since that time the species has continued a slow, but steady, re-colonization of New Jersey.

Atlas surveys found American Oystercatchers to be well established along New Jersey's coasts. One of the more significant changes in the range of this species is their colonization of the Delaware and Raritan Bay shores. It is important to note that this species nests relatively early in the season, and observers collecting breeding information on American Oystercatchers should begin their work in April.

Fall: American Oystercatchers gather in large flocks along the coast after the breeding season. At this time numbers begin to build as migrants from the north join local breeding birds. **Maxima:** 375, Brigantine NWR, 13 September 1996; 350+, Hereford Inlet, 25 October 1994.

Winter: A notable change in the status of American Oystercatcher in New Jersey is the number of birds that remain throughout the winter. CBC totals have skyrocketed since the *continued on page 234*

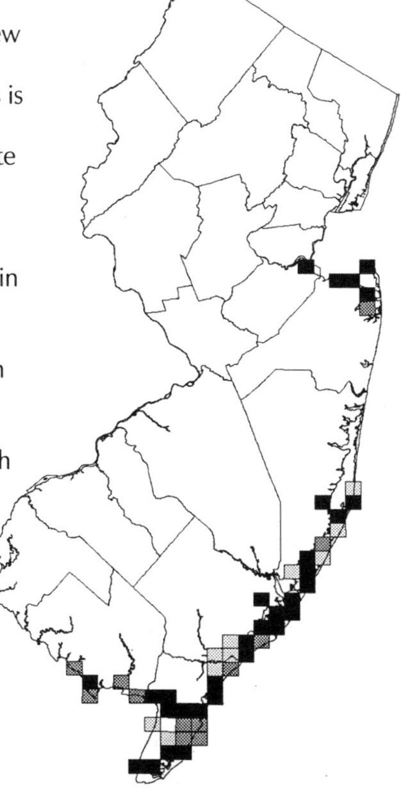

Statewide Summary	
Status	# of Blocks
Possible	10
Probable	12
Confirmed	31
Total	53

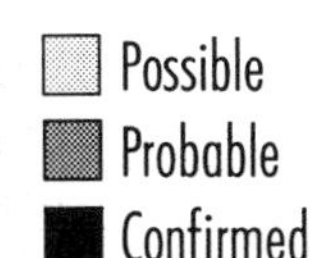

Physiographic Distribution American Oystercatcher	Number of blocks in province	Number of blocks species found breeding in province	Number of blocks species found in state	Percent of province species occupies	Percent of all records for this species found in province	Percent of state area in province
Inner Coastal Plain	128	4	53	3.1	7.5	15.0
Outer Coastal Plain	204	47	53	23.0	88.7	23.9
Pine Barrens	180	2	53	1.1	3.8	21.1

continued from page 233

American Oystercatcher

early 1980s, when statewide totals were fewer than ten. In severe winters numbers may drop during the coldest periods, but returning birds can be seen as early as late February. **CBC Statewide Stats:** Average: 161; Maximum: 498 in 1995; Minimum: 0 in 1978 and 1981. **CBC Maximum:** 313, Cape May, 1996.

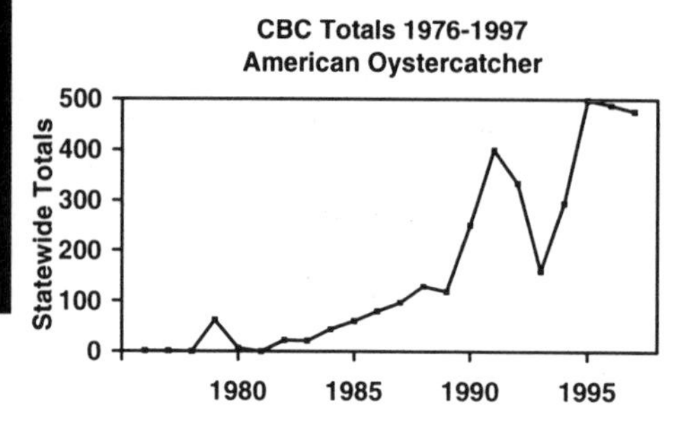

Spring: Migrant American Oystercatchers can be seen in late February, but more typically arrive in mid-March. Most have passed through by early April. ■

Black-necked Stilt

Himantopus mexicanus

Range: In the eastern United States, breeds from southern New Jersey south to Florida, and along the Gulf coast to Texas. Also breeds in the Mississippi Valley to Missouri. Winters from the Gulf Coast and southern Florida to South America.

NJ Status: Rare and very local summer resident, rare spring and very rare fall migrant.

Possible
Probable
Confirmed

Statewide Summary	
Status	# of Blocks
Possible	0
Probable	1
Confirmed	1
Total	2

Black-necked Stilt

continued

Breeding

Habitat: Nests in salt marshes, but requires open salt pans for feeding.

In the early 1800s Black-necked Stilts may have been fairly common breeding birds in the salt marshes of southern New Jersey. Wilson (1810) wrote of arriving breeding flocks of " 20 or 30 together," and nesting groups in salt pans on the marsh in clusters of "six or eight pairs." By the end of the 1800s, however, Black-necked Stilts had been extirpated as breeding birds and occurred in New Jersey as passage migrants only. The cause for the decline is unknown, but it is likely that hunting and marsh alteration for mosquito control combined to cause the extirpation. Stone (1937) knew of only one recent record, an individual collected in April 1894 in Cape May County

In the mid-1900s the story of Black-necked Stilt in New Jersey takes an unexpected turn. In 1952 Frank McLaughlin attempted to cross-foster Black-necked Stilts in Willet nests when he placed stilt eggs in Willet nests at Turkey Point in Cumberland County. The experiment was conducted for only one year, but may have successfully fledged young. Four eggs hatched in June 1952, but there was no evidence of young returning to breed in successive years (Fables 1955). This project was attempted again in 1976, but was also unsuccessful.

During the Atlas surveys Black-necked Stilts were discovered breeding in June 1993 at Goshen Landing in Cape May County for the first nesting record in New Jersey during the 1900s. The nest was closely watched and probably failed due to unusually high tides. The following year adults were seen again at Goshen Landing, but it is unlikely that they nested. Black-necked Stilts were also seen in courtship at one other location in New Jersey during the Atlas (Brigantine NWR). There were no further sightings there after the courtship was noted.

Fall: Black-necked Stilts are exceptionally rare in fall, with only a few records after mid-June.

Spring: Black-necked Stilts are annual visitors to New Jersey in spring, as breeders from Delaware and Maryland apparently overshoot their breeding grounds. They occur mainly from late April through mid-June, with most sightings reported in May. A large percentage of the reports are from the southern coastal counties. **Maximum:** 8, South Cape May Meadows, 20-21 May 1996. ■

Physiographic Distribution Black-necked Stilt	Number of blocks in province	Number of blocks species found breeding in province	Number of blocks species found in state	Percent of province species occupies	Percent of all records for this species found in province	Percent of state area in province
Outer Coastal Plain	204	2	2	1.0	100.0	23.9

American Avocet

Recurvirostra americana

American Avocet

Range: Nests from British Columbia to Manitoba south through the western United States. On the East Coast, winters from North Carolina to Central America.

NJ Status: Very rare spring and rare fall migrant, accidental in winter.

Historic Changes: In the 19th century, American Avocets nested on the salt marshes of Cape May County; Alexander Wilson confirmed nests with eggs on 20 May, 1810. In 1829 Audubon found a few birds, but no nests (Stone 1937). Thereafter, avocets were accidental in New Jersey with only five records in the first half of the 20th century. In the fall of 1954 a large flight of 40 birds at Fortescue marked a change in their occurrence in the state (Kunkle et al. 1959). Since the mid-1950s the species has been reported annually in fall.

Fall: American Avocets are rare but regular along the coast in autumn and accidental inland. Autumn migrants may arrive as early as July, but records are most likely from August through September. The species has been seen inland on at least four occasions, in both northern and southern New Jersey. **Maxima:** 15, Brigantine NWR, 20 October 1977; 15, Brigantine NWR, August 1980.

Winter: American Avocets have persisted into two recent winters. One was recorded on the Oceanville CBC in 1979, and another was seen at Mannington Marsh on 27 January 1991.

Spring: Spring sightings of American Avocets have also increased, although avocets remain far less than annual at that season. Most sightings occur in late April and May. A group of 14 at Brigantine NWR from 29-31 May 1992 was highly unusual. ■

Greater Yellowlegs

Tringa melanoleuca

Range: Breeds from southeastern Alaska east to Newfoundland. Winters along the coast from Massachusetts to Florida and the Gulf coast, south to South America.

NJ Status: Common spring and fall migrant, scarce to uncommon winter resident.

Fall: The southbound movement of Greater Yellowlegs is protracted, with the bulk of the migration occurring between mid-July and early November. Peak numbers are seen from early to mid-October, most notably at Brigantine NWR. Most birds are seen along the coast, although they are regular in small numbers inland. Adult Greater Yellowlegs precede juveniles and constitute most of the flight through August. Later flights contain a much higher number of juveniles. **Maxima:** Coastal: 3,000+, Brigantine NWR, 10 October 1997; 2,000, Brigantine NWR, 15 October 1993; Inland: 40, Duck Pond, 20 October 1994.

Winter: Greater Yellowlegs are generally restricted to the coast in winter. Numbers vary from year to year depending upon the severity of the season. CBC totals are likewise variable. **CBC Statewide Stats:** Average: 107; Maximum: 222 in 1997; Minimum: 20 in 1977 and 1981. **CBC Maximum:** 109, Cape May, 1997.

CBC Totals 1976-1997
Greater Yellowlegs

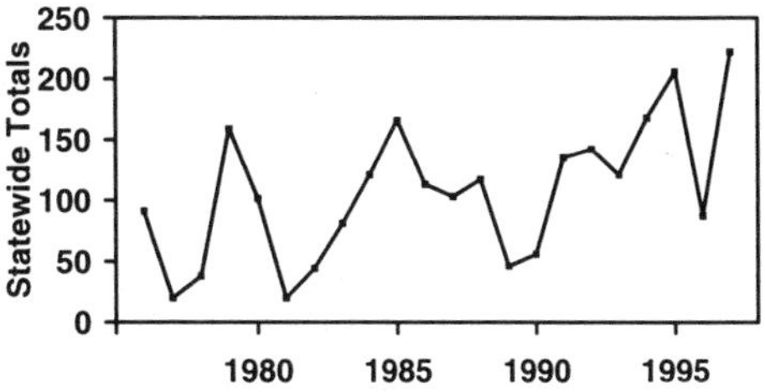

Spring: Greater Yellowlegs move north early in spring, with migrants arriving by mid-March. Peak flights occur in mid- to late April, and numbers decline through May. Although never plentiful inland, they are more common there in spring than in the fall. A few nonbreeders may spend the summer in New Jersey. **Maxima:** Coastal: 1,000, Salem City, 16 April 1985; 390, Hackensack Meadows, 27 April 1992; Inland: 45, Blackwells Mills, 17 April 1980. ■

Lesser Yellowlegs

Tringa flavipes

Range: Breeds from central Alaska to northern British Columbia east to James Bay. Winters from New Jersey to Florida and the Gulf Coast, south to South America.

NJ Status: Fairly common spring and common fall migrant, scarce winter resident.

Fall: Lesser Yellowlegs are one of the earliest returning shorebirds, with southbound migrants noted as early as late June. Adults migrate first and represent the bulk of the movement through July. In August and September adults become less common and a very high percentage of birds seen are juveniles. Migration is protracted, with a peak generally occurring from late July to mid-August. They are mainly found along the coast, but at times they can be fairly common inland. **Maxima:** Coastal: 1,000+, North Arlington, 26 July 1976, 1 August 1977, and 18 August 1983; Inland: 20, Paulinskill Lake, 27 July 1991.

Winter: Overall, Lesser Yellowlegs are less common in winter than Greater Yellowlegs. However, the listed statewide CBC high in 1991 (see below) is higher than that of Greater Yellowlegs. Outside of the 1991 season, no other statewide CBC total is over 100 birds. Numbers in winter vary with weather. **CBC Statewide Stats:** Average: 48; Maximum: 251 in 1991; Minimum: 4 in 1991. **CBC Maximum:** 131, Cape May, 1991.

CBC Totals 1976-1997
Lesser Yellowlegs

Statewide Totals (0–300) by year (1980, 1985, 1990, 1995)

Spring: Lesser Yellowlegs are early spring migrants and are noticeably less common than Greater Yellowlegs. Northbound birds are seen by mid-March and peak in mid-April, becoming less common by mid-May. They are scarce inland. Lesser Yellowlegs may be more common in spring than they were in the past. Stone (1937) recorded only three spring records, and Bull (1964) considered them "rare, but regular." However, Fables (1955) indicated that Lesser Yellowlegs were "much commoner in autumn than in spring," and that is still accurate. **Maxima:** Coastal: 50, Pedricktown, 7 April 1986 and 16 April 1983; Inland: 16, Harmony, 30 April 1980. ■

Spotted Redshank

Tringa erythropus

Range: Breeds from Scandinavia to Siberia. Winters from Europe to China.

NJ Status: Accidental. NJBRC Review List.

Occurrence: There have been seven state reports of Spotted Redshank, and three have been accepted by the NJBRC (all in fall). All are of single birds at coastal sites in the southern part of the state. There has been only one report since the 1970s. The three accepted records are:

Brigantine NWR	*14-28 September 1978*	*ph-RNJB 5:3; Fahey 1979*
Brigantine NWR	*28 September-8 October 1979*	*ph-RBPF*
Brigantine NWR	*22-23 October 1993*	*ph-RNJB 20:28*

Solitary Sandpiper

Tringa solitaria

Range: Breeds from Alaska south to British Columbia, east to Labrador. Winters mainly in South America.

NJ Status: Uncommon spring and fairly common fall migrant, reported on one CBC.

Fall: Southbound Solitary Sandpipers can arrive as early as late June, and a few trickle through into October. The peak flight is between mid-July and early September, and numbers diminish by early October. They are often found in locations where they may be the only shorebird present, such as the edges of wooded ponds, and are more common inland than on the coast. Highest numbers typically represent either a count done over a wide area, or a stationary observer noting migrants passing overhead. **Maxima:** 30, Paulinskill Lake, 27 July 1990; 25, Great Swamp, in late July 1975.

Winter: A Solitary Sandpiper was recorded on the Sussex CBC in 1991. They are very rarely seen after mid-October, and there are no wintering records.

Spring: The spring migration of Solitary Sandpipers is brief, with birds arriving in late April and departing by mid-May. A few continue to move throughout May, but there are no records of individuals summering. **Maxima:** 40, Great Swamp, 4 May 1983; 40, Black River, 7 May 1983. ■

Willet

Catoptrophorus semipalmatus

Range: Nominate *C. s. semipalmatus* breeds on the East Coast from Nova Scotia to Florida, and along the Gulf coast to Texas. Winters from Virginia to northern South America. Western *C. s. inornatus* breeds in the prairie marshes of western North America and some winter on the East Coast.

NJ Status: Common but local summer resident, common spring and fall migrant, very rare to rare winter resident.

Possible
Probable
Confirmed

Breeding

Habitat: Nests in Atlantic coast and Delaware Bay salt marshes.

Historically, Willets nested abundantly in the Atlantic and Delaware Bay salt marshes. Both Wilson (1812) and Turnbull (1869) recorded Willets as one of the most common breeding birds in the saltmarsh. The last nest was recorded on the New Jersey Atlantic Coast in 1889 (Fables 1955). From that time on, Willets were noted as occurring in small numbers or only occurring in spring and fall migration. Stone (1908) recounted the species' demise and considered them to be extirpated as breeding birds, but later he suggested they had probably survived as breeding birds on the Delaware Bay shore (Stone 1937). Willets began to recover in the mid-1900s, and the first New Jersey nest was found in 1952 (Fables1955).

Statewide Summary	
Status	# of Blocks
Possible	18
Probable	42
Confirmed	38
Total	98

Atlas observations indicated the recolonization of Willets has been remarkable. They have become broadly distributed breeding birds throughout appropriate habitat along the Atlantic Coast and Delaware Bay shore. The only section of the Atlantic Coast without Willets is the coastal area of Monmouth County.

Fall: The East Coast population of Willets migrates very early, beginning in late June, even before their young have fledged. Willets are almost entirely coastal migrants, and are very rarely seen inland. Most *C. s. semipalmatus*, the eastern subspecies, have moved through New Jersey by late July or early August, although some may continue migrating through the state into October. Those Willets seen after mid-August are as likely to be the western subspecies, *C. s. inornatus,* as *semipalmatus*. Willets are encountered in only small numbers after early August, and few observers distinguish between the two subspecies when they are found. **Maxima:** 1,000+, Holgate, 22 July 1979; 460, Villas, 16 July 1996.

Winter: Prior to 1990 there were only a handful of Willet records after December, although small numbers were sometimes recorded on CBCs. From 1990 to at least 1995, one bird (suspected to be the same individual) returned each year to winter in the Avalon area. In 1997-1998, five Willets spent the winter at Brigantine Island and four wintered at Hereford Inlet. All winter records are assumed to be the western subspecies *C. s. inornatus*. **CBC Statewide Stats:** Average: 2; Maximum: 14 in 1997; Minimum: 0 in seven years. **CBC Maximum:** 11, Cape May, 1997.

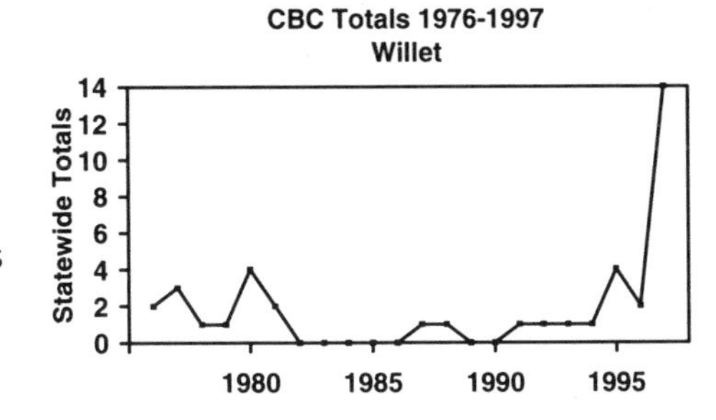

Spring: Willets return to the state in mid-April and quickly occupy nesting territories. They are very rarely seen inland. With so many local breeders present, it is difficult to distinguish local breeding birds from migrants. Most spring migrants are probably *C. s. semipalmatus*. **Maximum:** 120, over Higbee Beach, 26 April 1998. ■

Physiographic Distribution **Willet**	Number of blocks in province	Number of blocks species found breeding in province	Number of blocks species found in state	Percent of province species occupies	Percent of all records for this species found in province	Percent of state area in province
Piedmont	167	1	98	0.6	1.0	19.6
Inner Coastal Plain	128	6	98	4.7	6.1	15.0
Outer Coastal Plain	204	85	98	41.7	86.7	23.9
Pine Barrens	180	6	98	3.3	6.1	21.1

Spotted Sandpiper

Actitis macularia

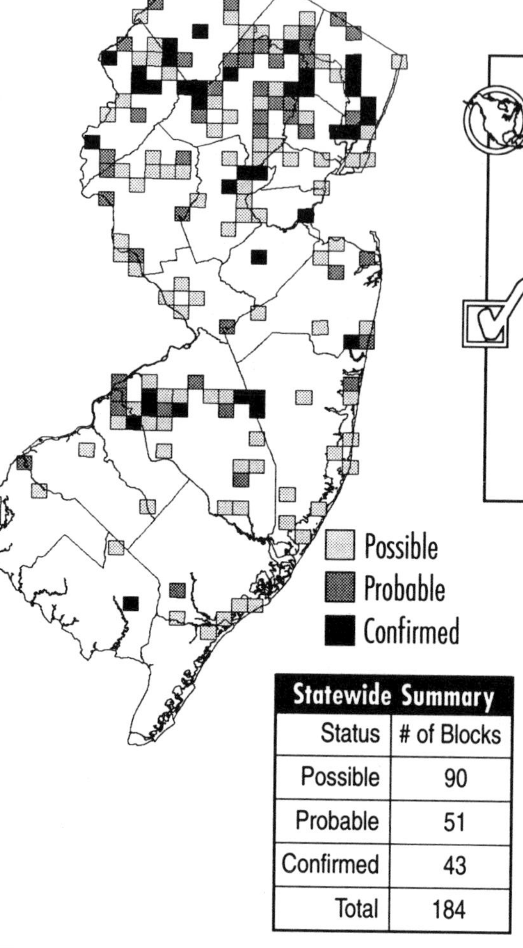

Range: Breeds locally throughout temperate North America, and winters from South Carolina and the Gulf states to South America.

NJ Status: Uncommon and somewhat local summer resident, common spring and fall migrant, reported on six CBCs.

Statewide Summary	
Status	# of Blocks
Possible	90
Probable	51
Confirmed	43
Total	184

Breeding

Habitat: Nests near fresh water in a variety of situations including lakes, ponds, rivers, and streams.

Physiographic Distribution Spotted Sandpiper	Number of blocks in province	Number of blocks species found breeding in province	Number of blocks species found in state	Percent of province species occupies	Percent of all records for this species found in province	Percent of state area in province
Kittatinny Mountains	19	8	184	42.1	4.3	2.2
Kittatinny Valley	45	20	184	44.4	10.9	5.3
Highlands	109	34	184	31.2	18.5	12.8
Piedmont	167	55	184	32.9	29.9	19.6
Inner Coastal Plain	128	30	184	23.4	16.3	15.0
Outer Coastal Plain	204	19	184	9.3	10.3	23.9
Pine Barrens	180	18	184	10.0	9.8	21.1

Early observers recorded Spotted Sandpipers as being quite common (Stone 1908, Griscom 1923), and it is likely they suffered less persecution from hunters and egg collectors than other shorebirds (see Willet, Black-necked Stilt, and American Oystercatcher). However, their habit of nesting near fresh water has probably caused declines due to the loss of freshwater wetlands. Although Stone (1937) knew of five nests on Cape May Island and reported several others along the Atlantic coast, neither Sibley (1997) nor the Atlas participants recorded any nests in the same area.

Historically, Spotted Sandpipers were considered common and were suggested to be abundant. Atlas data indicated their range was distributed among all provinces, but they only occurred in 22% of the blocks statewide. They were found in the lowest densities in the physiographic provinces south of the Piedmont. Surprisingly, there was only one Confirmed nest south of the Camden-Burlington county border, suggesting a marked decline for this species in southern New Jersey. Data from the Pennsylvania Atlas also indicated Spotted Sandpipers were less abundant than historical information suggested (Brauning 1992b).

Map Interpretation: Spotted Sandpipers begin southward migration early, and nonbreeders can linger until late spring. Therefore, the Atlas methods used a very short period of Safe Dates (1-30 June). This limited span should have eliminated migrants, but also may have reduced actual breeding reports.

Conservation Note: This species should be considered a good candidate for monitoring. Spotted Sandpipers have declined in New Jersey, and their patchy distribution could cause further declines to go undetected. Brauning (1992b) also suggested this species had declined in Pennsylvania and that the decline should be monitored.

Fall: Southbound Spotted Sandpipers can be seen by early July, and peak numbers pass from late July through early August. Most have moved through by mid-September. They occur both along the coast and inland. Like Solitary Sandpipers, they are usually seen alone, and maximum counts generally involve birds seen over a wide area. **Maxima:** 44, Sandy Hook, 21 July 1976; 26, Brigantine NWR, 17 August 1996.

Winter: Spotted Sandpipers have lingered late enough to be recorded on six CBCs since 1976 (i.e., 1976, 1978, 1980, 1984, 1985, and 1996), and there are a few other December records of lone individuals. There are, however, no recent reports of birds seen after the Christmas Bird Count season.

Spring: Spotted Sandpipers return in late April, and stragglers are seen into early June. Peak movements usually occur in mid-May. **Maxima:** 50+, Shark River, 29 May 1995; 20, Culvers Lake, 9 May 1988. ■

Upland Sandpiper

Bartramia longicauda

Range: Breeds from Alaska southeast to northern Oklahoma, east to New Brunswick and northern Virginia. Winters in South America.

NJ Status: Scarce and very local summer resident, scarce spring and uncommon fall migrant. Endangered Species in New Jersey.

Possible
Probable
Confirmed

Statewide Summary	
Status	# of Blocks
Possible	3
Probable	4
Confirmed	8
Total	15

Breeding

Habitat: Nests in grassland areas, dry meadows, fields, frequently around airports.

Like most other shorebirds, unrestricted hunting in the 1800s decimated the population of Upland Sandpipers. Unfortunately, at the same time substantial breeding habitat was also lost, and these factors combined to reduce the breeding population in the late 1800s and 1900s (Stone 1908, Griscom 1923,

Physiographic Distribution Upland Sandpiper	Number of blocks in province	Number of blocks species found breeding in province	Number of blocks species found in state	Percent of province species occupies	Percent of all records for this species found in province	Percent of state area in province
Kittatinny Valley	45	4	15	8.9	26.7	5.3
Piedmont	167	3	15	1.8	20.0	19.6
Inner Coastal Plain	128	1	15	0.8	6.7	15.0
Outer Coastal Plain	204	1	15	0.5	6.7	23.9
Pine Barrens	180	6	15	3.3	40.0	21.1

Stone 1937). It is likely that the breeding population has never recovered in New Jersey. Upland Sandpipers rely on an ephemeral habitat for breeding, and it is unsurprising that their current breeding locations differ from those listed in Fables (1955). His broad reference to breeding locations in "the central part of the state" and "Camden, Gloucester and Salem Counties" suggests a wider distribution in those areas in his time than indicated by the Atlas data. Interestingly, Upland Sandpipers may abandon what appears to be appropriate habitat, as was noted in Salem County in 1987 (Meritt 1987). It is unknown if there is a qualitative difference in the habitat that is apparent to the birds, but undetected by human observers, or if local breeding populations disappear from appropriate habitat for other reasons (e.g., hunting on the wintering grounds, poor reproduction, etc.). Pennsylvania Atlas volunteers noted a similar pattern of loss for this species, with birds abandoning what appears to be appropriate breeding habitat (Brauning 1992c).

Atlas data indicated that Upland Sandpipers are one of New Jersey's most rare breeding birds. They have declined dramatically and were recorded in only 15 blocks during five years of field surveys. They are almost wholly restricted to altered habitats (see Conservation Note), and their physiographic distribution is an artifact of the range of those habitats.

Conservation Note: The lack of protection for this species' breeding habitat, and the documented decline in their numbers and range indicate that, without a new strategy of management, Upland Sandpipers may disappear from New Jersey (see RNJB Region 4 reports 1983 through 1990). Currently, Upland Sandpipers' breeding range in New Jersey is almost completely restricted to airports and military facilities, and management at these facilities is critical to this species' survival in the state.

Fall: Southbound Upland Sandpipers typically arrive in mid-July and peak from early to mid-August. Only a few are seen after the end of August. In migration, they prefer large open grassy areas (i.e., sod farms or short-grass fields) either inland or along the coast. As breeding populations in eastern North America have generally declined, so have the numbers of migrants. **Maxima:** Inland: 75, Columbus Sod Farm, 17 August 1980; 66, Columbus Sod Farm, 11 August 1976. Coastal: 43, NAFEC, 13 August 1975.

Spring: Upland Sandpipers are encountered in far fewer numbers in spring than in fall. The first northbound migrants return in mid-April, and a few continue to drift through New Jersey into mid-May. **Maxima:** 6, Featherbed Lane, 26 April 1981; 4, Higbee Beach, 7 April 1993. ■

Eskimo Curlew

Numenius borealis

Occurrence: Eskimo Curlews were once present in large numbers throughout their historic range. In spring, they migrated north through the Mississippi Valley. In fall, they moved east across Canada and then south over the Atlantic to South America. They appeared along the coast only when easterly winds forced flocks to land.

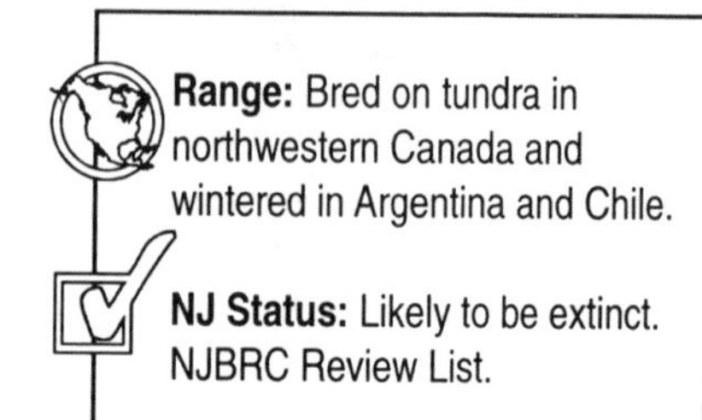

Range: Bred on tundra in northwestern Canada and wintered in Argentina and Chile.

NJ Status: Likely to be extinct. NJBRC Review List.

They declined rapidly during the 1870s and 1880s due to unrestricted hunting. Stone (1937) never saw an Eskimo Curlew in New Jersey, as they had become rare by 1869. A few were shot on the south shore of Long Island from 1875 to 1894, and there were infrequent sight reports after that. There is a specimen in the Denver Museum of Natural History (spec. #14716), taken in Manasquan in the summer of 1880 (Iversen and Kane 1975). Based on this specimen and other evidence, the NJBRC has reviewed their status and has accepted this species on the state list. The last United States record was from Galveston Island, Texas, in the spring of 1962 (Weston and Williams 1965). ■

Whimbrel

Numenius phaeopus

Range: Breeds from Alaska, to Hudson Bay. Winters on the coast from South Carolina to South America.

NJ Status: Common spring and fairly common fall migrant, accidental in winter.

Fall: The first migrant Whimbrels are seen in early July, and numbers peak later in the month. Most have passed through New Jersey by the end of August, but a few trickle through in September. They are rarely seen away from the coast at any season, and prefer the salt marshes to open beaches. In fall, many Whimbrels migrate far offshore. Interestingly, Stone (1937) and Bull (1964) both list fall maxima that exceed their spring totals, but both list spring peaks that are about the same as today. Sibley (1997) listed a maximum count for Cape May County of 1,500 on 8 August 1953 that exceeds all recent high counts. **Other maxima:** 120+, Sea Girt, 26 July 1995; 100+, Avalon, 18 July 1992.

Whimbrel

continued

Whimbrel

Winter: Whimbrels have been seen on two recent Cape May CBCs, in 1991 and in 1995. The bird seen on the 1995 count was present until at least 2 February 1995 in the Nummy Island area and may have successfully wintered.

Spring: Whimbrels are more common in spring than in fall, although northward migration is brief. Birds arrive in mid-April and peak from early to mid-May, with numbers diminishing rapidly thereafter. **Maxima:** 500+, Shellbay Landing, 6 May 1996; 500, Tuckerton, 21 April 1984; 500, Shellbay Landing, 14 May 1984. ■

Long-billed Curlew

Numenius americanus

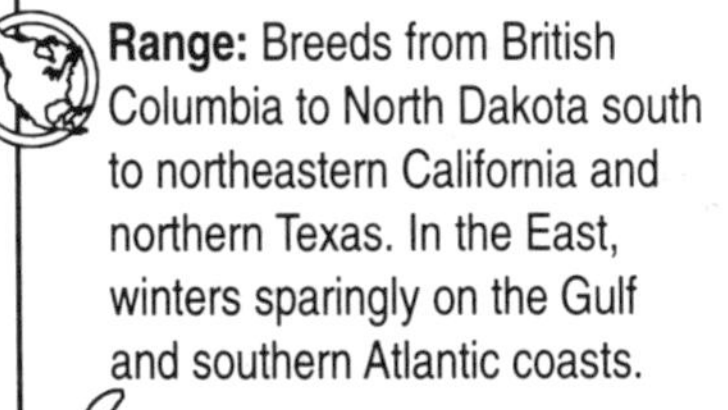

Range: Breeds from British Columbia to North Dakota south to northeastern California and northern Texas. In the East, winters sparingly on the Gulf and southern Atlantic coasts.

NJ Status: Accidental. NJBRC Review List.

Occurrence: Since 1937, there have been six state reports of Long-billed Curlews, and one has been accepted by the NJBRC. Long-billed Curlews were common migrants in the first half of the 1800s, and were found in coastal salt marshes from April-May and September-November. There are suggestions in early writings that a few birds may have summered in the state. By 1877 they had become rare (Stone 1937), and the last New Jersey specimens were single birds shot at:

*Five Mile Beach**	*14 September 1880*	*spec. ANSP*
*Cape May**	*c. 1890*	*spec. ANSP*
Five Mile Beach	*8 September 1898*	

The single recent record accepted by the NJBRC is: Cape May Point, 9 October 1987. ■

Black-tailed Godwit

Limosa limosa

Range: Breeds from Iceland and northwestern Europe east across Asia. Winters from the Mediterranean to Australia.

NJ Status: Accidental. NJBRC Review List.

Occurrence: There has been only one report and one accepted record of Black-tailed Godwit in New Jersey: Brigantine NWR, 22 May-13 September 1971. ■

Hudsonian Godwit

Limosa haemastica

Range: Breeds from Alaska to the shores of Hudson and James bays. Winters in South America.

NJ Status: Very rare spring and scarce to uncommon fall migrant.

Fall: Only a few Hudsonian Godwits are seen in migration prior to mid-August, and they become generally scarce after mid-September. Most migrate far offshore, flying nonstop from James Bay to northern South America. As with other shorebirds, adults precede juveniles. They are most consistently found at Brigantine NWR and are more likely seen after storms with easterly winds. They are rare away from the coast.
Maxima: Coastal: 55, from Cape May-Lewes Ferry, 26 August 1983; 33, South Cape May Meadows, 15 September 1988; Inland: 7, Wallkill sod farms, 17 August 1992.

Spring: Hudsonian Godwits migrate north through the Great Plains in spring; consequently, they are rarely seen along the East Coast. There have been eight spring records from 1975-1998, falling between 30 April and 30 May. Two of those were recorded inland. ■

Bar-tailed Godwit

Limosa lapponica

Range: Breeds from Scandinavia to Siberia and western Alaska. Winters south to Africa and Australia.

NJ Status: Accidental. NJBRC Review List.

Occurrence: There have been seven state reports of Bar-tailed Godwit, and five have been accepted by the NJBRC. All are from the Atlantic Coast. Most are of the nominate European subspecies, but one may have been *L. l. bauerii* which breeds in Siberia and Alaska. Records on both coasts of the United States have increased markedly since about 1970, possibly because of the increase in number of observers versed in the intricacies of shorebird identification.

The five accepted records include one record of what was probably the same individual seen at the Longport sod banks in spring. These sightings span the interval from late April to late May and the years 1972-1982. The records are:

19-24 May 1972	
6-7 May 1973	*ph-RBPF*
*6-20 May 1974**	
*14-19 May 1975**	
7-21 May 1977	*ph-RBPF*
*28 April-21 May 1978**	
20-27 May 1982	*ph-Cassinia 60:54*

The other accepted records are:

Absecon#	*18 July-14 August 1937*	
Beach Haven Inlet#	*"most of August 1951"*	*reported to be baueri*
*Brigantine NWR**	*26 June-28 August 1971*	
Nummy Island	*21 September 1985*	

Marbled Godwit

Limosa fedoa

Range: Breeds mainly in the northern Great Plains from Alberta south to Montana and the Dakotas. Winters on the coast from Virginia south to Central America.

NJ Status: Rare spring and scarce fall migrant, rare winter resident.

Fall: Migrant Marbled Godwits are most consistently recorded in late July and August. Most sightings involve only one or two birds, although groups may assemble at some locations in late fall. Sightings have increased somewhat in the 1990s. **Maxima:** 38, Brigantine NWR, 15 November 1997; 35, Brigantine Island, 26 October 1996.

Winter: Marbled Godwits will sometimes linger into early December and occasionally will winter. Until 1992 they were recorded only occasionally on CBCs, typically as individuals. Since that time numbers wintering have increased. **Maxima:** 12, Brigantine NWR, 12 December 1975; 10, Brigantine Island, 14 December 1983. **CBC Statewide Stats:** Average: 3; Maximum: 21 in 1997; Minimum: 0 in eight years. **CBC Maximum:** 21, Oceanville, 1997.

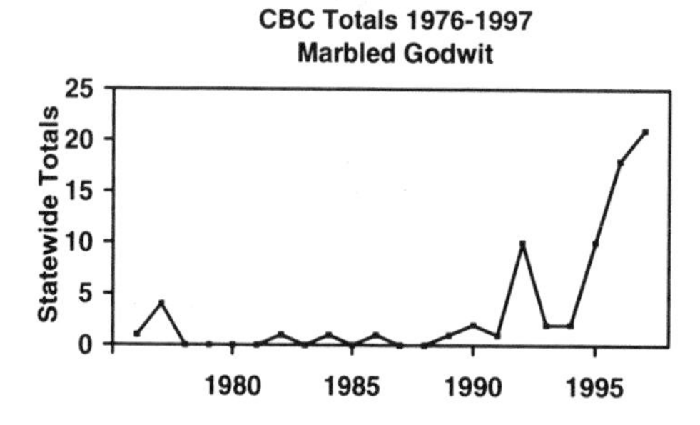

Spring: From 1975 through 1992, Marbled Godwits were recorded during the spring in only three years. However, one or two individuals have been recorded each spring between 1993 and 1998. Most records are in May, except for one at Tuckerton on 24 April 1993. **Maxima:** 3, Brigantine NWR, 20 May 1981; 3, Delaware Bay shore, 20 May 1981. ■

Ruddy Turnstone

Arenaria interpres

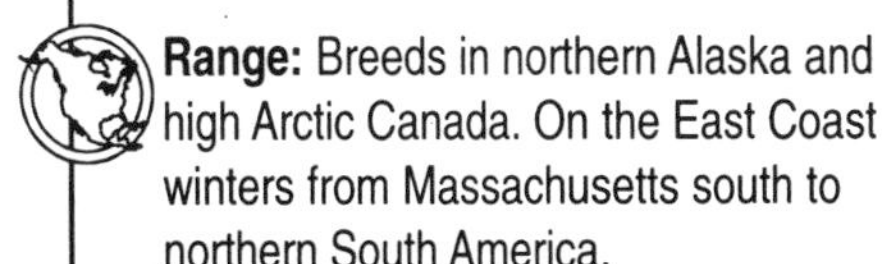

Range: Breeds in northern Alaska and high Arctic Canada. On the East Coast winters from Massachusetts south to northern South America.

NJ Status: Common spring and fall migrant, fairly common winter resident.

Fall: Ruddy Turnstones are present along the coast almost all year. Consequently, it is difficult to pinpoint peak movements in the fall, and maximum numbers generally go unreported. They are most scarce from mid-June to early July. Birds seen after early July are probably migrants rather than summering birds, and numbers of migrants continue to build throughout August. Numbers drop to typical wintering levels in early November. Migrants are only occasionally seen inland. **Maxima:** 500+, Thompson's Beach, 17 August 1997; 100, North Cape May, 10 August 1989.

Winter: Since 1976, CBC numbers of Ruddy Turnstones have been variable, although they have apparently increased as a winter resident since the mid-1960s. Stone (1937) and Bull (1964) considered them rare in winter, while Fables (1955) listed Ruddy Turnstones as casual. **CBC Statewide Stats:** Average: 160; Maximum: 333 in 1976; Minimum: 56 in 1992. **CBC Maximum:** 250, Cape May, 1976.

Spring: Ruddy Turnstone is one of the three main species associated with the Horseshoe Crab phenomenon on the shores of the Delaware Bay (along with Sanderling and Red Knot). Their northbound migration, from mid-May to early June, coincides with the abundant food source provided by the eggs of hundreds of thousands of Horseshoe Crabs. This food provides the Ruddy Turnstones with the fuel they need to complete their migration to the breeding grounds in the Arctic tundra. The density of Ruddy Turnstones and Red Knots along the lower Delaware Bay beaches is arguably the most awesome natural history spectacle in New Jersey. New Jersey ENSP aerial surveys in the 1990s, however, showed a decline in Ruddy Turnstone abundance, possibly related to years of Horseshoe Crab harvesting by bait fishermen. **Maximum:** 67,185, Delaware Bay shore, 27 May 1982. ■

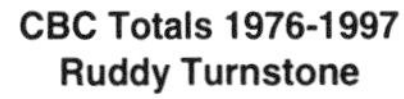

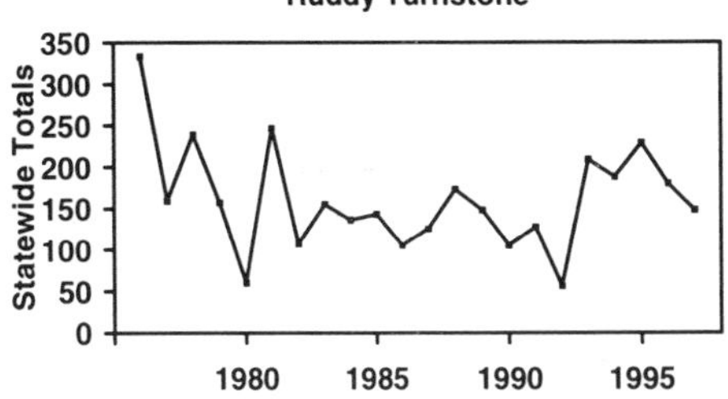

Red Knot
Calidris canutus

Range: Breeds in northern Alaska, and the Canadian Arctic Islands. Winters mainly in South America, but small numbers winter north to Massachusetts and California.

NJ Status: Common spring and fairly common fall migrant, scarce winter resident.

Fall: Southbound Red Knots are present in varying numbers on Atlantic coast beaches and salt marshes from early July into winter. The highest concentrations are generally seen in late July and August. **Maxima:** 1,311, Longport, 4 August 1979; 725, Longport, mid-August 1978.

Winter: Numbers of Red Knots on CBCs have varied considerably, but counts have been distinctly lower since the late 1980s. From 1976 to 1986, the statewide CBCs averaged 75 knots per year, and from 1987 to 1997, the counts averaged three birds per year. Red Knots are typically scarcest in mid-winter, although a few can usually be found around southern beaches and sandbars. **Maxima:** 200, Longport, winter 1978-1979; 150, Longport, winter 1976-1977. **CBC Statewide Stats:** Average: 43; Maximum: 221 in 1976; Minimum: 0 in three years. **CBC Maximum:** 161, Oceanville, 1983.

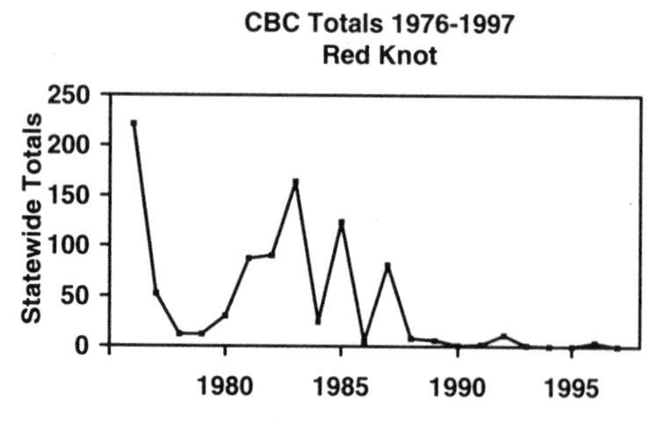

Spring: Along with Sanderling and Ruddy Turnstone, Red Knot is one of the main species whose migration coincides with the abundant food source provided by the egg-laying of hundreds of thousands of Horseshoe Crabs on the shores of Delaware Bay. Estimates indicate that as much as 80% of the North American breeding population of Red Knots use this resource, mainly from mid-May to early June. The New Jersey ENSP aerial surveys in the 1990s showed a decline in this species, and a Threatened Species listing is currently proposed because of the decline. **Maximum:** 54,090, Delaware Bay shore, 21 May 1982. ■

Sanderling
Calidris alba

Range: In North America, breeds in high Arctic Canada. On the East Coast winters from Massachusetts south to South America.

NJ Status: Common spring and fall migrant, common winter resident.

Fall: Sanderlings are present year-round in the state, becoming scarce only from mid- to late June. Returning migrants are noted early in July, and numbers build throughout the late summer and early fall. Peaks in numbers are hard to discern, as Sanderlings seem to be ever-present on sandy beaches, although the highest concentrations probably occur in late September and October. Sanderlings are seen only occasionally inland, and most inland records occur in mid-August to early September. **Maxima:** Coastal: 4,500, Hereford Inlet, 10 September 1989; 3,500+, Stone Harbor Point, 27 September 1993; Inland: 7, Spruce Run Res., 9 September 1983.

Winter: CBC totals of Sanderlings are variable, and some birds may move farther south during particularly harsh winters. **CBC Statewide Stats:** Average: 4,120; Maximum: 10,379 in 1991; Minimum: 1,481 in 1981. **CBC Maximum:** 7,690, Cape May, 1991.

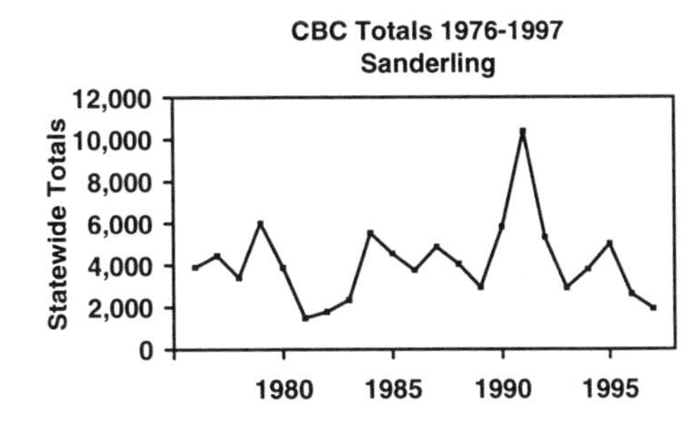

Spring: Sanderlings, along with Ruddy Turnstones and Red Knots, are one of the three main species that take advantage of the food source supplied by the egg-laying of hundreds of thousands of Horseshoe Crabs on the shores of Delaware Bay in May and early June. Sanderlings are never seen in numbers inland, and are even scarcer inland in spring than in fall. **Maximum:** 32,190, Delaware Bay shore, 3 June 1882. ■

Semipalmated Sandpiper

Calidris pusilla

Range: Breeds from Alaska across Canada to northern Labrador. Winters in South America.

NJ Status: Common spring and fall migrant.

Fall: Semipalmated Sandpipers are one of the most common shorebirds seen in fall migration in the state. They arrive from early to mid-July, with peak numbers seen from late July through early August. All July birds, and most early August birds, are adults. Juveniles arrive in mid-August and become more common than adults in September. Numbers diminish through October, with very few lingering into November. Most are seen along the coast, but they can be fairly common inland. Past reports of Semipalmated Sandpipers on CBCs are now attributed to Western Sandpiper. **Maxima:** Coastal: 10,000+, North Arlington, 29 July 1991; 10,000+, Brigantine NWR, 12 August 1995; 10,000+, Brigantine NWR, 29 August 1998; Inland: 150, Spruce Run Res., 25 August 1995.

Spring: The timing of spring migration of Semipalmated Sandpiper is condensed, with the bulk of the birds passing from mid-May to early June. The highest concentrations are found along the Delaware Bay shore, where they take advantage of the abundant food source provided by Horseshoe Crab eggs. They are generally scarce inland in spring. **Maxima:** Coastal: 57,650, Delaware Bay shore, 21 May 1982; 50,000, Hay Neck, 20 May 1992; Inland: 12, Harmony, 23 May 1990. ■

Western Sandpiper

Calidris mauri

Range: In North America breeds in Arctic Alaska. On the East Coast, winters from southern New Jersey to Florida, south to South America.

NJ Status: Very rare spring and common fall migrant, rare to scarce winter resident.

Fall: Western Sandpipers typically arrive from early to mid-July, but highest concentrations are seen from late August through early September when adult and juvenile migrations overlap. They occur into late fall, with birds lingering into December. Westerns are scarce inland, but they do occur with some regularity (e.g., dozens in the Allentown/

Western Sandpiper

continued

New Sharon area in August 1989). **Maxima:** 2,500 Brigantine NWR, 7 September 1975; 800, Brigantine NWR, 28 August 1987.

Winter: CBC totals of Western Sandpipers vary widely from year to year, seemingly with the weather conditions prior to and during the count period. Even in years with high CBC totals westerns are difficult to find in mid-winter, as they may be forced farther south. In the southern part of the state, there are records of birds that have spent the winter, but numbers are low and irregular. **CBC Statewide Stats:** Average: 81; Maximum: 492 in 1988; Minimum: 3 in 1981. **CBC Maximum:** 484, Cape May, 1988.

Spring: Most Western Sandpipers migrate north through the interior of the United States. At best, they may occur in the state only as vagrants in spring. Even if all published records of spring migrants in New Jersey are accurate, Western Sandpipers are less than annual in occurrence. Reports from April probably represent wintering birds and not passage migrants. Reports from mid- to late May coincide with peak movements of Semipalmated Sandpipers and have prompted Sibley (1997) to state "despite published reports there are no documented spring records" of Western Sandpiper for Cape May County. ■

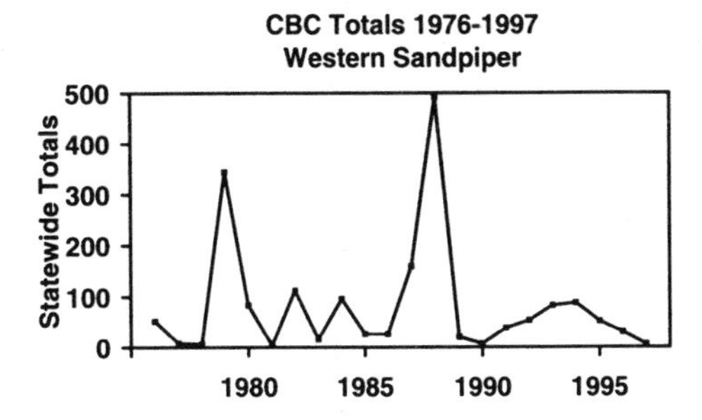

Little Stint

Calidris minuta

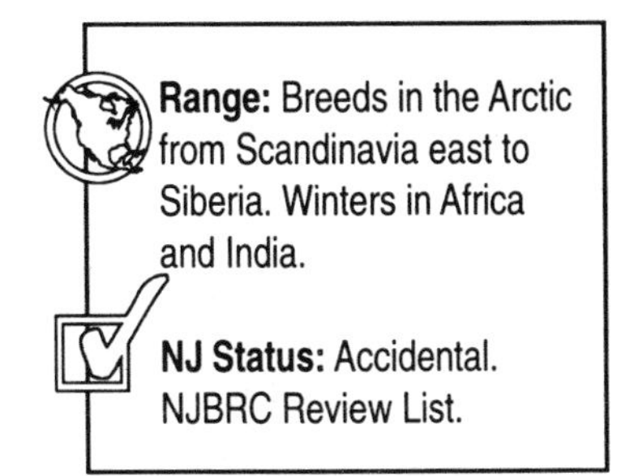

Range: Breeds in the Arctic from Scandinavia east to Siberia. Winters in Africa and India.

NJ Status: Accidental. NJBRC Review List.

Occurrence: There have been eight state reports of Little Stint, and two have been accepted by the NJBRC. The two accepted records, noted to be separate individuals, are:

Brigantine NWR	*22 July 1985*	
Brigantine NWR	*24 July 1985*	*Barber 1985*

Least Sandpiper

Calidris minutilla

Range: Breeds from Alaska to Newfoundland. In the East, winters from North Carolina and northern Texas south to South America.

NJ Status: Common spring and fall migrant, very rare winter resident.

Fall: Southbound adult Least Sandpipers arrive in early July, with numbers building to a peak from late July through early August, when they are joined by the first juveniles. Numbers begin to decline after mid-September, although some may remain past November. Least Sandpipers are quite common inland. **Maxima:** Coastal: 4,000 to 8,000, Brigantine NWR, 28 August 1992; 2,000, Kearny, 7 August 1982; Inland: 287, Spruce Run Res., 14 August 1998.

Winter: Least Sandpipers have been recorded on 11 CBCs since 1976, but rarely have birds successfully wintered. Recent records include eight that wintered at Nummy Island in 1993, and eight that were seen until at least 28 January 1995 at Wildwood Crest. **CBC Statewide Stats:** Average: 3; Maximum: 14 in 1992; Minimum: 0 in 12 years. **CBC Maximum:** 14, Cumberland County, 1992.

Spring: The northward migration of Least Sandpipers begins in early April, peaks from early to mid-May, and ends in early June. They are fairly common inland at this season, but less common than in fall. **Maxima:** Coastal: 1,000s, Moore's Beach, 6 May 1987; 1,000, Mannington Marsh, 18 May 1990; Inland: 30, Great Swamp, 16 May 1983; 30, Lake Watchung, 6 May 1980. ■

Least Sandpiper

White-rumped Sandpiper

Calidris fuscicollis

Range: Breeds in Arctic Alaska and Canada, south and east to Baffin Island. Winters in South America.

NJ Status: Uncommon spring and fairly common fall migrant, reported on two CBCs.

Fall: Southbound White-rumped Sandpipers arrive in early August, with peak movements noted from late August through early September. They can be found in declining numbers into November. Much of their fall migration is well offshore. White-rumped Sandpipers can be common after storms with easterly winds, as offshore migrants are presumably blown to the mainland. They are regular but generally uncommon inland. **Maxima:** Coastal: 294, Brigantine NWR, 21 August 1990; 200, Brigantine NWR, 18 August 1995; Inland: 170+, New Sharon, 22 August 1994.

Winter: Since 1976 there have been two reports of White-rumped Sandpipers on CBCs (i.e., 1979 and 1982). There are no other winter reports.

Spring: Most White-rumped Sandpipers return north through the Great Plains or the Mississippi River Valley. Those that pass through New Jersey are seen from mid-May to early June. In some years they occur in good numbers along the Delaware Bay shore, mixed with the large flocks of Semipalmated Sandpipers. They are rare to scarce inland. **Maxima:** 150, Mannington Marsh, 20 May 1992; 100+, Brigantine NWR, 25 May 1995. ■

Baird's Sandpiper

Calidris bairdii

Range: Breeds in Arctic Alaska and Canada, southeast to Baffin Island. Winters in South America.

NJ Status: Accidental spring and scarce fall migrant, reported on one CBC.

Fall: Most Baird's Sandpipers migrate through the Great Plains in both spring and fall. They occur in New Jersey between mid-August and mid-September. Adults are very rare. **Maxima:** Coastal: 10, Brigantine NWR, 8 September 1992; 6, Brigantine NWR, 27 August 1995; Inland: 4, Spruce Run Res., 17 September 1980.

continued on page 258

continued from page 257

Baird's Sandpiper

Winter: The most unusual record of a Baird's Sandpiper in New Jersey was one seen on the Cape May CBC in 1987. There are no other winter records for this species.

Spring: There are a few reports of Baird's Sandpipers in spring, but their extreme rarity in the northeastern United States at that season would preclude accepting any sightings without sufficient documentation. ■

Pectoral Sandpiper

Calidris melanotos

Range: Breeds in Arctic Alaska and Canada east to Hudson Bay. Winters in South America.

NJ Status: Fairly common spring and common fall migrant.

Fall: Southward migration of Pectoral Sandpipers is protracted, with two distinct peaks. Adults generally arrive in late July, and peak from mid- to late August. Juveniles peak much later, from late September to mid-October, and migration continues to early November. Given their preference for wet fields and meadows, they are also quite common inland. **Maxima:** Coastal: 100s, Cape May Point, 17 October 1991; 150+, Brigantine NWR, 23 October 1994; Inland: 200, Clarkesville Sod Farm, 24 August 1991.

Spring: Most Pectoral Sandpipers migrate north along the Mississippi River Valley. Stone (1937) never recorded a Pectoral Sandpiper in spring in Cape May County, but the species has become more common since that time. Pectoral Sandpipers are early migrants, with a few arriving in the state in late March, and peak in mid-April. They become scarce after early May. Pectorals are regular inland, but less common inland in spring than in the fall. **Maxima:** Coastal: 621, Pedricktown, 7 April 1986; 400, Pedricktown, 9 April 1983; Inland: 43, Dutch Neck, 9 April 1978. ■

Purple Sandpiper

Calidris maritima

Range: In North America, breeds in high Arctic Canada south to northern Hudson Bay. Winters along the coast from Newfoundland to North Carolina.

NJ Status: Fairly common spring and fall migrant, common winter resident.

Fall: The first Purple Sandpipers can arrive along the coast as early as the beginning of October, but they become more regular in early November. **Maximum:** 300, Barnegat Inlet, 30 November 1996.

Winter: Purple Sandpipers are present along the coast throughout the winter. They confine themselves to jetties and breakwaters, and they did not winter in the state prior to the building of rock jetties in the early 1920s (Stone 1937). **Maxima:** 350, Cold Spring Jetty, 9 March 1991; 250+, Cape May Point, 30 March 1991. **CBC Statewide Stats:** Average: 400; Maximum: 903 in 1977; Minimum: 109 in 1992. **CBC Maximum:** 450, Cape May, 1984.

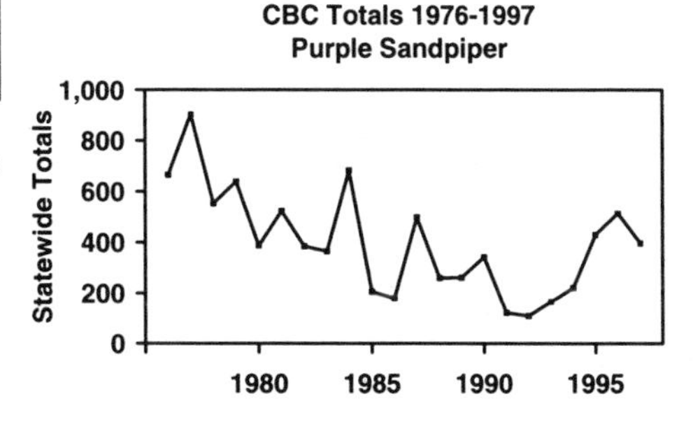

Spring: Purple Sandpipers are present into mid-May or rarely into early June. There are few records of Purple Sandpipers summering in New Jersey. ■

Dunlin

Calidris alpina

Range: In North America breeds in high Arctic Canada, south to Hudson Bay. On the East Coast, winters from Massachusetts to Florida, and along the Gulf coast to Texas.

NJ Status: Common spring and fall migrant, common winter resident.

Fall: Only a few Dunlin are seen before mid-September, and numbers peak from late October to early November. Southbound migrants are regularly seen inland in small numbers. **Maxima:** Coastal: 16,000, Hereford Inlet, 17 November 1993; 13,000, Brigantine NWR, 16 November 1985; Inland: 18, Spruce Run Res., 22 October 1982.

continued on page 260

continued from page 259

Dunlin

Winter: Large numbers of Dunlin remain throughout the winter along New Jersey's coast where they are the most common shorebird. Statewide CBC totals are variable, with years of high counts probably related to mild weather prior to the count period. Numbers drop somewhat in mid-winter as birds continue to move south. **Maxima:** 4,000, Avalon, winter 1991-1992; 4,000, Stone Harbor Point, 2 January 1990. **CBC Statewide Stats:** Average: 12,576; Maximum: 38,791 in 1984; Minimum: 5,503 in 1981. **CBC Maximum:** 34,440, Cape May, 1984.

CBC Totals 1976-1997
Dunlin

Statewide Totals: 40,000; 35,000; 30,000; 25,000; 20,000; 15,000; 10,000; 5,000; 0
1980 1985 1990 1995

Spring: The northward migration of Dunlin peaks in New Jersey in early May. Some Dunlin avail themselves of the rich food source created by egg-laying Horseshoe Crabs, but they occur in relatively small numbers on the Delaware Bay beaches and seem to prefer tidal mudflats. They are much rarer inland in spring than in fall. **Maxima:** Coastal: 10,000+, Thompson's Beach, 22 March 1998; 10,000, Hay Neck, 14 April 1992; 10,000, Shellbay Landing, 1 May 1992; Inland: 11, Stewartsville, 16 April 1983. ■

Curlew Sandpiper

Calidris ferruginea

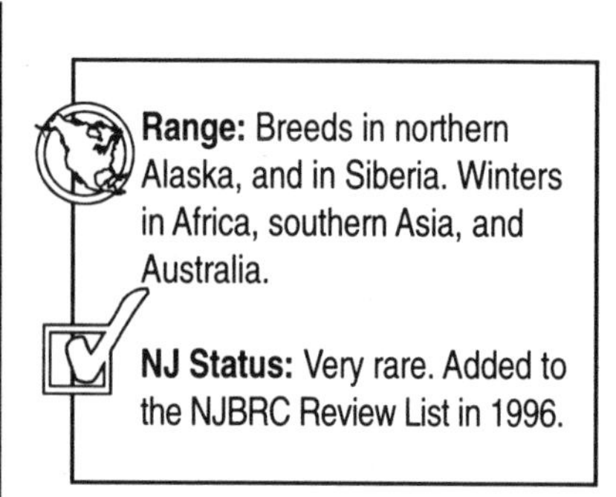

Range: Breeds in northern Alaska, and in Siberia. Winters in Africa, southern Asia, and Australia.

NJ Status: Very rare. Added to the NJBRC Review List in 1996.

Occurrence: Since the addition of Curlew Sandpiper to the NJBRC Review List in 1996 there have been five state reports, although none have been accepted by the NJBRC. The NJBRC has not undertaken a review of all historic reports. Curlew Sandpipers have been reported in New Jersey in all but one or two years since 1950, and the first state report was a specimen taken in 1829 (Stone 1937). Most spring reports are from May, and fall movement is mainly from July through September, with a few reports into November. The only winter report was of one from Jersey City, 15 December 1985. There is only one certain record of a juvenile Curlew Sandpiper from Columbus, 8 September 1996 (ph-RNJB 22:105). There is a decline in the number of reports in the 1990s. ■

Stilt Sandpiper

Calidris himantopus

Range: Breeds from Alaska southeast to northern Ontario. Winters in the southeastern United States to South America.

NJ Status: Rare spring and common fall migrant.

Fall: Adult Stilt Sandpipers begin their southbound passage in early July, and numbers peak from late July to early August. Kaufman (1996) indicated that juveniles peak about a month after adults, and in New Jersey a second peak from late August to early September involves mainly juveniles. Stilt Sandpipers numbers dwindle by the end of September. They are scarce inland, and, given the dates of occurrence, many of the inland records are probably of juveniles. **Maxima:** Coastal: 465, Brigantine NWR, 30 July 1981; 270, Brigantine NWR, 21 August 1990; Inland: 6, Spruce Run Res., 24 September 1985.

Spring: Most Stilt Sandpipers migrate north through the Great Plains. As of 1937, Stone knew of only one spring record for the state. There are now a few records each spring, typically of individual birds. Most records are from May, but there are a few from April, and two from late March. **Maxima:** 8-10, Goshen Landing, 11 May 1989; 6, Moore's Beach, 7 May 1984. ■

Buff-breasted Sandpiper

Tryngites subruficollis

Range: Breeds in high Arctic Alaska and Canada. Winters in South America.

NJ Status: Accidental spring and scarce to uncommon fall migrant.

Fall: Most Buff-breasted Sandpipers migrate through the Great Plains in both spring and fall. Their occurrence along the East Coast is mainly restricted to fall, and most birds seen are juveniles. Southbound migration occurs mainly between mid-August and mid-September, with a peak in early September. The species is regular inland, particularly on sod farms. Sibley (1997) listed only three occurrences of adults in Cape May County, one of which involved a flock of 17 on 2 August 1981. **Maxima:** 89, Brigantine NWR, 8 September 1995; 66, South Cape May Meadows, 2 September 1981.

Spring: There is one recent report of a Buff-breasted Sandpiper for spring, on 29 May 1972 in West Cape May. This species is extremely rare on the East Coast in spring. ■

Ruff

Philomachus pugnax

Fall: The occurrence of Ruffs in New Jersey goes back to a specimen from the late 1800's (Fables 1955), and the first sight record is of two on 2 October 1932 at Tuckerton (Stone 1937). Sightings of southbound Ruffs occur mainly along the Atlantic coast, between late June and mid-September. Most records are of single individuals.

Range: Breeds across northern Europe and Asia. Winters in southern Europe and Africa.

NJ Status: Rare to scarce spring and rare fall migrant.

Spring: Ruffs are more often encountered in spring than fall, and records span the dates 12 March to 29 May, with a peak from early to mid-April. The recent history of Ruff centers on the marshes of Pedricktown, where a string of spring sightings in the late 1970s led to an annual Ruff Watch at that location. Numbers peaked there in the mid-1980s when there were estimates of as many as 12 birds during spring 1985. **Seasonal maxima** (all at Pedricktown): 12 in spring 1985, 8 in spring 1984, 8 in spring 1992. ■

Short-billed Dowitcher

Limnodromus griseus

Range: Three subspecies breed in three distinct areas: southern Alaska (*L. g. caurinus*), northern Yukon east to Hudson Bay (*L. g. hendersoni*), and northern Quebec and Labrador (*L. g. griseus*). On the East Coast, winters from North Carolina south to South America.

NJ Status: Common spring and fall migrant, very rare winter resident.

Fall: Southbound adult Short-billed Dowitchers arrive in late June and peak from mid- to late July. A second peak of juveniles occurs in August. Numbers diminish by mid-September, although a few Short-billed Dowitchers linger much later. They are occasionally seen inland, but are generally scarce. The subspecies *L. g. griseus* is the predominant migrant in the state, although *L. g. hendersoni* occurs in fall in small numbers. Sibley (1997) estimated *L. g.*

Short-billed Dowitcher

continued

hendersoni at 10-20% of all dowitchers. **Maxima:** Coastal: 10,000, Brigantine NWR, 26 July 1981; 7,000, Brigantine NWR, 2 August 1990; Inland: 9, Harmony, 23 August 1975.

Winter: Sightings of dowitchers in mid-winter are rare and could be either short-billed or long-billed. Long-billed Dowitchers are generally considered to be more likely, but because only calling birds are safely identifiable, most seen are left unidentified. One Short-billed Dowitcher (identified by voice) on Nummy Island was present to at least 10 February 1995. **CBC Statewide Stats:** Average: 1; Maximum: 6 in 1985; Minimum: 0 in 13 years. **CBC Maxima:** 3, Lower Hudson, 1985; 3, Cape May, 1992.

Spring: Northbound Short-billed Dowitchers arrive in mid-April, peak in early May, and some continue through the month. Most spring birds are considered to be *L. g. griseus*. **Maxima:** Coastal: 1,500, Nummy Island, 7 May 1990; 1,000+, Grassy Sound, 4 May 1995; Inland: 20+, Culver's Lake, 24 May 1989. ■

Long-billed Dowitcher

Limnodromus scolopaceus

Range: In North America breeds in northern and western Alaska and the northern Northwest Territories. Winters from Virginia south to Central America.

NJ Status: Very rare spring and uncommon fall migrant, very rare winter resident.

Fall: Long-billed Dowitchers begin their migration at least a month later than Short-billed Dowitchers. Adults migrate first, but are scarce before the end of July; juveniles are first seen in early September. Peak Long-billed Dowitcher numbers occur from late September through early October. Brigantine NWR is the most consistent location to see Long-billed Dowitchers in high numbers, as they are scarce elsewhere along the coast, and rare inland. **Maxima:** 1,000, Brigantine NWR, 15 October 1993; 310, Brigantine NWR, 11 October 1994.

Winter: Outside of a recent high count (see below), Long-billed Dowitchers are seen only occasionally on CBCs. In mid-winter any dowitchers seen could be either short-billed or long-billed, although Long-billed Dowitchers are generally considered more likely. Five seen and heard throughout the winter of 1991-1992 near Wildwood Crest constitute one positive wintering record. Nevertheless, winter dowitcher sightings are rare, and only calling birds are

continued on page 264

continued from page 263

Long-billed Dowitcher

safely identifiable. **CBC Statewide Stats:** Average: 2; Maximum: 17 in 1995; Minimum: 0 in 11 years. **CBC Maximum:** 17, Oceanville, 1995.

Spring: Long-billed Dowitchers are very rare in spring, but there are a few well-documented records from late March through mid-April. The Short-billed Dowitcher sub-species *L. g. hendersoni*, which is very similar in plumage to Long-billed Dowitcher, may be present in spring and could cause complications in identification. ■

Common Snipe

Gallinago gallinago

Range: In eastern North America, breeds from Manitoba east to Newfoundland, south to northern Oklahoma and northern New Jersey. On the East Coast winters from Massachusetts south to northern South America.

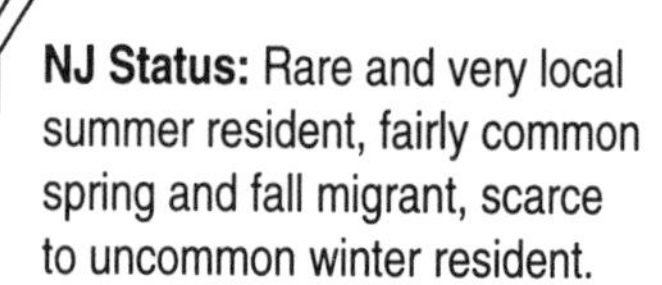

NJ Status: Rare and very local summer resident, fairly common spring and fall migrant, scarce to uncommon winter resident.

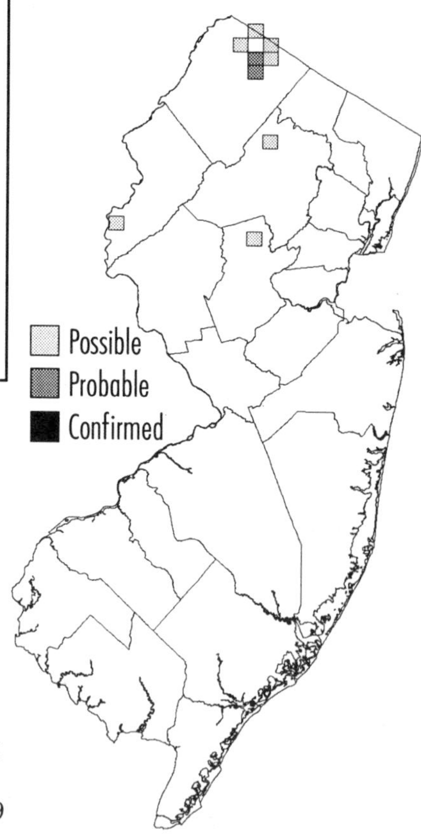

Breeding

Habitat: Breeds in wet meadows, and around freshwater marshes and bogs.

Historically, there have only been a few Common Snipe nests found in New Jersey. All historic nests were found in northern New Jersey, including a sketchy account of injured birds breeding at Chatham in Morris County in 1879

Common Snipe

continued

(Bull 1964), and an undated account from Newfoundland in Passaic County (Stone 1908). A more recent breeding record of an adult with young was reported in Franklin in 1950 (Fables 1955). In 1989 a nest with eggs was found and photographed at Naval Weapons Station Earle in Monmouth County (Radis 1990).

One of New Jersey's rarest breeding birds, Common Snipe were not Confirmed breeding during the Atlas surveys. The inland-nesting shorebirds - American Woodcock and Common Snipe - are very difficult to locate on the nest. Their nests and young are cryptically colored and notoriously difficult to find. The most promising breeding locations for this species are along the marshes of the Wallkill River, where the two Probable blocks were located during the Atlas research period. Birds lingering past early May should be considered potential nesting birds.

Fall: A few southbound Common Snipe arrive in late July. They become more numerous by mid-September and continue to move through early November, without a well-defined peak in numbers. They are widespread in fall, and usually occur in only small concentrations. **Maxima:** 39, Elmer Lake, 19 November 1984; 25, Moorestown, 15 November 1983.

Winter: Common Snipe are usually present in fair numbers throughout the CBC season, but numbers drop later in winter after hard freezes. CBC numbers are variable, but appear to be declining. **CBC Statewide Stats:** Average: 100; Maximum: 242 in 1976; Minimum: 37 in 1997. **CBC Maximum:** 69, Trenton Marsh, 1981.

continued on page 266

Statewide Summary	
Status	# of Blocks
Possible	7
Probable	2
Confirmed	0
Total	9

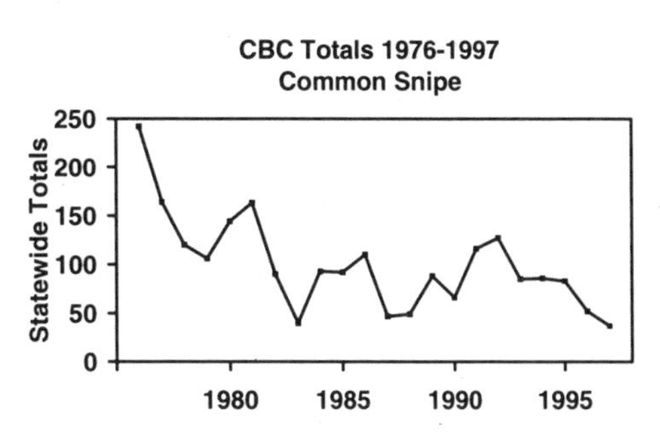

Physiographic Distribution Common Snipe	Number of blocks in province	Number of blocks species found breeding in province	Number of blocks species found in state	Percent of province species occupies	Percent of all records for this species found in province	Percent of state area in province
Kittatinny Valley	45	6	9	13.3	66.7	5.3
Highlands	109	2	9	1.8	22.2	12.8
Piedmont	167	1	9	0.6	11.1	19.6

continued from page 265

Common Snipe

Spring: Northward migration of Common Snipe is early, beginning in mid-March and peaking from early to mid-April, and numbers diminish rapidly after early May. Movements are widespread throughout the state. Common Snipe are more often seen in larger concentrations in spring than in fall. **Maxima:** 200, Mannington Marsh, 31 March 1990; 100, Pedricktown, 3 April 1979; 100, South Cape May Meadows, 15 April 1996. ■

Eurasian Woodcock

Scolopax rusticola

Range: Breeds across most of Europe, east to central Asia. Winters from western Europe and northern Africa to China and Japan.

NJ Status: Accidental. NJBRC Review List.

Occurrence: There have been three state reports of Eurasian Woodcocks, and two have been accepted by the NJBRC. According to Stone (1937), the following Shrewsbury specimen was a bird bought in the Washington Market in New York City. In addition to the Goshen record, the only other 20th century record from the United States was one in Ohio in 1937 (Peterjohn 1989).The two accepted records are:

Shrewsbury	*6 December 1859*	*spec. AMNH #45603*
Goshen	*2-9 January 1956*	

American Woodcock

Scolopax minor

Range: Breeds from southeastern Manitoba east to southern Newfoundland, south to eastern Texas and Georgia. On the East Coast, winters from Massachusetts to Florida

NJ Status: Fairly common but somewhat local summer resident, uncommon spring and fairly common fall migrant, uncommon winter resident.

Breeding

Habitat: Breeds along wooded edges of open fields.

Accounts of the status of the American Woodcock population in New Jersey post-1900 all suggested a general downward trend. Stone (1908) reported American Woodcocks had declined as breeding birds. Griscom (1923) indicated they were still fairly common breeding birds, but decreasing. Cruickshank (1942) contended that they were only decreasing slightly,

American Woodcock

continued

Statewide Summary	
Status	# of Blocks
Possible	51
Probable	168
Confirmed	38
Total	257

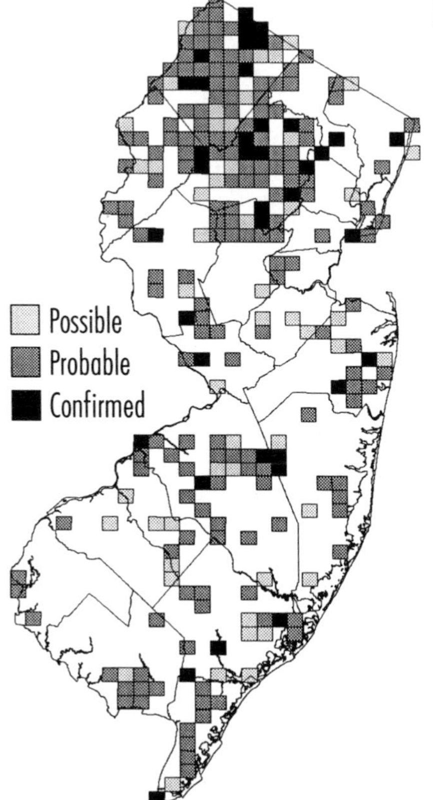

but he was writing 30 years after Stone reported their decline, and his baseline for the population was probably lower than Stone's. The largest declines probably predated the end of summer hunting and prior to increased hunting management during migration. Modern observers may be unable to appreciate the scale of the take prior to management actions: Bull (1964) reported that one individual shot 120 birds on 4 July 1868 near Chatham.

American Woodcocks were found in all provinces, however, their distribution was skewed to the provinces north of the Piedmont. They were found in 53-89% of the blocks in the Kittatinny Mountains, Kittatinny Valley, and Highlands. The Highlands is an important area for this species. Although the province only accounts for 13% of the state's

continued on page 268

Physiographic Distribution — American Woodcock	Number of blocks in province	Number of blocks species found breeding in province	Number of blocks species found in state	Percent of province species occupies	Percent of all records for this species found in province	Percent of state area in province
Kittatinny Mountains	19	17	257	89.5	6.6	2.2
Kittatinny Valley	45	30	257	66.7	11.7	5.3
Highlands	109	58	257	53.2	22.6	12.8
Piedmont	167	48	257	28.7	18.7	19.6
Inner Coastal Plain	128	26	257	20.3	10.1	15.0
Outer Coastal Plain	204	35	257	17.2	13.6	23.9
Pine Barrens	180	43	257	23.9	16.7	21.1

continued from page 267

American Woodcock

area, it holds 23% of the blocks occupied by American Woodcocks. The southern provinces had lower percentages of blocks occupied (from 17-29%).

Fall: Woodcocks are present all year, particularly in southern and coastal sections of the state. Additionally, they migrate at night and are secretive during the day, which makes it difficult to determine peak periods of movements. Concentrations of migrants at Cape May occur from early to mid-November. **Maxima:** 100s, Cape May Point, 30 October 1988; 120 in 1/2 hour, Villas, 9 November 1995.

CBC Totals 1976-1997
American Woodcock

Statewide Totals: 0, 50, 100, 150, 200
1980, 1985, 1990, 1995

Winter: CBC numbers vary considerably, as deep freezes are especially hard on woodcocks. When the ground freezes American Woodcocks are unable to feed easily. Under such stress, they can then be seen along roadsides feeding in sunny patches, something they normally would not do. **CBC Statewide Stats:** Average: 63; Maximum: 187 in 1990; Minimum: 31 in 1987. **CBC Maximum:** 160, Cape May, 1990.

Spring: Spring migration of American Woodcocks is difficult to detect, as breeders begin to move back into the state as soon as weather permits, usually by late February. **Maximum:** 100, Great Swamp, 28 February 1997. ■

Wilson's Phalarope

Phalaropus tricolor

Range: Breeds from British Columbia east to Ontario, south to northern California and Kansas. Winters in South America.

NJ Status: Rare spring and scarce to uncommon fall migrant.

Fall: Most Wilson's Phalaropes migrate through the Great Plains in fall, although small numbers are seen along the East Coast. Southbound adult females can move very early, by mid-June, followed shortly thereafter by adult males. Juveniles, however, are more commonly encountered than adults. Most birds seen after mid-August are juveniles, and they may be present into late September. **Maxima:** 11, Brigantine NWR, 13 August 1988; 9, South Cape May Meadows, 11 August 1982; 9, Brigantine NWR, early August 1987.

Wilson's Phalarope

continued

Spring: Most northbound Wilson's Phalaropes move through the Great Plains. Very few are seen in New Jersey, and those that have been recorded are generally found in mid-May. **Maxima:** 5, North Arlington, 23 May 1976; 4, South Cape May Meadows, 18 May 1987. ■

Red-necked Phalarope

Phalaropus lobatus

Range: Breeds from Alaska east across northern Canada to northern Labrador. Winters at sea; wintering areas poorly defined.

NJ Status: Rare spring and rare to scarce fall migrant onshore; apparently much more regular offshore.

Fall: Red-necked Phalaropes are primarily pelagic outside of the breeding season. Other than one report from early July, fall records span the dates 24 July to 8 October, with a peak from late August through early September. A majority of the onshore records come from Brigantine NWR. Most other sightings come from elsewhere along the coast, but there are a few records inland. They are probably much more common offshore than records indicate, but relatively few observers are present offshore during peak movements. Also, since they typically sit on the water, they can be difficult to detect unless flushed. **Maxima:** 13, North Arlington, 7 August 1975; 11, Brigantine NWR, 26 August 1995.

Spring: Outside of one mid-April report, spring records of Red-necked Phalaropes span the dates 1 May to 6 June, peaking from mid- to late May. Onshore sightings are rare, usually involving individual birds. Offshore sightings, typically from pelagic trips, produce higher counts. These sightings are restricted to the few times each year when birders charter pelagic trips, and it is likely that if there were more trips there would be more sightings. **Maxima:** 35, pelagic trip to Hudson Canyon, 29 May 1982; 18, pelagic trip to Hudson Canyon, 31 May 1976. **Maxima onshore:** 12, Kearny Marsh, 20 May 1979; 8, North Arlington, 17 May 1976. ■

Red Phalarope

Phalaropus fulicaria

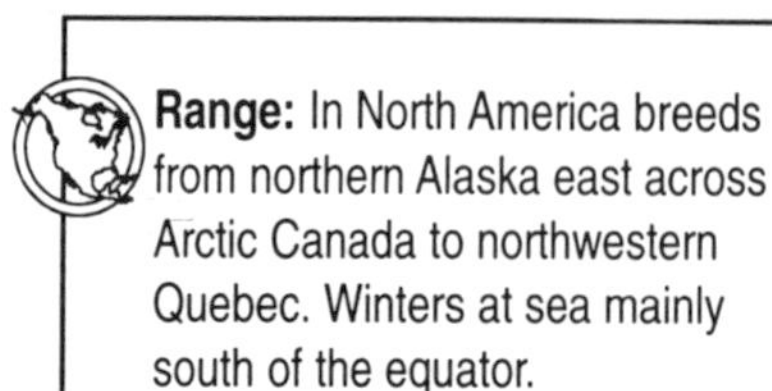

Range: In North America breeds from northern Alaska east across Arctic Canada to northwestern Quebec. Winters at sea mainly south of the equator.

NJ Status: Rare spring and fall migrant, more regular offshore.

Spring: In spring, Red Phalaropes are recorded from late March to mid-May, with a few records extending to late-May. Most onshore records are of single individuals, and there are at least four recent records inland. They are more regular offshore. One offshore report from 18 April 1980 had a staggering 17,000 about 50 miles east of Atlantic City. **Other maximum:** 45, 70 miles east of Cape May, 27 March 1989. ■

Fall: Red Phalaropes are pelagic outside of the breeding season. They occur later in fall than Red-necked Phalaropes. Most occur from September to early November, although a few may linger into December. They are very rarely seen on inland lakes. **Maximum:** 130, pelagic trip to Hudson Canyon, 20 November 1977.

Great Skua

Catharacta skua

Range: Breeds in high latitudes from Greenland to Norway. Pelagic while immature and during the nonbreeding season, ranging at sea throughout the North Atlantic.

NJ Status: Accidental. NJBRC Review List.

Occurrence: There have been 27 reports of Great Skua or skua sp. (17 in fall/winter, ten in May/June) since the first report off Avalon, 13 June 1969 (Leck 1984). Three records have been accepted by the NJBRC as Great Skua, and four have been accepted as skua sp. Identification of skuas is difficult, and there is also the possibility that additional species of skua might occur in New Jersey waters (Brady 1988; Lehman 1998a). Skuas occur regularly only far offshore, and the small number of reports reflects the limited number of the times that observers have been at the continental shelf. Rowlett (1980b) conducted pelagic surveys in the northern Chesapeake Bight including waters off the mouth of Delaware Bay and east of the Cape May Peninsula. He found

Great Skua

continued

skua sp. to be regular from December to March, but was unable to document a Great Skua record for New Jersey.

The three Great Skua records are:

100 miles E of the mouth of Delaware Bay	*1 December 1991*
pelagic trip to Hudson Canyon	*14 December 1991*
28 miles SE of Cape May	*19 February 1995*

The four accepted as skua sp. are:

pelagic trip to Hudson Canyon	*5 June 1976*	*reported as Great Skua*
pelagic trip to Hudson Canyon	*28 May 1977*	*phs- AB 31:1108, 1117; RNJB 23:78*
60-70 miles E of Cape May	*30 May 1987*	*ph-RBPF; reported as Great Skua*
Manasquan Inlet	*2 February 1991*	

South Polar Skua

Catharacta maccormicki

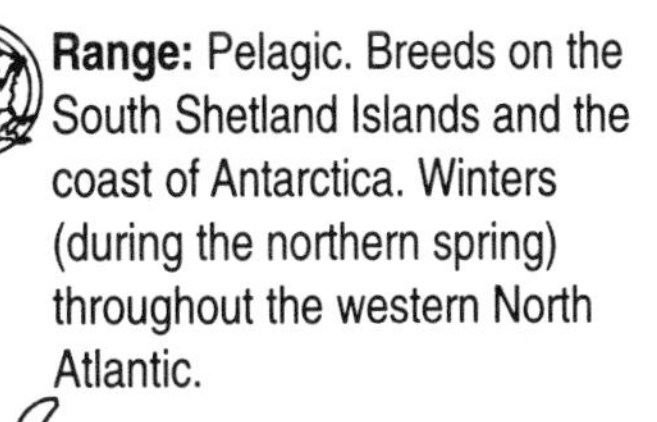

Range: Pelagic. Breeds on the South Shetland Islands and the coast of Antarctica. Winters (during the northern spring) throughout the western North Atlantic.

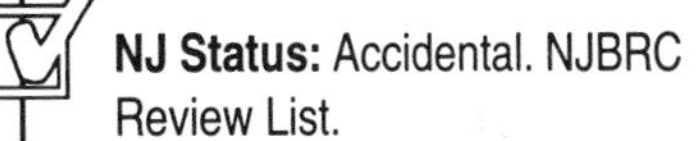

NJ Status: Accidental. NJBRC Review List.

Occurrence: Since 1976, there have been 14 state reports of South Polar Skuas, and nine have been accepted by the NJBRC (eight in spring, one in summer). Even with the current understanding of skua taxonomy and identification, information on skua distribution is spotty. Identification problems within this complex group of wide-ranging pelagic birds abound. South Polar Skuas are probably more common in New Jersey's waters than the following records indicate. The nine accepted records are:

	pelagic trip to Hudson Canyon	*29 May 1976*	*ph-RNJB 2:2, Smith 1976*
	pelagic trip to Hudson Canyon	*28 May 1977*	*ph-RBPF*
	*pelagic trip to Hudson Canyon**	*27 May 1978*	
	*60 miles E of Island Beach**	*26 May 1979*	
2	*pelagic trip to Hudson Canyon**	*28 May 1983*	
	70 miles east of Barnegat Inlet	*30 May 1987*	*ph-RNJB 13:49, ph-RBPF*
4	*pelagic trip to Hudson Canyon**	*29 May 1988*	
	pelagic trip to Hudson Canyon	*25 May 1991*	*ph-RNJB 17:45*
	54 miles ESE of Barnegat Inlet	*25 August 1996*	*ph-RNJB 23:79*

Pomarine Jaeger

Stercorarius pomarinus

Range: Breeds in northern Alaska and high Arctic Canada to northern Quebec. Winters at sea mainly in southern oceans.

NJ Status: Uncommon spring and fall migrant (generally far offshore), possibly a very rare winter resident. Rare from shore.

Fall: Records of Pomarine Jaegers in fall, both onshore and offshore, are generally from late September through mid-November. Determining their status is complicated by the difficulty of identification. They are highly pelagic, more so than Parasitic Jaegers, and Pomarine Jaegers begin migrating later than either Parasitic or Long-tailed Jaegers (Kaufman 1996). They are much less common from shore than Parasitic Jaegers. **Maxima:** 128, pelagic trip to Hudson Canyon, 16 September 1991; 50, pelagic trip to Hudson Canyon, 24-27 September 1987.

Winter: Although most Pomarine Jaegers migrate south to tropical oceans, some birds remain in the North Atlantic all winter. There are few winter reports of jaegers in New Jersey, although there are several reports of this species into mid-December. They have been reported on four CBCs from 1976 to 1997 (i.e., 1984, 1985, 1992 – two counts), with three of those reports coming on open ocean counts. In late January and early February of 1976, up to five Pomarine Jaegers were reported near fishing fleets 60 to 100 miles off the coast of New Jersey.

Spring: Most records of Pomarine Jaegers in spring are from pelagic trips far offshore, from late April through May. Although rarely seen from shore in any season, they are even less likely from shore in spring than in fall. **Maxima:** 15-20, pelagic trip to Hudson Canyon, 27 May 1985; 12, 65 miles off Cape May, 30 May 1987. ■

Parasitic Jaeger

Stercorarius parasiticus

Range: In North America breeds from northern Alaska across Arctic Canada to northern Labrador. Winters at sea mainly in southern oceans.

NJ Status: Rare to scarce spring and uncommon fall migrant from shore, more regular offshore.

Fall: Parasitic Jaegers migrate closer to shore than either Pomarine or Long-tailed Jaegers. Southbound birds can be seen by mid- to late August and

Parasitic Jaeger
continued

movements continue into early December. At the Avalon Sea Watch, the highest daily counts are noted in late October and early November. They can be found as far offshore as Hudson Canyon, but are less common there than Pomarine or Long-tailed Jaegers, becoming more common closer to shore. **Maxima:** 43, Cape May Point, 25 October 1980; 30+, Cape May, 1 November 1997. **ASW Single-Day Maximum:** 21 on 31 October 1997. **ASW Seasonal Stats:** Average: 144; Maximum: 224 in 1997.

Avalon Sea Watch: Parasitic Jaeger

Total: 250, 200, 150, 100, 50, 0

93 94 95 96 97

Winter: Parasitic Jaegers have been reported on four CBCs from 1976 to 1997 (i.e., 1980, 1984, 1986, and,1988). There are no reports after the count period.

Spring: Sightings of Parasitic Jaegers are less frequent in spring than in fall, with most records occurring in May. **Maxima:** 5, five miles off Cape May, 19 May 1995; 4, pelagic trip to Hudson Canyon, 29 May 1976. ■

Long-tailed Jaeger
Stercorarius longicaudus

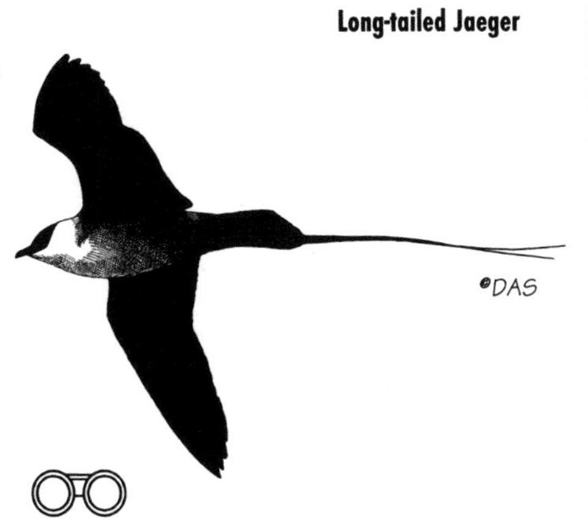

Range: In North America breeds from Alaska east to northern Quebec. Winters at sea in southern Oceans.

NJ Status: Very rare spring and fall migrant.

Occurrence: Long-tailed Jaeger was first reported in New Jersey 80 miles off Barnegat Inlet, 6 May 1894 (Stone 1937). Since then there have been about 45 state reports. Reports of northbound migrants occur mainly during May. Fall migrants are reported from late August through mid-October. Most sightings come from observers on pelagic birding trips. They are probably more common offshore than reports indicate, but there are few observers present offshore during peak movements. There have been 18 onshore reports, none of those inland. **Maximum:** 4, pelagic trip to Hudson Canyon, 16 September 1991. ■

Table 2: New Jersey ENSP Coastal Colonial Waterbird Survey

Species	1979 # of adults	1983 # of adults	1995 # of adults
Laughing Gull	*54,384*	*58,307*	*39,085*
Herring Gull	*5,891*	*5,237*	*6,828*
Great Black-backed Gull	*140*	*260*	*781*
Gull-billed Tern	*13*	*2*	*62*
Caspian Tern	*0*	*0*	*4*
Common Tern	*9,608*	*5,566*	*6,928*
Forster's Tern	*1,328*	*1,624*	*7,894*
Least Tern	*1,750*	*2,144*	*1,789*
Black Skimmer	*2,135*	*1,681*	*2,400*

From: D. Jenkins, NJ ENSP, pers. com.

Laughing Gull

Larus atricilla

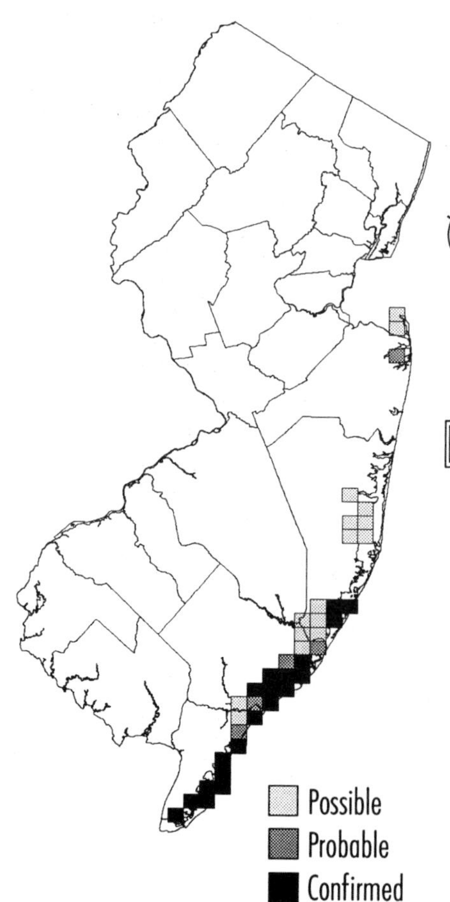

Range: Breeds on the East Coast from Nova Scotia to Florida, and along the Gulf coast to Texas. Winters from North Carolina south to South America.

NJ Status: Common but local breeding bird, common spring and fall migrant, very rare winter resident.

Breeding

Habitat: Breeds on coastal salt marshes.

Laughing Gulls are the birds that best embody "summer" for many of New Jersey's human residents. In the late 1800s the

Laughing Gull

continued

population of Laughing Gulls crashed due to egging and shooting for the millinery trade (Burger 1996). Stone (1908) reported that they had been reduced to only two breeding colonies statewide. Griscom (1923) reported that they were extirpated from Long Island, New York by 1888, although a single clutch was collected from Cedar Island, New York in 1890 (Bull 1964). After the passage of the Migratory Bird Treaty Act in 1918, the population of Laughing Gulls increased quickly. Several developments during the mid- to late 1900s – from a range increase of competitive Herring Gulls, to large "control" projects at airports that have shot thousands of breeding adult Laughing Gulls – are likely to have caused declines in the number of breeding pairs in New Jersey (Burger 1996).

During the Atlas surveys, Laughing Gull colonies were found only in Cape May, Atlantic, and southern Ocean counties. Even though their range is restricted to the southern portion of the state, the number of pairs of Laughing Gulls nesting in New Jersey is impressive: New Jersey ENSP Coastal Colonial Waterbird Survey estimates indicated 39,085 Laughing Gull adults on

continued on page 276

Map Interpretation: Nonbreeding adult and sub-adult Laughing Gulls can be seen virtually anywhere in the South Jersey on any day in the summer. Breeding adults on foraging flights can regularly travel from the colonies in the Atlantic coastal salt marshes to the Delaware Bay shore to forage on Horseshoe Crab eggs. Atlas observers were asked to confirm species only when nests or dependent young were found. Records of "roaming" individuals were downgraded from Possible to Observed. Locations recorded as Possible should not be considered as part of this species' breeding range.

Statewide Summary

Status	# of Blocks
Possible	16
Probable	5
Confirmed	20
Total	41

Physiographic Distribution

Laughing Gull	Number of blocks in province	Number of blocks species found breeding in province	Number of blocks species found in state	Percent of province species occupies	Percent of all records for this species found in province	Percent of state area in province
Inner Coastal Plain	128	2	41	1.6	4.9	15.0
Outer Coastal Plain	204	35	41	17.2	85.4	23.9
Pine Barrens	180	4	41	2.2	9.8	21.1

continued from page 275

their 1995 aerial survey of the colonies along the Atlantic coast salt marshes (Table 2).

Conservation Note: New Jersey ENSP Coastal Colonial Waterbird surveys along the Atlantic coast salt marshes showed a decline of adult Laughing Gulls from 54,384 in 1979 to 39,085 in 1995. Counts vary from year to year, and some previously occupied sites in Barnegat Bay (e.g., Clam Island) are now under water. It is important to establish reliable estimates of the size of the Laughing Gull colonies in New Jersey. This species may be a good indicator of changes in the marine and estuarine environments, and they present an opportunity for relatively easy data collection.

Fall: The abundance of Laughing Gulls as breeders makes it difficult to discern southbound movements of birds from the north. It appears that most Laughing Gulls move south from late September to mid-November. Their numbers decrease markedly thereafter, and typically they become scarce after the first of December. High counts at the Avalon Sea Watch are 2,094 on 29 September 1995 and 1,824 on 18 October 1996. It is possible the daily maximum is higher, but it is difficult to discern local movement from migration in this species. Numbers of migrants are not usually recorded elsewhere.

Winter: In most years Laughing Gulls linger long enough to be recorded in fair numbers on CBCs. They are very rare in winter after the count period, however. **CBC Statewide Stats:** Average: 18; Maximum: 84 in 1977; Minimum: 3 in four years. **CBC Maximum:** 76, Lower Hudson, 1977.

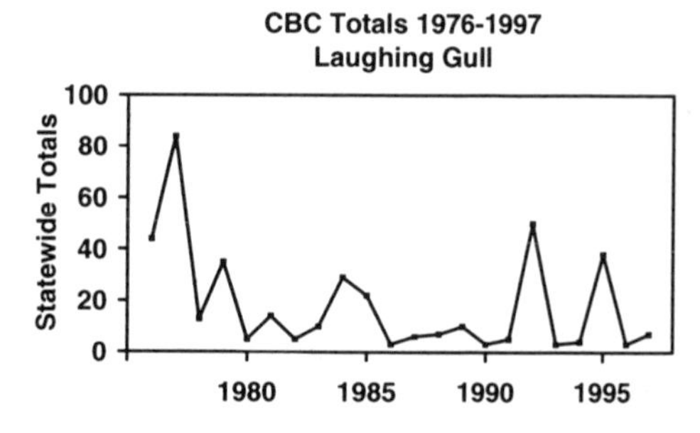

Spring: The return of Laughing Gulls in early March is one of the obvious signs of spring along the New Jersey coast. By late March and into April, hundreds can be seen streaming north across Delaware Bay and up the coast. ■

Franklin's Gull

Larus pipixcan

Range: Breeds in prairie marshes in the western United States and Canada. Winters off the Pacific coast of South America.

NJ Status: Very rare. NJBRC Review List.

Occurrence: There have been 27 state reports of Franklin's Gulls, and 12 have been accepted by the NJBRC (eight in fall, two in winter, two in spring). There was an invasion of Franklin's Gulls in November 1998, with over 40 individuals reported from the Avalon Sea Watch alone. Those reports, however, have not yet been reviewed by the NJBRC. The 12 accepted records are:

North Arlington	*9-20 February 1975*	*Kane and Roche 1975*
*Cape May Island**	*5-26 August 1979*	
Cape May Island	*28 September-6 October 1980*	
Cape May Point	*24 September 1981*	
Cold Spring Inlet	*6 November 1982*	*Sibley 1997*
Roxbury	*18 April 1992*	
Cape May	*11 September 1993*	
Atlantic City	*28 January-12 February 1995*	*ph-RNJB 21:38*
Avalon	*15 October 1995*	
Avalon	*2 November 1996*	
South Amboy	*21 April 1997*	*ph-RNJB 23:66*
Florence	*5 November 1997*	

Franklin's Gull

Little Gull

Larus minutus

Range: Breeds across northern Europe and Asia. In North America breeds at several sites around the Great Lakes and Hudson Bay. On the East Coast winters from Massachusetts to North Carolina.

NJ Status: Rare to scarce spring and fall migrant, rare to scarce winter resident.

Fall: There is a small movement of southbound Little Gulls from mid-November into early December. A few are seen at the Avalon Sea Watch, with dates spanning 12 November to 9 December. Little Gulls are most often seen among flocks of Bonaparte's Gulls. **ASW Single-Day Maximum:** 2 on 9 December 1995; 2 on 26 November 1996. **ASW Seasonal Stats:** Average: 3; Maximum: 6 in 1993.

Winter: Little Gulls are occasionally recorded on CBCs, but numbers drop in mid-winter. They have been recorded in only two years from 1987 to 1997. **CBC Statewide Stats:** Average: 1; Maximum: 4 in 1983; Minimum: 0 in ten years. **CBC Maximum:** 3, Lower Hudson, 1976.

CBC Totals 1976-1997
Little Gull

Statewide Totals (0–4); 1980, 1985, 1990, 1995

Spring: Little Gulls are most regularly seen from late February into May, and these sightings are probably of northbound birds. Sub-adult birds can linger well into May or even through much of the summer. **Maxima:** 17, South Amboy, 14 May 1972; 12, Jersey City, 21 May 1980; 8, Reed's Beach, 7 March 1992. ■

Black-headed Gull

Larus ridibundus

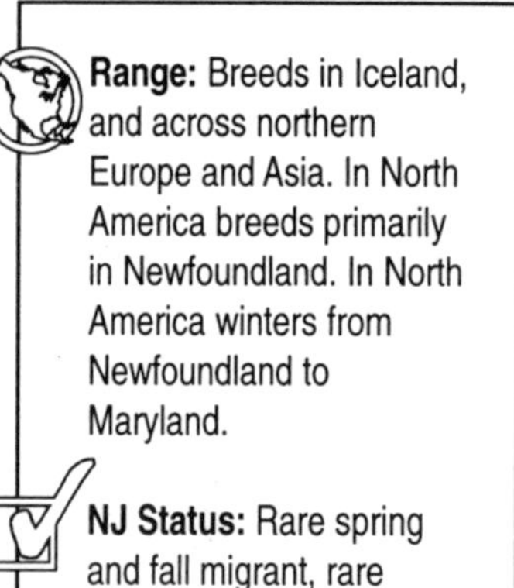

Range: Breeds in Iceland, and across northern Europe and Asia. In North America breeds primarily in Newfoundland. In North America winters from Newfoundland to Maryland.

NJ Status: Rare spring and fall migrant, rare winter resident.

Historic Changes: Black-headed Gull was first recorded in New Jersey on 21 November 1948. Numbers appear to have peaked in the mid- to late 1970s, and declined since.

Fall: Southbound Black-headed Gulls are occasionally noted from late November through early December. They have been recorded three times at the Avalon Sea Watch.

Black-headed Gull

continued

Winter: Statewide CBC totals for Black-headed Gulls were higher in the mid- to late 1970s; however, the CBC average for the state since 1978 is about five per year. Overall they are less common than Little Gulls, although they are probably more likely in mid-winter. Also, they appear to be more often found with Ring-billed or Laughing Gulls rather than with Bonaparte's Gulls. **Maximum:** 9, Caven Cove, winter 1977-1978. **CBC Statewide Stats:** Average: 5; Maximum: 26 in 1976; Minimum: 0 in four years. **CBC Maximum:** 24, Lower Hudson, 1976.

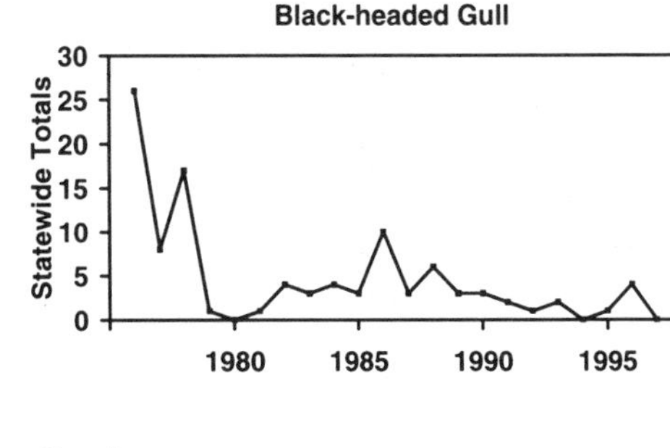

Spring: Northbound Black-headed Gulls are occasionally noted in March. They are much less likely to linger into spring than Little Gulls. ■

BLACK-HEADED GULL

Bonaparte's Gull

Larus philadelphia

Range: Breeds from Alaska south to British Columbia, east to central Ontario. On the East Coast winters from Maine to Florida, and along the Gulf coast to Texas.

NJ Status: Common spring and fall migrant, common winter resident.

Fall: Southbound Bonaparte's Gulls can be found in small numbers beginning in late August, although they arrive in numbers in late October. Peak flights occur from late November through early December. They occur regularly inland on large bodies of water, although generally in small numbers. **Maxima:** Coastal: 3,000, Sandy Hook, 25 December 1975; 2,748, Avalon Sea Watch, 11 December 1995; Inland: 50, Round Valley Res., 18 November 1976. **ASW Seasonal Stats:** Average: 5,964; Maximum: 8,647 in 1995.

continued on page 280

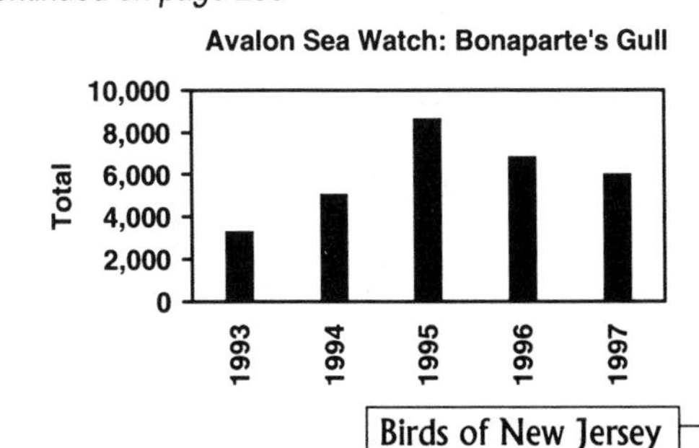

BONAPARTE'S GULL

continued from page 279

Bonaparte's Gull

Winter: CBC totals of Bonaparte's Gulls vary substantially from year to year. Numbers were highest in the late 1970s, when counts totaled over 10,000 birds from 1976 to 1978. The CBC average since then is just over 3,300. **CBC Statewide Stats:** Average: 4,454; Maximum: 12,286 in 1976; Minimum: 497 in 1996. **CBC Maximum:** 7,331, Lower Hudson, 1977.

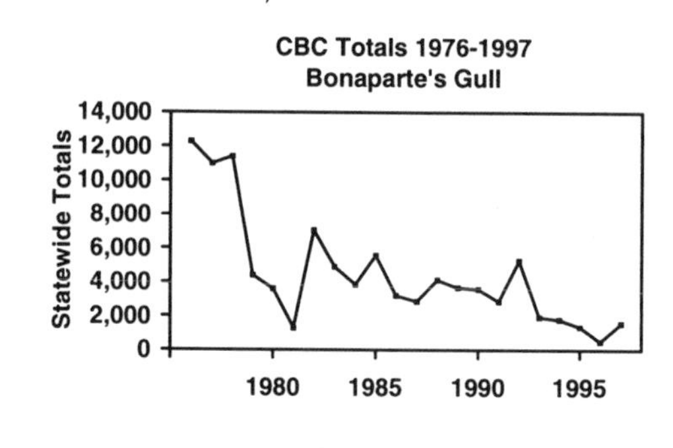

Spring: Northward movements of Bonaparte's Gulls can be noted beginning in late February, with numbers peaking in mid-April. They are more common in spring than in fall at large inland lakes and reservoirs. Sub-adults occasionally spend the summer along the coast. **Maxima:** Coastal: 500, Jersey City, 17 April 1977; 400, Jersey City , 9 April 1983; Inland: 300, Spruce Run Res., 17 April 1975. ■

Ring-billed Gull

Larus delawarensis

Fall: Ring-billed Gulls are present all year in New Jersey, but are most abundant between October and April. Adults can arrive from northern breeding grounds as early as late July, although peak movements occur in late October or early November. The variability in the Avalon Sea Watch numbers most likely reflect a difference in counting methods, and not a difference in the number of migrants. **Maxima:** 9,081, 10 December 1995; 5,672, 13 November 1996, both at the Avalon Sea Watch. **ASW Single-Day Maximum:** 9,081 on 10 December 1995. **ASW Seasonal Stats:** Average: 15,570; Maximum: 29,376 in 1995.

Winter: Influxes of Ring-billed Gulls can occur during mid-winter in response to harsh conditions farther north and

Range: In eastern North America, breeds around the Great Lakes and along the coasts of Quebec, Labrador, Newfoundland, and New Brunswick. On the East Coast winters from Nova Scotia to Florida.

NJ Status: Common spring and fall migrant, common winter resident.

Ring-billed Gull
continued

inland. Statewide CBC totals increased substantially from the mid-1970s to the mid-1980s, but appear to have leveled-off since then. **CBC Statewide Stats:** Average: 32,046; Maximum: 51,299 in 1992; Minimum: 10,478 in 1980. **CBC Maximum:** 23,063, Lower Hudson, 1984.

Spring: A return flight of Ring-billed Gulls in spring peaks from late March to early April. This is the gull most commonly found at inland lakes and reservoirs at any season. **Maxima:** 8,000, Sharptown, 4 April 1983; 5,000, Flemington, 9 March 1997. ■

Herring Gull
Larus argentatus

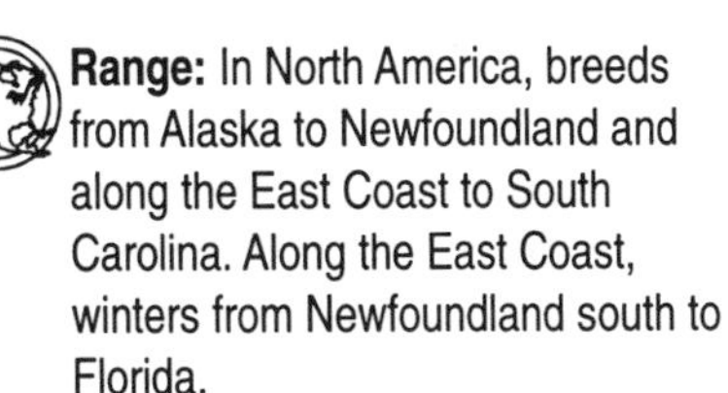

Range: In North America, breeds from Alaska to Newfoundland and along the East Coast to South Carolina. Along the East Coast, winters from Newfoundland south to Florida.

NJ Status: Common but local summer resident, common spring and fall migrant, common winter resident.

Breeding

Habitat: Nests on dredge spoil and salt marsh islands, or on barrier islands.

Herring Gull was first recorded nesting in New Jersey in 1946 at Stone Harbor (Fables 1955). Their colonization of New Jersey was part of a large southward range expansion fueled by increased conservation measures, an increase in food available from fisheries waste, and an increase in food available from land-fills (Pierotti and Good 1994). The species has continued a slow but steady colonization of New Jersey, and surveys show an increase from 5,891 to 6,828 breeding adults from 1979 to 1995 (Table 2). Herring Gulls and Great Black-backed Gulls are suspected of being responsible for forcing Laughing Gulls to move into sub-optimal nesting habitat in the salt marsh, where the Laughing Gulls are subject to nest loss by tidal flooding (Burger 1996).

Herring Gulls have become regular breeding birds in New Jersey, and Atlas data indicated
continued on page 282

continued from page 281

Herring Gull

Statewide Summary	
Status	# of Blocks
Possible	17
Probable	6
Confirmed	23
Total	46

that they occupy most blocks that have suitable breeding habitat. Their colonies were located in the Atlantic coast salt marsh in Cape May, Atlantic, and Ocean counties. The northern-most colony was located along the Arthur Kill near the border of Union and Middlesex counties.

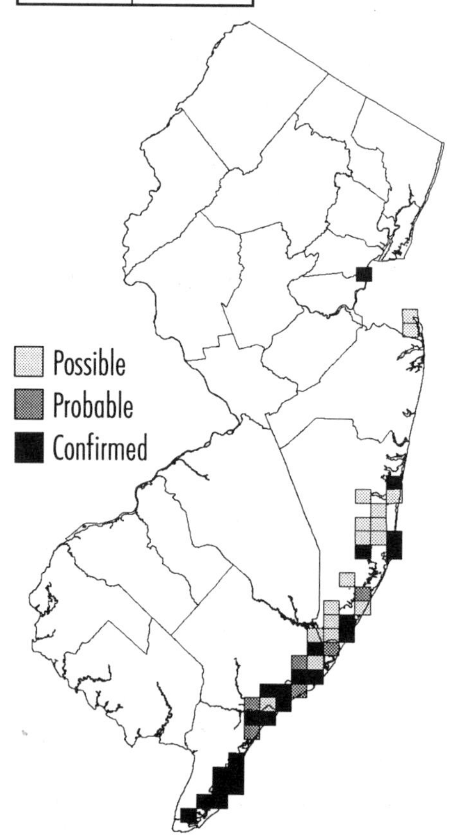

Fall: Herring Gulls are common throughout the year in New Jersey, and consequently it is difficult to discern movement of local birds from an influx of migrants. The variability in the

Map Interpretation:
Nonbreeding adult and sub-adult Herring Gulls can be seen virtually anywhere in the state on any day in the summer. Breeding adults on foraging flights can regularly go from the colonies in the Atlantic coastal salt marshes to the Delaware Bay shore to forage on Horseshoe Crab eggs. Records of suspected "roaming" individuals were downgraded from Possible to Observed. Locations mapped as Possible should not be considered as part of this species' breeding range.

Physiographic Distribution Herring Gull	Number of blocks in province	Number of blocks species found breeding in province	Number of blocks species found in state	Percent of province species occupies	Percent of all records for this species found in province	Percent of state area in province
Piedmont	167	1	46	0.6	2.2	19.6
Inner Coastal Plain	128	2	46	1.6	4.3	15.0
Outer Coastal Plain	204	37	46	18.1	80.4	23.9
Pine Barrens	180	6	46	3.3	13.0	21.1

Herring Gull

continued

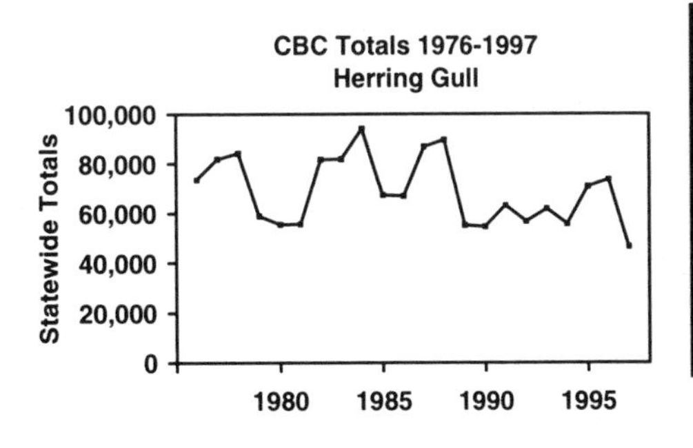

Avalon Sea Watch numbers most likely reflect a difference in counting methods, and not a difference in the number of migrants. **ASW Single-Day Maximum:** 8,309 on 5 November 1996. **ASW Seasonal Stats:** Average: 9,083; Maximum: 24,363 in 1996.

Winter: The highest numbers of Herring Gulls are found in winter. Numbers build throughout late fall and early winter, and statewide CBC totals exceed 55,000 birds. CBC totals do vary from year to year, however, probably due to weather conditions both within the state as well as to the north and inland. **CBC Statewide Stats:** Average: 68,875; Maximum: 94,013 in 1984; Minimum: 46,539 in 1997. **CBC Maximum:** 29,339, Long Branch, 1996.

Spring: A northward movement of Herring Gulls is sometimes discernable in March, although it usually goes unnoticed. Many subadults summer in New Jersey, and large numbers of subadult Herring Gulls forage on Horseshoe Crab eggs along the Delaware Bay shore in May and June. ■

Thayer's Gull

Larus thayeri

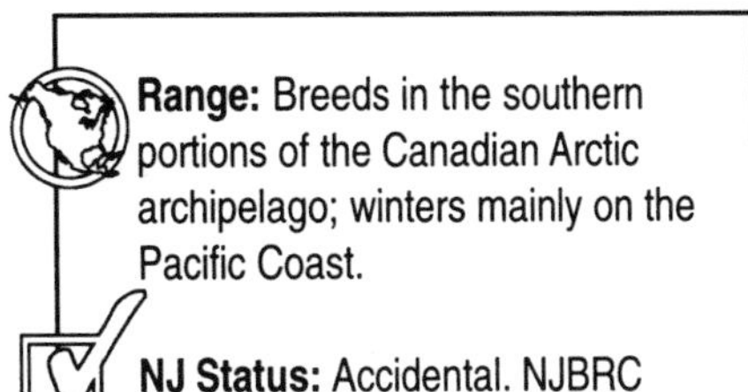

Range: Breeds in the southern portions of the Canadian Arctic archipelago; winters mainly on the Pacific Coast.

NJ Status: Accidental. NJBRC Review List.

Occurrence: There have been about 25 state reports of Thayer's Gull, but only one has been accepted by the NJBRC. Reports extend from December through May. All reports are from the Atlantic Coast or the Delaware River. The one accepted record is: Thompson's Beach, 24-27 May 1997 (phs-RNJB 24:2, 24:3; Bardon and Lehman 1998).

Among the reports that were not accepted is a specimen collected at Mt. Ephraim near the Delaware River, on 9 March 1888 (Stone1937). However, a recent examination of the specimen eliminated the possibility that this specimen was a Thayer's Gull, and suggests it is a Glaucous x Herring Gull hybrid (L. Bevier, pers. com.). ■

Iceland Gull

Larus glaucoides

Range: In North America, breeds on southeastern Baffin Island and in northern Quebec. Winters along the eastern Great Lakes and from Newfoundland to Virginia.

NJ Status: Rare to scarce spring and fall migrant, rare to scarce winter resident.

Fall: Iceland Gulls are rarely seen before November, and in some years they are not seen until December. First sightings each year are often in the northern part of the state. Most birds seen in New Jersey are first-year birds, and reports of adults are unusual. Iceland Gulls were recorded only five times from 1993 -1997 at the Avalon Sea Watch.

Winter: Iceland Gulls are typically seen among concentrations of other large gulls, and they are most often seen in numbers at landfills. They are more regularly seen in the northern part of the state than in the south. CBC totals have decreased since the late 1970s and early 1980s. However, CBC totals are not a good indicator of winter numbers for this species, as more may be present in late January and February. **Maxima:** 40, Florence, 1 February 1997; 25+, North Arlington, 6 February 1977. **CBC Statewide Stats:** Average: 7; Maximum: 18 in 1977; Minimum: 0 in 1994. **CBC Maximum:** 11, Lower Hudson, 1976.

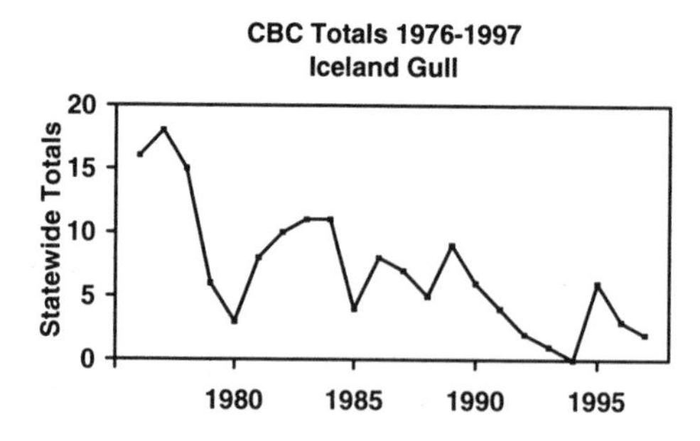

Spring: Iceland Gull numbers decline through March, although they will sometimes linger into May and even more rarely into early June. ■

Lesser Black-backed Gull

Larus fuscus

Range: *L. f. graellsii* breeds in Iceland, the Faroes, the British Isles and northern France. Winters south to North Africa, with small numbers reaching eastern North America.

NJ Status: Scarce spring and fall migrant, scarce to uncommon winter resident.

Historic Changes: The first North American record of Lesser Black-backed Gull came from New Jersey, when a bird was identified at Beach Haven on 9 September 1934 (Stone 1937). This European species has been occurring in increasing numbers along the East Coast.

Fall: Migrant Lesser Black-backed Gulls appear early in the fall, usually by mid-September. Lesser Black-backed Gulls have been recorded eight times from 1993-1997 at the Avalon Sea Watch, with a maximum of four on 10 December 1995 (the only date with multiple sightings). **Maximum:** 29, Florence, 10 November 1997.

Winter: Lesser Black-backed Gulls are most common in winter. Statewide CBC totals reflect their increasing presence, with a noticeable jump in numbers beginning in the late 1980s. The listed maximum at Florence (near a landfill), with its tremendous con-centration of large gulls, is many times higher than of any other location. **Maximum:** 53, Florence, 20 March 1997. **CBC Statewide Stats:** Average: 6; Maximum: 17 in 1997; Minimum: 0 in 1981. **CBC Maximum:** 6, Sandy Hook, 1989.

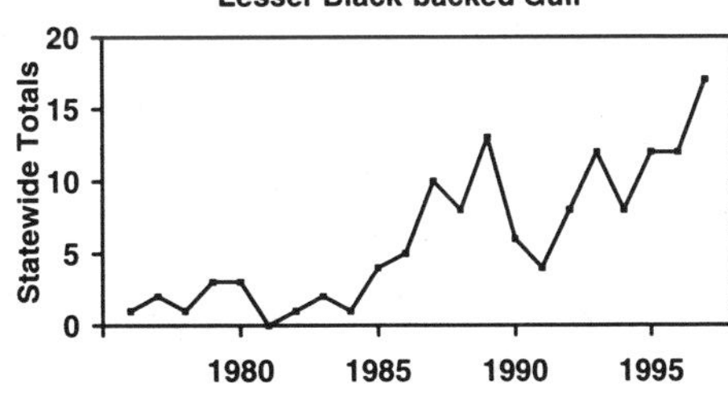

Spring: Sibley (1997) noted that small numbers of northbound Lesser Black-backed Gulls are seen at Cape May from March through May. ■

Glaucous Gull

Larus hyperboreus

Range: In North America breeds in the high Arctic from northern Alaska east to northern Labrador. On the East Coast, winters from Newfoundland to North Carolina.

NJ Status: Rare spring and fall migrant, rare winter resident.

Fall: Glaucous Gulls only occasionally appear before November, and in many years not until December. Most birds seen in New Jersey are first-year birds. They were recorded only

continued on page 286

continued from page 285

Glaucous Gull

once from 1993-1997 at the Avalon Sea Watch.

Winter: Glaucous Gulls occur in the largest numbers in winter. Although CBC totals are low they show a decrease since the early 1980s, and numbers have been particularly low in the 1990s. As with Iceland Gulls, they are more regular later in the winter. They are typically seen among concentrations of other large gulls, with the largest aggregations associated with landfills. They are more regular in the northern part of the state. **Maxima:** 10, Florence, 1 February 1997; 6, North Arlington, winter 1976-1977. **CBC Statewide Stats:** Average: 4; Maximum: 9 in 1982 and 1983; Minimum: 0 in 1992 and 1996. **CBC Maximum:** 5, Lower Hudson, 1976; 5, Lower Hudson, 1984.

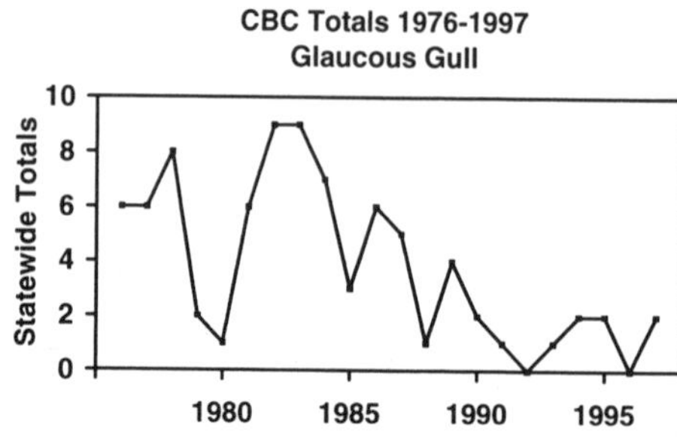

Spring: Glaucous Gulls rarely linger after March, although there are a few records in April and May. ■

Great Black-backed Gull

Larus marinus

Range: In North America, breeds along the coast from northern Labrador south to North Carolina. Winters from Newfoundland to Florida.

NJ Status: Fairly common but local summer resident, common spring and fall migrant, common winter resident.

Breeding

Habitat: Nests on dredge spoil and salt marsh islands, or on barrier islands.

The breeding history of Great Black-backed Gull in New Jersey is similar to that of Herring Gull. The first breeding

Physiographic Distribution Great Black-backed Gull	Number of blocks in province	Number of blocks species found breeding in province	Number of blocks species found in state	Percent of province species occupies	Percent of all records for this species found in province	Percent of state area in province
Inner Coastal Plain	128	2	37	1.6	5.4	15.0
Outer Coastal Plain	204	32	37	15.7	86.5	23.9
Pine Barrens	180	3	37	1.7	8.1	21.1

Great Black-backed Gull

continued

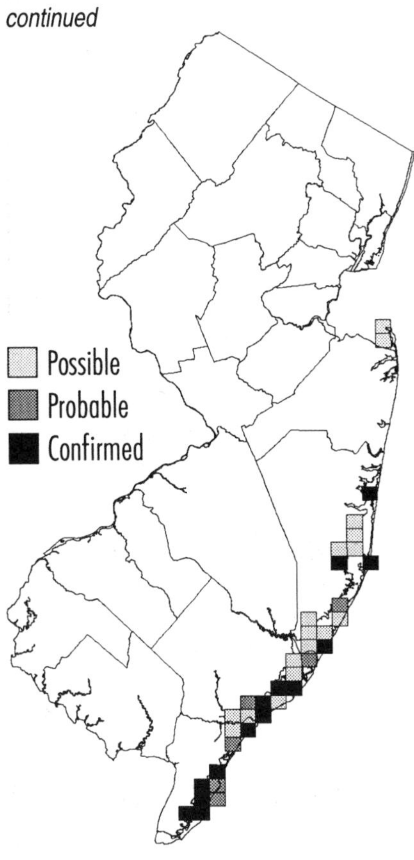

Statewide Summary	
Status	# of Blocks
Possible	17
Probable	6
Confirmed	14
Total	37

Map Interpretation: Nonbreeding adult and subadult Great Black-backed Gulls can be seen almost anywhere in New Jersey on any day in the summer. Breeding adults regularly fly from the colonies in the Atlantic coastal salt marshes to the Delaware Bay shore to forage on Horseshoe Crab eggs. Records of "roaming" individuals were downgraded from Possible to Observed. Locations recorded as Possible should not be considered as part of this species' breeding range.

record in New Jersey is of two nests from Absecon Bay in 1966 (Choate 1966). Like Herring Gulls, Great Black-backed Gulls have continued to expand their breeding range in New Jersey, possibly at the expense of Laughing Gulls. The New Jersey ENSP Coastal Colonial Waterbird Surveys found that Great Black-backed Gulls increased from 140 to 781 breeding adults between 1979 and 1995 (Table 2).

Atlas surveys found Great Black-backed Gulls nesting on salt marsh islands and barrier beaches in Cape May, Atlantic, and Ocean counties. In most cases they were found breeding in mixed-species colonies, often with Herring Gulls, Forster's Terns, and American Oystercatchers. It is likely that Great Black-backed Gulls will continue to expand as breeding birds in New Jersey.

Fall: The high number of subadults and nonbreeding adults that are found throughout the summer and fall complicates the assessment of the fall migration of Great Black-backed Gulls. The variability in the Avalon Sea Watch numbers most likely reflect a difference in counting methods, and not a difference in the number of migrants. **ASW Single-Day Maximum:** 184 on 24 September 1995. **ASW Seasonal**

continued on page 288

continued from page 287

Great Black-backed Gull

Stats: Average: 852; Maximum: 2,490 in 1995.

Winter: Although they are common year-round, concentrations of Great Black-backed Gulls are highest in winter. Outside of the CBCs, observers rarely report high counts. This species is mainly coastal, and when seen inland, it is often associated with landfills. **CBC Statewide Stats:** Average: 11,599; Maximum: 17,561 in 1991; Minimum: 8,050 in 1976. **CBC Maximum:** 7,644, Cape May, 1991.

CBC Totals 1976-1997
Great Black-backed Gull

Statewide Totals: 20,000; 15,000; 10,000; 5,000; 0
1980 1985 1990 1995

Spring: Spring concentrations of Great Black-backed Gulls along the Delaware Bay shore (most foraging on Horseshoe Crab eggs) can be impressive. Counts of mixed-species flocks of Herring and Great Black-backed Gulls at Reeds Beach alone totaled 8,500 on 19 May 1992; 4,908 on 31 May 1992; and 7,050 on 2 June 1992 (C. Sutton and J. Walsh, pers. obs.). ■

Sabine's Gull

Xema sabini

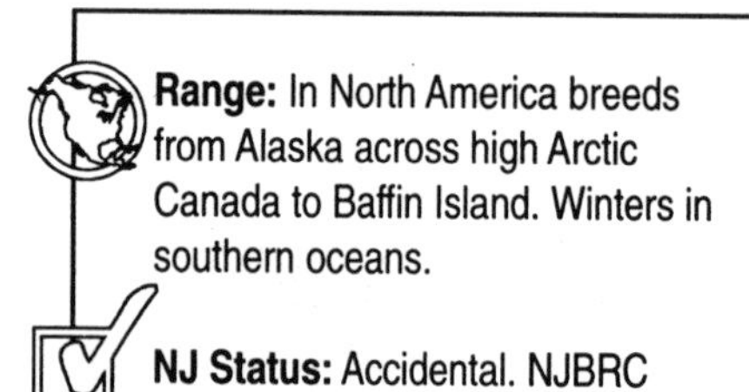

Range: In North America breeds from Alaska across high Arctic Canada to Baffin Island. Winters in southern oceans.

NJ Status: Accidental. NJBRC Review List.

Occurrence: There have been 15 state reports of Sabine's Gull, and six have been accepted by the NJBRC (four in fall, one in spring, one in summer). The six accepted records are:

*24 miles off Cape May**	*14 October 1979*	
*Cape May**	*12 November 1986*	
Avalon	*8 December 1987*	
Cape May	*21 August 1989*	
Avon	*1 August 1990*	*ph-RNJB 16:71*
Raritan Bay	*25 April 1993*	

3lack-legged Kittiwake

?issa tridactyla

Range: In North America, breeds on northern Baffin Island, northern Labrador, Newfoundland and around the Gulf of St. Lawrence. Winters at sea south to North Carolina.

NJ Status: Irregular spring and fall migrant from shore, common winter visitor offshore.

'all: Black-legged Kittiwakes ıre rarely recorded before early Vovember. They are most often ɜncountered on offshore pelagic rips, however they can some-imes be seen in fair numbers rom shore in migration. They ıre typically recorded only in ,mall numbers at the Avalon Sea Watch. **ASW Single-Day Aaximum:** 57 on 19 November 1996 (with 55 the following lay). **ASW Seasonal Stats:** \verage: 50; Maximum: 201 in 1996.

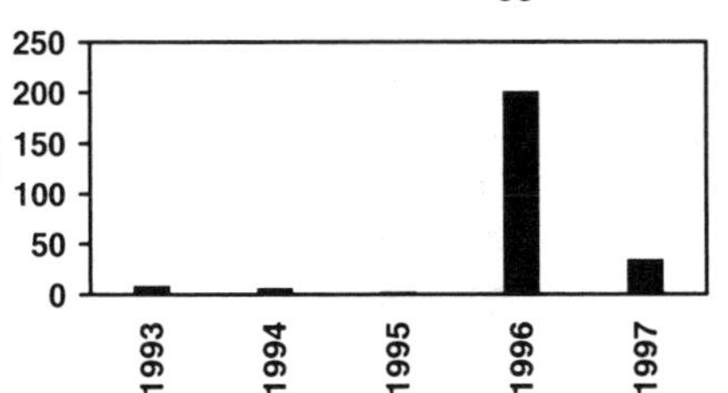

Winter: Offshore aggregations of Black-legged Kittiwakes in winter, particularly around fishing fleets, can number in the thousands. They are only irregularly seen from shore. CBC totals are variable and high numbers depend on the success of offshore counts (e.g., the Atlantic Ocean count). **Maxima:** 15,000, 75 miles east of Sea Isle City, 14-16 January 1977; 6,000, 60-100 miles offshore, late January-early February 1976; From shore: 205 on 9 January 1993 Cape May. **CBC Statewide Stats:** Average: 278; Maximum: 937 in 1985; Minimum: 2 in 1996. **CBC Maximum:** 751, Barnegat, 1980.

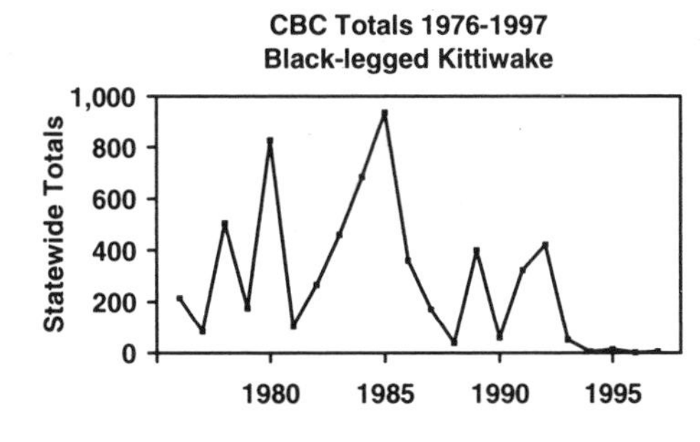

Spring: Onshore encounters with Black-legged Kittiwakes are so infrequent and offshore trips so irregular that discerning the period of spring migration is difficult. The highest numbers of birds in spring off Massachusetts occurs in March (Veit and Petersen 1993), and it is possible that this is true off New Jersey as well. ■

Ross's Gul

Rhodostethia rose

Range: Breeds in northern Siberia, northern Manitoba and Greenland. Probably winters on open Arctic waters, but range poorly known.

NJ Status: Accidental. NJBRC Review List.

Occurrence: There has been only one documented and accepted record of Ross's Gull in New Jersey: 5 miles E of Manasquan Inlet, 27 November 1993 (phs-RNJB 20:1, 22:23). ■

Ivory Gul

Pagophila eburne

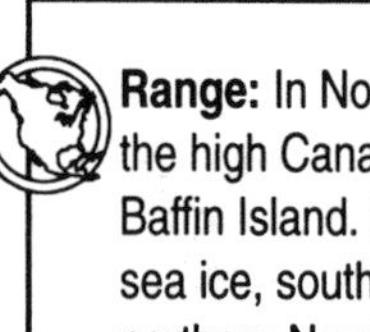

Range: In North America breeds in the high Canadian Arctic, south to Baffin Island. Winters primarily amid sea ice, south regularly only to northern Newfoundland.

NJ Status: Accidental. NJBRC Review List.

Occurrence: There have been seven state reports of Ivory Gull, and four have been accepted by the NJBRC (all in late January to mid-February). The two records from 1986 may have involved the same individual. The four accepted records are:

Island Beach	*3 February 1940*	*spec. ANSP*
Manasquan Inlet#	*28 January-5 February 1955*	
Lake Como	*10 February 1986*	*ph-RNJB 12:33*
Liberty SP	*16 February 1986*	*phs-RNJB 12:20, 12:36; Freiday 1986*

Gull-billed Tern

Sterna nilotica

Range: In North America breeds along the East coast from Long Island to Florida and along the Gulf coast to Texas. Winters from the Gulf Coast south to Central and South Americas.

NJ Status: Scarce and very local summer resident, uncommon spring and fall migrant.

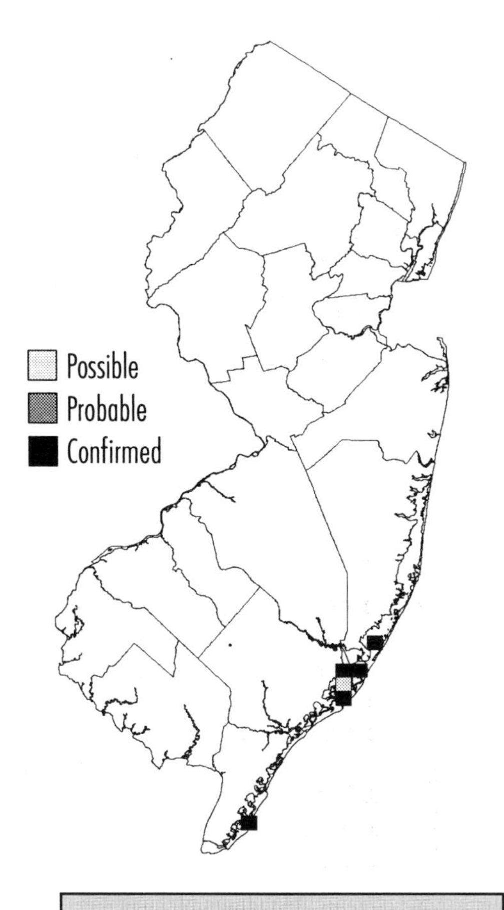

Statewide Summary	
Status	# of Blocks
Possible	1
Probable	0
Confirmed	5
Total	6

Breeding

Habitat: Nests mainly on beaches or salt marsh islands.

Gull-billed Terns have an enigmatic history in New Jersey. There is evidence this species bred in New Jersey early in the

continued on page 292

Map Interpretation: Only Confirmed breeding sites should be considered as the species' active breeding range. Like most other terns, Gull-billed Terns can wander far from breeding areas on foraging flights, and this could cause birds to be listed as Possible or Probable breeders in areas where they do not breed.

Physiographic Distribution Gull-billed Tern	Number of blocks in province	Number of blocks species found breeding in province	Number of blocks species found in state	Percent of province species occupies	Percent of all records for this species found in province	Percent of state area in province
Outer Coastal Plain	204	6	6	2.9	100.0	23.9

continued from page 291

19th Century, but there were no other breeding records from that time until a nest was found at Stone Harbor in 1926 (Stone 1937, Fables 1955). The next breeding records for New Jersey were at Brigantine NWR in 1956 (Leck 1984) and Stone Harbor in 1958 (Bull 1964, Leck 1984). From 1979 through 1995 the Gull-billed Tern population in New Jersey grew from 13 to 62 adults (Table 2).

Atlas volunteers Confirmed Gull-billed Terns in three blocks, and the 1995 New Jersey ENSP Coastal Colonial Waterbird Surveys found six colonies in two blocks. It is likely that these two surveys located most of the colonies. All Confirmed locations were located on the Atlantic Coast, although there are locations on the Delaware Bay where Gull-billed Terns are frequently seen in summer, but where they are not known to breed (e.g., Goshen Landing). During the Atlas surveys, they were seen regularly stealing food from Common Terns at Champagne Island in Hereford Inlet (D. Githens, pers. com.). This parasitic behavior became so common that observers suspected the Gull-billed Terns were getting most of their food from the Common Terns.

Fall: Few Gull-billed Terns nest north of New Jersey, so most fall sightings come from birds dispersing from local nesting colonies. Concentrations are noted in summer at Whitesbog (an inland site west of Barnegat Bay) and at Brigantine NWR. They are seen in much smaller numbers elsewhere along the coast. Most have departed by the end of August. **Maxima:** 70, Whitesbog, 10 August 1981; 63, Whitesbog, 8 August 1986.

Spring: Gull-billed Terns arrive at breeding locations in late April or early May. **Maxima:** 30, Brigantine NWR, 15 May 1986; 22, Brigantine NWR, 16 May 1982. ■

Gull-billed Tern

Caspian Tern
Sterna caspia

Range: In eastern North America breeds from Manitoba to the Great Lakes; along the north coast of the Gulf of St. Lawrence; and along the East Coast from Virginia to Texas. Winters from North Carolina south to Central America and parts of the Caribbean.

NJ Status: Rare and very local summer resident, uncommon spring and common fall migrant.

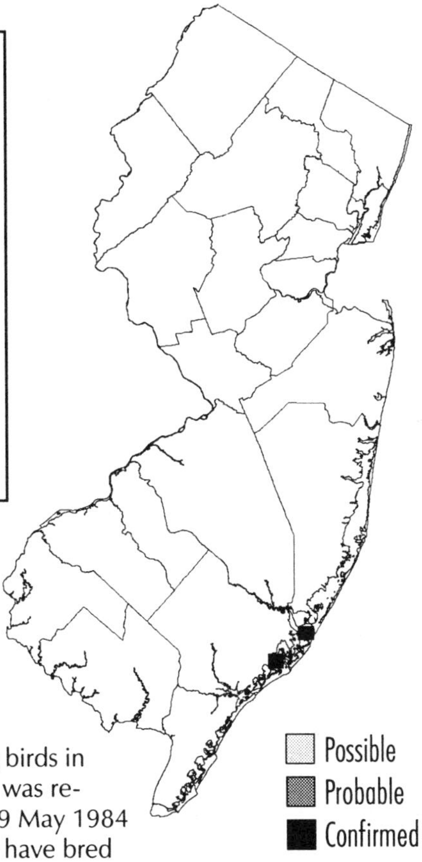

Possible
Probable
Confirmed

Breeding

Habitat: Nests on barrier and salt marsh islands.

Caspian Terns are new as breeding birds in New Jersey. The first nest in the state was recorded at Vol Sedge, Barnegat Bay, 29 May 1984 (Burger et al. 1984). Since then, they have bred regularly but in small numbers, most consistently at Brigantine NWR. During the Atlas surveys, three pairs were Confirmed, all on saltmarsh islands near Brigantine NWR. Their regular pattern of occurrence coupled with the extremely low population size suggests the population is maintained by immigration rather than by production.

continued on page 294

Statewide Summary	
Status	# of Blocks
Possible	0
Probable	0
Confirmed	2
Total	2

Physiographic Distribution Caspian Tern	Number of blocks in province	Number of blocks species found breeding in province	Number of blocks species found in state	Percent of province species occupies	Percent of all records for this species found in province	Percent of state area in province
Outer Coastal Plain	204	2	2	1.0	100.0	23.9

continued from page 293

Caspian Tern

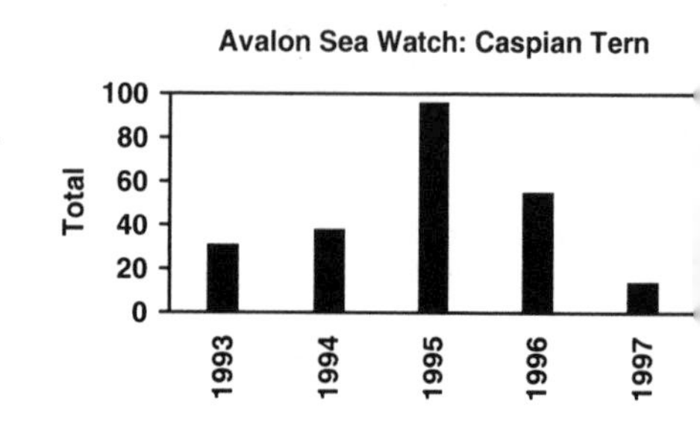

Fall: Small numbers of Caspian Terns are present in August, but the bulk of their southward migration occurs from September to October. They are regular inland in small numbers. Highest concentrations come from the lower Delaware River, although they are also found in numbers around the major coastal inlets. **Maxima:** Coastal: 200, Salem Cove, 10 September 1988; 200, Salem Cove, 15 October 1992; Inland: 24, Spruce Run Res., 22 August 1994. **ASW Single-Day Maximum:** 25 on 24 September 1995. **ASW Seasonal Stats:** Average: 47; Maximum: 96 in 1995.

Spring: Caspian Terns are considerably less common in spring than in fall. Highest concentrations occur along the lower Delaware River from mid- to late April. They are scarce elsewhere along the coast and only occasionally seen inland. Migration continues through May, with a few lingering into early June. **Maxima:** 30, Mannington Marsh, 22 April 1992; 30, Mannington Marsh, April 1984. ■

Royal Tern

Sterna maxima

Range: In the eastern United States, breeds along the East coast from Maryland to Florida and along the Gulf coast to Texas. Winters from North Carolina south to South America.

NJ Status: Rare and very local summer resident, uncommon spring and common fall migrant, reported on four CBCs.

Breeding

Habitat: Nests on barrier and salt marsh islands.

Royal Terns reach the northern edge of their breeding range in New Jersey. In June 1988 researchers in Barnegat Bay recorded the first confirmed nest of Royal Terns in New Jersey (Gochfeld et al. 1989). However, Atlas volunteers did not Confirm any Royal Tern nests during the five years of surveys.

Royal Tern

continued

Possible
Probable
Confirmed

Historic Changes: The historic status of this species is clouded, as early observers may have had difficulty separating Royal Terns from Caspian Terns (Stone 1908, Stone 1937). In the late 1800s, Royal Terns were not recorded from the northern part of their current range, possibly due to a population crash related to egging at their breeding colonies (Kaufman 1996). They began to reappear along the coast of New Jersey in 1933 (Stone 1937). Their numbers slowly increased; Fables in 1955 still considered them rare stragglers, but by 1956, 350 were recorded in Cape May, and the species has been occurring regularly since that time (Sibley 1997).

Fall: Royal Terns disperse north from their southern breeding colonies beginning in late June, and they occur in increasing numbers as summer progresses. Numbers build to a peak

continued on page 296

Map Interpretation: As with most other terns, Royal Terns can be seen feeding young for a long period after the young are able to fly, and many miles from nesting sites. All Atlas reports scored as Possible were excluded from mapping for those reasons. The only mapped Atlas record is of courting birds on Champagne Island in Hereford Inlet during June 1994. During summer, this species regularly occurs in large numbers (50+) on Champagne Island and often engages in courtship.

Statewide Summary	
Status	# of Blocks
Possible	0
Probable	1
Confirmed	0
Total	1

Physiographic Distribution Royal Tern	Number of blocks in province	Number of blocks species found breeding in province	Number of blocks species found in state	Percent of province species occupies	Percent of all records for this species found in province	Percent of state area in province
Outer Coastal Plain	204	1	1	0.5	100.0	23.9

continued from page 295

Royal Tern

from early to mid-October before the return flight south. Most are gone by mid-November. **Maxima:** 1,000s, Cape May Point, 22 October 1988; 1,520 Avalon Sea Watch, 18 October 1996. **ASW Seasonal Stats:** Average: 1,515; Maximum: 2,631 in 1996.

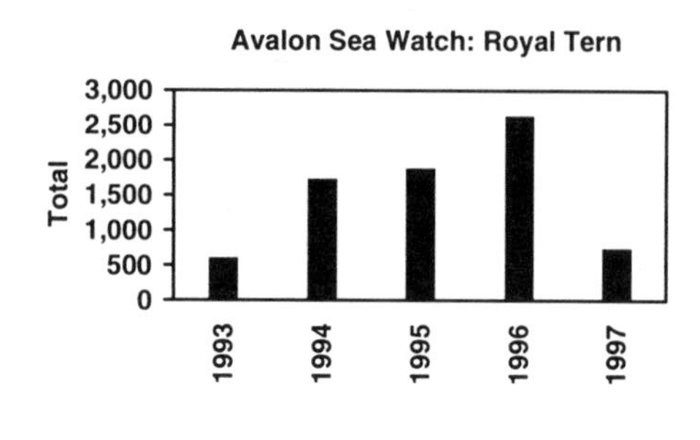

Winter: Individual Royal Terns have lingered long enough to be counted on four CBCs since 1976 (i.e., 1979, 1983, 1992, and 1994). There is no evidence they have ever successfully wintered.

Spring: Royal Terns are less likely to wander north of their breeding colonies in spring than in fall. They are found in small numbers from late April into May, with few present by late May. **Maxima:** 30+, Cape May Point, 24 April 1998; 17, South Cape May Meadows, 30 April 1988. ■

Sandwich Tern

Sterna sandvicensis

Range: In North America, breeds along the East coast from Virginia to Florida and along the Gulf coast to Texas. Winters from Florida and Texas south to Central and South America and the Caribbean.

NJ Status: Very rare spring and rare summer and fall visitor.

Historic changes: As of 1955, Fables reported only two records of Sandwich Terns for the state. The increase in records since 1955 mirrors the rise in Royal Tern numbers in New Jersey, although the number of Sandwich Terns is much lower.

Fall: Most Sandwich Terns are seen from late June through early September, although some occasionally linger beyond mid-September. The majority of the records come from Hereford Inlet and Cape May. **Maxima:** 12, South Cape May Meadows, 26 September 1985; 8, Hereford Inlet, 23-27 August 1991.

Spring: Sandwich Terns are very rare in spring, with a few records in May and early June. ■

Roseate Tern

Sterna dougallii

Range: In North America breeds locally from Nova Scotia south to New York also in Florida and the West Indies.

NJ Status: Rare to scarce spring migrant and summer visitor, very rare fall migrant. Endangered Species in New Jersey.

Fall: Roseate Terns are only occasionally seen in fall, as their southward migration takes place well offshore. Most southbound birds are seen from August through mid-September

Spring: Although about 90% of the North American population of Roseate Terns nests in the Cape Cod-Long Island area (Veit and Petersen 1993), they occur only in small numbers in New Jersey, primarily from mid-May to mid-July. The majority of sightings come from Hereford Inlet and Cape May, with only a few scattered sightings farther north along the coast. Individuals identified by distinct leg bands, presumably nonbreeders from colonies in Long Island Sound, sometimes remain in the same area over a period of weeks. **Maxima:** 9, Cape May Point, 12 May 1998; 6, Cape May Point, 13 May 1995; 6, Cape May, 11 May 1981. ■

Common Tern

Sterna hirundo

Range: In North America, breeds from the Northwest Territories south to Montana, east to the Great Lakes and Labrador and south along the coast to North Carolina. Winters mainly in Central and South America.

NJ Status: Common but local summer resident, common spring and fall migrant, reported on one CBC.

Breeding

Habitat: Nests on barrier and salt marsh islands.

The status of Common Tern in New Jersey has varied from periods of abundance to near extirpation. Early records indicated the species was common as a breeding bird along the Atlantic coast of the United States (Bent 1921). During the late 1800s, Common Terns were hunted extensively for use by the millinery trade and were nearly extirpated from New

continued on page 298

continued from page 297

Common Tern

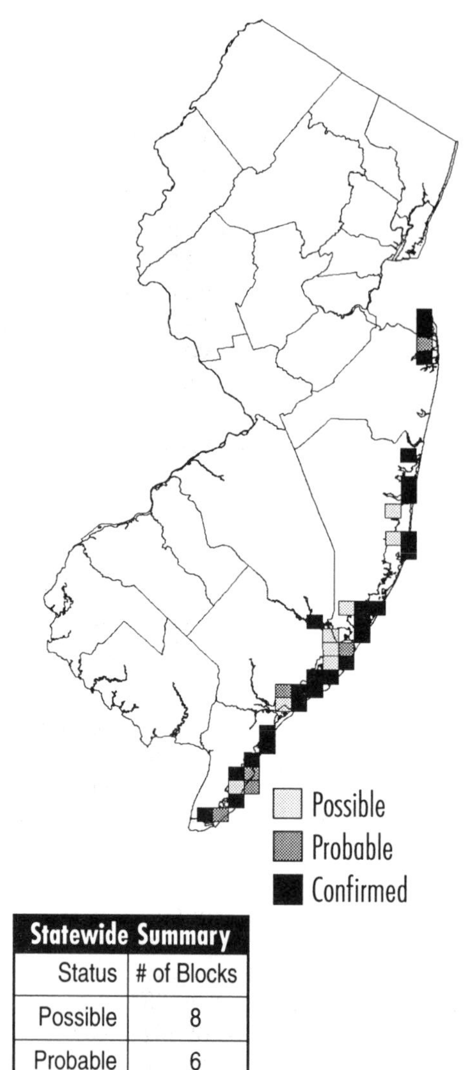

Map Interpretation: Many terns have an extended pre-nesting courtship and an extended period of post-fledging parental care. Many of the Atlas breeding codes are too liberal for these species, and an accurate map of their breeding range is best estimated by using Confirmed breeding locations only.

Jersey. The scale of this decline may be difficult for modern observers to appreciate – by 1883, there were no nests found in New Jersey (Shriner 1896), and Stone (1908) was "astonished " to find two nesting pairs near Atlantic City in 1893. Following protection from egging and the take for the millinery trade, the species recovered. Stone (1937) recounted several colonies in southern New Jersey, some numbering in the hundreds of nests. Since that time the species has, range-wide, gone through periods of decline and recovery, and it is currently declining in New Jersey.

Statewide Summary

Status	# of Blocks
Possible	8
Probable	6
Confirmed	25
Total	39

Physiographic Distribution

Common Tern	Number of blocks in province	Number of blocks species found breeding in province	Number of blocks species found in state	Percent of province species occupies	Percent of all records for this species found in province	Percent of state area in province
Inner Coastal Plain	128	2	39	1.6	5.1	15.0
Outer Coastal Plain	204	36	39	17.6	92.3	23.9
Pine Barrens	180	1	39	0.6	2.6	21.1

Common Terns were once the most common nesting terns in New Jersey, being more widespread and more abundant than Forster's Terns. Atlas data, combined with the New Jersey ENSP Coastal Colonial Waterbird Survey data, indicated that Common Terns are less abundant, but have more colonies, than Forster's Terns. The ENSP surveys also indicated Common Terns have been in a period of decline in New Jersey (Table 2). All Atlas Confirmed blocks for Common Terns were along the Atlantic coast

Conservation Note: Many of New Jersey's barrier beach islands have been developed. Prior to that development, Common Terns nested primarily on sandy beaches. Beach development, and possibly a range expansion by the predatory large gulls (Herring and Black-backed Gulls), have combined to limit the productivity of Common Terns and force them into the salt marsh for breeding. Common Terns reproduce poorly in the salt marshes, as their nests do not withstand tidal flooding. This habitat shift from the barrier islands into the salt marshes may be one of the reasons the Common Tern population is declining in New Jersey.

Fall: Dispersal of Common Terns from local breeding grounds begins in mid-July. The peak numbers move south from late August through early September, with diminishing numbers noted into early October. A few Common Terns may linger into early November and very rarely into December. They are generally rare inland in fall. **Maxima:** 2,000+, Hereford Inlet, 24 August 1992; 2,000, Cape May Point, 15 September 1988. **ASW Single-Day Maximum:** 2,363 on 25 September 1997. **ASW Seasonal Stats:** Average: 1,271; Maximum: 2,803 in 1997.

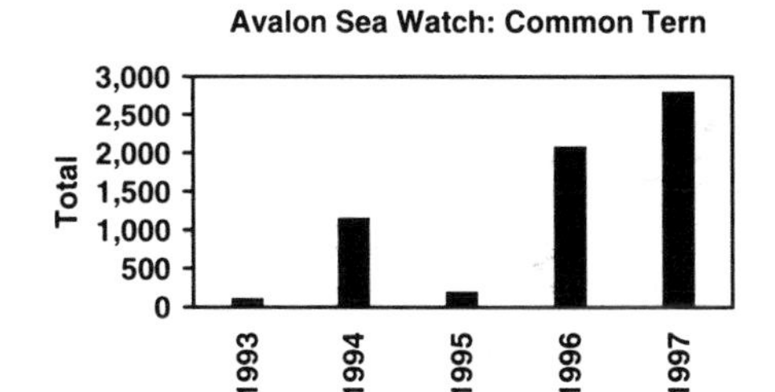

Winter: A Common Tern was reported on the Cape May CBC in 1985, although no details were submitted. There is no evidence Common Terns have ever successfully wintered.

Spring: Common Terns return at the end of April, with numbers moving north throughout May. Their abundance as a breeding species makes it difficult to identify peak numbers of migrants. In spring, they are found inland in small numbers. **Maxima:** Coastal: 1,400, Cape May Point, 11 May 1981; 1,000, Cape May Point, 20 May 1992; Inland: 13, Merrill Creek Res., 25 May 1989. ■

Arctic Tern

Sterna paradisaea

Range: In North America breeds from Alaska to Nova Scotia, and locally to Maine and Massachusetts. Winters in the southern oceans.

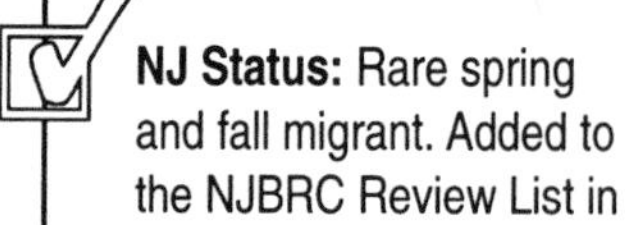

NJ Status: Rare spring and fall migrant. Added to the NJBRC Review List in 1996.

Occurrence: Since the addition of Arctic Tern to the NJBRC Review List in 1996 there has been two state reports, but none have been accepted to the NJBRC. There are about 54 previous state reports of Arctic Tern, although the NJBRC has not undertaken a review of all historic sightings. Reports span the months May to November, with 24 reports in May. Twenty-two of them are pelagic reports. The first record was a specimen of an adult male labeled "NJ," taken June 1848 (spec. USNM #58990). The species has been reported annually since 1975. **Maximum:** 20-30 on a pelagic trip out of Barnegat Inlet, 27 May 1995. ■

Forster's Tern

Sterna forsteri

Range: In eastern North America, breeds from Manitoba southeast to the Great Lakes, along the East coast from New Jersey to North Carolina, and along the Gulf coast to Texas. Winters from Virginia south to Central America.

NJ Status: Common but local summer resident, common spring and fall migrant, very rare winter resident.

Breeding

Habitat: Nests on salt marsh islands.

The change in the status of Forster's Tern from rarity to locally common breeding bird is well recounted in Sibley (1997). There is some uncertainty on the historic status of the species, as Forster's Terns were not easily separated from Common Terns by the early ornithologists (Stone 1937). Summer records from New Jersey in the late 1800s and early 1900s suggest Forster's Terns may have been breeding in New Jersey, but nesting was not confirmed (Stone 1937). There was a long period with no summer records, ending with the first

Forster's Tern

continued

Map Interpretation: Many of the terns have an extended pre-nesting courtship and an extended period of post-fledging parental care. Many of the Atlas breeding codes are too liberal for these species, and an accurate map of their breeding range is best estimated by using Confirmed breeding locations only.

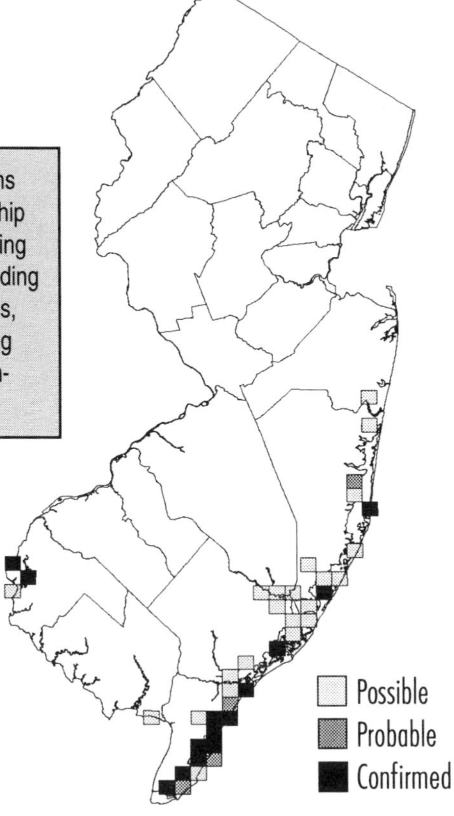

confirmed breeding record in 1955 at Brigantine NWR (Leck 1984). Forster's Terns rapidly gained a foothold in New Jersey at that point, and they soon were established as breeding birds along the salt marshes of the state.

Atlas data indicated Forster's Terns are broadly distributed in the salt marshes of Cape May County. In Atlantic, Ocean, and Salem counties, Forster's Terns were Confirmed in two blocks in each county. Their distribution is skewed more heavily to southern New Jersey than the distribution of Common Terns. Also, unlike Common Terns, Forster's Terns are beginning to expand their range and colonize the Delaware Bay shore.

Statewide Summary	
Status	# of Blocks
Possible	22
Probable	4
Confirmed	14
Total	40

Fall: The highest concentrations of Forster's Terns occur from October into early November. In fall, local populations are augmented by dispersing breeders

continued on page 302

Physiographic Distribution Forster's Tern	Number of blocks in province	Number of blocks species found breeding in province	Number of blocks species found in state	Percent of province species occupies	Percent of all records for this species found in province	Percent of state area in province
Inner Coastal Plain	128	2	40	1.6	5.0	15.0
Outer Coastal Plain	204	35	40	17.2	87.5	23.9
Pine Barrens	180	3	40	1.7	7.5	21.1

continued from page 301

Forster's Tern

and young from colonies to the south, and possibly by southbound breeding birds from much farther inland. Forster's Terns are present in large numbers much later into the season than Common Terns. Although they will wander inland for short distances in New Jersey, they are rare as migrants well away from the coast. **Maxima:** 3,284, Avalon Sea Watch, 5 November 1996; 1,550, Avalon Sea Watch, 26 October 1988. **ASW Seasonal Stats:** Average: 7,760; Maximum: 14,372 in 1995.

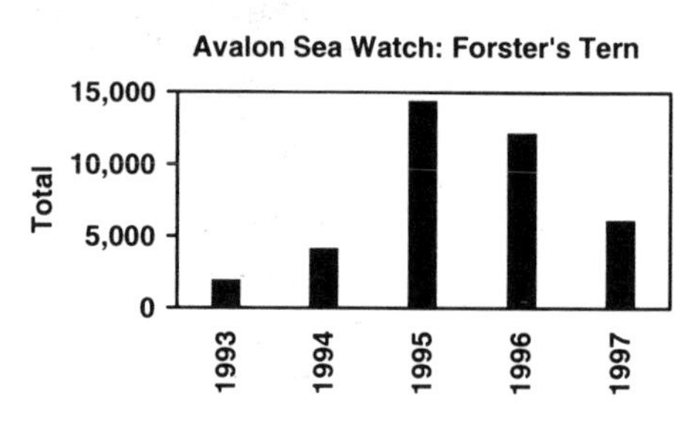

Winter: Forster's Terns frequently linger into December in the southern part of the state, sometimes long enough to be found in fair numbers on CBCs. On rare occasions they have spent the winter around Cape May County (e.g., 50, Norbury's Landing, to at least 15 February 1995). **CBC Statewide Stats:** Average: 9; Maximum: 56 in 1985; Minimum: 0 in seven years. **CBC Maximum:** 54, Cape May 1985.

Spring: Forster's Terns return north very early, usually arriving by mid- to late March. **Maximum:** 285, South Cape May Meadows, 10 May 1990. ■

Least Tern

Sterna antillarum

Range: In the eastern United States, breeds along the East coast from Maine to Florida, along the Gulf coast to Texas, and locally in the Mississippi River Valley. Winters in South America.

NJ Status: Fairly common but local summer resident, uncommon spring and fall migrant. Endangered Species in New Jersey.

Breeding

Habitat: Nests on open, sandy beaches.

Least Terns have suffered a fate similar to that of Common Terns and currently are in a tenuous position in New Jersey. Historically, they were a locally abundant breeding bird, but were hunted to near extinction by commercial collectors for the millinery trade. The scale of the plume hunting trade is difficult to imagine by

Least Tern

continued

Physiographic Distribution — **Least Tern**	Number of blocks in province	Number of blocks species found breeding in province	Number of blocks species found in state	Percent of province species occupies	Percent of all records for this species found in province	Percent of state area in province
Piedmont	167	4	30	2.4	13.3	19.6
Inner Coastal Plain	128	2	30	1.6	6.7	15.0
Outer Coastal Plain	204	23	30	11.3	76.7	23.9
Pine Barrens	180	1	30	0.6	3.3	21.1

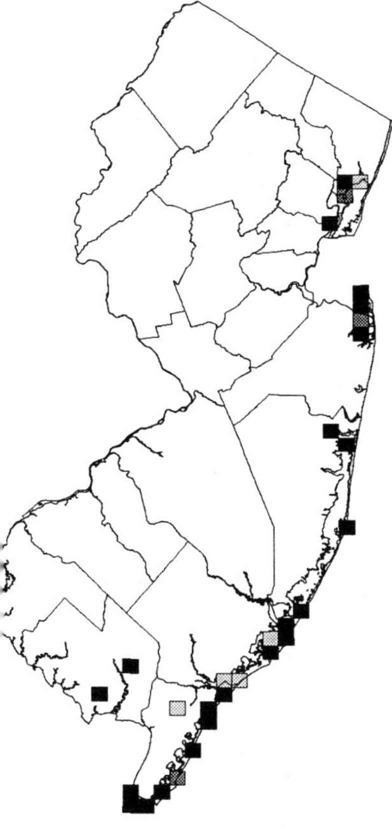

Possible
Probable
Confirmed

Statewide Summary	
Status	# of Blocks
Possible	5
Probable	3
Confirmed	22
Total	30

modern standards of wildlife conservation. Stone (1908) related a chilling 1885 encounter with two collectors who were standing *knee-deep* in Common and Least Terns carcasses – the sale of which brought 12 cents per bird. He followed that story with a second recollection of two collectors killing 75 breeding Least Terns from a colony on Brigantine Island in 1883. Indeed, the population became so reduced that the species was declared extirpated from New Jersey by Shriner in 1896. Leck (1984) found no breeding reports in New Jersey from 1890 through 1919.

Stone (1937) recounted Least Tern's recolonization of southern New Jersey, and suggested the species had persisted, in low numbers, as a breeding bird at Brigantine prior to its return to Cape May County as a breeder in 1924. Even in 1937, Stone lamented that recovery for this species was precarious, as the development of the barrier islands introduced too much human interference.

continued on page 304

continued from page 303

Least Tern

Atlas volunteers found Least Terns in two different habitats. Most were found in typical locations nesting along the high-beach wrack line of the barrier islands. Least Terns were also Confirmed breeding at two inland sand mining plants in Cumberland County. One inland colony was unsuccessful due to disturbance by all-terrain vehicle riders. Many coastal colonies, although they persist, are unable to fledge many young due to human disturbance, off-road vehicles, and predation by foxes and raccoons.

Conservation Note: Current management and regulatory actions taken in the state are ineffective for sustaining the population of Least Terns in New Jersey. One important aspect of the relationship between the distribution and the productivity of this species should be elucidated. Many of the colonies in New Jersey are unsuccessful – they either fledge very few or no young. Those colonies with very intense protection, particularly those at Sandy Hook (a portion of Gateway NWR), are able to be most effectively managed and consistently fledge the highest numbers of young. If the colonies in southern New Jersey do not receive the type of support the colonies at Sandy Hook receive, it is possible they will remain population "sinks" and may eventually disappear. Another problem Least Terns face is the ephemeral nature of their breeding habitat. Spoil islands and naturally created barrier islands are suitable when newly deposited, but once vegetated they no longer support breeding Least Terns.

Fall: Least Terns depart suddenly in late August or early September, with very few still present by mid-September. The peak of their southward movement is difficult to detect as migrants blend with local breeders.

Spring: Northward migration of Least Terns is no more discernable in spring than southbound flights are in fall. Breeders return to nesting areas in early May. ■

Bridled Tern

Sterna anaethetus

Range: Off eastern North America breeds throughout the West Indies. Winters mainly in the Caribbean and south Atlantic.

NJ Status: Very rare. NJBRC Review List.

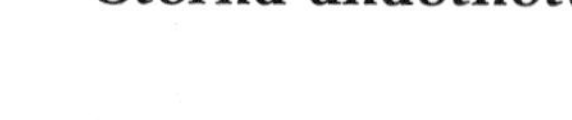

Occurrence: There have been 27 state reports of Bridled Tern, and 12 have been accepted by the NJBRC (six in fall, five in summer,

Bridled Tern

continued

one in winter). Most records are from shore following hurricanes. The 12 accepted records are:

	Location	Date	Notes
	Island Beach#	*24 February 1951*	*spec. ANSP #167592,- found dead*
	Lavallette	*13 August 1955*	*Woolfenden 1957, after Hurricane Connie*
	*Seaside Park**	*12 September 1960*	*spec. AMNH #708766, after Hurricane Donna*
2	*Stone Harbor**	*12 September 1960*	
	*Wildwood**	*12 September 1960*	
	*Holgate**	*5 August 1961*	*spec. AMNH, found dead*
	15 mi.off Barnegat Inlet	*15 August 1976*	*after Hurricane Belle*
	So. Cape May Meadows	*7 September 1979*	*after Hurricane David*
	*Atlantic City**	*8 October 1979*	*found dead*
	70 miles SE of Cape May	*12 September 1992*	*not certainly in New Jersey waters*
	Cape May Point	*13 July 1996*	*after Hurricane Bertha*
	41 mi. ESE of Barnegat Inlet	*25 August 1996*	*ph-RBPF*

Sooty Tern

Sterna fuscata

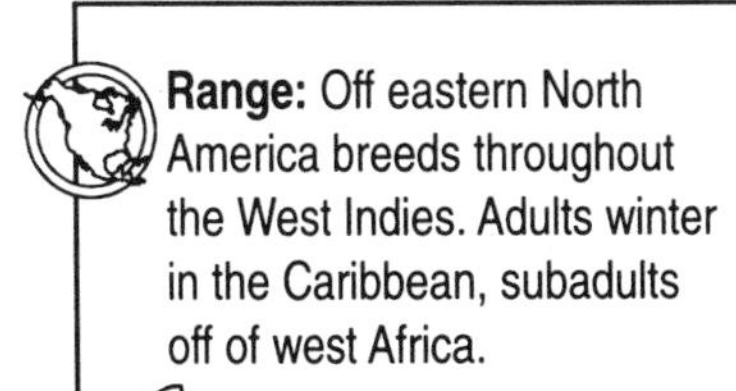

Range: Off eastern North America breeds throughout the West Indies. Adults winter in the Caribbean, subadults off of west Africa.

NJ Status: Very rare, usually following hurricanes. NJBRC Review List.

Occurrence: There have been 42 state reports of Sooty Tern, and 33 have been accepted by the NJBRC. Sightings invariably occur during or immediately after hurricanes. Most of the records have come from five storms: Connie (1955); Donna (1960); David (1979); and Bertha and Fran (1996). None of the state reports are pelagic; all were from shore. The 33 accepted records include five from inland. ■

Large-billed Tern

Phaetusa simplex

Range: Breeds in South America.

NJ Status: Accidental. NJBRC Review List.

Occurrence: There has been only one reported and accepted record of Large-billed Tern in New Jersey: Hackensack Meadowlands, 30 May 1988 (ph-RNJB 14:55), an adult. This sighting also represents the first North American record for this species (Kane et al. 1989). ■

White-winged Tern

Chlidonias leucopterus

Range: Breeds from eastern Europe to Asia. Winters in Africa, Southeast Asia, and Australia.

NJ Status: Accidental. NJBRC Review List.

Occurrence: There have been three state reports of White-winged Tern, and two have been accepted by the NJBRC. The two records are:

South Cape May Meadows	*10 May 1983*	*Sibley 1997*
South Cape May Meadows	*4 June-25 August 1989*	*phs-RNJB 15:61, 15:73; first summer plumage*

Whiskered Tern

Chlidonias hybridus

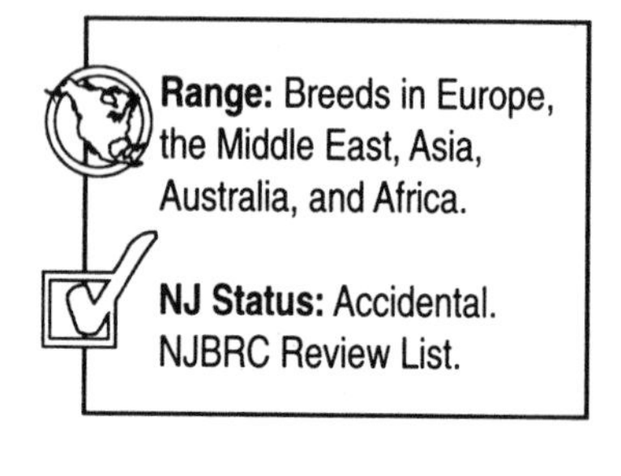

Range: Breeds in Europe, the Middle East, Asia, Australia, and Africa.

NJ Status: Accidental. NJBRC Review List.

Occurrence: There have been two state reports of Whiskered Tern, and both have been accepted by the NJBRC. The bird seen in 1993 was probably present in Cape May for some time prior to the listed sighting dates, but it was not identified until12 July. It eventually moved across the bay to Delaware. These are the only two records for North America. The two accepted records are:

Cape May Island	*12-15 July 1993*	*phs-RNJB 14:73, 14:88*
Cape May Point	*8-12 August 1998*	*ph-RBPF*

Black Tern

Chlidonias niger

Range: In eastern North America breeds from southern Manitoba east to New Brunswick, south to northern Kansas, and southern Maine. Winters off the coast from Mexico to northern South America.

NJ Status: Rare spring and uncommon fall migrant.

Historic Changes: Black Terns have declined markedly, at least since the 1960s, probably due to wetland destruction on the breeding grounds as well as along the migration route (Dunn and Agro 1995). Sibley (1997) reported historic maxima of hundreds of fall migrants at Cape May in several years from 1922-1934.

Fall: Black Terns may reach New Jersey surprisingly early; migrants are known from late June, although mid- to late July is the typical arrival period. Peak numbers are usually recorded between mid-August and early September. Few birds are recorded after early October. They are passage migrants through coastal wetlands and offshore, but are also recorded inland. **Maxima:** 50, Hancock's Bridge, 14 August 1994; 30, South Amboy, 28 July 1979.

Spring: Black Terns are less evident in spring than in fall, as the main flight is well to the west of New Jersey. At present an average of 5-10 sightings are made each year between early May and early June. Given the large decline in their numbers it is striking to note that spring transients have actually increased compared to the early part of the century. Stone (1908) knew of no spring records, and Cruickshank (1942) wrote "until recently the Black Tern was of casual occurrence anywhere in our region in spring." **Maxima:** 45, Wildwood Crest, 8 May 1981; 22, Mannington Marsh, 6 May 1995. ■

Brown Noddy

Anous stolidus

Occurrence: There have been three state reports of Brown Noddy; and one has been accepted by NJBRC: Cape May Point, 8 September 1979, after Hurricane David. ■

Range: Pelagic. Breeds in the Gulf-Caribbean region from Dry Tortugas and the Bahamas south through the Antilles to islands off South America.

NJ Status: Accidental. NJBRC Review List.

Black Skimmer

Rynchops niger

Range: Breeds on the East Coast from Massachusetts to Florida, and along the Gulf coast to Texas. Winters from North Carolina south to Central and South Americas.

NJ Status: Fairly common but local summer resident, fairly common spring and fall migrant, very rare winter resident. Endangered Species in New Jersey.

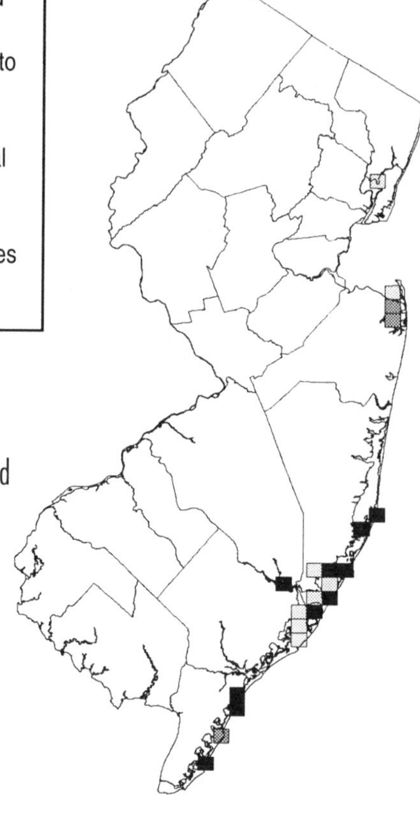

Possible
Probable
Confirmed

Statewide Summary	
Status	# of Blocks
Possible	8
Probable	3
Confirmed	10
Total	21

Map Interpretation: The Possible locations shown on the map should not be considered part of the breeding range. Only Confirmed colony sites represent breeding locations. Other Possible and Probable sites may represent nonbreeding subadults or adults.

Breeding

Habitat: Nests on open, sandy beaches.

As with the other beach nesting species, Black Skimmers suffered a period of near or

Physiographic Distribution

Black Skimmer	Number of blocks in province	Number of blocks species found breeding in province	Number of blocks species found in state	Percent of province species occupies	Percent of all records for this species found in province	Percent of state area in province
Piedmont	167	1	21	0.6	4.8	19.6
Inner Coastal Plain	128	1	21	0.8	4.8	15.0
Outer Coastal Plain	204	19	21	9.3	90.5	23.9

complete extirpation from New Jersey in the late 1800s and early 1900s. Wilson (1810) knew the species to be locally abundant, and recounted a huge amount of egg taking from the beaches in Cape May County. By 1890 Black Skimmers had become a rarity. There were no breeding records from Cape May County from 1895 to 1915, but at that time the species persisted in some small colonies in Atlantic County (Stone 1937). During the mid- and late 1900s there was an increase in the abundance and range of Black Skimmers on the United States Atlantic coast, with a probable stabilization of the species in the late 1900s (Gochfeld and Burger 1994).

Black Skimmers rarely nest in single-species colonies, and are often found in mixed colonies with Common Terns or Least Terns. They prefer sandy islands or beaches with little vegetation, and usually commence breeding after tern colonies have been established (Gochfeld and Burger 1994). During the series of ENSP Coastal Colonial Waterbird Surveys (Table 2), the New Jersey population has been quite variable, and it is difficult to predict the future for this species.

Atlas volunteers found the center of the Black Skimmer's population to be in southern Ocean County, although they were also Confirmed in Cape May and Atlantic counties. The largest Cape May County colony was located on Champagne Island in Hereford Inlet. However, a series of winter storms during 1997 and 1998 over-washed the island, and left no sand above the tide. The island may be rebuilt, but in 1998 the skimmers moved to nearby Stone Harbor Point (a nest site from the late 1980s).

Fall: Black Skimmers are often seen roosting near their breeding colonies after the nesting season, or seen wandering to nearby feeding areas. Numbers begin to decline in late September and they become scarce by late October. **Maxima:** 1,500, Hereford Inlet, 4 October 1986; 1,200, Hereford Inlet, 6 September 1991.

Winter: Black Skimmers occasionally linger into early December, and they have been recorded three times on CBCs since 1976 (e.g., 1986, 1987, 1988). There are also several recent records in mid-winter: 1, Holgate, 30 January 1980; 2, Cape May Point, 5 January 1993; 1, Brigantine Island, winter of 1997-1998; and 1, Hereford Inlet, winter of 1997-1998.

Spring: Black Skimmers return fairly early in spring, with the first seen by mid-April. Most are seen near known breeding locations. ■

Dovekie

Alle alle

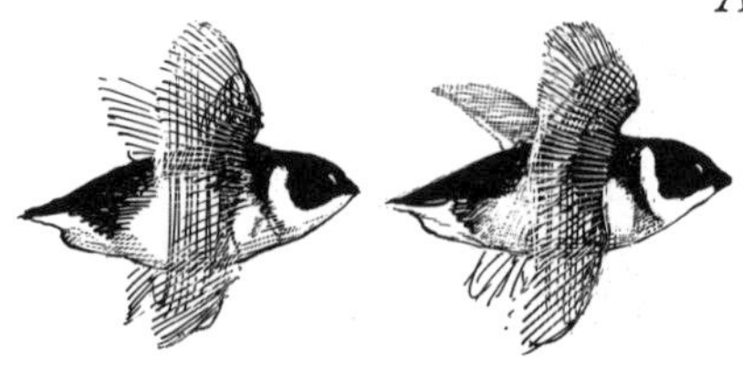

Dovekie

Range: In North America breeds in the high Arctic to southern Greenland and Iceland. Winters from the breeding range south to North Carolina.

NJ Status: Irregular winter visitor offshore. Rare from shore.

Occurrence: Assessing the status of Dovekie off of New Jersey is hampered by the lack of offshore observations in late fall and winter. Dovekies are probably present in New Jersey waters from mid-November through late March, and apparently numbers vary from year to year. Although they are sometimes seen from shore, most are found more than five miles offshore. An incredible count of 733, found 20 to 45 miles southeast of Cape May on 19 February 1995, may have been outside New Jersey waters. Among a handful of records from shore is one of a bird found alive on a highway near Cape May Court House on 27 February 1996, about 8 to 10 miles from the coast. They have been reported six times on CBCs since 1976, three times on the offshore Atlantic Ocean count. **Maxima:** 80+, 60-90 miles off Brielle, 14 January 1995; 50, 50 miles off Brielle, 11 March 1996. ■

Common Murre

Uria aalge

Range: In eastern North America breeds from Labrador and Quebec south to Newfoundland and Nova Scotia. In the Atlantic winters south to Maine, occasionally as far as Virginia.

NJ Status: Very rare. NJBRC Review List.

Occurrence: There have been 28 state reports of Common Murre, and 15 have been accepted by the NJBRC (14 in winter, one in spring). Most reports are from shore,

Common Murre

continued

with only five pelagic reports. The 15 accepted records are:

	Avon#	*3 February 1946*	*spec. AMNH #408,896, found dead*
	Shark River Inlet#	*8 December 1951*	
	Little Egg Inlet#	*15 February 1959*	*spec. AMNH #707773, found dead*
	*Sea Girt**	*13-24 February 1965*	*Bull 1970*
	*Island Beach**	*8 April 1966*	*found dead*
	Beach Haven	*7 March 1973*	*ph-RBPF, found dead*
	*Cape May Point**	*24 December 1973*	*found oiled*
2	*Holgate**	*5 February 1977*	*both found dead*
	32 miles off Cape May	*8 March 1987*	
	*Atlantic City**	*17 December 1988*	
	Manasquan Inlet	*21 January 1991*	*ph-RBPF*
	four miles off Brielle	*7 February 1993*	
	30-35 miles off Brielle	*20 February 1994*	
	Manasquan Inlet	*23-26 February 1995*	
	26 miles ESE of Wildwood	*16 January 1997*	*ph-RBPF*

Thick-billed Murre

Uria lomvia

Range: In eastern North America breeds from the high Arctic islands south to Hudson Bay and Newfoundland. In the East, winters from the breeding range along the coast to New York.

NJ Status: Rare winter visitor. Added to the NJBRC Review List in 1996.

Occurrence: Since the addition of Thick-billed Murre to the NJBRC Review List in 1996 there have been two state reports, and one has been accepted by NJBRC: Spring Lake, 26 February 1998, spec. Princeton.

There are at least 60 previous state reports of Thick-billed Murres, with most from December through March, however a historic review of all sightings has not been undertaken by the NJBRC. There are three spring and four fall reports but only one summer record, that from Sandy Hook (spec. AMNH, Bull 1970), one of five taken in the New York City region during late July-late August 1966. They have been reported on seven CBCs since 1976, three times on the offshore Atlantic Ocean count.

continued on page 312

continued from page 311

Thick-billed Murre

Most of the reports occurred prior to 1900, but reports have dropped off substantially since the 1950s. Only nine of the reports are from offshore, where it is likely that Thick-billed Murres are more regular, but winter pelagic birding trips are infrequent. Onshore reports are well distributed along the coast from Sandy Hook to Cape May. There are six inland reports, all of which occurred from 1894 to 1901. ■

Razorbill

Alca torda

Range: In North America breeds from Labrador to Maine. Winters off the coast from the breeding range south to North Carolina.

NJ Status: Uncommon to fairly common offshore winter visitor. Rare to scarce from shore.

Fall: Razorbills are the most frequently encountered alcid in New Jersey, and the one most regularly seen from shore. Southbound movements seem to be protracted, beginning in late October and sometimes continuing into January. **ASW Single-Day Maximum:** 9 on 11 December 1993. **ASW Seasonal Stats:** Average: 6; Maximum: 13 in 1993.

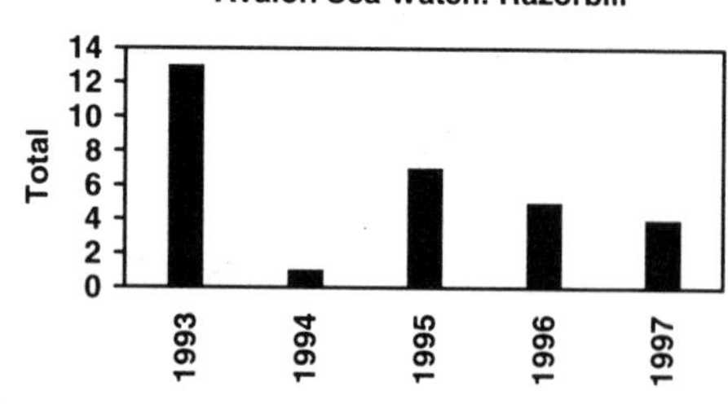

Winter: Razorbills are recorded in variable numbers from year to year. Most occur more than five miles offshore, but they tend to be recorded more often inshore than other large alcids. **CBC Statewide Stats:** Average: 2; Maximum: 9 in 1986; Minimum: 0 in nine years. **CBC Maximum:** 6, Atlantic Ocean, 1986.

Spring: Apparently, a northward movement of Razorbills occurs from late February through mid-March. **Maxima:** 88, three miles off Sea Isle, 25 February 1991; 81, off Cape May, 8 March 1987. ■

Black Guillemot

Cepphus grylle

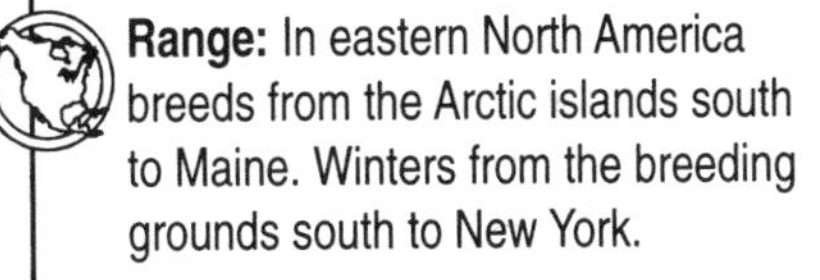

Range: In eastern North America breeds from the Arctic islands south to Maine. Winters from the breeding grounds south to New York.

NJ Status: Accidental. NJBRC Review List.

Occurrence: There have been 19 state reports of Black Guillemot, and seven have been accepted by the NJBRC (all in late fall/winter). The two sightings on 20 January 1991 were accepted as one record. The seven accepted records are:

Location	Date	Source
Cold Spring Inlet, Cape May	*10 December 1929*	*Stone 1937*
Newark Bay#	*27 December 1936*	
Boonton Res.#	*26 November 1939*	
Spring Lake#	*27 December 1958*	
*Stone Harbor**	*19 December 1962-13 January 1963*	
Point Pleasant	*27 December 1986*	
Sandy Hook	*20 January 1991*	
Manasquan Inlet	*20 January 1991*	

Atlantic Puffin

Fratercula arctica

Range: In eastern North America breeds from Labrador south to Maine. Winters offshore from Labrador south to Maryland.

NJ Status: Very rare. NJBRC Review List.

Occurrence: There have been 28 state reports of Atlantic Puffins; and 13 have been accepted by the NJBRC (nine in winter, two in fall, two in spring). The 13 accepted records are:

Number	Location	Date	Source
	Barnegat Inlet#	*19 December 1926*	
2	*16 miles off Long Beach Island#*	*1 January 1933*	
	Jarvis Sound#, Cape May	*24 December 1933*	
	Wreck Pond#	*21 January 1951*	
	Cape May#	*3 January 1954*	
	pelagic trip to Hudson Canyon	*8 November 1975*	
	*pelagic trip to Hudson Canyon**	*16 November 1975*	
2	*25 miles SE of Cape May*	*9 March 1985*	
	8 miles off Cape May	*23 February 1991*	
8	*20 miles off Barnegat Inlet*	*30 May 1992*	*ph-AB 46:401*
	29 miles ESE of Manasquan Inlet	*7 December 1996*	
	31 miles ESE of Manasquan Inlet	*7 December 1996*	
2	*60 miles SE Wildwood*	*16 February 1997*	*RBPF*

Rock Dove

Columba livia

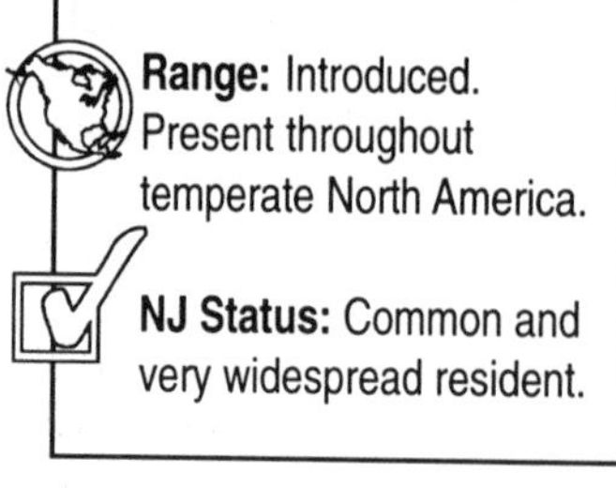

Range: Introduced. Present throughout temperate North America.

NJ Status: Common and very widespread resident.

Breeding

Habitat: Nesting is associated with man-made structures, particularly bridges and building ledges.

Possible
Probable
Confirmed

Rock Doves were introduced to North America, and the stock that was released represented domesticated stock used by pigeon racers and fanciers. (Rock Doves do have a wild population in Europe – the ancestral stock of the current domesticated stock.) Some of the introduced stock, through successive generations, has reverted to forms that resemble wild

Statewide Summary

Status	# of Blocks
Possible	122
Probable	212
Confirmed	332
Total	666

Physiographic Distribution

Rock Dove	Number of blocks in province	Number of blocks species found breeding in province	Number of blocks species found in state	Percent of province species occupies	Percent of all records for this species found in province	Percent of state area in province
Kittatinny Mountains	19	13	666	68.4	2.0	2.2
Kittatinny Valley	45	43	666	95.6	6.5	5.3
Highlands	109	98	666	89.9	14.7	12.8
Piedmont	167	149	666	89.2	22.4	19.6
Inner Coastal Plain	128	118	666	92.2	17.7	15.0
Outer Coastal Plain	204	160	666	78.4	24.0	23.9
Pine Barrens	180	85	666	47.2	12.8	21.1

Rock Dove

continued

Rock Doves, although it is still common to see individuals with domestic pigeon patterns. Rock Doves have frequently been overlooked in historic ornithological literature, and consequently, the details of this species' pattern of colonization are undocumented.

Atlas volunteers found Rock Doves breeding throughout New Jersey, but the population is probably also augmented by continued releases of homing pigeons. Rock Doves are partial to human structures and are usually found nesting near buildings, barns, and bridges. They are widespread in New Jersey, found breeding in all physiographic provinces. Their absence from the heart of the Pine Barrens is probably due to the scarcity of appropriate nesting substrate.

Fall: Rock Doves are permanent residents. There is no published information on the occurrence of fall migration of Rock Doves in New Jersey.

Winter: After a low period in the late 1970s, statewide CBC totals for Rock Doves have been remarkably consistent. **CBC Statewide Stats:** Average: 18,392; Maximum: 27,748 in 1988; Minimum: 7,092 in 1976. **CBC Maximum:** 13,123, Lower Hudson, 1985.

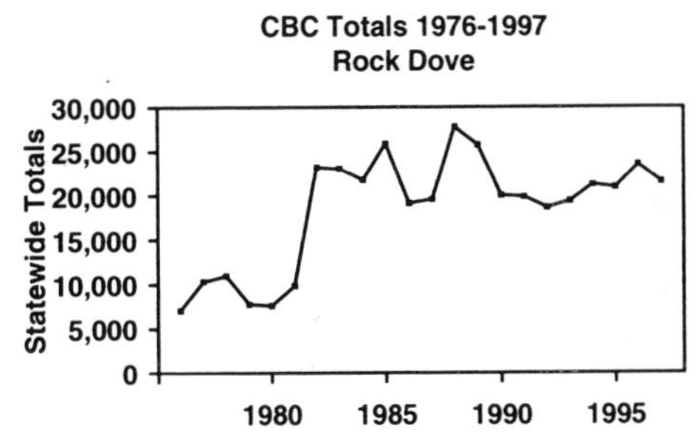

Spring: Rock Doves are permanent residents. There is no published information on the occurrence of spring migration of Rock Doves in New Jersey. ■

Band-tailed Pigeon

Columba fasciata

Occurrence: There has been only one report and one accepted record of Band-tailed Pigeon in New Jersey: Rattlesnake Mt., 17 September 1980. ■

Range: Breeds from western British Columbia south to California, east to Colorado and western Texas, and south to Central America. Winters from central California east to Texas and south through the breeding range.

NJ Status: Accidental. NJBRC Review List.

Eurasian Collared-Dove

Streptopelia decaocto

Range: Now resident throughout much of Europe and the Middle East to North Africa, with remarkable range expansion since the 1930s. Recently established as a breeder in the southeastern United States via the Bahamas.

NJ Status: Accidental. NJBRC Review List.

Occurrence: There has been only one report and one accepted record of Eurasian Collared-Dove in New Jersey: Cape May Point, 7 September 1997 (Lehman 1998b). ■

White-winged Dove

Zenaida asiatica

Range: Breeds from southern California east to Texas and in south Florida, south to the Caribbean and South America. Winters within the breeding range, but northern birds are migratory.

NJ Status: Very rare. NJBRC Review List.

Occurrence: There have been 21 state reports of White-winged Doves, and 13 have been accepted by the NJBRC (five in fall, five in spring, two in winter, one in summer). The 13 accepted records are:

West Cape May	*24 May 1981*	*ph-RBPF*
*Cape May Point**	*6 September 1983*	
Cape May	*24 May 1986*	
Tuckerton	*31 December 1990-1 January 1991*	*ph-RBPF*
Avalon	*4 November 1992*	*ph-RBPF*
Rio Grande	*3-7 May 1993*	
Avalon	*28 April 1994*	*ph-RBPF*
Cape May	*6 November 1994*	
Heislerville	*28 November-2 December 1995*	
Cape May Point	*5 May 1996*	
Cape May Point	*8 July 1996*	
Cape May	*13-18 November 1996*	
Mantoloking	*21 December 1996*	

Mourning Dove

Zenaida macroura

Range: Breeds throughout southern Canada and all of the United States. Winters throughout most of the breeding range.

NJ Status: Common and nearly ubiquitous resident.

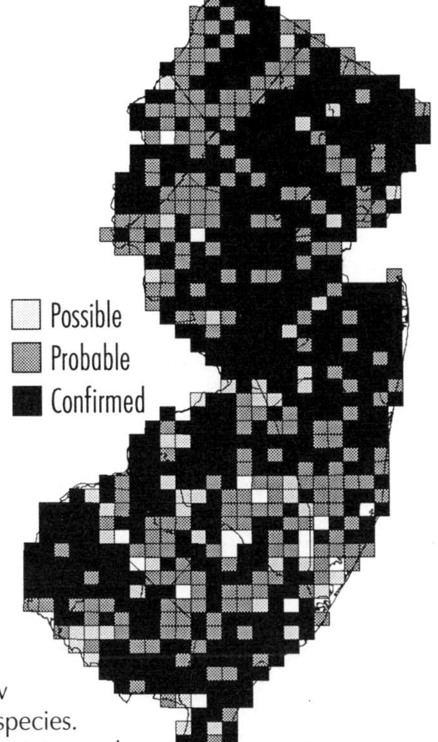

Breeding

Habitat: Breeds in almost any semi-open habitat with enough trees for cover.

Mourning Doves are one of New Jersey's most widespread nesting species. Details of Mourning Dove's historic status and range in New Jersey are lacking, although Griscom (1923) indicated the species was absent from the extreme northwest corner of the state, and from the areas around New York City.

Atlas volunteers found Mourning Doves in all but 19 blocks statewide. Mourning Doves may double brood and are conspicuous while nest

continued on page 318

Statewide Summary

Status	# of Blocks
Possible	47
Probable	245
Confirmed	541
Total	833

Physiographic Distribution

Mourning Dove	Number of blocks in province	Number of blocks species found breeding in province	Number of blocks species found in state	Percent of province species occupies	Percent of all records for this species found in province	Percent of state area in province
Kittatinny Mountains	19	19	833	100.0	2.3	2.2
Kittatinny Valley	45	44	833	97.8	5.3	5.3
Highlands	109	109	833	100.0	13.1	12.8
Piedmont	167	166	833	99.4	19.9	19.6
Inner Coastal Plain	128	128	833	100.0	15.4	15.0
Outer Coastal Plain	204	196	833	96.1	23.5	23.9
Pine Barrens	180	171	833	95.0	20.5	21.1

continued from page 317

Mourning Dove

building – the male may make 30-40 nest-material gathering trips in a morning (Jackson and Baskett 1964). The high frequency of this behavior gave Atlas volunteers ample opportunities to Confirm the species with the nest building code. Mourning Doves are flexible in their choice of nesting habitat and may nest along field edges or in suburban or urban neighborhoods. This, coupled with their conspicuous nest building behaviors, left few gaps in their mapped breeding range in New Jersey.

Fall: After the breeding season Mourning Doves congregate in large flocks, particularly around agricultural fields. Most of the New Jersey population is resident, although populations from the northern portions of the species' range do move south. Passage birds are rarely evident, however, as migration is masked by the presence of a large local population.

Winter: Statewide CBC totals of Mourning Doves indicated a slow rise in numbers since the mid-1970s. **CBC Statewide Stats:** Average: 18,366; Maximum: 24,332 in 1996; Minimum: 11,987 in 1978. **CBC Maximum:** 3,855, Elmer, 1996.

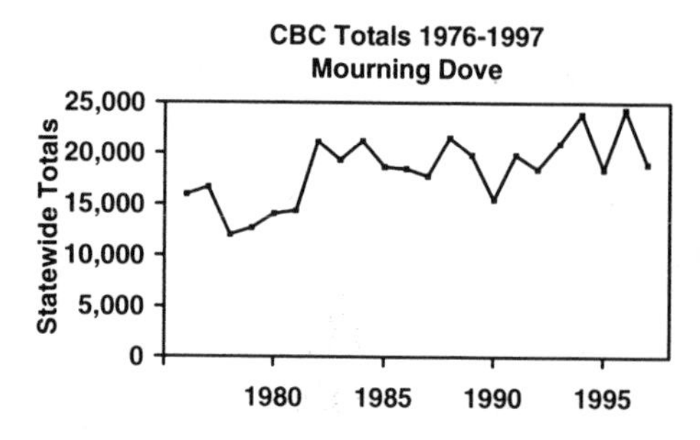

Spring: There is no noticeable return flight of northbound Mourning Doves. The large local population probably masks any movements that occur. ■

Passenger Pigeon

Ectopistes migratorius

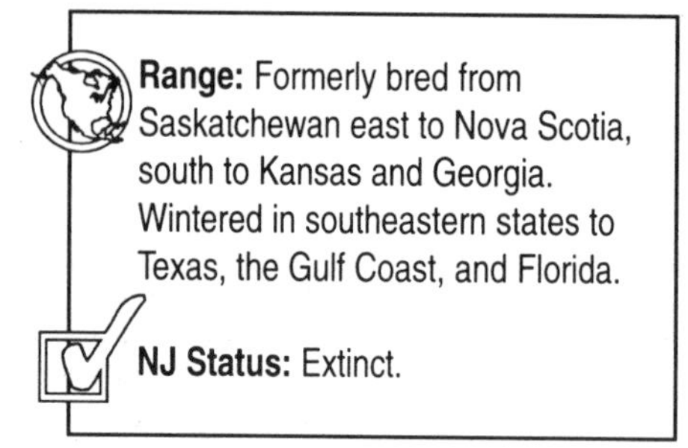

Range: Formerly bred from Saskatchewan east to Nova Scotia, south to Kansas and Georgia. Wintered in southeastern states to Texas, the Gulf Coast, and Florida.

NJ Status: Extinct.

Occurrence: Passenger Pigeons were once abundant in New Jersey, but were considered rare by the mid-1800s (Stone 1937). The last state record for the species was of one shot from a flock of ten, Morristown, 7 October 1893. Another reportedly shot in Englewood, 23 June 1896 (Fables 1955) turned out to be a Mourning Dove (Bull 1964). Two specimens are extant, both from Haddonfield, circa 1879 (ANSP). The last living Passenger Pigeon died in captivity in the Cincinnati Zoo in 1914 (Todd 1994). ■

Common Ground-Dove

Columbina passerina

Range: In the east, resident from Florida north to South Carolina.

NJ Status: Accidental. NJBRC Review List.

Occurrence: There have been four state reports of Common Ground-Doves, and two have been accepted by the NJBRC. The two accepted records are:

*near Camden**	*November 1858*	*shot, spec. lost*
Higbee Beach	*4 September 1984*	

Carolina Parakeet

Conuropsis carolinensis

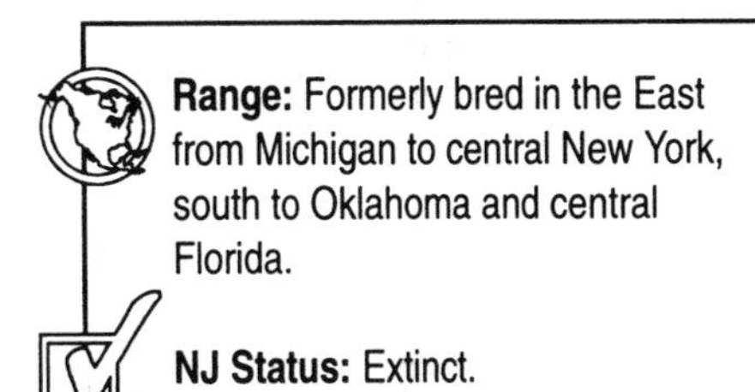

Range: Formerly bred in the East from Michigan to central New York, south to Oklahoma and central Florida.

NJ Status: Extinct.

Occurrence: While there are no New Jersey specimens of Carolina Parakeets, there are published references to their occurrence in the state in the 1850s in East Orange (Eaton 1936, Cruickshank 1942). The AOU Check-list includes New Jersey in the species' former range. On that basis, both Kunkle et al. (1959) and the NJBRC accorded it a place on the state list. The last specimen taken in the wild was from Florida, 12 March 1913; the last Carolina Parakeet died in the Cincinnati Zoo in 1918 (Todd 1994). ■

Black-billed Cuckoo

Coccyzus erythropthalmus

Range: Breeds from Alberta east to Nova Scotia, south to Oklahoma and northern Georgia. Winters in South America.

NJ Status: Uncommon and somewhat local summer resident, uncommon spring and fall migrant.

Statewide Summary	
Status	# of Blocks
Possible	120
Probable	125
Confirmed	41
Total	286

Breeding

Habitat: Breeds along woodland edges, in shrubby thickets and in second-growth woodlands.

Some early observers in New Jersey did not separate the range or abundance of Black-billed and Yellow-billed Cuckoos from one another (Shriner 1896), and frequently historic discussions of Black-billed Cuckoos centered on identification of this species, not on its range.

Griscom (1923) listed both cuckoos as common throughout northern New Jersey, but noted that Yellow-billed Cuckoos were more numerous. Fables (1955) indicated

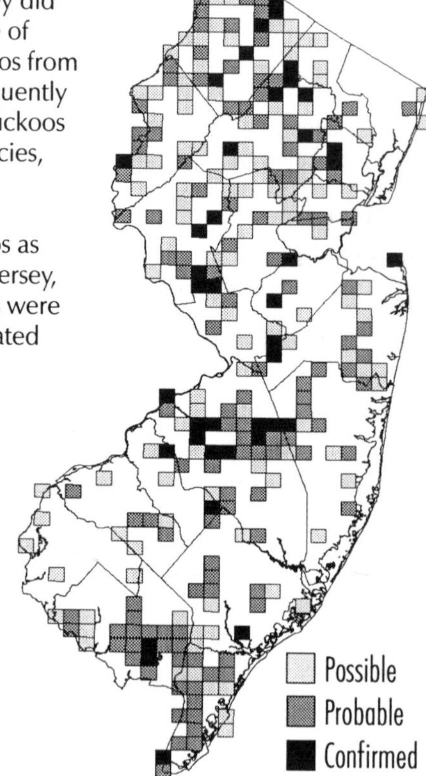

Map Interpretation: Black-billed Cuckoos appear to undergo erratic patterns of dispersal during the breeding season. Individuals may appear in an area, sing for a short time, and move on, and this may occur at any point in the summer (D. Sibley, pers. com.). This suggests that the some of the Atlas sightings that are scored as Possible may be floaters, or prospecting individuals.

both species were well distributed throughout the state, although not found in salt marshes, barrier islands, or urbanized regions. He also suggested Yellow-billed Cuckoos were more common in the Pine Barrens. Bull (1964) suggested that Black-billed Cuckoos were more common in the higher elevations and the interior of northern New Jersey. Leck (1984) contended that Black-billed Cuckoos were present throughout the state, but bred most commonly in northern New Jersey.

Black-billed Cuckoos prefer large woodland tracts for nesting, and Atlas results indicated that their distribution closely matches the areas of the state with the greatest forest cover. Atlas data also indicated the species is nearly absent from salt marshes and barrier islands on the Outer Coastal Plain. They were nearly absent from Bergen County and Salem County (areas with little forest cover), but had some strong pockets of occurrence in Cape May, Cumberland, and Burlington counties, as well as in most of the central and western counties. These southern New Jersey strongholds either represent a new pattern of distribution for this species, or were historically overlooked.

Fall: Southbound Black-billed Cuckoos can arrive by late July and most have moved through by late September. They become rare by the beginning of October. There are usually no more than a few migrant Black-billed Cuckoos seen at any specific locality on a given day, owing at least in part to their secretive nature. **Maxima:** 10, Higbee Beach, 16 August 1982; 4, Higbee Beach, 20 September 1987.

Spring: Black-billed Cuckoos are rarely seen before the beginning of May and most move through from mid-May into early June. **Maxima:** 20, Vincentown, 13 May 1976; 10, Sherman-Hoffman Sanctuary, 16 May 1981. ■

Physiographic Distribution

Black-billed Cuckoo	Number of blocks in province	Number of blocks species found breeding in province	Number of blocks species found in state	Percent of province species occupies	Percent of all records for this species found in province	Percent of state area in province
Kittatinny Mountains	19	15	286	78.9	5.2	2.2
Kittatinny Valley	45	28	286	62.2	9.8	5.3
Highlands	109	42	286	38.5	14.7	12.8
Piedmont	167	54	286	32.3	18.9	19.6
Inner Coastal Plain	128	36	286	28.1	12.6	15.0
Outer Coastal Plain	204	59	286	28.9	20.6	23.9
Pine Barrens	180	52	286	28.9	18.2	21.1

Yellow-billed Cuckoo

Coccyzus americanus

Range: In eastern North America, breeds from eastern South Dakota east to Maine, south to Texas and Florida. Winters in South America.

NJ Status: Fairly common and widespread summer resident, fairly common spring and fall migrant.

Statewide Summary	
Status	# of Blocks
Possible	161
Probable	274
Confirmed	91
Total	526

Possible
Probable
Confirmed

Breeding

Habitat: Breeds in tall dense thickets, second-growth woodlands, and woodland edges.

Griscom (1923) listed both Black-billed and Yellow-billed Cuckoos as common throughout northern New Jersey, but noted

Physiographic Distribution Yellow-billed Cuckoo	Number of blocks in province	Number of blocks species found breeding in province	Number of blocks species found in state	Percent of province species occupies	Percent of all records for this species found in province	Percent of state area in province
Kittatinny Mountains	19	16	526	84.2	3.0	2.2
Kittatinny Valley	45	33	526	73.3	6.3	5.3
Highlands	109	67	526	61.5	12.7	12.8
Piedmont	167	77	526	46.1	14.6	19.6
Inner Coastal Plain	128	66	526	51.6	12.5	15.0
Outer Coastal Plain	204	123	526	60.3	23.4	23.9
Pine Barrens	180	144	526	80.0	27.4	21.1

Yellow-billed Cuckoo

continued

that Yellow-billed Cuckoos were more numerous. Fables (1955) suggested both species were well distributed throughout New Jersey, although absent from the salt marshes, barrier islands, and urbanized regions. He also suggested that Yellow-billed Cuckoos were more common in the Pine Barrens. Bull (1964) contended that Black-billed Cuckoos were more common in the higher elevations and the interior of northern New Jersey.

Atlas data indicated Yellow-billed Cuckoos are more densely and more widely distributed in New Jersey then are Black-billed Cuckoos. Like Black-billed Cuckoos, they are nearly absent from the barrier islands. Unlike Black-billed Cuckoos, they are found along the wooded upland edge of the Atlantic coast salt marshes. Yellow-billed Cuckoos were encountered most frequently in the Outer Coastal Plain, Pine Barrens, and the heavily wooded areas in northern New Jersey. This distribution pattern of Yellow-billed Cuckoos included the areas of the state with the greatest forest cover, but also certain areas with less forest cover, such as the Inner Coastal Plain (e.g., Salem County) and the Piedmont.

Fall: Southbound Yellow-billed Cuckoos arrive by late July. Fewer pass through after mid-September, although a few continue to filter through during October. Yellow-billed Cuckoos are more frequently encountered in migration than Black-billed Cuckoos. **Maxima:** 15, Higbee Beach, 31 July 1988; 15, Higbee Beach, 26 August 1993.

Spring: Yellow-billed Cuckoos are generally not seen before the beginning of May and most move through from mid-May into early June. **Maxima:** 10, West Cape May, 25 May 1989; 8, Sherman-Hoffman Sanctuary, 25 May 1977. ■

Smooth-billed Ani/Groove-billed Ani

Crotophaga ani/Crotophaga sulcirostris

Range: Two similar species ranging from southern Texas east to southern Florida.

NJ Status: Accidental. NJBRC Review List

There has been one reported and one accepted record of Ani sp. for New Jersey: Sandy Hook, 9 October 1997 (ph-RNJB 24:1). These two species are very similar in appearance, and this records remains accepted by the NJBRC as Ani sp. ■

Barn Owl

Tyto alba

Possible
Probable
Confirmed

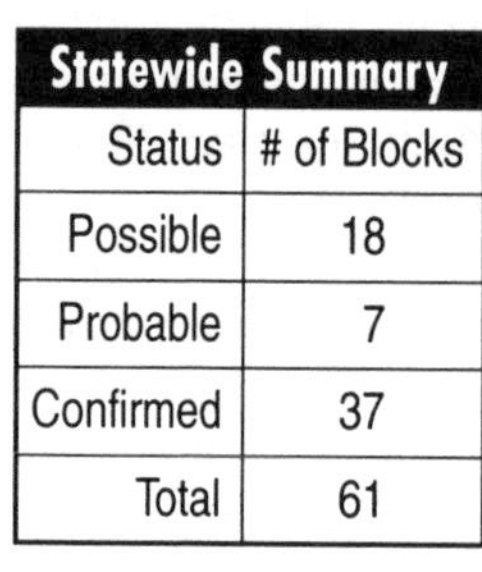

Statewide Summary	
Status	# of Blocks
Possible	18
Probable	7
Confirmed	37
Total	61

Breeding

Habitat: A cavity nester preferring open country; frequently uses man-made structures such as old barns, silos, etc.

Early ornithologists indicated the distribution of Barn Owls in New Jersey was skewed to southern New Jersey (Stone 1908, 1937). Many lamented that

Range: In the eastern United States, resident from South Dakota east to Massachusetts, south to Texas and Florida.

NJ Status: Uncommon and local summer resident, scarce to uncommon fall migrant, uncommon winter resident.

Physiographic Distribution Barn Owl	Number of blocks in province	Number of blocks species found breeding in province	Number of blocks species found in state	Percent of province species occupies	Percent of all records for this species found in province	Percent of state area in province
Kittatinny Valley	45	4	61	6.6	8.9	5.3
Highlands	109	8	61	13.1	7.3	12.8
Piedmont	167	12	61	19.7	7.2	19.6
Inner Coastal Plain	128	7	61	11.5	5.5	15.0
Outer Coastal Plain	204	27	61	44.3	13.2	23.9
Pine Barrens	180	3	61	4.9	1.7	21.1

the species' status was under-reported due to difficulties in detecting this owl (Griscom 1923, Cruickshank 1942). Barn Owl population trends are difficult to track, as focused searches invariably find more nests in a wider range than expected (Cruickshank 1942; see below). Barn Owls are able to coexist with humans, perhaps better than any other owl. Unfortunately, their habit is to nest in derelict buildings, and their nest sites are frequently destroyed.

Barn Owls, unlike many other owls, are inconspicuous even during their nesting period. Many owl species are detected from long distances by their habit of calling on territory (e.g., Great Horned Owl, Barred Owl, and Eastern Screech-Owl), but Barn Owls do not engage in this activity. To complicate matters, Barn Owls nest at almost any time of year, and young have been found in New Jersey in every month but February (Colvin and Hegdal 1995).

During Atlas surveys researchers from The Barn Owl Research Foundation conducted surveys for breeding Barn Owls in Gloucester, Salem and Cumberland counties. They confirmed breeding in 11 blocks for which Atlas volunteers had only located four Possible sites, and not recorded any Barn Owls in the remaining seven blocks (B. Colvin, pers. com.). Data from the private survey were included in the Atlas. If similar surveys had been conducted statewide, or in other counties, it is likely that the physiographic distribution of Barn Owls could be similarly concentrated in other areas as well.

Conservation Note: There is evidence that Barn Owls occur in all physiographic provinces of New Jersey, although we know little about the precise size and trends of the population. Despite five years of Atlas surveys, the true status of this species remains enigmatic for much of New Jersey. Focused nest searches, like those conducted by Colvin and Hegdal, would increase our understanding of the size and range of the Barn Owl population. Preservation of structures used by Barn Owls for nesting, and increasing the use of owl nest boxes should also be encouraged.

Fall: The migratory habits of Barn Owls are not well known. Northern populations are thought to be partially migratory, and there have been a few recoveries of banded birds well south of their banding location. However, Marti (1992) suggested that there is no evidence of migration in most studies of marked individuals in either North America or Europe. It is contended that immature birds disperse in all directions, sometimes to great distances, which is sometimes confused with migration (Marti 1992). However, the results of a study from an owl-banding project at Cape May (Duffy and Kerlinger 1992) appear to indicate otherwise. A total of 180 Barn Owls were captured from 1980-1988. Nearly 20 % of those captured were adults, indicating that the species may be at least partly migratory. **Maxima:** 16, 26 October 1979; 7, 6 October 1980; and 7, 9 October 1980, all Cape May Point (banded, K. Duffy, pers. com.).

continued on page 326

continued from page 325

Barn Owl

Winter: Although never numerous on CBCs, statewide totals show a decline in Barn Owl numbers beginning in the mid-1980s. **CBC Statewide Stats:** Average: 13; Maximum: 23 in 1977; Minimum: 2 in 1991. **CBC Maximum:** 11, Lower Hudson, 1982.

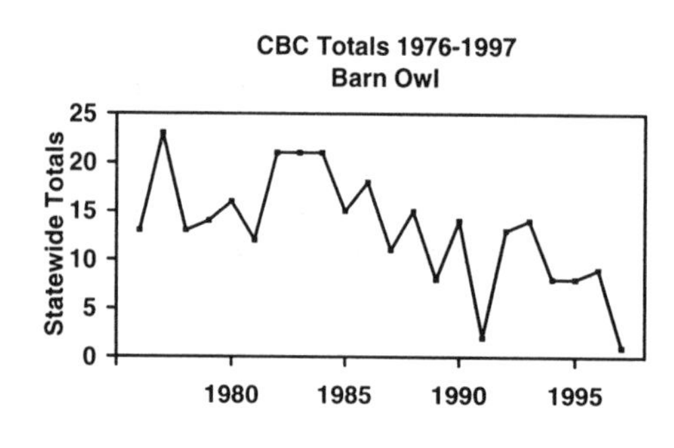

Spring: There is no discernable return flight of Barn Owls in spring. ■

Eastern Screech-Owl

Otus asio

Possible
Probable
Confirmed

Statewide Summary	
Status	# of Blocks
Possible	97
Probable	214
Confirmed	47
Total	358

Range: Resident from southeastern Manitoba east to southern New Hampshire, south to Texas and Florida.

NJ Status: Fairly common and fairly widespread resident.

Eastern Screech-Owl

continued

Breeding

Habitat: A cavity nester found in a variety of wooded habitats, generally near open ground; uses nest boxes.

Map Interpretation: Eastern Screech-Owls breed as yearlings, have relatively short dispersal flights from their natal territories, and there is little evidence of any true migration for this species (Gehlbach 1995). For these reasons Eastern Screech-Owls were scored as Possible breeders anywhere they were herd calling from April through September. This allowed Atlas volunteers a long period to find this species. Atlas volunteers were asked not to use tapes to elicit a calling response from territorial birds, but some volunteers did mimic screech-owl calls to locate birds.

Historic references to the distribution and abundance of Eastern Screech-Owls in New Jersey indicated they have been considered common throughout the 20th century. Most authors described them as absent from heavily wooded areas and from the upland edges of salt marshes (Stone 1908, Griscom 1923, Fables 1955). Gehlbach (1995) suggested population cycles may be mistaken for declines and doubted human influence had contributed to any range-wide, long-term decline.

Atlas surveys showed Eastern Screech-Owls are distributed throughout all the counties of New Jersey, but they were found most commonly north of the Piedmont. The three southern New Jersey physiographic regions – the Inner Coastal Plain, Outer Coastal Plain, and Pine Barrens – recorded the species in 28-29% of the blocks in each province. This contrasts with the northern New Jersey provinces – Kittatinny Mountains, Kittatinny Valley, and Highlands – where the species was recorded in 73-79% of the blocks of each province. The Piedmont also has a high frequency of

continued on page 328

Physiographic Distribution

Eastern Screech-Owl	Number of blocks in province	Number of blocks species found breeding in province	Number of blocks species found in state	Percent of province species occupies	Percent of all records for this species found in province	Percent of state area in province
Kittatinny Mountains	19	15	358	78.9	4.2	2.2
Kittatinny Valley	45	33	358	73.3	9.2	5.3
Highlands	109	82	358	75.2	22.9	12.8
Piedmont	167	83	358	49.7	23.2	19.6
Inner Coastal Plain	128	35	358	27.3	9.8	15.0
Outer Coastal Plain	204	60	358	29.4	16.8	23.9
Pine Barrens	180	50	358	27.8	14.0	21.1

continued from page 327

Eastern Screech-Owl

occurrence, with Eastern Screech-Owls found in 50% of the blocks. Perhaps the most notable aspect of this species' distribution is its absence from much of the Pine Barrens and Inner Coastal Plain.

Fall: Eastern Screech-Owls are residents, although in periods of food stress they may engage in long dispersal flights (Gehlbach 1995).

Winter: Statewide CBC totals of Eastern Screech-Owls have increased notably since the late 1970s and early 1980s. This is probably the result of an increased effort to survey for owls rather than a true increase in the overall population. Counts from the late 1970s were generally well under 200 birds, but they have been much higher since then (e.g., see maximum below). **CBC Statewide Stats:** Average: 265; Maximum: 379 in 1992; Minimum: 122 in 1978. **CBC Maximum:** 161, Cumberland, 1992.

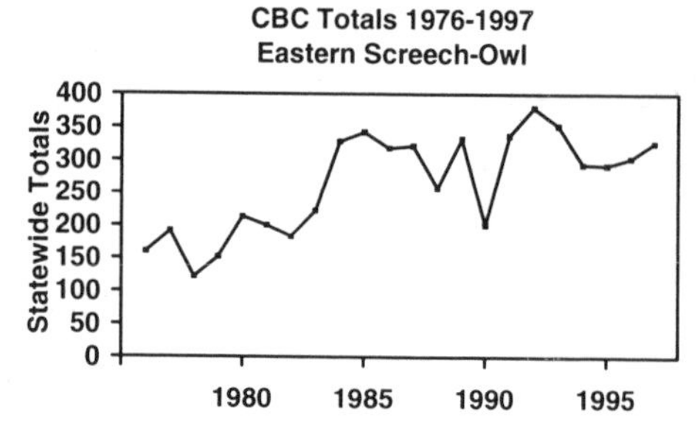

Spring: Eastern Screech-Owls are nonmigratory, permanent residents. There is no published information on the occurrence of spring migration of Eastern Screech-Owl in New Jersey. ■

Eastern Screech-Owl

Great Horned Owl

Bubo virginianus

Range: Resident throughout most of Canada and the United States

NJ Status: Fairly common and widespread resident.

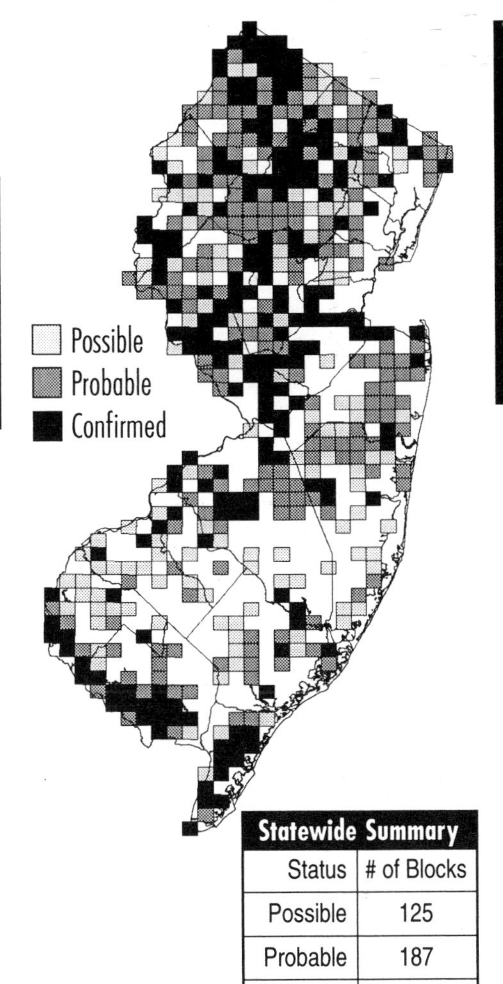

Breeding

Habitat: Breeds in a variety of woodland habitats; uses old hawk and crow nests.

During the 20th century Great Horned Owls have made a remarkable recovery in New Jersey. Stone (1908, 1937) indicated the species was reduced over much of its range, owing mostly to persecution as a "pest" species. Griscom (1923) indicated they were rare in northeastern New Jersey. By 1942, Cruickshank wrote that the species was increasing in some areas and was adapting to

continued on page 330

Statewide Summary	
Status	# of Blocks
Possible	125
Probable	187
Confirmed	198
Total	510

Physiographic Distribution

Great Horned Owl	Number of blocks in province	Number of blocks species found breeding in province	Number of blocks species found in state	Percent of province species occupies	Percent of all records for this species found in province	Percent of state area in province
Kittatinny Mountains	19	19	510	100.0	3.7	2.2
Kittatinny Valley	45	37	510	82.2	7.3	5.3
Highlands	109	94	510	86.2	18.4	12.8
Piedmont	167	113	510	67.7	22.2	19.6
Inner Coastal Plain	128	68	510	53.1	13.3	15.0
Outer Coastal Plain	204	106	510	52.0	20.8	23.9
Pine Barrens	180	73	510	40.6	14.3	21.1

continued from page 329

Great Horned Owl

advancing civilization. This pattern of adaptation was also echoed by Bull (1964).

This species' distribution is similar to that of the Eastern Screech-Owl: their distribution is most dense north of the Piedmont, and they were found least frequently in the Pine Barrens and Inner Coastal Plain. Great Horned Owls are found in coniferous woodlands, but the Pine Barrens may not provide enough open space for hunting.

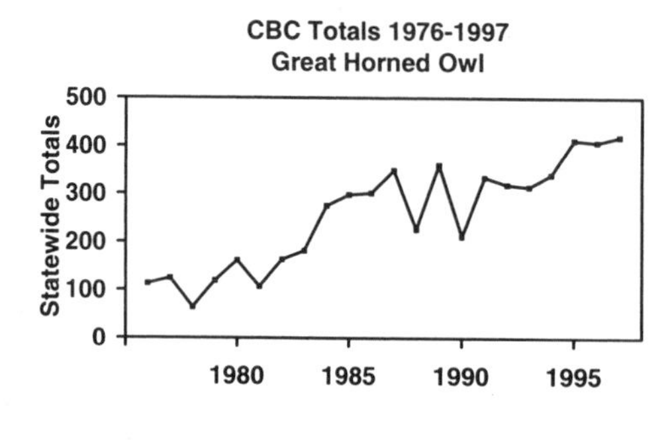

Fall: Great Horned Owls are nonmigratory, permanent residents. There is no published information on the occurrence of fall migration of Great Horned Owls in New Jersey.

Winter: Statewide CBC totals of Great Horned Owls have increased substantially since the early 1980s. This may be the result of an increased effort to survey for owls rather than an actual rise in overall numbers. Counts from the mid-1990s more than doubled counts from the early 1980s. **CBC Statewide Stats:** Average: 254; Maximum: 419 in 1997; Minimum: 64 in 1978. **CBC Maximum:** 151, Cumberland, 1992.

Spring: Great Horned Owls are nonmigratory, permanent residents. There is no published information on the occurrence of spring migration of Great Horned Owls in New Jersey. ■

Snowy Owl

Nyctea scandiaca

Range: In North America breeds from Alaska east across Arctic Canada. In the Northeast winters south regularly to New England and, irregularly, to the Mid-Atlantic states.

NJ Status: Very rare to rare migrant and winter visitor.

Fall: The earliest arriving Snowy Owls reach New Jersey in November, especially in years that have the largest influx of Snowy Owls. Although they are irregular visitors, it is an unusual year in which none of these birds are seen in the state. They are found most often along the coast where sand dunes, salt marsh, and even rocky

Snowy Owl

continued

jetties provide hunting or roosting sites. Inland, they are often found in agricultural fields.

Winter: Occasionally Snowy Owls do not arrive until December or January. Some individuals remain for only a brief period before continuing their dispersal, although others remain throughout the winter. They are sometimes recorded on CBCs. Recent flights have occurred in 1980-1981, 1981-1982, 1986-1987, and 1991-1992. The flight of 1991-1992 had at least 13 reports, a recent seasonal maximum. Probably the largest influx of Snowy Owls was in 1926-1927 when at least 150 birds were shot and many others seen from Long Island to northern New Jersey (Bull 1964). Only 15 birds were documented in New Jersey during that flight, but far fewer observers were afield 70 years ago than are today. **Maxima:** 3, Bayonne, January 1985; 3, Bayonne, February 1987.

Spring: Wintering Snowy Owls normally depart by late February although some birds occasionally linger into March. ■

Northern Hawk Owl

Surnia ulula

Range: In North America breeds from the limit of trees from Alaska east across Canada to Newfoundland. Winters within the breeding range irregularly farther south in the East to New England.

NJ Status: Accidental. NJBRC Review List.

Occurrence: There have been four state reports of Northern Hawk Owls, and two have been accepted by the NJBRC. The two accepted records are:

Essex County#	*winter 1904*	*spec. lost*
New Brunswick	*19 December 1926*	*Brooks 1927*

Barred Owl

Strix varia

Possible
Probable
Confirmed

Range: In eastern North America, resident from central Manitoba east to Nova Scotia, south to eastern Texas and Florida.

NJ Status: Uncommon and somewhat local resident. Threatened Species in New Jersey.

Statewide Summary	
Status	# of Blocks
Possible	35
Probable	96
Confirmed	18
Total	149

Breeding

Habitat: A cavity nester preferring swampy woods of at least moderate size and maturity.

Barred Owls, like most wetland-dependent species, went through a period of decline as wetland acreage was lost during the 1900s. The principal cause for this decline was the combined effect of habitat loss and loss of appropriate trees for nesting. Prior to protective measures enacted in the 1920s, Barred Owls were also shot by hunters and taken by pole traps (Stone 1937).

There has been a modest recovery in the statewide population of Barred Owls, particularly in areas where core populations remained even throughout the period of lowest abundance. Atlas surveys found that Barred Owls occupied the Kittatinny Mountains, Kittatinny Valley, and Highlands provinces with the greatest frequency. Sussex, Passaic,

Morris, Burlington, Cumberland, Atlantic, and Cape May counties have exceptional wetland areas with apparently stable or increasing populations of Barred Owls. In some cases, these new populations are radiating from core populations; in other areas, the birds are moving into territories that have not been occupied for many years, and are not connected to occupied areas.

Conservation Note:

Unfortunately, Barred Owls are nearly absent from Bergen, Essex, Union, Middlesex, Mercer, Hunterdon, Salem, Gloucester, and Camden counties. Due to development, these counties have small-sized or low-quality wetlands. This presents challenging management difficulties, as colonization of the sub-optimal wetlands in these counties is not likely without a strong recovery within their current range.

Fall: Barred Owls are nonmigratory, permanent residents. There is no published information on the occurrence of fall migration of Barred Owls in New Jersey.

Winter: Outside of the statewide maximum in 1991 (see below), all other CBC totals of Barred Owls since 1976 have tallied 20 or fewer birds. **CBC Statewide Stats:** Average: 14; Maximum: 30 in 1991; Minimum: 3 in 1977. **CBC Maximum:** 8, Cumberland, 1985.

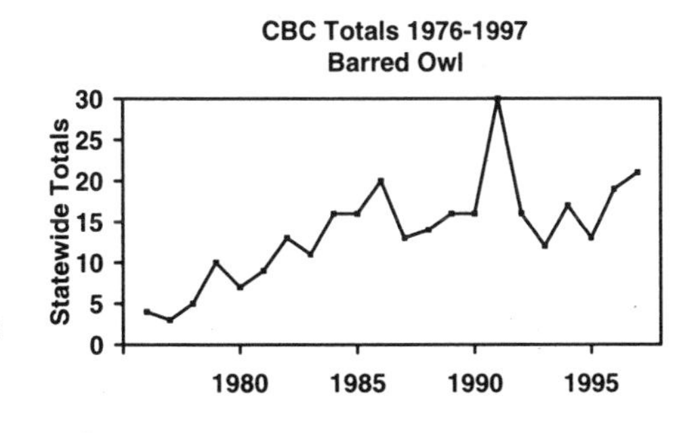

Spring: Barred Owls are nonmigratory, permanent residents. There is no published information on the occurrence of spring migration of Barred Owls in New Jersey. ■

Physiographic Distribution Barred Owl	Number of blocks in province	Number of blocks species found breeding in province	Number of blocks species found in state	Percent of province species occupies	Percent of all records for this species found in province	Percent of state area in province
Kittatinny Mountains	19	7	149	36.8	4.7	2.2
Kittatinny Valley	45	20	149	44.4	13.4	5.3
Highlands	109	42	149	38.5	28.2	12.8
Piedmont	167	15	149	9.0	10.1	19.6
Inner Coastal Plain	128	8	149	6.3	5.4	15.0
Outer Coastal Plain	204	29	149	14.2	19.5	23.9
Pine Barrens	180	28	149	15.6	18.8	21.1

Long-eared Owl

Asio otus

Possible
Probable
Confirmed

Range: In the east breeds from Ontario and Nova Scotia, south to Kansas and New Jersey. Winters from southern Canada to the Gulf Coast.

NJ Status: Scarce and local summer resident, uncommon migrant and winter resident.

Statewide Summary	
Status	# of Blocks
Possible	7
Probable	6
Confirmed	3
Total	16

Breeding

Habitat: Breeds in coniferous or mixed coniferous-deciduous woodlands, especially Red Cedar successional areas and pine groves; typically using old hawk, crow, or jay nests.

Long-eared Owls are, and have historically been, one of New Jersey's rarest regularly occurring breeding

Physiographic Distribution Long-eared Owl	Number of blocks in province	Number of blocks species found breeding in province	Number of blocks species found in state	Percent of province species occupies	Percent of all records for this species found in province	Percent of state area in province
Kittatinny Mountains	19	2	16	10.5	12.5	2.2
Highlands	109	5	16	4.6	31.3	12.8
Piedmont	167	3	16	1.8	18.8	19.6
Inner Coastal Plain	128	3	16	2.3	18.8	15.0
Pine Barrens	180	3	16	1.7	18.8	21.1

birds. Griscom (1923) suggested that there were breeding birds in the "wilder" sections of north New Jersey, and Stone (1937) listed several nests from Salem County. Long-eared Owls were reported breeding in Burlington County in 1939 (Haines 1942) and Mt. Laurel in the 1950s (Bosakowski et al. 1989). Most historic breeding records, however, are for the northern counties in New Jersey – Sussex, Essex, Middlesex, Hunterdon, and Morris (Bull 1964, Leck 1984). There is also an amazing report (by today's standards) of two nests and four breeding pairs in Kingwood, Hunterdon County, in 1978 (Hanisek 1978).

During five years of Atlas data collection this owl was found only in 16 blocks, with four of those reports from contiguous blocks. Seven of the Atlas blocks recorded Long-eared Owls as Possible breeders. Even if the breeding population is double the number of locations found, this would still put the statewide population at only 32 pairs. Studies on the population of Long-eared Owls in New Jersey indicated the breeding population was probably very low (Bosakowski et al. 1989). The question remains, how does this species maintain their population in the state, when they occur at such a low levels? Is this population maintained by reproduction from within the New Jersey breeding birds, or is it augmented by wintering birds remaining in the area to breed?

Map Interpretation: This species' secretive habits likely contributed to consistent underestimation of the number of nests in the state, and the results of the Atlas are also likely to be underestimates. Atlas volunteers in Pennsylvania also found few Long-eared Owls in their surveys, and suspected that they too had missed some nesting locations (Santner 1992a). It is likely that this species early nesting season and low population size combine to make detection difficult. It is also likely that, even with intensive searches, the species would still prove to be an incredibly rare breeding bird.

Conservation Note: Questions about the distribution of some breeding owls are not best addressed with Atlas methodology. Priority should also be placed on focused censuses for nocturnal breeding birds in river and swamp bottomlands – habitats used by both Barred and Long-eared Owls.

Fall: Migrant Long-eared Owls arrive in mid-October and continue moving through November. Results of an owl banding project at Cape May Point indicated that peak movements occur early November (Duffy and Kerlinger 1992). **Maxima:** 15, Cape May Point, 15 October 1988; 11, Cape May Point, 4 November 1979 (banded, K. Duffy, pers. com.).

Winter: Some Long-eared Owls remain throughout the winter in coniferous or mixed coniferous-deciduous woodlands adjacent to open fields. They sometimes form communal roosts. Unsurprisingly, CBC totals vary considerably from year to year. **Maxima:** 30, North Arlington,

continued on page 336

continued from page 335

Long-eared Owl

January 1972; 19, Croton, December 1987 (Bosakowski et al. 1989). **CBC Statewide Stats:** Average: 19; Maximum: 36 in 1982; Minimum: 8 in 1981. **CBC Maximum:** 18, Cumberland, 1977.

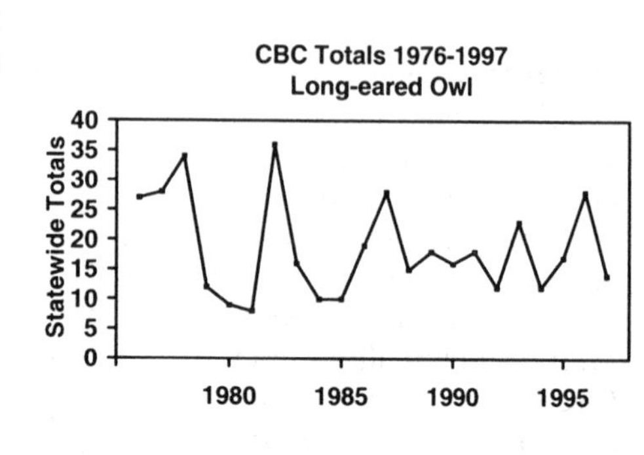

Spring: Most wintering birds have left winter roosts by the beginning of April, but the passage of Long-eared Owls through the state in spring is so low as to be undetected. ■

Short-eared Owl

Asio flammeus

Range: Breeds throughout southern Canada and the northern United States, in the East south to Nebraska and northern Massachusetts. Winters from the northern United States south to the Gulf Coast.

NJ Status: Probably extirpated as a breeder, uncommon migrant and winter resident.

Historic Changes: Short-eared Owls have nested in New Jersey in small numbers. Stone (1937) was aware of several nests in Salem and Cumberland counties, and north along the coast to Barnegat and Newark bays. By the mid-1950s, it was suggested that they were decreasing in number and were becoming rare (Fables 1955). The most recent indication of nesting occurred in 1989 when a pair was present at Supawna Meadows, Salem County from 28 March to 2 June. Also, there have been a handful of other sightings between May and August (outside the normal migration period), indicating the possibility that nesting may still occur. No nesting attempts were reported during the Atlas surveys.

Fall: Short-eared Owls are present from mid-October into early April. The peak of the southbound flight occurs from late October through mid-November. They are occasionally seen in migration during daylight hours. In 1995, at the Avalon Sea Watch, 13 migrants were seen between 1-18 November.

Short-eared Owl

continued

Winter: Numbers of Short-eared owls are variable from year to year, but highest numbers are noted in mid-winter. They are most frequently encountered hunting over open marshes or fields, just before sunrise and just after sunset. CBC totals are highly variable. **Maxima:** 30, Wallkill River, winter 1994-1995; 21, North Arlington, 21 December 1982. **CBC Statewide Stats:** Average: 42; Maximum: 90 in 1983; Minimum: 9 in 1997. **CBC Maximum:** 37, Barnegat, 1983.

Spring: There is no noticeable northward movement of Short-eared Owls as any migration would be masked by the presence of wintering birds. ■

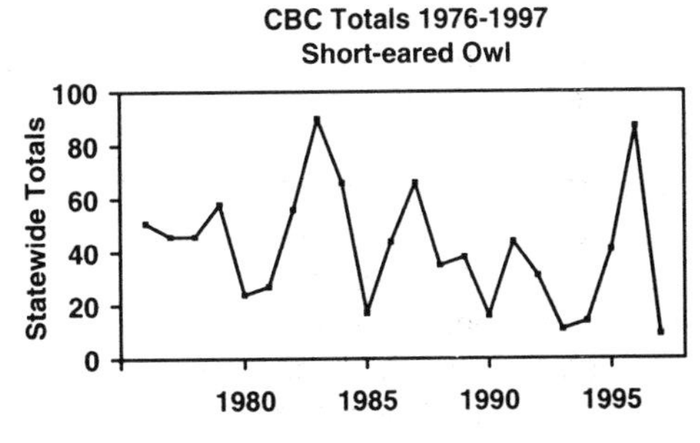

Short-eared Owl

Boreal Owl

Aegolius funereus

Range: In North America breeds from Alaska east across Canada to Newfoundland. Winters within the breeding range, and irregularly in the East south to New England.

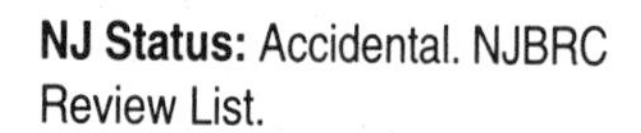

NJ Status: Accidental. NJBRC Review List.

Occurrence: There have been three state reports of Boreal Owl, and one has been accepted by the NJBRC: Bonhamtown, 1 November 1962 (spec. Newark Museum). ■

Northern Saw-whet Owl

Aegolius acadicus

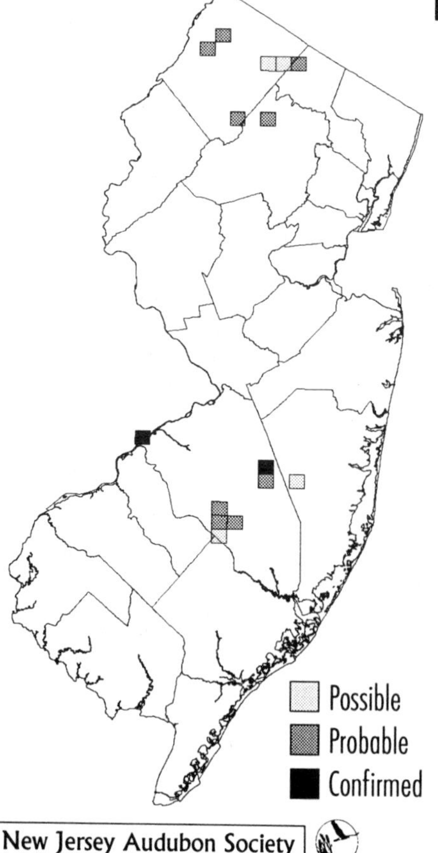

Range: In eastern North America, breeds from Manitoba east to Nova Scotia, south to northeastern Missouri and New Jersey. Winters from the southern part of the breeding range south to northern Texas and northern Florida.

NJ Status: Rare and very local summer resident, uncommon fall migrant and winter resident.

Northern Saw-whet Owl

continued

Breeding

Habitat: A cavity nester found in moist, mixed woods.

Saw-whet Owls were long suspected of being rare breeding birds in New Jersey (Fables 1955, Leck 1984). The first evidence of confirmed breeding in New Jersey was found on 7 June 1986 when a free-flying juvenile was seen with an adult in Passaic County (Benzinger 1987). There have been other instances where saw-whet owls were known to have summered, but definitive breeding evidence has always been difficult to obtain. Leck (1984) stated that five birds summered in the Great Swamp in 1973 but gave no details on any breeding activity. There have been reports of saw-whet owls present in the Pine Barrens in spring (Chatsworth: 1976, 1977, 1984, 1985; Moorestown: 1976; Vincentown: 1978; Gibbsboro: 1985; Lebanon State Forest: 1985, 1986, 1995, 1996; Medford: 1990; Wharton: 1996; Atsion: 1997), suggesting that breeding is probably occurring annually.

Statewide Summary	
Status	# of Blocks
Possible	4
Probable	9
Confirmed	2
Total	15

Atlas volunteers discovered an unexpectedly high number of Possible and Probable nesting locations, and Confirmed two nests (one in 1998). Despite these notable finds, this species still remains as one of our rarest, regularly-occurring breeding birds. Unfortunately this species' history in the state, and any changes in its abundance over time, is clouded by the difficulty in their detection. One study has suggested that there may be no natal site fidelity for this species (Cannings 1993). One possibility is that the New Jersey breeding population is periodically augmented by wintering individuals from farther north that remain to breed the following spring. This could cause the number of breeding pairs in New Jersey to increase following winters of saw-whet invasions.

Fall: Northern Saw-whet Owls are extremely secretive and rarely encountered in the field. Most of the information about migration comes from the Cape

continued on page 340

Physiographic Distribution — Northern Saw-whet Owl	Number of blocks in province	Number of blocks species found breeding in province	Number of blocks species found in state	Percent of province species occupies	Percent of all records for this species found in province	Percent of state area in province
Kittatinny Mountains	19	2	15	10.5	13.3	2.2
Highlands	109	5	15	4.6	33.3	12.8
Inner Coastal Plain	128	1	15	0.8	6.7	15.0
Pine Barrens	180	7	15	3.9	46.7	21.1

continued from page 339

Northern Saw-whet Owl

May Point Owl Banding Project. Banding results there indicated that numbers vary from year to year, but that in some years saw-whet owls are fairly common migrants. Banding captures show the peak from early to mid-November (Duffy and Kerlinger 1992). **Maxima:** 108, Cape May Point, 9 November 1995; 92, Cape May Point, 17 November 1995; (banded, K. Duffy, pers. com.).

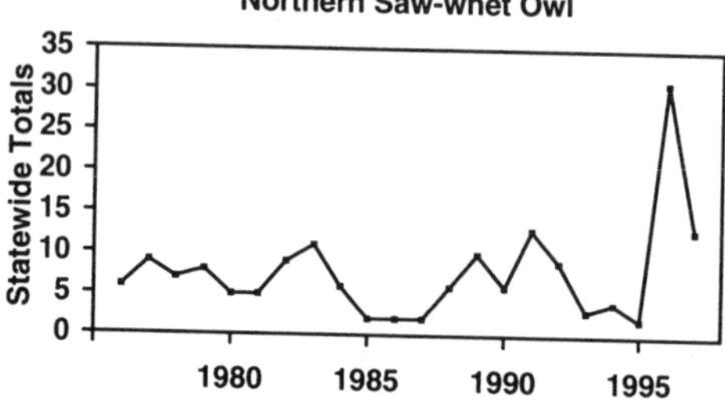

Winter: Northern Saw-whet Owls are difficult to locate in winter. However, recoveries of road kills found along the Garden State Parkway indicated that they may be fairly common in winter in some years. In the winter of 1995-1996 an amazing total of 82 dead saw-whets was found, 37 in Cape May County (Sutton 1996). The statewide high for all CBCs occurred in the same year. **CBC Statewide Stats:** Average: 8; Maximum: 31 in 1996; Minimum: 2 in four years. **CBC Maximum:** 9, Moorestown, 1996.

Spring: Cannings (1993) indicated that spring migration of Northern Saw-whet Owls peaks in late March. ■

Common Nighthawk

Chordeiles minor

Range: Breeds locally throughout most of North America to the tree line. Winters in South America.

NJ Status: Uncommon and local summer resident, uncommon spring and fairly common fall migrant.

Breeding

Habitat: Nests on the ground in semi-open country, particularly in pine woods; also on rooftops in cities and towns.

Historically, Common Nighthawks nested in open areas of the Pine Barrens, in pastures, and barren fields; by the end of the 1800s they were found nesting on gravel rooftops in cities and towns (Griscom 1923, Bull 1964). Although they were rarely described as common, comparisons of historic distribution compared to current patterns indicate a

Common Nighthawk

continued

Statewide Summary	
Status	# of Blocks
Possible	65
Probable	36
Confirmed	6
Total	107

decline. This decline is echoed in other areas of North America as well (Poulin et al. 1996).

Stone (1908) described Common Nighthawks as a common summer resident, but by 1937 he called them "local or very rare breeding birds" in the northern counties. Griscom (1923) considered them to be rare and local, and Cruickshank (1942) reported that they had been drastically reduced in numbers. Bull (1964) noted that although Common Nighthawks still nested

continued on page 342

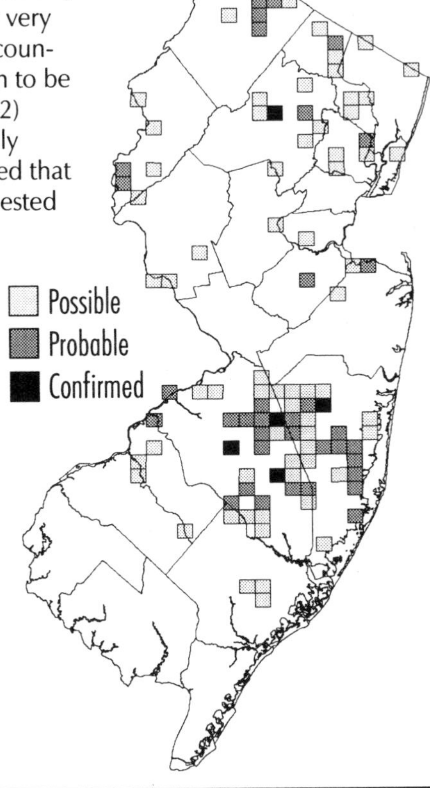

Map Interpretation: Common Nighthawks are cryptic in their coloration and difficult to locate on nests, although their evening and early morning display makes their presence easy to observe. Overall, just over 60% of the blocks where nighthawks were found were categorized as Possible breeding locations. This high percentage of Possible sightings may be an indication of low density, or may also be the result of low coverage in the crepuscular hours.

Physiographic Distribution

Common Nighthawk	Number of blocks in province	Number of blocks species found breeding in province	Number of blocks species found in state	Percent of province species occupies	Percent of all records for this species found in province	Percent of state area in province
Kittatinny Valley	45	12	107	26.7	11.2	5.3
Highlands	109	12	107	11.0	11.2	12.8
Piedmont	167	18	107	10.8	16.8	19.6
Inner Coastal Plain	128	14	107	10.9	13.1	15.0
Outer Coastal Plain	204	4	107	2.0	3.7	23.9
Pine Barrens	180	47	107	26.1	43.9	21.1

continued from page 341

Common Nighthawk

regularly on rooftops, they had declined markedly as ground nesters. Leck (1984) and Boyle (1986) found them confined to the Pine Barrens and to urban areas of the northern part of the state. The decline in Common Nighthawks has been postulated to coincide with mosquito control practice of nonselective pesticide spraying. Also, the switch from gravel to smooth rubber-like substances for roofing has probably caused declines of nighthawks in some areas (Poulin et al. 1996).

Atlas surveys found Common Nighthawks thinly distributed in most physiographic regions. The Pine Barrens holds 44% of the blocks occupied by Common Nighthawks. The Kittatinny Valley, although only holding 11% of the occupied blocks statewide, had Common Nighthawks in 27% of the blocks in the province. Statewide, Common Nighthawks were Confirmed breeding in only six of the 107 blocks in which they were located during Atlas surveys.

Fall: The vanguard of southbound Common Nighthawks arrives by mid-August. Peak flights are recorded in late August and early September, with numbers diminishing by mid-October. They are most frequently seen at sunrise or sunset, although they are sometimes seen moving at midday. They are more common inland and along ridges than along the coast. **Maxima:** 1,500, Trenton, 22 August 1986; 1,200, Montclair, 2 September 1988.

Spring: Common Nighthawks are less common in spring than in fall, especially along the coast. The first northbound birds are seen in late April and most have moved on by late May. **Maxima:** 100s, Greenbrook Sanctuary, 17 May 1986; 100, Great Swamp, 29 April 1983. ■

CHUCK-WILL'S-WIDOW

Chuck-will's-widow

Caprimulgus carolinensis

Range: Breeds from eastern Nebraska east to Long Island, south to eastern Texas and Florida. Winters from southern Florida south to northern South America.

NJ Status: Uncommon and local summer resident, uncommon spring and fall migrant.

Breeding

Habitat: Nests on the ground in deciduous or mixed woods.

New Jersey is near the northern limit of Chuck-will's-widow's breeding range. The first breeding record in New Jersey occurred at Cape May

Chuck-will's-widow

continued

Possible
Probable
Confirmed

Map Interpretation: Chuck-will's-widows are secretive, and usually they are detected only by their nocturnal vocalizations. It is likely they were not found in blocks that received little nocturnal coverage, and the Atlas data probably represents a low-end estimate of their distribution.

Statewide Summary	
Status	# of Blocks
Possible	11
Probable	32
Confirmed	2
Total	45

Point, when a female with two young was observed on 21 May 1921 (Fables 1955). From that point on they expanded their range slowly along the Atlantic coast. By 1954, approximately 20 birds could be heard calling on the lower half of the Cape May peninsula (Fables 1955). They had reached Oceanville, Atlantic County by 1973, and Island Beach, Ocean County by 1978 (Leck 1984).

Along the Atlantic coast, Atlas surveys indicated that the range of Chuck-will's-widows had changed little after reaching the area around Barnegat Bay in the late 1970s. Over 86% of this species' statewide range is in the Outer Coastal Plain province. They were also found in several blocks in Cumberland and eastern Salem counties, probably documenting a recent colonization. Further expansion of Chuck-will's-widows may be limited by their habitat preferences. They prefer moist deciduous woodlands, which in southern New Jersey occur

continued on page 344

Physiographic Distribution

Chuck-will's-widow	Number of blocks in province	Number of blocks species found breeding in province	Number of blocks species found in state	Percent of province species occupies	Percent of all records for this species found in province	Percent of state area in province
Inner Coastal Plain	128	1	45	0.8	2.2	15.0
Outer Coastal Plain	204	39	45	19.1	86.7	23.9
Pine Barrens	180	5	45	2.8	11.1	21.1

continued from page 343

Chuck-will's-widow

mainly near the upland edges of the salt marshes along both coasts. They may be blocked from expanding by a lack of that habitat in three directions – the Pine Barrens to the north and west; the extensive farmland and urban sprawl of the Inner Coastal Plain to the northwest; and heavily developed eastern Monmouth County to the north.

Fall: Most Chuck-will's-widows have probably moved out of New Jersey by mid-September. They are strictly nocturnal and are encountered only accidentally during migration.

Spring: Chuck-will's-widows return by late April, but, as in fall, they are rarely seen in migration. ■

Whip-poor-will

Caprimulgus vociferus

Range: In the East breeds from central Saskatchewan east to Nova Scotia, south to eastern Oklahoma and northern Georgia. Winters from Florida south to Central America.

NJ Status: Fairly common and somewhat local summer resident, uncommon spring and fall migrant.

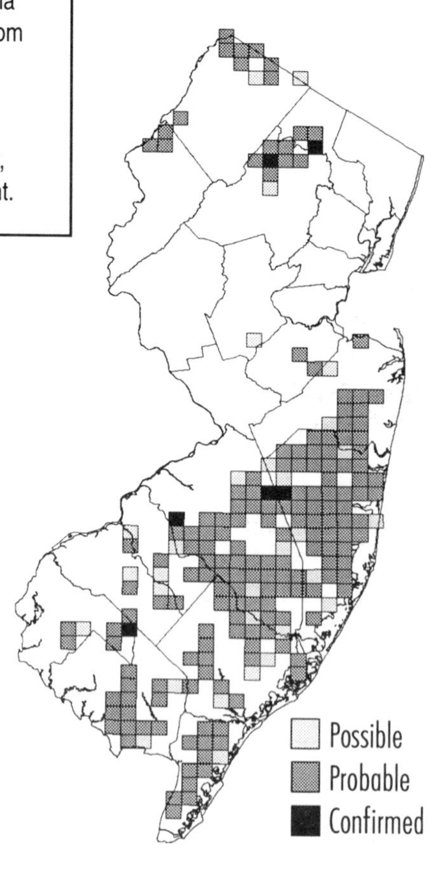

Breeding

Habitat: Nests on the ground, typically in open, mixed or pine woodlands.

A common theme in the historic accounts of Whip-poor-wills is the contention that they are unable to live within close proximity to civilization (Griscom 1923, Cruickshank 1942, Bull 1964). Griscom found them common in what he termed the "hill country" of northern New Jersey, and Cruickshank (1942) spoke of hearing dozens in some northern

Whip-poor-will

continued

New Jersey locales. Fables (1955) described them as "a summer resident of the wilder regions of the state," specifically noting their preference for the Pine Barrens.

In the past, Whip-poor-wills were more common in the southern part of the state than in the north. However, a "sudden decline" of Whip-poor-wills in northern New Jersey was noted in the mid-1970s (Wolfarth 1975b). The decline apparently continued into the mid-1990s. The two most likely explanations are the succession of farmland and old fields to secondary woodlands, and urban and suburban sprawl (Benzinger and Van De Venter 1995).

Atlas data showed that the 83% of the blocks in which Whip-poor-wills were found occurred in the Pine Barrens and on the Outer Coastal Plain. They were nearly absent from the Inner Coastal Plain and the Piedmont. They were found locally in the Highlands, particularly near Picatinny Arsenal, where they are fairly numerous (Benzinger and Van De Venter 1995), and along the Kittatinny Ridge.

Fall: Whip-poor-wills are later migrants than Chuck-will's-widows, sometimes lingering into early November. Migration peaks from late September through early October, as evidenced by 20 captured 7-9 October 1987 during the owl-banding project at Cape May Point. They are strictly nocturnal, and are only very rarely encountered during migration.

Spring: Whip-poor-wills return to breeding territories in late April, but are far more often heard than seen. ■

Map Interpretation: Whip-poor-wills, like Chuck-will's-widows, are most often detected by their nocturnal vocalizations. It is likely they were not found in blocks that got little nocturnal coverage, and that the Atlas data represens a low-end estimate of their range.

Statewide Summary

Status	# of Blocks
Possible	30
Probable	172
Confirmed	6
Total	208

Physiographic Distribution

Whip-poor-will	Number of blocks in province	Number of blocks species found breeding in province	Number of blocks species found in state	Percent of province species occupies	Percent of all records for this species found in province	Percent of state area in province
Kittatinny Mountains	19	6	208	31.6	2.9	2.2
Kittatinny Valley	45	5	208	11.1	2.4	5.3
Highlands	109	13	208	11.9	6.3	12.8
Piedmont	167	1	208	0.6	0.5	19.6
Inner Coastal Plain	128	11	208	8.6	5.3	15.0
Outer Coastal Plain	204	59	208	28.9	28.4	23.9
Pine Barrens	180	113	208	62.8	54.3	21.1

Chimney Swift
Chaetura pelagica

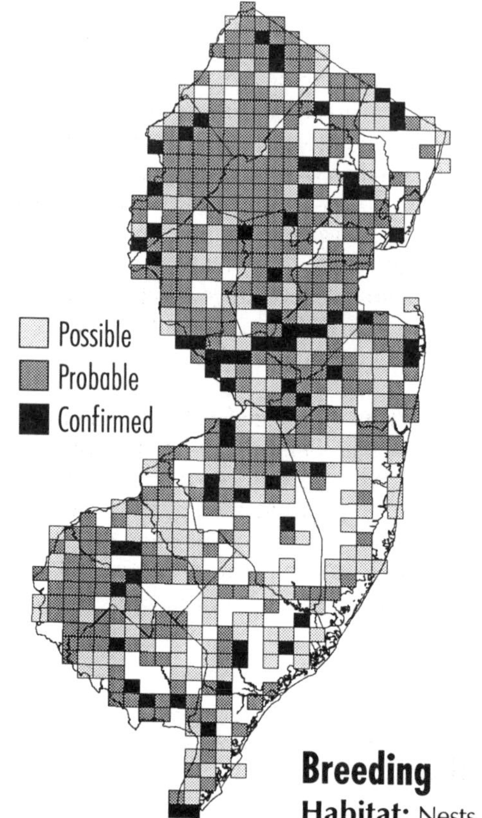

Range: Breeds from eastern Saskatchewan east to Nova Scotia, south to Texas and northern Florida. Winters in South America.

NJ Status: Common and very widespread summer resident, common spring and fall migrant.

Statewide Summary	
Status	# of Blocks
Possible	209
Probable	342
Confirmed	73
Total	624

Breeding

Habitat: Nests in chimneys or other similar man-made structures.

At one time Chimney Swifts could be found nesting in hollow trees, but most authors agreed that chimneys and chimney-like structures were

Physiographic Distribution Chimney Swift	Number of blocks in province	Number of blocks species found breeding in province	Number of blocks species found in state	Percent of province species occupies	Percent of all records for this species found in province	Percent of state area in province
Kittatinny Mountains	19	16	624	84.2	2.6	2.2
Kittatinny Valley	45	43	624	95.6	6.9	5.3
Highlands	109	94	624	86.2	15.1	12.8
Piedmont	167	124	624	74.3	19.9	19.6
Inner Coastal Plain	128	111	624	86.7	17.8	15.0
Outer Coastal Plain	204	136	624	66.7	21.8	23.9
Pine Barrens	180	100	624	55.6	16.0	21.1

Chimney Swift

continued

the nearly exclusive choice of Chimney Swifts throughout most of the 20th century (Griscom 1923, Leck 1984). They have long been a widespread and highly visible resident in New Jersey. Griscom (1923) stated that "few people are so unobservant as to overlook the bow-and-arrow-like form" of the Chimney Swift.

Overall, their status in the state has changed very little during the course of the 20th century. Atlas results indicated that Chimney Swifts occurred in 67% or more of every province, excepting the Pine Barrens.

Fall: Discerning the onset of Chimney Swift migration is difficult given the number of local birds, but peak numbers probably move through in early September. Most have left by mid-October, with a few stragglers remaining until the end of October or early into November.
Maxima: 4,000, Ridgewood (roost), 13 September 1976; 2,500, Blairstown (roost), 19 August 1978.

Spring: Chimney Swifts return in mid-April. Numbers build from late April into early May, with movements beyond that point generally masked by the large numbers of local breeding birds.
Maxima: 100s, Trenton, 26 April 1981; 100s, Trenton, 6 May 1982. ■

Ruby-throated Hummingbird

Archilochus colubris

Range: Breeds from Alberta east to Nova Scotia, and south to eastern Texas and Florida. Winters from Florida to Central America.

NJ Status: Fairly common and fairly widespread summer resident, fairly common spring and fall migrant.

Breeding

Habitat: Nests in a variety of woodland habitats, frequently near water.

In New Jersey, Ruby-throated Hummingbirds have been considered fairly common and widespread breeding birds during most of the 20th century (Stone 1908, Bull 1964). Leck (1984) suggested there was a decline in Ruby-throated Hummingbirds throughout the eastern United States, and specifically in New Jersey, during what he termed "recent decades." They were placed on the National Audubon Society's Blue List from 1979 to 1986 (Ricciardi 1996). However, there appears

continued on page 348

continued from page 347

Ruby-throated Hummingbird

Physiographic Distribution

Ruby-throated Hummingbird	Number of blocks in province	Number of blocks species found breeding in province	Number of blocks species found in state	Percent of province species occupies	Percent of all records for this species found in province	Percent of state area in province
Kittatinny Mountains	19	18	426	94.7	4.2	2.2
Kittatinny Valley	45	39	426	86.7	9.2	5.3
Highlands	109	88	426	80.7	20.7	12.8
Piedmont	167	55	426	32.9	12.9	19.6
Inner Coastal Plain	128	39	426	30.5	9.2	15.0
Outer Coastal Plain	204	87	426	42.6	20.4	23.9
Pine Barrens	180	100	426	55.6	23.5	21.1

to be no lingering effects of declines that were reported in the 1970s and 1980s (Robinson et al. 1996).

During the Atlas surveys, Ruby-throated Hummingbirds were present throughout the state and found in all physiographic provinces. They were least common in the Inner Coastal Plain and the Piedmont. They were patchy in the Pine Barrens and almost absent from the barrier islands. Ruby-throated Hummingbirds are inconspicuous, quick in their movements, and quiet in their vocalizations, making detection during the breeding season difficult. This is evidenced by the high percentage (i.e., 43%) of occupied blocks categorized as Possible. Atlases from surrounding states experienced similar difficulties. Percentages of occupied

Possible
Probable
Confirmed

Statewide Summary

Status	# of Blocks
Possible	184
Probable	153
Confirmed	89
Total	426

Ruby-throated Hummingbird
continued

blocks scored as Possible from New York, Pennsylvania, and Maryland were all over 45%.

Map interpretation: It is likely that breeding range of Ruby-throated Hummingbird included all Possible, Probable, and Confirmed locations. In fact, given their difficulty of detection, it is reasonable to assume that their range may be under-represented by the Atlas map.

Fall: Ruby-throated Hummingbirds are early migrants with some southbound movement noted in late July. Movements peak from late August through early September, although a few birds may linger until mid-October. **Maxima:** 35, Cape May Point, 31 August 1986; 18, West Cape May, 8 September 1992.

Spring: Northbound Ruby-throated Hummingbirds arrive in mid-April. Spring movements are rarely concentrated, and birds headed further north are difficult to distinguish from local breeding birds. **Maximum:** 8, Higbee Beach, 25 April 1992. ■

Black-chinned Hummingbird
Archilochus alexandri

Range: Breeds from southern British Columbia south to California, east to Colorado and western Texas. Winters from southern Texas south to Mexico.

NJ Status: Accidental. NJBRC Review List.

Occurrence: There has been only one reported and one accepted record of Black-chinned Hummingbird in New Jersey: Villas, 10-15 November 1996 (Crossley 1997), at a feeder. The record was part of an unprecedented fall for hummingbirds in New Jersey, which included two new species of hummingbirds for the state (the other Calliope), and reports of four *Selasphorus* sp. hummingbirds. ■

Calliope Hummingbird
Stellula calliope

Occurrence: There has been only one reported and one accepted record of Calliope Hummingbird in New Jersey: Wildwood Crest, 23 November-5 December 1996 (ph-RNJB 23:54, Lehman 1997), at a feeder. In the field this bird was identified as a *Selasphorus* hummingbird, but further study confirmed that it was a Calliope Hummingbird (Lehman 1997). ■

Range: Breeds from British Columbia south to California and east to Wyoming, and Utah. Winters in Mexico.

NJ Status: Accidental. NJBRC Review List.

Rufous Hummingbird
Selasphorus rufus

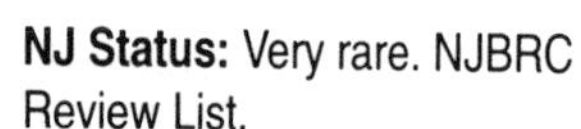

Range: Breeds from southern Alaska south to northern California, east to eastern Alberta. Winters mainly in Mexico.

NJ Status: Very rare. NJBRC Review List.

Occurrence: There have been 17 state reports of *Selasphorus* (sp.) hummingbirds, five have been accepted by the NJBRC as Rufous Hummingbirds (four in fall, one in summer), and six have been accepted as Rufous/Allen's Hummingbirds (all from fall). Immature and female Rufous and Allen's Hummingbirds are nearly inseparable from each other in the field, and birds reported in these plumages are accepted by NJBRC only as Rufous/Allen's Hummingbirds. All New Jersey's accepted records of *Selasphorus* (sp.) hummingbirds have come in the 1990s, with five reports in 1996.

The five accepted records of Rufous Hummingbird are:

New Lisbon	*2-3 July 1991*	*rufous-backed male*
Oaklyn	*15-22 November 1996*	*ph-RBPF, rufous-backed male*
Oakland	*4 December 1996*	*ph-RBPF*
Blairstown	*30 July 1997*	*ph-RBPF*
Denville	*31 October 1997*	

The six accepted records of *Selasphorus* sp. are:

Chester	*25-26 September 1994*	*ph-RBPF*
Woodbine	*14-15 October 1994*	*ph-RNJB 21:20*
Cape May	*14-15 October 1995*	*ph-RBPF*
Cape May	*17-18 September 1996*	*ph-RBPF*
Hopatcong	*5-17 October 1996*	
Villas	*21 July 1998*	

Belted Kingfisher

Ceryle alcyon

Range: In eastern North America breeds from Manitoba east to Labrador, south to northern Texas and northern Florida. Winters from the Great Lakes and southern New England south to Central America.

NJ Status: Uncommon but widespread summer resident, fairly common spring and fall migrant, uncommon winter resident.

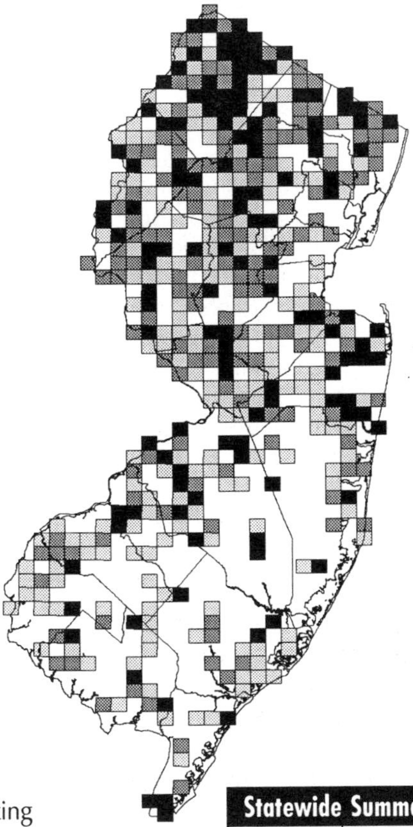

Possible
Probable
Confirmed

Statewide Summary	
Status	# of Blocks
Possible	178
Probable	145
Confirmed	130
Total	453

Breeding

Habitat: A cavity nester, excavating holes in any vertical bank near water.

During the 20th century, Belted Kingfishers have been, as Cruickshank (1942) stated, a "characteristic summer bird of our waterways." Their

continued on page 352

Physiographic Distribution Belted Kingfisher	Number of blocks in province	Number of blocks species found breeding in province	Number of blocks species found in state	Percent of province species occupies	Percent of all records for this species found in province	Percent of state area in province
Kittatinny Mountains	19	17	453	89.5	3.8	2.2
Kittatinny Valley	45	40	453	88.9	8.8	5.3
Highlands	109	84	453	77.1	18.5	12.8
Piedmont	167	104	453	62.3	23.0	19.6
Inner Coastal Plain	128	84	453	65.6	18.5	15.0
Outer Coastal Plain	204	74	453	36.3	16.3	23.9
Pine Barrens	180	50	453	27.8	11.0	21.1

continued from page 351

distribution was known to be governed by two factors: the availability of vertical banks or cliffs for excavating their nest sites, and a nearby source of food. Consequently, Belted Kingfishers were often referred to as local breeding birds (Bull 1964). They are intolerant of human disturbance and may avoid or vacate nest sites if the area is frequented by humans. Prior to protection afforded by migratory bird laws, Belted Kingfishers were often shot, particularly near fish hatcheries and along trout streams (Hamas 1994).

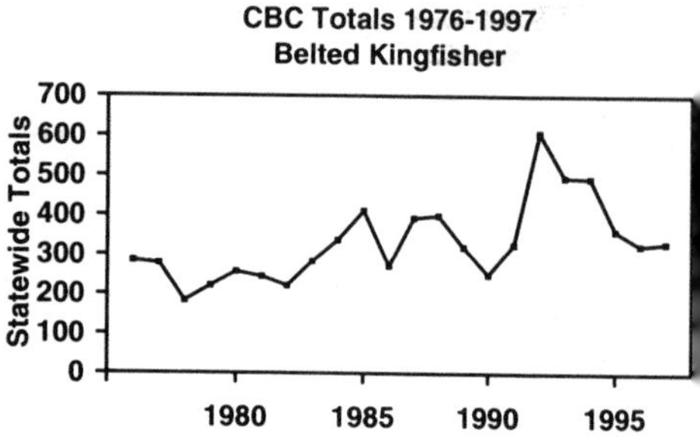

CBC Totals 1976-1997
Belted Kingfisher

Statewide Totals: 0, 100, 200, 300, 400, 500, 600, 700
1980, 1985, 1990, 1995

Atlas volunteers found Belted Kingfishers in all the physiographic provinces in the state. They were more often encountered in the northern half of the state than in the southern part; likely the product of the availability of appropriate nest sites. North of the Piedmont they were found in at least 77% of the blocks in each physiographic province, although they were found in only 41% of the blocks south of the Piedmont. They were absent from large sections of the relatively dry Pine Barrens and from many blocks on the Outer Coastal Plain. Although broadly distributed throughout the state, the limited number of appropriate nesting sites assures they will always be patchy in their distribution in southern New Jersey.

Fall: The southbound migration of Belted Kingfishers is protracted, and occurs from late August through mid-October. They are usually encountered individually.

Winter: CBC totals of Belted Kingfishers are variable, with numbers dependent on the presence of open water. They are particularly scarce in mid-winter when much of the fresh water in the state may be frozen. **CBC Statewide Stats:** Average: 331; Maximum: 607 in 1992; Minimum: 183 in 1978. **CBC Maximum:** 143, Cumberland, 1992.

Spring: Some Belted Kingfishers return as soon as open water is available, with migration probably peaking in April. ■

Red-headed Woodpecker

Melanerpes erythrocephalus

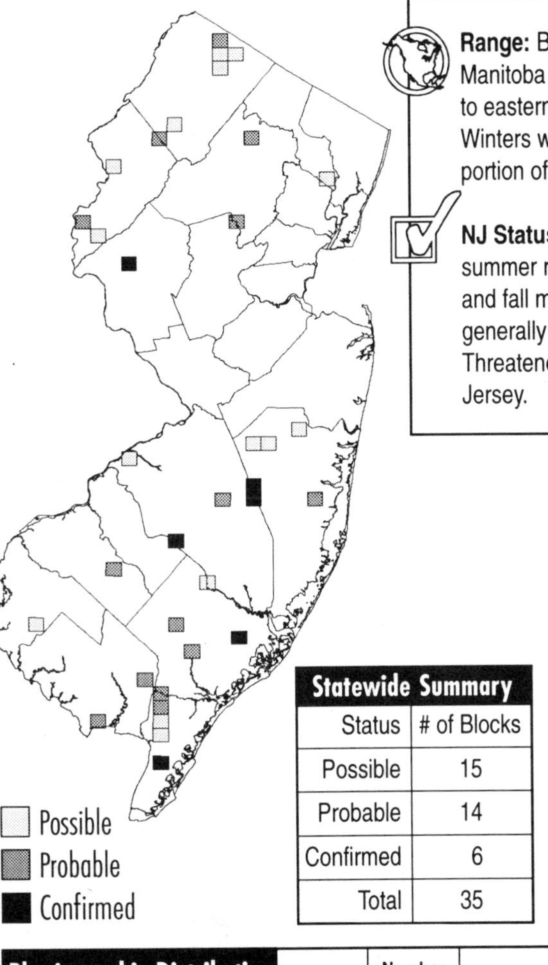

Range: Breeds from southern Manitoba east to New York, south to eastern Texas and Florida. Winters within the southern portion of the breeding range.

NJ Status: Scarce and local summer resident, scarce spring and fall migrant, irregular but generally rare winter resident. Threatened Species in New Jersey.

Statewide Summary	
Status	# of Blocks
Possible	15
Probable	14
Confirmed	6
Total	35

Breeding

Habitat: Nests in cavities in open, dry, mixed woodlands with fairly mature trees, or in swamps and river bottoms.

Red-headed Woodpeckers were once common breeding birds throughout much of

continued on page 354

Physiographic Distribution

Red-headed Woodpecker	Number of blocks in province	Number of blocks species found breeding in province	Number of blocks species found in state	Percent of province species occupies	Percent of all records for this species found in province	Percent of state area in province
Kittatinny Valley	45	7	35	15.6	20.0	5.3
Highlands	109	3	35	2.8	8.6	12.8
Piedmont	167	3	35	1.8	8.6	19.6
Inner Coastal Plain	128	1	35	0.8	2.9	15.0
Outer Coastal Plain	204	7	35	3.4	20.0	23.9
Pine Barrens	180	14	35	7.8	40.0	21.1

continued from page 353

eastern North America, but suffered serious declines by the turn of the 20th century (Bull 1964, Kaufman 1996). Whether they were ever numerous as breeding birds in New Jersey, however, is less clear. Writing in 1908, Stone considered Red-headed Woodpeckers local summer residents and made no mention of any historic decline. In 1937 he stated, quite unequivocally, that this species "has always been rare and exceedingly erratic in its occurrence east of the Delaware and Hudson Rivers." Griscom (1923) described Red-headed Woodpecker's status and distribution in northern New Jersey as "defying logical interpretation," deciding not to list breeding localities since they were apt to fail to appear at a given site in following years.

Although Bull (1964) identified Red-headed Woodpeckers as erratic and local, he contended that they had declined in northern New Jersey. He cited competition with European Starlings and collisions with automobiles as the chief reasons for the decline in New Jersey – and these same reasons are also cited for their decline in other areas of their range (Kaufman 1996). By the mid-1980s, there were three principal nesting areas identified in the state: northwestern New Jersey, the Pine Barrens, and Cape May County (Leck 1984).

The results of the Atlas surveys showed that the New Jersey population of Red-headed Woodpeckers is small and broadly distributed. They were found in only 35 blocks, yet were found in six of seven provinces, but never occupied more than 15% of any one province. Statewide they were Confirmed in only six blocks. They were found in only 13 of 340 blocks north of the Coastal Plain. The Kittatinny Valley, although occupying only 5% of the state, hosted 20% of the occupied blocks. The Pine Barrens held 40% of the occupied blocks in the state. The only other province with a notable presence of Red-headed Woodpeckers was the Outer Coastal Plain, which had 20% of the statewide occupied blocks.

Conservation Note: Several locations in New Jersey have had declines in local populations of breeding Red-headed Woodpeckers. For example the Cape May County Park had up to 10 adults present in 1977 and had breeding birds regularly at the park. They were found early during Atlas surveys at the park, but had disappeared from there by the end of the survey period (V. Elia, pers. obs.). Similar patterns of site occupation and abandonment were noted in areas within Belleplain State Forest also. If the declines of Red-headed Woodpeckers in Cape May County are symptomatic of the population statewide, Red-headed Woodpeckers are worthy of expanded monitoring methods.

Fall: Southbound Red-headed Woodpeckers are seen between early September and early November, with the heaviest concentration of records from late September through early October. They are infrequently encountered in migration,

Red-headed Woodpecker

continued

although they are conspicuous diurnal migrants. **Maxima:** 5, East Point, 16 October 1990; 5, Sunrise Mt., 12 September 1976.

Winter: Many Red-headed Woodpeckers are migratory, although in some areas they are considered to be permanent residents (Kaufman 1996). In New Jersey they are seen only rarely in winter. An influx to the Great Swamp during the late fall of 1983 produced a sizable and atypical wintering population – a phenomenon which was repeated in 1984. Breeding, at this site, followed both incursions (R. Kane, pers. obs.). Outside of those two years, statewide CBC totals usually number fewer than twenty. **CBC Statewide Stats:** Average: 11; Maximum: 52 in 1984; Minimum: 1 in 1979. **CBC Maximum:** 47, Great Swamp, 1984.

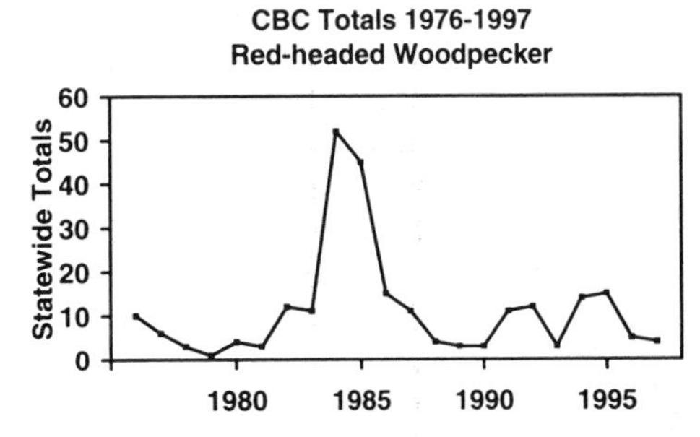

Spring: Northbound Red-headed Woodpeckers are seen in late April and May. Sibley (1997) indicated a spring average at Cape May of about five birds per season. **Maxima:** 5, Cape Island, 11 May 1996; 4, Cape May, 3 May 1975. ■

Red-bellied Woodpecker

Melanerpes carolinus

Range: Resident from southeastern Minnesota east to Massachusetts, south to eastern Texas and Florida.

NJ Status: Fairly common and nearly ubiquitous resident.

Breeding

Habitat: Nests in cavities in a variety of semi-open mixed or deciduous woodland habitats, frequently near water.

During the first half of the 20th century, Red-bellied Woodpeckers were known only as accidental stragglers from the south (Stone 1937, Fables 1955). Sightings gradually became more regular in the southern counties, and the first

continued on page 356

continued from page 355

Red-bellied Woodpecker

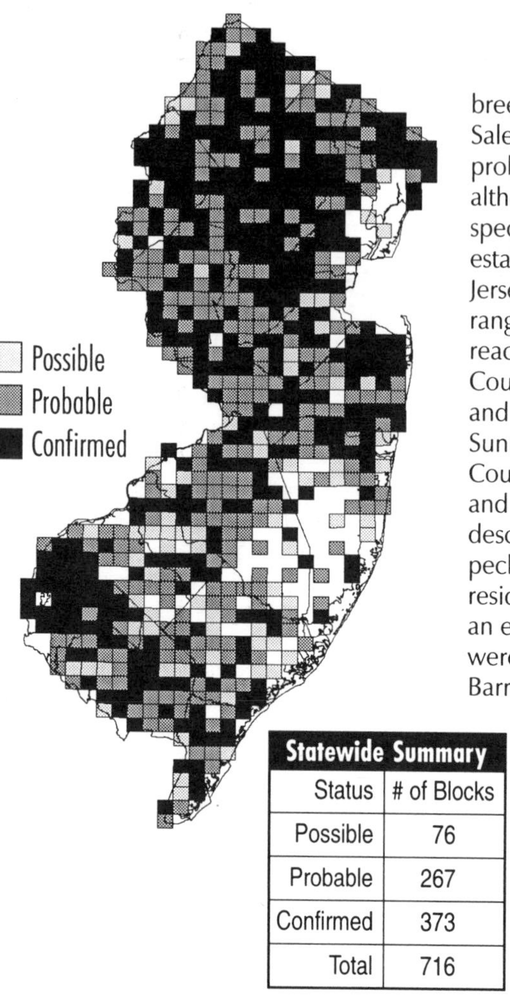

breeding records occurred in Salem and Cape May counties, probably in the early 1950s, although Fables (1955) was not specific about the dates. Once established in southern New Jersey, Red-bellied Woodpeckers range expanded rapidly. They reached Princeton, Mercer County by 1962 (Leck 1984), and were confirmed breeding at Sunrise Mountain, Sussex County on 9 May 1976 (Decker and Decker 1976). Boyle (1986) described Red-bellied Woodpeckers as fairly common residents that were continuing an expansion in the north, but were still uncommon in the Pine Barrens. Sibley (1997) suggested that the increase in the population was continuing.

The Atlas surveys were conducted at the peak of Red-bellied Woodpecker's abundance in the state, which is also evident by CBC totals (see

Statewide Summary

Status	# of Blocks
Possible	76
Probable	267
Confirmed	373
Total	716

Physiographic Distribution

Red-bellied Woodpecker	Number of blocks in province	Number of blocks species found breeding in province	Number of blocks species found in state	Percent of province species occupies	Percent of all records for this species found in province	Percent of state area in province
Kittatinny Mountains	19	19	716	100.0	2.7	2.2
Kittatinny Valley	45	45	716	100.0	6.3	5.3
Highlands	109	108	716	99.1	15.1	12.8
Piedmont	167	148	716	88.6	20.7	19.6
Inner Coastal Plain	128	114	716	89.1	15.9	15.0
Outer Coastal Plain	204	158	716	77.5	22.1	23.9
Pine Barrens	180	124	716	68.9	17.3	21.1

Red-bellied Woodpecker

continued

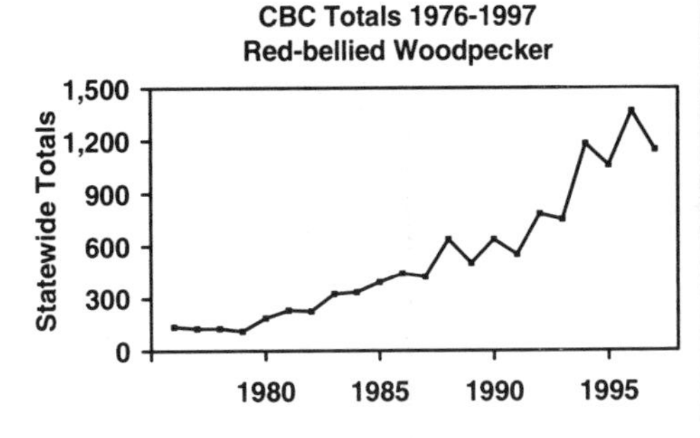

below). Atlas data showed that Red-bellied Woodpeckers were broadly distributed, and were found in 84% of the blocks in the state. They occurred in all the physiographic provinces, although they were absent from sections of the Pine Barrens and most of the barrier islands of the Outer Coastal Plain. This species' efficient colonization of New Jersey may be the fastest and most thorough colonization of any newly arrived native species.

Fall: Red-bellied Woodpeckers are mainly a resident species, but some migration is noted at Cape May from mid-September through October (Sibley 1997).

Winter: CBC totals of Red-bellied Woodpeckers have increased dramatically since the late 1970s – an indication of the population's growth. **CBC Statewide Stats:** Average: 531; Maximum: 1,365 in 1996; Minimum: 138 in 1976. **CBC Maximum:** 160, Great Swamp, 1994.

Spring: Although this is usually considered a resident species, some migration of Red-bellied Woodpeckers is seen in Cape May during May (Sibley 1997). ■

Yellow-bellied Sapsucker

Sphyrapicus varius

Range: In eastern North America breeds from Manitoba east to Newfoundland, south to northern Iowa and northern New Jersey and along the Appalachians to North Carolina. Winters from the central United States to Central America, north along the East coast to Massachusetts.

NJ Status: Rare and very local summer resident, uncommon spring and fall migrant, uncommon winter resident.

Breeding

Habitat: Deciduous or mixed deciduous/evergreen forest.

New Jersey is on the extreme southeast margin of Yellow-bellied Sapsucker's breeding range. There was one confirmed nesting record in New Jersey prior to the Atlas survey period:

continued on page 358

continued from page 357

Yellow-bellied Sapsucker

Physiographic Distribution Yellow-bellied Sapsucker	Number of blocks in province	Number of blocks species found breeding in province	Number of blocks species found in state	Percent of province species occupies	Percent of all records for this species found in province	Percent of state area in province
Highlands	109	1	2	0.9	50.0	12.8
Kittatinny Mountains	19	1	2	5.3	50.0	2.2

a pair feeding three young at Franklin Lakes, in the summer of 1957 (NJNN). There are two other reports of possible breeding attempts in New Jersey prior to the Atlas surveys: from the Watchung Reservation and the Pequannock Watershed, and both in the summer of 1992. Although not regularly occurring as breeders, it is likely that Yellow-bellied Sapsuckers have escaped detection and nested on several occasions in the northern section of the state.

There were only two reports of breeding Yellow-bellied Sapsuckers in the state during the Atlas surveys, although one record was from 1998. In the summer of 1995, Yellow-bellied Sapsuckers were observed on several occasions in appropriate habitat at Wanaque Reservoir, Passaic County; however, no further evidence of breeding was obtained. The second record during the Atlas surveys was of a pair feeding young in the nest at High Point State Park during June 1998.

Possible
Probable
Confirmed

Fall: Yellow-bellied Sapsuckers begin to arrive in New Jersey in mid- to late September and peak flight days occur from late September to mid-October. Movement continues into early November. They can be common along the coast on a few big flight days each fall. They are less numerous inland, where birds are usually found alone. **Maxima:** 30-35, Higbee Beach, 13 October 1991; 27, Higbee Beach, 28 September 1975.

Statewide Summary	
Status	# of Blocks
Possible	0
Probable	1
Confirmed	1
Total	2

Yellow-bellied Sapsucker

continued

Winter: Yellow-bellied Sapsuckers are uncommon statewide in winter and are most likely to be encountered inland and to the north. Numbers vary from year to year, and very rarely do they become locally common – e.g., 40, wintering in the Princeton area, winter 1985-1986. More typically, however, they are found singly. CBC numbers in the mid-1990s were consistently higher than in most previous years. **CBC Statewide Stats:** Average: 55; Maximum: 78 in 1986; Minimum: 4 in 1979. **CBC Maximum:** 25, Great Swamp, 1980.

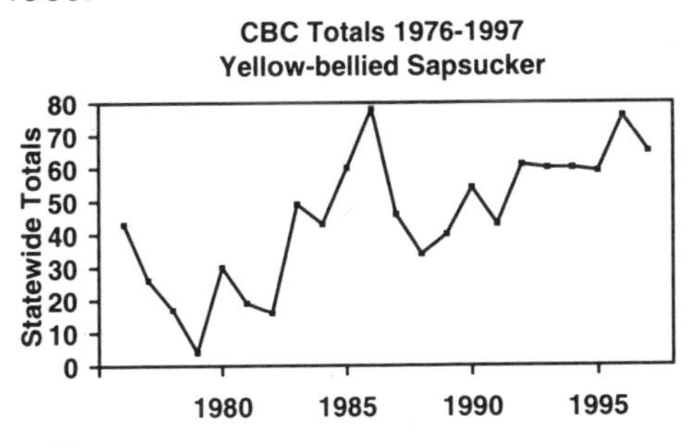

Spring: The main passage of northbound Yellow-bellied Sapsuckers is from late March through early May, with most birds noted in April. The number of spring reports fluctuates from one year to the next, and in some years they may be rare. It is unusual to see more than one Yellow-bellied Sapsucker at a time at this season, so the historic high of 15, Englewood, 15 April 1927 (Bull 1964) is extraordinary. **Maxima:** 4, Bernardsville, 13 April 1996; 4, Somerville, 13 April 1996. ■

Downy Woodpecker

Picoides pubescens

Range: Resident throughout most wooded areas of North America.

NJ Status: Common and nearly ubiquitous resident.

Breeding

Habitat: Nests in cavities in a variety of woodland habitats.

Downy Woodpeckers have long been common and widespread breeding birds in New Jersey. Stone (1908) described them as "universally distributed" and found their abundance second only to Northern Flicker among New Jersey's woodpeckers. In New York, it was suggested that Downy Woodpeckers had increased in abundance during the 20th century as abandoned farmland returned to forest (Confer 1988). This would seem a likely scenario in New Jersey, too.

continued on page 360

continued from page 359

Downy Woodpecker

Atlas volunteers discovered a pattern of distribution similar to that reported by Stone (1908). Volunteers found Downy Woodpeckers in 91% of the blocks in the state. Downy Woodpeckers will use small patches of woods for nesting, and they even inhabit the forest-poor, urbanized northeast counties, and the Inner Coastal Plain. Like the other woodpeckers, they were absent from most of the barrier islands, especially in southern New Jersey.

Fall: Although Downy Woodpeckers are considered to be nonmigratory, some migration is noted in fall, possibly passage birds from north of New Jersey. Griscom (1923) and Cruickshank (1942) suggested movements occurred most commonly in October. Veit and Petersen (1993) also noted October migration in Massachusetts.

Statewide Summary	
Status	# of Blocks
Possible	77
Probable	210
Confirmed	492
Total	779

Possible
Probable
Confirmed

Physiographic Distribution Downy Woodpecker	Number of blocks in province	Number of blocks species found breeding in province	Number of blocks species found in state	Percent of province species occupies	Percent of all records for this species found in province	Percent of state area in province
Kittatinny Mountains	19	19	779	100.0	2.4	2.2
Kittatinny Valley	45	45	779	100.0	5.8	5.3
Highlands	109	108	779	99.1	13.9	12.8
Piedmont	167	162	779	97.0	20.8	19.6
Inner Coastal Plain	128	121	779	94.5	15.5	15.0
Outer Coastal Plain	204	165	779	80.9	21.2	23.9
Pine Barrens	180	159	779	88.3	20.4	21.1

Downy Woodpecker

continued

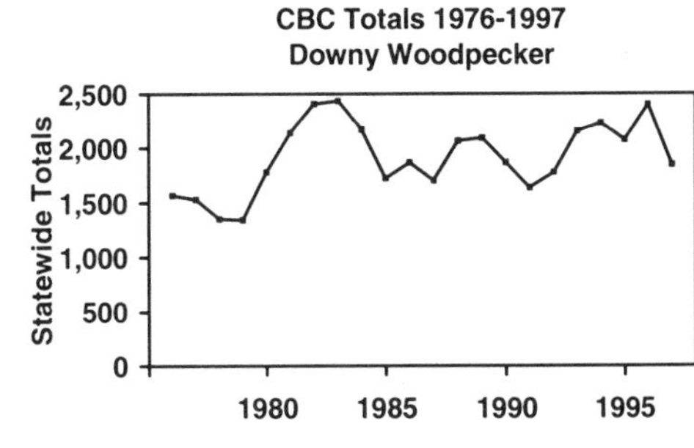

Winter: Christmas Bird Count totals of Downy Woodpeckers are somewhat variable, but are seemingly without obvious trends. **CBC Statewide Stats:** Average: 1,918; Maximum: 2,436 in 1983; Minimum: 1,344 in 1979. **CBC Maximum:** 317, Boonton, 1981.

Spring: There is no published information on the occurrence of spring migration of Downy Woodpeckers in New Jersey. ■

Hairy Woodpecker

Picoides villosus

Range: Resident throughout most wooded areas of North America.

NJ Status: Fairly common and very widespread resident.

Breeding

Habitat: Nests in cavities in a variety of mature woodland habitats.

The historic accounts of Hairy Woodpecker pointed out that, although fairly common and widely distributed, they were less common than Downy Woodpecker (Stone 1908, Leck 1984). The reason for this was also universally agreed upon – Hairy Woodpeckers were found in larger, more mature woodlands with larger trees. Kaufman (1996) indicated that they were believed to have decreased in numbers in many areas of their overall range. In New Jersey, Hairy Woodpeckers were suspected to have declined somewhat by the mid-1980s (Boyle 1986).

Atlas data, however, indicated that the distribution of Hairy Woodpeckers appears to have changed very little in New Jersey during the course of the 20th century. The species is more common in northern than southern New Jersey, and their distribution becomes more patchy from north to south. Hairy Woodpeckers were found in over 90% of the blocks north of the Piedmont, but in less than 70% of the blocks from the Piedmont southward. The Pine Barrens and Outer Coastal Plain were the most sparsely populated, and, not surprisingly, the barrier islands hosted few Hairy Woodpeckers.

Fall: The New Jersey population of Hairy Woodpeckers is essentially nonmigratory, although they are somewhat migratory at the northern edge of their overall range. Several authors have suggested Hairy Woodpeckers were subject to very rare fall

continued on page 362

continued from page 361

Hairy Woodpecker

Possible
Probable
Confirmed

flights, particularly in October (Griscom 1923, Bull 1964). Elsewhere, some post-breeding dispersal has been noted.

Winter: CBC totals for Hairy Woodpeckers are fairly consistent. Counts for this year-round resident, from 1976 to 1997, did not show a marked decline. **CBC Statewide Stats:** Average: 323; Maximum: 394 in 1996; Minimum: 241 in 1977. **CBC Maximum:** 60, Boonton, 1992.

CBC Totals 1976-1997
Hairy Woodpecker

Statewide Totals
400
350
300
250
200
150
100
50
0
1980
1985
1990
1995

Statewide Summary	
Status	# of Blocks
Possible	132
Probable	225
Confirmed	226
Total	583

Spring: There is no published information on the occurrence of spring migration of Hairy Woodpeckers in New Jersey. ■

Physiographic Distribution

Hairy Woodpecker	Number of blocks in province	Number of blocks species found breeding in province	Number of blocks species found in state	Percent of province species occupies	Percent of all records for this species found in province	Percent of state area in province
Kittatinny Mountains	19	19	583	100.0	3.3	2.2
Kittatinny Valley	45	44	583	97.8	7.5	5.3
Highlands	109	104	583	95.4	17.8	12.8
Piedmont	167	117	583	70.1	20.1	19.6
Inner Coastal Plain	128	85	583	66.4	14.6	15.0
Outer Coastal Plain	204	104	583	51.0	17.8	23.9
Pine Barrens	180	110	583	61.1	18.9	21.1

Three-toed Woodpecker

Picoides tridactylus

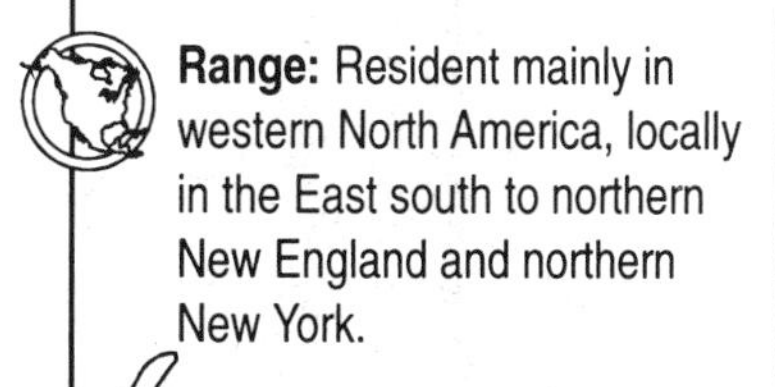

Range: Resident mainly in western North America, locally in the East south to northern New England and northern New York.

NJ Status: Accidental. NJBRC Review List.

Occurrence: There have been two state reports of Three-toed Woodpeckers, and one has been accepted by the NJBRC: West Englewood, 5 February 1918. Fables (1955) and Bull (1964) listed this record as hypothetical. However, the circumstances and the description compelled both Cruickshank (1942) and the NJBRC to accept the record. ■

Black-backed Woodpecker

Picoides arcticus

Range: In eastern North America, resident from Manitoba east to Newfoundland, south to the Great Lakes, northern New York, and northern New England.

NJ Status: Very rare. NJBRC Review List.

Occurrence: There have been 22 state reports of Black-backed Woodpeckers, and 17 have been accepted by the NJBRC. This is a species of the boreal forests, and incursions have occurred in New Jersey in the 1920s, and again from the late 1950s into the 1960s. Of the accepted records, only one has occurred since 1969. Although seven reports come from Bergen County, and four of those from Oradell Res., the remaining reports are scattered around the state.

The 17 accepted records include ten accepted by Fables (1955), Kunkle et al. (1959), and/or Cruickshank (1942), the first of which was one from Englewood#, 29 November 1923 (spec. AMNH #181127).

Records since 1960 are:

	*Oradell Res.**	*11 December 1960-January 1961*	
	*Fairton**	*9-11 October 1962*	*ph-RBPF; film-RBPF*
1-2	*Cape May**	*5-6 October 1963*	
	*Stanton Station**	*11 October-11 November 1963*	
	Island Beach	*28 September 1965*	*ph-RBPF, banded male*
	*Salem**	*late October-early November 1969*	
	Princeton	*5-9 April 1983*	*ph-RNJB 9:60*

Range: Breeds throughout most wooded areas of North America. Generally winters south of Canada.

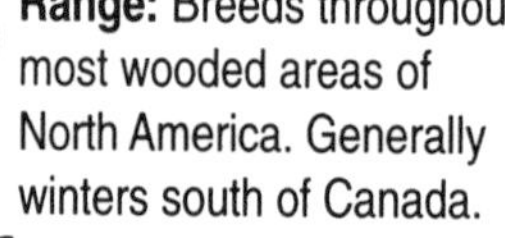

NJ Status: Common and nearly ubiquitous summer resident, common spring and fall migrant, fairly common winter resident.

Northern Flicker

Colaptes auratus

Breeding

Habitat: Nests in cavities in a variety of wooded habitats.

Stone (1908) described Northern Flickers as "one of our most familiar and abundant birds." Cruickshank (1942) noted their adaptability as breeding birds because he found them

Statewide Summary	
Status	# of Blocks
Possible	71
Probable	253
Confirmed	484
Total	808

Possible
Probable
Confirmed

Physiographic Distribution Northern Flicker	Number of blocks in province	Number of blocks species found breeding in province	Number of blocks species found in state	Percent of province species occupies	Percent of all records for this species found in province	Percent of state area in province
Kittatinny Mountains	19	19	808	100.0	2.4	2.2
Kittatinny Valley	45	44	808	97.8	5.4	5.3
Highlands	109	107	808	98.2	13.2	12.8
Piedmont	167	162	808	97.0	20.0	19.6
Inner Coastal Plain	128	126	808	98.4	15.6	15.0
Outer Coastal Plain	204	178	808	87.3	22.0	23.9
Pine Barrens	180	172	808	95.6	21.3	21.1

nesting in city parks and suburban yards. In these environments, however, they were in direct competition with European Starlings for nest cavities, and Fables (1955) was the first to note the appropriation of newly excavated Northern Flicker nest cavities by European Starlings. Although Northern Flickers have continued to be broadly distributed and common breeding birds throughout their overall range, declines in their abundance have been noted since the late 1960s. Loss of habitat has been noted as a cause, in addition to competition with European Starlings. This downward trend is of particular concern, as many other cavity-nesting species rely on Northern Flicker cavities that were excavated in previous years (Moore 1995).

Atlas volunteers found Northern Flickers to be one of the most broadly distributed breeding birds in New Jersey. They were found in 95% of the blocks in the state and were evenly distributed throughout the physiographic provinces. Like the other woodpeckers, they were absent from some of the barrier islands – a significant indicator of the nearly complete loss of woodland habitats along the Atlantic coast.

Fall: Large southbound flights of Northern Flickers occur along the coast. Peak movements occur from late September through early October, with migrants thinning out by early November. Stone (1937) recounted the large-scale gunning of Northern Flickers at Cape May in the fall, before the practice was made illegal. Gunners would attach posts to the tops of small pines, which the flickers would find to be irresistible perches. They were then "raked" off with ease. Stone related that "piles of dead birds as high as a man's knees were frequent sights." One gunner shot four hundred flickers in an hour and a half. Fortunately, those events ended even before Stone's time. **Maxima:** 5,000+, Higbee Beach, 13 October 1991; 1,000, Higbee Beach, 30 September 1982.

Winter: Statewide CBC totals of Northern Flickers are variable from year to year, but counts have averaged higher since 1982 than in prior years. **CBC Statewide Stats:** Average: 894; Maximum: 1,444 in 1988; Minimum: 289 in 1978. **CBC maximum:** 201, Princeton, 1995.

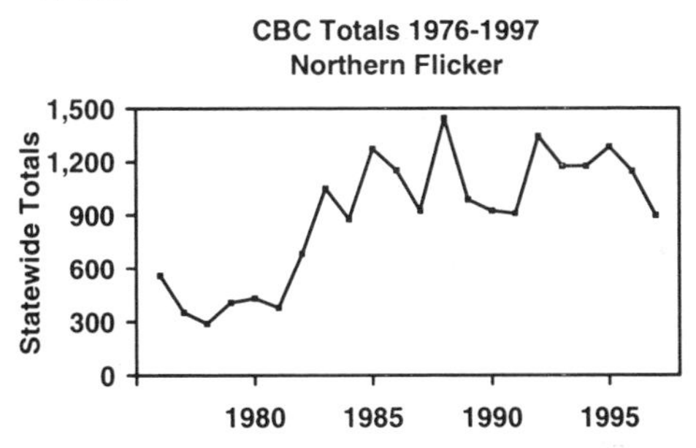

Spring: Northern Flickers return northward early in the spring, peaking from late March through early April. An estimate of 10,000 flickers at Sandy Hook on 28 March 1988 is the largest flight recorded in spring. **Other maxima:** 45, Higbee Beach, 5 April 1988; 30+, Hardwick, 5 April 1985.

Subspecies: *C. a. auratus* ("Yellow-shafted Flicker") is the subspecies seen in New Jersey. Sibley (1997) estimated that

continued on page 366

continued from page 365

Northern Flicker

sight records of intergrades between C. a. *auratus* and C. a. *cafer* ("Red-shafted Flicker") at Cape May averaged about one per fall, but that those might actually be variants of C. a. *auratus*, rather than intergrades. Veit and Petersen (1993), however, referred to a study at the Manomet Bird Observatory that investigated the presence of intergrades between C. a. *auratus* and C. a. *cafer* during migration. They reported no intergrades were found in spring, but 24% of the 91 birds trapped in fall were identified as intergrades. There are no records of pure C. a. *cafer* in New Jersey. ■

Pileated Woodpecker

Dryocopus pileatus

Range: Resident In eastern North America, locally from central Manitoba to Nova Scotia south to eastern Texas and Florida.

NJ Status: Uncommon and somewhat local resident.

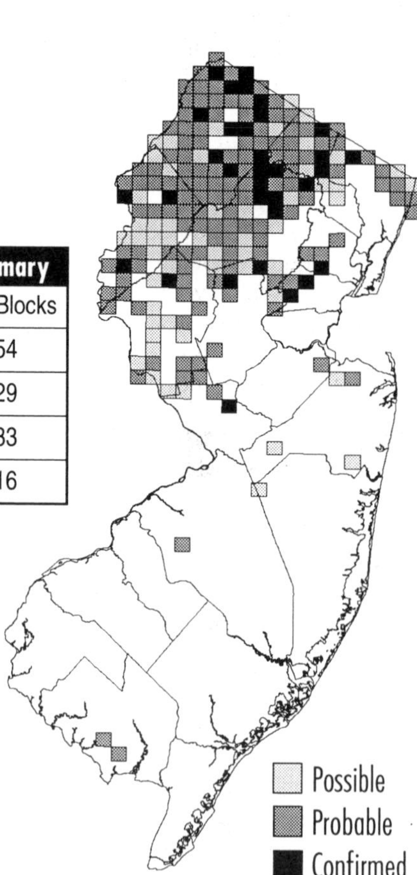

Statewide Summary	
Status	# of Blocks
Possible	54
Probable	129
Confirmed	33
Total	216

Breeding

Habitat: Nests in cavities in mature mixed or deciduous woods.

Stone (1937) suspected that, at one time, Pileated Woodpeckers were common breeding birds in New Jersey. However, by the turn of the 20th century he considered them to be extirpated from most of the state. It was believed that Pileated Woodpeckers disappeared in the face of encroaching civilization (Griscom 1923, Stone 1937). Historically they were also shot for

Pileated Woodpecker

continued

sport (Bull and Jackson 1995), but it is not known what effect this had on the local population. Griscom (1923) was heartened by their rediscovery in Passaic and Sussex counties in the early 1920s. By the middle of the 20th century, Pileated Woodpecker numbers were slowly increasing in the northern part of the state (Fables 1955), and by the mid-1960s they were described as having "increased greatly" (Bull 1964).

During the 1900s, the presence of Pileated Woodpeckers on the Coastal Plain has been enigmatic, usually noted in terms of isolated sightings. It is difficult to determine if these were vagrants from the north, or, if some of the sightings represented local breeding birds (Stone 1908). Pileated Woodpeckers require woodlands with mature trees that have enough girth to support their sizable cavities (Bull and Jackson 1995); such mature woodlands are more prevalent in northern New Jersey than in southern New Jersey. During the 1980s, there was some evidence that Pileated Woodpeckers were, on a small scale, attempting to establish themselves in southern New Jersey. Bear Swamp in Cumberland County has supported a few pairs of Pileated Woodpeckers since the mid-1980s. In the late 1980s they were also present at Corbin City WMA in Atlantic County, although they were not found there during the Atlas surveys. Pileated Woodpecker sightings have occurred sporadically in adjacent Atlantic County Park, indicating they may still be present in that area (C. Sutton, pers. com.).

Atlas observers found that more than 95% of Pileated Woodpecker's range was from the Piedmont northward. In the Kittatinny Mountains, Kittatinny Valley, and in the Highlands, Pileated Woodpeckers were found in 89% of the blocks. The percentage of blocks occupied dropped to 30% in the Piedmont. Pileated Woodpeckers continued to occupy the Bear Swamp area of Cumberland County, where they were listed as Probable in two blocks.

continued on page 368

Physiographic Distribution **Pileated Woodpecker**	Number of blocks in province	Number of blocks species found breeding in province	Number of blocks species found in state	Percent of province species occupies	Percent of all records for this species found in province	Percent of state area in province
Kittatinny Mountains	19	19	216	100.0	8.8	2.2
Kittatinny Valley	45	38	216	84.4	17.6	5.3
Highlands	109	98	216	89.9	45.4	12.8
Piedmont	167	51	216	30.5	23.6	19.6
Inner Coastal Plain	128	4	216	3.1	1.9	15.0
Outer Coastal Plain	204	4	216	2.0	1.9	23.9
Pine Barrens	180	2	216	1.1	0.9	21.1

continued from page 367

Pileated Woodpecker

Fall: Pileated Woodpeckers are permanent, nonmigratory residents. There is no published information on the occurrence of fall migration of Pileated Woodpeckers in New Jersey.

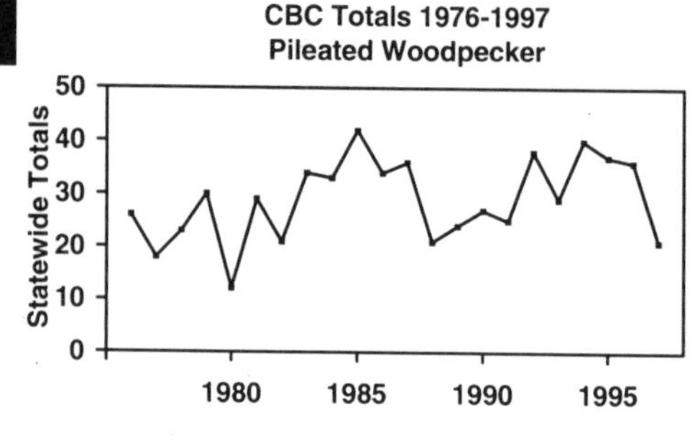

Winter: CBC totals of Pileated Woodpeckers seem to vary without showing obvious trend, and statewide totals are fairly low. **CBC Statewide Stats:** Average: 29; Maximum: 42 in 1985; Minimum: 12 in 1980. **CBC Maximum:** 14, Walnut Valley, 1987.

Spring: Pileated Woodpeckers are permanent, nonmigratory residents. There is no published information on the occurrence of spring migration of Pileated Woodpeckers in New Jersey. ■

Olive-sided Flycatcher

Contopus cooperi

Olive-sided Flycatcher

Range: In eastern North America breeds from Manitoba east to Newfoundland, south to the Great Lakes and northern New York, and sporadically south along the Appalachians to Tennessee. Winters in South America.

NJ Status: Scarce spring and uncommon fall migrant.

Olive-sided Flycatcher

continued

Fall: Olive-sided Flycatchers are typically found singly, fly-catching from the tip of a dead tree, often near water. Most pass through New Jersey between early August and mid-September. More exceptional are three reports from July and one from early November, the latter an injured bird. **Maxima:** 3, several times.

Spring: Olive-sided Flycatchers are most prevalent inland and northward in spring. Passage occurs between mid-May and early June. **Maximum:** 3, Higbee Beach, 30 May 1982. ■

Eastern Wood-Pewee

Contopus virens

Range: Breeds from southern Manitoba east to Nova Scotia, south to eastern Texas and northern Florida. Winters mainly in northern South America.

NJ Status: Common and very widespread summer resident, fairly common spring and fall migrant.

Breeding

Habitat: Breeds in mixed or deciduous woodlands, favoring areas near clearings.

Eastern Wood-Pewees were described as common and widespread breeding birds in New Jersey throughout the 20th century (Stone 1908, Boyle 1986). An analysis of BBS data from 1966-1993 indicated a significant range-wide decline for this species (Price et al 1995). This decline appears to be patchy, however, with some areas of the country affected more than others.

Atlas volunteers found Eastern Wood-Pewees occurred throughout all the physiographic provinces, and located them in 78% of the blocks statewide. They use mixed hardwood or pine forests for breeding, which is indicated by the high density of occupied blocks in the Kittatinny Valley, Kittatinny Mountains, Highlands, and the Pine Barrens. Forest fragmentation does not appear to be a hindrance to the selection of nesting habitat for Eastern Wood-Pewees (McCarty 1996). They were absent from much of the highly urbanized northeastern Piedmont, sections of the Outer

continued on page 370

continued from page 369

Eastern Wood-Pewee

Coastal Plain (especially the barrier islands), and the northeastern Inner Coastal Plain.

Fall: Most Eastern Wood-Pewees move south between late August and early October, and peak numbers are seen in mid-September. They are usually seen in relatively small numbers, even at locations that concentrate other migrant songbirds. **Maxima:** 29, Higbee Beach, 11 September 1988; 20+, Bull's Island, 2 September 1981.

Spring: Eastern Wood-Pewees arrive on their breeding grounds in early to mid-May. They are late migrants, with northbound birds noted well into June. Spring migrants are usually seen in ones and twos, with no concentrated flights. **Maxima:** 10, Higbee Beach, 16 May 1994; 10, Higbee Beach, 24 May 1994 (Sibley 1997). ■

Statewide Summary	
Status	# of Blocks
Possible	76
Probable	402
Confirmed	183
Total	661

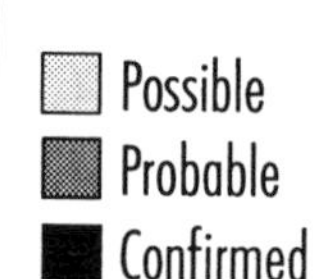

Physiographic Distribution Eastern Wood-Pewee	Number of blocks in province	Number of blocks species found breeding in province	Number of blocks species found in state	Percent of province species occupies	Percent of all records for this species found in province	Percent of state area in province
Kittatinny Mountains	19	18	661	94.7	2.7	2.2
Kittatinny Valley	45	41	661	91.1	6.2	5.3
Highlands	109	107	661	98.2	16.2	12.8
Piedmont	167	119	661	71.3	18.0	19.6
Inner Coastal Plain	128	87	661	68.0	13.2	15.0
Outer Coastal Plain	204	129	661	63.2	19.5	23.9
Pine Barrens	180	160	661	88.9	24.2	21.1

Yellow-bellied Flycatcher

Empidonax flaviventris

Range: Breeds from British Columbia east across Canada to Labrador and southeast to Minnesota. In the East, breeds south to New York, and, in the mountains, irregularly to North Carolina. Winters in Central America and southern Mexico.

NJ Status: Scarce spring and uncommon fall migrant.

Fall: Yellow-bellied Flycatchers favor woodlands, hedgerows, and thickets of smaller trees, especially near water. Most birds pass through New Jersey in late August and early September, although the typical range of reports runs from mid-August to late September. **Maxima:** 10, Trenton, 1 September 1984; 7, Hopewell, 14 September 1986, banded.

Spring: The spring migration of Yellow-bellied Flycatchers is relatively late, in the very concentrated period from mid- to late May. **Maxima:** 5, Garret Mountain, 26 May 1997; 4, West Cape May, 20 May 1988. ■

Acadian Flycatcher

Empidonax virescens

Range: Breeds from southeastern Minnesota east to southeastern Massachusetts, south to eastern Texas and northern Florida. Winters in Central and South America.

NJ Status: Fairly common but somewhat local summer resident, scarce spring and fall migrant.

Breeding

Habitat: Nests in stands of hemlock, and swampy or wet woods.

Acadian Flycatchers have been summer residents in southern New Jersey since the turn of the 20th century (Stone 1908). Fables (1955) specifically noted a well-established population in Cumberland and Cape May counties, a pattern that still persists. This species declined dramatically in the northern part of the state around 1900, for unknown reasons (Griscom 1923, Bull 1964). Stone (1908) reported that Acadian Flycatchers were common throughout New Jersey, except in the northernmost counties. By 1942 Cruickshank knew them only as transients in the north, and by the mid-1960s

continued on page 372

continued from page 371

Acadian Flycatcher

Statewide Summary	
Status	# of Blocks
Possible	69
Probable	144
Confirmed	40
Total	253

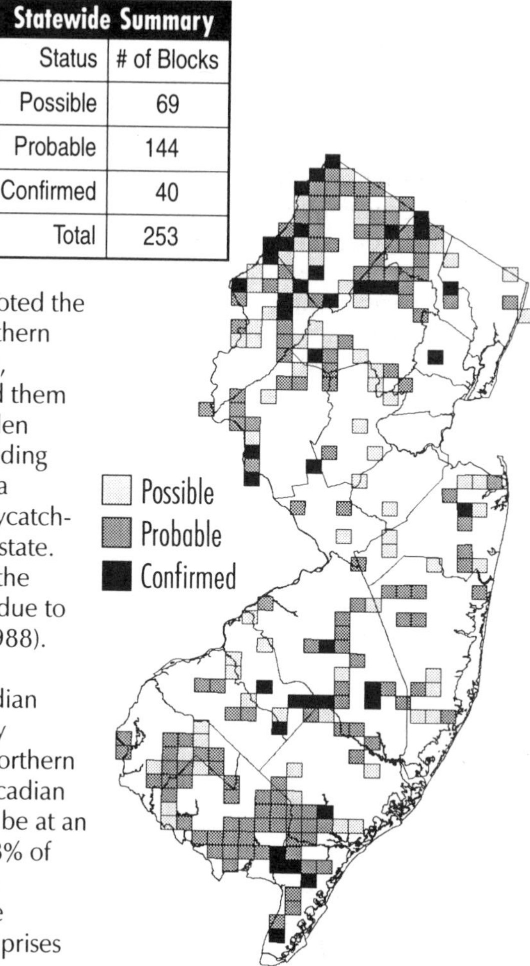

they were rare anywhere north of the Raritan River (Bull 1964). The return of Acadian Flycatchers to the northern areas of the state is not well documented. Leck (1984) noted the expansion of an *existing* northern population in the late 1970s, although Boyle (1986) found them fairly common in hemlock glen habitats. The New York Breeding Bird Atlas also documented a recolonization of Acadian Flycatchers into some regions of the state. The authors postulated that the recovery of this species was due to forest regeneration (Eaton 1988).

Atlas surveys showed Acadian Flycatchers occurred in every physiographic province. In northern New Jersey, it is likely that Acadian Flycatchers' population may be at an all-time high. Surprisingly, 38% of the blocks reporting Acadian Flycatchers were north of the Piedmont, and this area comprises

Physiographic Distribution Acadian Flycatcher	Number of blocks in province	Number of blocks species found breeding in province	Number of blocks species found in state	Percent of province species occupies	Percent of all records for this species found in province	Percent of state area in province
Kittatinny Mountains	19	19	253	100.0	7.5	2.2
Kittatinny Valley	45	26	253	57.8	10.3	5.3
Highlands	109	51	253	46.8	20.2	12.8
Piedmont	167	24	253	14.4	9.5	19.6
Inner Coastal Plain	128	16	253	12.5	6.3	15.0
Outer Coastal Plain	204	62	253	30.4	24.5	23.9
Pine Barrens	180	55	253	30.6	21.7	21.1

Acadian Flycatcher

continued

only 20% of the state. In the north, they were found in all of the Kittatinny Mountain blocks and in 46% of the Highland blocks, and in the Highlands, they were concentrated around the Wawayanda Plateau.

Atlas surveys in southern New Jersey found Acadian Flycatchers were well distributed in Cumberland and Cape May counties. Boyle (1986) suggested that Acadian Flycatchers were mainly absent from the Pine Barrens, but Atlas observers found them in over 30% of the Pine Barrens blocks. This, in conjunction with their return to the northern counties, suggests that Acadian Flycatchers expanded their distribution in the state from the mid-1970s to the mid-1990s.

Fall: Acadian Flycatchers have a southerly breeding distribution, with relatively small numbers nesting north and northwest of New Jersey. In addition, the difficulty of identification among the five eastern species of *Empidonax* flycatchers is a well-known problem. It is therefore not surprising that few are reported during migration. Most migrants apparently occur between mid-August and early September. **Maximum:** 3, Higbee Beach, 9 August 1989.

Spring: Acadian Flycatchers arrive on their breeding grounds from late April through mid-May, although migrants can still be found in early June. Northbound birds are usually encountered as lone individuals. **Maximum:** 3, Higbee Beach, 2 June 1998. ■

Alder Flycatcher

Empidonax alnorum

Range: In eastern North America breeds from Manitoba east to Newfoundland, south to northern Ohio and northern New Jersey, and in the Appalachians locally to northern North Carolina. Winters in South America.

NJ Status: Uncommon and local summer resident, probably a rare to scarce spring and uncommon fall migrant.

Breeding

Habitat: Nests in thickets of small trees and shrubs, generally near water, often in swamps.

Specific historical information on the distribution of Alder Flycatchers goes back only to the 1970s, when *E. traillii* (then called Traill's Flycatcher) was officially split into *E. alnorum* (Alder

continued on page 374

continued from page 373

Alder Flycatcher

Flycatcher) and *E. traillii* (Willow Flycatcher). Within their overall range, Alder Flycatchers have a more northerly distribution than Willow Flycatchers, and it is almost certain that alders have never nested much farther south in the state than the Atlas map indicates. Bull (1964) reported that both willow and alder song types were broadly, but locally, distributed north of the Coastal Plain, although he considered the *"fitz-bew"* song of the Willow Flycatcher to be the prevailing form. Stone (1937) makes no mention of *E. traillii* breeding in Cape May County. Fables' (1955) references to breeding *E. traillii* (then called Alder Flycatcher) along the Delaware River near Camden, and rarely in the Pine Barrens, surely refer to Willow Flycatcher. By the mid-1980s, Boyle (1986) described Alder Flycatchers as rare and local breeding birds in the north.

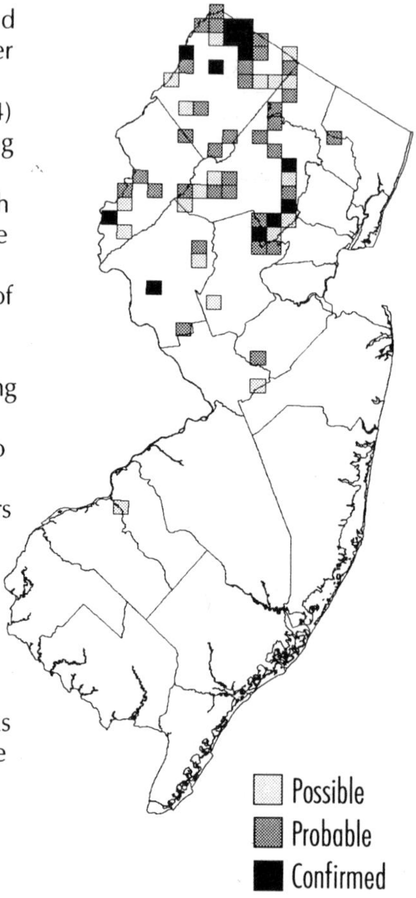

The distribution of Alder Flycatcher was patchy and local in New Jersey, a pattern similar to that found in Pennsylvania (Mulvihill 1992a). New Jersey Atlas surveys found over 70% of the statewide range of Alder Flycatcher to be north of the Piedmont. Alder Flycatchers were found in 34% of the blocks in the Kittatinny Mountains and Kittatinny

Possible
Probable
Confirmed

Physiographic Distribution

Alder Flycatcher	Number of blocks in province	Number of blocks species found breeding in province	Number of blocks species found in state	Percent of province species occupies	Percent of all records for this species found in province	Percent of state area in province
Kittatinny Mountains	19	8	65	42.1	12.3	2.2
Kittatinny Valley	45	14	65	31.1	21.5	5.3
Highlands	109	23	65	21.1	35.4	12.8
Piedmont	167	17	65	10.2	26.2	19.6
Inner Coastal Plain	128	3	65	2.3	4.6	15.0

Alder Flycatcher
continued

Statewide Summary	
Status	# of Blocks
Possible	19
Probable	33
Confirmed	13
Total	65

Valley, within a cluster of blocks in the Wallkill River valley, and along the Delaware River. They were also located in 21% of the Highlands blocks. On the Piedmont, Alder Flycatchers were concentrated in Morris County blocks that contained the Great Swamp and Troy Meadows, and their distribution followed a swath northward that roughly approximates the boundaries of Glacial Lake Passaic. There were only six blocks statewide that hosted breeding Alder Flycatchers but not Willow Flycatchers.

Fall: Alder Flycatchers are notoriously difficult to separate from Willow Flycatchers other than by voice or close examination in the hand. These flycatchers rarely call during fall migration; so migration periods are not well known. Southbound birds appear to move between mid-August and late September, probably peaking from late August through mid-September. **Maximum:** 3, Cape May Point, 7 September 1987.

Spring: Most records of migrant Alder Flycatchers occur from mid-May into early June. The records are typically of lone singing individuals. Breeding birds arrive on territory in mid-May. ■

Willow Flycatcher
Empidonax traillii

Range: In eastern North America breeds from Michigan to coastal Maine, south to northern Oklahoma and northern Virginia. Winters in Central America.

NJ Status: Fairly common and fairly widespread summer resident, probably an uncommon spring and fall migrant.

Breeding

Habitat: Nests in thickets of small trees and shrubs, often near streams or in fresh and saltwater marshes; may be found in drier habitats than Alder Flycatcher.

Historic information on the distribution of Willow

continued on page 376

continued from page 375

Willow Flycatcher

Physiographic Distribution Willow Flycatcher	Number of blocks in province	Number of blocks species found breeding in province	Number of blocks species found in state	Percent of province species occupies	Percent of all records for this species found in province	Percent of state area in province
Kittatinny Mountains	19	14	362	73.7	3.9	2.2
Kittatinny Valley	45	38	362	84.4	10.5	5.3
Highlands	109	78	362	71.6	21.5	12.8
Piedmont	167	100	362	59.9	27.6	19.6
Inner Coastal Plain	128	68	362	53.1	18.8	15.0
Outer Coastal Plain	204	57	362	27.9	15.7	23.9
Pine Barrens	180	7	362	3.9	1.9	21.1

Flycatchers is complicated by the fact that this species was lumped with Alder Flycatcher until the 1970s (see discussion under Alder Flycatcher). As of the mid-1930s, Stone found Acadian Flycatcher to be the only flycatcher of the *Empidonax* genus nesting in Cape May County (Stone 1937). Fables' (1955) references to breeding "Alder" Flycatchers along the Delaware River near Camden, and rarely in the Pine Barrens, are likely to have referred to Willow Flycatchers, and probably represented an extension of Willow Flycatcher's range into southern New Jersey. In a breeding bird survey of the Great Swamp, Morris County, in 1982 and 1983, Willow Flycatchers were found to be the most common flycatchers there and were described as "an increasing species in New Jersey" (Kane et al. 1985). Leck (1984) suggested that Willow Flycatchers were expanding their range onto the Coastal Plain, but still described them as local breeding birds.

Statewide Summary

Status	# of Blocks
Possible	49
Probable	199
Confirmed	114
Total	362

Possible
Probable
Confirmed

Willow Flycatcher

continued

In New Jersey, Willow Flycatchers have apparently undergone a north-to-south range expansion during the second half of the 20th century. Atlas data indicated that they were widely distributed throughout the northern half of the state, occurring in 68% of the blocks from the Piedmont northward. They were located in 80% of the Kittatinny Mountain and Valley blocks, 72% of the Highlands blocks, and 60% of the Piedmont blocks. South of the Piedmont, Willow Flycatchers clearly avoided the Pine Barrens and the eastern section of the Outer Coastal Plain, with the exception of the upland edges of the salt marshes. They were well distributed on the Inner Coastal Plain, where they occupied 53% of the blocks.

Fall: Willow Flycatchers are extremely difficult to separate from Alder Flycatchers other than by voice, so their period of migration is difficult to pinpoint. Willows probably move south mainly in August and into early September.

Spring: Willow Flycatchers typically arrive on breeding grounds in the northern part of the state by mid- to late May. Interestingly, local breeding birds do not reach the Cape May peninsula until later in the month. **Maximum:** 8, Sandy Hook, 25 May 1998. ■

Least Flycatcher

Empidonax minimus

Range: In eastern North America breeds from Manitoba to Newfoundland, south to South Dakota and northern New Jersey and along the Appalachians to northern Georgia. Winters in Central America.

NJ Status: Uncommon and local summer resident, uncommon spring and fairly common fall migrant.

Breeding

Habitat: Nests in open deciduous woodlands, preferring edges and clearings.

Stone (1908) identified the range of Least Flycatcher as the "northern counties," which Griscom (1923) specified as Sussex, Warren, Passaic, and Morris counties. The New Jersey breeding population apparently decreased in the late 1970s (Leck 1984, Boyle 1986), as was the case in eastern Massachusetts

continued on page 378

continued from page 377

Least Flycatcher

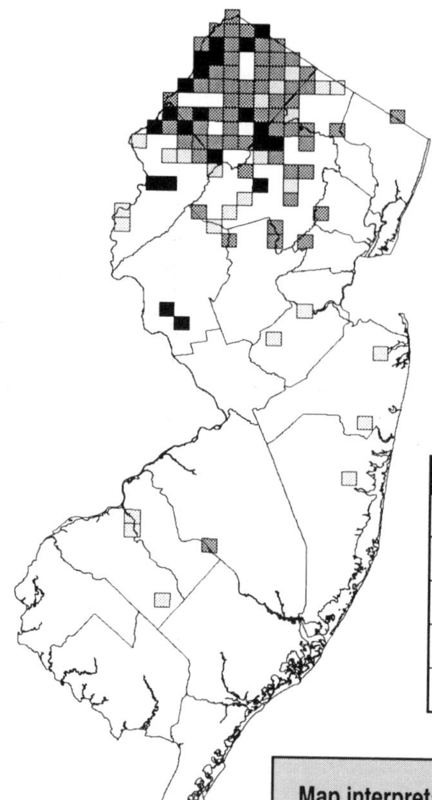

and New Hampshire (Veit and Petersen 1993). A breeding bird survey of the Great Swamp, Morris County, in 1983 and 1984, found only two pairs each year, prompting the observers to describe Least Flycatcher as a "declining species" in the state (Kane et al. 1985). Declines have also been noted in the other eastern states, but the

Statewide Summary

Status	# of Blocks
Possible	25
Probable	61
Confirmed	21
Total	107

Map interpretation: Least Flycatchers are notoriously late migrants. Even though they may have nested very rarely on the Coastal Plain in the past, it is more likely that the Possible or Probable locations south of the Piedmont represent late migrants rather than breeding birds.

Physiographic Distribution

Least Flycatcher	Number of blocks in province	Number of blocks species found breeding in province	Number of blocks species found in state	Percent of province species occupies	Percent of all records for this species found in province	Percent of state area in province
Kittatinny Mountains	19	18	107	94.7	16.8	2.2
Kittatinny Valley	45	31	107	68.9	29.0	5.3
Highlands	109	40	107	36.7	37.4	12.8
Piedmont	167	9	107	5.4	8.4	19.6
Inner Coastal Plain	128	4	107	3.1	3.7	15.0
Outer Coastal Plain	204	1	107	0.5	0.9	23.9
Pine Barrens	180	4	107	2.2	3.7	21.1

reasons are uncertain (Briskie 1994). In Pennsylvania, a drop in the breeding population in some areas of the state was noted in the early to mid-1980s (Mulvihill 1992b).

Atlas surveys found that 82% of their range was north of the Piedmont. The distribution of Least Flycatchers in northern New Jersey appears to be very similar to that identified by Griscom (1923). Within northern New Jersey, they were broadly distributed and occupied 95% of the blocks within the Kittatinny Mountains and 69% of the Kittatinny Valley. Least Flycatchers have been found only very rarely breeding in southern New Jersey. Stone (1908) noted a record from the late 1800s near Haddonfield, and Fables reported a nest in Burlington County near Batsto in 1950.

Fall: Probably the most common migrant *Empidonax*, Least Flycatchers are also easier to identify than other *Empidonax*. Migrants can be seen quite early, with a few present by late July. They peak from late August through mid-September, and most are gone before October. **Maxima:** 40, Higbee Beach, 29 August 1982 (Sibley 1997); 20+, Higbee Beach, 1 September 1988.

Spring: Least Flycatchers arrive on their breeding grounds in early May. Most migrants move through in the middle of May. **Maxima:** 8+, Culvers Lake, 15 May 1982; 6, Palmyra, 9 May 1997. ■

Least Flycatcher

Pacific-slope/Cordilleran Flycatcher

Empidonax difficilis/occidentalis

Range: Western United States and western Canada from southeastern Alaska to central California and east to Colorado.

NJ Status: Accidental. NJBRC Review List.

Occurrence: There has been only one documented and accepted record of Pacific-slope/Cordilleran Flycatcher in New Jersey: Brigantine NWR, 16 November 1981. This record was originally accepted by the NJBRC in 1990 as Western Flycatcher. After the acceptance, Western Flycatcher was split into Pacific-slope and Cordilleran Flycatcher. During the State List revision in 1996, this record was accepted as Pacific-slope/Cordilleran Flycatcher. ■

Eastern Phoebe

Sayornis phoebe

Breeding

Habitat: Often nests under bridges over streams; also on other ledges, either man-made or natural, usually near water.

Eastern Phoebe's distribution in New Jersey has changed over the course of the 20th century and has slowly expanded southward. Although several ornithologists from the early 1900s described them as common summer residents in northern New Jersey (Griscom 1923, Cruickshank 1942), Stone (1937) knew of no Eastern Phoebe nests south of the central Pine Barrens or Lower Delaware River.

Range: Breeds from southern Northwest Territories east to Nova Scotia, south to eastern Texas and northern Georgia. Winters from the southeastern United States south to Central America.

NJ Status: Fairly common and very widespread summer resident, fairly common spring and common fall migrant, rare winter resident.

Eastern Phoebe

continued

Atlas surveys found that Eastern Phoebes were well distributed throughout most physiographic provinces, but were conspicuously absent from the urbanized northeast, large sections of Cape May and Cumberland counties, and from the barrier islands. Eastern Phoebes occupied 99% of the blocks north of the Piedmont, and from 73-80% of the blocks in the Piedmont, Inner Coastal Plain, and Pine Barrens. Their absence from southern Cape May County and sections of Cumberland County remains a mystery, just as their absence from sections of the Coastal Plain on Long Island puzzled Cruickshank (1942). This distributional anomaly seems to be characteristic of Eastern Phoebes –for the most part phoebes avoid coastal wetlands throughout their range. This may be due to a lack of appropriate nesting substrates near the coast.

continued on page 382

Possible
Probable
Confirmed

Statewide Summary	
Status	# of Blocks
Possible	58
Probable	97
Confirmed	466
Total	621

Physiographic Distribution Eastern Phoebe	Number of blocks in province	Number of blocks species found breeding in province	Number of blocks species found in state	Percent of province species occupies	Percent of all records for this species found in province	Percent of state area in province
Kittatinny Mountains	19	19	621	100.0	3.1	2.2
Kittatinny Valley	45	44	621	97.8	7.1	5.3
Highlands	109	108	621	99.1	17.4	12.8
Piedmont	167	133	621	79.6	21.4	19.6
Inner Coastal Plain	128	93	621	72.7	15.0	15.0
Outer Coastal Plain	204	86	621	42.2	13.8	23.9
Pine Barrens	180	138	621	76.7	22.2	21.1

continued from page 381

Eastern Phoebe

Fall: Migrant Eastern Phoebes arrive in mid-September, with peak numbers moving south in early to mid-October. Movements can continue well into November, and a few linger into December. **Maxima:** 100s, Higbee Beach, 8 October 1987; 100s, Higbee Beach, 8 October 1991.

Winter: In mild Decembers, Eastern Phoebes are frequently found on CBCs, and at least a few are tallied statewide every year, usually in the southern part of the state. Mid-winter records are unusual, however, as shown by the few deep-winter records. **CBC Statewide Stats:** Average: 9; Maximum: 49 in 1996; Minimum: 0 in 1982. **CBC Maximum:** 11, Cape May, 1996.

CBC Totals 1976-1997
Eastern Phoebe

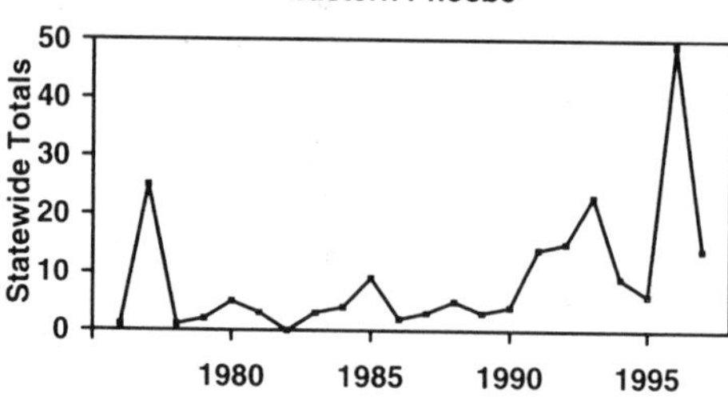

Spring: Phoebes return early in spring, sometimes in late February. More typically they arrive in early to mid-March and peak in early to mid-April. Most migrants have moved on by early May. **Maxima:** 30, Higbee Beach, 4 April 1993; 25, Watchung Reservation, 29 March 1975. ■

Say's Phoebe

Sayornis saya

Range: Breeds from Alaska east to the central plains and south throughout much of western North America. Winters from California east to Texas, south to Mexico.

NJ Status: Accidental. NJBRC Review List.

Occurrence: There have been ten state reports of Say's Phoebe, and eight have been accepted by the NJBRC (seven in fall, one in winter). All but one of the records are coastal, and three are from Island Beach. Two of the records came in 1977, an extraordinary flight year, with an unprecedented nine records in the Northeast. The eight accepted records are:

Tuckerton#	*30 September 1948*	
Loveladies#	*28 January-12 February1956*	
Brigantine NWR	*2 October 1960*	*movie film-RBPF*
Island Beach	*27 September 1975*	*ph-RBPF; Smith 1976*
Oakland	*24-25 September 1977*	*Kokorsky and Schultze 1978*
Island Beach	*15 October 1977*	*ph-RNJB 4:37*
Island Beach	*14 October 1990*	
Higbee Beach	*1 October 1995*	*ph-RNJB 22:18*

Ash-throated Flycatcher

Myiarchus cinerascens

Range: Breeds from Washington southeast to Texas and west to California. Winters from California and Arizona to Mexico.

NJ Status: Very rare. NJBRC Review List.

Occurrence: There have been 19 state reports of Ash-throated Flycatcher, and 11 have been accepted by the NJBRC (nine in fall, two in winter). All but one of the reports were coastal and most were in November. The 11 accepted records are:

Assunpink	*9 December 1984-9 January 1985*	*ph-RNJB 11:39*
West Cape May	*24 November-14 December 1985*	*ph-RNJB 12:15*
Sandy Hook	*24-31 October 1987*	*ph-RNJB 14:17, banded*
Cape May	*17-19 November 1989*	
Higbee Beach	*28 November 1992*	*ph-RBPF*
Higbee Beach	*22 November 1993*	*ph-RBPF*
South Cape May Meadows	*28 November 1995*	*ph-RNJB 22:19*
West Cape May	*11-17 November 1996*	*ph-RNJB 23:50*
West Cape May	*12-16 November 1997*	
Hidden Valley Ranch	*26-28 November 1997*	
Long Branch	*3-10 January 1998*	*ph-RNJB 24:50*

Great Crested Flycatcher

Myiarchus crinitus

Range: Breeds from central Saskatchewan east to southern Nova Scotia, south to east Texas and Florida. Winters mainly in Central and South America.

NJ Status: Fairly common and nearly ubiquitous summer resident, fairly common spring and fall migrant, reported on two CBCs.

Breeding

Habitat: Nests in cavities in mixed or deciduous woods, often along edges or near clearings.

Great Crested Flycatchers have been common breeding birds in New Jersey throughout the 20th century (Stone 1908, Boyle 1986). Fables (1955) described them as

continued on page 384

continued from page 383

Great Crested Flycatcher

Statewide Summary	
Status	# of Blocks
Possible	82
Probable	404
Confirmed	247
Total	733

summer residents in "both thin and dense woodlands, deciduous and coniferous," indicating their wide distribution. As a cavity-nesting species they compete with European Starlings for nest sites. There does not seem to be any indication that this has an effect on their status or distribution in New Jersey.

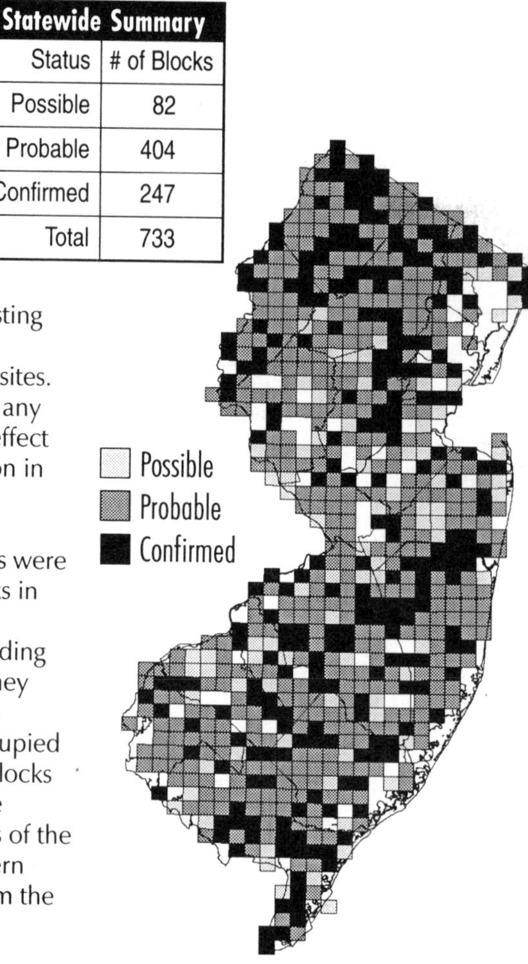

Great Crested Flycatchers were located in 86% of the blocks in the state, making them the second most common breeding flycatcher in New Jersey. They were found in all the physiographic provinces and occupied from 76% to 100% of the blocks in the provinces. They were absent only from large parts of the highly urbanized northeastern portion of the state and from the barrier islands.

Physiographic Distribution Great Crested Flycatcher	Number of blocks in province	Number of blocks species found breeding in province	Number of blocks species found in state	Percent of province species occupies	Percent of all records for this species found in province	Percent of state area in province
Kittatinny Mountains	19	19	733	100.0	2.6	2.2
Kittatinny Valley	45	43	733	95.6	5.9	5.3
Highlands	109	108	733	99.1	14.7	12.8
Piedmont	167	127	733	76.0	17.3	19.6
Inner Coastal Plain	128	109	733	85.2	14.9	15.0
Outer Coastal Plain	204	156	733	76.5	21.3	23.9
Pine Barrens	180	171	733	95.0	23.3	21.1

Great Crested Flycatcher
continued

Fall: The number of migrant Great Crested Flycatchers in a given location is not much different from the number of local nesting birds. This seems odd, given their status as a broadly distributed and fairly common breeding bird throughout the northeastern United States. They rarely linger beyond mid-October. **Maxima:** 25, Higbee Beach, 6 September 1981; 12, Higbee Beach, 29 August 1996.

Winter: Between 1976 and 1997, there were two reports of Great Crested Flycatchers on CBCs (both of which were supported by good details, AB). However, Ash-throated Flycatcher, although a rarity in the state, is more likely during the late fall and early winter. There are no other winter reports.

Spring: Great Crested Flycatchers return to their breeding grounds in the last few days of April. Movements are usually inconspicuous, as migrants are difficult to distinguish from local breeding birds. ■

Western Kingbird
Tyrannus verticalis

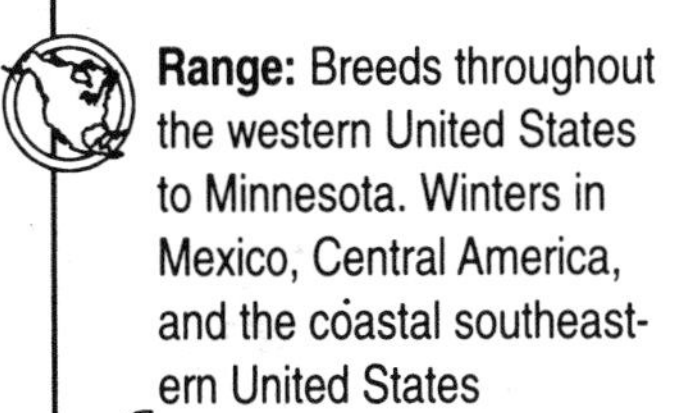

Range: Breeds throughout the western United States to Minnesota. Winters in Mexico, Central America, and the coastal southeastern United States

NJ Status: Rare to scarce fall and very rare spring migrant, accidental in winter.

Fall: Western Kingbirds are most often reported between mid-September and early December. Sightings come mainly from the coast in fall, and they are rare inland. Seasonal totals vary from just a few to more than 20. In the first third of the 20th century, Western Kingbirds were rarer than at present. Stone (1937) knew of only a single Cape May County record, but they have become more regular since that time (Sibley 1997). The increased number of records correlates well with the extension of the breeding range eastward (Bull 1964). **Maximum:** 8, West Cape May, 24 November 1984.

Winter: In the southern part of the state Western Kingbirds occur into December, and were reported on six CBCs between 1976 and 1997. The only mid-winter record is Tom's River, 29 January 1952 (Fables 1955).

Spring: Spring migrant Western Kingbirds are very unusual with only about ten reports known, usually from late spring into early summer. ■

Eastern Kingbird

Tyrannus tyrannus

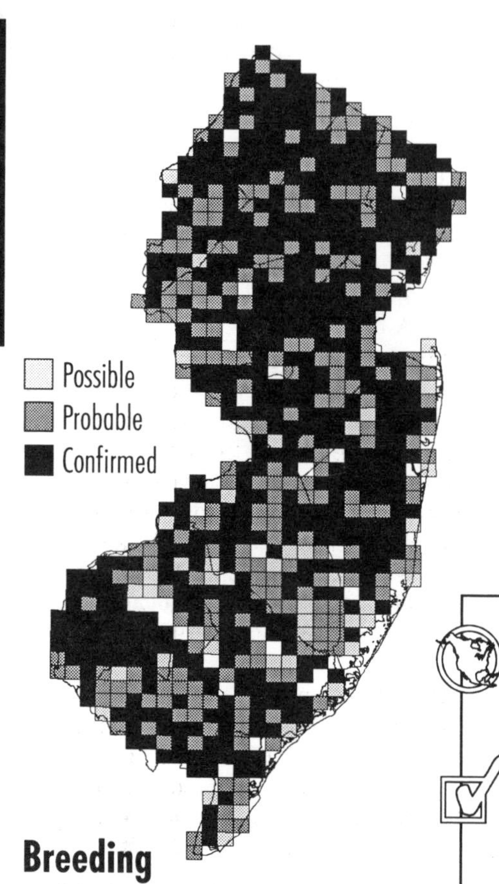

Statewide Summary	
Status	# of Blocks
Possible	44
Probable	233
Confirmed	512
Total	789

Range: Breeds throughout much of temperate Canada and the United States. Winters in Central and South America.

NJ Status: Common and nearly ubiquitous summer resident, fairly common spring and common fall migrant.

Breeding

Habitat: Nests in a variety of open woodland habitats and forest edges.

Stone (1908) found Eastern Kingbirds common enough that they should be "familiar to everyone." Griscom (1923) and Cruickshank (1942) contended that Eastern Kingbirds were slowly disappearing as suburbs were developed

Physiographic Distribution Eastern Kingbird	Number of blocks in province	Number of blocks species found breeding in province	Number of blocks species found in state	Percent of province species occupies	Percent of all records for this species found in province	Percent of state area in province
Kittatinny Mountains	19	19	789	100.0	2.4	2.2
Kittatinny Valley	45	44	789	97.8	5.6	5.3
Highlands	109	109	789	100.0	13.8	12.8
Piedmont	167	154	789	92.2	19.5	19.6
Inner Coastal Plain	128	126	789	98.4	16.0	15.0
Outer Coastal Plain	204	168	789	82.4	21.3	23.9
Pine Barrens	180	169	789	93.9	21.4	21.1

Eastern Kingbird

continued

around New York City, but that they were still common outside of developed areas. An analysis of BBS data indicated that from 1966 through 1991 Eastern Kingbird numbers have declined in much of eastern North America, and the decline was statistically significant in New Jersey (Murphy 1996). Development, loss of small farms, and forest succession are the main factors associated with the decline (Murphy 1996).

Atlas volunteers located Eastern Kingbirds in 93% of the blocks statewide, making them one of the most widely distributed species in the state, and the commonest flycatcher. As an edge-nesting species they are able to use a variety of habitats for nesting. Their broad distribution on the Inner Coastal Plain and in the highly developed northeastern section of the state is evidence of their affinity for open areas. Their strong presence in both the Kittatinny Mountains and the Pine Barrens (two strikingly different provinces) speaks to the adaptability of Eastern Kingbird.

Fall: Eastern Kingbirds are early southbound migrants, and concentrations around Cape May from late August to early September can be spectacular. Numbers dwindle rapidly after mid-September, with few birds seen during October. Unlike most other flycatchers, they are diurnal migrants. **Maxima:** 5,000, Higbee Beach, 20 August 1987; 2,300, Cape May Point, 29 August 1986.

Spring: The northward movements of Eastern Kingbirds are never as concentrated as those in fall. The first birds arrive in late April, with most passing through in mid-May. **Maximum:** 100, Higbee Beach, 16 May 1989. ■

Gray Kingbird

Tyrannus dominicensis

Range: In North America, breeds in Florida and along the Gulf coast to Alabama. Winters in southern breeding range.

NJ Status: Accidental. NJBRC Review List.

Occurrence: There have been eight state reports of Gray Kingbird, and seven have been accepted by the NJBRC (six in fall, one in spring). The seven accepted records are:

Cape May Point	*30 May 1923*	*Potter 1923*
Point Pleasant#	*18 September 1946*	
Bound Brook	*30 September 1962*	*Bull 1970*
South Cape May Meadows	*18 September 1988*	
Brigantine NWR	*9 September 1993*	
South Cape May Meadows	*29 September-3 October 1993*	*ph-RNJB 20:29*
Sandy Hook	*7 October 1997*	*ph-RBPF*

Scissor-tailed Flycatcher

Tyrannus forficatus

Occurrence: There have been over 48 state reports of Scissor-tailed Flycatcher, and 23 have been accepted by the NJBRC. Reports have been annual since 1988. Although the reports span the period 15 April to 6 November, over half have occurred from May through June. There is another cluster of reports from September and October.

Range: Breeds from New Mexico to Missouri and south. Winters mainly from Mexico south to Central America.

NJ Status: Very rare. NJBRC Review List.

New Jersey's first record of a Scissor-tailed Flycatcher was a specimen obtained at Crosswicks Meadow, south of Trenton, on 15 April 1872 (Stone 1937). It was 69 years before the next report at Cold Spring, 2 September 1941 (Fables 1955). Since that time most reports were from the central or southern part of the state, and coastal observations have outnumbered inland observations nearly two to one. **Maxima:** 2, Cape May Point, 13 June 1984; 2, Cinnaminson, 14 May 1994. ■

Fork-tailed Flycatcher

Tyrannus savana

Range: Breeds from Mexico south to South America. Winters in Central and South America.

NJ Status: Very rare. NJBRC Review List.

Occurrence: There have been 15 state reports of Fork-tailed Flycatcher, and 13 have been accepted by the NJBRC (nine in fall, three in spring, one in summer). Spring records on the Atlantic Coast may represent overshoots in the first austral fall migration (McCaskie and Patten 1994). Fall records represent a more complex migration anomaly which is yet to be understood.

Fork-tailed Flycatcher

continued

The 13 accepted records are:

Bridgeton	*early December, ca.1820*	*spec. location unknown*
Camden	*June 1832*	*Audubon painted, spec. lost*
Trenton#	*fall 1900*	
Cape May#	*1-3 November 1939*	
*Cape May**	*23 August 1968*	
Brigantine NWR	*4 September 1972*	
South Cape May Meadows	*11 October 1978*	*ph-NJA/RNJB 5:1*
Cape May	*18-20 May 1984*	*ph-RNJB 10:68*
Cape May	*29 September 1991*	*ph-RNJB 18:17*
Overpeck Park	*11 October 1994*	
West Cape May	*12-16 December 1994*	*ph-RNJB 21:41*
Brigantine NWR	*8 October 1995*	*ph-RNJB 22:19*
Cape May Point	*18 May 1998*	

Loggerhead Shrike

Lanius ludovicianus

Range: Breeds in the Canadian prairie provinces as well as most of the United States. Winters in the southern half of the United States, regularly in the east north to Virginia.

NJ Status: Very rare spring and fall migrant, accidental in winter. Endangered Species in New Jersey. Added to the NJBRC in 1996.

Breeding

Habitat: Nests in trees at the edges of fallow pasturelands or old fields.

The historic breeding status of Loggerhead Shrike in New Jersey is unclear. While Bent (1950) noted that Loggerhead Shrikes bred at Elizabeth and Cape May, Stone (1908, 1937) and Fables (1955) make no mention of Loggerhead Shrikes as breeding birds in the state, and Leck (1984) specifically stated that "we have no records of breeding in New Jersey." Fables (1955) does make the cryptic suggestion that the species "winters on the Delaware Bay shore and should be sought there during the breeding season."

Loggerhead Shrikes have undergone a nearly range-wide decline, so a sighting during the Atlas period on

continued on page 390

continued from page 389

Loggerhead Shrike

Physiographic Distribution Loggerhead Shrike	Number of blocks in province	Number of blocks species found breeding in province	Number of blocks species found in state	Percent of province species occupies	Percent of all records for this species found in province	Percent of state area in province
Pine Barrens	180	1	1	0.5	100.0	21.1

2 June 1995 in southern Burlington County was intriguing. On that date, Loggerhead Shrikes would normally be nesting or feeding young, but it is nearly certain that this individual was not a mated bird.

Statewide Summary	
Status	# of Blocks
Possible	1
Probable	0
Confirmed	0
Total	1

Possible
Probable
Confirmed

Historic Changes: Present-day observers have noted a steady ebb in reports of migrants: e.g., from 1975 to 1984 an average of eight birds per year were reported; the next decade produced only three per year. In 1993, for the first time, there were no reports at all. This steep decline mirrors this species disappearance as a breeding species from much of the northeastern United States, and prompted the NJBRC to add the species to the Review List in 1996. Since then there has been only one reported and one accepted record of Loggerhead Shrike in New Jersey: Great Swamp NWR, 5 April 1997.

Fall: Presently, Loggerhead Shrikes are very rare birds in New Jersey at any season. In former years Loggerhead Shrikes were regular, though uncommon, coastal migrants from mid-August through October. Stone (1937) reported that at Cape May "we usually see but one at a time but in the course of a day's walk we may come upon two, three or five while Conrad Roland saw six in the Cape May Point region on 16 September 1934."

Winter: Historically, Loggerhead Shrikes were seldom seen in the colder months, though they were regular in the southern counties and even present in the north during mild winters

Loggerhead Shrike

continued

(Fables 1955). Statewide CBC totals from 1976 to 1987 averaged one or two Loggerhead Shrikes per year, but none have been recorded in the state since 1987.

Spring: Historically, Loggerhead Shrikes were less common in spring than in fall and more likely to be seen inland from mid-March to mid-April. Cruickshank (1942) cited a spring record from Plainfield on the late date of 3 May 1906. ■

Loggerhead Shrike

Northern Shrike

Lanius excubitor

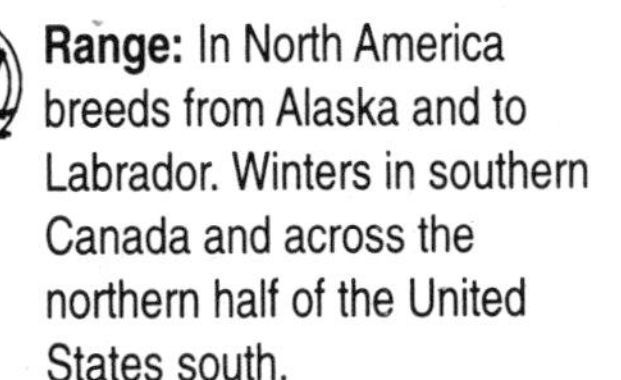

Range: In North America breeds from Alaska and to Labrador. Winters in southern Canada and across the northern half of the United States south.

NJ Status: Rare and irruptive migrant and winter resident.

Occurrence: Northern Shrikes are irruptive and occur in varying numbers each year. They have been recorded from 28 October to 20 April, although November to March appearances are most typical. In most years, at least a few Northern Shrikes are reported, but in three years from 1975-1998 there were no winter sightings. Although Northern Shrikes are far more likely to be found in northern New Jersey than in southern New Jersey, they have occurred in all regions of the state.

continued on page 392

continued from page 391

Northern Shrike

The most impressive flight year on record was the winter of 1926-1927. On 22 January 1927, C. Urner saw an extraordinary total of 16 Northern Shrikes at Beach Haven (Stone 1937). Other irruptions in the first half of the century were 1930-1931 and 1949-1950. Since 1975 there have been four major flight years (> ten reports): 1978-1979, 1990-1991, 1991-1992 and 1995-1996. By far the largest of the recent incursions was in 1995-1996, when at least 60 different individuals were noted across the state (Kane 1996). **CBC Statewide Stats:** Average: 3; Maximum: 29 in 1996; Minimum: 0 in six years. **CBC maximum:** 6, Sussex County, 1996. ■

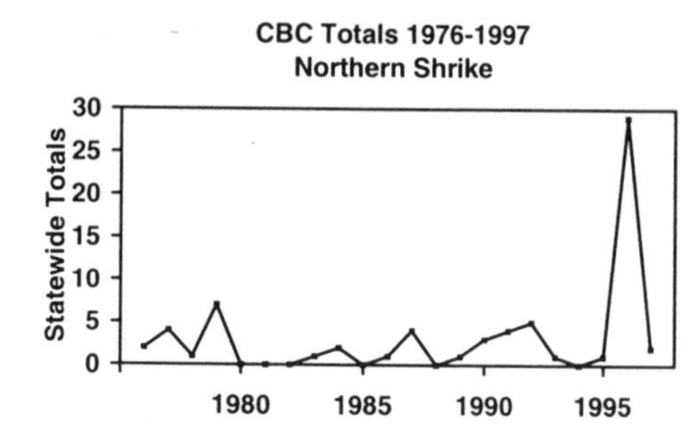

White-eyed Vireo

Vireo griseus

Range: Breeds from southern Iowa east to Massachusetts, south to eastern Texas and Florida. Winters from the coast of Virginia south to Central America.

NJ Status: Fairly common and widespread summer resident, and fairly common spring and fall migrant, accidental in winter.

Breeding

Habitat: Nests in shrubby fields, thickets, and hedgerows.

White-eyed Vireos went through a period of decline in the late 1800s and retreated from the northern limit of their range by the turn of the 20th century. Griscom (1923) noted that they had shown a marked decrease in numbers throughout northern New Jersey and were absent at higher altitudes. In Massachusetts, where they were once widespread breeding birds, they had nearly disappeared by 1930 (Veit and Petersen 1993). Bull (1964) remarked that, after their drop in

White-eyed Vireo

continued

numbers in the New York City region around 1900 their status had not improved, and numbers remained low. White-eyed Vireo's status in southern New Jersey has remained more stable. Stone (1908) and Fables (1955) both considered the species a common bird in southern New Jersey. By the mid-1980s, Boyle (1986) described White-eyed Vireos as fairly common summer residents, except at the higher elevations of northern New Jersey.

The Atlas results showed that the distribution of White-eyed Vireos had changed little during the latter half of the 20th century. From the Piedmont northward they occurred in only 37% of the blocks, but occurred in 73% of the

continued on page 394

Possible
Probable
Confirmed

Statewide Summary	
Status	# of Blocks
Possible	72
Probable	319
Confirmed	108
Total	499

Physiographic Distribution

White-eyed Vireo	Number of blocks in province	Number of blocks species found breeding in province	Number of blocks species found in state	Percent of province species occupies	Percent of all records for this species found in province	Percent of state area in province
Kittatinny Mountains	19	4	499	21.1	0.8	2.2
Kittatinny Valley	45	18	499	40.0	3.6	5.3
Highlands	109	42	499	38.5	8.4	12.8
Piedmont	167	61	499	36.5	12.2	19.6
Inner Coastal Plain	128	83	499	64.8	16.6	15.0
Outer Coastal Plain	204	150	499	73.5	30.1	23.9
Pine Barrens	180	141	499	78.3	28.3	21.1

continued from page 393

blocks south of the Piedmont. They were nearly absent from areas of high elevation, from the northeastern Piedmont, and from the barrier islands of Atlantic and Cape May counties.

Fall: Due to the presence of resident birds and the relatively small population of White-eyed Vireos breeding north of New Jersey, it is difficult to pin down precise periods of their passage and peak numbers of migrants. Fall departure takes place mainly from August through September, with only stragglers remaining after early October.

Winter: White-eyed Vireos were reported on three CBCs between 1976 and 1997 (i.e.,1985, 1995, and 1997). There have also been at least four other recent winter reports. Remarkably, an individual may have survived the winter of 1992-1993 in the Cape May area.

Spring: The arrival of White-eyed Vireos in spring is expected after mid-April. Passage migrants are difficult to detect among the numbers of breeding birds. ■

White-eyed Vireo

Bell's Vireo

Vireo bellii

Range: Breeds from southern California to Texas, north to North Dakota and southern Wisconsin, and east to Ohio. Winters mainly in Mexico and Central America.

NJ Status: Accidental. NJBRC Review List.

Occurrence: There have been nine state reports of Bell's Vireo, and three have been accepted by the NJBRC (two in fall, one in winter). The three accepted records are:

Island Beach	*15 September 1959*	*Jehl 1960, spec. AMNH #708118*
Higbee Beach	*30 October-4 November 1994*	*ph-RNJB 21:21*
Hidden Valley Ranch	*4 December 1996-3 January 1997*	

Yellow-throated Vireo

Vireo flavifrons

Range: Breeds from southern Manitoba to Maine, south to eastern Texas and northern Florida. Winters from Central America to northern South America.

NJ Status: Uncommon and somewhat local summer resident, scarce to uncommon spring and uncommon fall migrant, reported on one CBC.

Breeding

Habitat: Nests in semi-open, mixed or deciduous woodlands.

As breeding birds, Yellow-throated Vireos were restricted to the northern part of the state during at least the first half of the 20th century (Fables 1955). Their numbers in "suburban" areas of northern New Jersey declined sharply around 1917, when birds retreated to more rural sections of the state (Griscom 1923). This was likely the result of spraying to control Dutch Elm disease (Rodewald and James 1996). By the mid-1980s, Leck (1984) suggested there was a "marked decline in recent decades." Apparently, they have decreased locally throughout their overall range wherever forest clearing or forest fragmentation has occurred (Rodewald and James 1996).

Atlas observers found that Yellow-throated Vireos occurred throughout wooded areas of northern New Jersey. In fact, they were found in 92% of all blocks north of the Piedmont, as well as in 33% of the Piedmont blocks. On

continued on page 396

continued from page 395

Yellow-throated Vireo

the Coastal Plain, they were thinly distributed. Sufficient deciduous forest cover is an important factor influencing Yellow-throated Vireo's distribution. Even though they use edges of forests for nesting, they may be sensitive to the total amount of forest near their nest sites (Rodewald and James 1996). This is probably the reason Yellow-throated Vireos were absent from a large part of the Inner and Outer Coastal Plain as well as from the highly developed northeastern Piedmont, where little forest remains. Their patchy distribution in the Pine Barrens indicated their avoidance of purely coniferous forests, and their adherence to appropriate habitat, particularly along some of the river courses in the Pine Barrens.

Although declining in some parts of their overall range, Yellow-throated Vireos have extended their range

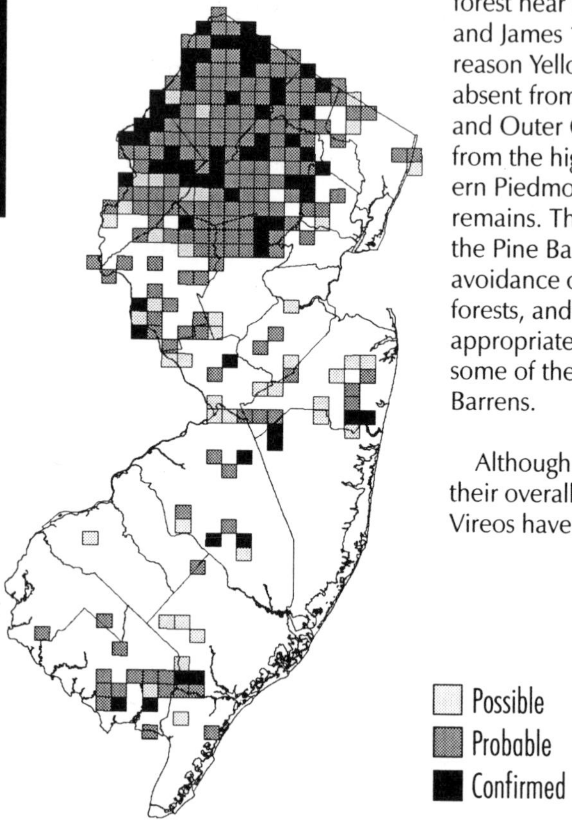

Possible
Probable
Confirmed

Statewide Summary	
Status	# of Blocks
Possible	42
Probable	171
Confirmed	66
Total	279

Physiographic Distribution

Yellow-throated Vireo	Number of blocks in province	Number of blocks species found breeding in province	Number of blocks species found in state	Percent of province species occupies	Percent of all records for this species found in province	Percent of state area in province
Kittatinny Mountains	19	19	279	100.0	6.8	2.2
Kittatinny Valley	45	44	279	97.8	15.8	5.3
Highlands	109	97	279	89.0	34.8	12.8
Piedmont	167	55	279	32.9	19.7	19.6
Inner Coastal Plain	128	17	279	13.3	6.1	15.0
Outer Coastal Plain	204	28	279	13.7	10.0	23.9
Pine Barrens	180	19	279	10.6	6.8	21.1

Yellow-throated Vireo

continued

southward in New Jersey. They were unknown in the southern part of the state until the 1970s, when they were first found breeding in Cumberland County. While Atlas surveys did not find Yellow-throated Vireo in the central or eastern sections of the Pine Barrens, they were found in scattered blocks in the western Pine Barrens. They may have used that region as a "corridor" to establish themselves in the southern counties.

Fall: Migrant Yellow-throated Vireos are typically seen in small numbers. Most pass southward in late August and early September, and only very few are present by the end of September. **Maximum:** 5, Cape Island, 6 September 1981.

Winter: A Yellow-throated Vireo was reported on the Belleplain CBC in 1996, although no details were submitted. This species that should not be expected after late September.

Spring: The first northbound Yellow-throated Vireos generally arrive in the last days of April or early May. Most migrants are gone by the end of May. **Maximum:** 5, Scherman-Hoffman Sanctuary, 27 April 1988. ■

Blue-headed Vireo

Vireo solitarius

Range: In the East, breeds from Manitoba east to southern Newfoundland, south to northern Minnesota and northern New Jersey and along the Appalachians to northern Georgia. Winters from North Carolina and the Gulf coast to Central America and Cuba.

NJ Status: Uncommon and local summer resident, uncommon spring and fairly common fall migrant, accidental in winter.

Breeding

Habitat: Nests in semi-open coniferous or mixed woods, especially where hemlock is present.

Blue-headed Vireos have nested in northwestern New Jersey since at least the 1890s (Stone 1908). Both Griscom (1923) and Cruickshank (1942) noted their presence as breeding birds in northern New Jersey, but estimated that Blue-headed Vireo numbers were low. Bull (1964) knew of only two confirmed nests, one in Warren County and one in Sussex County, but assumed that Blue-headed Vireos bred elsewhere in the Highlands. Boyle (1986) described their distribution as local.

continued on page 398

continued from page 397

Blue-headed Vireo

Blue-headed Vireos have expanded their range southward in some parts of the East (Kaufman 1996). However, Atlas surveys found that the Blue-headed Vireo's distribution in New Jersey was similar to their reported range during the first half of the 20th century. The core of the population occurred in the higher elevations along the Kittatinny Mountains and in the Highlands. Although they occupied only 9% of the blocks in the state, they were found in all the Kittatinny Mountain blocks and 40% of the Highlands blocks. Thus 78% of Blue-headed Vireo's range in New Jersey is concentrated in 15% of the state.

Fall: Blue-headed Vireos are later fall migrants than other vireos. They are scarce before mid-September and peak from late September through early October. Late migrants occasionally linger into December. **Maxima:** 50, Princeton, 9 October 1981; 20+, Sandy Hook, 23 October 1989.

Possible
Probable
Confirmed

Statewide Summary	
Status	# of Blocks
Possible	18
Probable	38
Confirmed	25
Total	81

Physiographic Distribution Blue-headed Vireo	Number of blocks in province	Number of blocks species found breeding in province	Number of blocks species found in state	Percent of province species occupies	Percent of all records for this species found in province	Percent of state area in province
Kittatinny Mountains	19	19	81	100.0	23.5	2.2
Kittatinny Valley	45	14	81	31.1	17.3	5.3
Highlands	109	44	81	40.4	54.3	12.8
Piedmont	167	3	81	1.8	3.7	19.6
Pine Barrens	180	1	81	0.6	1.2	21.1

Blue-headed Vireo

continued

Winter: Blue-headed Vireos were reported on eight CBCs between 1976 and 1997 (with three reported in 1997). One individual successfully wintered at Overpeck Park in the winter of 1991-1992. Another apparently attempted to do so in Belleplain State Forest, and was seen on 10 January 1997.

Spring: The arrival of the Blue-headed Vireos begins between mid- to late April, and most have moved on by mid-May.
Maxima: 20+, Cape May Point, 3 May 1975; 20, Garret Mt., 6 May 1986. ■

Blue-headed Vireo

Warbling Vireo

Vireo gilvus

Range: In eastern North America breeds from southern Manitoba east to Nova Scotia, south to eastern Texas and extreme western North Carolina. Winters in Central America.

NJ Status: Fairly common and fairly widespread summer resident, uncommon spring and fall migrant.

Breeding

Habitat: Nests in open mixed or deciduous woods, typically in large trees along streams and ponds.

Stone (1908) found Warbling Vireos to be common but local summer residents of the northern part of the state, favoring the shade trees of villages and towns. Their history is similar to that of Yellow-throated Vireo, in that a population decline was noted early in the 1900s in northern

continued on page 400

continued from page 399

Warbling Vireo

New Jersey, possibly due to spraying for Dutch Elm disease (Bull 1964). This spraying may have had a greater impact on Warbling Vireos than Yellow-throated Vireos because of their habit of frequenting open areas in and around towns. Fables (1955) noted that Warbling Vireos were found south along the Delaware River Valley to Burlington and Camden counties.

Leck (1984) stated that Warbling Vireos had a "very local distribution" in New Jersey, but Atlas volunteers found them well distributed throughout much of the northern and central parts of the state, probably indicating an increase. They were found in 73% of the blocks from the Piedmont northward, representing 78% of the blocks occupied statewide. The southernmost Confirmed breeding location was in Camden County, near the southern extent of

Possible
Probable
Confirmed

Statewide Summary	
Status	# of Blocks
Possible	31
Probable	176
Confirmed	118
Total	325

Physiographic Distribution

Warbling Vireo	Number of blocks in province	Number of blocks species found breeding in province	Number of blocks species found in state	Percent of province species occupies	Percent of all records for this species found in province	Percent of state area in province
Kittatinny Mountains	19	16	325	84.2	4.9	2.2
Kittatinny Valley	45	42	325	93.3	12.9	5.3
Highlands	109	87	325	79.8	26.8	12.8
Piedmont	167	105	325	62.9	32.3	19.6
Inner Coastal Plain	128	47	325	36.7	14.5	15.0
Outer Coastal Plain	204	23	325	11.3	7.1	23.9
Pine Barrens	180	5	325	2.8	1.5	21.1

Warbling Vireo

continued

the range noted by Fables (1955). Warbling Vireos avoided the Pine Barrens, which may explain their slow colonization of southern New Jersey. There is ample riparian habitat in the south, and the two Probable locations near the Salem/ Gloucester county border, coupled with the presence of birds within "safe dates" in Cumberland County suggests the possibility of continued range expansion in southern New Jersey.

Historic Changes: Stone (1937) was unaware of any records of Warbling Vireos in Cape May County, and Bull (1964) considered them "rare and little known" migrants in the north. Warbling Vireos are more numerous as migrants in the present-day, but are encountered in only small numbers.

Fall: Southbound Warbling Vireos arrive from mid- to late August and peak in early September. Numbers diminish after mid-September. **Maxima:** 15, Taylor's Refuge, 23 August 1995; 10, Higbee Beach, 2 September 1992.

Spring: Although the spring and fall maxima are similar, Warbling Vireos are seemingly less common in spring than in fall. Most are seen from early to mid-May. **Maxima:** 12, Palmyra, 11 May 1991; 10, Cape Island, 10 May 1996. ■

Philadelphia Vireo

Vireo philadelphicus

Range: Breeds primarily from northeastern British Columbia to Newfoundland south, in the Northeast, to northern New York, and northern New England. Winters largely in Central America.

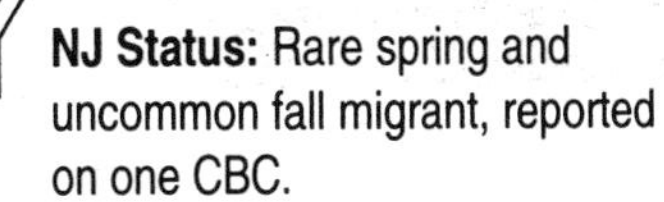

NJ Status: Rare spring and uncommon fall migrant, reported on one CBC.

Fall: Philadelphia Vireos are most often encountered along the coast during southward migration. They begin to arrive in late August, the peak movement is in September, and most have passed through by early October. Reports of Philadelphia Vireos have increased substantially during the 20th century as Stone (1908, 1937) knew of only a few records. **Maxima:** 18, Higbee Beach, 21 September 1987 (Sibley 1997); 15+, Higbee Beach, 16 September 1983 (Sibley 1997).

Winter: Amazingly, a Philadelphia Vireo was recorded on the Sandy Hook CBC in 1993 (good details submitted, AB). There are no other reports after October.

Spring: In most years, there are only one or two reports of northbound Philadelphia Vireos in the state from mid- to late May. However, in May of 1998 there were five reported on Cape May Island alone. ■

Red-eyed Vireo

Vireo olivaceus

Range: In eastern North America breeds from Manitoba east to Nova Scotia, south to eastern Texas and central Florida. Winters in South America.

NJ Status: Common and very widespread summer resident, fairly common spring and common fall migrant.

Possible
Probable
Confirmed

Statewide Summary	
Status	# of Blocks
Possible	55
Probable	370
Confirmed	249
Total	674

Breeding

Habitat: Nests in a variety of mature woodland habitats, often in moist or wet woods.

Red-eyed Vireos have long been considered one of the most common nesting birds in the state (Stone 1908, Bull 1964). During the 20th century however they have declined, and BBS data indicated significant rangewide declines for this species (Price et al. 1995). By the mid-1980s, Leck (1984) suggested that Red-eyed Vireos had "decreased considerably" in the state.

Atlas data showed Red-eyed Vireos were broadly distributed throughout the state. They were found in 79% of the blocks statewide, although they were patchy in the Pine Barrens, and absent from sections of the urbanized northeast and from many barrier islands. While they remain common and widespread in the state, it is possible they are less abundant than in years past.

Fall: Red-eyed Vireos are one of the more common Neotropical migrants encountered in fall. Migrants begin to appear in mid-August, with a peak from early to mid-September. Numbers diminish after late September, with most gone by mid-October. A few may linger into early November. **Maxima:** 550, Higbee Beach, 11 September 1988; 200, Higbee Beach, 11 September 1995.

Red-eyed Vireo

continued

Spring: Red-eyed Vireos are much less common in spring than in fall. Northbound birds are first encountered in the last few days of April, with migration continuing into early June. **Maxima:** 20, Higbee Beach, 2 June 1992; 10, Higbee Beach, 8 May 1994. ■

Physiographic Distribution **Red-eyed Vireo**	Number of blocks in province	Number of blocks species found breeding in province	Number of blocks species found in state	Percent of province species occupies	Percent of all records for this species found in province	Percent of state area in province
Kittatinny Mountains	19	19	674	100.0	2.8	2.2
Kittatinny Valley	45	44	674	97.8	6.5	5.3
Highlands	109	109	674	100.0	16.2	12.8
Piedmont	167	136	674	81.4	20.2	19.6
Inner Coastal Plain	128	104	674	81.3	15.4	15.0
Outer Coastal Plain	204	136	674	66.7	20.2	23.9
Pine Barrens	180	126	674	70.0	18.7	21.1

Blue Jay

Cyanocitta cristata

Range: In the East breeds from central Manitoba east to Newfoundland, south to eastern Texas and Florida. Winters throughout most of the breeding range.

NJ Status: Common and nearly ubiquitous summer resident, fairly common spring and common fall migrant, common winter resident.

Breeding

Habitat: Nests in deciduous or mixed woods, often in suburbs, towns, and parks.

Blue Jays have been common breeding birds in the state during the 20th century. However, as Stone (1908) suggested, they are "by no means so conspicuous an object as one might suppose" during the

continued on page 404

continued from page 403

Blue Jay

breeding season. Cruickshank (1942) was struck by their adaptability, noting that they could be found from mountainous woodlands to the suburbs. Fables (1955) noted an increase in Blue Jay numbers in the Pine Barrens and in southwestern New Jersey during the 1940s and 1950s.

Atlas observers found Blue Jays to be one of the most broadly distributed breeding birds in the state, occurring in 93% of the blocks. They were well distributed throughout all the physiographic provinces; however, they were most conspicuously absent from some blocks on the barrier islands and

Statewide Summary

Status	# of Blocks
Possible	60
Probable	145
Confirmed	588
Total	793

Physiographic Distribution

Blue Jay	Number of blocks in province	Number of blocks species found breeding in province	Number of blocks species found in state	Percent of province species occupies	Percent of all records for this species found in province	Percent of state area in province
Kittatinny Mountains	19	19	793	100.0	2.4	2.2
Kittatinny Valley	45	44	793	97.8	5.5	5.3
Highlands	109	106	793	97.2	13.4	12.8
Piedmont	167	156	793	93.4	19.7	19.6
Inner Coastal Plain	128	121	793	94.5	15.3	15.0
Outer Coastal Plain	204	176	793	86.3	22.2	23.9
Pine Barrens	180	171	793	95.0	21.6	21.1

Blue Jay

continued

adjacent areas of salt marsh, and in the blocks adjacent to the lower Delaware River.

Fall: The general misconception that Blue Jays are strictly resident birds is easily dispelled by spending a day at Cape May Point from late September through October, when large numbers can be seen migrating over the Point in loose flocks. Interestingly, Stone (1937) did not find Blue Jays to be common in passage in Cape May. He regarded flocks of 15 and 40 in fall 1927 as "our most notable Jay year." **Maxima:** 5,000, Cape May Point, 5 October 1988; 2,384, Cape May Point, 12 October 1992.

Winter: Statewide CBC totals for Blue Jays are fairly consistent, typically numbering between 8,000 and 10,000 birds. **CBC Statewide Stats:** Average: 7,836; Maximum: 12,192 in 1990; Minimum: 3,790 in 1981. **CBC Maximum:** 1,621, Belleplain, 1990.

Spring: There is a noticeable influx of northbound Blue Jays in late April and May. Movements continue even into early June. **Maxima:** 500, Sandy Hook, 1 May 1976; 300, Jockey Hollow, 10 May 1975. ■

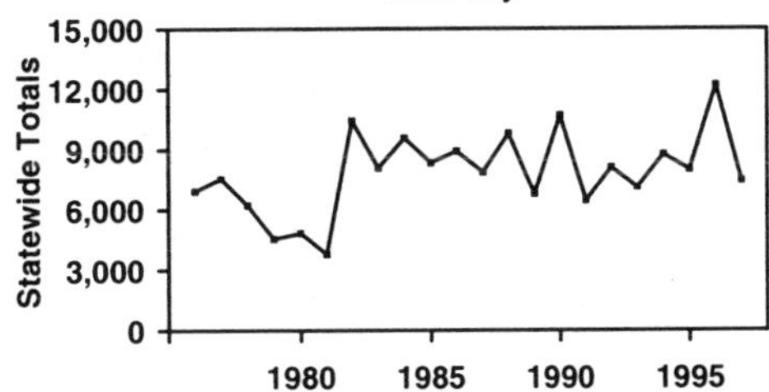

American Crow

Corvus brachyrhynchos

Range: Breeds throughout most of Canada and the United States to the tree line. Winters mainly within the United States.

NJ Status: Common and nearly ubiquitous summer resident, fairly common migrant, common winter resident.

Breeding

Habitat: Nests in a variety of semi-open woodland habitats.

Although Stone (1908) described American Crows as abundant residents, he was concerned that that their numbers were declining due to "persecution" by farmers. He suggested that scarecrows or other methods of frightening the crows

continued on page 406

continued from page 405

American Crow

away from crops would be preferable to "attempted extermination." It is still possible to hunt American Crows during a legal hunting season, and it is legal to kill them (without a limit) both in and out of season if they are deemed an agricultural pest. Nonetheless, they have continued to be common and broadly distributed breeding birds in the state during the 20th century.

Statewide Summary	
Status	# of Blocks
Possible	101
Probable	161
Confirmed	549
Total	811

Atlas volunteers found American Crows in 95% of the blocks in the state. They were present in all 340 blocks north of the Outer Coastal Plain, and in 85% of the blocks in the Pine Barrens and Outer Coastal Plain. The New Jersey Atlas had a high Confirmation rate (68%) compared to several other Atlas projects from nearby states (e.g., New York, Maryland, Pennsylvania). The reason for this is not clear, but it may be related to the density of the species rather than to effort of observers.

Fall: Many American Crows in New Jersey are permanent residents. However, migration is apparent from October to December, mainly along mountain ridges and at Cape May. Flights of several hundred birds in a day occur every fall along northwestern New Jersey ridges. Maxima are rarely reported.

Winter: Outside of the breeding season, American Crows are highly social, almost always occurring in flocks. Large nighttime roosts can form in winter, with thousands of birds present at a given location. Statewide CBC totals appear fairly stable. **Maxima:** 9,000, Piscataway, 6 February 1977; 5,000-10,000, Flemington, winter 1975-1976.

CBC Totals 1976-1997
American Crow

Statewide Totals: 0, 10,000, 20,000, 30,000, 40,000, 50,000
1980 1985 1990 1995

American Crow

continued

CBC Statewide Stats: Average: 31,712; Maximum: 47,655 in 1979; Minimum: 19,803 in 1977. **CBC Maximum:** 21,725, Raritan Estuary, 1980.

Spring: Migrant American Crows have been noted along the ridges of northwestern New Jersey in late February and early March. ■

Physiographic Distribution

American Crow	Number of blocks in province	Number of blocks species found breeding in province	Number of blocks species found in state	Percent of province species occupies	Percent of all records for this species found in province	Percent of state area in province
Kittatinny Mountains	19	19	811	100.0	2.3	2.2
Kittatinny Valley	45	45	811	100.0	5.5	5.3
Highlands	109	109	811	100.0	13.4	12.8
Piedmont	167	167	811	100.0	20.6	19.6
Inner Coastal Plain	128	128	811	100.0	15.8	15.0
Outer Coastal Plain	204	177	811	86.8	21.8	23.9
Pine Barrens	180	166	811	92.2	20.5	21.1

Fish Crow

Corvus ossifragus

Breeding

Habitat: Nests in a variety of semi-open woodland habitats, typically near water.

Stone (1908) found the range of Fish Crow to be restricted to the Atlantic Coast and the lower Delaware River. Fables (1955)

continued on page 408

Range: Breeds along the East Coast in small numbers in Maine, New Hampshire, and Vermont, and more commonly from Massachusetts south to Florida, along the Gulf coast and north along the Mississippi River to central Illinois.

NJ Status: Common and widespread summer resident, fairly common spring and fall migrant, fairly common winter resident.

continued from page 407

Fish Crow

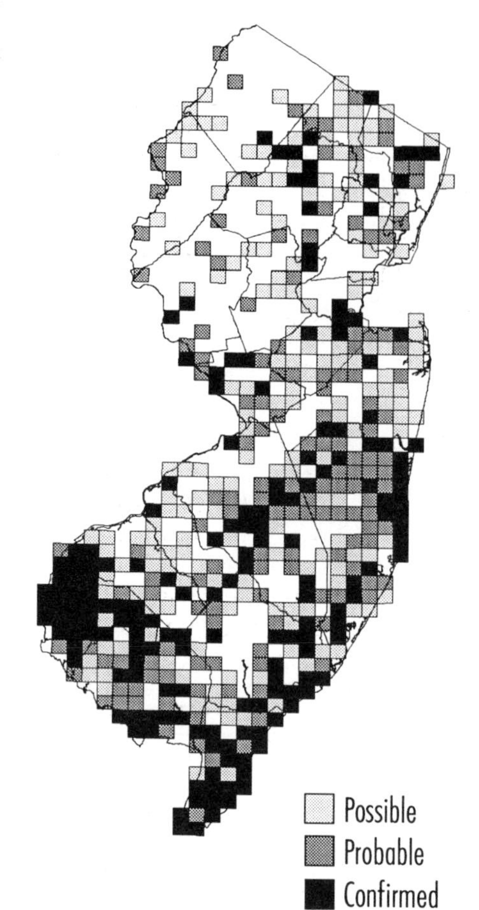

Statewide Summary	
Status	# of Blocks
Possible	181
Probable	147
Confirmed	172
Total	500

reiterated this distribution, but noted that they also bred at a few scattered inland sites, though only near lakes and streams. Bull (1964) was skeptical of inland reports, and contended that inland reports, away from water, were misidentified American Crows. By 1986, Boyle noted they were uncommon, but increasing. It is still possible to hunt Fish Crows during the legal season, and it is also legal to kill them (without a limit) both in and out of season if they are deemed an agricultural pest.

Physiographic Distribution Fish Crow	Number of blocks in province	Number of blocks species found breeding in province	Number of blocks species found in state	Percent of province species occupies	Percent of all records for this species found in province	Percent of state area in province
Kittatinny Mountains	19	7	500	36.8	1.4	2.2
Kittatinny Valley	45	8	500	17.8	1.6	5.3
Highlands	109	44	500	40.4	8.8	12.8
Piedmont	167	64	500	38.3	12.8	19.6
Inner Coastal Plain	128	87	500	68.0	17.4	15.0
Outer Coastal Plain	204	169	500	82.8	33.8	23.9
Pine Barrens	180	121	500	67.2	24.2	21.1

Atlas results indicated continued inland expansion for Fish Crows, and similar results were noted by the Pennsylvania and Maryland Atlas projects. Fish Crows were fairly widespread in the southern portion of the state, although absent from large areas of the Pine Barrens and parts of the Inner Coastal Plain. From the Piedmont north, they were local, occurring in 36% of the blocks. They were particularly scarce in the Kittatinny Ridge and Valley regions.

Interestingly, in a high percentage of blocks (36%) the breeding status of Fish Crow did not exceed the Possible category. Where they occur, Fish Crows are conspicuous, and are not difficult to relocate on follow-up visits. The high percentage of Possible sightings is an indication that some of the blocks may have had either a very low density of breeding Fish Crows, or that sightings may have included wandering, nonbreeding individuals.

Fall: Fish Crows appear to be more migratory than American Crows. Some migration is evident from September through November, especially along the Delaware River, the ridges, and at Cape May. Sibley (1997) suggested that the migration peak is earlier than that of American Crows, citing flights at Cape May of 50 on 30 August 1994 and 50 on 5 September 1994.

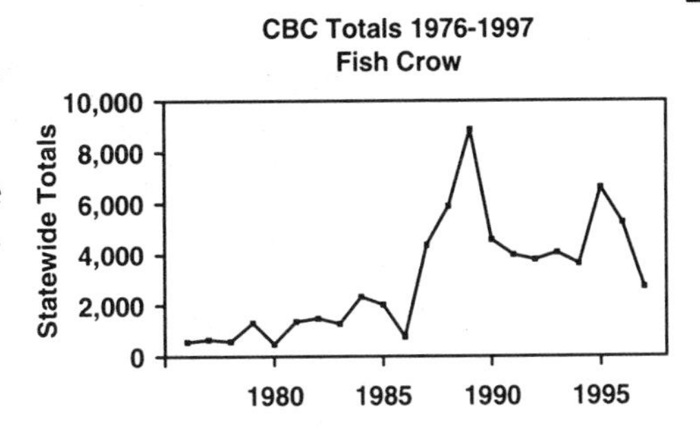

Winter: Like American Crows, Fish Crows are highly social and are almost always found in flocks, with large roosts occurring in winter. During the winter they seem to be absent from certain areas, withdrawing from parts of the immediate coast and from parts of northern New Jersey. Statewide CBC totals have shown an overall increase as the birds have expanded their range inland. **Maxima:** 5,000, Stone Harbor, September 1987; 1,300, Stone Harbor, 30 September 1992. **CBC Statewide Stats:** Average: 3,031; Maximum: 8,884 in 1989; Minimum: 478 in 1980. **CBC Maximum:** 7,021, Trenton Marsh, 1989.

Spring: Fish Crows withdraw from large areas of the state in winter, and their return in spring is more easily detected than other species that are present all year. Migrants are noted in March and April. ■

Common Raven

Corvus corax

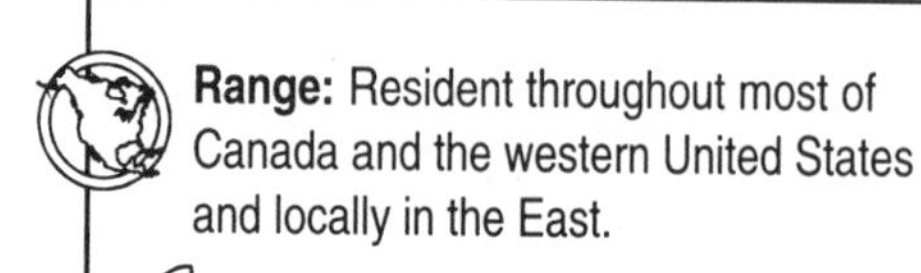

Range: Resident throughout most of Canada and the western United States and locally in the East.

NJ Status: Rare and very local summer resident, rare spring and fall migrant, rare winter resident.

Physiographic Distribution **Common Raven**	Number of blocks in province	Number of blocks species found breeding in province	Number of blocks species found in state	Percent of province species occupies	Percent of all records for this species found in province	Percent of state area in province
Kittatinny Mountains	19	6	9	31.6	66.7	2.2
Kittatinny Valley	45	2	9	4.4	22.2	5.3
Highlands	109	1	9	0.9	11.1	12.8

Breeding

Statewide Summary	
Status	# of Blocks
Possible	4
Probable	2
Confirmed	3
Total	9

Habitat: Nests in mountainous woods near cliffs.

Common Ravens have never been common breeding birds in New Jersey, but in the late 1800s and early 1900s they were apparently more widespread than at present. Stone (1908) referred to a few nesting pairs from the Pine Barrens during the late 1800s, and he indicated the birds had a habit of flying to the beaches on foraging trips from these nesting sites. He had no evidence of breeding in southern New Jersey after 1905, when a pair nested near Tuckerton, and he considered the Pine Barrens to have been the last bastion for the species in the state. Griscom (1923) suggested that two birds seen on 21 September 1918 near Culvers Gap, Sussex County might have been a local breeding pair. He suggested

Possible
Probable
Confirmed

Common Raven

continued

that it was a "remote possibility" that a pair or two might still be present in the mountainous northwestern section of the state. Raven populations also suffered serious declines in both New York (Peterson 1988a) and Pennsylvania (Mulvihill 1992c) in the late 1800s and early 1900s. Among other factors, encroaching civilization and lumbering were considered to be the main culprits. Both of those states had much larger raven populations than did New Jersey, and they held on to a core breeding group despite the population's decline.

In the spring of 1991, a Common Raven was seen carrying nest material on the New Jersey side of the Delaware Water Gap, Warren County. A small population quickly became established in New Jersey along the Kittatinny Mountains after an absence of about 86 years. Pennsylvania BBS data showed that Common Ravens had begun to recover in that state in the late 1970s (Mulvihill 1992), and the New York population also began to recover at that time (Peterson 1988). During the Atlas surveys, Common Ravens were Confirmed in three blocks and listed as Probable in two more.

Fall: The occurrence of migrant Common Ravens along the Kittatinny Mountains predates their renewed nesting by decades. Bull (1964) cited a record of four at Raccoon Ridge on 22 October 1944, and subsequently small numbers of migrants continued to be seen annually. Sightings have increased at hawk watching locations along the Kittatinny Mountains, but numbers are still low. They are very rare on the Coastal Plain.

Winter: The resident population of Common Ravens on the mountain ridges in the northwestern part of the state produces the bulk of the state's Common Raven sightings in winter. The Walnut Valley CBC recorded ravens on four counts in the 1990s (i.e., 1992, 1993, 1994, and 1997)

Spring: There has been only one recent record of a Common Raven in spring away from the ridges, a bird at Sandy Hook on 20 May 1991. Surprisingly, the bird was watched as it flew in to shore from over the ocean and landed on the beach. ■

Horned Lark

Eremophila alpestris

Breeding

Habitat: Nest in short grasses in fallow fields, airports, sand dunes, etc.

Horned Larks were found nesting in small numbers in the northwestern part of the state in the late 1800s (Griscom 1923). Cruickshank (1942) noted a southward spread of breeding sites, beginning in the early 1930s. They continued to expand their range rapidly, and by the mid-1950s had been found breeding in every county except Union

continued on page 412

continued from page 411

Horned Lark

Range: Nests throughout most of North America except the Gulf coast and Florida. Winters throughout most of the United States.

NJ Status: Scarce and local summer resident, scarce spring and uncommon fall migrant, uncommon to fairly common winter resident.

and Hudson (Fables 1955). The timing of Horned Lark's initial occurrence as breeding birds at the end of the 19th century, and their spread thereafter, was closely paralleled in Pennsylvania (Reid 1992c) and Maryland (Fletcher 1996).

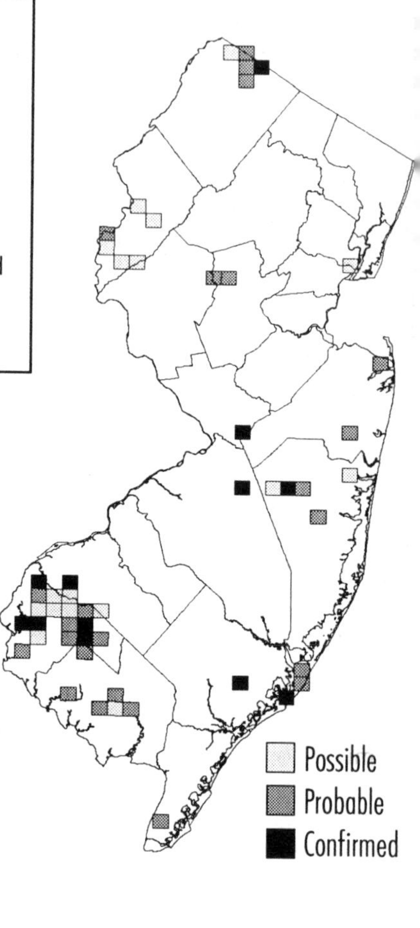

Statewide Summary	
Status	# of Blocks
Possible	17
Probable	24
Confirmed	12
Total	53

Physiographic Distribution

Horned Lark	Number of blocks in province	Number of blocks species found breeding in province	Number of blocks species found in state	Percent of province species occupies	Percent of all records for this species found in province	Percent of state area in province
Kittatinny Mountains	19	1	53	5.3	1.9	2.2
Kittatinny Valley	45	7	53	15.6	13.2	5.3
Highlands	109	3	53	2.8	5.7	12.8
Piedmont	167	3	53	1.8	5.7	19.6
Inner Coastal Plain	128	9	53	7.0	17.0	15.0
Outer Coastal Plain	204	23	53	11.3	43.4	23.9
Pine Barrens	180	7	53	3.9	13.2	21.1

The eastward expansion of Horned Lark's overall range occurred during a narrow window of opportunity, as numbers were already declining in some areas of the eastern United States by the late 1940s (Beason 1995). Although Horned Larks became fairly widespread breeding birds in New Jersey, by the mid-1960s they were described as local, especially inland (Bull 1964). Leck (1984) echoed this sentiment and described their status as "uncommon and local." Their reliance on man-made short grass habitats, such as farm fields, left Horned Larks susceptible to the disappearance of those areas through succession and development. Likewise, natural habitats such as coastal sand dunes have vanished as development has encroached along the coast.

Atlas surveys showed how alarmingly local Horned Larks have become. The areas that have retained multi-block clusters of Horned Lark are few – the farmlands of Salem and Cumberland counties, the Wallkill River Valley, a series of blocks in Warren County, and Lakehurst Naval Air Station, Ocean County. Aside from these locations, Horned Larks were very local and scattered. They were only found in three blocks along the barrier islands, a surprisingly low total, and were absent, or nearly absent, from ten counties.

Conservation Note: As farm fields and similar open areas are lost to development and succession, Horned Larks are increasingly relegated to fewer nesting areas. They appear to be able to find new breeding areas if they are made available, but this type of habitat is rarely created. If this species is to survive in New Jersey, the areas that currently support existing populations must be managed to maintain short-grass habitat.

Fall: Most of New Jersey's breeding Horned Larks probably leave New Jersey (Beason 1995) and are replaced in winter by the northern subspecies, *E. a. alpestris*. Those that arrive to spend the winter are late fall migrants, usually noted moving from mid-October into December. The largest flocks are seen inland. **Maximum:** 90, Alpha Grasslands, 24 November 1996.

Winter: Horned Larks are most regularly found in winter on barren ground such as dunes and plowed farm fields, where they may be seen in large flocks. CBC totals are highly variable. **Maxima:** 650, Sayre's Neck, 28 December 1988; 500, Fostertown Road, 16 February 1986. **CBC Statewide Stats:** Average: 988; Maximum: 2,882 in 1996; Minimum: 129 in 1992. **CBC Maximum:** 1,008, Elmer 1994.

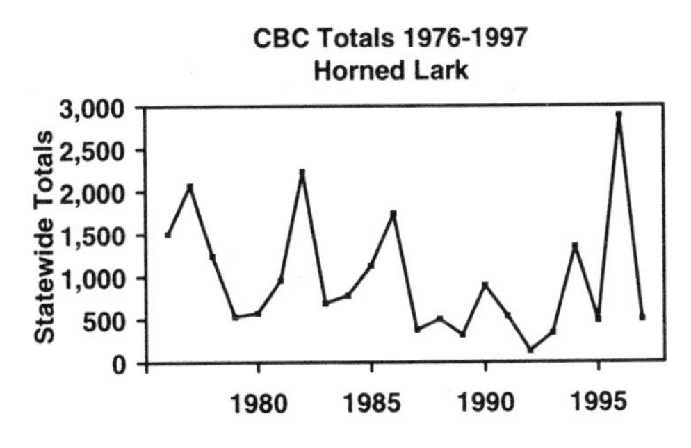

Spring: Horned Larks are very early spring migrants, with many leaving by late February. ■

Purple Martin

Progne subis

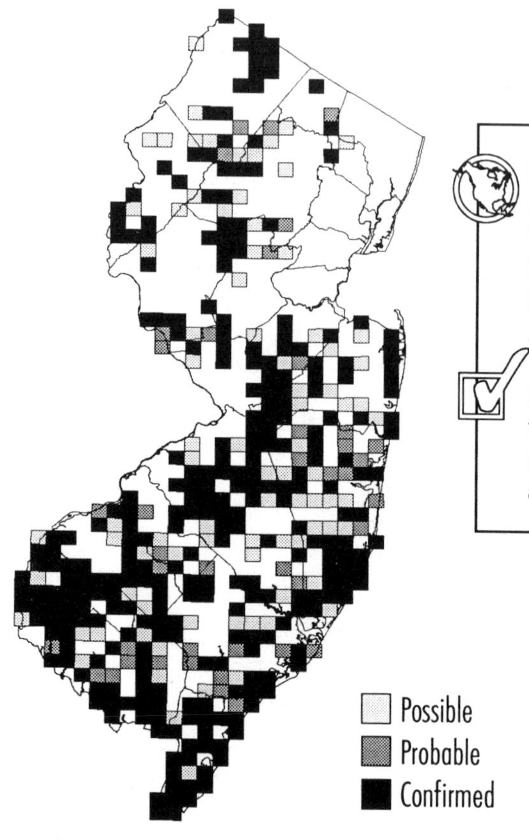

Range: In eastern North America breeds from Manitoba east to Nova Scotia, south to Texas and Florida. Winters in South America.

NJ Status: Common and fairly widespread summer resident, common spring and fall migrant.

Statewide Summary	
Status	# of Blocks
Possible	84
Probable	41
Confirmed	283
Total	408

Breeding

Habitat: Nests in open country near water, almost exclusively in colonial martin houses.

Stone (1908) indicated Purple Martins were much more common in southern New Jersey than in northern New Jersey. There population in northern New Jersey, while historically lower than that in southern New Jersey, is recovering from a crash in the early 20th century. Griscom (1923) indicated their population in northern New Jersey became so low that he could only list six breeding locations. He cited competition with House Sparrows and European Starlings as a reason for the decline. By 1942, Cruickshank listed more locations with breeding Purple Martins, but also expressed concern that the species could be extirpated from northern New Jersey. Even as recently as 1955, Fables suggested that the population was declining in some sections of the state.

During a large part of the 20th century, Purple Martins relied on the presence of man-made, multi-compartment nest-houses for breeding. Stone (1908) noted that the birds would use other structures when martin houses were not present. Fables (1955) suggested they were still using natural cavities in the Pine Barrens, but that nest-houses augmented Purple Martin populations in a given area. Bull (1964), however, suspected that they used martin houses almost exclusively.

Although Purple Martins were found to be quite common in much of New Jersey, 79% of their statewide range was south of the Piedmont. On the Inner Coastal Plain and Outer Coastal Plain, the Purple Martin strongholds in the state, their distribution probably corresponds to the distribution of nest houses as Atlas observers did not report a single martin colony in a natural cavity.

In northern New Jersey, the three ingredients required for nesting Purple Martins – nest-houses, water, and open space – occurred in pockets and, likewise, so did Purple Martins. The Kittatinny Valley had Purple Martins in 46% of the blocks, and the Highlands

continued on page 416

Purple Martin

Physiographic Distribution **Purple Martin**	Number of blocks in province	Number of blocks species found breeding in province	Number of blocks species found in state	Percent of province species occupies	Percent of all records for this species found in province	Percent of state area in province
Kittatinny Mountains	19	2	408	10.5	0.5	2.2
Kittatinny Valley	45	21	408	46.7	5.1	5.3
Highlands	109	37	408	33.9	9.1	12.8
Piedmont	167	27	408	16.2	6.6	19.6
Inner Coastal Plain	128	65	408	50.8	15.9	15.0
Outer Coastal Plain	204	142	408	69.6	34.8	23.9
Pine Barrens	180	114	408	63.3	27.9	21.1

continued from page 415

Purple Martin

had them in 34%. They were least common in the Kittatinny Mountains and Piedmont, where they occurred in 16% or fewer of the blocks. Areas with heavy urbanization, such as those in northeastern New Jersey, were completely devoid of nesting Purple Martins, much as they were in Griscom's (1923) and Cruickshank's (1942) days.

Fall: Purple Martins are early migrants, often leaving from local breeding colonies by mid-August. They can sometimes then be found in large concentrations at staging areas in late August and early September. One of the largest known staging areas is near the town of Mauricetown along the Maurice River in Cumberland County, where thousands can be present. Nearly all have departed the by the end of September. **Maxima:** 30,000, Mauricetown, 30 August 1995; 11,000, Mauricetown, 4 September 1992.

Spring: On occasion, male Purple Martins can return to southern New Jersey by late February, but it is doubtful if they survive late season cold snaps. Most begin to return in early April. ■

Brown-chested Martin

Progne tapera

Range: Breeds from northern South America south. Winters from Brazil north to Panama.

NJ Status: Accidental. NJBRC Review List.

Occurrence: There has only been one documented and accepted record of Brown-chested Martin in New Jersey: Cape May, 6-15 November 1997 (ph-RNJB 24:67, 68). This is the second confirmed North American record. ■

Tree Swallow

Tachycineta bicolor

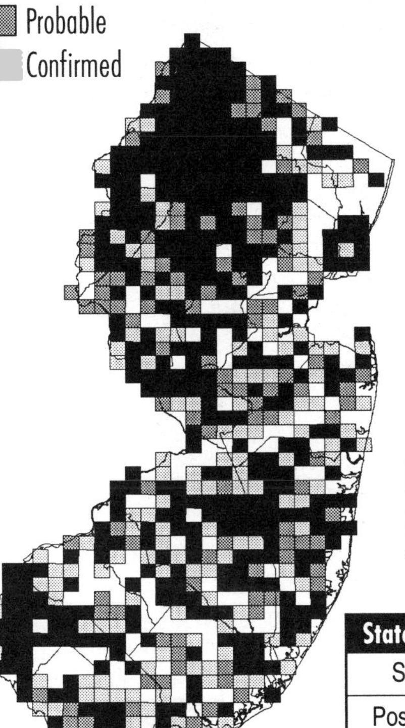

Range: In the East breeds from Manitoba east to Newfoundland, south to northern Arkansas and northern Georgia. Winters along the Atlantic coast from Virginia to Florida and along the Gulf coast, south to Central America and parts of the Caribbean.

NJ Status: Fairly common and very widespread summer resident, common spring and fall migrant, rare to scarce winter resident.

Breeding

Habitat: Nests in tree cavities, and other natural or man-made cavities, in a variety of open wooded habitats near water.

Statewide Summary	
Status	# of Blocks
Possible	143
Probable	115
Confirmed	407
Total	665

During much of the 20th century, the term "local" was most often used to describe

continued on page 418

Physiographic Distribution

Tree Swallow	Number of blocks in province	Number of blocks species found breeding in province	Number of blocks species found in state	Percent of province species occupies	Percent of all records for this species found in province	Percent of state area in province
Kittatinny Mountains	19	19	665	100.0	2.9	2.2
Kittatinny Valley	45	44	665	97.8	6.6	5.3
Highlands	109	102	665	93.6	15.3	12.8
Piedmont	167	117	665	70.1	17.6	19.6
Inner Coastal Plain	128	106	665	82.8	15.9	15.0
Outer Coastal Plain	204	136	665	66.7	20.5	23.9
Pine Barrens	180	141	665	78.3	21.2	21.1

continued from page 417

Map Interpretation: Tree Swallows do not nest in colonies. This makes nest sites harder to find, and in areas of low density may make Confirmed sightings less likely than for the colonially nesting swallows.

Tree Swallows breeding status (Griscom 1923, Bull 1964, Leck 1984). Indeed, modern observers may be unaware that Tree Swallows were quite rare in northern New Jersey as breeding birds. The first breeding record for northern New Jersey was either in 1905 near Mount Horeb, or at Culvers Lake in 1919 (Griscom 1923). Their status in New Jersey has changed dramatically during the 1900s. Apparently, the availability of nest boxes, especially bluebird and Wood Duck nest boxes, have increased their numbers in many areas (Robertson et al. 1992), although they still frequently use natural cavities.

Atlas data showed that Tree Swallows occurred throughout all the physiographic provinces, and occurred in 78% of the state. They were found in 95% of the blocks north of the Piedmont; from the Piedmont south, the number dropped to 77% of the blocks. A high percentage (i.e., 22%) of Tree Swallow breeding reports were scored as Possible. The reasons for this are unclear, but may be a associated with their low density in the Pine Barrens, on the Inner Coastal Plain, and in areas of extensive farmland.

Fall: The huge concentrations of Tree Swallows along the Atlantic coast are some of the most spectacular sights of the fall season. The buildup begins by late July, but numbers peak from late

Tree Swallow

Tree Swallow

continued

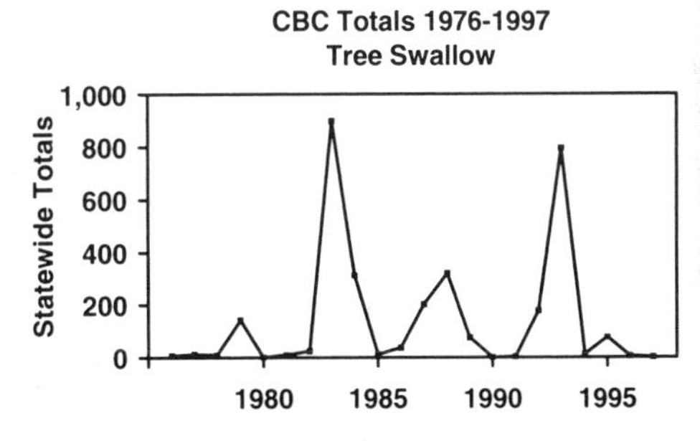

September to mid-October. Numbers diminish through November and early December. **Maxima:** 500,000, Cape Island, 30 September-1 October 1974; 110,000, coastal Cape May County, October 1987.

Winter: Tree Swallow totals on CBCs are highly variable and entirely weather dependent. A few individuals attempt to winter in the southern part of the state, and they are sometimes successful in mild winters. **CBC Statewide Stats:** Average: 142; Maximum: 899 in 1983; Minimum: 0 in 1980 and 1990. **CBC Maximum:** 627, Barnegat, 1993.

Spring: Tree Swallows herald the arrival of spring, typically returning in early to mid-March. Peak northward movements occur from early to mid-April. **Maxima:** 1,000+,Culvers Lake, 12 April 1986; 1,000, Culvers Lake, 11 April 1985. ■

Violet-green Swallow

Tachycineta thalassina

Range: Breeds from Alaska, south to west Texas and Mexico. Winters from California to Central America.

NJ Status: Accidental. NJBRC Review List.

Occurrence: There have been two state reports of Violet-green Swallow, and both have been accepted by the NJBRC. The two accepted records are:

Cape May Point	*7-13 November 1992*
Cape May Point	*17-29 October 1997*

Northern Rough-winged Swallow

Stelgidopteryx serripennis

Range: Breeds throughout most of the United States and southern Canada. Winters from Florida and the Gulf Coast south to South America.

NJ Status: Fairly common and widespread summer resident, uncommon spring and fairly common fall migrant.

Breeding

Habitat: Nests in existing cavities, but avoids tree cavities and nest boxes. Found in open country near water, using stream banks, gravel pits, bridges, natural or man-made holes and crevices, etc.

Northern Rough-winged Swallows have become more widespread in New Jersey, and appear to have shifted their range northward during the course of the 20th century. Stone (1908) found them "tolerably common" in the southern part of the state, but rare in the northern counties. Griscom (1923) found them

Map Interpretation: Northern Rough-winged Swallows are limited by nest site availability, and many adults may not breed in a given year if all cavities in an area are occupied (Dejong 1996). This could create a large population of "floaters" and suggests that the current breeding range may be best represented by only the Confirmed sightings.

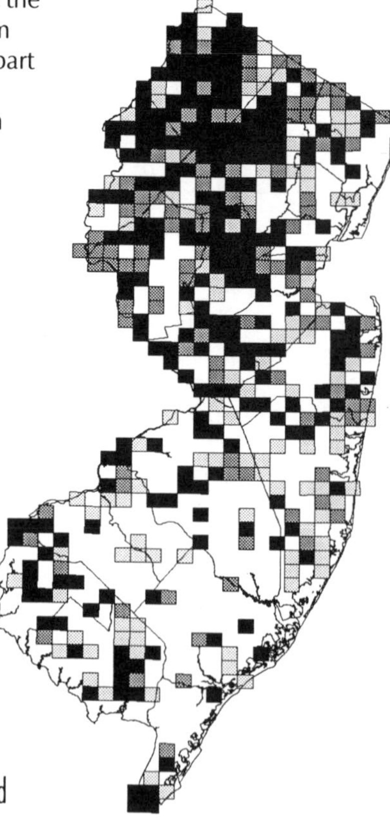

Statewide Summary	
Status	# of Blocks
Possible	107
Probable	102
Confirmed	238
Total	447

Physiographic Distribution Northern Rough-winged Swallow	Number of blocks in province	Number of blocks species found breeding in province	Number of blocks species found in state	Percent of province species occupies	Percent of all records for this species found in province	Percent of state area in province
Kittatinny Mountains	19	17	447	89.5	3.8	2.2
Kittatinny Valley	45	40	447	88.9	8.9	5.3
Highlands	109	93	447	85.3	20.8	12.8
Piedmont	167	98	447	58.7	21.9	19.6
Inner Coastal Plain	128	68	447	53.1	15.2	15.0
Outer Coastal Plain	204	71	447	34.8	15.9	23.9
Pine Barrens	180	60	447	33.3	13.4	21.1

local in the northern counties, but suggested that they were locally common in a few of the areas. Cruickshank (1942) wrote that rough-winged swallows had spread considerably in the north in the years between Griscom's writings and his own. Both Fables (1955) and Bull (1964) considered them fairly common breeding birds, although Bull noted that they were limited by the availability of nest holes.

The Atlas results showed that Northern Rough-winged Swallows were widespread in the state, occurring throughout all the physiographic provinces. They have clearly shifted the center of their population northward during the 20th century. Interestingly, they were recorded most regularly north of the Piedmont, where they were found in 87% of the blocks. They are less common in southern New Jersey, occurring in 33% of the blocks in the Pine Barrens and 35% of the blocks on the Outer Coastal Plain. There are sections of southern New Jersey where rough-winged swallows are fairly common. For example, they were well represented in southern Cumberland County, which is rife with sand and gravel pits, but they were nearly absent in the northern half of neighboring Cape May County, where there are fewer sand and gravel pits.

Fall: Northern Rough-winged Swallows are early migrants, beginning their move south in mid-July, with a noticeable peak from late July through early August. They become scarce by the end of August; however, late movements are sometimes seen at Cape May Point (e.g., 40 on 12 October 1996; 30+ on 18 October 1988). Rarely a few may linger into early November. **Maxima:** 100, Lambertville, early August 1996; 50, Cape May Point, 31 July 1986; 50, Cape May Point, 28 July 1992.

Spring: The northward movement of Northern Rough-winged Swallows is inconspicuous. The first birds can arrive by late March, but most probably move through from early April to mid-May. **Maximum:** 20, Spruce Run Res., 12 May 1983. ■

Bank Swallow

Riparia riparia

Range: In eastern North America breeds from Manitoba east to Labrador, south to Texas and North Carolina. Winters in South America.

NJ Status: Fairly common but somewhat local summer resident, fairly common spring and fall migrant.

Breeding

Habitat: Colonial. Excavates cavities for nesting in river banks, gravel pits, sand banks, etc.

Stone's (1908) statement that Bank Swallows were "rather local in distribution" has held up into

Statewide Summary	
Status	# of Blocks
Possible	56
Probable	26
Confirmed	99
Total	181

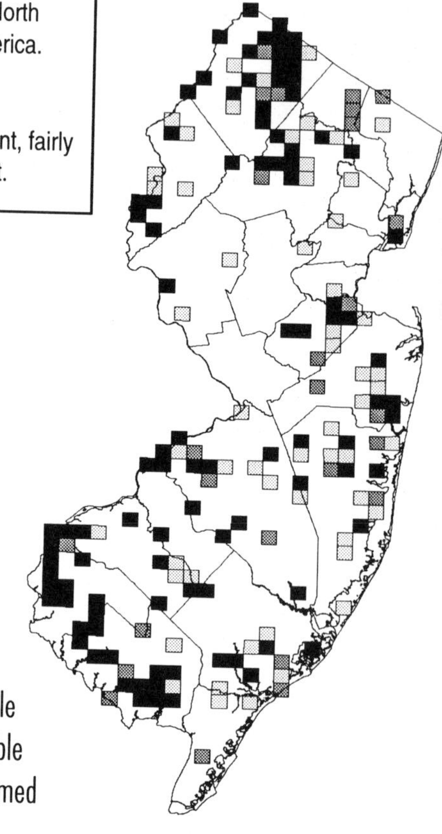

Physiographic Distribution Bank Swallow	Number of blocks in province	Number of blocks species found breeding in province	Number of blocks species found in state	Percent of province species occupies	Percent of all records for this species found in province	Percent of state area in province
Kittatinny Mountains	19	7	181	36.8	3.9	2.2
Kittatinny Valley	45	21	181	46.7	11.6	5.3
Highlands	109	27	181	24.8	14.9	12.8
Piedmont	167	10	181	6.0	5.5	19.6
Inner Coastal Plain	128	35	181	27.3	19.3	15.0
Outer Coastal Plain	204	43	181	21.1	23.8	23.9
Pine Barrens	180	38	181	21.1	21.0	21.1

Map interpretation: Bank Swallows are colonial breeding birds, with many pairs present at the nesting colonies. None of the locations scored as Possible or as Probable were at locations where a colony was found. These probably represented birds either foraging or wandering, and some could even have been early southbound migrants. The actual breeding distribution of Bank Swallows is best represented only by the blocks shown as Confirmed.

the 1990s. Unlike other swallows, Bank Swallows avoid using man-made structures for nesting, although they use temporary habitats created by human activities – such as the steep sides of a sand pit created during excavation. These habitats tend to be ephemeral, and Bank Swallow colonies often appear and disappear from year to year. Stream- and river-bank colonies tend to be more stable, or at least less susceptible to human disturbance.

Bank Swallows were patchy in their distribution throughout the state during the Atlas surveys. They were found in all provinces, but they did not occupy more than 46% of any one province and were found in only 21% of the blocks statewide. Over 31% of the occupied blocks were located north of the Piedmont, and 64% were south of that region. They were conspicuous in their near absence from the Piedmont itself. Much of the population north of the Piedmont was along the Delaware River, in the Kittatinny Valley, and in central Morris County. The population in southern New Jersey was broadly spaced with clusters primarily in Salem and Cumberland counties. Interestingly, as noted by Stone (1937), Bank Swallows were not Confirmed nesting in Cape May County.

Fall: An early migrant, southbound or dispersing Bank Swallows are noted in early July. Most migrants pass between mid-July and mid-August. However, large aggregations in the mid-1980s near Harmony in late August and early September may have represented a staging area. Few remain after late September or early October. **Maxima:** 5,000-10,000 swallows (mostly Bank), Harmony, 22 August 1985; 5,000+ swallows (mostly Bank), Harmony, 11 September 1986.

Spring: Bank Swallows begin to return north from early to mid-April, with most passing from early to mid-May. **Maxima:** 800, Mannington Marsh, 29 May 1986; 100s, Mannington Marsh, 6 May 1994. ■

Cliff Swallow

Petrochelidon pyrrhonota

Range: In eastern North America breeds from Manitoba to southern Newfoundland south to Texas and North Carolina; absent from most of the Southeast. Winters in South America.

NJ Status: Scarce and local summer resident, uncommon spring and fall migrant. Threatened Species in New Jersey.

Possible
Probable
Confirmed

Breeding

Habitat: Colonial. Nests in open country, often near water, typically under bridges.

Historically, Cliff Swallows were birds of the western United States where they nested on rocky cliff ledges. They expanded eastward during the 19th and 20th centuries, utilizing the increasing numbers of artificial nest-sites provided by the construction of bridges, culverts, barns, and other buildings. They had colonized numerous locations in New Jersey by the early 1900s (Stone 1908), but numbers declined precipitously within two decades (Griscom 1923). Their continuing decline may be caused by competition with House Sparrows for nest space (Brown and Brown 1995).

By 1979, there were reported to be only 13 breeding pairs of Cliff Swallows in the state (Leck

Map interpretation: Cliff Swallows are colonial breeding birds. The locations scored as Possible and Probable were in blocks where no colony was found. These sightings likely represent individuals or pairs that were either foraging or wandering. The actual breeding distribution of Cliff Swallows is best represented only by the blocks shown as Confirmed.

1984), and they were officially listed as Threatened. A resurgence in the population was noted in 1982, when a colony with 184 nests was found at Lambertville on the Delaware River, Hunterdon County, and another colony of 134 nests was discovered along the river at Bull's Island State Recreation Area, Hunterdon County. Smaller colonies were also found in Sussex and Warren counties (Welton 1983). Boyle (1986) described Cliff Swallows as "local (but increasing)."

Atlas observers found Cliff Swallows to have two main population centers in the state. Over 66% of the occupied blocks were located in the Kittatinny Valley and Piedmont provinces. The Kittatinny Valley holds 34% of the state's occupied blocks, but occupies only 5% of the state's area. The Cliff Swallows in the Piedmont are clustered along the Delaware River in Hunterdon County, and they occupy only 8% of that province. Most of the other blocks where Cliff Swallows were found were scattered throughout the northern half of the state.

Conservation Note: Cliff Swallows are far from having recovered in New Jersey. Stone (1908) indicated that Cliff Swallows were a local breeding birds in the Pine Barrens and that they were also found breeding in Cape May, Cumberland, and Burlington counties, as well as at locations in northern New Jersey. Despite five years of censusing, no colonies were found south of Trenton.

Fall: Cliff Swallows begin migration by late July, most move between late August and late September, with a peak in mid-September. They become rare by mid-October. **Maxima:** 1,200, Cape May Point, 11 September 1993; 70, Cape May Point, 16 September 1986.

Spring: Cliff Swallows generally arrive later in spring than other swallows, usually appearing in mid-April. Most northbound birds are seen between late April and mid-May. **Maxima:** 350-450, Alpine Lookout, 19 May 1978; 100+, Rio Grande, 12 May 1984. ■

Statewide Summary

Status	# of Blocks
Possible	10
Probable	5
Confirmed	29
Total	44

Physiographic Distribution

Cliff Swallow	Number of blocks in province	Number of blocks species found breeding in province	Number of blocks species found in state	Percent of province species occupies	Percent of all records for this species found in province	Percent of state area in province
Kittatinny Mountains	19	3	44	15.8	6.8	2.2
Kittatinny Valley	45	15	44	33.3	34.1	5.3
Highlands	109	7	44	6.4	15.9	12.8
Piedmont	167	14	44	8.4	31.8	19.6
Inner Coastal Plain	128	4	44	3.1	9.1	15.0
Outer Coastal Plain	204	1	44	0.5	2.3	23.9

Cave Swallow

Petrochelidon fulva

Range: Breeds in New Mexico, Texas, and south Florida, south. Winter range of northern birds unknown, southern breeding birds are resident.

NJ Status: Accidental. NJBRC Review List.

Occurrence: There have been nine state reports of Cave Swallow, and seven have been accepted by the NJBRC (six in fall, one in spring). The seven accepted records are:

	Cape May Point	*20 April-4 June 1990*
4	*Cape May Point*	*7-15 November 1992*
	Cape May Point	*20 November 1993*
2	*Wildwood*	*8 November 1994*
	Cape May Point	*2-3 November 1996*
5	*Cape May Point*	*7-17 November 1997*
2	*East Point*	*9 November 1997*

Barn Swallow

Hirundo rustica

Range: Breeds throughout much of temperate North America. Winters in Central and South America.

NJ Status: Common and nearly ubiquitous summer resident, common spring and fall migrant, reported on two CBCs.

Breeding

Habitat: Nests in barns, under bridges, under eaves in fairly open country.

Barn Swallows have long been the most abundant breeding swallow in New Jersey. Griscom (1923) contended that Barn Swallow populations had declined in the late 1800s and early 1900s due to suburban expansion into rural areas. Aside

Barn Swallow

continued

from that comment on changing status, most other authors considered Barn Swallows to be abundant and common breeding birds (Stone 1908, Stone 1937, Cruickshank 1942, Fables 1955, Leck 1984).

Barn Swallows remain broadly distributed breeding birds in all physiographic provinces. Atlas surveys found Barn Swallows in 93% of the blocks statewide, making them one of New Jersey's most common breeding birds. They use man-made structures for nesting where there is little or no competition for nest sites from other this species. The only area from which Barn Swallows were absent was the heart of the Pine Barrens, and it is possible they may occur in that area, but only at a very low density.

Fall: The constant, nearly all-day movements of Barn Swallows that can occur from late August through

continued on page 428

Possible
Probable
Confirmed

Statewide Summary	
Status	# of Blocks
Possible	74
Probable	79
Confirmed	638
Total	791

Physiographic Distribution Barn Swallow	Number of blocks in province	Number of blocks species found breeding in province	Number of blocks species found in state	Percent of province species occupies	Percent of all records for this species found in province	Percent of state area in province
Kittatinny Mountains	19	18	791	94.7	2.3	2.2
Kittatinny Valley	45	42	791	93.3	5.3	5.3
Highlands	109	108	791	99.1	13.7	12.8
Piedmont	167	154	791	92.2	19.5	19.6
Inner Coastal Plain	128	123	791	96.1	15.5	15.0
Outer Coastal Plain	204	191	791	93.6	24.1	23.9
Pine Barrens	180	155	791	86.1	19.6	21.1

continued from page 427

Barn Swallow

early September at Cape May were first noted by Stone (1937) in the late 1920s, and persist to this day. Numbers diminish by late September, although a few can sometimes linger into November. **Maxima:** 12,000, Cape May Point, 19 August 1996; 3,000, Great Swamp, 20 August 1979.

Winter: Barn Swallows were reported on two CBCs between 1976 and 1997 (i.e., two counts in 1985), but are not known to winter.

Spring: Barn Swallows arrive in the last few days of March, with most of the northbound birds passing from late April to mid-May. Although common as migrants, actual numbers are not frequently reported in spring. **Maximum:** 200+, Black River, 12 May 1983. ■

Carolina Chickadee

Poecile carolinensis

Range: Resident from southeastern Kansas east to New Jersey, south to eastern Texas and northern Florida.

NJ Status: Common and widespread resident.

Statewide Summary	
Status	# of Blocks
Possible	26
Probable	94
Confirmed	379
Total	499

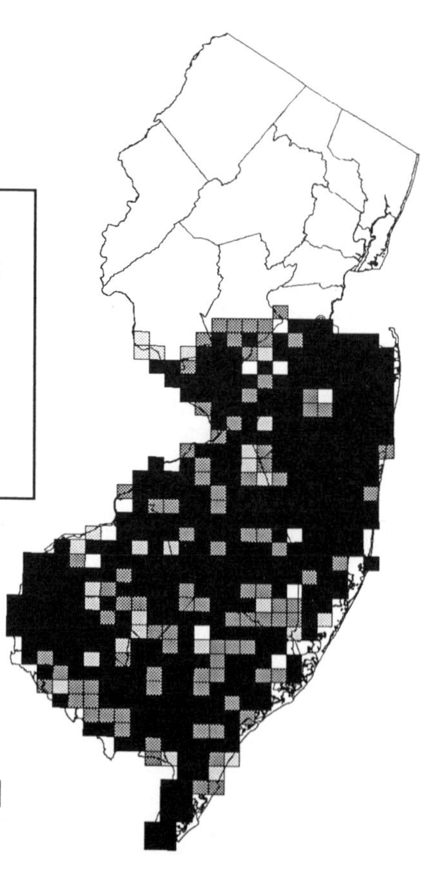

Possible

Probable

Confirmed

Carolina Chickadee

continued

Breeding

Habitat: Nests in mixed or deciduous woodlands.

One of New Jersey's most intriguing patterns of bird distribution is that shown by Black-capped and Carolina Chickadees. Historically, the Raritan River was described as the dividing line between the ranges of Carolina and Black-capped Chickadees (Stone 1908, Fables 1955). Boyle (1986) redefined that line as South Amboy, Middlesex County on Raritan Bay, to Lambertville, Hunterdon County on the Delaware River. Although there is a small population of Black-capped Chickadees on Sandy Hook, the breeding chickadee on the south shore of Raritan Bay is Carolina Chickadee. The mechanisms that maintain the sharp range separation of these two closely related species are unknown – but there has never been a New York State record of Carolina Chickadee, and Black-capped Chickadee is, at best, a scarce vagrant in the New Jersey south of their breeding range.

The ranges of both Carolina and Black-capped Chickadees have changed little during the 20th century. Carolina Chickadees were widespread south of the contact zone with Black-capped Chickadees and were found in 92% of the blocks south of there. Stone (1908) suggested that Carolina Chickadees were more common in the Pine Barrens than elsewhere. During the Atlas surveys, however, they were found to be nearly equally distributed through the Inner Coastal Plain and Pine Barrens, but were absent from many of the barrier island blocks of the Outer Coastal Plain. There are no documented records of Carolina Chickadees north of Raritan Bay's south shore.

The mechanism that separates Carolina and Black-capped Chickadees is fascinating and begs further study. There were only 19 blocks reporting both species, but only three blocks where both species were Confirmed (near Hopewell, New Brunswick, and Princeton). In areas of overlap, chickadees may sing the other species' song; so the best estimate of the true area of overlap is the blocks where both were Confirmed.

continued on page 430

Physiographic Distribution

Carolina Chickadee	Number of blocks in province	Number of blocks species found breeding in province	Number of blocks species found in state	Percent of province species occupies	Percent of all records for this species found in province	Percent of state area in province
Piedmont	167	28	499	16.8	5.6	19.6
Inner Coastal Plain	128	119	499	93.0	23.8	15.0
Outer Coastal Plain	204	175	499	85.8	35.1	23.9
Pine Barrens	180	177	499	98.3	35.5	21.1

continued from page 429

Carolina Chickadee

Fall: Carolina Chickadees are nonmigratory, permanent residents. There is no published information on the occurrence of fall migration of Carolina Chickadees in New Jersey.

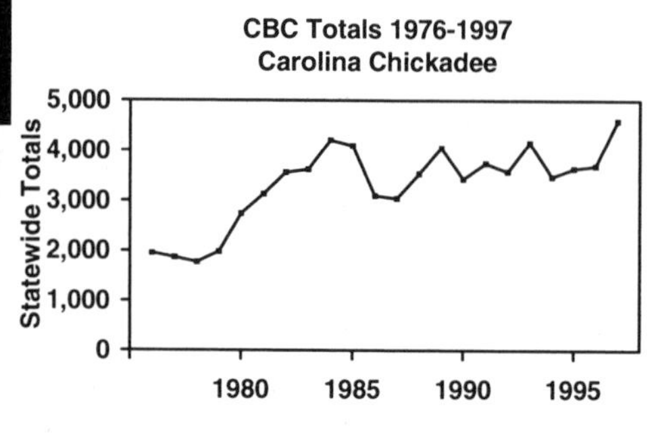

Winter: Statewide CBC totals of Carolina Chickadees are stable. **CBC Statewide Stats:** Average: 3,316; Maximum: 4,598 in 1997; Minimum: 1,772 in 1978. **CBC Maximum:** 797, Pinelands, 1990.

Spring: Carolina Chickadees are nonmigratory, permanent residents. There is no published information on the occurrence of spring migration of Carolina Chickadees in New Jersey. ■

Black-capped Chickadee

Poecile atricapillus

Range: In eastern North America resident from Manitoba east to Newfoundland, south to Kansas and northern New Jersey, and in the Appalachians south to North Carolina.

NJ Status: Common and fairly widespread resident.

Statewide Summary	
Status	# of Blocks
Possible	13
Probable	67
Confirmed	243
Total	323

Possible
Probable
Confirmed

Black-capped Chickadee

continued

Breeding

Habitat: Nests in cavities in open mixed or deciduous woodlands.

Black-capped and Carolina Chickadees present one of the most intriguing patterns of distribution of all breeding species in the state (see Carolina Chickadee for a discussion). It has been suggested that the contact zone between the two species might be shifting slowly northward. The evidence for this is scant; however there are a few examples of Carolina Chickadees moving into new areas. In the mid-1980s Carolina Chickadees arrived at Hopewell, Mercer County and coexisted with Black-capped Chickadees into the mid-1990s. A second known location where a shift in the resident chickadee population occurred was at Princeton, where both Carolina and Black-capped Chickadees were found until about 1980, but by the mid-1990s only Carolina Chickadees occurred (Sibley 1994).

Black-capped Chickadees were widespread, occurring in nearly all the blocks north of the contact zone and were Confirmed in 75% of the blocks where they occurred. Over 97% of their range is from the Piedmont northward. Within their range they were absent only from some of the highly urbanized blocks in the northeastern section of the state. Although Black-capped and Carolina Chickadees are known to hybridize (Smith 1993), no evidence of this was found in New Jersey during the Atlas surveys.

Atlas data suggested that if any changes are taking place within the overlap zone of the two chickadees, it is occurring at an extremely slow rate. The overlap area occurred specifically in southern Hunterdon, Somerset, and Union counties, and in northern Mercer and Middlesex counties. Historic descriptions

continued on page 432

Physiographic Distribution **Black-capped Chickadee**	Number of blocks in province	Number of blocks species found breeding in province	Number of blocks species found in state	Percent of province species occupies	Percent of all records for this species found in province	Percent of state area in province
Kittatinny Mountains	19	19	323	100.0	5.9	2.2
Kittatinny Valley	45	44	323	97.8	13.6	5.3
Highlands	109	109	323	100.0	33.7	12.8
Piedmont	167	140	323	83.8	43.3	19.6
Inner Coastal Plain	128	11	323	8.6	3.4	15.0

continued from page 431

Black-capped Chickadee

of the extent of the ranges of both species were close enough to Atlas results to show that there was very little change during the 20th century. Sibley (1994) pointed out that the contact zone is probably irregular and might vary from year to year. Another complicating factor is that the chickadees learn to imitate each other's song, making some identifications uncertain (Kaufman 1996).

Fall: New Jersey's breeding Black-capped Chickadees are permanent, nonmigratory residents. However, irruptions of birds from farther north occur at irregular intervals, augmenting the resident population. These southward flights are usually the result of a poor seed crop in the north (Smith 1993). The most recent notable incursions occurred in the falls of 1982,1984, and 1995.

CBC Totals 1976-1997
Black-capped Chickadee

Statewide Totals: 0, 1,000, 2,000, 3,000, 4,000, 5,000, 6,000
1980, 1985, 1990, 1995

Winter: The highest statewide CBC totals of Black-capped Chickadees were tallied in two incursion years, 1982 and 1984. Leck (1984) referred to a southern invasion of Black-capped Chickadees in 1961, when 34 were reported on the Cape May CBC. Sibley (1997), however, considered Black-capped Chickadees hypothetical in Cape May County, stating that they were extremely rare at best. **CBC Statewide Stats:** Average: 3,595; Maximum: 5,190 in 1984; Minimum: 2,414 in 1997. **CBC Maximum:** 874, Boonton, 1982.

Spring: There is no published information on the occurrence of spring migration of Black-capped Chickadees in New Jersey. ■

Boreal Chickadee

Poecile hudsonicus

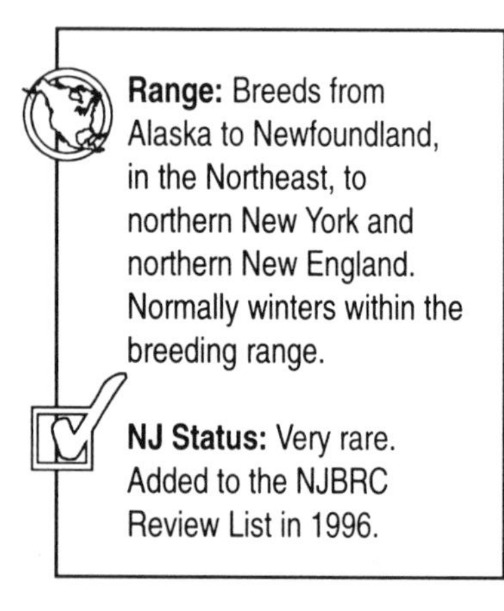

Range: Breeds from Alaska to Newfoundland, in the Northeast, to northern New York and northern New England. Normally winters within the breeding range.

NJ Status: Very rare. Added to the NJBRC Review List in 1996.

Occurrence: An irruptive species, Boreal Chickadees are irregular and unpredictable in New Jersey. In most years there are no reports. In a major flight year, birds may arrive as early as mid-October, although November is more typical. They usually depart by late

Boreal Chickadee
continued

March, although there is one report at Bearfort Mountain on 24 April 1976. The first known record from New Jersey was a specimen obtained at Ramsey, 1 November 1913 (Fables, 1955). Four years later, in 1916-1917, at least nine birds were noted in the Princeton and Plainfield areas (Stone 1937). After this, there were no records for 35 years. Beginning in 1952, the pattern of occurrence changed. For the next 35 years Boreal Chickadees were reported, although often in small numbers, in about half of the years. From 1987-1998 the previous pattern returned and there were no reports of Boreal Chickadees. There have been three major flight years (>20 birds) in New Jersey: 1961-1962, 1969-1970, and 1975-1976. Moderate invasion occurred in 1916-1917,and 1981-1982. The most extensive incursion, however, was in 1975-1976 when at least 50 Boreal Chickadees appeared in the state. Five were tallied on the Boonton CBC on 28 December 1975, but they have been reported on only four other counts since (i.e., 1980, two counts in 1982, and 1984). There have been no reports of Boreal Chickadees since their addition to the Review List in 1996. **Maxima:** 10, Hopewell area, 16 November 1969 (Cassinia); 5, Pequannock Watershed, 13 October 1975. ■

Tufted Titmouse
Baeolophus bicolor

Range: Breeds throughout the eastern United States northeast to Quebec and Maine. Winters within the breeding range.

NJ Status: Common and nearly ubiquitous resident.

Breeding

Habitat: Deciduous or, less commonly, mixed woodlands, yards, orchards, etc., with trees sufficiently large to provide nest cavities.

The northward range expansion of Tufted Titmouse during the 1900s is well documented in the literature. Early in the century, they were common only in the southern half of New Jersey, breeding locally north to Orange, Plainfield, and Morristown (Stone 1908). Griscom (1923) listed their range as expanding slightly north of Stone's 1908 range description, but allowed that the species had become more common within that range. Cruickshank (1942) indicated that they were continuing to

continued on page 434

continued from page 433

Tufted Titmouse

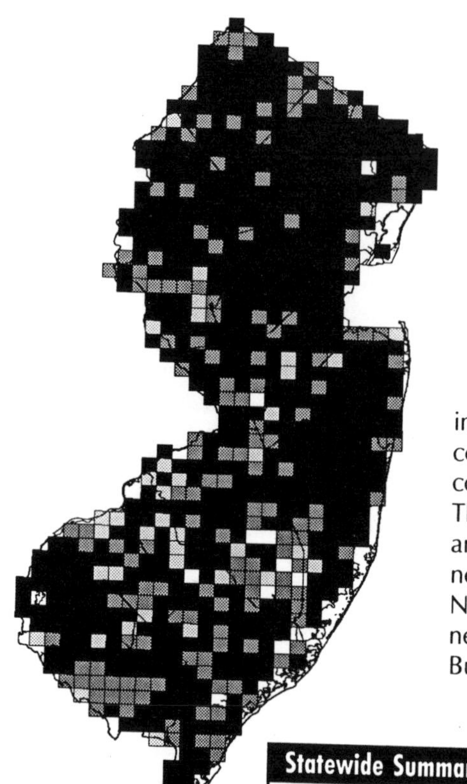

increase and had begun to colonize Rockland and Orange counties in southern New York. The subsequent range expansion and population explosion in northern New Jersey, southern New York, and western Connecticut is well documented in Bull (1964).

Statewide Summary	
Status	# of Blocks
Possible	38
Probable	154
Confirmed	599
Total	791

Possible
Probable
Confirmed

Physiographic Distribution

Tufted Titmouse	Number of blocks in province	Number of blocks species found breeding in province	Number of blocks species found in state	Percent of province species occupies	Percent of all records for this species found in province	Percent of state area in province
Kittatinny Mountains	19	19	791	100.0	2.4	2.2
Kittatinny Valley	45	44	791	97.8	5.6	5.3
Highlands	109	109	791	100.0	13.8	12.8
Piedmont	167	154	791	92.2	19.5	19.6
Inner Coastal Plain	128	122	791	95.3	15.4	15.0
Outer Coastal Plain	204	169	791	82.8	21.4	23.9
Pine Barrens	180	174	791	96.7	22.0	21.1

Tufted Titmice have become common throughout most of New Jersey. During Atlas surveys they were found in more than 92% of the blocks in all physiographic provinces except the Outer Coastal Plain. The Outer Coastal Plain lags behind the rest of the state only because titmice avoid nesting on the barrier islands. For most species, the percentage of Possible, Probable, and Confirmed sightings are quite similar among the Breeding Bird Atlases of New York, Pennsylvania, and New Jersey. For this species, the New Jersey Confirmation rate of 76% exceeds that of any of the neighboring states by a large margin. This may be due to a higher density of Tufted Titmice in New Jersey than in the neighboring states.

Fall: Occasionally Tufted Titmice appear in areas where they do not breed. This illustrates that some dispersal, probably of juveniles, takes place in this otherwise sedentary species (Grubb and Pravosudov 1994). At times, however, more massive, extensive, and poorly understood movements take place. In autumn 1978, as part of an unprecedented irruption over the whole Northeast (Post 1979), flocks of Tufted Titmice entered normally titmice-free coastal habitats from Sandy Hook to Cape May – e.g., groups of 8-15 birds at Cape May in late October 1978. Another great movement occurred in the Northeastern states in fall 1995, when a remarkable count of 700+ Tufted Titmice was noted flying east to west over Overpeck Park on 10 October 1995.

Winter: CBC numbers have gradually increased since the mid-1970s, with counts in the 1990s being more than double those of the 1980s. **CBC Statewide Stats:** Average: 3,754; Maximum: 6,670 in 1996; Minimum: 2,154 in 1979. **CBC Maximum:** 931, Lower Hudson, 1996.

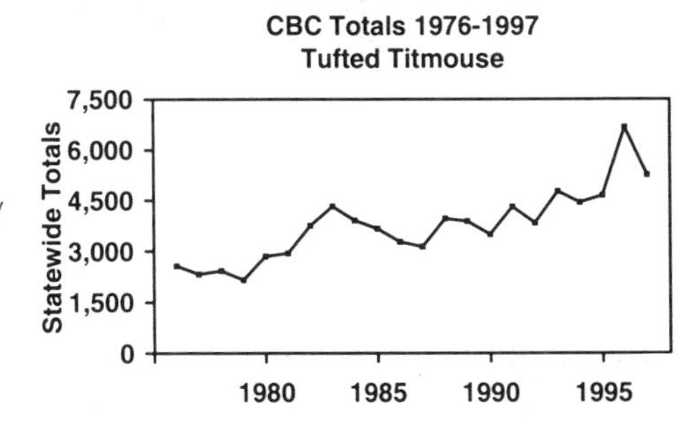

Spring: Movements of Tufted Titmice are very rarely noted away from breeding areas – e.g., 10, Sandy Hook, spring 1979. ■

Red-breasted Nuthatch

Sitta canadensis

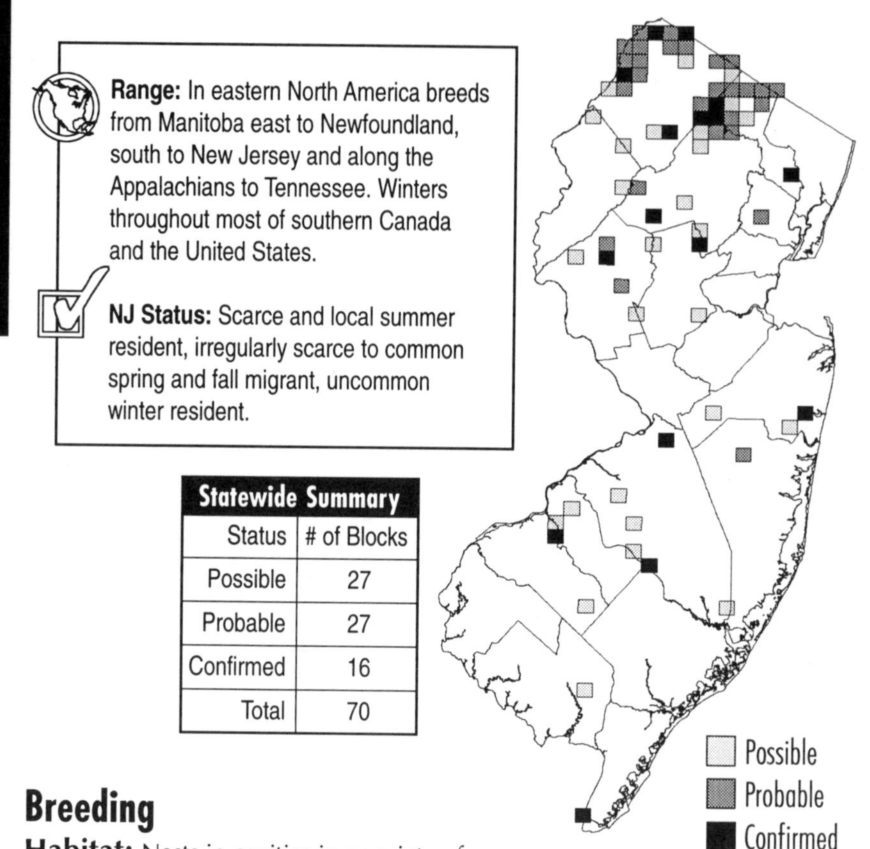

Range: In eastern North America breeds from Manitoba east to Newfoundland, south to New Jersey and along the Appalachians to Tennessee. Winters throughout most of southern Canada and the United States.

NJ Status: Scarce and local summer resident, irregularly scarce to common spring and fall migrant, uncommon winter resident.

Statewide Summary	
Status	# of Blocks
Possible	27
Probable	27
Confirmed	16
Total	70

Breeding

Habitat: Nests in cavities in a variety of woodland habitats, but prefers spruce groves and other coniferous woodlands.

Historically Red-breasted Nuthatches were birds of the boreal forests in the eastern United States, and their colonization of New Jersey as breeding birds is a recent event. During the first half of the 20th century, they were known only as transients and winter visitors in New Jersey (Stone 1908, Cruickshank 1942). Fables (1955) noted two summer records in 1954, one from Ocean County on 23 June and one from Burlington County on 12 July, which might have represented local breeding birds. The first state nesting occurred at Newfoundland, Morris County in 1971 (Kane and Marx 1972). Another breeding record came in 1974, at Moorestown, Burlington County, where two adults were seen feeding young (Meritt 1974), and a similar sighting was made at Dividing Creek, Cumberland County in 1977. Red-breasted Nuthatches have been increasing their range southward in other states as well. New York (Peterson 1988b) and Pennsylvania (Santner 1993) Atlas projects recount a similarly timed range expansion.

Physiographic Distribution **Red-breasted Nuthatch**	Number of blocks in province	Number of blocks species found breeding in province	Number of blocks species found in state	Percent of province species occupies	Percent of all records for this species found in province	Percent of state area in province
Kittatinny Mountains	19	12	70	63.2	17.1	2.2
Kittatinny Valley	45	6	70	13.3	8.6	5.3
Highlands	109	28	70	25.7	40.0	12.8
Piedmont	167	8	70	4.8	11.4	19.6
Inner Coastal Plain	128	5	70	3.9	7.1	15.0
Outer Coastal Plain	204	4	70	2.0	5.7	23.9
Pine Barrens	180	7	70	3.9	10.0	21.1

Atlas data showed Red-breasted Nuthatch's were found in only 8% of the blocks statewide, and their pattern of distribution was variable among regions: clumped in the north and patchy in the south. They occupied a contiguous series of blocks in the Kittatinny Mountains and the Wawayanda Plateau of the northern Highlands, particularly where Norway Spruce groves are concentrated. In fact, 65% of the blocks where they were found were north of the Coastal Plain. South of the Piedmont, Red-breasted Nuthatches were Confirmed in only five blocks, none of which were even in the same county. Throughout their range in New Jersey they have never been numerous, and rarely is more than one pair found in an area. Oddly, Breeding Bird Atlas volunteers repeatedly reported an influx of Red-breasted Nuthatches, beginning in late July, into areas with no known breeding pairs. These sightings probably represent post-breeding dispersal.

Some of the earliest records of breeding Red-breasted Nuthatches in New Jersey came from the Coastal Plain, but Atlas data indicated that they were very local in that area. Red-breasted Nuthatches are known to wander widely in search of food (Kaufman 1996), and it is likely that their occurrence on the Coastal Plain is ephemeral. They may be present at a location one year and are gone the next. This is evidenced by the Confirmation of breeding in southern Cape May County in 1997, a first county record in an intensely covered county. Veit and Petersen (1993) indicated that Red-breasted Nuthatch's irregular presence as a breeding bird in eastern Massachusetts is related to influxes of migrants from the previous fall.

Fall: The magnitude of the southward movement of Red-breasted Nuthatches is variable from year to year. In some years, good numbers appear by early to mid-August, with a peak occurring from mid- to late September. In other years only small numbers are seen, beginning in October and peaking in November. **Maxima:** 500, Cape May Point, 28 September 1995; 400, Higbee Beach, 21 September 1981.

continued on page 438

continued from page 437

Red-breasted Nuthatch

Winter: The numbers of Red-breasted Nuthatches encountered in winter are based on the size of the fall flight. Statewide CBC totals are variable. **CBC Statewide Stats:** Average: 210; Maximum: 702 in 1982; Minimum: 36 in 1995. **CBC Maximum:** 162, Princeton, 1982.

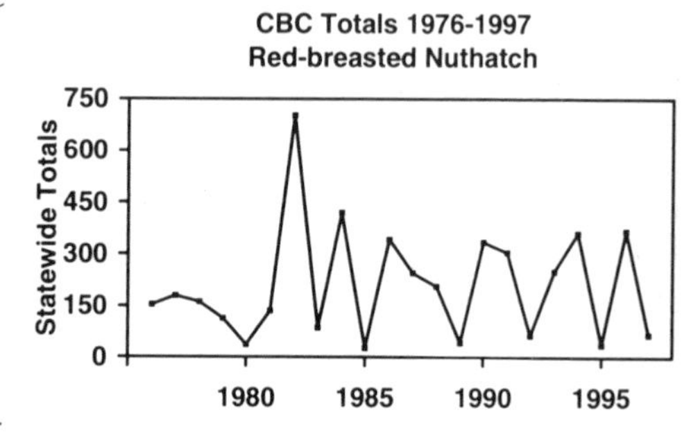

Spring: In years when there has been a fall incursion of Red-breasted Nuthatches, a return flight is detected in late April or early May. **Maximum:** 15, Higbee Beach, 27 April 1990. ■

White-breasted Nuthatch

Sitta carolinensis

Possible
Probable
Confirmed

Range: In eastern North America resident from southern Manitoba east to Nova Scotia, south to east Texas and northern Florida.

NJ Status: Fairly common and very widespread resident.

Breeding

Habitat: Nests in cavities in a variety of mixed or deciduous woodland habitats.

White-breasted Nuthatch

continued

Early authors found White-breasted Nuthatches to be more common as fall migrants and winter residents than as breeding birds (Griscom 1923, Bull 1964). In the southern part of the state, Stone (1937) described White-breasted Nuthatches as rare migrants on the Cape May Peninsula, but did not know them to breed. Fables (1955) wrote that they were rare breeding birds in the Pine Barrens, but more common in the western part of the state. He cited evidence of breeding in Camden and Burlington counties.

Atlas data indicated that White-breasted Nuthatches were more widely distributed than historic accounts suggest, and volunteers found them in 75% of the blocks statewide. They were found in all but one block north of the Piedmont. They were absent from the highly urbanized northeast and from sections of the largely deforested Inner Coastal Plain. They were also absent from interior sections of the Pine Barrens, from the lower Cape May Peninsula, and absent from most of the barrier islands and salt marsh edges.

Fall: White-breasted Nuthatches are generally nonmigratory permanent residents. Irruptive southward movements from northern and western sections of their North American range occur irregularly (Pravosudov and Grubb 1993). This was seen on 5 October 1977, when 63 White-breasted Nuthatches were counted passing Sunrise Mountain.

continued on page 440

Statewide Summary

Status	# of Blocks
Possible	114
Probable	243
Confirmed	284
Total	641

Physiographic Distribution

White-breasted Nuthatch	Number of blocks in province	Number of blocks species found breeding in province	Number of blocks species found in state	Percent of province species occupies	Percent of all records for this species found in province	Percent of state area in province
Kittatinny Mountains	19	19	641	100.0	3.0	2.2
Kittatinny Valley	45	44	641	97.8	6.9	5.3
Highlands	109	109	641	100.0	17.0	12.8
Piedmont	167	136	641	81.4	21.2	19.6
Inner Coastal Plain	128	81	641	63.3	12.6	15.0
Outer Coastal Plain	204	111	641	54.4	17.3	23.9
Pine Barrens	180	141	641	78.3	22.0	21.1

continued from page 439

White-breasted Nuthatch

Winter: The listed statewide CBC maximum for White-breasted Nuthatches occurred after a fall irruption and was nearly twice the average number. **CBC Statewide Stats:** Average: 1,226; Maximum: 2,002 in 1996; Minimum: 784 in 1977. **CBC Maximum:** 220, Great Swamp, 1978.

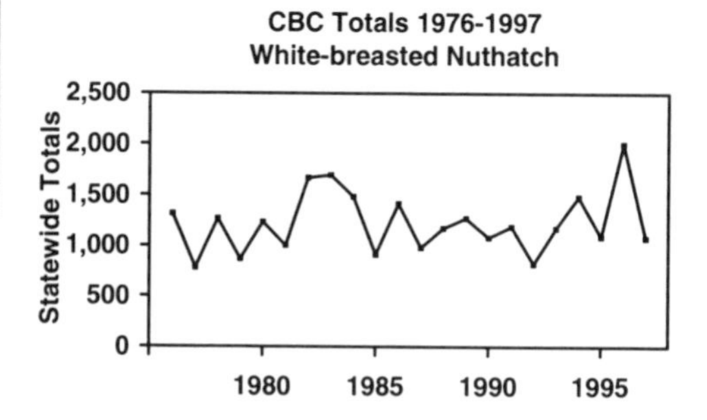

Spring: There is no published information on the occurrence of spring migration of White-breasted Nuthatches in New Jersey. ■

Brown Creeper
Certhia americana

Breeding

Habitat: Typically nests in crevices, behind strips of bark, in mature coniferous or deciduous woodlands, often in dead or dying trees.

There is little information on breeding Brown Creepers in New Jersey during the first half of the 20th century. As of 1942, there was only one known nesting location, near Springdale, Sussex County (Cruickshank 1942). At that time they were suspected of being more broadly distributed, as summer sightings had occurred at a few other locations in the northern counties. In 1954, a nest was found near Princeton, which Fables (1955)

Range: In eastern North America, breeds from southern Manitoba east to Newfoundland; south to northern Wisconsin, Missouri, Illinois, northern New Jersey and along the Appalachians to Tennessee. Winters throughout most of southern Canada and the United States.

NJ Status: Scarce and local summer resident, scarce to uncommon spring and uncommon fall migrant, uncommon winter resident.

Brown Creeper

continued

considered an extension of Brown Creeper's range onto the Coastal Plain. In 1972, 15 pairs were found nesting in the western Pequannock Watershed in Sussex and Passaic counties (Kane and Marx 1972).

In 1980, in the southern part of the state, there were breeding reports from Ocean, Burlington, Atlantic, and Cumberland counties (Leck 1984). They were also found on surveys of Bear Swamp, Cumberland County in 1981 and 1983 (Sutton and Sutton 1986). By the mid-1980s, Leck (1984) evaluated the status of Brown Creeper as local in northern New Jersey, although Boyle (1986) described them as uncommon.

continued on page 442

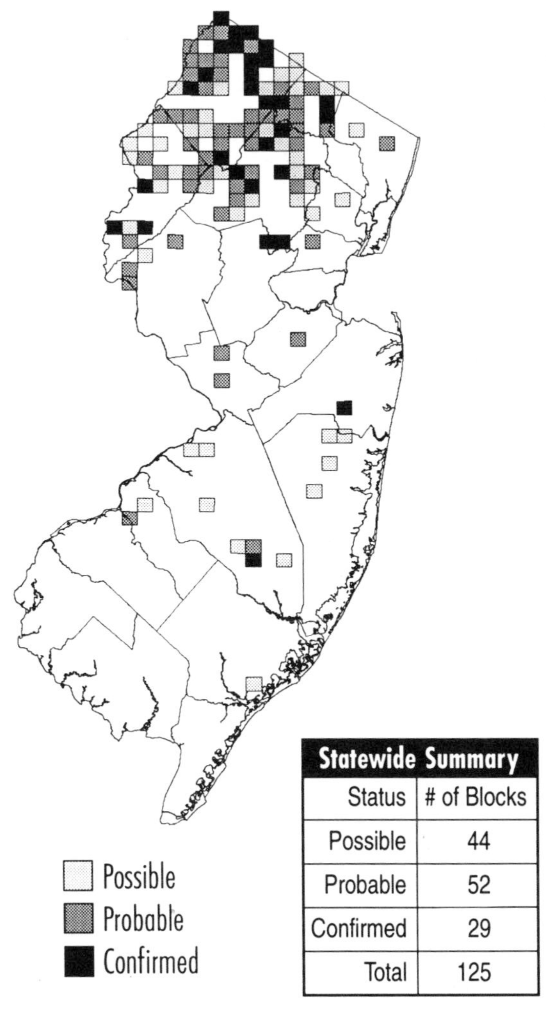

Statewide Summary	
Status	# of Blocks
Possible	44
Probable	52
Confirmed	29
Total	125

Physiographic Distribution

Brown Creeper	Number of blocks in province	Number of blocks species found breeding in province	Number of blocks species found in state	Percent of province species occupies	Percent of all records for this species found in province	Percent of state area in province
Kittatinny Mountains	19	16	125	84.2	12.8	2.2
Kittatinny Valley	45	23	125	51.1	18.4	5.3
Highlands	109	55	125	50.5	44.0	12.8
Piedmont	167	14	125	8.4	11.2	19.6
Inner Coastal Plain	128	7	125	5.5	5.6	15.0
Outer Coastal Plain	204	1	125	0.5	0.8	23.9
Pine Barrens	180	9	125	5.0	7.2	21.1

continued from page 441

Atlas results showed the distribution of Brown Creepers in New Jersey is similar to that of Red-breasted Nuthatches – clumped in contiguous blocks in the north, although patchy among the southern counties. Brown Creepers are quiet and unobtrusive, and they rely on dead or mature trees for nesting habitat. The intensive efforts of the Atlas surveys were especially well suited for the discovery of new breeding locations for this species. One of the highlights of the surveys was the number of new nesting sites found for Brown Creepers, especially when compared to those found in the historic accounts. Data from the surveys showed that 75% of Brown Creeper's statewide range is north of the Piedmont, where they occupied 54% of the blocks in the Kittatinny Valley, Kittatinny Mountains, and Highlands. From the Piedmont south, Brown Creepers were found at scattered locations, including nest sites within the Pine Barrens.

Fall: Few southbound Brown Creepers are seen before late September, and peak numbers move from mid- to late October. In 1995, at Island Beach SP, 388 were banded for the season, with 101 on 26 October and 98 on 13 October. There were no comparable reports elsewhere in the state that season, indicating that they can be inconspicuous and that large numbers can pass unnoticed. **Other maxima:** 20+, Sandy Hook, 23 October 1989; 20+, Sandy Hook, 19 October 1991.

Winter: Brown Creepers are often found in mixed feeding flocks with chickadees, Tufted Titmice, nuthatches, and kinglets. Statewide CBC totals are variable, probably due to the severity of the weather before and during the count period. **CBC Statewide Stats:** Average: 228; Maximum: 365 in 1980; Minimum: 100 in 1995. **CBC Maximum:** 43, Cumberland, 1979.

CBC Totals 1976-1997
Brown Creeper

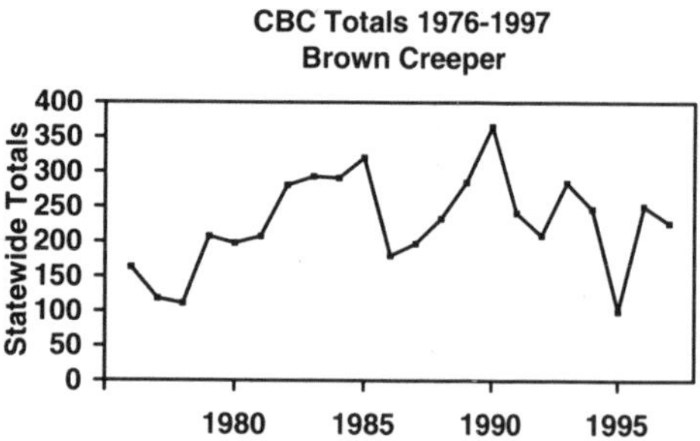

Spring: Brown Creepers move north in early April, with most having passed through by the end of the month. **Maxima:** 7, Garret Mt., 14 April 1996; 7, Turkey Swamp Park, 7 April 1984. ■

Rock Wren

Salpinctes obsoletus

Range: Breeds from southern British Columbia east to southern Saskatchewan, south to California and western Texas. Winters from California east to Texas, south to Central America.

NJ Status: Accidental. NJBRC Review List.

Occurrence: There has been only one report and one accepted record of Rock Wren in New Jersey: Cape May Point, 2 December 1992-31 March 1993 (phs-RNJB 19:1, 19:48). ■

Carolina Wren

Thryothorus ludovicianus

Range: Resident from southeastern Nebraska east to Massachusetts, south to central Texas and Florida.

NJ Status: Common and widespread resident.

Breeding

Habitat: Nests in the tangles of undergrowth in mixed or deciduous woods, along woodland edges and in gardens; also uses items commonly found in yards, such as flower pots, shelves in barns, etc.

Carolina Wrens have been established breeding birds in southern New Jersey throughout the 20th century (Stone 1908, Boyle 1986). Historically their range north of the Piedmont has been variable. Fables (1955) described a range remarkably similar to that found by the Atlas volunteers, although he was writing at a time when they were recolonizing northwestern New Jersey. Carolina Wren populations flourish during strings of mild winters, only to have their numbers severely diminished during harsh winters. Although those changes can be seen statewide, they are most apparent in the northern part of the state.

The distribution of Carolina Wrens found during the Atlas surveys showed a population that had profited by mild

continued on page 444

continued from page 443

Carolina Wren

winter conditions during the early 1990s. They were well distributed in most provinces, occupying over 58% of the blocks in each provinces with the exception of the Kittatinny Mountains. The wide distribution found during the surveys, combined with steadily increasing numbers on CBCs (see below), may indicate that they were near a historic high in abundance during the early Atlas survey period. A series

Possible
Probable
Confirmed

Statewide Summary	
Status	# of Blocks
Possible	126
Probable	220
Confirmed	202
Total	548

Map Interpretation: Carolina Wrens are quite vocal and easy to detect. Like the other wrens that breed in New Jersey, Carolina Wrens may build dummy nests. This eliminated the use of one of the most frequently used Confirmation codes (nest building). This may have lowered the Confirmation rate for this species.

Physiographic Distribution

Carolina Wren	Number of blocks in province	Number of blocks species found breeding in province	Number of blocks species found in state	Percent of province species occupies	Percent of all records for this species found in province	Percent of state area in province
Kittatinny Mountains	19	6	548	31.6	1.1	2.2
Kittatinny Valley	45	28	548	62.2	5.1	5.3
Highlands	109	71	548	65.1	13.0	12.8
Piedmont	167	103	548	61.7	18.8	19.6
Inner Coastal Plain	128	101	548	78.9	18.4	15.0
Outer Coastal Plain	204	134	548	65.7	24.5	23.9
Pine Barrens	180	105	548	58.3	19.2	21.1

Carolina Wren

continued

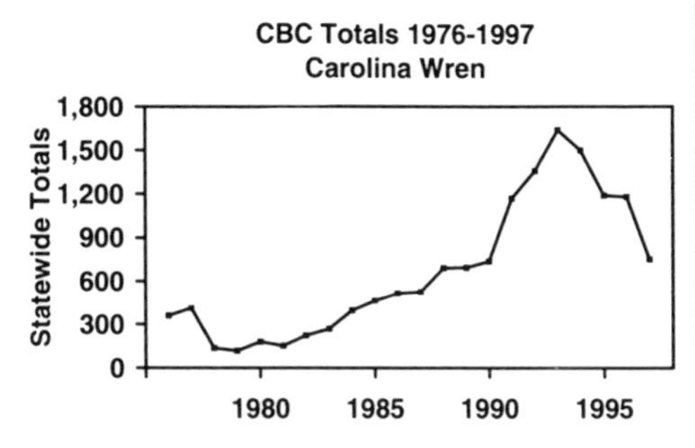

of harsh winters late in the Atlas period caused them to retreat from some areas of northwestern New Jersey (T. Halliwell, pers., com.). From 1994 to 1997 few Carolina Wrens were found there.

Fall: Carolina Wrens are nonmigratory, permanent residents. There is no published information on the occurrence of fall migration of Carolina Wrens in New Jersey.

Winter: The overall population of Carolina Wrens is reduced in severe winters, particularly in the northern part of the state. Statewide CBC totals show a steady increase from the late 1970s to a peak in 1993, but counts have dropped since then. **CBC Statewide Stats:** Average: 667; Maximum: 1,639 in 1993; Minimum: 118 in 1979. **CBC Maximum:** 383, Cape May, 1996.

Spring: There is no published information on the occurrence of spring migration of Carolina Wrens in New Jersey. ■

Bewick's Wren

Thryomanes bewickii

Range: Breeds in the East from Oklahoma and Texas north to eastern Iowa, southern Missouri, and Kentucky. Winters in the southern breeding range.

NJ Status: Accidental. NJBRC Review List.

Occurrence: There have been eight state reports of Bewick's Wren, and five have been accepted by NJBRC (two in spring, two in fall, one in summer). There have been no reports in recent decades, and given their severe range contraction in the East, future regular occurrence is unlikely. The five accepted records are:

Sunrise Mt.#	*20 April 1958*	
Cape May Point	*13 October 1962*	*banded*
West Orange	*June 1964*	
*Island Beach**	*11 October 1969*	*banded*
Island Beach	*4 May 1977*	*ph-NJA/RNJB 3:201, banded*

House Wren

Troglodytes aedon

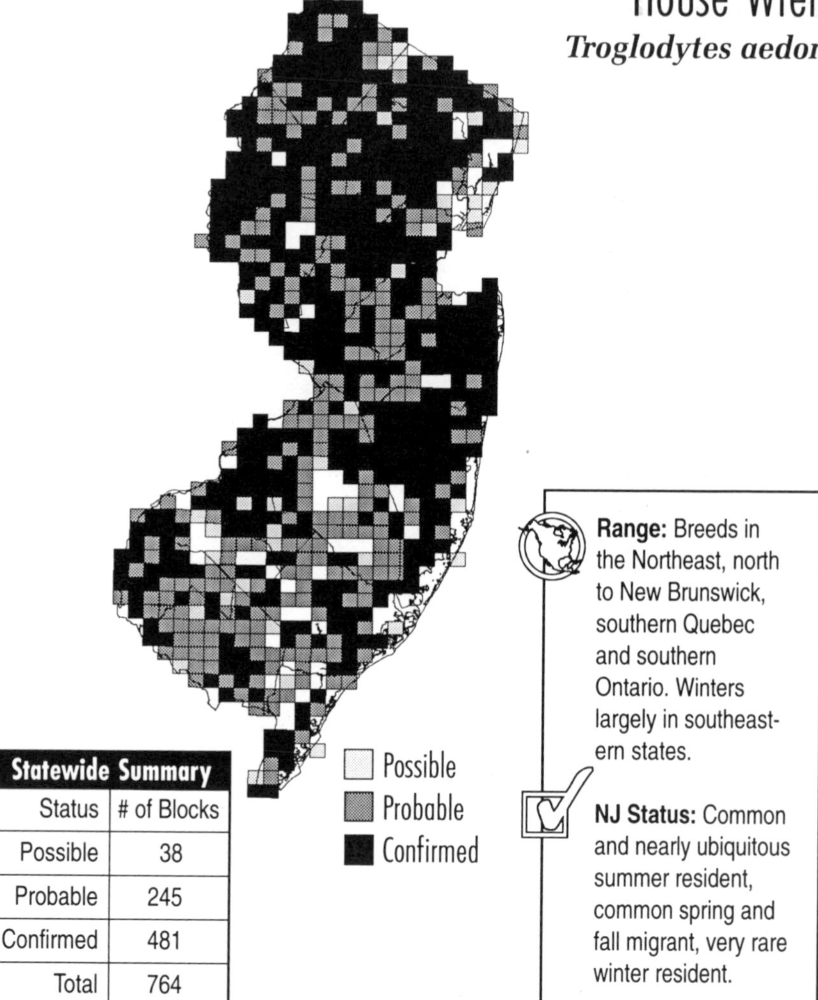

Statewide Summary	
Status	# of Blocks
Possible	38
Probable	245
Confirmed	481
Total	764

Range: Breeds in the Northeast, north to New Brunswick, southern Quebec and southern Ontario. Winters largely in southeastern states.

NJ Status: Common and nearly ubiquitous summer resident, common spring and fall migrant, very rare winter resident.

Physiographic Distribution

House Wren	Number of blocks in province	Number of blocks species found breeding in province	Number of blocks species found in state	Percent of province species occupies	Percent of all records for this species found in province	Percent of state area in province
Kittatinny Mountains	19	19	764	100.0	2.5	2.2
Kittatinny Valley	45	45	764	100.0	5.9	5.3
Highlands	109	107	764	98.2	14.0	12.8
Piedmont	167	150	764	89.8	19.6	19.6
Inner Coastal Plain	128	125	764	97.7	16.4	15.0
Outer Coastal Plain	204	160	764	78.4	20.9	23.9
Pine Barrens	180	158	764	87.8	20.7	21.1

House Wren

continued

Breeding

Habitat: Breeds most often in edge habitat altered by man such as backyards, farms, orchards, etc., where artificial cavities are often utilized, including pots, porches, and bird houses.

House Wrens suffered a period of decline toward the end of the 19th and early 20th centuries (Stone 1908), possibly as a result of competition for nest sites with House Sparrows (Kaufman 1996). However, by 1937 House Wrens had regained their former widespread status (Stone 1937). A similar increase in population was noted in Pennsylvania and was attributed to an increase in nest boxes (Schutsky 1992).

Statewide, House Wrens were found in 90% of the blocks and Confirmed in 63% of the blocks in which they were found. They were conspicuously absent from the barrier islands south of Monmouth County, but otherwise they were broadly distributed throughout the rest of the state.

Fall: Southbound movement of House Wrens begins in August and peak numbers are reached in September. By mid-October only stragglers remain in northern New Jersey. A low-density migration continues into November in the southern part of the state. **Maxima:** 25, Sandy Hook, 3 September 1978; 10, Higbee Beach, 14 October 1989.

Winter: House Wrens are usually found on at least one CBC; in mild Decembers there may be several reports. Although there are records of birds surviving the winter, they do so very rarely, and usually only in the southern part of the state. **CBC Statewide Stats:** Average: 5; Maximum: 17 in 1997; Minimum: 0 in three years. **CBC Maximum:** 3, five different counts.

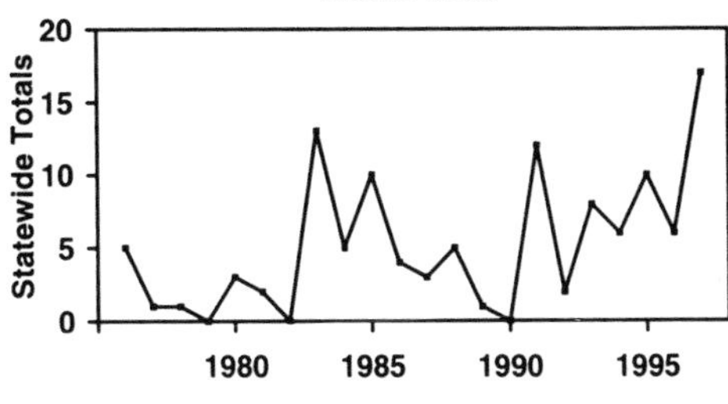

Spring: Northbound House Wrens are usually noted in mid-April. Migration peaks in late April and continues to mid-May; it levels off as resident birds stake out territories. ■

Winter Wren

Troglodytes troglodytes

Physiographic Distribution **Winter Wren**	Number of blocks in province	Number of blocks species found breeding in province	Number of blocks species found in state	Percent of province species occupies	Percent of all records for this species found in province	Percent of state area in province
Kittatinny Mountains	19	7	38	36.8	18.4	2.2
Kittatinny Valley	45	5	38	11.1	13.2	5.3
Highlands	109	19	38	17.4	50.0	12.8
Piedmont	167	7	38	4.2	18.4	19.6

Range: In eastern North America breeds from central Manitoba east to Newfoundland, south to central Wisconsin and northern New Jersey and along the Appalachians to Georgia. Winters throughout most of the central and southeastern United States.

NJ Status: Scarce and local summer resident, scarce to uncommon spring and uncommon fall migrant, uncommon winter resident.

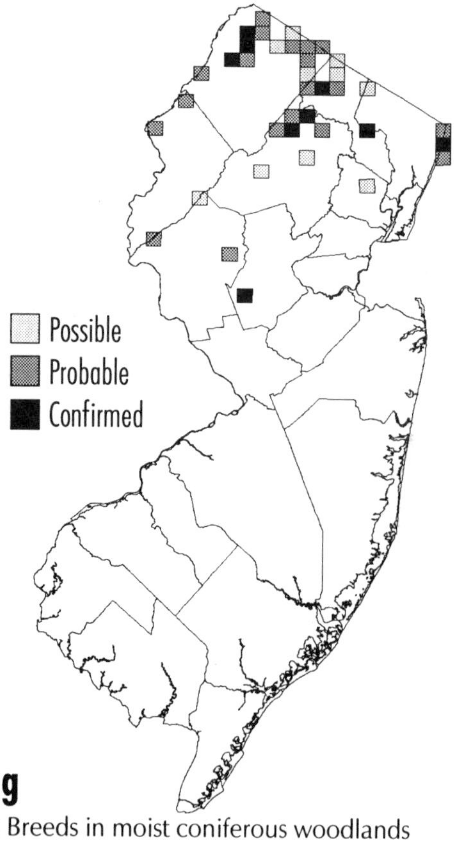

Possible
Probable
Confirmed

Statewide Summary	
Status	# of Blocks
Possible	10
Probable	19
Confirmed	9
Total	38

Breeding

Habitat: Breeds in moist coniferous woodlands with thick understory, often on talus slopes.

Cruickshank (1942) described Winter Wrens as transients and winter residents. He predicted that a few might someday be found breeding in the mountains of northwestern New Jersey. Singing males were,

Winter Wren

continued

in fact, found in the early 1950s at Bearfort Mountain, Passaic County, and at Green Pond Mountain, Morris County (Fables 1955). The first confirmation of breeding Winter Wrens occurred in June of 1962 at Lake Girard, Sussex County, with an adult feeding three young (Bull 1964). By 1986, Boyle described their breeding status as rare and local in the mountainous northwest.

Winter Wrens were found breeding in only 38 blocks over the five years of data collection, and their range was restricted to only a small section of the state. All of the breeding Winter Wrens were found from the Piedmont northward, and 82% were found in the Kittatinny Valley, Kittatinny Mountains, and Highlands – an area comprising only 20% of the state. There were two isolated breeding pockets of Winter Wrens found along the Delaware River in Sussex and Warren counties, and along the Hudson River in Bergen County.

Fall: Southbound Winter Wrens are scarce before late September, with peak numbers passing from mid- to late October into early November. They are shy and reclusive and normally found by their call note. **Maxima:** 40+, Cape Island, 5 November 1995; 30+, Sandy Hook, 23 October 1998.

Winter: Winter Wrens are shy and solitary in winter. Numbers are dependent upon the severity of the weather. This is generally reflected in the variability of statewide CBC totals, but counts show an increase in the mid-1990s. **CBC Statewide Stats:** Average: 57; Maximum: 167 in 1997; Minimum: 22 in 1979. **CBC Maximum:** 40, Cape May, 1997.

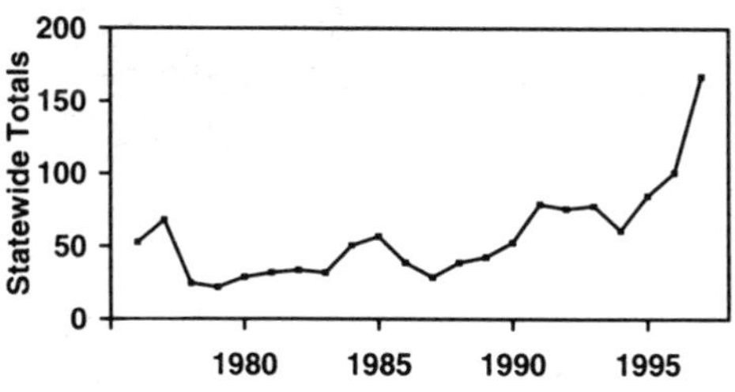

Spring: Small movements of northbound Winter Wrens are noted from late March through early April, with few still present by the end of April. **Maxima:** 8, West Cape May, 27 March 1992; 7, Higbee Beach, 18 April 1992. ■

Sedge Wren

Cistothorus platensis

Breeding

Habitat: Moist meadows of grass and/or sedge with a few scattered bushes. Historically the upland edge of salt marsh has been a preferred nesting zone.

Sedge Wrens are extremely rare and occur only sporadically as breeding birds in New Jersey. Although always uncommon, they have almost disappeared

continued on page 450

continued from page 449

Sedge Wren

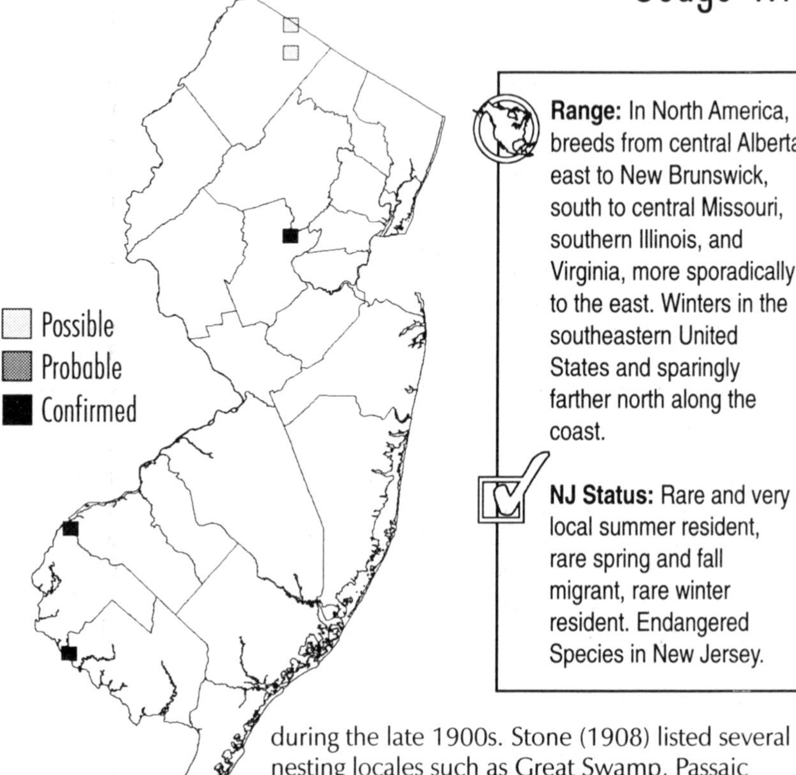

Range: In North America, breeds from central Alberta east to New Brunswick, south to central Missouri, southern Illinois, and Virginia, more sporadically to the east. Winters in the southeastern United States and sparingly farther north along the coast.

NJ Status: Rare and very local summer resident, rare spring and fall migrant, rare winter resident. Endangered Species in New Jersey.

Statewide Summary	
Status	# of Blocks
Possible	2
Probable	0
Confirmed	3
Total	5

during the late 1900s. Stone (1908) listed several nesting locales such as Great Swamp, Passaic Meadows near Chatham, Wallkill Valley, along the Delaware Bay, and in Salem County. Stone (1937) reported Sedge Wrens from Cape May, Burlington, Salem, Morris and Sussex counties, and Fables (1955) recorded them in Essex County. During the summer of 1947, eight nests were reported from Troy Meadows, but the same locale hosted no nests by 1962 (Bull 1964). Sedge Wrens are opportunistic breeding birds – several years may pass with no breeding records in the state, only to have a small

Physiographic Distribution Sedge Wren	Number of blocks in province	Number of blocks species found breeding in province	Number of blocks species found in state	Percent of province species occupies	Percent of all records for this species found in province	Percent of state area in province
Kittatinny Valley	45	1	5	2.2	20.0	5.3
Highlands	109	1	5	0.9	20.0	12.8
Piedmont	167	1	5	0.6	20.0	19.6
Inner Coastal Plain	128	1	5	0.8	20.0	15.0
Outer Coastal Plain	204	1	5	0.5	20.0	23.9

Sedge Wren
continued

colony discovered in a location subject to regular scrutiny. The next year there may be no wrens again. Their overall decline has been linked to draining of wetlands and succession. There does appear to be some appropriate habitat remaining, but few Sedge Wrens to occupy it.

Atlas participants recorded Sedge Wrens in only one location each year, and Confirmed the species only three times. The species is difficult to detect, nomadic, and may breed relatively late in the season – all characteristics that may contribute to their being overlooked. They are declining over much of their range in the eastern United States (Kaufman 1996), and protection for Sedge Wrens is difficult owing to the ephemeral nature of their preferred breeding habitats.

Fall: Sedge Wrens may occur in any month, but the fall migration "peak" appears to be in October. They are most often found along the southern coast and Delaware Bay shore, especially at the upper edge of the salt marsh, and are very rarely found inland. The species is notoriously irregular in occurrence and often inconsistent in its arrival times.

Winter: Most Sedge Wrens are reported from December to January. They were formerly more common in winter, as evidenced by the reduced CBC totals in recent years. The Cape May CBC had three double-figure counts in the 1930s, with a high of 16 in 1934. On counts from 1965 to 1992 the Cape May count averaged one every four years (Sibley 1997). **Winter Maxima:** 5, Turkey Point, 1 January-February 1992; 3-6, Brigantine NWR, 30 November-December 1980. **CBC Statewide Stats:** Average: 1; Maximum: 9 in 1992; Minimum: 0 in 12 years. **CBC Maximum:** 6, Cumberland, 1992.

Spring: Sedge Wrens are rarely encountered in spring, most often in late April and May. ■

Marsh Wren
Cistothorus palustris

Range: Breeds across North America from southern Canada south to the central United States. Disjunct populations nest farther south, especially along the coasts. Winters in Mexico and the southern United States, very rarely farther north along the coasts.

NJ Status: Common but somewhat local summer resident, fairly common spring and fall migrant, rare to scarce winter resident.

Breeding

Habitat: Inland, nests in extensive cattail marshes or *Phragmites*. In coastal marshes they are less restricted, selecting Marsh Elder or tall marsh grasses, including *Spartina* and *Phragmites*.

continued on page 452

continued from page 451

Marsh Wren

Marsh Wren's habit of nesting in both freshwater and saltwater marshes has left New Jersey with one of the most robust populations compared to our neighboring states. A century ago, before the beginning of extensive draining of New Jersey's largest cattail marshes, Marsh Wrens were far more abundant inland than they are today, even enabling one collector to secure 400-500 eggs in a single day at Elizabeth (Stone 1937). Along with this inland population, the coastal population may have declined early in the 1900s, as Stone (1937) remarked that Marsh Wrens were the most reduced breeding bird in Cape May County. He related the decline to habitat destruction (e.g., draining of marshes for mosquito control and filling of marshes to create building lots). Fables (1955) indicated that although Marsh

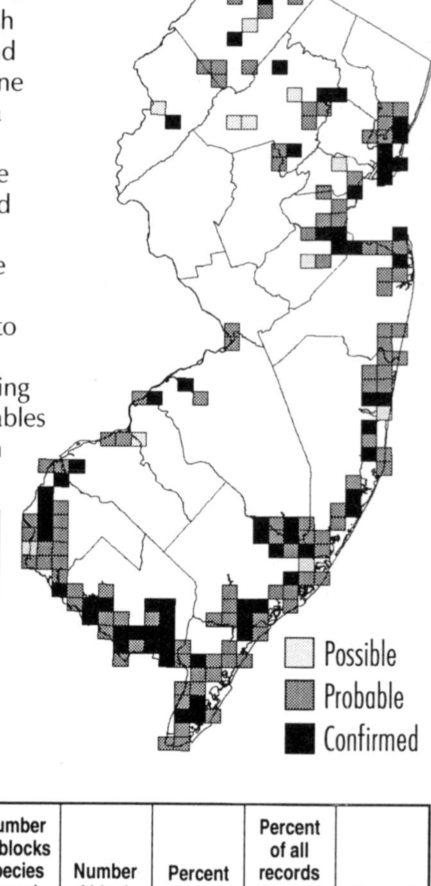

Statewide Summary	
Status	# of Blocks
Possible	11
Probable	108
Confirmed	68
Total	187

Physiographic Distribution Marsh Wren	Number of blocks in province	Number of blocks species found breeding in province	Number of blocks species found in state	Percent of province species occupies	Percent of all records for this species found in province	Percent of state area in province
Kittatinny Valley	45	14	187	31.1	7.5	5.3
Highlands	109	8	187	7.3	4.3	12.8
Piedmont	167	24	187	14.4	12.8	19.6
Inner Coastal Plain	128	31	187	24.2	16.6	15.0
Outer Coastal Plain	204	95	187	46.6	50.8	23.9
Pine Barrens	180	15	187	8.3	8.0	21.1

Wrens were still common, they were declining due to habitat loss. A 1984 census of Troy Meadows found 64 pairs, where a 1947 count had found 160 (Kane 1985).

Atlas data indicated that Marsh Wrens nest in a high percentage of the coastal blocks from Trenton to Jersey City. These core populations of coastal nesting birds extend inland along watersheds that flow into the Delaware River and Atlantic coastal bays. This coastal population may act as a source population for populating freshwater and brackish marshes "upstream" (i.e., the Hackensack, Mullica, Great Egg, Maurice, Cohansey, and Salem rivers, and Rancocas Creek). "Land-locked" populations of Marsh Wrens in New Jersey are few, and remain centered at some of the state's premier freshwater wetlands: the Wallkill River Valley, Great Swamp, Troy Meadows, and Vernon Crossing Marsh.

Fall: Marsh Wrens are rarely seen away from their breeding habitat. The greater part of the autumn movement takes place from September through early October. Marsh Wrens are unexpected in northern New Jersey after October, although low density movement continues through the fall in the south-coastal region. In the 1920s and 1930s, flights of about 100 birds were noted at Cape May in late September-early October (Stone 1937). Recent years have produced nothing of this magnitude (Sibley 1997).

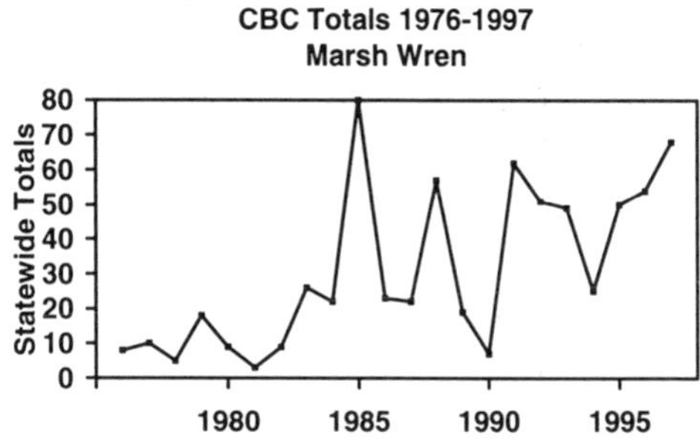

Winter: Marsh Wrens are more regular in the southern part of the state in winter than in the north, where they are rare. A few stragglers are usually found in the north through December, but they do not normally survive the winter. In southern New Jersey, Marsh Wren numbers may be depleted by winter's end, but the winter must be unusually severe for all to succumb. CBC numbers are variable, but have increased markedly since the early 1980s. **CBC Statewide Stats:** Average: 31; Maximum: 80 in 1985; Minimum: 3 in 1981. **CBC Maximum:** 47, Cape May, 1985.

Spring: Northbound Marsh Wrens are not expected before late April. Often it is mid-May before birds arrive in northern New Jersey. As in fall, there is no discernible peak to the flight. ■

Golden-crowned Kinglet

Regulus satrapa

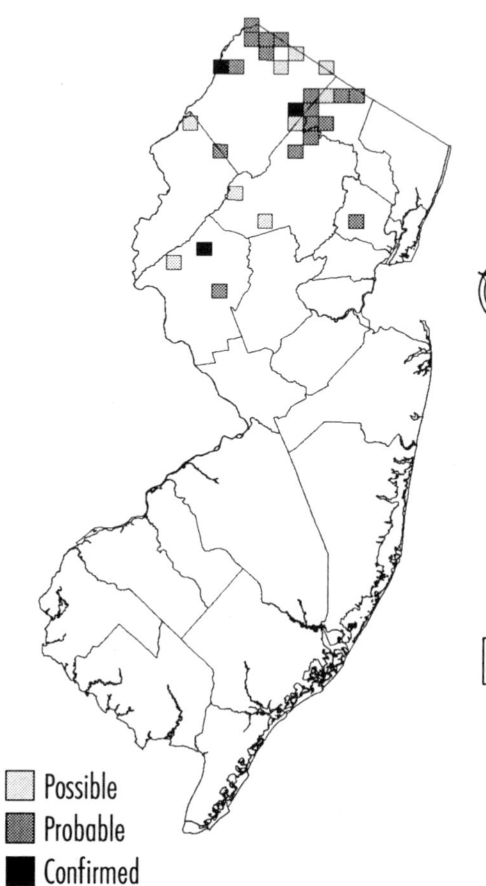

Statewide Summary	
Status	# of Blocks
Possible	9
Probable	17
Confirmed	3
Total	29

Range: In eastern North America breeds from Manitoba east to Newfoundland, south to northern Illinois, northern New Jersey and along the Appalachians to North Carolina. Winters from the southern part of the breeding range south to Texas and Florida.

NJ Status: Scarce and local summer resident, fairly common spring and common fall migrant, uncommon to fairly common winter resident.

Breeding

Habitat: Nests in dense coniferous woods, particularly spruce, fir, and hemlock.

The first nesting of Golden-crowned Kinglets in New Jersey occurred in 1971 at Vernon, Sussex County, when ten pairs, four of them feeding young, were discovered in the Norway Spruce groves. Additional pairs were found nesting in other spruce groves in 1972 (Kane and Marx 1972). A range extension into New Jersey and southern New York followed the maturation of Norway Spruce planted for watershed protection in the 1930s (Andrle 1971, Kane 1973). The mature spruces create a moist, cool micro-climate usually available only at higher elevations (Kane 1973). By 1986, Boyle considered Golden-crowned Kinglets to be rare and local breeding birds.

Physiographic Distribution Golden-crowned Kinglet	Number of blocks in province	Number of blocks species found breeding in province	Number of blocks species found in state	Percent of province species occupies	Percent of all records for this species found in province	Percent of state area in province
Kittatinny Mountains	19	6	29	31.6	20.7	2.2
Kittatinny Valley	45	5	29	11.1	17.2	5.3
Highlands	109	16	29	14.7	55.2	12.8
Piedmont	167	2	29	1.2	6.9	19.6

Atlas surveys showed that Golden-crowned Kinglets were still one of the scarcest, regularly occurring nesting songbirds in the state. Observers located Golden-crowned Kinglets in only 29 blocks over the five years of surveys, and they were classed as Possible in nine of those blocks. Most were found in the Kittatinny Mountains and on the Waywayanda Plateau of the northern Highlands. It has been suggested that Golden-crowned Kinglets may be decreasing in northern New Jersey spruce groves because of competition with Blackburnian Warblers (Harrison 1993), as the warblers had been noted harassing the kinglets. The suggestion that Blackburnian Warblers may exclude Golden-crowned Kinglets from a nesting area warrants further study.

Fall: The first southbound Golden-crowned Kinglets are encountered in late September with peak numbers moving from mid- to late October. The number of migrants can vary from year to year. In Massachusetts, Veit and Petersen (1993) attribute this to two factors: birds may stay north when food supplies are good, or numbers may be reduced when previous winters were especially severe. **Maxima:** 1,000s, Higbee Beach, 30 October 1988; 1,000s, Higbee Beach, 23 October 1989; 1,000s, Sandy Hook, 19 October 1991.

Winter: The relative abundance of Golden-crowned Kinglets in winter is also variable and for the same reasons as in fall. This is reflected in the statewide range of CBC numbers. **CBC Statewide Stats:** Average:729; Maximum: 1,445 in 1985; Minimum: 121 in 1978. **CBC Maximum:** 218, Cape May, 1997.

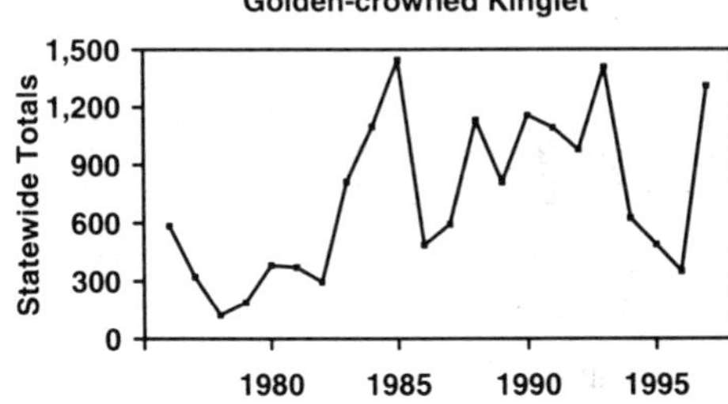

Spring: Return flights of Golden-crowned Kinglets are early, usually peaking from late March through mid-April. Nearly all have moved on by early May. **Maxima:** 200+, Cape May Point, 22 March 1991; 100s, Upper Montclair, 14 April 1992. ■

Ruby-crowned Kinglet

Regulus calendula

Range: Breeds in the mountains of the West and across boreal North America from Alaska to Labrador. In the East, nests south to northern New York and rarely to Massachusetts. Winters in Mexico and the southern United States north along the Atlantic coast very rarely to Massachusetts.

NJ Status: Common spring and fall migrant, scarce winter resident.

Fall: Ruby-crowned Kinglets arrive in numbers in late September, although individuals have appeared as early as late August. Colossal flights sometimes occur along the coast during mid- to late October. Numbers gradually diminish throughout the remainder of the fall. **Maxima:** 5000+, Sandy Hook, 23 October 1989; 1,000s, Higbee Beach, 30 October 1988.

Winter: CBC totals for Ruby-crowned Kinglets are variable, depending on the severity of the weather prior to and during the count period. In southern New Jersey, Ruby-crowned Kinglets successfully winter, though in small numbers. In the north they are regular through December, but only in mild winters do they survive the season. Early in the century, wintering birds were quite rare anywhere in the state. **CBC Statewide Stats:** Average: 86; Maximum: 191 in 1985; Minimum: 29 in 1978. **CBC Maximum:** 26, Cape May, 1993.

CBC Totals 1976-1997
Ruby-crowned Kinglet

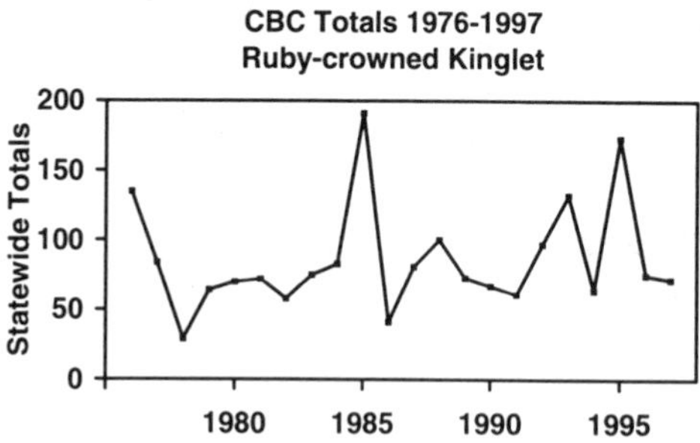

Spring: Northbound Ruby-crowned Kinglets are more common inland than along the coast. Numbers build from late March to a maximum from mid-April to early May. After mid-May only rare stragglers are found; so a Ruby-crowned Kinglet seen 17-18 June 1998 in Cape May Point is difficult to explain. **Maxima:** 100s Upper Montclair, 14 April 1992; 100s, Princeton, 2 May 1987. ■

Blue-gray Gnatcatcher

Polioptila caerulea

Range: In the eastern United States breeds from Minnesota to Maine, south to Texas and Florida. Winters from the southeastern United States south to Central America.

NJ Status: Fairly common and widespread summer resident, common spring and fall migrant, reported on seven CBCs.

Possible
Probable
Confirmed

Breeding

Habitat: Nests in successional and older growth deciduous forest.

In the first decade of the 20th century, Blue-gray Gnatcatchers were rare and local as breeding birds, even in southern New Jersey (Stone 1908). Only two Blue-gray Gnatcatcher nests had been found by 1910, and specimens were only known north to Princeton. The first breeding record for northern New Jersey was from Swartswood Lake in 1928,

continued on page 458

Statewide Summary

Status	# of Blocks
Possible	67
Probable	183
Confirmed	276
Total	526

Physiographic Distribution

Blue-gray Gnatcatcher	Number of blocks in province	Number of blocks species found breeding in province	Number of blocks species found in state	Percent of province species occupies	Percent of all records for this species found in province	Percent of state area in province
Kittatinny Mountains	19	19	526	100.0	3.6	2.2
Kittatinny Valley	45	42	526	93.3	8.0	5.3
Highlands	109	100	526	91.7	19.0	12.8
Piedmont	167	83	526	49.7	15.8	19.6
Inner Coastal Plain	128	43	526	33.6	8.2	15.0
Outer Coastal Plain	204	107	526	52.5	20.3	23.9
Pine Barrens	180	132	526	73.3	25.1	21.1

continued from page 457

Blue-gray Gnatcatcher

although no further nesting was documented until 1946 (Bull 1964). This range expansion was a part of a broader range expansion for this species taking place in eastern North America (Ellison 1992).

Atlas data showed Blue-gray Gnatcatchers have dramatically increased to the point where they are now found in 62% of the blocks statewide. North of the Piedmont, they were found in 90% or more of the blocks in the Kittatinny Valley, Kittatinny Mountains, and Highlands. They were found in 73% of the Pine Barrens blocks, where they are using patches of deciduous trees within that province. Their distribution closely follows the regions of New Jersey with good forest cover. Like other forest obligates, Blue-gray Gnatcatchers were conspicuous in their absence from the barrier islands and saltmarsh edges of the Outer Coastal Plain, from much of the Inner Coastal Plain, and from the highly urbanized northeastern section of the Piedmont.

Fall: Movements of Blue-gray Gnatcatchers may begin before August, with notable flights occurring from mid-August through September. After mid-October only the very rare straggler is found. **Maxima:** 123, Higbee Beach, 22 August 1988 (Sibley 1997); 93, Higbee Beach, 11 September 1988 (Sibley 1997).

Winter: There are a number of reports of Blue-gray Gnatcatcher in December, and they were reported on seven CBCs between 1976 and 1997. Individuals are not known to successfully winter.

Spring: Blue-gray Gnatcatchers are early northbound migrants, although not expected before April. Peak flights occur from mid-April through early May. **Maxima:** 50+, Hidden Valley Ranch, 15 April 1997; 35, Bull's Island, 26 April 1986. ■

Northern Wheatear

Oenanthe oenanthe

Range: In North America breeds in Alaska and east across northern Canada south to northern Quebec and Labrador. Winters in Asia and Africa.

NJ Status: Very rare. NJBRC Review List.

Occurrence: There have been 18 state reports of Northern Wheatears, and 13 have been accepted by the NJBRC (12 in fall, one in

Northern Wheatear

continued

spring). Of the 12 fall records, 11 are in September and October. The 13 accepted records are:

Cape May Point#	*7-14 October 1951*	
Brigantine NWR	*19 September-11 October 1970*	*ph-RBPF*
Brigantine NWR	*1 October 1974*	
Cape May Point	*23 September 1978*	
Thompson's Beach	*1 June 1981*	*ph-RNJB 7:73*
Cape May Point	*27-28 September 1981*	*ph-RNJB 8:17*
Brigantine NWR	*8-15 October 1983*	*ph-RNJB 10:1*
*Cape May**	*12 November 1985*	
Cape May Point	*11 September 1988*	*phs-RNJB 15:1, 15:19*
Rosedale Park	*8-11 September 1993*	*ph-RNJB 20:22*
North Wildwood	*6-11 October 1995*	*ph RNJB 22:20*
Sergeantsville	*30 September 1996*	
Cape May Point	*5 October 1996*	*phs-RBPF*

Eastern Bluebird

Sialia sialis

Range: Breeds from southern Manitoba east to Nova Scotia, south to Texas and Florida. Winters north to southern New England.

NJ Status: Fairly common and widespread summer resident, fairly common spring and common fall migrant, uncommon winter resident.

Breeding

Habitat: Nests in cavities, both natural and man-made, on woodland edge habitats, especially farmland and open swamps with standing dead trees.

Eastern Bluebirds have long been widespread breeding birds throughout New Jersey, although their numbers have declined during the 20th century. In 1908, Stone was already lamenting that bluebirds were one of the "chief sufferers" from competition with House Sparrows for nesting cavities. Eventually, European Starlings became major competitors (Griscom 1923, Fables 1955). Fables (1955) wrote that numbers were still decreasing, but noted that erecting nest boxes could aid Eastern Bluebirds in their struggle to find suitable nesting sites. However, it was some time

continued on page 460

continued from page 459

Eastern Bluebird

before that practice became common. Consequently, the presence of both House Sparrows and European Starlings served to limit Eastern Bluebird's access to nest cavities, except in more remote swamps, on open ridgetops, and Pine Barrens openings (Kane 1982b). Eastern Bluebird "trails," a series of boxes erected specifically for bluebirds, eventually became more common and widespread. As a result of these extensive nest box programs, the number of nesting Eastern Bluebirds has rebounded dramatically.

Atlas volunteers found Eastern Bluebirds in 53% of the blocks statewide, although there were some large, contiguous areas without bluebirds. They were well distributed in northern New Jersey where they were located in 91% of the blocks north of the Piedmont. They were generally absent from the eastern Piedmont, most of which is urbanized, from much of the Inner Coastal Plain,

Possible
Probable
Confirmed

Statewide Summary	
Status	# of Blocks
Possible	46
Probable	89
Confirmed	317
Total	452

Physiographic Distribution Eastern Bluebird	Number of blocks in province	Number of blocks species found breeding in province	Number of blocks species found in state	Percent of province species occupies	Percent of all records for this species found in province	Percent of state area in province
Kittatinny Mountains	19	19	452	100.0	4.2	2.2
Kittatinny Valley	45	45	452	100.0	10.0	5.3
Highlands	109	95	452	87.2	21.0	12.8
Piedmont	167	79	452	47.3	17.5	19.6
Inner Coastal Plain	128	25	452	19.5	5.5	15.0
Outer Coastal Plain	204	75	452	36.8	16.6	23.9
Pine Barrens	180	114	452	63.3	25.2	21.1

Eastern Bluebird

continued

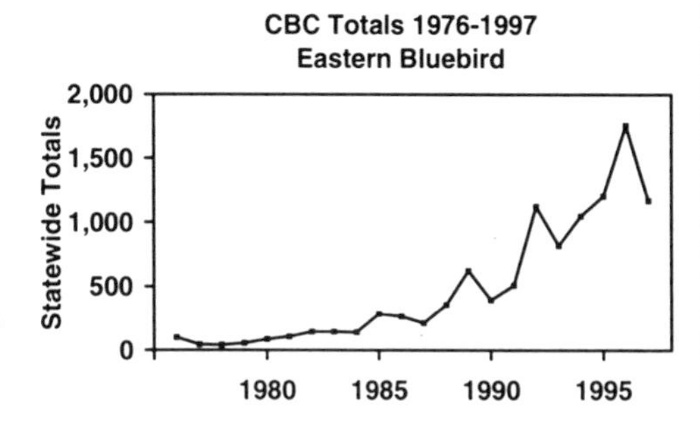

and from much of the Atlantic Coast. Elsewhere, Eastern Bluebirds were present in 63% of the Pine Barrens blocks and were well established in Salem, Cumberland, and Cape May counties. The major factors controlling the distribution of these birds seem to be suitable habitat for nesting and a low density of humans. Eastern Bluebirds were Confirmed at a high rate (70%), as most nests are located in easy-to-find nest boxes.

Fall: Eastern Bluebird migration is usually underway by early October, and peaks from late October to mid-November. At the peak of migration large flights may occur at coastal watches. **Maxima:** 2,500+, Cape May, 13 November 1992; 1,000s, Higbee Beach, 6 November 1993.

Winter: As the population of Eastern Bluebird has recovered, numbers have begun to increase on CBCs. Numbers in the 1990s have shown notable increases. In mild winters the species may be locally common in favored habitats. **CBC Statewide Stats:** Average: 484; Maximum: 1,754 in 1996; Minimum: 40 in 1978. **CBC Maximum:** 223, Belleplain, 1992.

Spring: Northward migration of Eastern Bluebirds begins in February, appears to peak in March, with some birds continuing to move in April. They are seen in much smaller concentrations than those of fall. **Maximum:** 40, Cape May Court House, 5 March 1980. ■

Mountain Bluebird

Sialia currucoides

Range: Breeds in western Canada and western United States east to the western Dakotas, south to California, New Mexico, and Arizona. Winters in western states and Mexico.

NJ Status: Accidental. NJBRC Review List.

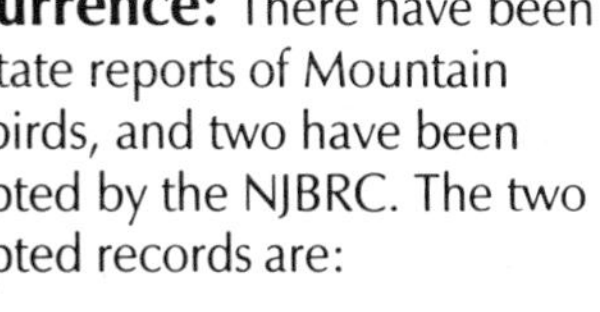

Occurrence: There have been five state reports of Mountain Bluebirds, and two have been accepted by the NJBRC. The two accepted records are:

Brigantine NWR	*21 November 1982*	*phs-RNJB 9:14, 9:15*
Higbee Beach	*12 November 1988*	

Townsend's Solitaire

Myadestes townsendi

Range: Breeds from southern Alaska through western Canada, south to California, Arizona, and New Mexico, and east to Colorado. Winters in southwestern Canada and the western United States east to southwestern Saskatchewan and western Texas.

NJ Status: Accidental. NJBRC Review List.

Occurrence: There have been five state reports of Townsend's Solitaires, and four have been accepted by the NJBRC (all in fall). Three of the records are from the Kittatinny Ridge, the other from the Highlands. The four accepted records are:

Sunrise Mt.	*17 November-14 December 1980*
Mt. Tabor	*19 October 1981*
Sunrise Mt.	*15 November 1987*
Raccoon Ridge	*18 November 1989*

Veery

Catharus fuscescens

Range: In eastern North America breeds from southern Manitoba east to southern Newfoundland, south to Iowa, New Jersey, and along the Appalachians to northern Georgia. Winters in South America.

NJ Status: Fairly common and fairly widespread summer resident, uncommon spring and common fall migrant.

Breeding

Habitat: Nests in moist deciduous woodlands and wooded swamps.

Stone (1908) described Veeries as "common summer residents" in the northern counties, a fact echoed by succeeding authors, including Boyle (1986), who termed them "very common." Fables (1955) suggested that Veeries nested as far south as Monmouth County, and Leck (1984) also found evidence of summering birds in Monmouth County. Unfortu-

Veery
continued

nately, Breeding Bird Survey data indicated that Veeries are declining across the continent (Moskoff 1995).

Atlas results from the northern part of the state indicated Veeries occupied 94% of the blocks north of the Piedmont and were found in 57% of the blocks within that province. They were largely absent from the highly urbanized northeastern section of the state, and they remain scarce or absent from the southernmost counties. Atlas data suggested that Veeries have extended their range in southern New Jersey since Fables' (1955) and Leck's (1984) publications. Veeries were present in 18% of the blocks in the Pine Barrens, with
continued on page 464

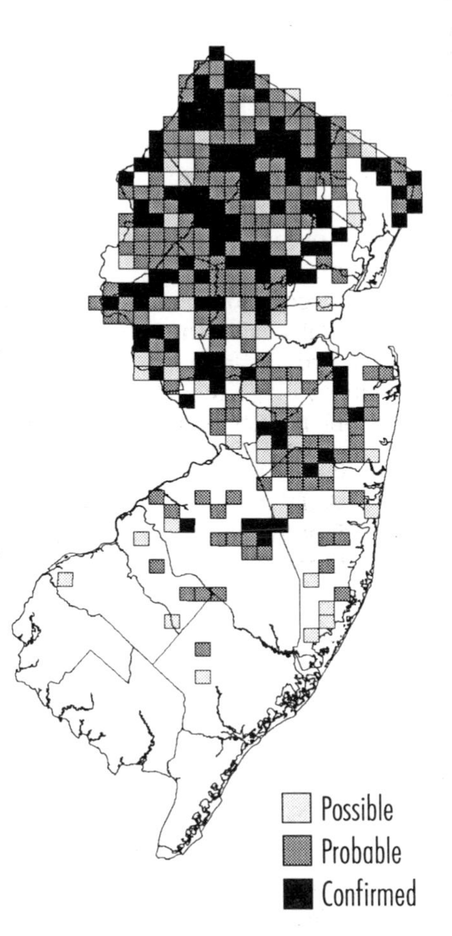

Statewide Summary	
Status	# of Blocks
Possible	46
Probable	184
Confirmed	123
Total	353

Physiographic Distribution

Veery	Number of blocks in province	Number of blocks species found breeding in province	Number of blocks species found in state	Percent of province species occupies	Percent of all records for this species found in province	Percent of state area in province
Kittatinny Mountains	19	19	353	100.0	5.4	2.2
Kittatinny Valley	45	38	353	84.4	10.8	5.3
Highlands	109	107	353	98.2	30.3	12.8
Piedmont	167	96	353	57.5	27.2	19.6
Inner Coastal Plain	128	35	353	27.3	9.9	15.0
Outer Coastal Plain	204	26	353	12.7	7.4	23.9
Pine Barrens	180	32	353	17.8	9.1	21.1

continued from page 463

many of the sightings in northern Ocean and central Burlington counties, although some were found as far south as central Atlantic County. Their presence in southern New Jersey goes beyond the Pine Barrens, however, as birds were also found on both the Inner and Outer Coastal Plain, north and west of the Pine Barrens.

Fall: Some southbound Veeries can be found in early August, but they become more common later in the month. They peak in early to mid-September, and a few linger into early October. They are vocal nocturnal migrants and are often heard overhead during the night. **Maxima:** 400, Higbee Beach, 4 September 1980; 100s, Higbee Beach, 8 September 1979.

Spring: Northbound Veeries are seen mainly in May, and rarely form any large concentrations. The maximum count listed below occurred during the night and was based on nocturnal flight calls. **Maxima:** 20, Villas, 15 May 1995 (heard); 15, Garret Mt., 12 May 1997. ■

Veery

Gray-cheeked Thrush

Catharus minimus

Range: In eastern North America, breeds from Hudson Bay east to Newfoundland. Winters in South America.

NJ Status: Scarce spring and uncommon fall migrant, reported on one CBC.

Historic Changes: Reports of Gray-cheeked Thrushes have declined in the past few decades. The pre-1970s literature regarded this species as a common or fairly common migrant – e.g., 53 were banded at Island Beach SP on 27 September 1963 (Leck 1984). Present-day observers are lucky if they see a few Gray-cheeked Thrushes in an entire season.

Fall: Gray-cheeked Thrushes are reclusive and inconspicuous migrants, generally seen from mid-September into early October. Like other thrushes, they are vocal nocturnal migrants, and nocturnal counts are actually a better indication of their movements than ground counts. The historic numbers cited above and the maxima listed below were counted prior to the 1996 split of Bicknell's Thrush and Gray-cheeked Thrush, and undoubtedly include some Bicknell's Thrushes. Although the two species cannot yet be separated reliably in the field by sight, they can be separated by voice. Most observers normally report only the complex, not the species. **Maxima:** 25, Higbee Beach, 23 September1983; 14, Higbee Beach, 7 October 1985 (banded).

Winter: Gray-cheeked Thrush was reported on the Sussex CBC in 1981, however no details were submitted and the sighting was questioned by the count editor (AB).

Spring: Most Gray-cheeked Thrushes are encountered from mid- to late May. They are less commonly encountered in spring than in fall, although maxima are similar. **Maximum:** 25, Villas, 15 May 1995 (heard). ■

Bicknell's Thrush

Catharus bicknelli

Range: Breeds on mountain tops from Quebec east to Nova Scotia south to central New York. Winters in the West Indies.

NJ Status: Poorly known, but probably a regular spring and fall migrant.

Fall: The status of Bicknell's Thrush in New Jersey, a recent (1996) split from Gray-cheeked Thrush, is poorly known. Field identification is very difficult unless a bird vocalizes. A small sampling of banding records from Cape May indicated that southward movement of Bicknell's Thrushes is similar to that of Gray-cheeked Thrushes, with several records from early October (P. Hodgetts, pers. com.). Sibley (1997) noted a sight record at Higbee Beach on 2 October 1994.

Spring: The timing of spring migration for Bicknell's Thrushes is probably similar to that of Gray-cheeked Thrushes. Sibley (1997) noted a sight record at Higbee Beach on 8-9 May 1984, seen in direct comparison with a gray-cheeked. In the spring of 1998, there were three reports of Bicknell's Thrushes on Cape May Island in mid-May, one of which was heard singing. ■

Swainson's Thrush

Catharus ustulatus

Fall: Swainson's Thrushes usually arrive in early September, and peak numbers occur from mid-September to early October. The species normally departs by mid-October. The highest numbers are noted by their nocturnal flight calls given while passing overhead, in both fall and spring. Formerly a common migrant – e.g., 700, Cape May Point, 1 October 1974 (AB) – most observers believe that the species declined during

Range: In eastern North America, breeds from Manitoba east to Newfoundland south to Wisconsin, Michigan, Pennsylvania, and West Virginia. Winters from Mexico to Argentina.

NJ Status: Uncommon spring and fall migrant, reported on five CBCs.

Swainson's Thrush
continued

the 1980s and 1990s. **Other maxima:** 100s, Bernardsville, 18 September 1982 (heard); 60, Higbee Beach, 23 September 1988 (Sibley 1997).

Winter: There are several reports of Swainson's Thrushes into early winter and they were reported on five CBCs between 1976 and 1997 (i.e., 1984, 1986, 1993, 1995, and 1996). The 1986 and 1993 reports included details that were noted as "thorough" and "good" respectively (AB). The others had less complete details, and confusion with Hermit Thrush is at least a possibility. There are no reports after the CBC season.

Spring: Swainson's Thrushes are unexpected before early May and after early June. Peak numbers occur from mid- to late May. Although they are uncommon statewide on northward migration, they are more common inland rather than along the coast. **Maxima:** 60, Jockey Hollow, 22 May 1975; 50+, Garrett Mt., 13 May 1987. ■

Hermit Thrush
Catharus guttatus

Range: In eastern North America breeds from Manitoba east to Newfoundland, south to central New Jersey, and south along the Appalachians to North Carolina. Winters from Oklahoma to Massachusetts south to Texas, Florida, and Mexico.

NJ Status: Scarce and local summer resident, fairly common spring and common fall migrant, uncommon winter resident.

Breeding

Habitat: Breeds in moist woodlands.

Stone (1908) suggested that Hermit Thrushes might "possibly be found to breed" in parts of Sussex County. It took 13 years before that prediction bore fruit, although it was in Passaic, not Sussex County, where a pair was found breeding on Bearfort Mountain in July 1921 (Griscom 1923). There is little information on further breeding until the first nest was discovered in June 1951 near Sunfish Pond, Warren County (Fables 1955). Fables identified additional breeding sites for Hermit Thrushes, noting ten singing males in Stokes State Forest and High Point State Park, Sussex County in 1954. Breeding Bird Survey data indicated that Hermit Thrushes are probably increasing over much of their North American range (Jones and Donovan 1996).

continued on page 468

continued from page 467

Hermit Thrush

Physiographic Distribution Hermit Thrush	Number of blocks in province	Number of blocks species found breeding in province	Number of blocks species found in state	Percent of province species occupies	Percent of all records for this species found in province	Percent of state area in province
Kittatinny Mountains	19	17	83	89.5	20.5	2.2
Kittatinny Valley	45	14	83	31.1	16.9	5.3
Highlands	109	30	83	27.5	36.1	12.8
Piedmont	167	2	83	1.2	2.4	19.6
Inner Coastal Plain	128	2	83	1.6	2.4	15.0
Outer Coastal Plain	204	4	83	2.0	4.8	23.9
Pine Barrens	180	14	83	7.8	16.9	21.1

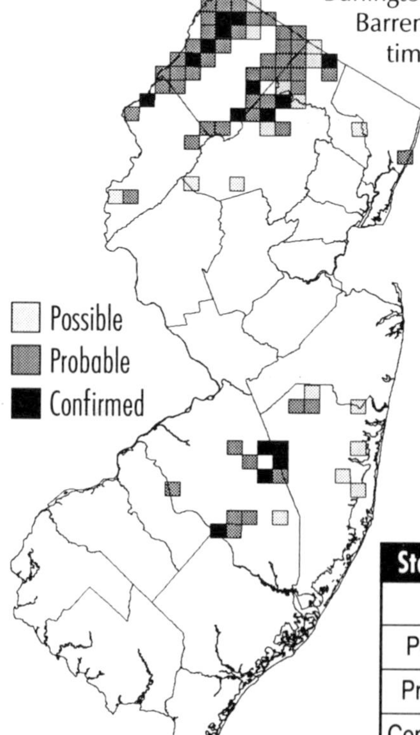

Hermit Thrushes were first discovered nesting in the Pine Barrens in 1981, when birds were found in three locations in Wharton State Forest, Burlington County. Their presence in the Pine Barrens may have gone unnoticed for some time, as Griscom (1923) found them to be common in the Pine Barrens of Long Island during the first half of the 20th century. In the north, Boyle (1986) described Hermit Thrushes as uncommon and local, describing their habitat as hemlock glens or ridges.

Atlas observers found Hermit Thrushes principally in four physiographic provinces: the Kittatinny Mountains and Valley, the Highlands, and the Pine Barrens. They are broadly distributed in the Kittatinny Mountains, occupying 89% of the blocks. Their distribution in the Highlands is more local and is confined to the northern

Statewide Summary	
Status	# of Blocks
Possible	17
Probable	50
Confirmed	16
Total	83

Hermit Thrush

continued

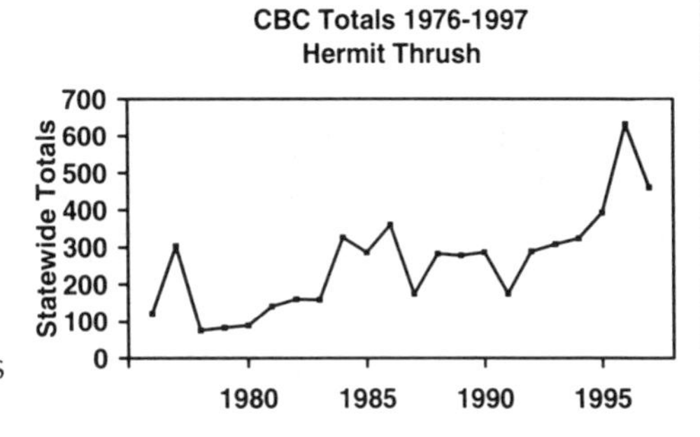

Highlands. Hermit Thrushes were patchy in the Pine Barrens and only occupied 8% of the blocks in that province – but this accounted for about 17% of their statewide range. Like most forest nesting thrushes, they are most frequently detected by call, and, due to their shy habits, are rarely Confirmed.

Fall: Hermit Thrushes are later migrants than the other thrushes, with few seen before October. Peak numbers pass from mid- to late October, with movements continuing through much of November. They are generally the most often seen thrush in migration. **Maxima:** 100s, Higbee Beach, 30 October 1988; 40+, Higbee Beach, 26 October 1996.

Winter: Hermit Thrushes are often present in good numbers during CBCs, but numbers probably decline in mid-winter, especially when the weather is severe. CBC numbers are variable, and the listed statewide maximum (see below) is notably higher than any other count. **CBC Statewide Stats:** Average: 259; Maximum: 631 in 1996; Minimum: 75 in 1978. **CBC Maximum:** 179, Cape May,1996.

Spring: Most Hermit Thrushes move north in April, with numbers diminishing quickly after early May. **Maxima:** 50+, Garret Mt., 29 April 1989; 35, Stokes State Forest, 8 May 1995. ■

Wood Thrush

Hylocichla mustelina

Range: Breeds from eastern Minnesota to New Brunswick, south to eastern Texas and extreme northern Florida. Winters in Central America.

NJ Status: Fairly common and nearly ubiquitous summer resident, scarce to uncommon spring and fall migrant, reported on seven CBCs.

Breeding

Habitat: Nests in the understory of deciduous woodlands preferring moist woods.

Throughout the 20th century, Wood Thrushes have been described as common birds in New

continued on page 470

continued from page 469

Wood Thrush

Jersey. Fables (1955), Bull (1964), and Leck (1984) all indicated increases for this species, particularly in the Pine Barrens. New Jersey Breeding Bird Survey data suggested that there was little change in breeding numbers between 1966 and 1996, but this is contrary to declines documented elsewhere in North America since the late 1970s. Among other factors, it is contended that their behavior of nesting in small, fragmented woods, may cause lower reproductive success (Roth et al. 1996). In Pennsylvania, Breeding Bird Survey data showed a significant increase in Wood Thrush numbers between 1965 and 1979, but surveys since then failed to maintain that trend (Leberman 1992b). In Maryland, Breeding Bird Survey information indicated a steady decline from 1966 to 1989 (Solem 1996).

Wood Thrushes were found throughout all the physiographic provinces during the Atlas surveys and were located in 86% of the blocks statewide. They were only absent from the highly urbanized areas of the northeastern Piedmont, from some sections of the Pine Barrens, from the Barrier Islands, and from certain areas along the lower Delaware River. Like other forest nesting thrushes, Wood Thrushes are easily detected by voice, but are difficult to Confirm as breeding birds.

Possible
Probable
Confirmed

Statewide Summary	
Status	# of Blocks
Possible	51
Probable	337
Confirmed	341
Total	729

Fall: Wood Thrushes move south in September and early October. Although declining in some areas, they are still broadly distributed and relatively common breeding birds in many eastern woodlands north of New Jersey. Consequently, it seems odd that they are recorded in relatively low numbers in migration, particularly on the Coastal Plain. **Maximum:** 20, Higbee Beach, 23 September 1983.

Winter: Wood Thrushes were reported on seven CBCs between

Wood Thrush

continued

Physiographic Distribution **Wood Thrush**	Number of blocks in province	Number of blocks species found breeding in province	Number of blocks species found in state	Percent of province species occupies	Percent of all records for this species found in province	Percent of state area in province
Kittatinny Mountains	19	19	729	100.0	2.6	2.2
Kittatinny Valley	45	43	729	95.6	5.9	5.3
Highlands	109	109	729	100.0	15.0	12.8
Piedmont	167	141	729	84.4	19.3	19.6
Inner Coastal Plain	128	112	729	87.5	15.4	15.0
Outer Coastal Plain	204	150	729	73.5	20.6	23.9
Pine Barrens	180	155	729	86.1	21.3	21.1

1976 and 1997. Two were reported statewide in both 1992 and 1993, and the submitted details were noted as "well described" in all four instances (AB). The others had less complete details, and confusion with Hermit Thrush is at least a possibility. There are no reports after the CBC season.

Spring: Wood Thrushes arrive on their breeding grounds beginning in late April, with northbound migrants passing from early to mid-May. **Maximum:** 15+, Higbee Beach, 5 May 1990. ■

American Robin

Turdus migratorius

Breeding

Habitat: Nests in woodlands, field edges, suburbia, as well as deeper deciduous forest.

Stone (1908) referred to American Robin as "perhaps, our best known bird." At that time they were shot for raiding cultivated cherry trees, but Stone suggested that this was futile as "it is impossible to exterminate them." Most references during the 1900s continued to echo Stone's assertion that American Robins were ubiquitous breeding birds in New Jersey. Breeding Bird Surveys indicated significant positive population increases for this species throughout the range of the surveys (Price et al. 1995).

continued on page 472

continued from page 471

American Robin

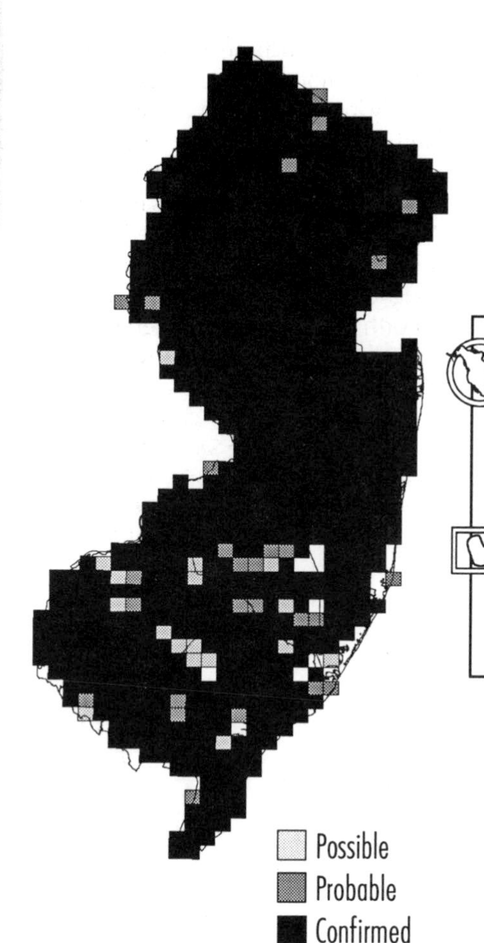

Range: Breeds over the whole of North America south of the Canadian Arctic. Withdraws from the northern portion of the breeding range in winter.

NJ Status: Common and nearly ubiquitous summer resident, abundant migrant, and common winter resident.

Statewide Summary

Status	# of Blocks
Possible	17
Probable	27
Confirmed	788
Total	832

Physiographic Distribution

American Robin	Number of blocks in province	Number of blocks species found breeding in province	Number of blocks species found in state	Percent of province species occupies	Percent of all records for this species found in province	Percent of state area in province
Kittatinny Mountains	19	19	832	100.0	2.3	2.2
Kittatinny Valley	45	45	832	100.0	5.4	5.3
Highlands	109	109	832	100.0	13.1	12.8
Piedmont	167	167	832	100.0	20.1	19.6
Inner Coastal Plain	128	128	832	100.0	15.4	15.0
Outer Coastal Plain	204	189	832	92.6	22.7	23.9
Pine Barrens	180	175	832	97.2	21.0	21.1

Atlas surveys located American Robins in 98% of the blocks in the state – putting them in a tie with Common Grackles and Mourning Doves as the second most commonly recorded species statewide. They were absent only from some barrier islands and from blocks consisting entirely of salt marsh habitats. Their ability to coexist, even flourish, within close proximity to human habitation has allowed them to become one of the most broadly distributed and numerous breeding songbirds in North America. Although most visible in suburban yards and farmland fields, American Robins were also found in areas of undeveloped forest.

Fall: Southward movements of American Robins may begin by August, but most of the fall flight occurs much later, peaking from late October to early November. Huge diurnal flights may occur anywhere in the state. The magnitude of flights along the coast may be staggering. **Maxima:** 200,000+, Cape May, 4 November 1995; uncountable 1,000s, Cape May, 30 October, 1988.

Winter: Although American Robins are locally common in winter, they are normally less numerous northward and inland. Numbers vary from year-to-year, and this variability is reflected in CBC totals. Roosts of several thousand birds may occasionally be established anywhere in the state, often persisting throughout the winter. Movements from the north (after severe weather) or the south (after a balmy spell) may occur at any time. **Maximum:** 80,000 in one roost, Spruce Run Res., early December 1997. **CBC Statewide Stats:** Average: 12,109; Maximum: 29,408 in 1992; Minimum: 2,478 in 1979. **CBC Maximum:** 7,964, Cumberland, 1988.

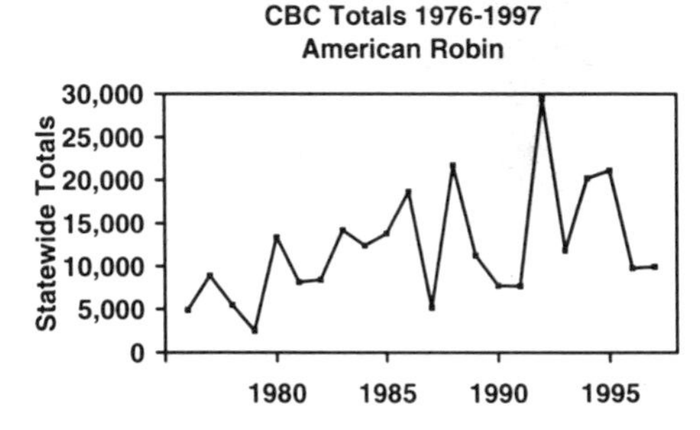

Spring: Numbers of American Robins are less concentrated in spring than in fall. Migration begins in February and continues through May. Most New Jersey breeding birds are on territory by early April, even though significant numbers of migrants still continue to pass – e.g., 2,493, Alpine, 26 April 1970 (AFN). **Other maxima:** 2,000, Jake's Landing, 27 February 1994; 1,000+, Madison, 5 March 1995. ■

Varied Thrush

Ixoreus naevius

Range: Breeds from Alaska to Montana and Washington south to northwestern California. Winters from southern Alaska to Washington and Idaho south to California.

NJ Status: Very rare. NJBRC Review List.

Occurrence: There have been 23 state reports of Varied Thrush, and 15 have been accepted by the NJBRC (all from late fall and winter). There are many extralimital records of the species in the Northeast, but there have been no state reports since 1988. The 15 accepted records are:

Location	Date	Documentation
New Jersey#	*March 1848*	*spec. in Boston*
Hoboken#	*December 1851*	*spec. AMNH, missing*
Pine Valley#	*26 November 1936-20 March 1937*	
*Moorestown**	*27 November 1965-4 February 1966*	
Tenafly	*23 November 1971*	*spec. AMNH #803013*
Sandyston Twp.	*19 December 1975-29 January 1976*	*ph-RBPF*
Franklin Lakes	*14 January-19 March 1978*	*ph-RBPF*
Newfoundland	*25 January-4 April 1978*	*ph-RBPF*
Allamuchy SP	*15-16 November 1980*	
Pine Lake	*17-21 December 1980*	*ph-RNJB 17:26*
Hamilton Square	*26 November 1982-12 April 1983*	*ph-RNJB 19:38*
Rifle Camp Park	*26 November 1983*	*ph-RBPF*
*Norwood Scout Camp**	*9 November 1985*	
Absecon	*26 January-10 February 1987*	*ph-RBPF*
Whittingham WMA	*28 February 1987*	*ph-RBPF*

Gray Catbird

Dumetella carolinensis

Breeding

Statewide Summary	
Status	# of Blocks
Possible	16
Probable	71
Confirmed	752
Total	839

Habitat: Nests in dense thickets, shrubby edges, old fields, and gardens.

Stone (1908) wrote that Gray Catbirds were "equally at home in the swampy thickets or in the shrubbery of the garden... familiar to all." Their status in New Jersey

Gray Catbird

continued

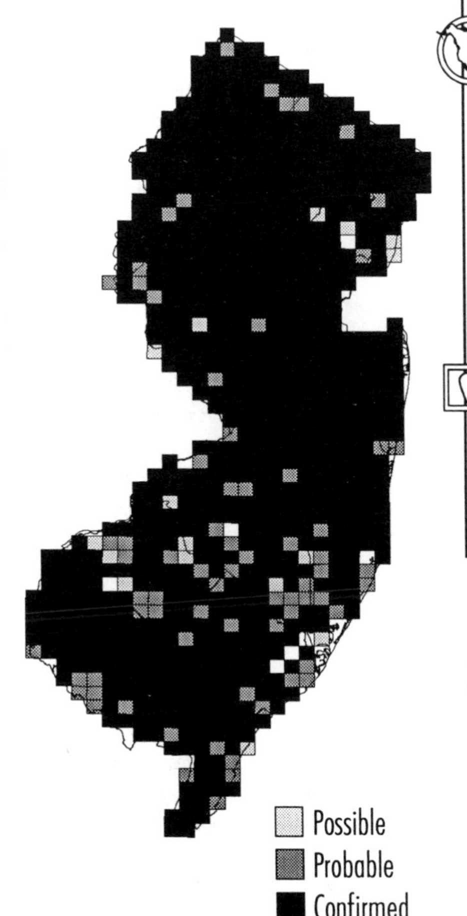

Range: In eastern North America, breeds from southern Manitoba east to Nova Scotia, south to northeastern Texas and northern Florida. Winters along the East coast from Massachusetts to Florida west to Arkansas and Texas, south to the West Indies and Central America.

NJ Status: Common and nearly ubiquitous summer resident, common spring and fall migrant, scarce to uncommon winter resident.

has changed little since that account was written. Gray Catbirds were listed as common breeders by Griscom (1923), Cruickshank (1942), Fables (1955), and Leck (1984). However, Breeding Bird Survey data indicated that Gray Catbirds are declining in some portions of their North American range (Cimprich and Moore 1995).

continued on page 476

Physiographic Distribution **Gray Catbird**	Number of blocks in province	Number of blocks species found breeding in province	Number of blocks species found in state	Percent of province species occupies	Percent of all records for this species found in province	Percent of state area in province
Kittatinny Mountains	19	19	839	100.0	2.3	2.2
Kittatinny Valley	45	45	839	100.0	5.4	5.3
Highlands	109	109	839	100.0	13.0	12.8
Piedmont	167	166	839	99.4	19.8	19.6
Inner Coastal Plain	128	128	839	100.0	15.3	15.0
Outer Coastal Plain	204	194	839	95.1	23.1	23.9
Pine Barrens	180	178	839	98.9	21.2	21.1

continued from page 475

Gray Catbird

Atlas observers found Gray Catbirds were the most widely distributed breeding birds in the state, occurring in 98% of the blocks. They were absent only from a few barrier island blocks and a few salt marsh blocks along the lower Delaware River. Gray Catbirds have generally benefited from human activities, as they prefer the early successional habitats created by development. Gray Catbird is also one of few species that recognizes and rejects cowbird eggs (Cimprich and Moore 1995). Of the 95 incidents of cowbird parasitism reported to the Atlas, only one involved Gray Catbird as a host species.

Fall: The magnitude of Gray Catbirds' migration is often difficult to estimate due to the presence of local breeding birds, but peak flights are noted from mid- to late September. Movements diminish by mid-October. **Maxima:** 400, Higbee Beach, 1 October 1974 (Sibley 1997); 100s, Cape Island, 9 August 1989 (Sibley 1997).

Winter: Gray Catbirds winter in relatively small numbers along the coast and in the southern part of the state. CBC totals are variable, but have shown an overall increase. **CBC Statewide Stats:** Average: 77; Maximum: 166 in 1997; Minimum: 23 in 1976. **CBC Maximum:** 58, Cape May, 1996.

Spring: In some locations, the presence of Gray Catbirds that have remained throughout the winter may obscure the arrival of northbound migrants. Most probably arrive in early May, with movements continuing at least through mid-May. **Maximum:** 79, Island Beach, 11 May 1991 (banded). ■

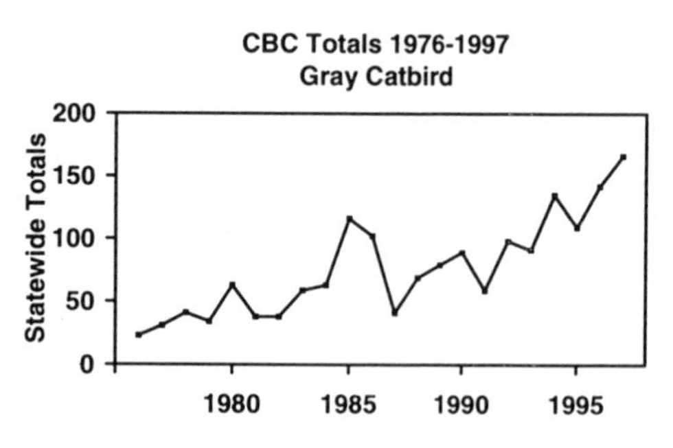

Northern Mockingbird
Mimus polyglottos

Range: In the eastern United States breeds from southern Nebraska east to southern Maine, south to Texas and Florida. Winters throughout most of the breeding range.

NJ Status: Common and nearly ubiquitous summer resident, uncommon migrant and common winter resident.

Statewide Summary	
Status	# of Blocks
Possible	38
Probable	218
Confirmed	533
Total	789

Breeding

Habitat: Found most often in yards, hedgerows, thickets, and forest edge.

Northern Mockingbirds have undergone a remarkable range expansion since the early 1900s. Stone (1908) considered them a "very rare summer resident." Prior to that time, sporadic nesting was known from the northeast, southwest, and coastal portions of New Jersey. Stone (1908) noted that a colony still existed at Sandy Hook in 1892, but that it "suffered severely" in the blizzard of 1888. Their failure to maintain a stable population in the early years of colonization may have been the result of human interference. Stone (1908) recounted that Northern Mockingbird young were often collected and raised as cage birds. Cruickshank (1942) later reported that sightings of Northern Mockingbirds increased after the cage-bird trade became illegal. During the early 1950s, the species was thinly distributed in southern and northeastern New Jersey (Fables 1955). The following decade saw

continued on page 478

continued from page 477

a further increase in the range extension and population growth of Northern Mockingbirds, and they colonized Sussex County in 1958 (Bull 1964, Leck 1985).

Atlas surveys found Northern Mockingbirds in 93% of the blocks in the state. They were notably absent from some of the higher elevations and forested regions of northwestern New Jersey and from the heart of the Pine Barrens. Their distribution throughout the remainder of New Jersey is impressively broad.

Fall: Despite a widespread perception to the contrary, Northern Mockingbirds are somewhat migratory. However, the presence of resident birds makes it difficult to judge the full period of passage. Movement begins from mid- to late summer, but most migrants are noted from September to October. During the fall of 1982 at Alpine Lookout, counters averaged three birds per ten hours and found a great increase over the 1968-1972 average of one bird per 20 hours (Paxton et al. 1983). At Cape May Point, small groups of mockingbirds are often noted migrating overhead (Sibley 1997).

Winter: The abundance and availability of winter fruit from ornamental yard plantings (especially the widely escaped *Rosa multiflora*) appear to have been important factors in aiding Northern

CBC Totals 1976-1997
Northern Mockingbird

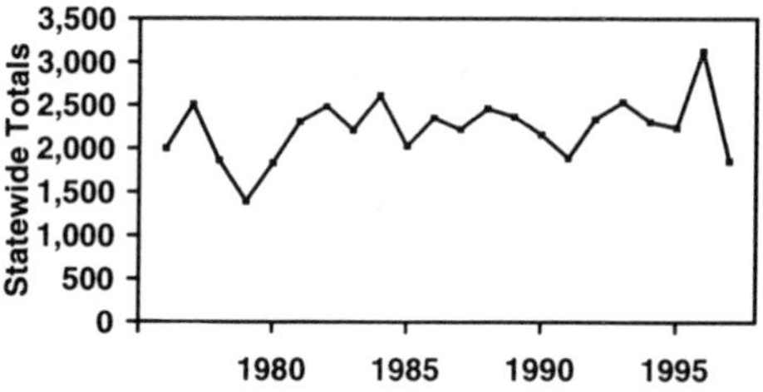

Physiographic Distribution **Northern Mockingbird**	Number of blocks in province	Number of blocks species found breeding in province	Number of blocks species found in state	Percent of province species occupies	Percent of all records for this species found in province	Percent of state area in province
Kittatinny Mountains	19	14	789	73.7	1.8	2.2
Kittatinny Valley	45	44	789	97.8	5.6	5.3
Highlands	109	105	789	96.3	13.3	12.8
Piedmont	167	163	789	97.6	20.7	19.6
Inner Coastal Plain	128	127	789	99.2	16.1	15.0
Outer Coastal Plain	204	186	789	91.2	23.6	23.9
Pine Barrens	180	150	789	83.3	19.0	21.1

Northern Mockingbird

continued

Mockingbirds to expand and consolidate their range. CBC totals from 1976 to 1997 were fairly consistent. **CBC Statewide Stats:** Average: 2,229; Maximum: 3,120 in 1996; Minimum: 1,387 in 1979. **CBC Maximum:** 357, Cape May, 1996.

Spring: The small spring migration of Northern Mockingbirds is usually overlooked against the background of resident birds. On the Palisades, Boyajian (1973) determined that movement takes place from April to mid-May. His daily high count at the Palisades was 11 on 7 April 1973. ■

Sage Thrasher

Oreoscoptes montanus

Range: Breeds from southernmost British Columbia east to Montana, south to northern Arizona and northern New Mexico. Winters from the southern portion of breeding range to Mexico.

NJ Status: Accidental. NJBRC Review List.

Occurrence: There have been three state reports of Sage Thrashers, and two have been accepted by the NJBRC. The two accepted records are:

Barnegat #	*27 November 1949*	
Spring Lake	*30 October 1990*	*ph-RNJB 17:16*

Brown Thrasher

Toxostoma rufum

Range: Breeds from southeastern Alberta east to central Maine, south to eastern Texas and Florida. Winters in the southern third of the United States, north along the Atlantic coast to Massachusetts.

NJ Status: Fairly common and very widespread summer resident, fairly common spring and fall migrant, scarce winter resident.

Breeding

Habitat: Breeds in dense thickets and shrubbery, especially along edges of mixed or deciduous woodlands.

continued on page 480

continued from page 479

Brown Thrasher

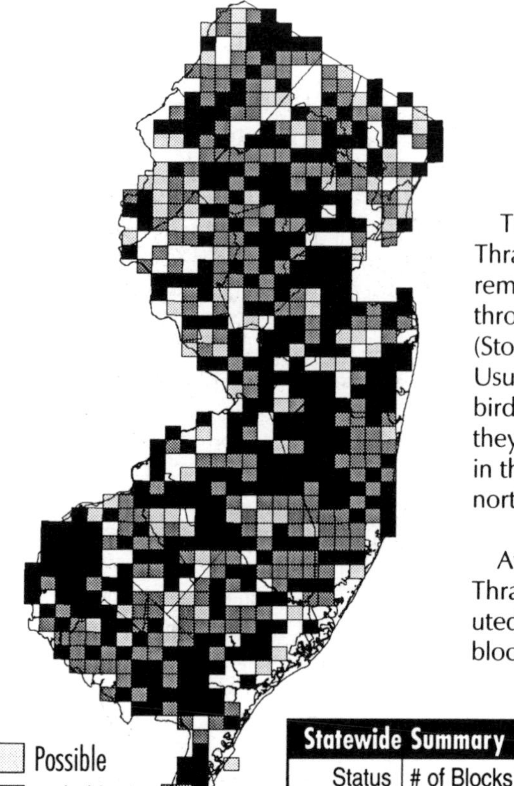

The distribution of Brown Thrashers in New Jersey has remained essentially unchanged throughout the 20th century (Stone 1908, Leck 1984). Usually referred to as a common bird, Griscom (1923) noted that they were "relatively uncommon in the hilly country" of the northwestern part of the state.

Atlas volunteers found Brown Thrashers were widely distributed and located in 81% of the blocks statewide, from the upper reaches of the Kittatinny Valley to the southernmost tip of the Cape May peninsula. They were one of the most widespread species in the Pine Barrens, occupying 89% of the blocks. Echoing Griscom's (1923)

Statewide Summary

Status	# of Blocks
Possible	81
Probable	234
Confirmed	374
Total	689

Physiographic Distribution

Brown Thrasher	Number of blocks in province	Number of blocks species found breeding in province	Number of blocks species found in state	Percent of province species occupies	Percent of all records for this species found in province	Percent of state area in province
Kittatinny Mountains	19	11	689	57.9	1.6	2.2
Kittatinny Valley	45	40	689	88.9	5.8	5.3
Highlands	109	87	689	79.8	12.6	12.8
Piedmont	167	133	689	79.6	19.3	19.6
Inner Coastal Plain	128	110	689	85.9	16.0	15.0
Outer Coastal Plain	204	147	689	72.1	21.3	23.9
Pine Barrens	180	161	689	89.4	23.4	21.1

omments on distribution, Brown Thrashers were more thinly distributed in northern New Jersey. They occupied only 8% of the Kittatinny Mountain blocks and were absent from some parts of the northern Highlands, especially around the Wawayanda Plateau. They were conspicuously absent from the barrier islands of southern Ocean, Atlantic, and Cape May counties.

Conservation Note:

Although Brown Thrashers occurred throughout all the physiographic provinces in the state, there is some evidence that their numbers may be declining nationwide. Breeding Bird Survey data from 1966-1993 showed that their numbers declined significantly on survey routes in the United States (Price et al. 1995). This trend was also seen in Maryland between 1966 and 1989 (Hitchner 1996), and in Pennsylvania between 1965 and 1990 (Ickes 1992).

Fall: The arrival of southbound Brown Thrashers is obscured by the presence of local breeding birds. Peak flights occur from mid-September into mid-October. Movements can be inconspicuous, and typically involve only small numbers in a given area. **Maxima:** 65, Sandy Hook, 14 September 1991; 30+, Higbee Beach, 9 October 1995.

Winter: The status of Brown Thrasher in winter is similar to that of Gray Catbird. Thrashers are more often found along the coast and south. Their abundance during and after the CBC season is based on the severity of the weather.

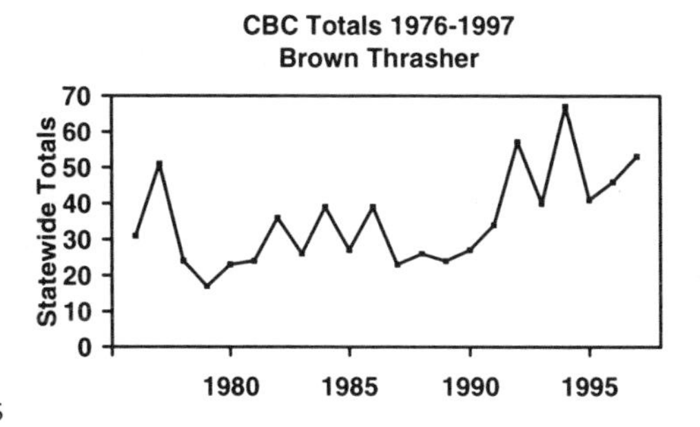

CBC Statewide Stats: Average: 39; Maximum: 67 in 1994; Minimum: 17 in 1979. **CBC Maximum:** 40, Cumberland, 1994.

Spring: A northbound movement of Brown Thrashers is discernable from late March to mid-April. The presence of wintering birds and migrants obscures the timing of the arrival of local breeding birds. **Maxima:** 15, Higbee Beach, 5 April 1988; 15, Higbee Beach, 11 April 1992; 15, Higbee Beach, 4 April 1993. ■

European Starling

Sturnus vulgaris

Range: Introduced. Breeds throughout much of Canada and the United States

NJ Status: Common and nearly ubiquitous resident.

Breeding

Habitat: Nests in cavities, man-made or natural, in a variety of wooded, open, and urban habitats.

On 6 March 1890, 80 European Starlings were released in Central Park, New York City. An additional 40 were released on 25 April 1891 (Stone 1908). These releases have

Statewide Summary	
Status	# of Blocks
Possible	25
Probable	29
Confirmed	757
Total	811

Physiographic Distribution European Starling	Number of blocks in province	Number of blocks species found breeding in province	Number of blocks species found in state	Percent of province species occupies	Percent of all records for this species found in province	Percent of state area in province
Kittatinny Mountains	19	18	811	94.7	2.2	2.2
Kittatinny Valley	45	45	811	100.0	5.5	5.3
Highlands	109	109	811	100.0	13.4	12.8
Piedmont	167	166	811	99.4	20.5	19.6
Inner Coastal Plain	128	126	811	98.4	15.5	15.0
Outer Coastal Plain	204	189	811	92.6	23.3	23.9
Pine Barrens	180	158	811	87.8	19.5	21.1

ffected North America's bird life on a massive scale. Starlings quickly spread north to Ossining, New York, by 1899 and Stamford, Connecticut, by 1900, and west to Morristown, New Jersey, by 1907 (Bull 1964). By 1908, Stone noted that they had spread along the coast southward in New Jersey to Tuckerton, to Vineland in the interior, and to the Philadelphia area. They reached Cape May by 1909, and by the mid-1930s, European Starlings were one of the most abundant birds in southern New Jersey (Stone 1937). Since then, their spread across the entire North American continent, has been astounding. The North American population is now estimated at 200 million – all descendents of birds originally released in 1890 and 1891 (Cabe 1993).

A cavity-nesting species, European Starlings compete aggressively with other cavity-nesters. Although it is generally believed that they have a detrimental effect on these species, no conclusive studies have been done (Cabe 1993). In New Jersey, woodpeckers, Great Crested Flycatchers, Tree Swallows, Purple Martins, and Eastern Bluebirds may all be affected by competition with starlings.

Map Interpretation: European Starlings were Confirmed in 93% of the blocks where they were found – the highest Confirmation rate of any species. This is probably due to their high density, coupled with their conspicuous nesting behaviors. In addition, they have a long nesting period; so Atlas volunteers had many opportunities to Confirm this species.

Not surprisingly, European Starlings were found to be one of the most widespread species in the state, nesting in 95% of the blocks. They were only absent from some parts of the Pine Barrens in areas with large, unbroken tracks of woodlands.

Fall: Although some migration of European Starlings occurs, it is poorly understood. Apparently, their migration varies from region to region, from year to year, among individuals, and even among young from the same nest (Cabe 1993). Starlings gather in huge flocks after the breeding season, constantly moving from place to place in search of food.

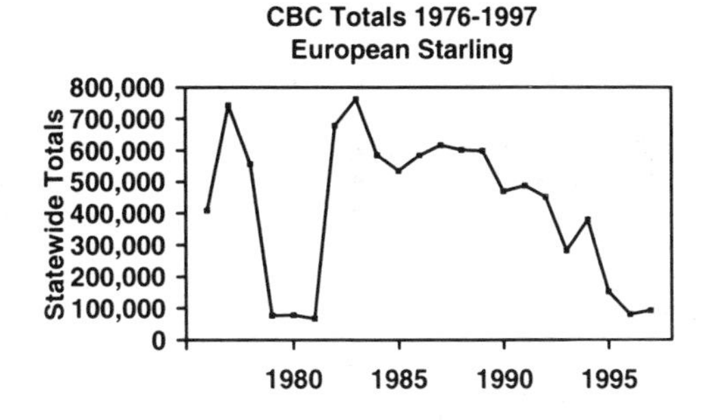

Winter: Numbers of European Starlings counted on CBCs vary, but, statewide, hundreds of thousands are usually recorded. However, totals show a steady decline from the early 1980s through the mid-1990s. **CBC Statewide Stats:** Average: 422,234; Maximum: 762,826 in 1983; Minimum: 67,938 in 1981. **CBC Maximum:** 647,000, Lower Hudson, 1977.

Spring: Almost any return flight of European Starlings in spring is masked by large local populations. ■

American Pipi

Anthus rubescens

Range: Breeds from Alaska to Labrador, in the east south on scattered mountaintops to New Hampshire. Winters across the southern states, north along the coast to southern New England.

NJ Status: Uncommon to common spring and fall migrant, uncommon winter resident.

Fall: American Pipits are unexpected before late September, with the largest numbers recorded in late October through November. They are most often noted while in flight by their distinctive flight calls. The number of reports and the size of flocks appeared to decline during the 1980s and 1990s – e.g., the last report of 1,000 birds was at Cape May, 10 November 1973 (AB). **Other maxima:** 500, Alpha Grasslands, late October 1978; 400, Sharptown, 25 October 1989.

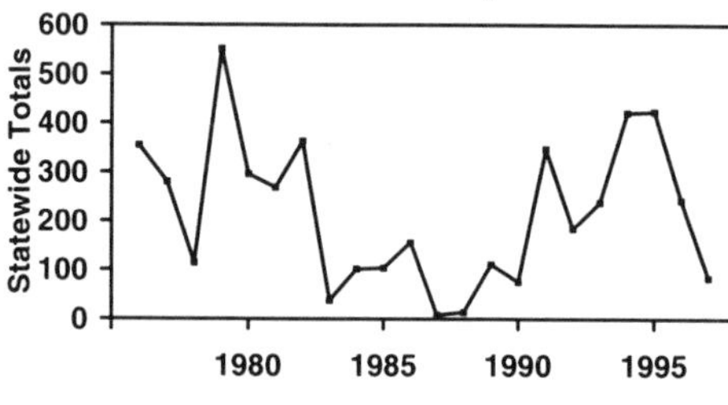

Winter: After early winter, American Pipits are most often found in southern New Jersey rather than in the north. CBC totals are highly variable. **CBC Statewide Stats:** Average: 217; Maximum: 551 in 1979; Minimum: 8 in 1987. **CBC Maximum:** 250, Cape May, 1979.

Spring: Although American Pipits tend to be uncommon throughout most of New Jersey in spring, they are rather rare along the coast. The peak flight in spring occurs from early to late April. Only stragglers remain after early May. **Maxima:** 300, Harmony, 6 April 1975; 250, Mannington Marsh, 18 April 1982. ■

Bohemian Waxwing
Bombycilla garrulus

Range: In North America breeds from Alaska east to northern Manitoba and south to central British Columbia and central Alberta.

NJ Status: Accidental. NJBRC Review List.

Occurrence: There have been 16 state reports of Bohemian Waxwings, and seven have been accepted by the NJBRC (six in winter, one in spring). The seven accepted records are:

	Princeton	*3-9 February 1962*	
	Riverton	*17 March 1962*	
	*Flemington Jct. **	*10-22 April 1962*	
3	*Barnegat*	*1 December 1968*	
	Ringwood	*6 February to early March 1977*	*ph-RNJB 3:94; Kane 1977b*
	Sandy Hook	*3-18 February 1991*	*ph-RNJB 17:2*
	Erma	*29 January 1998*	*ph-RNJB 24:52*

Cedar Waxwing
Bombycilla cedrorum

Range: In eastern North America breeds from Manitoba east to Newfoundland, south to Missouri and Georgia. Winters from the southern portion of breeding range to Mexico.

NJ Status: Fairly common and very widespread summer resident, common spring and fall migrant, common winter resident.

Breeding

Habitat: Nests in mixed or deciduous woodlands.

In 1908, Stone eloquently portrayed the habits of Cedar Waxwings as roving flocks feeding on fruit trees well into June, with most disappearing and "leaving only a few nesting pairs which are not very conspicuous in our summer bird life." Indeed this description could

continued on page 486

continued from page 485

Cedar Waxwing

have been written at any point during the 20th century. Bull (1964) claimed that Cedar Waxwings were less common and more local breeding birds on the Coastal Plain than in northern New Jersey. Boyle (1986) described them as more common in the north. The term

Possible
Probable
Confirmed

Map Interpretation: It is likely that the map underestimates the range of Cedar Waxwing in New Jersey. Cedar Waxwings can be difficult to detect, as they are fairly late-season breeding birds and sing an atypical "song."

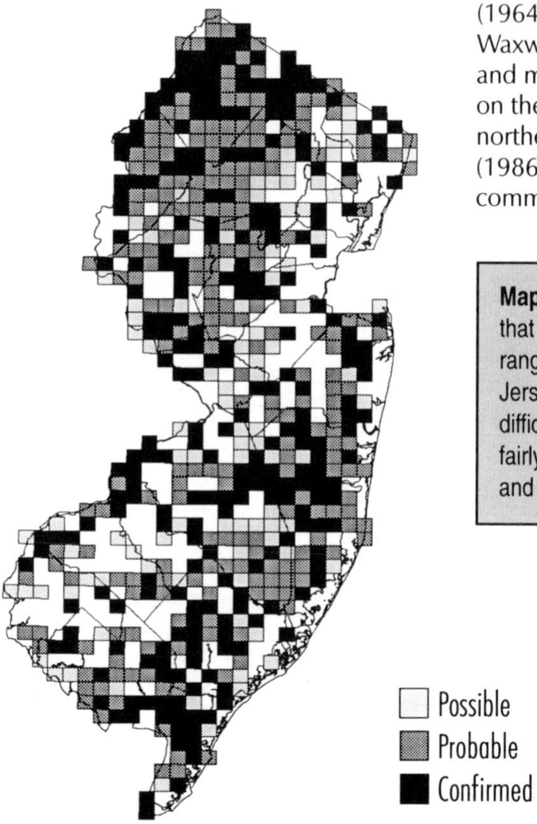

Statewide Summary	
Status	# of Blocks
Possible	94
Probable	233
Confirmed	258
Total	585

Physiographic Distribution

Cedar Waxwing	Number of blocks in province	Number of blocks species found breeding in province	Number of blocks species found in state	Percent of province species occupies	Percent of all records for this species found in province	Percent of state area in province
Kittatinny Mountains	19	18	585	94.7	3.1	2.2
Kittatinny Valley	45	40	585	88.9	6.8	5.3
Highlands	109	98	585	89.9	16.8	12.8
Piedmont	167	107	585	64.1	18.3	19.6
Inner Coastal Plain	128	74	585	57.8	12.6	15.0
Outer Coastal Plain	204	107	585	52.5	18.3	23.9
Pine Barrens	180	141	585	78.3	24.1	21.1

most frequently used to describe Cedar Waxings is "erratic" (Griscom 1923, Boyle 1986), whether in or out of the breeding season. They are among the latest nesting songbirds, arriving during June and sometimes beginning nest preparations even later in the summer.

On the Atlas surveys, Cedar Waxwings were found to be very widespread throughout the state. North of the Piedmont, they were especially well distributed, occurring in 88% of the blocks. Waxwings occurred in 64% of the Piedmont blocks, but were absent from large parts of the urbanized eastern Piedmont. In the southern part of the state, they were thinly distributed on the Inner Coastal Plain, but were well represented in the Pine Barrens, occurring in 78% of the blocks. Waxwings were also found in many of the blocks in Cumberland and Cape May counties, although they were absent from most of the barrier islands.

Fall: Cedar Waxwings are erratic in the timing of their southward movements. Peak numbers may occur anytime from late August into November, although most often from September to October. Huge flights are annually recorded along the coast. **Maxima:** 1,000s, Higbee Beach, 3 November 1994; 800, Spruce Run Res., 31 October 1992.

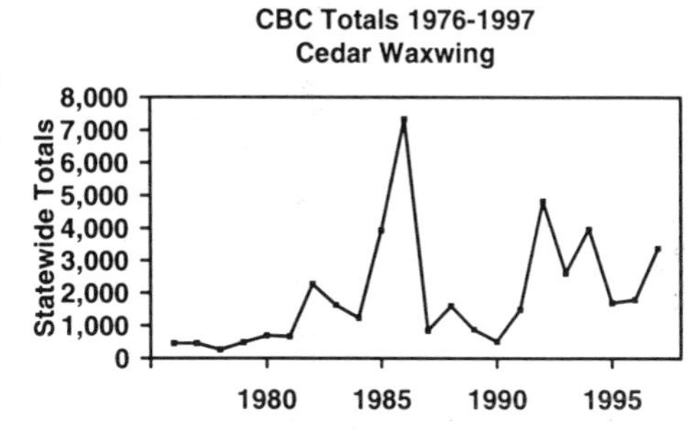

Winter: Cedar Waxwings are scarce to locally common in northern New Jersey, probably depending on the fruit crop, but are more regular southward. CBC totals are variable, consistent with the waxwing's nomadic nature. **CBC Statewide Stats:** Average: 1,953; Maximum: 7,329 in 1986; Minimum: 262 in 1978. **CBC Maximum:** 1,153, Raritan Estuary, 1986.

Spring: Substantial northward movements of Cedar Waxwings can occur from early March to June. True migration appears to reach a peak from mid-May to early June. Large numbers observed prior to May probably represent nomadic feeding flocks rather than actual spring migrants (Cruickshank 1942). **Maxima:** 3,000, Princeton, 17 May 1975 (AB); 1,000s, Cape May, 27 May 1988 (Sibley 1997). ■

Blue-winged Warbler

Vermivora pinus

Range: Breeds in the east from Maine to Delaware. Winters in Central America.

NJ Status: Fairly common and widespread summer resident, fairly common spring and common fall migrant.

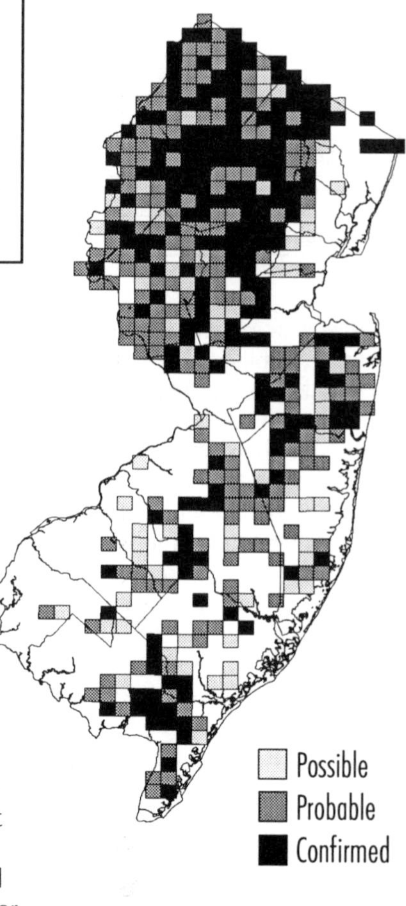

Statewide Summary	
Status	# of Blocks
Possible	66
Probable	185
Confirmed	207
Total	458

Breeding

Habitat: Nests in open, second-growth woodlands, and along woodland edges.

The distribution of Blue-winged Warblers in the state has changed markedly since the early 1900s. Stone (1908) found them to be common breeding birds in the central and north-eastern counties of the state, but absent from the northwest, the southwest, and the Pine Barrens. Griscom (1923) stated that he never saw a Blue-winged Warbler in Sussex County, finding them absent from "the higher sections of northwestern New Jersey." In 1942 Cruickshank noted their presence in the Kittatinny Valley, but not at higher altitudes. Bull (1964) wrote that they were common breeding birds in lowland areas of the northern counties, and Fables (1955) indicated that they were local in the Pine Barrens and on the Cape May peninsula. All the early authors seem to agree that Blue-winged Warblers were absent from the Highlands, and the Kittatinny Mountains.

Physiographic Distribution **Blue-winged Warbler**	Number of blocks in province	Number of blocks species found breeding in province	Number of blocks species found in state	Percent of province species occupies	Percent of all records for this species found in province	Percent of state area in province
Kittatinny Mountains	19	19	458	100.0	4.1	2.2
Kittatinny Valley	45	43	458	95.6	9.4	5.3
Highlands	109	107	458	98.2	23.4	12.8
Piedmont	167	103	458	61.7	22.5	19.6
Inner Coastal Plain	128	31	458	24.2	6.8	15.0
Outer Coastal Plain	204	60	458	29.4	13.1	23.9
Pine Barrens	180	95	458	52.8	20.7	21.1

Atlas data indicated that Blue-winged Warblers nest in 98% of the blocks in the Highlands and the Kittatinny Mountains, and can be found in 80% of the blocks north of the Coastal Plain. This expansion of their range may be due, at least in part, to the presence of an elaborate system of power-line cuts that has provided Blue-winged Warblers with the edge habitat that they require. This has brought them into direct contact with Golden-winged Warblers throughout that species' range in northwestern New

continued on page 490

Blue-winged Warbler

continued from page 489

Jersey, apparently to the detriment of Golden-winged Warblers (see Golden-Winged Warbler, below).

In northeastern New Jersey, Blue-winged Warblers have apparently declined as that area has become highly urbanized. During the Atlas they were thinly distributed in most of the Inner Coastal Plain, and found in only 27% of the blocks there. They were present in 53% of the blocks in the Pine Barrens, which appears to be a notable increase when compared to the first half of the 20th century. They are well established in Cape May County and in the southern portion of Cumberland County.

Blue-winged Warbler

Fall: The first southbound Blue-winged Warblers can be found in early August. Numbers peak from mid- to late August and few remain after mid-September. **Maxima:** 65, Higbee Beach, 16 August 1988; 40, Higbee Beach, 16 August 1982.

Spring: The first Blue-winged Warblers encountered in spring are usually local breeding birds arriving back on territory in late April. Most migrants move through from early to mid-May. **Maxima:** dozens, Princeton, 13 May 1983; 10+, Fairview Farm, 8 May 1993. ■

Golden-winged Warbler

Vermivora chrysoptera

Breeding

Habitat: Nests in shrubby, brushy overgrown openings with scattered trees.

Golden-winged Warblers expanded their range in the east in the late 1800s due to the clearing of forests (Confer 1992, Kaufman 1996). Stone (1908) knew that they bred at locations in Sussex, Passaic, and Morris counties, but inferred they were rare. Griscom's (1923) assessment of their distribution differed from Stone's, and he found them common at higher altitudes of the northern counties, southward to Warren and Essex counties. That status remained unchanged by the mid-1960s, as Bull (1964) noted

Physiographic Distribution

Golden-winged Warbler	Number of blocks in province	Number of blocks species found breeding in province	Number of blocks species found in state	Percent of province species occupies	Percent of all records for this species found in province	Percent of state area in province
Kittatinny Mountains	19	12	66	63.2	18.2	2.2
Kittatinny Valley	45	12	66	26.7	18.2	5.3
Highlands	109	39	66	35.8	59.1	12.8
Piedmont	167	3	66	1.8	4.5	19.6

Golden-winged Warbler

continued

that they were fairly common, though local, in the northern and northwestern parts of the state. Boyle (1986), however, found their numbers decreasing in the state, and other studies suggest their range has been decreasing throughout the northeastern United States (Confer 1992).

Range: Breeds from southeastern Manitoba southeast to Illinois and Michigan, east to Massachusetts, south along the Appalachians to northern Georgia. Winters in Central and northern South America.

NJ Status: Fairly common but local summer resident, rare spring and uncommon fall migrant.

Atlas data indicated that the distribution of Golden-winged Warblers in New Jersey has changed considerably since the early 1900s. Over 98% of their statewide range was north of the Piedmont, and they were no longer found in Essex and Warren counties. Nearly 75% of their statewide range is concentrated in the Kittatinny Mountains and in the Highlands, but they occupy only 39% of the blocks in those provinces. This species' range in the state is becoming extremely limited, especially since these two provinces represent only 15% of the state's area.

Statewide Summary

Status	# of Blocks
Possible	13
Probable	28
Confirmed	25
Total	66

Possible

Probable

Confirmed

Conservation Note: In New Jersey, the range of Golden-winged Warbler overlaps completely with the range of Blue-winged Warbler. These species will hybridize and this is suspected to be at least partly responsible for a decrease in the numbers of Golden-winged Warblers (Confer 1992). There are, however, additional possibilities to consider, including succession and reforestation, loss of wintering habitat, and parasitism by cowbirds (Confer 1992). Golden-winged Warblers have a limited range in New Jersey, and pressure from Blue-winged Warblers in addition to other factors suggest their continued

continued on page 492

continued from page 491

Golden-winged Warbler

presence as a breeding bird in the state is tenuous.

Fall: Golden-winged Warblers can occasionally be seen in early August, but most move south from late August to early September. Nearly all are gone before October. It is unusual for more than one or two migrant Golden-winged Warblers to be present at the same location on the same day. **Maxima:** 5, Higbee Beach, 29 August 1992; 4, Higbee Beach, 4 September 1992.

Spring: Very few Golden-winged Warblers are noted passing through New Jersey in spring, with most recorded from early to mid-May. Breeding birds arrive on territory in early May. **Maxima:** 2, Princeton, 15 May 1978; 2, Princeton, 4 May 1986; 2, Higbee Beach, 9 May 1992. ■

Blue-winged x Golden-winged Warbler Hybrid

Breeding

Blue-winged and Golden-winged Warblers hybridize where their ranges overlap, as is the case in northern New Jersey. Stone (1937) referred to records of hybrids as far back as 1859. The two primary hybrid types, "Brewster's" and "Lawrence's" Warblers, are scarce and local, but occur regularly both in breeding areas and during migration. Benzinger and Angus (1992) reported a ratio of 9:2 in favor of Brewster's Warblers in breeding areas in the New Jersey Highlands. It is interesting to note that only two hybrids were reported by Atlas volunteers.

Fall: Most southbound Blue-winged X Golden-winged Warbler hybrids are seen from mid-August to mid-September. Sightings have increased since the mid-1980s, but this may be the result of a real increase in the numbers of hybrids, an increase in observer awareness, or both.

Spring: Northbound Blue-winged X Golden-winged Warbler hybrids are seen in early to mid-May. ■

Tennessee Warbler
Vermivora peregrina

Range: Breeds from southeastern Alaska across Canada to Labrador south; in the Northeast, to northern New York, Vermont, New Hampshire, and central Maine. Winters from Mexico to northern South America.

NJ Status: Uncommon spring and fairly common fall migrant, reported on one CBC.

Historic Changes: Stone (1908) described this species as a "rare transient... more common in autumn. Very rare in spring." While numbers have increased considerably since that time, they continue to fluctuate. Historic highs were reached in the 1970s and 1980s when the species was commonly found in both spring and fall, however, a decline has been noted in the 1990s. Tennessee Warblers (along with Cape May and Bay-breasted Warblers) have shown dramatic population swings in response to spruce budworm cycles in the north (Kaufman 1996).

Fall: The first migrant Tennessee Warblers arrive by mid-August, with peak numbers reached from late August to mid-September. After early October only stragglers remain. **Maxima:** 250, Higbee Beach, 11 September 1988 (Sibley 1997); 120, Higbee Beach, 19 August, 1982.

Winter: A closely observed and well described Tennessee Warbler was recorded on the Lower Hudson CBC in 1976. There are no other winter reports.

Spring: Northbound Tennessee Warblers typically arrive in late April, are unexpected after late May, and the peak flight is usually in mid-May. There have been four recent late June-early July reports of solitary, singing birds, but no other evidence of breeding. **Maxima:** 75+, Allaire SP, 17 May 1975; 50+, Bernardsville, 14 May 1975. ■

Orange-crowned Warbler

Vermivora celata

Range: In eastern North America, breeds from Manitoba to Labrador. Winters mainly from the southern United States south to Central America.

NJ Status: Rare spring and scarce fall migrant, rare winter visitor.

Fall: Orange-crowned Warblers are the latest of our transient warblers, normally appearing during late September. The bulk of records are of lone birds between mid-October and mid-November. In recent years, New Jersey has averaged about 20 reports for the season. Although rare statewide, Orange-crowned Warblers are far more likely to appear along the coast than inland. **Maximum:** 4, Higbee Beach, 22 October 1982.

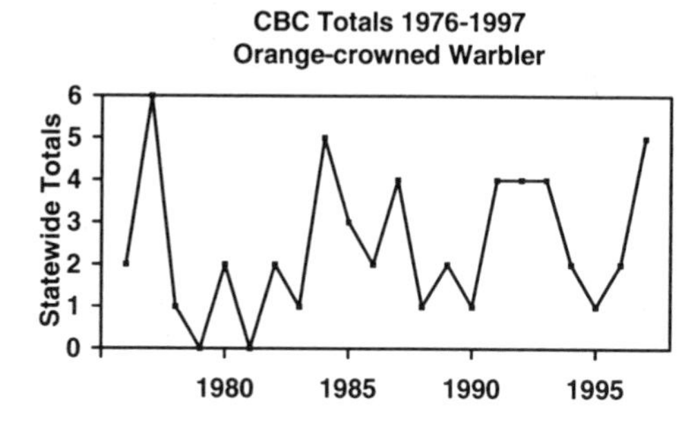

Winter: Although small numbers of Orange-crowned Warblers are found on CBCs, those numbers dwindle as the season advances. A few birds have wintered in the south-coastal region of the state. The 1954-1955 season set a record for winter Orange-crowned Warblers in New Jersey – e.g., 11 were on the Cape May CBC, 26 December 1954, as well as eight (six in one group) in the Shark River area, 2 January 1955 (Bull 1964). **CBC Statewide Stats:** Average: 2; Maximum: 6 in 1977; Minimum: 0 in 1979 and 1981. **CBC Maximum:** 3, Oceanville, 1997.

Spring: In most years, there are fewer than five reports of Orange-crowned Warblers from March through mid-May. March reports may represent wandering winter visitors rather than returning migrants. Reports are inevitably of single individuals. ■

Nashville Warbler

Vermivora ruficapilla

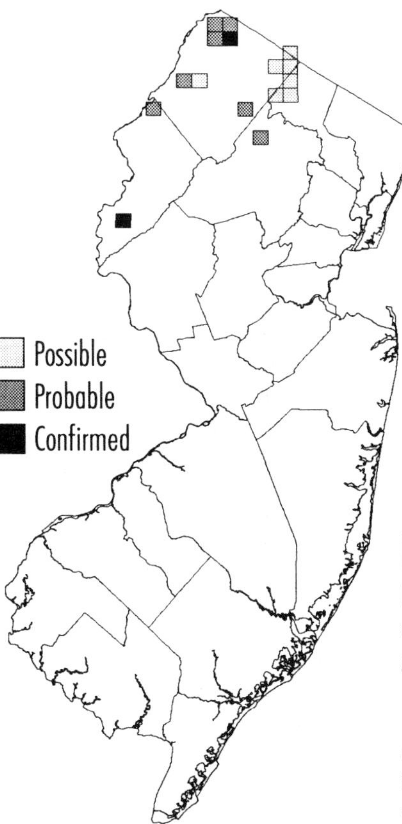

Range: In eastern North America breeds from Manitoba east to Newfoundland, south to Minnesota and northwestern New Jersey. Winters in Central America.

NJ Status: Scarce and local summer resident, uncommon spring and fairly common fall migrant, reported on ten CBCs.

Statewide Summary	
Status	# of Blocks
Possible	7
Probable	7
Confirmed	2
Total	16

Breeding

Habitat: Nests in riparian woodlands and brushy bogs; also open second-growth woodlands.

Nashville Warblers have always been rare breeding birds in New Jersey and their distribution seems to have changed little during the 20th century. There have historically been conflicting opinions about their status. Stone (1908) described Nashville Warblers as rare breeding birds and knew of only one breeding record, in 1887. Griscom (1923) contended that Nashville Warblers were common breeding birds within habitat in the higher sections of

continued on page 496

Physiographic Distribution Nashville Warbler	Number of blocks in province	Number of blocks species found breeding in province	Number of blocks species found in state	Percent of province species occupies	Percent of all records for this species found in province	Percent of state area in province
Kittatinny Mountains	19	5	16	26.3	31.3	2.2
Kittatinny Valley	45	2	16	4.4	12.5	5.3
Highlands	109	9	16	8.3	56.3	12.8

continued from page 495

Nashville Warbler

Sussex and Passaic counties, but he listed no additional nesting records. It is possible that Griscom's estimate of the density of this species as a breeding bird was high, as Cruickshank (1942), Bull (1964), Leck (1984), and Boyle (1986) all record Nashville Warblers as rare and local.

Atlas volunteers found that Nashville Warblers remained one of the scarcest breeding songbirds in the state. During the surveys they were found in only 16 blocks, almost half of which were recorded as only Possible breeding locations. They continue to occur only at scattered sites in the Kittatinny Mountains, Kittatinny Valley, and northern Highlands.

Fall: A few southbound Nashville Warblers arrive in late August. Peak numbers occur in mid-September, and they become scarce by mid-October. While they occur regularly, they are not numerous. **Maxima:** 20, Higbee Beach, 13 September 1997; 18, Higbee Beach, 21 September 1976.

Winter: Occasionally Nashville Warblers will linger into December, and they were reported on ten CBCs between 1976 and 1997.

Spring: Many of the northbound Nashville Warblers migrate inland, and they are usually encountered in only small numbers along the East coast. **Maxima:** 15, Higbee Beach, 14 May 1992; 10, Princeton, 12 May 1978. ■

Virginia's Warbler

Vermivora virginiae

Range: Breeds in the southwestern United States east to western Texas and southwestern South Dakota. Winters in Mexico.

NJ Status: Accidental. NJBRC Review List.

Occurrence: There have been two state reports of Virginia's Warblers, and one has been accepted by NJBRC: Island Beach SP, 6 October 1962 (ph-RBPF), banded. ■

Northern Parula

Parula americana

Range: Breeds from southeastern Manitoba east to Nova Scotia, south to east Texas and northern Florida. Winters from south Florida and Texas to the West Indies and Central America.

NJ Status: Uncommon and local summer resident, common spring and fall migrant, reported on three CBCs.

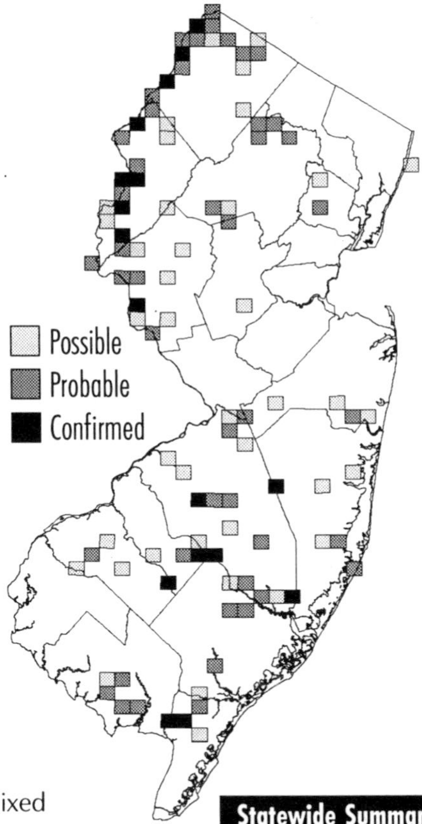

Possible
Probable
Confirmed

Breeding

Habitat: Nests in wet or moist mixed or deciduous woodlands; also in spruce plantations.

Historically, the range of Northern Parulas as breeding birds has been linked to availability of the pendant lichen, *Usnea*, which they use for

continued on page 498

Statewide Summary

Status	# of Blocks
Possible	39
Probable	45
Confirmed	17
Total	101

Physiographic Distribution

Northern Parula	Number of blocks in province	Number of blocks species found breeding in province	Number of blocks species found in state	Percent of province species occupies	Percent of all records for this species found in province	Percent of state area in province
Kittatinny Mountains	19	13	101	68.4	12.9	2.2
Kittatinny Valley	45	12	101	26.7	11.9	5.3
Highlands	109	15	101	13.8	14.9	12.8
Piedmont	167	12	101	7.2	11.9	19.6
Inner Coastal Plain	128	8	101	6.3	7.9	15.0
Outer Coastal Plain	204	15	101	7.4	14.9	23.9
Pine Barrens	180	26	101	14.4	25.7	21.1

continued from page 497

nesting (Moldenhauer and Regelski 1996). However, where *Usnea* is absent, Northern Parulas will use a variety of other substrates for nesting. Stone (1908) found Northern Parulas to be common breeding birds in the Pine Barrens, where *Usnea* was common. In 1937 he wrote that he had never seen them "so abundantly" as in the Dennisville area of Cape May County in the late 1890s, where *Usnea* also grew. However, both Griscom (1923) and Cruickshank (1942) noted that parulas nested locally in the northern part of the state, where the lichen did not grow.

By 1937 Stone wrote that Northern Parulas were disappearing from Cape May County as *Usnea* disappeared, probably due to air pollution (Moldenhauer and Regelski 1996). Fables (1955) indicated that Northern Parulas were extirpated from the state's northern breeding grounds and were rare in the south. He also attributed this decline in large part to be due to the disappearance of *Usnea*, although he was aware that they did not absolutely require it for nesting. By the mid-1970s, Northern Parulas were considered "former breeding birds" in the mountainous northwest, and, reports to RNJB suggested they were extirpated from the Coastal Plain.

In the late 1970s, there were indications that Northern Parulas were trying to re-establish a

Northern Parula

breeding population, and in the early 1980s, singing males were noted at several locations in the state. This marked the beginning of their comeback as breeding birds that continued through the 1990s. Although *Usnea* is now nearly absent from the state (K. Anderson, pers. com.), Northern Parulas have re-established a breeding population that uses an alternate nesting substrate.

Atlas surveys found Northern Parulas in only 12% of the blocks statewide. They have a broad distribution and were found in every physiographic province in the state. They were well established along the upper reaches of the Delaware River in the Kittatinny Mountains, where they were present in 68% of the blocks. Elsewhere, they appeared to be increasing in the Highlands, and in the Pine Barrens and adjacent areas of Cumberland and Cape May counties. It remains to be seen if Northern Parulas are capable of continuing to expand their range in the absence of *Usnea*. Another limiting factor in the recolonization of New Jersey may be their apparent requirement for large tracts of forests (Moldenhauer and Regelski 1996).

Conservation Note: Little is known about alternative nest substrates use by Northern Parulas. They are rapidly recolonizing New Jersey, and this offers an opportunity to gather information on their nesting behavior in the absence of *Usnea*. The two most frequently used nest sites in northern New Jersey are Sycamore branches with accumulated debris, and Norway Spruce branches (R. Kane, pers. obs.). Sycamores are abundant along the upper Delaware River where there is a concentration of Northern Parulas. Another substrate identified in the literature is the "the drooping boughs of live hemlock" (Davie 1898). In southern New Jersey, Northern Parulas have been observed nest-building in the drooping boughs of pine trees (V. Elia, pers. obs.), and other evergreens may serve the same purpose.

Fall: Although a few Northern Parulas move south in August, most pass through in September. They can still be present in good numbers in early October, but numbers diminish by mid-month. **Maxima:** 300, Higbee Beach, 18 September 1995; 250, Higbee Beach, 12 September 1992.

Winter: Northern Parulas were reported on three CBCs between 1976 and 1997 (i.e., 1982, 1985, and 1986). There are no other winter reports.

Spring: Northern Parulas are one of the more common migrant warblers in New Jersey in spring. They arrive in late April and peak in early to mid-May. **Maxima:** 100, Princeton, 13 May 1983; 40, Palmyra, 12 May 1995. ■

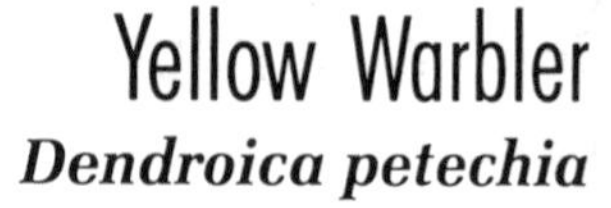

Range: In eastern North America breeds from Manitoba to Newfoundland, south to Oklahoma and northern Georgia. Winters from Central America and the West Indies to northern South America.

NJ Status: Fairly common and very widespread summer resident, common spring and fall migrant, reported on two CBCs.

Habitat: Nests in brushy or shrubby areas adjacent to marshes, ponds, streams, etc.

The distribution of Yellow Warblers has changed little during the 20th century. Stone (1908) contended that Yellow Warblers were "our best-known breeding warbler." Griscom (1923) described them as common and "somewhat local." Cruickshank (1942) used

Statewide Summary	
Status	# of Blocks
Possible	47
Probable	177
Confirmed	451
Total	675

Physiographic Distribution Yellow Warbler	Number of blocks in province	Number of blocks species found breeding in province	Number of blocks species found in state	Percent of province species occupies	Percent of all records for this species found in province	Percent of state area in province
Kittatinny Mountains	19	19	675	100.0	2.8	2.2
Kittatinny Valley	45	45	675	100.0	6.7	5.3
Highlands	109	109	675	100.0	16.1	12.8
Piedmont	167	157	675	94.0	23.3	19.6
Inner Coastal Plain	128	113	675	88.3	16.7	15.0
Outer Coastal Plain	204	150	675	73.5	22.2	23.9
Pine Barrens	180	82	675	45.6	12.1	21.1

Yellow Warbler

continued

the term "very common" to describe their status, and Fables (1955) indicated that they were found widely throughout the state, although less commonly in the Pine Barrens.

During the Atlas surveys, Yellow Warblers were found breeding in 79% of the blocks statewide, and in 97% of the blocks from the Piedmont northward. They were found in 46% of the blocks in the Pine Barrens, and many of the occupied blocks were around the edges of that province where the Pine Barrens blends with coastal upland habitats. Yellow Warblers were widely distributed on the Inner Coastal Plain, a testament to their need for brushy growth rather than mature woodlands. On the Outer Coastal Plain, they are especially common in the upland habitats that border the salt marshes.

Fall: Yellow Warblers are one of the earliest warbler migrants. The first birds in passage can be seen by mid-July, with a peak from early to mid-August. Although numbers decline by early September, a few continue to move into early October. **Maxima:** 200, Higbee Beach, 18 August 1989; 200, Higbee Beach, 20 August 1998.

Winter: There are a few scattered records of Yellow Warblers lingering into December, and they were reported on two CBCs between 1976 and 1997 (i.e., 1980 – with no details; and 1988 – with excellent details, AB). There are no reports after the CBC season.

Spring: Yellow Warblers arrive in mid- to late April, with most northbound birds moving through in early to mid-May. **Maxima:** 100, Tuckahoe, 26 April 1988; 50, Old Mine Road, 1 May 1983. ■

Chestnut-sided Warbler

Dendroica pensylvanica

Range: Breeds from Alberta east to Nova Scotia, south to northern Illinois and northern New Jersey and along the Appalachians to northern Alabama. Winters in Central and northern South America.

NJ Status: Fairly common but somewhat local summer resident, fairly common spring and fall migrant.

Breeding

Habitat: Nests in second-growth woodlands, overgrown fields, and on woodland edges.

Chestnut-sided Warblers experienced an expansion of their overall range during the 19th century as old growth forests were cut, and brushy second-growth habitats were created. They

continued on page 502

continued from page 501

Chestnut-sided Warbler

have apparently declined somewhat since the 1960s (Richardson and Brauning 1995). In New Jersey, Stone (1908) described them as common summer residents of the northern counties, a finding echoed by Griscom (1923), Cruickshank (1942), Bull (1964), and Leck (1984).

Atlas data indicated that 79% of Chestnut-sided Warbler's statewide range was north of the Piedmont, where they were found in 80% of the blocks. The Piedmont is a transitional area and Chestnut-sided Warblers occupy only 17% of the blocks in that province. Based on the range and abundance descriptions of the earlier authors, this suggests that Chestnut-sided Warblers may have declined in the Piedmont.

Historic Changes: Stone (1937) considered Chestnut-sided Warblers as "rather rare" transients. The numbers of migrants has increased in the second half of the 20th century, as second-growth habitats have become more abundant in eastern North America (Kaufman 1996).

Fall: Southbound Chestnut-sided Warblers arrive in mid-August, with peak numbers passing from late August through mid-September. Most are gone by late September. **Maxima:** 40, Higbee Beach, 30 August 1992; 35, Higbee Beach, 11 September 1988.

Map Interpretation: Chestnut-sided Warblers were found in nine blocks south of the Piedmont, and were Confirmed in northern Monmouth County. This find has precedent, as Fables (1955) referred to a breeding site in Monmouth County at Turkey Swamp. The other eight locations in southern New Jersey (particularly the six noted as Possible breeding), probably represent wandering, nonbreeding birds.

Statewide Summary	
Status	# of Blocks
Possible	28
Probable	79
Confirmed	72
Total	179

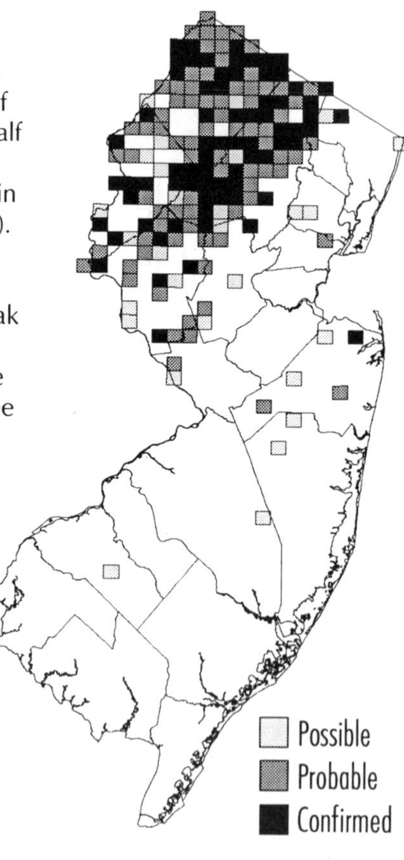

Chestnut-sided Warbler

continued

Spring: Most Chestnut-sided Warblers pass through New Jersey in early to mid-May on their way northward. Spring maxima from inland locales exceed both inland and coastal fall maxima. **Maxima:** 100, Princeton, 13 May 1983; 50, Princeton, 14 May 1988. ■

Physiographic Distribution — Chestnut-sided Warbler	Number of blocks in province	Number of blocks species found breeding in province	Number of blocks species found in state	Percent of province species occupies	Percent of all records for this species found in province	Percent of state area in province
Kittatinny Mountains	19	18	179	94.7	10.1	2.2
Kittatinny Valley	45	34	179	75.6	19.0	5.3
Highlands	109	89	179	81.7	49.7	12.8
Piedmont	167	29	179	17.4	16.2	19.6
Inner Coastal Plain	128	2	179	1.6	1.1	15.0
Outer Coastal Plain	204	5	179	2.5	2.8	23.9
Pine Barrens	180	2	179	1.1	1.1	21.1

Magnolia Warbler

Dendroica magnolia

Range: In eastern North America, breeds from central Manitoba east to Newfoundland to New Jersey and western North Carolina. Winters in the West Indies and in Central America.

NJ Status: Scarce and local summer resident, fairly common spring and common fall migrant, reported on one CBC.

Breeding

Habitat: Nests in fairly young stands of coniferous or mixed woodlands.

As of 1908, Stone considered Magnolia Warblers to be transient, nonbreeding birds in New Jersey. Griscom's only suggestion of breeding was a male seen in July 1922 on the Wawayanda Plateau in the northern Highlands (Griscom 1923). However, by 1942, Cruickshank found that they bred sparsely in the Kittatinny Mountains and on the Wawayanda Plateau, and suggested that they were not "as rare as formerly supposed." Fables (1955) called them local residents of hemlock and spruce in the Highlands. There was no appreciable change in that status through

continued on page 504

continued from page 503

Magnolia Warbler

the mid-1960s (Bull 1964). Kane (1973) called them rare breeders in the Highlands, and Leck (1984) wrote that their breeding status was uncertain. Benzinger (1988) and Benzinger and Angus (1992) found Magnolia Warblers primarily in spruce plantations but also in mixed hemlock and hardwood stands. They stated that the species had increased in the Pequannock Watershed (Sussex, Morris, and Passaic counties) since the 1970s.

Essentially boreal forest nesting birds, it is clear that Magnolia Warblers have never been numerous breeding birds in the state. Their current distribution is very similar to that previously noted by Cruickshank. The Atlas results showed that they were found in only 17 blocks. Nearly half of the blocks where they were found were only Possible breeding locations, and they were Confirmed breeding in only one block. The stronghold for Magnolia Warblers was in the Kittatinny Mountains, where birds were found in 53% of the blocks. They were also found in a few blocks on the Wawayanda Plateau of the northern Highlands. Of the breeding warblers, only Nashville and Yellow-rumped Warblers were found in fewer blocks.

Possible
Probable
Confirmed

Statewide Summary	
Status	# of Blocks
Possible	8
Probable	8
Confirmed	1
Total	17

Physiographic Distribution

Magnolia Warbler	Number of blocks in province	Number of blocks species found breeding in province	Number of blocks species found in state	Percent of province species occupies	Percent of all records for this species found in province	Percent of state area in province
Kittatinny Mountains	19	10	17	52.6	58.8	2.2
Kittatinny Valley	45	2	17	4.4	11.8	5.3
Highlands	109	5	17	4.6	29.4	12.8

Magnolia Warbler
continued

Fall: Only a few Magnolia Warblers arrive before late August, with peak numbers passing from early to mid-September. They continue to move in early October, with most passage migrants gone by mid-month. **Maxima:** 240, Higbee Beach, 11 September 1988; 150, Higbee Beach, 12 September 1992.

Winter: There is one report of a Magnolia Warbler on a CBC, on the Boonton count in 1985 (with good details, AB). There are no other winter reports.

Spring: Magnolia Warblers are one of the more common migrant spring warblers in the state, with most passing north in mid- to late May. **Maxima:** 150, Garret Mt., 19 May 1997; 100, Princeton, 13 May 1983; 100, Princeton, 14 May 1988. ■

Cape May Warbler
Dendroica tigrina

Range: Breeds from the Northwest Territories east to Nova Scotia south to Wisconsin and New Hampshire. Winters primarily in the West Indies.

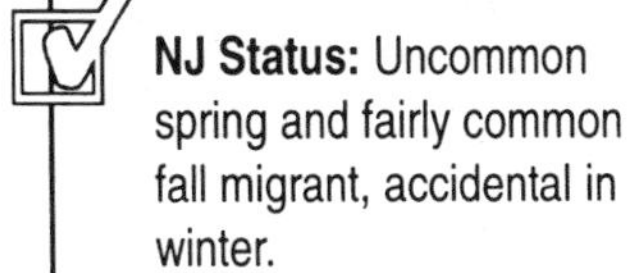

NJ Status: Uncommon spring and fairly common fall migrant, accidental in winter.

Historic Changes: Cape May Warblers are one of the boreal forest warblers which are subject to population variations tied to the spruce budworm cycles. Around the turn of the century, only a few specimens or sight records of the species were known from New Jersey (Stone 1908). However, by the middle of the 20th century, large flights were occasionally recorded – e.g., up to 500 in a day, Wenonah, late September 1951 (AFN).

Fall: Cape May Warblers' migration generally extends from late August through mid-October, although there are a few earlier and many later reports. Peak flights can occur from late August through late September. They are uncommon migrants statewide, although at times they can be quite common at coastal migrant traps. Current levels, while far greater than those of the early 20th century, are considerably lower than in the peak years. **Maxima:** 180, Higbee Beach, 29 August 1982 (Sibley 1997); 150, Higbee Beach, 11 September 1988 (Sibley 1997).

continued on page 506

continued from page 505

Cape May Warbler

Winter: Cape May Warblers occasionally persist into early winter and, between 1976 and 1997, were reported six times on CBCs. One survived the winter season at Princeton, 15 January-March 1990.

Spring: Cape May Warblers begin to arrive in early to mid-May, and migration is over by late May. Peak numbers occur in mid- to late May. **Maxima:** 1,000+, Sandy Hook, 19 May 1984; dozens, Princeton, 13 May 1983. ■

Black-throated Blue Warbler

Dendroica caerulescens

Range: Breeds from southwestern Ontario and northeastern Minnesota east to Nova Scotia and northern New Jersey, and south along the Appalachians to northern Georgia. Winters mainly in the West Indies.

NJ Status: Uncommon and local summer resident, fairly common spring and common fall migrant.

Possible
Probable
Confirmed

Breeding

Habitat: Nests in mixed or deciduous woodlands with a dense laurel or rhododendron understory.

The history of Black-throated Blue Warbler as a breeding bird in New Jersey dates back to 1909, when a pair was suspected of nesting near Wawayanda Lake (Stone 1908). Griscom (1923) found them to be local breeding birds in Sussex and Passaic

Black-throated Blue Warbler

continued

counties, and Cruickshank (1942) extended that range description to include northern Morris County. Bull (1964) included Warren County in his description of their range, and noted their preference for laurel-covered hillsides at higher elevations. Boyle (1986) considered Black-throated Blue Warblers to be rare and local breeding birds.

Map interpretation: The southernmost breeding location depicted on the breeding map probably refer to a wandering male or a late migrant. Black-throated Blue Warblers have nested in New Jersey for nearly all of the 20th century and only nest at he highest elevations in the northern part of the state.

Statewide Summary	
Status	# of Blocks
Possible	9
Probable	17
Confirmed	8
Total	34

Atlas surveys found 85% of Black-throated Blue Warblers' range confined to the Kittatinny Mountains and the Highlands, the same areas earlier authors had found birds throughout the 20th century. Combined, these two physiographic provinces represent only 15% of the area of the state. Even within these two physiographic regions, Black-throated Blue Warblers were not widespread. In the Highlands they occurred in only 17% of the blocks, mainly at the highest altitudes. In the Kittatinny Mountains they occupied 53% of the blocks.

Fall: Black-throated Blue Warblers arrive in late August, with peak numbers passing south in early to mid-September. Migration continues through early October, but diminishes by mid-month. **Maxima:** 1,000, Higbee Beach, 12 September 1992; 500, Higbee Beach, 31 August 1988; 500, Higbee Beach, 11 September 1995.

Spring: As with many spring migrants, northward movements of Black-throated Blue Warblers are more widespread and less concentrated than in fall. They pass through the state in good numbers in mid-May. **Maxima:** 100, Princeton, 13 May 1983; 50, Princeton, 30 April 1981 (early). ■

Physiographic Distribution

Black-throated Blue Warbler	Number of blocks in province	Number of blocks species found breeding in province	Number of blocks species found in state	Percent of province species occupies	Percent of all records for this species found in province	Percent of state area in province
Kittatinny Mountains	19	10	34	52.6	29.4	2.2
Kittatinny Valley	45	3	34	6.7	8.8	5.3
Highlands	109	19	34	17.4	55.9	12.8
Piedmont	167	2	34	1.2	5.9	19.6

Yellow-rumped Warbler

Dendroica coronata

Range: In eastern North America, the race *D. c. coronata*, "Myrtle Warbler," breeds from Manitoba east to Newfoundland, south to northern Minnesota, West Virginia, and northwestern New Jersey. Winters from Massachusetts and the central United States south to Central America and the West Indies.

NJ Status: Rare and local summer resident, common spring and fall migrant, common winter resident.

Statewide Summary	
Status	# of Blocks
Possible	6
Probable	8
Confirmed	2
Total	16

Possible
Probable
Confirmed

Breeding

Habitat: Nests in coniferous or mixed woodlands, preferring edges and openings.

Yellow-rumped Warblers were first confirmed breeding in New Jersey in the summer of 1979 along Clinton Road, West Milford in Passaic County (Bacinski 1980). Subsequently, eight individuals were found on a breeding bird survey of the Highlands in 1986.

During Atlas surveys, observers located Yellow-rumped Warblers in only 16 blocks, and only Confirmed the species in one block. Those results made this species one of the rarest, regularly occurring breeding songbirds in New Jersey. They were located mainly in the Kittatinny Mountains and on the Wawayanda Plateau in the northern Highlands. As a recent addition to New Jersey's fauna, it may be that Yellow-rumped Warblers will continue to expand their range in coniferous woods at higher altitudes. For instance, in the Kittatinny Mountains, they occupy only 42% of the blocks. It is likely that there are also unoccupied areas in the

Kittatinny Mountains and the Highlands that are suitable for colonization.

Fall: By far the most numerous migrant warbler, Yellow-rumped Warblers can stage massive flights from early to mid-October. The first southbound birds generally arrive from mid- to late September and migration continues into December. **Maxima:** 100,000, Higbee Beach, 16 October 1990; 75,000-100,000, Cape May Point, 18 October 1995.

Winter: Yellow-rumped Warbler is *the* winter warbler, subsisting largely on bayberries, poison ivy berries, and other fruits. They are found in the largest concentrations along the coast. CBC totals are variable depending on the severity of the winter, and numbers probably diminish further by late January and early February. **CBC Statewide Stats:** Average: 5,282;

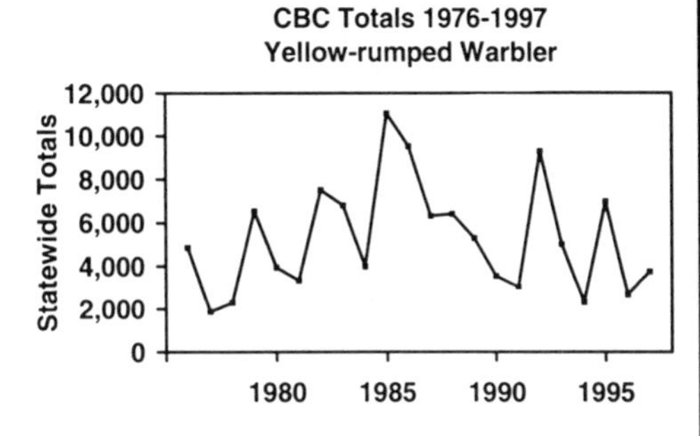

Maximum: 11,044 in 1985; Minimum: 1,867 in 1977. **CBC Maximum:** 4,250, Cape May, 1992.

Spring: An influx of northbound Yellow-rumped Warblers occurs in late April and early May, but numbers decline rapidly and most have moved northward by mid-May. **Maxima:** 3,000, Higbee Beach, 26 April 1990; 500-1,000, Manasquan Inlet, 4-5 May 1996.

Subspecies: Yellow-rumped Warbler has two races, "Myrtle" Warbler (*D. c. coronata*) group of the East, and "Audubon's" Warbler (*D. c. audubonii*) group of the West. The Myrtle is the resident race in New Jersey and the subspecies to be expected at all seasons. However, there are at least a dozen reports of Audubon's Warbler in New Jersey, and from all seasons except summer. The NJBRC added this race to the Review List in 1996. ■

Physiographic Distribution Yellow-rumped Warbler	Number of blocks in province	Number of blocks species found breeding in province	Number of blocks species found in state	Percent of province species occupies	Percent of all records for this species found in province	Percent of state area in province
Kittatinny Mountains	19	8	16	42.1	50.0	2.2
Kittatinny Valley	45	1	16	2.2	6.3	5.3
Highlands	109	7	16	6.4	43.8	12.8

Black-throated Gray Warbler

Dendroica nigrescens

Range: Breeds from southern British Columbia south to California, east to southwestern Wyoming and New Mexico. Winters from the southern-most United States to Mexico.

NJ Status: Occasional. NJBRC Review List.

Occurrence: There have been 22 state reports of Black-throated Gray Warblers, and 16 have been accepted by the NJBRC (13 in fall, one in winter, two in spring). Of the 13 fall records, which span the dates 30 August to 25 December, nine were photographed and four were banded at Island Beach. The winter bird was a male in a courtyard at Princeton University, 17 December 1982-11 January 1983 (phs-RNJB 9:22, 9:23). ■

Black-throated Green Warbler

Dendroica virens

Range: Breeds from northern Alberta east to Newfoundland, southeast across northern Illinois and southern Michigan, and south along the Appalachians to northern Alabama. Also from southeastern Virginia to South Carolina. Winters in the West Indies and in Central and northern South America.

NJ Status: Uncommon and local summer resident, fairly common spring and fall migrant, reported on one CBC.

Breeding

Habitat: Nests in coniferous and mixed woodlands often near spruce and hemlock groves, also in White Cedar swamps.

The status and distribution of Black-throated Green Warbler in New Jersey has changed during the 1900s. Stone (1908) noted a nest found at Demarest, Bergen County, in June of 1904, and supposed that they nested elsewhere in northern New Jersey. Griscom (1923) wrote of their presence in the higher parts of Sussex and Passaic counties, whereas Cruickshank (1942) described them as locally common south to the

Black-throated Green Warbler

continued

Watchung Mountains of Union and Somerset counties. Their distribution is quite different from that of any other warbler in New Jersey. Their range is broad and extends beyond the northern reaches of the state to a disjunct breeding population in the Pine Barrens, first recorded breeding in July 1935 (Stone 1937).

Atlas surveys found concentrations of breeding Black-throated Green Warblers in four areas: along the Kittatinny Mountains, the northern Kittatinny Valley, the northern Highlands, and the Pine Barrens. They were found in all of the Kittatinny Mountain blocks, and although they occupied only 26% of the Highlands blocks, they were found in most of the Wawayanda Plateau blocks. Their range has retracted

continued on page 512

Statewide Summary	
Status	# of Blocks
Possible	19
Probable	42
Confirmed	23
Total	84

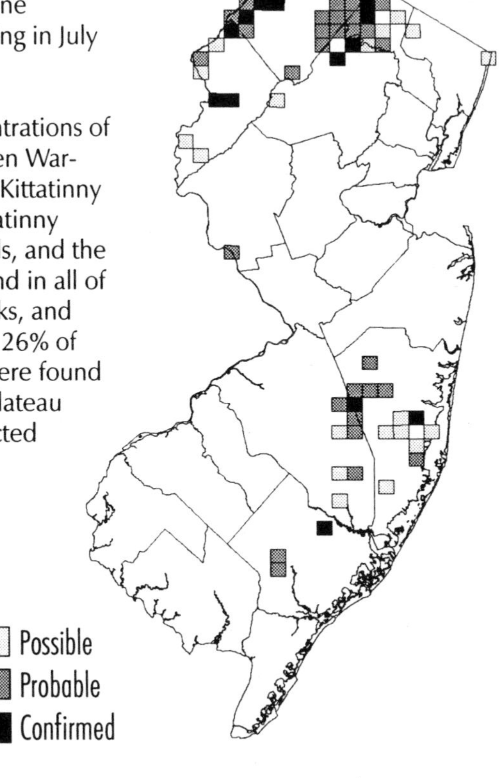

Physiographic Distribution Black-throated Green Warbler	Number of blocks in province	Number of blocks species found breeding in province	Number of blocks species found in state	Percent of province species occupies	Percent of all records for this species found in province	Percent of state area in province
Kittatinny Mountains	19	19	84	100.0	22.6	2.2
Kittatinny Valley	45	11	84	24.4	13.1	5.3
Highlands	109	29	84	26.6	34.5	12.8
Piedmont	167	2	84	1.2	2.4	19.6
Outer Coastal Plain	204	1	84	0.5	1.2	23.9
Pine Barrens	180	22	84	12.2	26.2	21.1

continued from page 511

Black-throated Green Warbler

somewhat in the north, as Cruickshank's range description included the Watchung Mountains, where they are no longer breeding. The main portion of the Highland's population extended no farther south than Sparta Mountain.

Black-throated Green Warblers were found in 12% of the Pine Barrens blocks. Their presence in that province was centered around watercourses, particularly White Cedar swamps.

Subspecies: The habitat used by Black-throated Green Warblers in the Pine Barrens is more similar to the habitat used by the southern Coastal Plain subspecies, *D. v. waynei*, which breeds in cypress and White Cedar swamps in Virginia and the Carolinas (Dunn and Garrett 1997), than to the nominate *D. v. virens* of northern New Jersey. However, there is no evidence supporting the occurrence of *waynei* in the Pine Barrens, but there is evidence they are referable to *virens* (Wander 1981). A specimen collected near Manahawkin, Ocean County, from a cedar swamp 29 June 1963 was thought to belong to the nominate race *virens* (Murray 1972). Research on song dialect in this population would be useful to establish the subspecific composition of the population in the Pine Barrens.

Historic Changes: Stone (1937) considered Black-throated Green Warblers to be "rather rare" transients in Cape May County, but both Fables (1955) and Bull (1964) described them as widespread and fairly common migrants statewide.

3lack-throated Green Warbler

continued

'all: The first migrant Black-throated Green Warblers arrive rom mid- to late August, but the nain movement is in mid-September. They become scarce y early October, although they ccasionally linger into November. **Maxima:** 180, Higbee Beach, 11 September 1988; 115, Tewksbury, 22 September 1997.

Winter: A Black-throated Green Warbler (with good details, RNJB) was reported on the Boonton CBC in 1983. There are no other winter reports.

Spring: Black-throated Green Warblers are seen regularly in the warbler waves moving north in mid-May. **Maxima:** 100, Princeton, 13 May 1983; 20+, Higbee Beach, 12 May 1988; 20+, Brigantine NWR, 7 May 1994. ■

Townsend's Warbler

Dendroica townsendi

Range: Breeds from Alaska south to northern California and northern Idaho. Winters from California south to Costa Rica.

NJ Status: Accidental. NJBRC Review List.

Occurrence: There have been eight state reports of Townsend's Warblers, and seven have been accepted by the NJBRC (six in fall/winter, one in spring). The seven accepted records are:

Princeton	*23 December 1971-15 January 1972*	
Vincentown	*5 December 1977-21 February 1978*	*ph.-NJA/RNJB 4:48; Meritt 1978*
Harmony	*11-14 December 1979*	*ph.-RBPF*
Sandy Hook	*16-18 December 1980*	
Island Beach	*31 October 1987*	*ph.-RNJB 14:1, banded*
Princeton	*28 April 1988*	
West Cape May	*11 November 1988*	*ph.-RBPF*

Blackburnian Warbler
Dendroica fusca

Range: Breeds from central Alberta east to southern Newfoundland, southeast across northern Wisconsin and Michigan, and south along the Appalachians to northern Georgia. Winters in northern South America.

NJ Status: Scarce and local summer resident, uncommon spring and fairly common fall migrant.

Statewide Summary	
Status	# of Blocks
Possible	10
Probable	16
Confirmed	14
Total	40

Breeding

Habitat: Nests in coniferous and mixed woodlands, often near spruce and hemlock.

Blackburnian Warblers have always had a limited breeding distribution in New Jersey, because there is only a small amount of appropriate breeding habitat in the state.

Physiographic Distribution — Blackburnian Warbler	Number of blocks in province	Number of blocks species found breeding in province	Number of blocks species found in state	Percent of province species occupies	Percent of all records for this species found in province	Percent of state area in province
Kittatinny Mountains	19	15	40	78.9	37.5	2.2
Kittatinny Valley	45	6	40	13.3	15.0	5.3
Highlands	109	18	40	16.5	45.0	12.8
Piedmont	167	1	40	0.6	2.5	19.6

Stone (1908) listed Blackburnian Warbler as a transient nonbreeder, although they may have occurred at such a low density that they were overlooked. In the early 1920s a "few pairs" nested in the hemlock woods of Sussex and Passaic counties (Griscom 1923). In the early 1940s Cruickshank (1942) described them as uncommon, and Bull (1964) found them "nowhere common" in the northern part of the state, but widely distributed where hemlock was present. Kane (1973) found an average of five to six pairs in each of four mature Norway Spruce plantings in the Pequannock Watershed. They were also found in White Cedar swamps in Kuser Bog and Wawayanda State Park (R. Kane, pers. obs.). Boyle (1986) noted that that they were uncommon and local in hemlock stands.

Some early authors made much of Blackburnian Warblers affinity for hemlocks, and it is their preferred nesting substrate throughout much of their range (Morse 1994). In New Jersey, however, Kane and Marx (1972) found 28 pairs of Blackburnian Warblers nesting in spruce, and only one pair nesting in hemlock. Interestingly, Benzinger (1994) estimated that less than 25% of the New Jersey population is found in hemlock.

Atlas data showed that the distribution of Blackburnian Warblers was restricted to the Kittatinny Mountains and the northern Highlands. As is the case with most of the breeding birds using high-elevation coniferous woods in New Jersey, they are limited in their distribution in the state, and patchy within the provinces they occupy. All but one of the breeding blocks was north of the Piedmont, and they occupied only 22% of the blocks in the provinces north of the Piedmont.

Fall: Southbound Blackburnian Warblers arrive in mid-August and peak from late August through early September. Most have moved on by mid-September. **Maxima:** 65, Higbee Beach, 29 August 1982; 40, Higbee Beach, 11 September 1988.

Spring: Blackburnian Warblers are generally widespread migrants in spring and are usually found in small numbers. Most pass through in mid-May. **Maxima:** dozens, Princeton, 13 May 1983; 12, Garret Mt., 19 May 1997. ■

Range: Breeds from eastern Nebraska east to New Jersey, south to east Texas and northern Florida. Winters from the Gulf Coast south to Central America.

NJ Status: Fairly common but local summer resident, scarce spring and fall migrant.

Statewide Summary	
Status	# of Blocks
Possible	11
Probable	26
Confirmed	15
Total	52

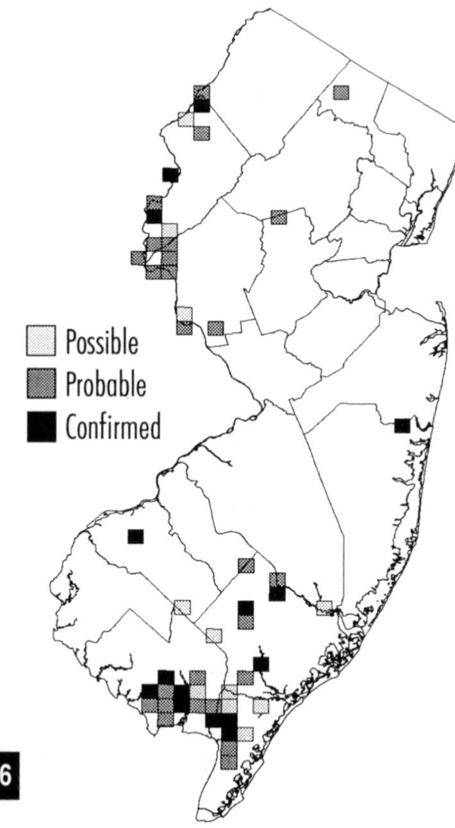

Yellow-throated Warbler

Dendroica dominica

Breeding

Habitat: Generally nests in moist mixed woodlands; the southern subspecies *D. d. dominica* prefers mixed oak-pine or pine plantations, although the Midwestern subspecies *D. d. albilora* prefers Sycamores.

The first breeding record of Yellow-throated Warblers in New Jersey was in May of 1922, when a nest with four young was found at Cape May Point (Fables 1955). This proved to be an extension of the range of the southern subspecies *D. d. dominica*. A nest found at Bull's Island in 1954 (Fables 1955) was a range extension of the Midwestern subspecies *D. d. albilora*. Yellow-throated Warblers expanded their range slowly through the mid-1970s, although they continued to be considered rare. By 1981, however, they had established a foothold in northern Cape May and southern Cumberland counties.

Atlas data indicated that Yellow-throated Warblers, although only found in 6% of the blocks in the state, are clumped into two distinct regions. Overall, 58% of the occupied blocks were located in the three southern counties (Atlantic, Cape May, and Cumberland), and 37% were found along the upper Delaware River. *D. d. albilora* is still concentrated around Bull's Island on the Delaware River in the north, and *D. d. dominica* is centered in the state's two southernmost counties – Cape

Yellow-throated Warbler

continued

May and Cumberland. *D. d. albilora*, although spreading along the Delaware River, has shown only a slight tendency to spread inland. In the south, *D. d. dominica* appears to be spreading into parts of Atlantic County, and was Confirmed in both Gloucester and Ocean counties.

Fall: Due to their southerly breeding distribution, Yellow-throated Warblers are infrequently encountered in migration. Those that are seen tend to occur early in the season, most in early August. **Maximum:** 2, Higbee Beach, 29 July 1989.

Spring: Yellow-throated Warblers are seen only occasionally in spring migration. Local breeding birds return very early, sometimes by late March. **Maximum:** 3, Cape May, 22 April 1982 (Sibley 1997). ■

Physiographic Distribution **Yellow-throated Warbler**	Number of blocks in province	Number of blocks species found breeding in province	Number of blocks species found in state	Percent of province species occupies	Percent of all records for this species found in province	Percent of state area in province
Kittatinny Mountains	19	3	52	15.8	5.8	2.2
Kittatinny Valley	45	4	52	8.9	7.7	5.3
Highlands	109	8	52	7.3	15.4	12.8
Piedmont	167	4	52	2.4	7.7	19.6
Inner Coastal Plain	128	1	52	0.8	1.9	15.0
Outer Coastal Plain	204	19	52	9.3	36.5	23.9
Pine Barrens	180	13	52	7.2	25.0	21.1

Pine Warbler

Dendroica pinus

Range: Breeds from southeastern Manitoba and northern Wisconsin east to Maine, south and west to east Texas and Florida. Winters mainly in the southeastern United States.

NJ Status: Common and fairly widespread summer resident, uncommon spring and scarce fall migrant, rare winter resident.

Breeding

Habitat: Nests in open pine or mixed woodlands; also in pine plantings.

Stone (1908) considered Pine Warblers to be one the most characteristic birds of the Pine Barrens. At that time, he knew of only one nesting

continued on page 518

continued from page 517

Pine Warbler

Physiographic Distribution — Pine Warbler	Number of blocks in province	Number of blocks species found breeding in province	Number of blocks species found in state	Percent of province species occupies	Percent of all records for this species found in province	Percent of state area in province
Kittatinny Mountains	19	13	376	68.4	3.5	2.2
Kittatinny Valley	45	8	376	17.8	2.1	5.3
Highlands	109	35	376	32.1	9.3	12.8
Piedmont	167	17	376	10.2	4.5	19.6
Inner Coastal Plain	128	23	376	18.0	6.1	15.0
Outer Coastal Plain	204	110	376	53.9	29.3	23.9
Pine Barrens	180	170	376	94.4	45.2	21.1

Statewide Summary	
Status	# of Blocks
Possible	26
Probable	127
Confirmed	223
Total	376

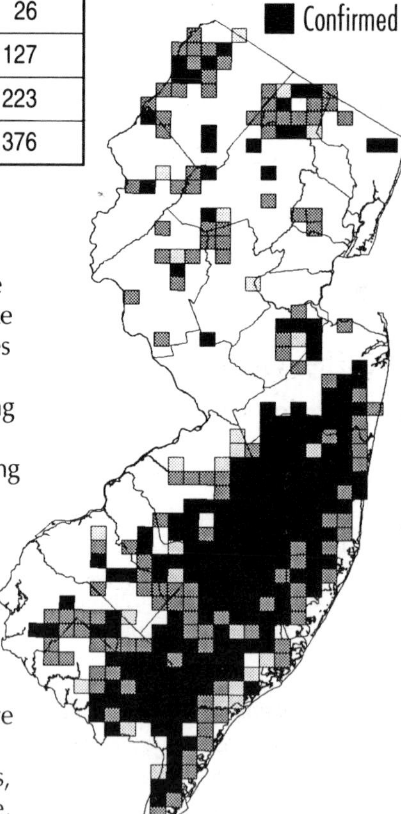

location outside of the Pine Barrens, at High Point, in Sussex County, where a "colony" was located in 1890. Subsequently he discovered Pine Warblers nesting near Cape May (Stone 1937). The High Point location was also noted by Griscom (1923), who added Round Pond on the Kittatinny Ridge as another breeding site in northern New Jersey. By 1955, Fables had added the Wawayanda Plateau in the northern Highlands to their breeding range. Bull (1964), however, noted the sites in the north as only sporadic nesting locations, and Boyle (1986) contended that Pine Warblers were uncommon in the northern section of the state.

Atlas observers found Pine Warblers to be patchy in the north, but more widely distributed than historical accounts suggested. They were well distributed on the Wawayanda Plateau and in the Kittatinny Mountains, and south into the Piedmont. Statewide,

Pine Warbler

continued

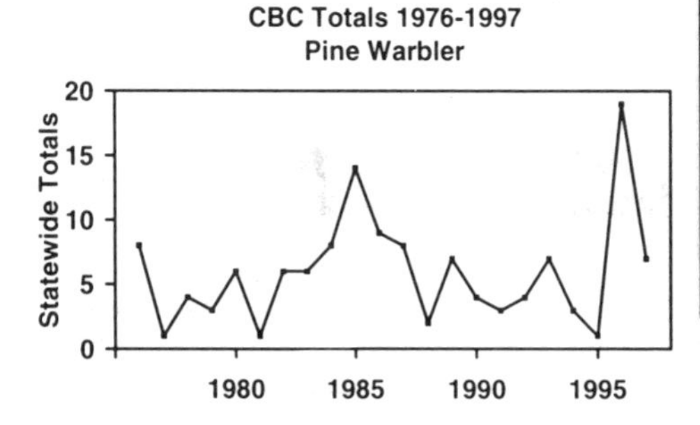

Pine Warblers remain concentrated in southern New Jersey, with 76% of their occupied blocks in the Pine Barrens and Outer Coastal Plain. Pine Warblers remained one of the indicator birds of the Pine Barrens and were found in 94% of the blocks in that province. They were also well distributed in Cape May and southeastern Cumberland counties. In southern New Jersey, they were conspicuously absent from the Inner Coastal Plain and from the barrier islands.

Fall: As a common and widespread breeding bird, it is unusual that Pine Warblers are normally encountered only in small numbers in fall migration. Those that are seen are found any time from late August through October. **Maxima:** 7, Cape May Point and 4, Higbee Beach, both on 6 October 1997.

Winter: Pine Warblers occur in small numbers on CBCs, usually with fewer than ten seen. A few probably survive the winter each year, particularly in years of mild weather. **CBC Statewide Stats:** Average: 6; Maximum: 19 in 1996; Minimum: one in three years. **CBC Maximum:** 13, Belleplain, 1996.

Spring: Northward migration is very early; small numbers of Pine Warblers are noted from mid-March to mid- April. Local breeding birds may be on territory as early as mid-March. **Maxima:** 16, Higbee Beach, 7 April 1992; 15, Rifle Camp Park, 4 April 1981. ■

Prairie Warbler

Dendroica discolor

Range: Breeds from Missouri east to southern Maine, south to extreme eastern Texas and Florida. Winters from Florida south to the West Indies and Central America.

NJ Status: Common and widespread summer resident, fairly common spring and fall migrant, accidental in winter.

Breeding

Habitat: Nests in dry, brushy clearings and forest edges.

Prairie Warbler's distribution in New Jersey has expanded during the 20th

continued on page 520

continued from page 519

Prairie Warbler

century. Stone (1908) knew them as a common summer resident in the Pine Barrens, but as a scarce transient elsewhere in the state. Griscom (1923) described Prairie Warblers only as transients in northern New Jersey, although he reported them as a common summer resident on Long Island, New York. Cruickshank (1942) noted an increase in breeding locations away from Long Island, and reported that they were spreading into parts of Bergen and Passaic counties. In addition to finding them common in the Pine Barrens, Fables (1955) suggested that they were continuing to expand into shrubby fields in the north. By the mid-1960s, Bull (1964) noted that Prairie Warblers had greatly expanded their range in the north over the preceding 40 years, and by the mid-1980s, they were fairly common in northern New Jersey (Boyle 1986).

Possible
Probable
Confirmed

Statewide Summary	
Status	# of Blocks
Possible	61
Probable	249
Confirmed	166
Total	476

Physiographic Distribution

Prairie Warbler	Number of blocks in province	Number of blocks species found breeding in province	Number of blocks species found in state	Percent of province species occupies	Percent of all records for this species found in province	Percent of state area in province
Kittatinny Mountains	19	14	476	73.7	2.9	2.2
Kittatinny Valley	45	42	476	93.3	8.8	5.3
Highlands	109	83	476	76.1	17.4	12.8
Piedmont	167	55	476	32.9	11.6	19.6
Inner Coastal Plain	128	21	476	16.4	4.4	15.0
Outer Coastal Plain	204	97	476	47.5	20.4	23.9
Pine Barrens	180	164	476	91.1	34.5	21.1

Prairie Warbler

continued

Atlas observers found that Prairie Warblers occupied 57% of the blocks north of the Coastal Plain, as well as 66% of the blocks from the Pine Barrens southward. Their expansion in the north has been noteworthy. Although absent from areas north of the Piedmont throughout much of the first half of the 20th century, they were located in 80% of the blocks there during the Atlas surveys. In the south, Prairie Warblers occupied 91% of the Pine Barrens blocks, and most of the blocks in Cumberland and Cape May counties. They were generally absent from the Inner Coastal Plain, and along a corridor through the Piedmont continuing to Bergen County. This area has been largely deforested, either by agricultural practices or by urban sprawl.

Fall: The arrival of migrant Prairie Warblers is often masked by local breeding populations. Peak movements occur from late August to mid-September, with most moving south by late September. Regularly, a few linger into early November. **Maxima:** 30, Higbee Beach, 11 September 1988; 18, Higbee Beach, 27 August 1982.

Winter: Prairie Warblers were reported on two CBCs between 1976 and 1997 (i.e., 1992 and 1993). Another was present at the Cape May National Golf Course from 4 December 1997 until at least mid-January 1998.

Spring: Northbound Prairie Warblers arrive in late April, with most moving through from early to mid-May. **Maxima:** 25, Higbee Beach, 1 May 1982; 15, Higbee Beach, 4 May 1988. ■

Palm Warbler

Dendroica palmarum

Range: Breeds from British Columbia east to Newfoundland south to northern Minnesota and central Maine. Winters from the southern United States to Central America and the West Indies and north along the Atlantic coast, to Long Island.

NJ Status: Fairly common spring and common fall migrant, rare to scarce winter resident.

Fall: In fall, the earliest Palm Warblers arrive from early to mid-September with maximum numbers found between mid-September and late October. Coastal movement continues into early December – e.g., 20-30, West Cape May, 4 December 1989. They favor the open ground of weedy fields, marsh edges,

continued on page 522

continued from page 521

Palm Warbler

beaches, etc. **Maxima:** 900, Higbee Beach, 4 October 1988; 600, Higbee Beach, 4 September 1988 (Sibley 1997).

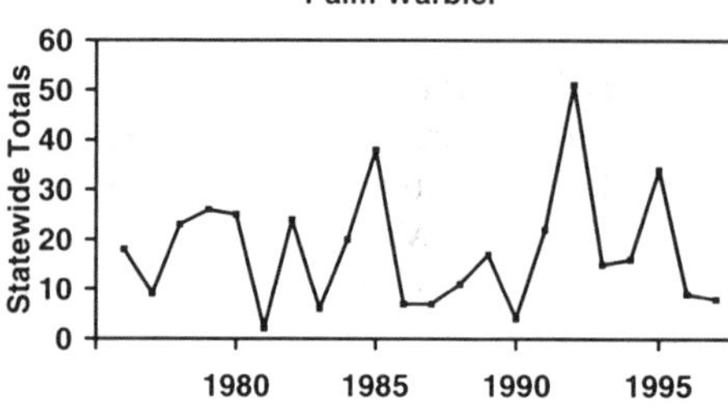

Winter: Palm Warblers are rare but regular in the southernmost areas of the state where a few birds, no doubt, winter during most years. In the north, they are occasionally noted early in the winter but rarely, if ever, survive to spring. Among warblers, only Yellow-rumped Warblers are found more often than palms on CBCs. **CBC Statewide Stats:** Average: 18; Maximum: 51 in 1992; Minimum: 2 in 1981. **CBC Maximum:** 22, Cape May, 1995.

Spring: Typical spring arrival is in early April, though there are a number of March records. Peak movement is from mid- to late April, with a few records of stragglers after early May. **Maxima:** 68 Palmyra, 12 April 1992; 50+, Trenton Marsh, 15 April 1986.

Subspecies: Most fall reports are of the browner, more westerly breeding race – *D. p. palmarum*. The "Yellow" Palm Warbler, *D. p. hypochrysea*, which breeds from Ontario east, migrates primarily west of the Appalachians in autumn (Bull 1974). They arrive later in fall and in far fewer numbers than the "Western" Palm Warbler (Sibley 1997). The relativ abundance of the two subspecies in spring is far different from that of fall. Nearly all spring birds are Yellow Palm Warblers. ■

Bay-breasted Warbler

Dendroica castanea

Range: Breeds from the southern Yukon and Northwest Territories east to southwestern Newfoundland, south to northern Minnesota and central Maine. Winters from Central to northern South America.

NJ Status: Uncommon spring and fall migrant.

Historic Changes: Bay-breasted Warblers were considerably less common at the turn of the century than they are today (Stone 1908), and are one of the species that exhibits large population swings resulting from cyclical outbreaks of the spruce budworm on the boreal breeding grounds

Bay-breasted Warbler

continued

(Kaufman 1996). The 1970s and 1980s saw migrant numbers build to record totals, but the 1990s showed a notable drop-off.

Fall: Passage of Bay-breasted Warblers begins in mid-August, and peaks in September. Only the occasional straggler is noted after early October. **Maxima:** 120, Higbee Beach, 11 September 1988 (Sibley 1997); 100, Princeton, 22 September 1983.

Spring: Bay-breasted Warblers are unexpected before May and after early June. Maximum numbers occur from mid- to late May. **Maxima:** 40, Princeton, 14 May 1981; 28, Marlton, 21 May 1984. ■

Blackpoll Warbler

Dendroica striata

Range: In eastern North America, breeds from northern Manitoba east to Labrador, south to Nova Scotia, and sporadically to parts of New England and New York. Winters in northern South America.

NJ Status: Common spring and fall migrant, reported on one CBC.

Fall: The earliest Blackpoll Warblers are normally seen in late August and the peak flight occurs from mid-September to mid-October. They will frequently linger into November. A large portion of the autumn passage takes place over the open Atlantic, and many birds fly nonstop from northeastern North America to northern South America (Nisbet 1970). Brady (1991) witnessed such a flight on 15 October, when between 2:45-4:45 a.m., an estimated 9,000 blackpolls flew through the light cast by the ship's lamps, 70 miles off Barnegat Inlet. **Other maxima:** 400, Higbee Beach, 11 September 1988 (Sibley 1997); 300, Higbee Beach, 4 October 1988.

Winter: A Blackpoll Warbler was reported on the Assunpink CBC in 1982, but no details were submitted (AB). There are no other winter reports.

Spring: Despite their deserved reputation as being one of the latest spring warblers, the earliest Blackpoll Warblers usually arrive in early May. Largest numbers, however, occur from mid- to late May, with migrants regularly seen through early June. **Maxima:** 100s, Higbee Beach, 25 May 1989 (Sibley 1997); 100+, Princeton, 13 May 1983. ■

Cerulean Warbler

Dendroica cerulea

Breeding

Habitat: Nests in wet, mature deciduous woodlands.

Range: Breeds from southeastern Minnesota east to Vermont, south to eastern Oklahoma and north-central North Carolina. Winters in northern South America.

NJ Status: Scarce and local summer resident, rare to scarce spring and fall migrant.

Cerulean Warblers have increased as breeding birds in New Jersey since about 1950. The first breeding record in the state was at Millington, Somerset County in 1947, and Fables (1955) listed several summer or breeding records from 1947-1952. Bull (1964) noted them to be a rare and local breeding bird in northern New Jersey, though increasing. Boyle (1986) described them as uncommon breeding birds in the north.

Statewide Summary	
Status	# of Blocks
Possible	23
Probable	49
Confirmed	7
Total	79

Possible
Probable
Confirmed

During the Atlas surveys, Cerulean Warblers were found in the Highlands and in the Kittatinny Ridge and Valley. South of the Highlands the species was found mainly around Bull's Island along the Delaware River in southern Hunterdon County. Cerulean Warblers use deciduous woods for nesting, making southward expansion possible. The Probable breeding site in Cumberland County was preceded by a pair suspected of nesting near Tarkiln Pond in northern Cape May County in the early 1990s. Leck (1984) also mentions nesting attempts by Cerulean Warblers in southern New Jersey.

Conservation Note: Although Cerulean Warblers have increased over the past 50 years in New Jersey, they are decreasing throughout their North American range. Cerulean Warbler is listed as a Species of National Concern by the U. S. Fish and Wildlife Service and was recently nominated for the status of "Special Concern" in New Jersey.

Cerulean Warbler

continued

Fall: Most sightings of southbound Cerulean Warblers occur in August and early September. At Cape May, Sibley (1997) estimated that only about five Cerulean Warblers are seen on average each fall. Stone (1937) considered Cerulean Warblers "exceedingly rare" and Bull (1964) described them as "very rare." Although they are encountered more regularly today, sightings are still infrequent. **Maximum:** 3, Cape May, 5 August 1993.

Spring: Breeding Cerulean Warblers arrive on territory from late April through early May. Migrants are more widespread in spring than fall. Most northbound birds are seen from early to mid-May. **Maximum:** 6, Island Beach, 9 May 1987 (banded). ■

Physiographic Distribution Cerulean Warbler	Number of blocks in province	Number of blocks species found breeding in province	Number of blocks species found in state	Percent of province species occupies	Percent of all records for this species found in province	Percent of state area in province
Kittatinny Mountains	19	15	79	78.9	19.0	2.2
Kittatinny Valley	45	20	79	44.4	25.3	5.3
Highlands	109	37	79	33.9	46.8	12.8
Piedmont	167	6	79	3.6	7.6	19.6
Outer Coastal Plain	204	1	79	0.5	1.3	23.9

Black-and-white Warbler

Mniotilta varia

Range: In eastern North America breeds from Manitoba east to Newfoundland, south to Texas and Alabama. Winters from central Texas and Florida south to Central and northern South America and the West Indies.

NJ Status: Fairly common and widespread summer resident, common spring and fall migrant, reported on three CBCs.

Breeding

Habitat: Nests in mature or second-growth deciduous or mixed woodlands, often in drier areas.

Throughout most of the 20th century, Black-and-white Warblers were noted as common and widespread woodland residents in northern New Jersey, but were generally considered uncommon

continued on page 526

continued from page 525

Black-and-white Warbler

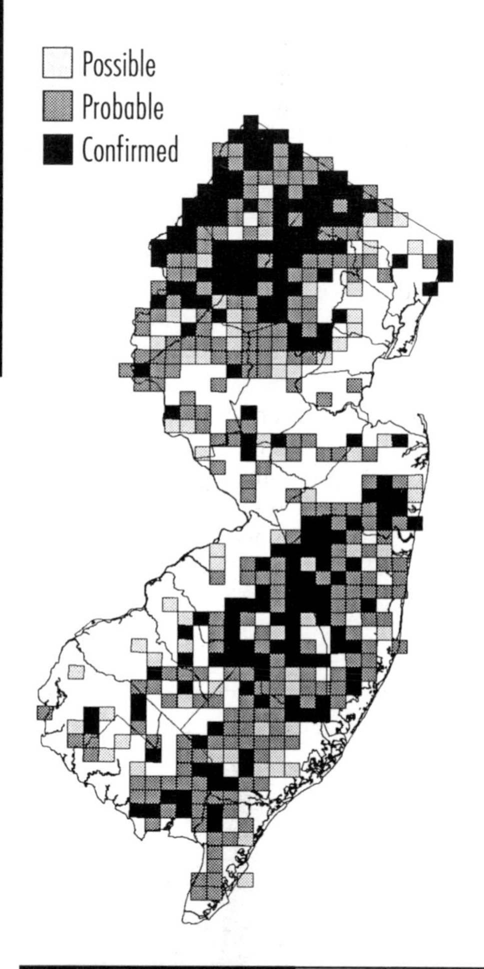

Statewide Summary	
Status	# of Blocks
Possible	67
Probable	237
Confirmed	199
Total	503

on the Coastal Plain. Stone (1908) estimated that they were most common in northern sections of the state and less so in southern New Jersey. Griscom (1923) suggested Black-and-white Warblers occurred in northern New Jersey "wherever there is woodland." Bull (1964) also found them common in the north, but described them as less common on the Coastal Plain, as did Leck (1984).

Atlas observers found Black-and-white Warblers to be widely distributed north of the Piedmont, where they were present in 95% of the blocks. However,

Physiographic Distribution **Black-and-white Warbler**	Number of blocks in province	Number of blocks species found breeding in province	Number of blocks species found in state	Percent of province species occupies	Percent of all records for this species found in province	Percent of state area in province
Kittatinny Mountains	19	19	503	100.0	3.8	2.2
Kittatinny Valley	45	41	503	91.1	8.2	5.3
Highlands	109	105	503	96.3	20.9	12.8
Piedmont	167	68	503	40.7	13.5	19.6
Inner Coastal Plain	128	29	503	22.7	5.8	15.0
Outer Coastal Plain	204	91	503	44.6	18.1	23.9
Pine Barrens	180	150	503	83.3	29.8	21.1

they were also well represented in the Pine Barrens and Outer Coastal Plain. In the Pine Barrens they were present in 83% the blocks, and they were well represented in Cumberland and Cape May counties. This suggests an expansion of their range in southern New Jersey during the second half of the 20th century. Black-and-white Warblers are scarce in the largely deforested corridor that includes the Inner Coastal Plain and a swath continuing through the Piedmont northward to Bergen County. This pattern supports the contention that they are sensitive to forest fragmentation (Kricher 1995), as the forests along that swath have been reduced mainly to small woodlots.

Fall: A few southbound Black-and-White Warblers can be seen by early August, but peak numbers pass from late August through mid-September. Small numbers continue to move into early October. **Maxima:** 500, Higbee Beach, 5 September 1993; 330, Higbee Beach, 7 September 1988.

Winter: Black-and-White Warblers were reported on three CBCs between 1976 and 1997 (i.e., 1976, 1980, and 1983). There are no mid-winter reports.

Spring: The first northbound Black-and-White Warblers can arrive by mid-April, but peak numbers pass in the first half of May. On 10-11 May 1978, 130 were banded at Island Beach. **Other maxima:** 100, Princeton, 13 May 1983; 100, Atsion, 7 May 1993. ■

Black-and-white Warbler

American Redstart

Setophaga ruticilla

Breeding

Habitat: Breeds in open mixed or deciduous woodlands, preferring moist woods with a dense understory.

Stone (1908) found American Redstarts to be common breeding birds in the northern counties, but much less common in southern New Jersey. Griscom (1923) wrote that, excepting Common Yellowthroat and Ovenbird, they were the most common breeding warbler in northern New Jersey. Cruickshank (1942), however, described them as uncommon breeding birds. This difference of opinion was probably unrelated to a true change in status, as Bull's (1964) impressions were similar Griscom's. In southern New Jersey, Fables (1955) noted that American Redstarts could be locally "abundant" in the Pine Barrens, a departure from the previous accounts of their scarce

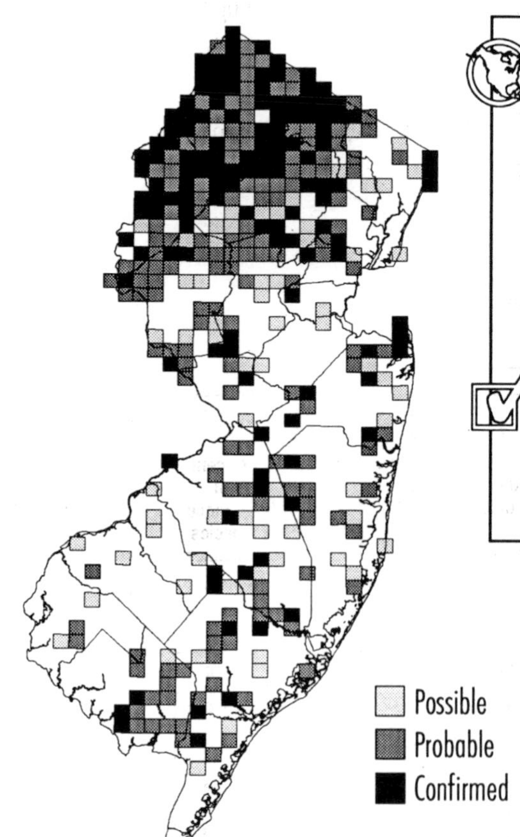

Range: In eastern North America breeds from Manitoba east to Newfoundland, south to extreme eastern Texas, central Georgia, and coastal South Carolina. Winters in Central and northern South America and the West Indies.

NJ Status: Fairly common and fairly widespread summer resident, common spring and fall migrant.

Statewide Summary	
Status	# of Blocks
Possible	67
Probable	155
Confirmed	135
Total	357

presence on the Coastal Plain. He also described them as well distributed in what he called the "southwestern part of the state."

Atlas observers located American Redstarts in 95% of all blocks north of the Piedmont, and in 42% of the Piedmont itself. South of the Piedmont, their distribution was patchy. They were found in 33% of the Pine Barrens blocks and were present in the northern Cape May and southern Cumberland county sections of the Outer Coastal Plain. While Fables (1955) asserted that American Redstarts were well distributed in southwestern New Jersey, Atlas data found them scarce in that area, and most of the sightings in Salem, Gloucester and Camden counties probably represent nonbreeding birds. If the difference between Fables' data and that collected during the Atlas represents a real decline, it is similar to declines that have been seen in several other states (Sherry and Holmes 1997).

Map Interpretation: American Redstart males are sexually mature in their first summer, and they acquire full adult plumage in their second summer. Some of these young males (more than 50%) will sing on territory, but remain unmated throughout the summer (Sherry and Holmes 1997). Given the particulars of Atlas data collection, the singing code (and most lower grades) could yield a map that includes nonbreeding, first-summer males, and not breeding adults.

Fall: Among the most numerous autumn migrant songbirds in the state, southbound American Redstarts can be seen from early August into early October. Peak numbers pass from late August through mid-September. **Maxima:** 3,600, Higbee Beach, 7 September 1986; 2,000+, Higbee Beach, 13 September 1997.

Spring: Northbound American Redstarts arrive in early May with peak numbers passing in mid-month. **Maxima:** 100+, Hazlet, 19 May 1996; 100, Princeton, 13 May 1983. ■

Physiographic Distribution

American Redstart	Number of blocks in province	Number of blocks species found breeding in province	Number of blocks species found in state	Percent of province species occupies	Percent of all records for this species found in province	Percent of state area in province
Kittatinny Mountains	19	19	357	100.0	5.3	2.2
Kittatinny Valley	45	41	357	91.1	11.5	5.3
Highlands	109	104	357	95.4	29.1	12.8
Piedmont	167	70	357	41.9	19.6	19.6
Inner Coastal Plain	128	25	357	19.5	7.0	15.0
Outer Coastal Plain	204	38	357	18.6	10.6	23.9
Pine Barrens	180	60	357	33.3	16.8	21.1

Prothonotary Warbler

Protonotaria citrea

Range: Breeds from southeastern Minnesota east to New Jersey, south to eastern Texas and northern Florida. Winters in Central and northern South America.

NJ Status: Fairly common but local summer resident, scarce spring and scarce to uncommon fall migrant.

Possible
Probable
Confirmed

Statewide Summary	
Status	# of Blocks
Possible	24
Probable	43
Confirmed	32
Total	99

Breeding

Habitat: Nests in cavities in the understory of swamps, wet deciduous woodlands, and river bottom lands.

Stone listed only two records of Prothonotary Warblers for the state, both from the late 1800s (Stone 1908). The first breeding records for New Jersey came in June 1924, one in Morris County and the other in Cape May County (Stone 1937). Their numbers increased slowly, and Fables (1955) found them increasing in the southern counties, and he noted that they were more common in parts of the Pine Barrens than was generally believed at that time.

During Atlas surveys, Prothonotary Warblers were found to be well distributed in the swampy woodlands of the lower third of the state, particularly in Cumberland and Cape May counties. Over 43% of blocks with Prothonotary Warblers were in the Pine Barrens.

Although Prothonotary Warblers have sporadically nested in northern New Jersey, they have yet to establish themselves there in any numbers. In fact they

Physiographic Distribution Prothonotary Warbler	Number of blocks in province	Number of blocks species found breeding in province	Number of blocks species found in state	Percent of province species occupies	Percent of all records for this species found in province	Percent of state area in province
Kittatinny Valley	45	2	99	4.4	2.0	5.3
Highlands	109	4	99	3.7	4.0	12.8
Piedmont	167	2	99	1.2	2.0	19.6
Inner Coastal Plain	128	11	99	8.6	11.1	15.0
Outer Coastal Plain	204	37	99	18.1	37.4	23.9
Pine Barrens	180	43	99	23.9	43.4	21.1

Map Interpretation: Unmated male Prothonotary Warblers will hold territories and even occasionally build dummy nests (Bent 1953), habits that increase the likelihood that the Possible and some of the Probable locations may be unmated, prospecting birds and not active breeding birds.

were found in only 2% of the blocks north of the Coastal Plain. Recently they have retreated from several traditional northern New Jersey sites in Bound Brook, Princeton Institute Woods, Great Swamp, and Bull's Island (R. Kane, pers. com.).

Fall: Few Prothonotary Warblers nest north of New Jersey, and, consequently, they are encountered only rarely as migrants. Dispersing and southbound birds can be seen by late July, with most having moved on by late August. **Maxima:** 15, Higbee Beach, 4 August 1986; 10, Higbee Beach, 31 July 1988.

Spring: Most Prothonotary Warblers encountered in spring are local breeding birds that return from late April to early May. There are only a few instances of more than one or two northbound migrants present in the same location on the same day. ■

Prothonotary Warbler ©DAS

Worm-eating Warbler

Helmitheros vermivorus

Range: Breeds from eastern Iowa east to Massachusetts, south to eastern Texas and central Georgia. Winters in Central America and the West Indies.

NJ Status: Uncommon and somewhat local summer resident, uncommon spring and fairly common fall migrant.

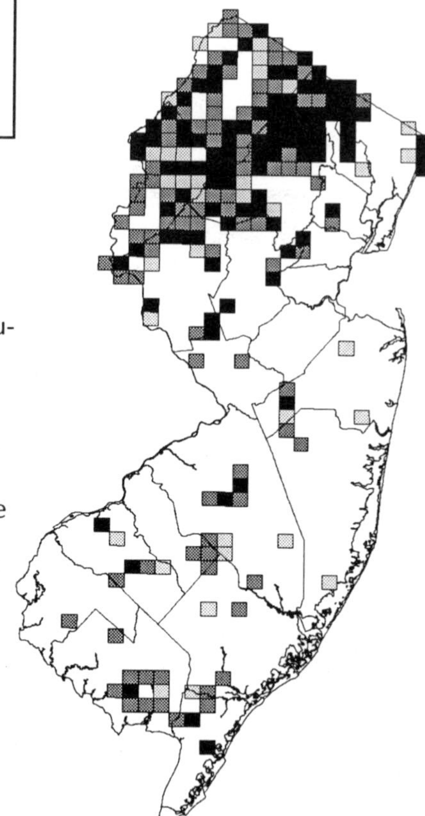

Statewide Summary	
Status	# of Blocks
Possible	35
Probable	92
Confirmed	97
Total	224

Breeding

Habitat: In northern New Jersey prefers the undergrowth of forested ravines and other wooded slopes; in the south prefers damp or wet deciduous woodlands.

Stone (1908) found Worm-eating Warblers to be scarce nesting birds in New Jersey and absent as breeding birds from the southern portion of the state. By 1937, he knew of only two records in Cape May County, both of fall migrants. Griscom (1923) noted that they were more common in northern New Jersey than had previously been reported and wrote that they were widespread on heavily wooded hillsides throughout the northern counties. Bull (1964) also found Worm-eating Warblers to be locally common in the north. They were, apparently, unknown as breeding birds in the southern part of the state until the early 1980s, when they were found breeding in Bear Swamp, Cumberland County during the June bird counts (Sutton and Sutton 1986). Boyle (1986) described them as

uncommon summer residents in the northern counties, and occasional breeding birds in Cumberland County.

Atlas observers found Worm-eating Warbler's range in northern New Jersey to be more broadly distributed than previously suspected. They were found in 82% of the blocks north of the Piedmont and in more than 84% of the blocks in both the Kittatinny Mountains and the Highlands provinces.

Leck (1984) contended that Worm-eating Warbler's population was in decline in the state, but Atlas data showed them to be continuing their spread southward and, although patchy, to be broadly distributed south of the Piedmont. They occupied 11% of the blocks in the Pine Barrens and the Outer Coastal Plain. Since first reported in southern Cumberland County in the early 1980s, they have continued to colonize both Cumberland and northern Cape May Counties.

continued on page 534

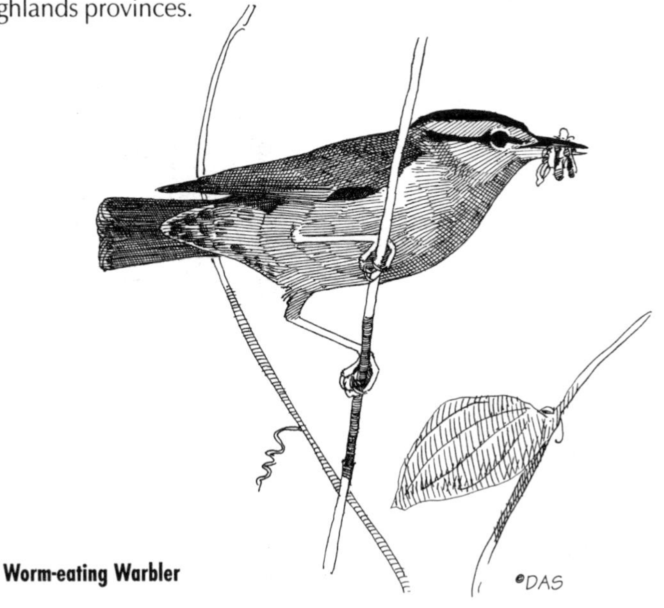

Worm-eating Warbler

Physiographic Distribution — **Worm-eating Warbler**	Number of blocks in province	Number of blocks species found breeding in province	Number of blocks species found in state	Percent of province species occupies	Percent of all records for this species found in province	Percent of state area in province
Kittatinny Mountains	19	16	224	84.2	7.1	2.2
Kittatinny Valley	45	34	224	75.6	15.2	5.3
Highlands	109	93	224	85.3	41.5	12.8
Piedmont	167	33	224	19.8	14.7	19.6
Inner Coastal Plain	128	6	224	4.7	2.7	15.0
Outer Coastal Plain	204	22	224	10.8	9.8	23.9
Pine Barrens	180	20	224	11.1	8.9	21.1

continued from page 533

Worm-eating Warbler

Fall: Worm-eating Warblers move south early, with the first southbound migrants seen in late July. Most move through from mid-August to early September, after which numbers dwindle rapidly. **Maxima:** 12, Higbee Beach, 30 August 1992; 10+, Higbee Beach, 4 September 1992.

Spring: Northbound Worm-eating Warblers arrive in late April, with small movements into mid-May. **Maxima:** 5, Princeton, 7 May 1980; 5, Princeton, 14 May 1990; 3, Higbee Beach, 6 May 1987. ■

Swainson's Warbler

Limnothlypis swainsonii

Possible
Probable
Confirmed

Range: Breeds from eastern-most Oklahoma east to Virginia, south to eastern Texas and northern Florida. Winters in the Bahamas, Cuba, the Caymans, Jamaica, Yucatan Peninsula, and Belize.

NJ Status: Accidental. NJBRC Review List.

Breeding

Habitat: Nests in wet or swampy thickets.

During mid-April to late June 1994, Swainson's Warblers were recorded singing in two blocks in Cape May. It is likely that

Physiographic Distribution Swainson's Warbler	Number of blocks in province	Number of blocks species found breeding in province	Number of blocks species found in state	Percent of province species occupies	Percent of all records for this species found in province	Percent of state area in province
Outer Coastal Plain	223	2	2	0.9	100.0	26.2

Swainson's Warbler

continued

Statewide Summary	
Status	# of Blocks
Possible	0
Probable	2
Confirmed	0
Total	2

the sightings represented only one bird that wandered from Cape May Point to Higbee Beach WMA. No further evidence of breeding was obtained. Observers are cautioned that Swainson's Warbler songs may be similar to some songs of Hooded Warbler and Louisiana Waterthrush, and efforts should be made to see singing birds to confirm the identification.

Occurrence: There have been 17 state reports of Swainson's Warblers, and nine have been accepted by the NJBRC (eight in spring, one in fall). Four of the reports were of banded birds. The nine accepted records are:

Linwood	*23 May 1968*	*ph-EBBA News 31:159, banded*
*Island Beach**	*5 May 1971*	*banded*
Greenbrook Sanctuary	*8 May 1977*	
*Island Beach**	*17 May 1979*	*banded*
Cape May Point	*5 October 1985*	*ph-RBPF, banded*
Higbee Beach	*May, 8-10 May 1992*	*ph-RBPF*
Cape Island	*17 April-30 June 1994*	*ph-RBPF*
Eatontown	*14-31 May 1994*	*ph-RBPF*
Higbee Beach	*1 May 1996*	

Ovenbird

Seiurus aurocapillus

Range: In eastern North America breeds from central Manitoba east to Newfoundland, south to eastern Oklahoma and northern Georgia. Winters from the Gulf Coast south to Central America and the West Indies.

NJ Status: Common and very widespread summer resident, fairly common spring and common fall migrant, reported on two CBCs.

Breeding

Habitat: Nests in mature, open, dry deciduous or mixed woodlands with little or no understory.

Ovenbirds have long been common and widespread breeding birds in New Jersey, and were described by Stone (1908) as being "one of the most characteristic birds of our woodlands." Almost 90

continued on page 536

continued from page 535

years later, Atlas observers found this to still be true throughout the state. Cruickshank (1942) noted that Ovenbirds could be found "wherever there are woods." However, although still very common throughout their North American breeding range, they have declined during the 20th century, largely because of forest fragmentation (Van Horn and Donovan 1994).

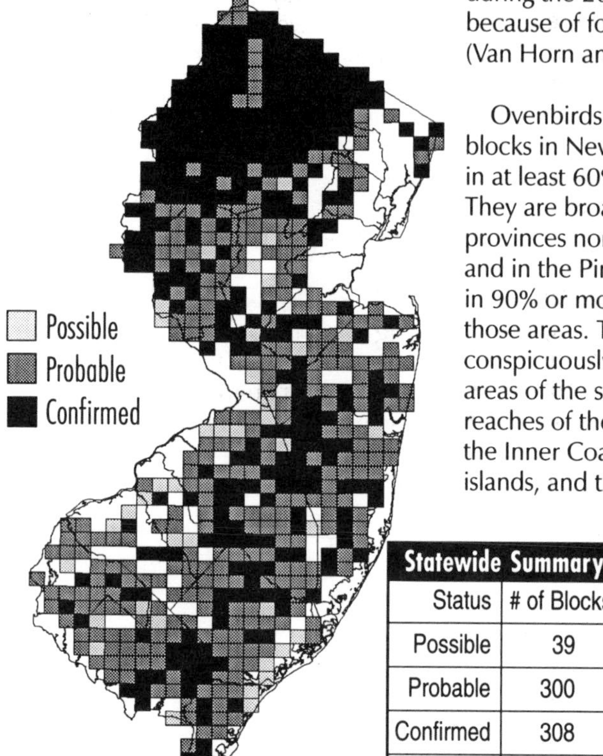

Ovenbirds occurred in 76% of all blocks in New Jersey and occurred in at least 60% of each province. They are broadly distributed in the provinces north of the Piedmont and in the Pine Barrens, occurring in 90% or more of the blocks in those areas. They are, however, conspicuously absent from some areas of the state, such as the lower reaches of the Delaware River on the Inner Coastal Plain, the barrier islands, and the highly urbanized northeastern Piedmont. Each of these areas have either fragmented woodlots, or no woodlots at all.

Statewide Summary

Status	# of Blocks
Possible	39
Probable	300
Confirmed	308
Total	647

Physiographic Distribution

Ovenbird	Number of blocks in province	Number of blocks species found breeding in province	Number of blocks species found in state	Percent of province species occupies	Percent of all records for this species found in province	Percent of state area in province
Kittatinny Mountains	19	19	647	100.0	2.9	2.2
Kittatinny Valley	45	43	647	95.6	6.6	5.3
Highlands	109	109	647	100.0	16.8	12.8
Piedmont	167	100	647	59.9	15.5	19.6
Inner Coastal Plain	128	81	647	63.3	12.5	15.0
Outer Coastal Plain	204	131	647	64.2	20.2	23.9
Pine Barrens	180	164	647	91.1	25.3	21.1

Ovenbird

continued

Conservation Note: There is evidence that, over part of their North American range, Ovenbirds are declining. There is also evidence that, as forests are fragmented, Ovenbirds either experience lower rates of reproduction or abandon areas altogether (Van Horn and Donovan 1994). They can occur at very high densities, and changes in density can go undetected when a species declines from "very abundant" to "abundant" – even though this decline could represent a large drop in the total population. In New Jersey, Ovenbirds occupy a range similar to that of 20 years ago, however their density may have declined. The Atlas data has defined their current range, but it is important to have density estimates at several locations to evaluate changes in density over time.

Fall: Ovenbirds begin their trek southward in mid-August with peak numbers in passage from early to mid-September. Their habit of staying on the ground in the interior of woodlands makes them inconspicuous in migration. **Maxima:** 150, Higbee Beach, 7 September 1988; 140, Higbee Beach, 11 September 1988.

Winter: Ovenbirds were reported on two CBCs between 1976 and 1997 (i.e., 1978 and 1986). There are no other winter reports.

Spring: The first breeding Ovenbirds return to their territories from mid- to late April. Birds bound for points farther north of New Jersey continue moving through into mid-May. **Maxima:** 100, Princeton, 13 May 1983; 50, Trenton Marsh, 16 May 1986. ■

Northern Waterthrush

Seiurus noveboracensis

Range: In eastern North America breeds from Manitoba east to Newfoundland, south to the Great Lakes and northern New Jersey, and south along the Appalachians to West Virginia. Winters in the West Indies and Central and South America.

NJ Status: Uncommon and local summer resident, fairly common spring and common fall migrant, reported on one CBC.

Breeding

Habitat: Nests in shrubby bogs or wet woodlands with standing or sluggish water.

Stone (1908) reported Northern Waterthrushes were only transients through the state. Griscom (1923), however, noted that they nested at higher elevation in the northernmost counties of the state. Fables

continued on page 538

continued from page 537

Northern Waterthrush

Physiographic Distribution Northern Waterthrush	Number of blocks in province	Number of blocks species found breeding in province	Number of blocks species found in state	Percent of province species occupies	Percent of all records for this species found in province	Percent of state area in province
Kittatinny Mountains	19	10	81	52.6	12.3	2.2
Kittatinny Valley	45	15	81	33.3	18.5	5.3
Highlands	109	39	81	35.8	48.1	12.8
Piedmont	167	8	81	4.8	9.9	19.6
Outer Coastal Plain	204	1	81	0.5	1.2	23.9
Pine Barrens	180	8	81	4.4	9.9	21.1

(1955) extended the estimate of their breeding range south to the Great Swamp of Morris County. Leck (1984) referred to additional nesting reports in Monmouth and Ocean counties.

Statewide Summary	
Status	# of Blocks
Possible	19
Probable	42
Confirmed	20
Total	81

Possible
Probable
Confirmed

Atlas data indicated that in the northern part of the state Northern Waterthrushes were concentrated in the Highlands, Kittatinny Valley, and Kittatinny Mountains. They occupied 40% of the blocks in the Kittatinny Mountains and Valley. Over 48% of their statewide range was in the Highlands where birds occupied 36% of the blocks. Their presence at scattered locations in the Pine Barrens, although without a Confirmation, is intriguing, given the precedent of a 1980 study which found two territorial birds in southern New Jersey cedar swamps (Wander 1981). Their preferred habitat of shrubby bogs occurs in the Pine Barrens in the proximity of White Cedar swamps, and this offers the possibility of continued range extension.

Fall: Among of the earliest songbird migrants of the fall, migrant Northern Waterthrushes can be seen in passage by mid-July. Their

Northern Waterthrush

continued

extended period of migration lasts through September. Peak movements are noted from mid-August through mid-September. **Maxima:** 200, Higbee Beach, 16 August 1988; 120, Higbee Beach, 7 September 1988.

Winter: A Northern Waterthrush was recorded on the Sussex CBC in 1979. There are no other winter reports.

Spring: Northbound Northern Waterthrushes arrive in late April and most have moved through by mid- to late May. **Maxima:** 100, Princeton, 12 May 1981; dozens, Princeton, 13 May 1983. ■

Louisiana Waterthrush

Seiurus motacilla

Range: Breeds from extreme southeastern Minnesota east to southern New Hampshire, south to northeastern Texas and central Georgia. Winters in Central and northern South America and the West Indies.

NJ Status: Fairly common but somewhat local summer resident, scarce spring and uncommon fall migrant.

Breeding

Habitat: Nests along wooded streams.

Louisiana Waterthrushes have long been established breeding birds throughout northern New Jersey. Griscom (1923) noted that they were found wherever there was appropriate habitat, and Leck (1984), writing 60 years later, found much the same thing. In 1955, Fables knew of only one nest in southern New Jersey, in Cumberland County. By 1978, there was a small but persistent population of Louisiana Waterthrushes in southern coastal swamps. Several pairs were found in a survey of the cedar swamps of southern New Jersey in 1980 (Wander 1981). This range expansion was supported by information that breeding pairs were present in small numbers in the early 1980s during surveys of Bear Swamp, Cumberland County (Sutton and Sutton 1986).

Atlas volunteers in northern New Jersey found Louisiana Waterthrushes in 90% of the blocks north of the Piedmont. South of the Highlands, their distribution was patchy. They were located in 28% of the Piedmont blocks, with much of their range within that province along the Delaware River. They were nearly absent

continued on page 540

continued from page 539

Louisiana Waterthrush

Possible
Probable
Confirmed

from the Inner Coastal Plain, which consists mainly of fragmented woodlots, agricultural areas, and housing developments.

The Atlas surveys found that Louisiana Waterthrushes had expanded their range in southern New Jersey, as compared to their status as rare breeding birds in the mid-1980s. They were well established throughout southern Cumberland and northern Cape May counties. The presence of Louisiana Waterthrushes in the Pine Barrens is restricted to western sections, where they occur in pockets of appropriate habitat.

Fall: A very early migrant, southbound Louisiana Waterthrushes are seen by mid-July. Peak numbers move through in early August and most

Statewide Summary	
Status	# of Blocks
Possible	42
Probable	110
Confirmed	111
Total	263

Physiographic Distribution Louisiana Waterthrush	Number of blocks in province	Number of blocks species found breeding in province	Number of blocks species found in state	Percent of province species occupies	Percent of all records for this species found in province	Percent of state area in province
Kittatinny Mountains	19	19	263	100.0	7.2	2.2
Kittatinny Valley	45	36	263	80.0	13.7	5.3
Highlands	109	101	263	92.7	38.4	12.8
Piedmont	167	47	263	28.1	17.9	19.6
Inner Coastal Plain	128	7	263	5.5	2.7	15.0
Outer Coastal Plain	204	31	263	15.2	11.8	23.9
Pine Barrens	180	22	263	12.2	8.4	21.1

Louisiana Waterthrush
continued

are gone by the end of that month. **Maxima:** 8+, Higbee Beach, 14 August 1992; 6, Cape Island, 1 August 1988; 6, Higbee Beach, 11 August 1991.

Spring: Louisiana Waterthrushes return to their breeding grounds very early, with birds sometimes on territory by late March. They are infrequently encountered in spring away from known nesting areas, with most sightings involving lone individuals. ■

Louisiana Waterthrush

Kentucky Warbler
Oporornis formosus

Range: Breeds from eastern Nebraska east to New Jersey, south to eastern Texas and northern Florida. Winters in Central and northern South America.

NJ Status: Uncommon and local summer resident, scarce spring and fall migrant.

Breeding
Habitat: Breeds in the dense understory of moist or wet deciduous woodlands.

In the early 1900s, Kentucky Warblers were known to breed in two areas of the state: along the Palisades in the Hudson Valley, and along the Delaware River near

continued on page 542

continued from page 541

Kentucky Warbler

Camden (Stone 1908). By 1923, Griscom reported they were gone from the Palisades and knew of no other locations that supported breeding Kentucky Warblers in northern New Jersey. Stone (1937) considered them a rare transient without a breeding population in Cape May. Cruickshank (1942) estimated that a pair or two were breeding in the Palisades and that there was perhaps another breeding location in Essex County. Fables (1955) also noted their presence in the Palisades, but suggested that they were mainly to be found in the southwestern section of the state. Bull (1964) suggested that they had disappeared as breeding birds in northern New Jersey and reported none breeding farther north than Somerset and Hunterdon

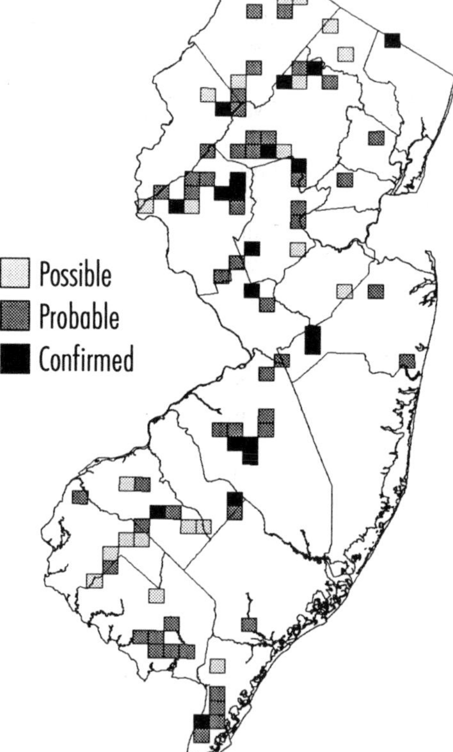

Statewide Summary	
Status	# of Blocks
Possible	21
Probable	51
Confirmed	20
Total	92

Physiographic Distribution Kentucky Warbler	Number of blocks in province	Number of blocks species found breeding in province	Number of blocks species found in state	Percent of province species occupies	Percent of all records for this species found in province	Percent of state area in province
Kittatinny Valley	45	7	92	15.6	7.6	5.3
Highlands	109	25	92	22.9	27.2	12.8
Piedmont	167	16	92	9.6	17.4	19.6
Inner Coastal Plain	128	12	92	9.4	13.0	15.0
Outer Coastal Plain	204	24	92	11.8	26.1	23.9
Pine Barrens	180	8	92	4.4	8.7	21.1

Kentucky Warbler

continued

counties. Their return to northern areas of the state occurred sometime between the mid-1960s and the mid-1970s, and is poorly documented. By the mid-1980s they could be found at scattered locations throughout the state, although more commonly in the south (Leck 1984, Boyle 1986).

Atlas volunteers found that since the first half of the 20th century, Kentucky Warblers have expanded their range in New Jersey, both in the north and in the south. They also expanded their range in neighboring states during the same time period (Sibley 1988b, Master 1992). Although their range has increased in New Jersey, their distribution remained patchy, and they were found in only 11% of the blocks statewide. They were absent from the Kittatinny Mountains, but otherwise occurred in 4% to 23% of the blocks in the other provinces.

Fall: Kentucky Warblers are near the northern limit of their breeding range in New Jersey, and migrants are seen in only small numbers, usually in mid-August. Few remain after late August. **Maxima:** 5, Higbee Beach, 17 August 1988; 3, Higbee Beach, 9 August 1988.

Spring: Kentucky Warblers are occasionally seen in late April, but most breeding birds return to their territories in early to mid-May. **Maximum:** 4, Higbee Beach, 5 May 1990. ■

Connecticut Warbler

Oporornis agilis

Range: Breeds from British Columbia to Quebec south to Minnesota, Wisconsin, and Michigan. Winters in northern and central South America.

NJ Status: Very rare spring and uncommon fall migrant.

Historic Changes: Early in the century, Stone (1908) regarded Connecticut Warbler as a "common transient visitant in autumn." As late as 1937, he stated that Connecticut Warblers were common north and west of the Pine Barrens.

Fall: The normal arrival of southbound Connecticut Warblers is in early September, although there are a number of late

continued on page 544

continued from page 543

Connecticut Warbler

August reports. The peak flight is usually in mid-September, but substantial flights may extend into early October. There are a number of reports throughout October but rarely into November. Sibley (1997) reported a remarkable count of six in the Cape May area on the very late dates of 26-28 October 1984. Banding studies (e.g., 56, Hidden Valley Ranch, during September 1991, Sibley 1997) suggest they are more common than many observers would expect, yet they have hardly regained their apparent former abundance. **Maxima:** 13, Higbee Beach, 11 and 14 September 1988 (Sibley 1997); 8, Hidden Valley Ranch, 12 September 1991.

Spring: The northward migration of Connecticut Warblers takes place west of the Alleghenies. Consequently, there have been few well-documented spring New Jersey records. Two specimens have been taken: Haddonfield, 20 May 1882 (Stone 1937) and Fort Lee, 25 May 1917 (Bull 1964). There have been at least three recent additional sight reports in spring. ■

Mourning Warbler

Oporornis philadelphia

Range: Breeds from northeastern British Columbia east to Newfoundland, south to Wisconsin, Michigan, and south along the Appalachians to north-central Virginia. Winters in southern Central America and northern South America.

NJ Status: Uncommon spring and fall migrant.

Breeding

Habitat: Nests in dense thickets of shrubs, brambles, and saplings.

Until the surveys for the New Jersey Breeding Bird Atlas, there was no evidence that Mourning Warblers nested any closer to New Jersey than the Catskill and

Physiographic Distribution — Mourning Warbler	Number of blocks in province	Number of blocks species found breeding in province	Number of blocks species found in state	Percent of province species occupies	Percent of all records for this species found in province	Percent of state area in province
Highlands	110	1	1	0.9	100.0	12.9

Statewide Summary	
Status	# of Blocks
Possible	0
Probable	1
Confirmed	0
Total	1

Pocono Mountains. From 2-20 June 1996, however, a singing male established a territory along a powerline cut in the Pequannock Watershed. The bird repeatedly sang from exposed perches, a behavior quite different from this species reclusive habits during migration. There was no further evidence of breeding.

Fall: Early southbound arrivals of Mourning Warblers are noted from early to mid-August, reaching a peak from late August to early September. Records drop off after mid-September, although stragglers have been observed into early October. The early literature regarded Mourning Warblers as rare or very rare transients, and Stone (1937) knew of no records at Cape May. **Maxima:** 12, Cape May, 27 August 1985 and 16 August 1988 (Sibley 1997).

Spring: Mourning Warblers are among the latest of our regular spring warbler transients. Their short migration period begins in mid- to late May, and ends after early June. The peak is normally in late May. **Maximum:** 8, Eagle Rock Reservation, 27 May 1978. ■

MACGILLIVRAY'S WARBLER

MacGillivray's Warbler
Oporornis tolmiei

Range: Breeds from southeastern Alaska south to the mountains of California, Arizona, and New Mexico, east to western South Dakota. Winters in Mexico and Central America.

NJ Status: Accidental. NJBRC Review List.

Occurrence: There have been five state reports of MacGillivray's Warbler, and one has been accepted by the NJBRC: West Cape May, 12 November 1997-10 January 1998 (ph-RNJB 24:51). ■

COMMON YELLOWTHROAT

Common Yellowthroat
Geothlypis trichas

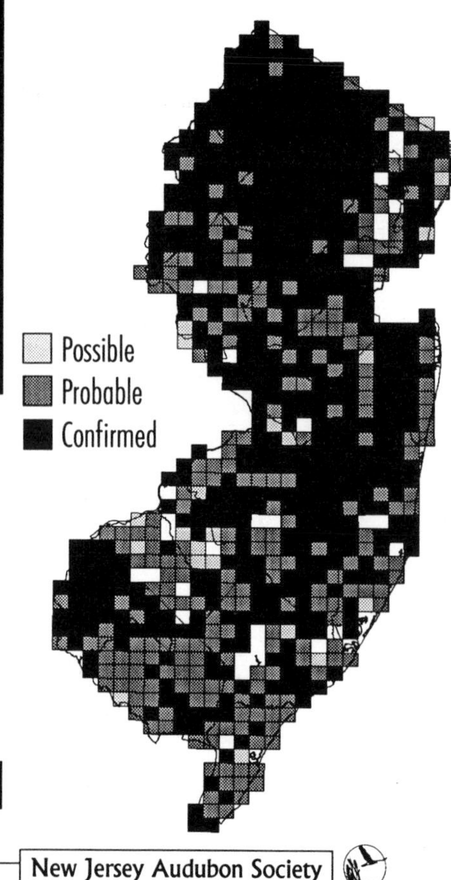

Range: In eastern North America breeds from Manitoba east to southern Newfoundland, south to Texas and Florida. Winters from the southeastern United States and the Gulf Coast to the West Indies and Central America.

NJ Status: Common and nearly ubiquitous summer resident, common spring and fall migrant, rare winter resident.

Breeding

Habitat: Nests in a variety of open, wet habitats such as marsh edges, the shrubby edges of

Common Yellowthroat

continued

damp or wet woods, in the understory of moist woods, etc.

In 1908 Stone wrote that "Common Yellowthroat is universally distributed from one end of the state to the other, as much at home in the Pine Barrens as in the mountains." Successive authors also reported that they were common breeding birds in New Jersey (Cruickshank 1942, Leck 1984).

Atlas surveys found Common Yellowthroats breeding in 95% of the blocks statewide, making them one of the most widely distributed birds in the state. They were broadly distributed in all physiographic regions and occurred in 93% or more of the blocks in all provinces. Their success is probably due to their ability to use a variety of wetland habitats for breeding. They are as likely to be found along the salt marsh edges as along the edges of small ponds in the Highlands. They are, however, clearly dependent upon wetlands for nesting. Many authors agree that, although still widely distributed, Common Yellowthroats have almost certainly been reduced in abundance throughout their range (Mulvihill 1992e, Kaufman 1996). It is remarkable therefore that, despite thousands of acres of wetlands loss, yellowthroats continue to persist in high numbers. Wetlands protection in New Jersey undoubtedly contributes to their local success.

Fall: Local populations of Common Yellowthroats linger into September, but are augmented by large movements of more northern breeding birds throughout

continued on page 548

Statewide Summary	
Status	# of Blocks
Possible	21
Probable	245
Confirmed	547
Total	813

Physiographic Distribution

Common Yellowthroat	Number of blocks in province	Number of blocks species found breeding in province	Number of blocks species found in state	Percent of province species occupies	Percent of all records for this species found in province	Percent of state area in province
Kittatinny Mountains	19	19	813	100.0	2.3	2.2
Kittatinny Valley	45	45	813	100.0	5.5	5.3
Highlands	109	109	813	100.0	13.4	12.8
Piedmont	167	156	813	93.4	19.2	19.6
Inner Coastal Plain	128	123	813	96.1	15.1	15.0
Outer Coastal Plain	204	192	813	94.1	23.6	23.9
Pine Barrens	180	169	813	93.9	20.8	21.1

continued from page 547

Common Yellowthroat

September and into early October. Numbers decline throughout October, but stragglers can be found through November. **Maxima:** 500+, Higbee Beach, 5 September 1993; 250+, Higbee Beach, 19 September 1981.

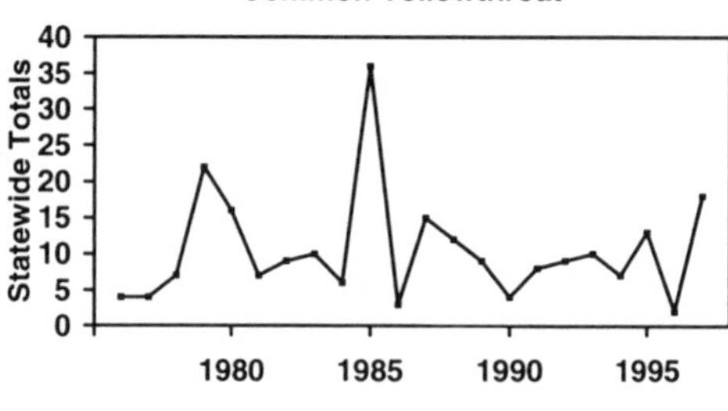

Winter: Common Yellowthroats are encountered regularly on CBCs, particularly along the coast and in the south. In most years, the statewide total is fewer than 20 birds. Numbers further drop by mid-winter, and wintering Common Yellowthroats are rare. **CBC Statewide Stats:** Average: 11; Maximum: 36 in 1985; Minimum: 2 in 1996. **CBC Maximum:** 7, Boonton, 1985.

Spring: Common Yellowthroats returning north arrive in late April, with most birds on territory by early May. Most passage birds probably move through in the first half of May, although it is difficult to distinguish birds in passage from local breeding birds. **Maximum:** 107, Island Beach, 12 May 1991 (banded). ■

Hooded Warbler

Wilsonia citrina

Range: Breeds from Iowa east to southern Rhode Island, south to easternmost Texas and northern Florida. Winters in Central America.

NJ Status: Fairly common but somewhat local summer resident, scarce spring and fall migrant.

Breeding

Habitat: Nests in the dense understory of moist or wet deciduous woodlands, especially in laurel.

In the early 1900s, Stone (1908) found Hooded Warblers mainly in two areas: in the mountains of northern New Jersey, and in the cedar swamps of the southern Pine Barrens. By 1937,

Hooded Warbler

continued

he also reported they were common breeding birds on the length of the Cape May peninsula. Griscom (1923) described Hooded Warbler's status in the northern counties as "abundant." Cruickshank (1942) wrote "in the best Hooded Warbler country of northern New Jersey I have recorded 23 individuals in a day." Leck (1984) stated that Hooded Warblers were found in three areas: the mountains of the northern part of the state, the cedar swamps in the Pine Barrens, and the wooded swamps of Cape May and Cumberland counties.

Atlas observers found Hooded Warblers to have a distribution similar to that cited in Leck (1984), although the species appears to have retreated from the southern part of the Cape May Peninsula. Overall, 43% of their range was north of the Piedmont, where they were well

continued on page 550

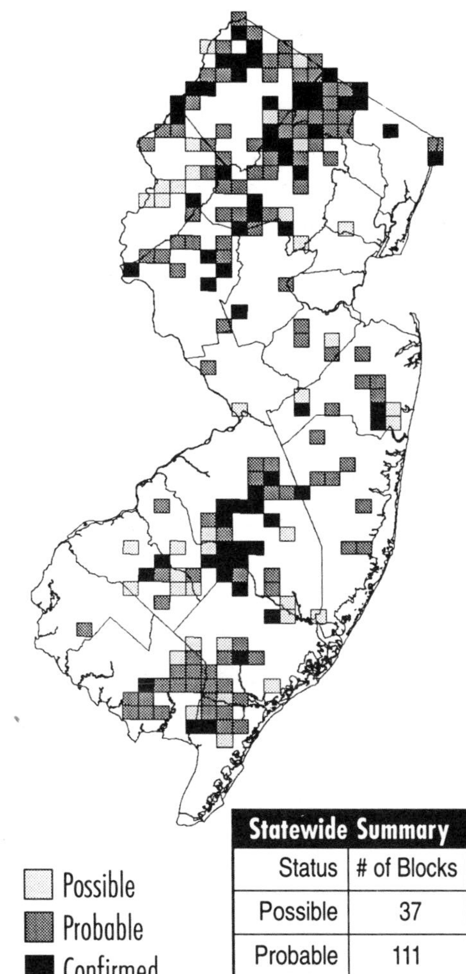

Statewide Summary	
Status	# of Blocks
Possible	37
Probable	111
Confirmed	64
Total	212

Physiographic Distribution Hooded Warbler	Number of blocks in province	Number of blocks species found breeding in province	Number of blocks species found in state	Percent of province species occupies	Percent of all records for this species found in province	Percent of state area in province
Kittatinny Mountains	19	16	212	84.2	7.5	2.2
Kittatinny Valley	45	15	212	33.3	7.1	5.3
Highlands	109	62	212	56.9	29.2	12.8
Piedmont	167	16	212	9.6	7.5	19.6
Inner Coastal Plain	128	11	212	8.6	5.2	15.0
Outer Coastal Plain	204	32	212	15.7	15.1	23.9
Pine Barrens	180	60	212	33.3	28.3	21.1

continued from page 549

Hooded Warbler

represented in both the Kittatinny Mountains and Highlands. They were also fairly well distributed throughout the Pine Barrens and were present in 33% of the blocks in that province. They occupy only a small percentage of either the Inner Coastal Plain or Piedmont. Their apparent disappearance from southern Cape May County is particularly troubling.

Fall: Primarily a southern breeding bird, New Jersey is near the northern edge of Hooded Warblers' breeding range. Consequently, they are encountered in only small numbers in migration, although they occur over a long period that runs from mid-August to early October. **Maxima:** 8, Cape May Point, 3 October 1976; 6, Higbee Beach, 6 September 1988.

Spring: Breeding Hooded Warblers return to territories in late April or early May. Only a few are encountered in migration, most from early to mid-May. **Maximum:** 4, Princeton, 2 May 1981. ■

Wilson's Warbler

Wilsonia pusilla

Range: In eastern North America, breeds from Manitoba to Newfoundland, south to northern New York, Vermont, New Hampshire, and Maine. Winters from the Gulf Coast to Mexico and Central America.

NJ Status: Uncommon spring and fall migrant, reported on one CBC.

Fall: The earliest arriving Wilson's Warblers usually reach New Jersey in late August, although an occasional individual may occur earlier. Peak numbers occur from early to mid-September, leaving only the occasional straggler after early October. Numbers vary from year to year, and sometimes they appear rare. **Maxima:** 17, Higbee Beach, 11 September 1988; 15, Sandy Hook, 8 September 1985.

Winter: A Wilson's Warbler (with good details, AB) was reported on the Long Branch CBC in 1985.

Wilson's Warbler

continued

Spring: Occasionally there are Wilson's Warbler records in early May and early June, but most of the migration occurs from mid- to late May. Despite this short period of peak passage, they are more easily found during spring than during fall. In spring, Wilson's Warblers are more likely in the northern rather than the southern part of the state. **Maxima:** 30+, Princeton-Trenton area, 21 May 1976; 15, Trenton, 14 May 1977. ■

Canada Warbler

Wilsonia canadensis

Range: Breeds from Alberta south to Wisconsin, east to Nova Scotia, south to northern Pennsylvania and along the Appalachians to northern Georgia. Winters in northern South America.

NJ Status: Uncommon and local summer resident, fairly common spring and fall migrant.

Breeding

Habitat: Nests in moist or wet woodlands with a thick understory.

Stone (1908) reported Canada Warblers were summer residents in Sussex and Passaic counties. By the early 1940s their breeding range had extended to include Warren and Morris counties (Cruickshank 1942), and the first nest on the Coastal Plain was found at Assunpink, Monmouth County in 1980 (Leck 1984). During a survey of southern New Jersey cedar swamps in the same year, Canada Warblers were found at four sites, once each in Atlantic, Burlington, Cumberland, and Ocean counties (Wander 1981). These discoveries showed Canada Warblers to be rare breeding birds in the Pine Barrens.

Atlas surveys found that Canada Warblers occurred mainly in the Kittatinny Mountains and in the northern Highlands, and 90% of their range was north of the Piedmont. Although not Confirmed in the Pine Barrens, they were found in one block in that province. There is little doubt that their numbers in the southern part of the state are very small. Their distribution in the Pine Barrens, however, may be broader than the map indicates. The population may be so low in this province that detection,

continued on page 552

continued from page 551

Canada Warbler

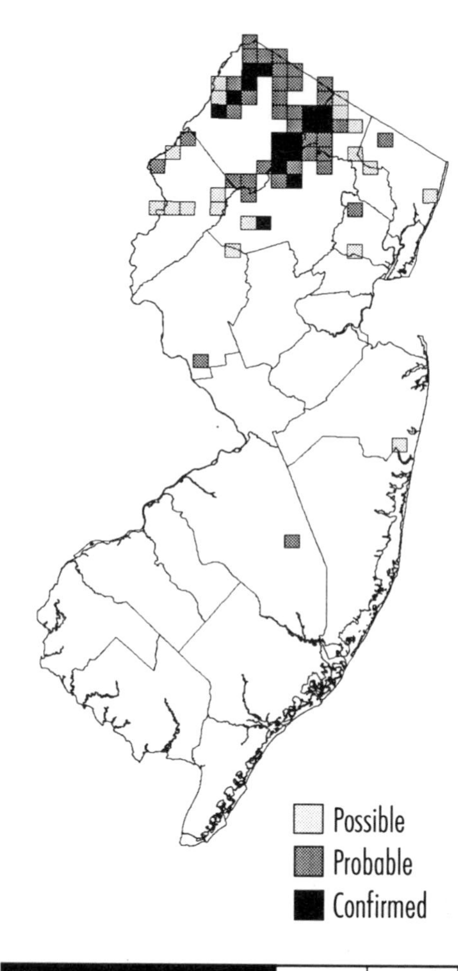

even within appropriate habitat, is unlikely without focused surveys.

Fall: Canada Warblers are early migrants, with southbound birds seen by early August. Peak numbers pass from mid- to late August, and after mid-September only stragglers are seen. **Maxima:** 95, Higbee Beach, 29 August 1982; 40, Higbee Beach, 30 August 1992.

Spring: Fairly late migrants in spring, most Canada Warblers pass from mid- to late May. **Maxima:** 52, Island Beach, 23-24 May 1987 (banded); 50, Princeton, 14 May 1988. ■

Statewide Summary	
Status	# of Blocks
Possible	18
Probable	35
Confirmed	16
Total	69

Physiographic Distribution Canada Warbler	Number of blocks in province	Number of blocks species found breeding in province	Number of blocks species found in state	Percent of province species occupies	Percent of all records for this species found in province	Percent of state area in province
Kittatinny Mountains	19	13	69	68.4	18.8	2.2
Kittatinny Valley	45	12	69	26.7	17.4	5.3
Highlands	109	36	69	33.0	52.2	12.8
Piedmont	167	6	69	3.6	8.7	19.6
Outer Coastal Plain	204	1	69	0.5	1.4	23.9
Pine Barrens	180	1	69	0.6	1.4	21.1

Yellow-breasted Chat

Icteria virens

Range: In eastern North America breeds from North Dakota east to Massachusetts, south to eastern Texas and northern Florida. Winters mainly in Central America.

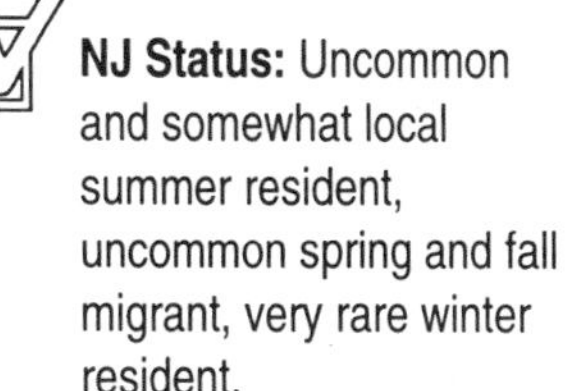

NJ Status: Uncommon and somewhat local summer resident, uncommon spring and fall migrant, very rare winter resident.

Breeding

Habitat: Breeds in open areas in dense shrubby tangles in hedgerows, overgrown fields, and at marsh edges.

Stone (1908) found Yellow-breasted Chats to be fairly well distributed throughout the southern, middle, and northeastern parts of the state, but absent from the Pine Barrens. Griscom (1923) added that the range included the northwestern sections of the state as well. Stone (1937) found chats to be familiar summer residents in Cape May County. Fables (1955) reiterated that they were absent from the Pine Barrens and does not mention their distribution south of that province. Boyle (1986) pointed out that, although local, the main distribution of Yellow-breasted Chats was in the south.

Yellow-breasted Chats were found to be broadly distributed throughout the state, patchy in the north, and occupying many contiguous blocks in southwestern

continued on page 554

Yellow-breasted Chat

continued from page 553

New Jersey. Cape May, Cumberland, and Salem counties offer a great expanse of successional and fallow farm fields, which are favored habitats for Yellow-breasted Chats. They were absent from most of the Pine Barrens and the barrier islands. North of the Coastal Plain their distribution was patchy, although they were found in over 30% of the Kittatinny Mountain and Kittatinny Valley blocks.

Statewide Summary	
Status	# of Blocks
Possible	34
Probable	105
Confirmed	25
Total	164

Possible
Probable
Confirmed

Fall: The period of Yellow-breasted Chat migration is difficult to pin down. Local breeding birds become quiet and inconspicuous by late July, creating the illusion that they have departed. Also, individuals are known to disperse to the northeast in fall (Sibley 1997), and birds seen after early August could be birds from the south and west. Nevertheless, outside of the breeding season, it is unusual to see more than a few Yellow-breasted Chats in any location on a given day. They are seen only occasionally after late September. **Maxima:** 7, Higbee Beach, 29 August 1988; 6, Higbee Beach, 16 August 1991.

Physiographic Distribution: Yellow-breasted Chat	Number of blocks in province	Number of blocks species found breeding in province	Number of blocks species found in state	Percent of province species occupies	Percent of all records for this species found in province	Percent of state area in province
Kittatinny Mountains	19	6	164	31.6	3.7	2.2
Kittatinny Valley	45	15	164	33.3	9.1	5.3
Highlands	109	15	164	13.8	9.1	12.8
Piedmont	167	18	164	10.8	11.0	19.6
Inner Coastal Plain	128	31	164	24.2	18.9	15.0
Outer Coastal Plain	204	69	164	33.8	42.1	23.9
Pine Barrens	180	10	164	5.6	6.1	21.1

Yellow-breasted Chat

continued

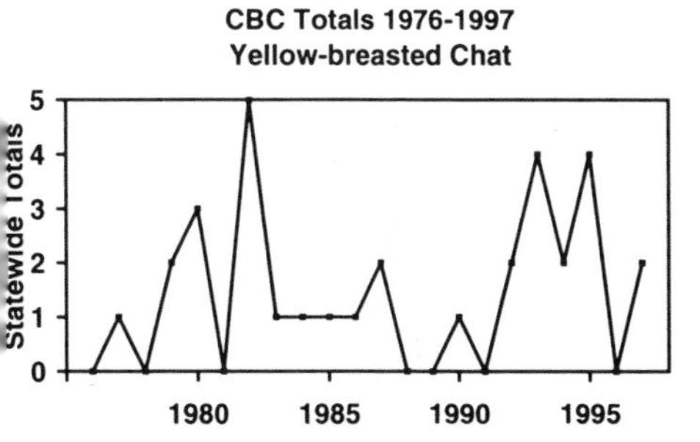

Winter: One or two Yellow-breasted Chats may linger long enough into December to be recorded on CBCs, but in some years none are seen. Even more rarely, chats will attempt to winter, usually along the coast. One did so successfully in the winter of 1992-1993 at Higbee Beach, when it was observed throughout the winter until at least 1 April 1993. **CBC Statewide Stats:** Average: 1; Maximum: 5 in 1982; Minimum: 0 in seven years. **CBC Maximum:** 2, Hackensack-Ridgewood, 1980; 2, Sandy Hook, 1995.

Spring: Most Yellow-breasted Chats seen in spring are local breeding birds that have returned to their breeding locales. Most are on territory by mid-May. ■

Summer Tanager

Piranga rubra

Range: In the eastern United States breeds from southeastern Nebraska east to southern New Jersey, south to Texas and Florida. Winters in Central and northern South America.

NJ Status: Uncommon and local summer resident, scarce spring and fall migrant, accidental in winter.

Breeding

Habitat: Nests in open, dry pine-oak woods.

Summer Tanagers bred in southern New Jersey in the first half of the 19th century, but by 1908 Stone considered them extirpated as breeding birds and listed them as rare stragglers from the south. The first breeding record in the 20th century was in 1955 near Springton, Cumberland County (Kunkle et al. 1959). There were no further breeding records until 1975, when they were found nesting near Dividing Creek, Cumberland County (Kunkle 1975). Wander and Brady (1980) reported further evidence of their successful recolonization, listing five singing males in the Pine Barrens during the summer of 1980. Boyle (1986) regarded them as uncommon and local summer residents in southern New Jersey.

continued on page 556

continued from page 555

Summer Tanager

Possible
Probable
Confirmed

Statewide Summary	
Status	# of Blocks
Possible	13
Probable	32
Confirmed	16
Total	61

Atlas volunteers found most of Summer Tanager's range clustered in the southernmost part of the state, although birds have begun to appear in other areas as well. Over 87% of their range was within the Outer Coastal Plain and Pine Barrens provinces, but they remained thinly distributed and did not occupy more than 14% of either region. Since their rediscovery in 1975 in Cumberland County, Summer Tanagers have expanded their range into northern Cape May and southern Atlantic counties. They have also become established on the western edge of the Pine Barrens. One of the most notable findings of the Atlas surveys was the discovery of breeding Summer Tanagers north of the Coastal Plain, where they were located in four blocks, with Confirmations in Essex and Hunterdon counties. Nationwide, Summer Tanager's range is expanding in some regions, yet contracting in other regions (Robinson 1996). Given the spread of their range in New Jersey, it seems plausible to expect that their range will continue to expand northward.

Physiographic Distribution Summer Tanager	Number of blocks in province	Number of blocks species found breeding in province	Number of blocks species found in state	Percent of province species occupies	Percent of all records for this species found in province	Percent of state area in province
Highlands	109	2	61	1.8	3.3	12.8
Piedmont	167	2	61	1.2	3.3	19.6
Inner Coastal Plain	128	4	61	3.1	6.6	15.0
Outer Coastal Plain	204	28	61	13.7	45.9	23.9
Pine Barrens	180	25	61	13.9	41.0	21.1

Summer Tanager

continued

Fall: Few Summer Tanagers nest north of southern New Jersey, and the species is encountered only in small numbers in migration. They are early migrants, and most have moved south by early September. **Maximum:** 3, Longport, 4 September 1980.

Winter: Remarkably, a Summer Tanager spent the winter of 1984-1985 at Cedar Run Refuge in Medford Township and returned to do the same in 1985-1986. This bird was recorded on the Pinelands CBC in both years. Another individual lingered until 2 January 1993 at Rancocas Nature Center, in Mount Holly.

Spring: Summer Tanagers return to their breeding grounds from late April to early May. Migrants are seen in May. **Maxima:** 4, Higbee Beach, 5 May 1989; 3, Cape May Point, 5 May 1980. ■

Scarlet Tanager

Piranga olivacea

Range: Breeds from southeastern Manitoba east to Maine, south to eastern Oklahoma and northwestern Georgia. Winters in northwestern South America.

NJ Status: Fairly common and very widespread summer resident, fairly common spring and common fall migrant.

Breeding

Habitat: Breeds in fairly mature, dry deciduous or mixed woodlands.

Throughout the 20th century, the distribution of Scarlet Tanagers in New Jersey has been weighted to the northern part of the state. Stone (1908) considered this species to be a "tolerably common summer resident … most abundant in the northern counties." Fables (1955) also noted that Scarlet Tanagers were more common in the northern counties than in the south. Leck's (1984) statement that they were found throughout the state, though primarily in north and central sections, suggests that there range was unchanged by the mid-1980s.

Atlas data showed Scarlet Tanagers remain most widely distributed in northern New Jersey, where they were reported in 98% of the blocks north of the Piedmont. They were less frequently found south of the Piedmont, where they only occupied 63% of the blocks. This is still a fairly high rate of occupation and suggests that they have become more common in the south during the last half of the 20th century. They were largely absent from the urbanized areas of the northeastern section of the Piedmont,
continued on page 558

continued from page 557

Scarlet Tanager

Physiographic Distribution — Scarlet Tanager	Number of blocks in province	Number of blocks species found breeding in province	Number of blocks species found in state	Percent of province species occupies	Percent of all records for this species found in province	Percent of state area in province
Kittatinny Mountains	19	19	596	100.0	3.2	2.2
Kittatinny Valley	45	43	596	95.6	7.2	5.3
Highlands	109	108	596	99.1	18.1	12.8
Piedmont	167	115	596	68.9	19.3	19.6
Inner Coastal Plain	128	79	596	61.7	13.3	15.0
Outer Coastal Plain	204	108	596	52.9	18.1	23.9
Pine Barrens	180	124	596	68.9	20.8	21.1

Statewide Summary	
Status	# of Blocks
Possible	72
Probable	327
Confirmed	197
Total	596

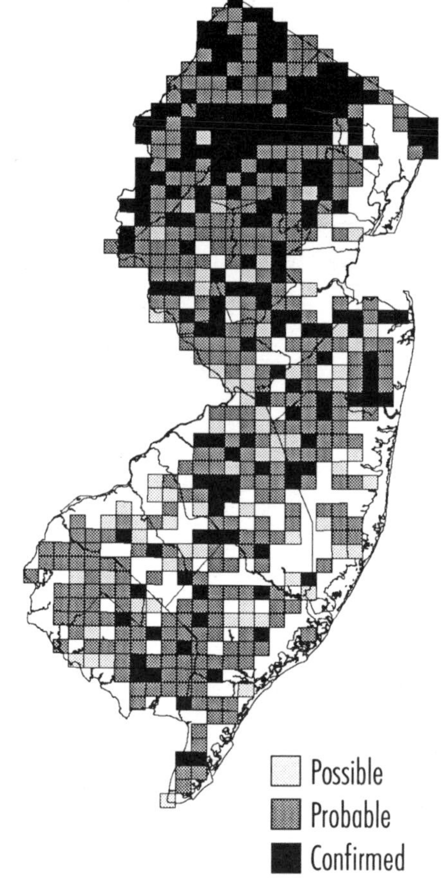

and only thinly distributed in areas of the Pine Barrens and the largely deforested corridor of the Inner Coastal Plain.

Fall: Scarlet Tanagers are primarily September migrants, peaking in mid-month. Numbers decline in early October with most having passed by mid-month. **Maxima:** 200, Higbee Beach, 11 September 1988; 125+, Higbee Beach, 23 September 1983.

Spring: Breeding Scarlet Tanagers arrive around the first of May, with most migrants passing in early to mid-May. **Maxima:** 100, Princeton, 12 May 1988; 50, Mercer County, 11 May 1977. ■

Western Tanager

Piranga ludoviciana

Range: Breeds from British Columbia to California, and east to western South Dakota and westernmost Texas. Winters mainly in Mexico and Central America.

NJ Status: Very rare. NJBRC Review List.

Occurrence: There have been 49 state reports of Western Tanagers, and 21 have been accepted by the NJBRC. Although the first state record was at a feeder at Island Beach, 10 March 1938 (Fables 1955), most of the records are from late September through January, and no particular pattern is evident. They often remain at one location over a period of days. This species is much less common in spring, when there are only three records. The most unusual record is of a singing male at Kinnelon from 5-22 June 1977. ■

Green-tailed Towhee

Pipilo chlorurus

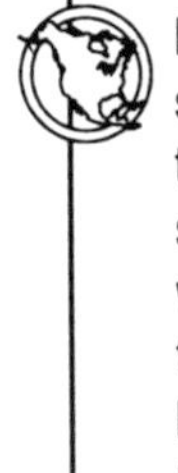

Range: Breeds from southern Washington east to Montana south to southern California and western Texas. Winters in the southern portion of breeding range south to Mexico.

NJ Status: Accidental. NJBRC Review List.

Occurrence: There have been seven state reports of Green-tailed Towhees, and six have been accepted by the NJBRC (all late fall/winter).
The six accepted records are:

Overpeck Creek	*23 December 1939-30 January 1940*	
Newton	*21 January-21 April 1961*	*ph-RBPF*
*Whitesville**	*25 November 1962-13 April 1963*	
*Flemington**	*28 November-December 1968*	*at a feeder*
Mickleton	*20 November 1975-10 April 1976*	*ph-RBPF, at a feeder*
*Pennington**	*20 March-12 April 1985*	*at a feeder.*

Spotted Towhee

Pipilo maculatus

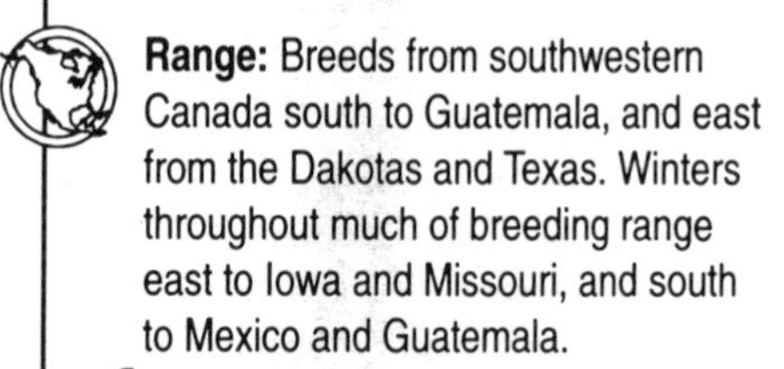

Range: Breeds from southwestern Canada south to Guatemala, and east from the Dakotas and Texas. Winters throughout much of breeding range east to Iowa and Missouri, and south to Mexico and Guatemala.

NJ Status: Accidental. Added to the NJBRC Review List in 1996.

Occurrence: There have been six state reports of Spotted Towhees, and four have been accepted by the NJBRC. Spotted Towhee was split from Rufous-sided Towhee *P. erythrophthalmus* in 1995, and the eastern subspecies became Eastern Towhee. The four accepted records are:

Metuchen	*24 December 1952*	*spec. USNM #421001, female*
*Ramsey**	*29 October 1959*	*banded*
Island Beach SP	*31 October 1987*	*ph-RNJB 14:19, banded*
Cape May Point	*1 December 1994-25 March 1995*	*ph-RNJB 22:96*

Eastern Towhee

Pipilo erythrophthalmus

Range: Breeds from southeastern Saskatchewan east to Nova Scotia and south through the eastern United States to Florida and Louisiana. Winters mainly from eastern Kansas east to Massachusetts, south to eastern Texas and Florida.

NJ Status: Common and nearly ubiquitous summer resident, common spring and fall migrant, uncommon winter resident.

Breeding

Habitat: Nest in dense thickets and dry, open woods with a shrubby understory.

Eastern Towhees have been common breeding birds in New Jersey throughout the 20th century. Stone (1908) found them "particularly plentiful in the Pine Barrens of which it is one of the characteristic species." In a three-year census of a four-square mile area of the Pine Barrens

Eastern Towhee

continued

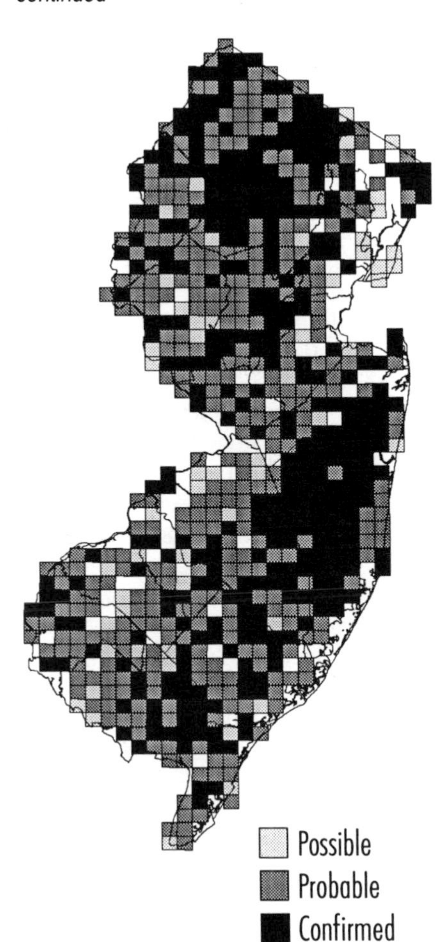

during the early 1940s, towhees were so abundant that they equaled all other resident species combined (Fables 1955). Conversely, Griscom (1923), while discussing Eastern Towhee's general distribution in northern New Jersey, noted their absence from rich, moist lowland areas, but described them as abundant in "the hills." Bull (1964) noted that they were most common at lower elevations, especially on the Coastal Plain.

Atlas data indicated that the distribution of Eastern Towhees had changed little through the 1900s. They were located in 87% of the blocks in the state, but were absent from areas where there is a dearth of woodland habitats – such as the

continued on page 562

Statewide Summary	
Status	# of Blocks
Possible	54
Probable	338
Confirmed	348
Total	740

Physiographic Distribution Eastern Towhee	Number of blocks in province	Number of blocks species found breeding in province	Number of blocks species found in state	Percent of province species occupies	Percent of all records for this species found in province	Percent of state area in province
Kittatinny Mountains	19	19	740	100.0	2.6	2.2
Kittatinny Valley	45	44	740	97.8	5.9	5.3
Highlands	109	109	740	100.0	14.7	12.8
Piedmont	167	136	740	81.4	18.4	19.6
Inner Coastal Plain	128	103	740	80.5	13.9	15.0
Outer Coastal Plain	204	155	740	76.0	20.9	23.9
Pine Barrens	180	174	740	96.7	23.5	21.1

continued from page 561

urbanized northeastern Piedmont, parts of the Inner Coastal Plain, and some of the barrier islands. Eastern Towhees were particularly common in the most heavily forested parts of the state, the Kittatinny Ridge and Valley, the Highlands, and the Pine Barrens, and occupied at least 96% of the blocks in these provinces.

Conservation Note: Although Eastern Towhees are nearly ubiquitous breeding birds in New Jersey, there is evidence that they may be declining in abundance in the state (Greenlaw 1996) and rangewide (Price et al. 1995). Similar declines in Maryland were noted from Breeding Bird Survey data (Farrell 1996), but reasons for the declines are as yet, unknown. This species should be carefully monitored for changes in abundance and overall range.

Fall: Southward migration of Eastern Towhees begins in September and continues through at least mid-November, when the species becomes difficult to find in northern New Jersey. The magnitude of migration is difficult to assess as transients mix with local residents. **Maximum:** 60, Sandy Hook, 4 October 1997.

CBC Totals 1976-1997
Eastern Towhee

Statewide Totals

400
350
300
250
200
150
100
50
0

1980 1985 1990 1995

Winter: Although uncommon in the southern part of the state, Eastern Towhees tend to be rare inland and to the north. There is evidence suggesting that they have become more common in winter, as Stone (1908) knew of only two winter reports. If the winter is mild, it is now possible for CBCs (even in northwestern New Jersey) to record several towhees on count day. In general, CBC numbers are variable, with higher counts being dependent on mild early-winter conditions. **CBC Statewide Stats:** Average: 147; Maximum: 366 in 1992; Minimum: 55 in 1979. **CBC Maximum:** 156, Cape May, 1996.

Spring: Eastern Towhees arriving from the south reach New Jersey by early April, with peak numbers occurring from mid-April to early May. Migrants are more evident in spring than autumn. **Maxima:** 30+, Higbee Beach, 18 April 1992; 30, Higbee Beach, 24 April 1985. ■

Cassin's Sparrow

Aimophila cassinii

Range: Breeds in the southwestern states and Mexico north to western Nebraska and Colorado. Winters in the southern portion of the breeding range.

NJ Status: Accidental. NJBRC Review List.

Occurrence: There have been two reports of Cassin's Sparrows, and one has been accepted by the NJBRC: Island Beach, 22 September 1961 (spec. AMNH #366768). ■

Bachman's Sparrow

Aimophila aestivalis

Range: Breeds locally in the southeastern states mostly from southern Missouri, Kentucky, and North Carolina south to the Gulf Coast and Florida. Winters in the southern portion of the breeding range.

NJ Status: Accidental. NJBRC Review List.

Occurrence: There have been three state reports of Bachman's Sparrows, and two have been accepted by the NJBRC. A substantial contraction in the breeding range of this species may make future occurrence even less likely than it was earlier in the 20th century. The two accepted records are:

Fort Lee#	*9 May 1918*	*spec. USNM #442569*
Atsion#	*16 June 1957*	

American Tree Sparrow

Spizella arborea

Range: Breeds from Alaska to Labrador. Winters in the East from southernmost Canada south to North Carolina.

NJ Status: Fairly common spring and common fall migrant, common winter resident.

Fall: The first American Tree Sparrows can normally be found in late October or early November. In some years a migratory peak occurs between late November and mid-December; in other years there is a steady buildup in numbers throughout the fall and early winter. They are most common in the northern part of the state, becoming uncommon in the south, especially in the southern coastal region. **Maximum:** 20, Rosedale Park, 21 November 1984.

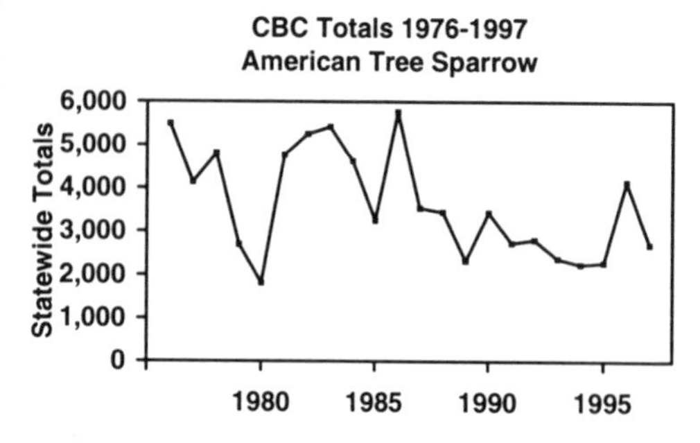

Winter: Numbers of American Tree Sparrows vary considerably from year to year depending upon the severity of the season. Tree Sparrows are most common in New Jersey when conditions are harsh to the north of the state. Stone (1937) found tree sparrows to winter commonly near Cape May, whereas Sibley (1997) documented an average of only five sightings per winter, and a drop in CBC numbers from the 1970s to the 1990s. **CBC Statewide Stats:** Average: 3,636; Maximum: 5,760 in 1986; Minimum: 1,813 in 1980. **CBC Maximum:** 1,517, Lower Hudson, 1982.

Spring: The light return flight of the relatively few American Tree Sparrows wintering to our south is usually masked by the presence of local wintering birds. These residents gradually depart and after early April only stragglers remain. ■

Chipping Sparrow
Spizella passerina

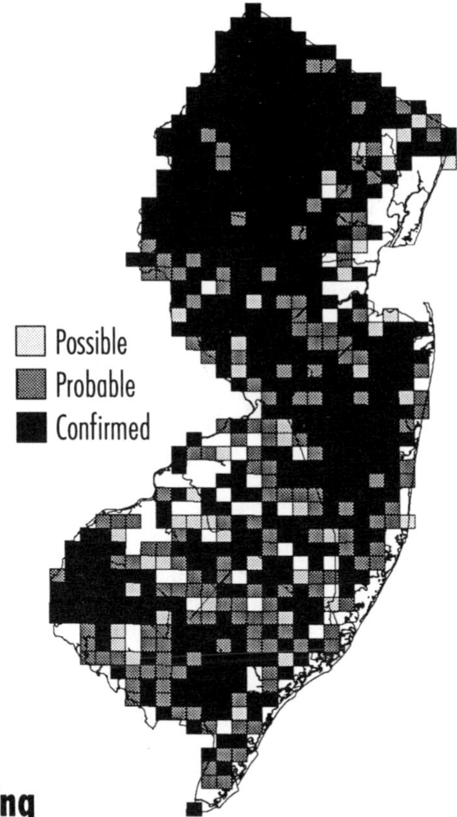

Range: In eastern North America, breeds from Manitoba east to southern Newfoundland, south to central Texas and Georgia. Winters from New Jersey south to the Gulf coast states and Central America.

NJ Status: Common and nearly ubiquitous summer resident, fairly common spring and fall migrant, scarce winter resident.

Statewide Summary	
Status	# of Blocks
Possible	42
Probable	164
Confirmed	519
Total	725

Breeding

Habitat: Nests in open or mixed pine woods, and in towns, parks, orchards, etc.

Chipping Sparrows have been common and broadly distributed breeding birds in New Jersey throughout the 20th century. Stone (1908) consid-

continued on page 566

Physiographic Distribution Chipping Sparrow	Number of blocks in province	Number of blocks species found breeding in province	Number of blocks species found in state	Percent of province species occupies	Percent of all records for this species found in province	Percent of state area in province
Kittatinny Mountains	19	19	725	100.0	2.6	2.2
Kittatinny Valley	45	45	725	100.0	6.2	5.3
Highlands	109	109	725	100.0	15.0	12.8
Piedmont	167	136	725	81.4	18.8	19.6
Inner Coastal Plain	128	96	725	75.0	13.2	15.0
Outer Coastal Plain	204	153	725	75.0	21.1	23.9
Pine Barrens	180	167	725	92.8	23.0	21.1

continued from page 565

Chipping Sparrow

ered them to be the "most familiar of our sparrows," and succeeding authors agreed (Fables 1955, Leck 1984).

Atlas volunteers found Chipping Sparrows to be widely distributed throughout the state, and found them in 85% of the blocks statewide. They were found in 100% of the blocks north of the Piedmont, and were Confirmed in 95% of those blocks. Chipping Sparrows were absent only from the most highly urbanized areas of New Jersey, and from most of the barrier islands and salt marsh blocks. Oddly, they were notably uncommon on the tip of the Cape May Peninsula, with very few pairs nesting south of the Cape May Canal (Sibley 1997).

Fall: Migrant Chipping Sparrows arrive in early October with peak numbers passing from late October to early November. Numbers have dwindled by mid-November. An unprecedented flight occurred on 25 October 1996, when 1,150 were tallied around Cape Island. **Other maxima:** 200+, Lake Muconetcong, 23 October 1995; 100s, Palmyra, 16 October 1996.

Winter: Statewide CBC totals of Chipping Sparrows are highly variable. They often become rare by mid-winter, especially in the harshest winters.

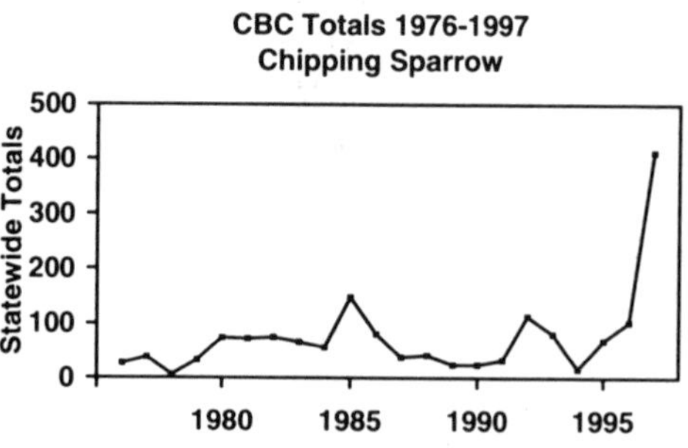

Maximum: 40+, West Cape May, winter 1996-1997. **CBC Statewide Stats:** Average: 74; Maximum: 413 in 1997; Minimum: 6 in 1978. **CBC Maximum:** 173, Cape May, 1997.

Spring: Chipping Sparrows start moving north beginning in late March and they continue to pass through into early May. Their numbers peak in mid- to late April. **Maxima:** 50+, Garret Mt., 26 April 1986; 50, Andover, 23 April 1995. ■

Clay-colored Sparrow
Spizella pallida

Range: Breeds throughout the prairie regions of Canada south to South Dakota, and east, and locally in western New York and southern Maine. Mainly winters from Texas to Mexico.

NJ Status: Very rare spring and rare to scarce fall migrant; very rare, but increasing, winter resident.

Fall: Clay-colored Sparrows occur mainly from mid-September to early November, and autumn totals range from just a few to nearly 20 reports. Although they are found inland, they are far more likely to appear along the coast. They have been more regular as migrants since the mid-1950s (Kunkle et al. 1959), probably a result of the eastward extension of their breeding range during the late 20th century (Knapton 1994).
Maximum: 3, Hidden Valley Ranch, 1 November 1996.

Winter: Until the 1990s, Clay-colored Sparrows were regarded as accidental in winter. However, there were 12 winter reports between 1990 and 1997, and a few birds successfully wintered. They were also reported on six CBCs between 1976 and 1997.

Spring: There have only been about 15 reports of Clay-colored Sparrows in spring. Three of these were males that sang into July, but there is no evidence that breeding occurred. ■

Field Sparrow
Spizella pusilla

Range: Breeds from eastern Montana east to Maine, south to central Texas and Georgia. Winters from Kansas, southern Michigan, and southern New England south to the Gulf Coast and Central America.

NJ Status: Common and very widespread summer resident, common spring and fall migrant, fairly common winter resident.

Breeding

Habitat: Nests in brushy, overgrown fields.

Throughout their range, Field Sparrows reached their greatest abundance late in the 19th

continued on page 568

continued from page 567

Field Sparrow

Statewide Summary	
Status	# of Blocks
Possible	43
Probable	240
Confirmed	375
Total	658

century following the clearing of eastern forests (Carey et al. 1994). In New Jersey, they have long been summer residents of overgrown fields from the Kittatinny Mountains to the tip of the Cape May Peninsula, and they have been regarded as common breeders by many authors during the 20th century (Stone 1908, Leck 1984). Fables (1955) specifically noted their absence from some urban and suburban areas.

During Atlas surveys Field Sparrows were found in over 90% of the blocks north of the Piedmont, and 76% of the blocks south of the Piedmont. They occupied only 61% of the Piedmont, and were nearly absent from the urbanized northeastern portion of that province. Despite some noticeable gaps in their distribution within the Pine Barrens, Field

Physiographic Distribution **Field Sparrow**	Number of blocks in province	Number of blocks species found breeding in province	Number of blocks species found in state	Percent of province species occupies	Percent of all records for this species found in province	Percent of state area in province
Kittatinny Mountains	19	18	658	94.7	2.7	2.2
Kittatinny Valley	45	45	658	100.0	6.8	5.3
Highlands	109	100	658	91.7	15.2	12.8
Piedmont	167	101	658	60.5	15.3	19.6
Inner Coastal Plain	128	105	658	82.0	16.0	15.0
Outer Coastal Plain	204	144	658	70.6	21.9	23.9
Pine Barrens	180	145	658	80.6	22.0	21.1

Field Sparrow

continued

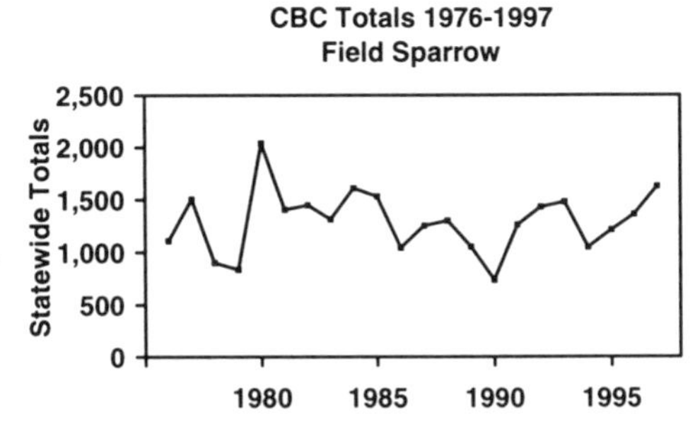

Sparrows still occupied 80% of the blocks in that province. They were absent from most of the barrier islands and salt marsh blocks.

Fall: An influx of migrant Field Sparrows is often noted in early October. Peak numbers move in late October-early November, but the flight continues into early December. **Maxima:** 500+, Sandy Hook, 23 October 1989; 200, Princeton, 8 November 1983.

Winter: Statewide CBC totals of Field Sparrows are fairly consistent. In most areas these numbers are probably constant throughout the winter. **CBC**

Statewide Stats: Average: 1,296; Maximum: 2,036 in 1980; Minimum: 734 in 1990. **CBC Maximum:** 806, NW Gloucester, 1980.

Spring: Northward movements of Field Sparrows are easily missed, because wintering birds, arriving migrants, and local breeding birds probably overlap. At Cape May, Sibley (1997) noted that migration is "sometimes evident in mid-April." Spring maxima are rarely reported. ■

Vesper Sparrow

Pooecetes gramineus

Range: In eastern North America, breeds from central Manitoba east to Nova Scotia, south to northern Nebraska and western North Carolina. Winters from southern Oklahoma, Kentucky, and Virginia south to Central America.

NJ Status: Rare and local summer resident, rare spring and scarce fall migrant, very rare winter resident. Endangered Species in New Jersey.

Breeding

Habitat: Nests in dry grassy or weedy fields, meadows or pastures.

Vesper Sparrows were fairly common summer residents throughout the state during the first half of the 20th century (Stone 1908, Cruickshank 1942). Modern observers would find the magnitude of their decline in New Jersey difficult to imagine if we were

continued on page 570

continued from page 569

Vesper Sparrow

Physiographic Distribution Vesper Sparrow	Number of blocks in province	Number of blocks species found breeding in province	Number of blocks species found in state	Percent of province species occupies	Percent of all records for this species found in province	Percent of state area in province
Kittatinny Mountains	19	1	16	5.3	6.3	2.2
Kittatinny Valley	45	7	16	15.6	43.8	5.3
Highlands	109	1	16	0.9	6.3	12.8
Piedmont	167	3	16	1.8	18.8	19.6
Inner Coastal Plain	128	1	16	0.8	6.3	15.0
Outer Coastal Plain	204	1	16	0.5	6.3	23.9
Pine Barrens	180	2	16	1.1	12.5	21.1

Statewide Summary	
Status	# of Blocks
Possible	6
Probable	7
Confirmed	3
Total	16

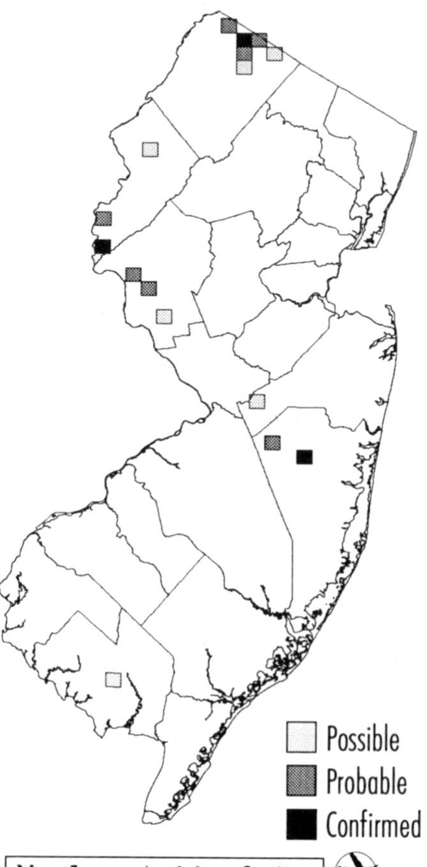

without Stone's description of Vesper Sparrows as "common summer residents" and "the characteristic Sparrow of the dry old fields" (Stone 1908). A statewide drop in numbers was noted by Fables (1955), which he attributed to habitat loss from expanding urbanization. By the mid-1960s Bull (1964) described Vesper Sparrows as uncommon and local. He wrote that that their decrease was related to a rapid decline in agriculture and that they were more dependent on farming than any other open country bird.

A survey of grassland birds conducted in 1982 found Vesper Sparrows at 17 locations statewide, and estimated the population at these sites to be from 32 to 44 territorial birds (Wander 1982). Most of the sites were concentrated in southern Warren and southern

Somerset counties, with other locations in Atlantic, Mercer, and Monmouth counties.

Atlas surveys documented that Vesper Sparrows have continued to decline. Observers found them to be one of the scarcest nesting songbirds in the state, located in only 16 blocks and Confirmed in only three blocks. Six of the blocks (38%) were scored as Possible breeding locations, which may have simply indicated unmated or wandering males. None were found in Somerset, Mercer, or Atlantic counties, where Wander had found them in 1982. The Kittatinny Valley, although a small province, held 44% of Vesper Sparrow's statewide range.

Conservation Note: Like most grassland species, Vesper Sparrows are dependent on human influenced landscapes, particularly farmland. This species is disappearing as a breeding bird in the state, concurrent with the rapid decline of farmland acreage. Although the decrease of Vesper Sparrow populations was noted by the authors of the atlases from neighboring states (i.e., New York, Pennsylvania, Maryland), those larger states have relatively robust populations compared to New Jersey's relict population. It is likely that, without a concentrated management effort, including farmland preservation, this Endangered Species will be extirpated as a breeding bird within a few decades.

Fall: Most Vesper Sparrows are seen from mid-October to early November. Due to their declines in the East, they are encountered only in small

continued on page 572

Vesper Sparrow

continued from page 571

Vesper Sparrow

numbers during migration. Apparently they have never been common as migrants, as Stone (1937) noted that they were "a regular, but not very abundant transient, more common in autumn than in spring." **Maxima:** 15, North Arlington, 19 October 1975; 10+, Overpeck Park, 18 October 1994.

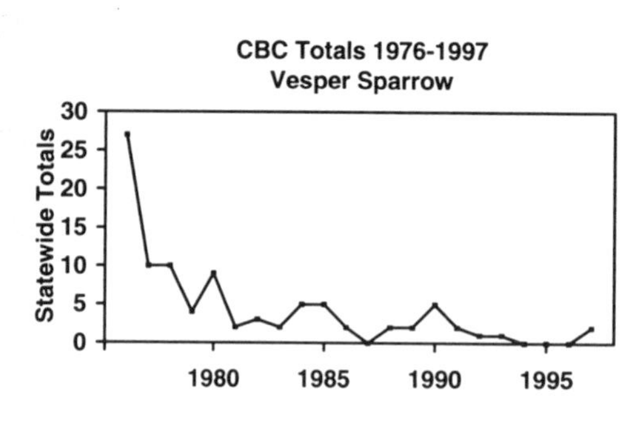

Winter: CBC totals of Vesper Sparrows have declined dramatically from the first half of the 20th century, when 50 birds were found on the 1942 and 1949 Cape May Christmas Counts (Sibley 1997). Today there are often no Vesper Sparrows found in the state, although in some years from one to five are tallied. **CBC Statewide Stats:** Average: 4; Maximum: 27 in 1976; Minimum: 0 in four years. **CBC Maximum:** 18, Cumberland, 1976.

Spring: Northbound Vesper Sparrows are sometimes encountered from late March to mid-April. **Maximum:** 7, Lincoln Park, 29 March 1981. ■

Lark Sparrow

Chondestes grammacus

Range: Breeds in central and western North America from southern Canada to Mexico; sparingly and sporadically recorded breeding east. Winters in the southern United States east to Louisiana, south to Mexico.

NJ Status: Very rare spring and rare fall migrant, accidental in winter.

Fall: Lark Sparrows' primary period of migration is from mid-August to late October, although there are a few earlier reports and an increasing number of later ones. Seasonal totals range from just one or two to as many as 12. They are rare statewide, but are far more likely in fall along the coast than inland. The early literature regarded them as extremely rare, but a subsequent eastward range expansion gave rise to annual records by the 1950s (Kunkle et al. 1959). **Maximum:** 4, Island Beach SP, mid-September 1975.

Lark Sparrow

continued

Winter: Between 1976 and 1997, Lark Sparrows have been reported lingering into mid-December in about half of the winters and were reported on nine CBCs. Successful wintering has occurred only a few times.

Spring: Reports of Lark Sparrows in spring are very unusual, and there are fewer than ten reports. ■

Black-throated Sparrow

Amphispiza bilineata

Range: Breeds in western states east to western Wyoming and western Colorado and south into Mexico. Winters in the southern part of range.

NJ Status: Accidental. NJBRC Review List.

Occurrence: There have been four state reports of Black-throated Sparrows, and three have been accepted by the NJBRC. The three accepted records are:

New Brunswick	*30 October 1961-23 April 1962*	*ph-Auk 80:380, at a feeder*
North Arlington	*14 December 1974-19 January 1975*	*ph-NJA/RNJB 1:3*
Cherry Hill	*12 December 1992-mid-February 1993*	*ph-RNJB 19:25, at a feeder.*

Lark Bunting

Calamospiza melanocorys

Range: Breeds from southern Alberta east to southwestern Manitoba and eastern North Dakota, south to northern Texas. Winters in southern portion of breeding range south into Mexico.

NJ Status: Accidental. NJBRC Review List.

Occurrence: There have been 12 state reports of Lark Buntings, and four have been accepted by the NJBRC (all in fall). The four accepted records are:

Cape May Point#	*16 September 1956*	*a female*
Island Beach	*7 September 1962*	*spec. Univ. Michigan #157599; Warburton1968, a female*
Johnson Park	*27 August-3 September 1989*	*ph-RNJB 15:69*
Cape May Point	*16 September 1993*	

Savannah Sparrow

Passerculus sandwichensis

Range: In eastern North America breeds from the Northwest Territories east to Newfoundland, south to South Dakota and New Jersey, and south along the Appalachians to North Carolina. Winters from Oklahoma and coastal New Hampshire south to Central America and Cuba.

NJ Status: Scarce and local summer resident, fairly common spring and common fall migrant, fairly common winter resident. Threatened Species in New Jersey.

Possible
Probable
Confirmed

Statewide Summary	
Status	# of Blocks
Possible	11
Probable	29
Confirmed	21
Total	61

Breeding

Habitat: Nests in open fields, meadows, and pastures.

In New Jersey, Savannah Sparrows have undergone a habitat shift from breeding along the coast to breeding at inland locations. Historic assessments of this species range in New Jersey indicated that they bred mainly close to the coast, particularly on recently filled areas of the saltmarsh. In 1921, Stone found them nesting on a filled salt marsh near Cape May, but by 1927 they had disappeared from that location (Stone 1937). By the 1940s, in the northern half of the state, Savannah Sparrows were apparently found to nest *only* near coastal salt marshes (Cruickshank 1942). Cruickshank related that in 1935, as filling and ditching progressed in the Newark Meadows, over 100 pairs were found nesting at that site. Fables (1955) identified Savannah Sparrow's distribution as ranging along the coast from the Newark Meadows to the Delaware Bay shore, and did not mention any inland nesting sites.

By the 1980s, however, their habitat shift away from the coastal salt marshes to inland breeding sites was nearly complete. Wander (1982) found 25 territorial birds at 11 sites statewide, ten of which occurred in northern New Jersey (six in southern Warren County) and one in Salem County. The reason for this habitat shift would appear to be that the historic diking, ditching, and filling of the salt marsh had provided an ongoing, but ephemeral habitat. When filling of salt marshes became illegal, Savannah Sparrows apparently lost their breeding habitat along the coast.

Atlas surveys indicated that Savannah Sparrows had a patchy distribution. They were found in only 7% of the blocks in the state, but they were present in all provinces. They occurred in over 26% of the Kittatinny Valley blocks; however, they did not occur in more than 12% of the blocks in any other province. They were nearly absent from the Pine Barrens as well as the rest of southern New Jersey, with the exception of the heavily farmed areas of Salem County.

Conservation Note: Breeding habitat for Savannah Sparrows occurs in only unnatural situations in the state. These sparrows appear to be reliant on farm fields, airports, and other man-made habitats. These habitats are disappearing from many areas, and Savannah Sparrow's are seriously threatened in the state. Their distribution is patchy, and, although rare, the breeding locations are fairly contiguous. This clumping of suitable breeding sites could aid managers in developing local habitat conservation plans for Savannah Sparrows.

Fall: Savannah Sparrows are one of the earliest migrant sparrows, with only a few seen by early September. The main movement occurs in October, peaking in mid-month. Although many will stay

continued on page 576

Physiographic Distribution

Savannah Sparrow	Number of blocks in province	Number of blocks species found breeding in province	Number of blocks species found in state	Percent of province species occupies	Percent of all records for this species found in province	Percent of state area in province
Kittatinny Mountains	19	2	61	10.5	3.3	2.2
Kittatinny Valley	45	12	61	26.7	19.7	5.3
Highlands	109	9	61	8.3	14.8	12.8
Piedmont	167	19	61	11.4	31.1	19.6
Inner Coastal Plain	128	10	61	7.8	16.4	15.0
Outer Coastal Plain	204	7	61	3.4	11.5	23.9
Pine Barrens	180	2	61	1.1	3.3	21.1

continued from page 575

through the winter, numbers decline by early December. **Maxima:** 1,000, Featherbed Lane ,10 October 1992; 700+, Overpeck Park, 10 October 1993.

Winter: Statewide CBC totals for Savannah Sparrows are variable, with higher numbers usually lingering in milder winters. **CBC Statewide Stats:** Average: 355; Maximum: 686 in 1985; Minimum: 196 in 1987. **CBC Maximum:** 421, Lower Hudson, 1983.

Spring: Savannah Sparrows move north mainly in April. Numbers diminish quickly after the end of the month. **Maxima:** 50-75, Burlington County Airpark, 26 April 1989; 30, Burlington County Airpark, 14 April 1990.

Subspecies: Local breeding birds are *P. s. savanna* (Wheelwright and Rising 1993). The larger, paler *P. s. princeps*, or "Ipswich" Sparrow, which nests on Sable Island, Nova Scotia, are an uncommon winter resident in dunes and dry saltmarsh edges. Ipswich Sparrows are present from late October to early April, but the highest numbers are seen in mid-winter. **Maxima:** 29, Brigantine Island, 28 January 1993; 25+, Brigantine Island, January 1975. ■

Grasshopper Sparrow

Ammodramus savannarum

Range: In eastern North America breeds from southern Manitoba east to southern Maine, south to central Texas and central Georgia. Winters from Texas and North Carolina south to Central America.

NJ Status: Uncommon and local summer resident, very rare spring and rare fall migrant, accidental in winter. Threatened Species in New Jersey.

Breeding

Habitat: Nests in dry weedy fields, pastures, and airports.

Grasshopper Sparrows were described as common summer residents in New Jersey during the first half of the 20th century, when old fields were far more prevalent than today (Stone 1908, Cruickshank 1942). By the mid-1960s, their numbers were in decline as their dry grassy habitats were destroyed for developments (Bull 1964). In

Grasshopper Sparrow

continued

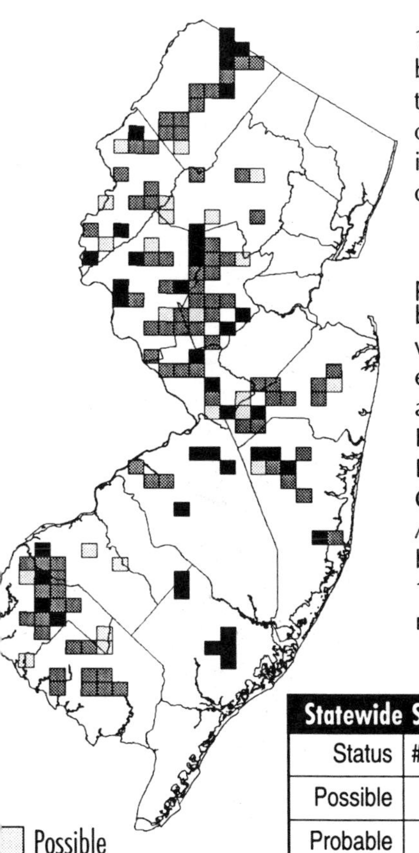

1982, during a grassland breeding bird study, Wander (1982) found them to be well distributed throughout the state with 90 pairs at 23 sites in 11 counties, but he noted that they continued to decline.

Atlas data indicated that Grasshopper Sparrows continued to be broadly, but thinly, distributed. They were absent from the urbanized eastern sections of the Piedmont, in areas with good forest cover (e.g., the Highlands, Kittatinny Mountains, and Pine Barrens), the barrier islands, and Cape May County. It is likely that the Atlas surveys discovered more breeding sites than Wander did in 1982 because the Atlas surveys were more intensive in both manpower and duration. The difference in the results probably does not reflect an increase in the population, but rather the greater scope of the Atlas surveys.

continued on page 578

Statewide Summary

Status	# of Blocks
Possible	23
Probable	82
Confirmed	39
Total	144

Physiographic Distribution

Grasshopper Sparrow	Number of blocks in province	Number of blocks species found breeding in province	Number of blocks species found in state	Percent of province species occupies	Percent of all records for this species found in province	Percent of state area in province
Kittatinny Valley	45	22	144	48.9	15.3	5.3
Highlands	109	17	144	15.6	11.8	12.8
Piedmont	167	35	144	21.0	24.3	19.6
Inner Coastal Plain	128	24	144	18.8	16.7	15.0
Outer Coastal Plain	204	30	144	14.7	20.8	23.9
Pine Barrens	180	16	144	8.9	11.1	21.1

continued from page 577

Grasshopper Sparrow

Conservation Note: Grasshopper Sparrows are declining throughout much of the eastern United States (Vickery 1996). Breeding Bird Survey data indicated a significant rangewide decline of 67% from 1966-1993 (Price et al. 1995). Like other grassland species, Grasshopper Sparrows have a patchy distribution and rely mainly on man-made habitats for breeding, such as fallow farmland. Farmland is subject to both development and succession, making many of these nesting areas tenuous. Grasshopper Sparrows often appear in areas for a year or two when suitable habitat presents itself. Airports and preserved pastureland/farmland represent the only stable grasslands available to this and other grassland birds in New Jersey.

Fall: Grasshopper Sparrows are infrequently encountered in migration, with most seen in October and November. Although Stone (1937) considered them common breeding birds, he indicated that he rarely encountered migrants. Bull (1964) also considered them rare migrants. **Maxima:** 5, Higbee Beach, 13 October 1980; 4, Higbee Beach, 5 November 1995.

Winter: Grasshopper Sparrows were reported on four CBCs between 1976 and 1997 (i.e., 1984, 1990, 1991, and 1994). They are exceedingly rare after the CBC period. One was present at Cape May from 18 December 1993-10 January 1994.

Spring: Away from known breeding areas, spring encounters with Grasshopper Sparrows are unusual. A few migrants are seen in late April and early May. ■

Henslow's Sparrow

Ammodramus henslowii

Range: Breeds mainly from eastern Kansas east to western New York, south locally to Tennessee and North Carolina. Winters from eastern Texas to southern North Carolina and northern Florida.

NJ Status: Rare and very local summer resident, otherwise a very rare visitor. Endangered Species in New Jersey. Added to the NJBRC Review List in 1996.

Breeding

Habitat: Nests in moist or dry old fields; historically well-known for nesting along the upland edge of the saltmarsh.

Formerly, Henslow's Sparrows were considered uncommon and local breeding birds throughout New Jersey. In

Henslow's Sparrow

continued

Physiographic Distribution Henslow's Sparrow	Number of blocks in province	Number of blocks species found breeding in province	Number of blocks species found in state	Percent of province species occupies	Percent of all records for this species found in province	Percent of state area in province
Kittatinny Valley	45	1	2	2.2	50.0	5.3
Pine Barrens	180	1	2	0.6	50.0	21.1

addition to widely scattered pairs, small colonies could be found at a number of places – e.g., near New Brunswick, Cape May, Great Swamp, Point Pleasant, and Lindenwold (Stone 1937, Bull 1964). They have always had an unpredictable pattern of occupation at breeding sites and, after a few years, might abandon what appeared to be prime breeding habitat (Bull 1964). They are now virtually extirpated as breeding birds in New Jersey.

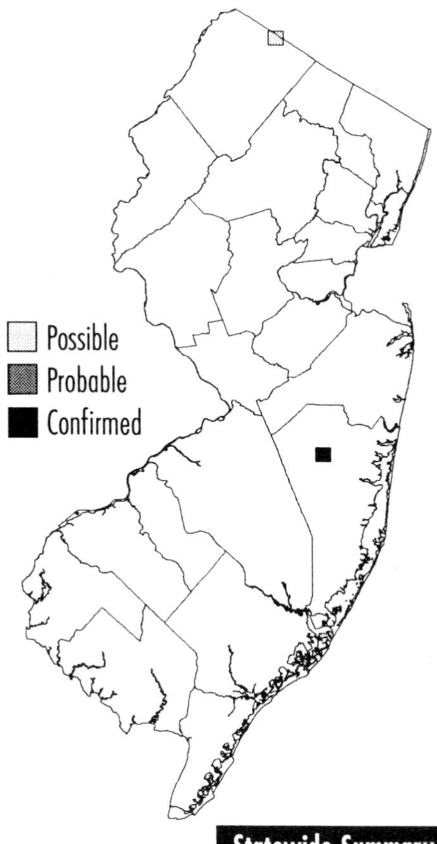

The only Confirmed breeding record during the Atlas survey period occurred at Lakehurst Air Engineering Center, where a bird was nest-building in June 1994. The species was sporadically present at this location from at least 1988 through 1994. Prior to this, the last confirmed nesting in the state was near Princeton in 1972 (AB).

Statewide Summary	
Status	# of Blocks
Possible	1
Probable	0
Confirmed	1
Total	2

Conservation Note: The decline of Henslow's Sparrows in New Jersey is part of a larger pattern encompassing much of the species' range. Breeding Bird Survey data showed a rangewide decline of 74% from 1966-1993 (Price et al. 1995). Loss and alteration of habitat may

continued on page 580

continued from page 579

Henslow's Sparrow

only be part of the explanation, since much seemingly optimal breeding habitat remains (i.e., upland edge of salt marsh). The Maryland Atlas project noted Henslow's Sparrows in only three blocks, all of which were abandoned after 1989. The Pennsylvania Atlas, however, discovered more pairs of Henslow's Sparrows than expected (Reid 1992d), lending a bit of hope for their future in the region. It has been appropriately suggested that this species is long overdue for consideration on the Federal Endangered Species List.

Fall: Most autumn reports of Henslow's Sparrows are from October. Formerly a regular but rare migrant, Henslow's Sparrows have become very rare, leading to their addition to the NJBRC Review List in 1996. A historical review of reports has not been undertaken, and while there have been one or two reports since the addition to the Review List, none have been reviewed.

Winter: There have been very few winter reports of Henslow's Sparrow, and they would have to be considered accidental at that season.

Spring: Henslow's Sparrows are even more rare in spring than they are in fall, with reports generally in early to mid-May. ■

Le Conte's Sparrow

Ammodramus leconteii

Range: Breeds from British Columbia east to Quebec and south to South Dakota and Michigan. Winters mainly from Kansas to South Carolina, south to eastern Texas and northern Florida.

NJ Status: Very rare. NJBRC Review List.

Occurrence: There have been 26 state reports of Le Conte's Sparrows, and 12 have been accepted by the NJBRC. The 12 accepted records are:

Tuckerton	*26 September-2 October 1976*	
Sandy Hook	*3 February-March 1985*	
Reed's Beach	*28-30 December 1986*	
Sandy Hook	*17-26 October 1987*	*ph.-RNJB 14:19, banded*
Overpeck Park	*14 November 1991-28 March 1992*	
Higbee Beach	*21 April 1992*	*ph-RBPF*
Haledon Res.	*10 October 1993*	*ph-RNJB 20:19*

Le Conte's Sparrow

continued

Higbee Beach	*16 November 1993*	
Bridgeton	*1 January 1994*	*ph-RNJB 20:64*
Palmyra	*30 December 1996-mid-January 1997*	
Higbee Beach	*26-28 October 1997*	*ph-RNJB 24:22*
Erma	*1-28 February 1998*	*ph-RNJB 24:52*

Nelson's Sharp-tailed Sparrow

Ammodramus nelsoni

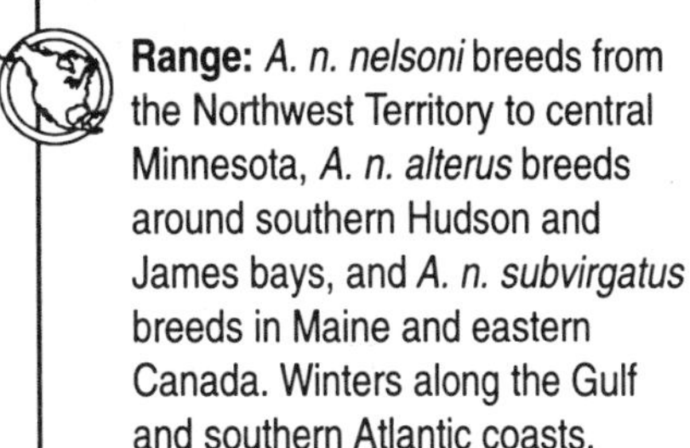

Range: *A. n. nelsoni* breeds from the Northwest Territory to central Minnesota, *A. n. alterus* breeds around southern Hudson and James bays, and *A. n. subvirgatus* breeds in Maine and eastern Canada. Winters along the Gulf and southern Atlantic coasts.

NJ Status: Probably a fairly common fall migrant, winter and spring status are poorly known.

Fall: Although the period of migration of Nelson's Sharp-tailed Sparrows appears to be similar to that of Saltmarsh Sharp-tailed Sparrows (i.e., October and early November), their status as a migrant is not well known. Nelson's Sharp-tailed Sparrows are more highly migratory than Saltmarsh Sharp-tailed Sparrows, and sharp-tailed sparrows seen away from the saltmarsh are likely to be Nelson's. **Maximum:** 12, Wildwood Crest, 22 October 1996.

Winter: The winter status of Nelson's Sharp-tailed Sparrow is poorly known, but they may be scarce or absent in mid-winter (Sibley 1997). They probably attempt to winter every year, and there is no evidence that they are more or less hardy than Saltmarsh Sharp-tailed Sparrows. Their true winter status, however, remains to be determined.

Spring: Sibley (1997) noted only one possible spring record of Nelson's Sharp-tailed Sparrow in Cape May County, 18 May 1989, but he presumed them to be regular migrants through coastal salt marshes in May.

Subspecies: Sibley (1997) indicated that all three subspecies of Nelson's Sharp-tailed Sparrow occur in migration in New Jersey, although there is little information on the relative status of each subspecies. ■

Saltmarsh Sharp-tailed Sparrow

Ammodramus caudacutus

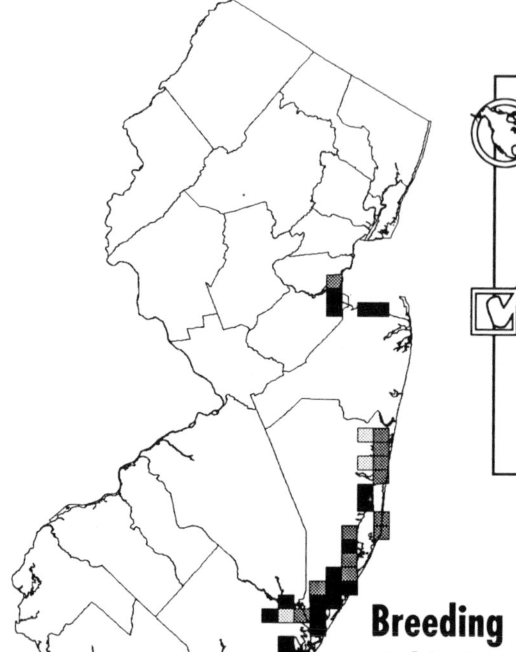

- Possible
- Probable
- Confirmed

Range: Breeds along the East coast from Maine to North Carolina. Winters along the coast from New Jersey to Florida.

NJ Status: Uncommon and local summer resident, uncommon spring and fairly common fall migrant, uncommon winter resident.

Statewide Summary	
Status	# of Blocks
Possible	6
Probable	21
Confirmed	29
Total	56

Breeding

Habitat: Nests in coastal salt marshes.

The large-scale ditching, draining, and filling of the salt marshes during the 20th century has reduced the numbers of breeding Saltmarsh Sharp-tailed Sparrows in New Jersey (Stone 1937, Cruickshank 1942). In the early 1900s, Stone (1908) found them abundant statewide along the coast, but by the mid-1930s

Physiographic Distribution Saltmarsh Sharp-tailed Sparrow	Number of blocks in province	Number of blocks species found breeding in province	Number of blocks species found in state	Percent of province species occupies	Percent of all records for this species found in province	Percent of state area in province
Inner Coastal Plain	128	5	56	3.9	8.9	15.0
Outer Coastal Plain	204	46	56	22.5	82.1	23.9
Pine Barrens	180	5	56	2.8	8.9	21.1

he bemoaned their disappearance from areas around Cape May due to changes in habitat. He suggested that the ditching and filling of salt marshes would lead to their extirpation from the state (Stone 1937). Cruickshank (1942) identified "too much so-called mosquito control work" as a reason for their decline, and even extirpation in some areas. Nonetheless, by the mid-1980s, Boyle (1986) identified their breeding status as fairly common.

Atlas volunteers located Saltmarsh Sharp-tailed Sparrows in appropriate habitat along the coast, including the lower Delaware Bay. They were found slightly inland along the Mullica River, but for the most part their distribution remained coastal. Their range covered most of coastal Ocean, Atlantic, Cape May, and Cumberland counties, but there were gaps in their distribution. They were absent from the east coast of Monmouth County, where development has left no suitable salt marsh habitat.

Although their range appears to be fairly large, it is likely that the loss of habitat during this century has resulted in an overall population decline. Unfortunately there were no estimates of the size of their population earlier this century, and tracking changes in their range without tracking changes in density, can be misleading.

Subspecies: Saltmarsh Sharp-tailed Sparrow is represented by two subspecies, *A. c. caudacutus* and *A. c. diversa*. Both breed in New Jersey. However, they are essentially inseparable to field observers. South of Atlantic County the breeding subspecies is *A.c. diversa* while *A. c. caudacutus* breeds north of there (Pyle 1997).

Fall: From September through November, local Saltmarsh Sharp-tailed Sparrows are joined by migrants, with peak numbers occurring in October and early November. **Maximum:** 10, Sandy Hook, 13 October 1997.

Winter: Migrant and wintering Saltmarsh Sharp-tailed Sparrows are secretive and are rarely found away from their salt marsh habitats. Prior to 1996, Saltmarsh Sharp-tailed Sparrow (with two subspecies) and Nelson's Sharp-tailed Sparrow (with three subspecies – see above) were represented by one species called Sharp-tailed Sparrow. Statewide CBC totals reflect numbers prior to the split. Nonetheless, the totals are highly variable. **CBC Statewide Stats:** Average: 33; Maximum: 123 in 1985; Minimum: 8 in 1993. **CBC Maximum:** 101, Oceanville, 1985.

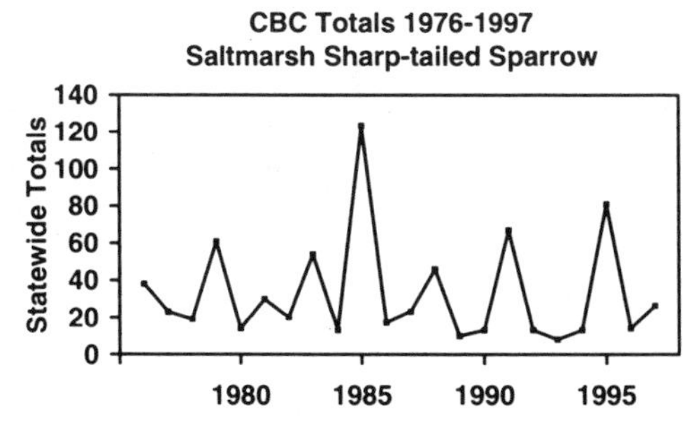

Spring: The timing of the departure of New Jersey's wintering Saltmarsh Sharp-tailed Sparrows and the arrival of local breeding birds is not well known. Local nesting birds probably begin to return in late April. ■

Seaside Sparrow

Ammodramus maritimus

Statewide Summary	
Status	# of Blocks
Possible	5
Probable	36
Confirmed	38
Total	79

Range: Breeds along the Atlantic coast from New Hampshire south to northern Florida and west along the Gulf coast to Texas. Winters along the Atlantic coast north to New York.

NJ Status: Common but local summer resident, fairly common spring and fall migrant, uncommon winter resident.

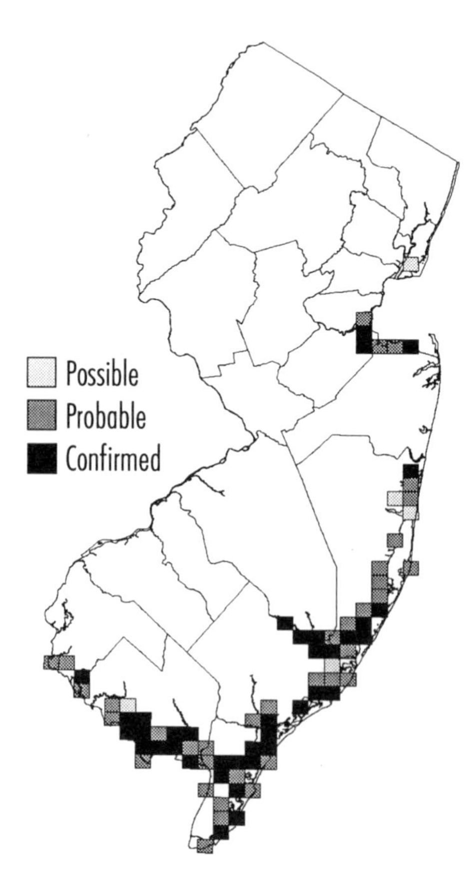

Breeding

Habitat: Nests in salt marshes.

Seaside Sparrows declined during the 20th century as the ditching and filling of much of the salt marsh degraded and destroyed their habitat (Stone 1937, Bull 1964). In 1908 Stone called Seaside Sparrows common nesting birds, and suggested they prefer wetter areas of the salt marsh than sharp-tailed sparrows. Stone (1937) suggested that Seaside Sparrows, along with sharp-tailed sparrows and Marsh Wrens, might be in danger of extinction along the New Jersey coast due to habitat changes. Cruickshank (1942) noted that "constant ditching and diking" of salt marshes had nearly extirpated Seaside Sparrows from areas around Raritan and Newark bays. By the mid-1980s, despite a reduction in numbers, they were considered a common breeding bird in the salt marsh on both coasts (Leck 1984).

Physiographic Distribution Seaside Sparrow	Number of blocks in province	Number of blocks species found breeding in province	Number of blocks species found in state	Percent of province species occupies	Percent of all records for this species found in province	Percent of state area in province
Piedmont	167	1	79	0.6	1.3	19.6
Inner Coastal Plain	128	6	79	4.7	7.6	15.0
Outer Coastal Plain	204	67	79	32.8	84.8	23.9
Pine Barrens	180	5	79	2.8	6.3	21.1

Seaside Sparrow

Seaside Sparrows are more widely distributed, and more easily seen, than Saltmarsh Sharp-tailed Sparrows. Atlas volunteers located Seaside Sparrows in appropriate habitat along both the Atlantic and Delaware Bay coasts. Their range extended farther north along the Delaware Bay shore than did Saltmarsh Sharp-tailed Sparrow's range. They were conspicuously absent from the east coast of Monmouth County, where development has destroyed appropriate salt marsh habitat. Although their range appears to be extensive, it is likely that the loss of habitat during the 20th century has resulted in an overall population decline.

Fall: In migration, Seaside Sparrows are rarely found away from their coastal salt marsh habitats. The timing of the departure of local breeding birds is not well known, and movements of migrants from the north are almost unnoticeable.

Winter: CBC numbers of Seaside Sparrows are highly variable. Although they appear to be less numerous in winter, they are present in the state

continued on page 586

continued from page 585

Seaside Sparrow

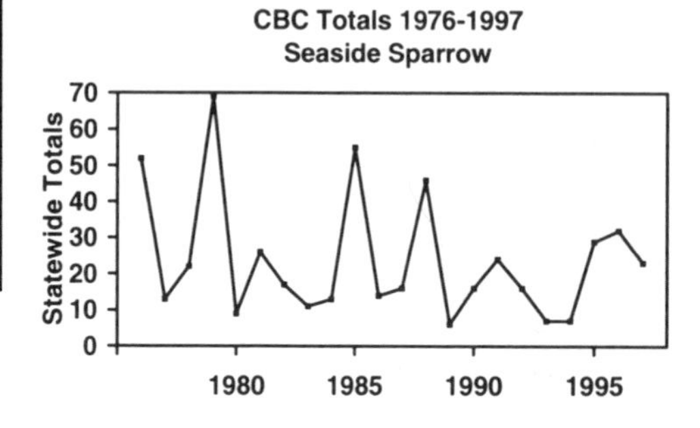

year-round. **CBC Statewide Stats:** Average: 24; Maximum: 69 in 1979; Minimum: 6 in 1989. **CBC Maximum:** 48, Barnegat, 1979.

Spring: Returning Seaside Sparrows arrive on the breeding grounds in mid- to late April. ■

Fox Sparrow

Passerella iliaca

Range: In eastern North America, breeds mainly from northern Manitoba east across Canada to Newfoundland. Winters in the southeastern United States north to coastal New England.

NJ Status: Fairly common spring and common fall migrant, uncommon winter resident.

Fall: Fox Sparrow numbers vary noticeably from one year to the next. Normally the earliest arrivals appear from mid- to late October with highest numbers usually noted in November. **Maxima:** 50, Palmyra, 14 November 1993 ; dozens, Higbee Beach, 22 November 1987 (Sibley 1997).

Winter: Fox Sparrows are more likely in southern New Jersey than in northern New Jersey in winter. CBC totals are quite variable. **CBC Statewide Stats:** Average: 163; Maximum: 306 in 1997; Minimum: 57 in 1987. **CBC Maximum:** 130, Cape May, 1997.

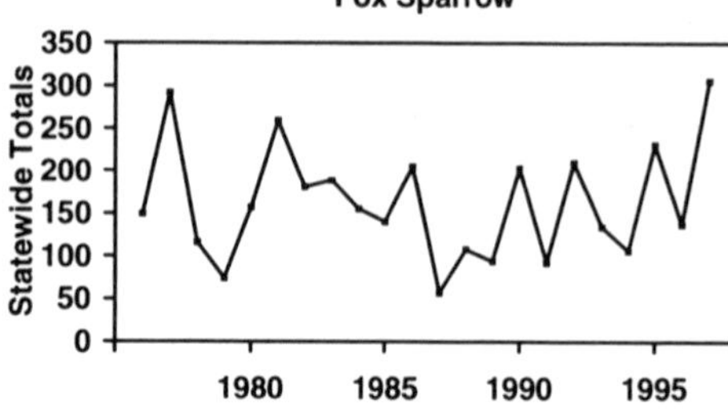

Fox Sparrow

continued

Spring: The northbound movement of Fox Sparrows can easily be missed due to the early and tightly concentrated period of passage. The earliest movements may be noted by late February, but the peak flight generally occurs from mid- to late March. Only the occasional straggler remains after early April. Very rarely, astounding numbers of migrants may be grounded: e.g., 700+, Franklin Lakes, 25 March 1933 (Cruickshank 1942). **Other maxima:** 85-100, Sandy Hook, 11 March 1987; 40, Jakes Landing, 9 March 1996. ■

Song Sparrow

Melospiza melodia

Range: In eastern North America, breeds from Manitoba east to Newfoundland, south to northern Arkansas and northern Georgia. Winters mainly south of the Great Lakes and along the coast from Nova Scotia to Florida.

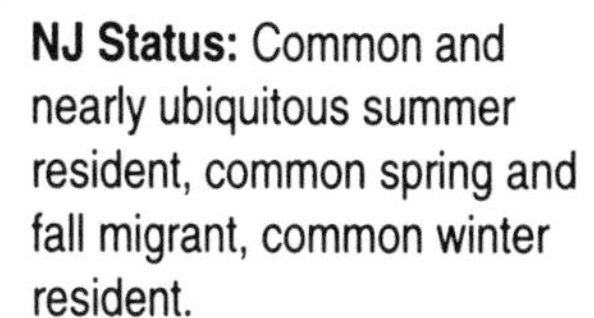

NJ Status: Common and nearly ubiquitous summer resident, common spring and fall migrant, common winter resident.

Breeding

Habitat: Nests in a wide variety of shrubby, brushy edge habitats from woodland clearings to overgrown fields and backyards. Somewhat moist conditions are favored.

Song Sparrows have been a common and broadly distributed nesting bird throughout New Jersey during the 20th century (Stone 1908, Boyle 1986). Atlas data indicated that Song Sparrows were the most broadly distributed sparrows breeding in the state, occurring in 92% of the blocks statewide. They were found in 100% of the blocks in all the physiographic provinces, except the Pine Barrens and the Outer Coastal Plain. In the Pine Barrens, they were restricted to widely scattered patches of appropriate habitat in the dry Pitch Pine forest. It is unknown if their current patchy distribution in the Pine Barrens is a new development, or if it has been overlooked in the past. They were also absent from areas of eastern Cumberland and northwestern Cape May counties. While these areas are part of the Outer Coastal Plain, they contain very Pine Barrens-like habitat.

continued on page 588

continued from page 587

Song Sparrow

Physiographic Distribution Song Sparrow	Number of blocks in province	Number of blocks species found breeding in province	Number of blocks species found in state	Percent of province species occupies	Percent of all records for this species found in province	Percent of state area in province
Kittatinny Mountains	19	19	783	100.0	2.4	2.2
Kittatinny Valley	45	45	783	100.0	5.7	5.3
Highlands	109	109	783	100.0	13.9	12.8
Piedmont	167	167	783	100.0	21.3	19.6
Inner Coastal Plain	128	128	783	100.0	16.3	15.0
Outer Coastal Plain	204	187	783	91.7	23.9	23.9
Pine Barrens	180	128	783	71.1	16.3	21.1

Statewide Summary	
Status	# of Blocks
Possible	30
Probable	180
Confirmed	573
Total	783

Subspecies: "Eastern" Song Sparrow, *M. m. melodia*, is the breeding bird across most of New Jersey, although the "Atlantic" Song Sparrow, *M. m. atlantica*, apparently nests on the barrier islands (Fables 1955).

Fall: Song Sparrows migrate from September through at least early December. The actual dates for passage migrants are difficult to determine due to confusion with local birds. Maximum numbers are noted from October through mid-November. **Maxima:** 2,000+, Sandy Hook, 23 October 1989; 1,000+, Higbee Beach, 30 October 1988.

Song Sparrow

continued

Winter: CBC totals for Song Sparrows are fairly consistent. They are one of the most common winter birds throughout the state. **CBC Statewide Stats:** Average: 5,350; Maximum: 6,784 in 1997; Minimum: 3,766 in 1978. **CBC Maximum:** 988, Lower Hudson, 1982.

Spring: The northward movement of Song Sparrows begins by early March and peaks late in the month. Spring migrants are not as conspicuous as autumn birds. **Maximum:** 89, Island Beach SP, 31 March 1991, (banded). ■

Lincoln's Sparrow

Melospiza lincolnii

Range: Nests from Alaska to Labrador, and in the Northeast south to northern New England and northern New York, occasionally to western Massachusetts. Winters from the southern United States to Central America.

NJ Status: Scarce spring and uncommon fall migrant, accidental in winter.

Fall: Early migrant Lincoln's Sparrows arrive from mid- to late September, with numbers peaking from early to mid-October. A low-density movement in southern New Jersey may persist through mid-November. Lincoln's Sparrows are usually more numerous inland than on the coast. They are more widely noted today than in the past. Stone (1937) regarded them as rare transients statewide and knew of only one record from Cape May. **Maxima:** 80, Overpeck Park, 2 October 1996; 25, Lyons, 2 October 1994.

Winter: Although Lincoln's Sparrows are increasingly noted into December, there is only one mid-winter record from Woodbine, 26 January 1987. They were reported on nine CBCs between 1976 and 1997.

Spring: Virtually all spring records of Lincoln's Sparrows are in May, with mid-May providing most reports. Although migrants are usually less common at this season than in fall, occasionally remarkable weather-related fallouts occur along the coast (see maxima). **Maxima:** 30-50, Sandy Hook, 19 May 1984; 10, Sandy Hook, 20 May 1997. ■

Swamp Sparrow
Melospiza georgiana

Range: Breeds from the southern Northwest Territories east to Newfoundland, south in the east to eastern Nebraska and Maryland. Winters from southern Wisconsin and southern New England, south to Mexico and Florida.

NJ Status: Fairly common and fairly widespread summer resident, fairly common spring and common fall migrant, uncommon to common winter resident.

Breeding

Habitat: Nests in open freshwater marshes, the upper edge of tidal salt marsh, and other wetlands.

Although historically described as common breeding birds in New Jersey (Stone 1908, Boyle 1986), the distribution of Swamp Sparrows has always been restricted by the distribution of freshwater wetlands. Bull (1964) noted that they could sometimes nest "semicolonially." For example, he cited an instance of 120 pairs present at Troy Meadows in the summer of 1947. Fables (1955), although noting that Swamp Sparrows bred throughout the state, found them absent as breeding birds from the Cape May Peninsula. Kane et al. (1985) found 114 and 110 pairs respectively in 1983 and 1984 censuses of Great Swamp NWR, and a 1984 study of Troy Meadows found Swamp Sparrows to be the commonest breeding birds with 209 pairs nesting at that site (Kane 1985).

Statewide Summary	
Status	# of Blocks
Possible	35
Probable	171
Confirmed	98
Total	304

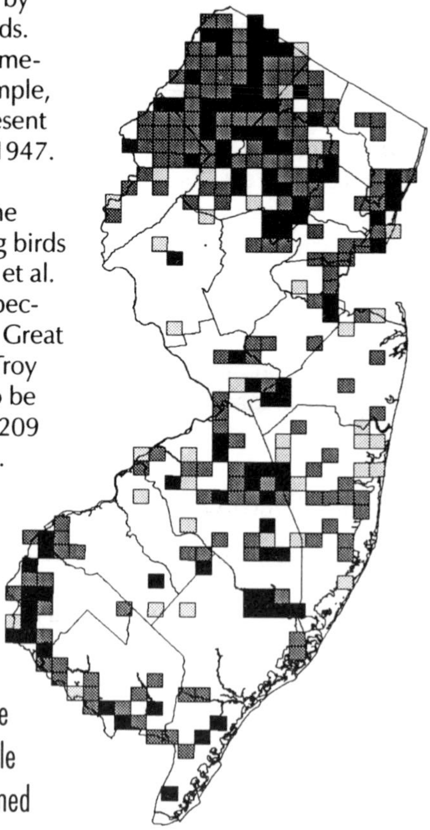

Possible
Probable
Confirmed

Atlas data showed that Swamp Sparrows were broadly distributed throughout the state, although more uniformly distributed in the north. They were found in 36% of blocks statewide and 48% of the blocks from the Piedmont northward. South of the Piedmont they were found in only 27% of the blocks. They were, however, located in nearly all the Delaware Bay shore blocks from southern Gloucester County to northern Cape May County, indicating their preference for the salt/brackish marsh edges. Swamp Sparrows were more broadly distributed in the Pine Barrens than might be suspected. This is likely due to their use of old and abandoned cranberry bogs, which commonly occur throughout the Pine Barrens. Contrary to Fables (1955) findings, they were located at a few locations in Cape May County, but remain thinly distributed in the county.

Subspecies: Most of the breeding Swamp Sparrows in New Jersey are the widespread "Eastern" Swamp Sparrow, *M. g. georgiana*. The nesting birds along Delaware Bay are the darker, larger-billed race *M. g. nigrescens*, the "Coastal Plain" Swamp Sparrow.

Fall: Southward migration of Swamp Sparrows begins by late September and continues through at least November. Largest numbers arrive from mid-October to early November. **Maxima:** 5,000+, Sandy Hook, 23 October 1989; 1,000+, Higbee Beach, 30 October 1988.

Winter: CBC totals for Swamp Sparrows are fairly consistent, with variations probably the result of harsh winter conditions. They may be quite rare inland and northward at the end of a severe winter. **Maxima:** 900, Artificial Island, 29 December 1993; 500 Artificial Island, 7 February 1993. **CBC Statewide Stats:** Average: 701; Maximum: 1,300 in 1997; Minimum: 264 in 1978. **CBC Maximum:** 282, Cumberland, 1995.

continued on page 592

Physiographic Distribution Swamp Sparrow	Number of blocks in province	Number of blocks species found breeding in province	Number of blocks species found in state	Percent of province species occupies	Percent of all records for this species found in province	Percent of state area in province
Kittatinny Mountains	19	13	304	68.4	4.3	2.2
Kittatinny Valley	45	42	304	93.3	13.8	5.3
Highlands	109	61	304	56.0	20.1	12.8
Piedmont	167	48	304	28.7	15.8	19.6
Inner Coastal Plain	128	46	304	35.9	15.1	15.0
Outer Coastal Plain	204	45	304	22.1	14.8	23.9
Pine Barrens	180	49	304	27.2	16.1	21.1

continued from page 591

Swamp Sparrow

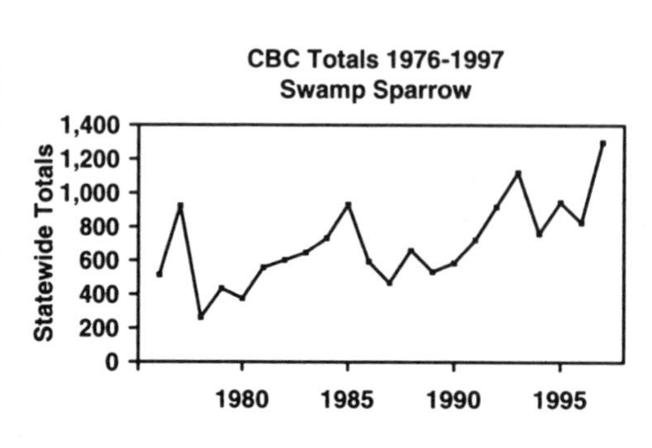

Spring: Swamp Sparrow's migration north begins in late March and peaks from mid-April to early May. **Maximum:** 60, Chester, 28 April 1984. ■

White-throated Sparrow

Zonotrichia albicollis

Possible
Probable
Confirmed

Range: Breeds from northwest Canada to Newfoundland southeast through Canada to the Great Lakes and northern New Jersey. In the East, winters from the southern Great Lakes and southern New England south to Texas and Florida.

NJ Status: Scarce and very local summer resident, common spring and fall migrant, common winter resident.

Breeding

Habitat: Open areas in damp, high-elevation Eastern Hemlock-northern hardwood forest.

Northwestern New Jersey is on the extreme southern edge of White-throated

White-throated Sparrow

continued

Physiographic Distribution — White-throated Sparrow	Number of blocks in province	Number of blocks species found breeding in province	Number of blocks species found in state	Percent of province species occupies	Percent of all records for this species found in province	Percent of state area in province
Kittatinny Mountains	19	2	10	10.5	20.0	2.2
Kittatinny Valley	45	5	10	11.1	50.0	5.3
Highlands	109	2	10	1.8	20.0	12.8
Piedmont	167	1	10	0.6	10.0	19.6

Map Interpretation: This rare and very local breeding species may not nest in New Jersey every year. Some individuals may linger quite late into the summer, and these should not be mistaken for breeding birds. Until a nest is confirmed elsewhere, the potential breeding range of this species in New Jersey should only include areas over 1,200 feet in elevation.

Statewide Summary

Status	# of Blocks
Possible	6
Probable	3
Confirmed	1
Total	10

Sparrow's breeding range. Fables (1955) noted a few records that were suggestive of breeding attempts. One of these reports was of a set of eggs collected in Essex County in1894, but doubt was later cast on the accuracy of the collection site. Confirmation of breeding eluded observers until 18 June 1972, when an adult was found feeding a dependent fledgling on Cherry Ridge, near the Sussex-Passaic County line (Kane and Marx 1972).

During the Atlas surveys, White-throated Sparrows were found in only ten blocks, making them one of the rarest nesting songbirds in the state. They were Confirmed in only one block, in the Highlands of Passaic County. Over the years, singing White-throated Sparrows have been recorded into July in many parts of the state, but proven nesting has been confined to the high elevations of the northern Highlands and Kittatinny Ridge.

Fall: The earliest southbound White-throated Sparrows typically arrive in mid- to late September, with peak numbers from mid-October through November. Occasional coastal fallouts can be astonishingly large. **Maxima:** 100,000+, Sandy Hook, 23 October 1989; 1,000+, Higbee Beach, 30 October 1988 .

Winter: White-throated Sparrows are one of the most common passerines in the state in winter, although they can be

continued on page 594

continued from page 593

White-throated Sparrow

rather uncommon northward in some years, especially by midwinter. CBC totals are fairly consistent. **CBC Statewide Stats:** Average: 11,979; Maximum: 17,661 in 1997; Minimum: 8,553 in 1979. **CBC Maximum:** 2,800, Cape May, 1980.

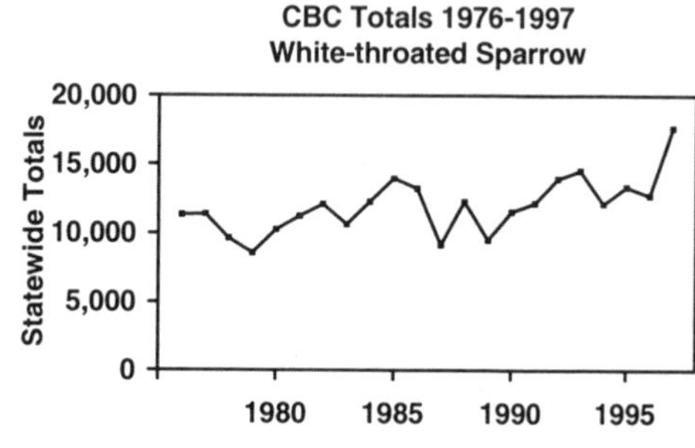

Spring: White-throated Sparrows begin their migration in early April and continue through mid-May. Although normally less numerous than in fall, huge numbers are occasionally encountered from mid- to late April. **Maxima:** 10,000+, Sandy Hook, 29 April 1989; 1,500+, Garret Mt., 29 April 1989. ■

Harris's Sparrow

Zonotrichia querula

Range: Breeds in north central Canada. Winters from South Dakota and Minnesota south to Texas.

NJ Status: Very rare. NJBRC Review List.

Occurrence: There have been 24 state reports of Harris's Sparrows, and 11 have been accepted by the NJBRC (six in winter, three in spring, two in fall). The 11 accepted records are:

Troy Meadows#	*7 May 1935*	
*Princeton**	*28 March-13 May 1966*	
*Sand Brook**	*2 January-19 February 1967*	*at a feeder*
Island Beach	*7 October 1967*	*ph-RBPF, adult male banded*
*Grovers Mill**	*11 November 1968-19 January 1969*	*at a feeder*
*Holmdel**	*22 February-1 March 1969*	
Mt. Pleasant	*25 February-mid-April 1975*	*phs-RBPF, at a feeder*
Flanders	*19 January-mid-March 1986*	*phs-RNJB 12:17, 12:26*
Mendham	*8 November 1989-mid-March 1990*	
Higbee Beach	*3 May 1992*	
Pennington	*14-18 November 1993*	*ph-RNJB 20:23*

White-crowned Sparrow

Zonotrichia leucophrys

Range: Breeds from Alaska across northern Canada to Newfoundland, south through the western United States. Winters in the southern United States mainly west of the Appalachians.

NJ Status: Scarce spring and uncommon fall migrant, uncommon winter resident.

Fall: White-crowned Sparrow numbers fluctuate dramatically from year-to-year. Though normally uncommon, migrants occasionally occur in considerable numbers following large coastal passerine fallouts. The earliest birds may arrive in late September, but the peak flight is from mid- to late October. **Maxima:** 500-700, Sandy Hook, 23 October 1989; 250, Island Beach, 15 October 1988.

Winter: In winter, White-crowned Sparrows are most numerous in southwestern New Jersey. For the first half of the 20th century, they were considered accidental in winter, and the first documented occurrence of wintering in New Jersey was during 1953-1954 (Fables 1955). Numbers quickly climbed in the following decade – e.g., 200 banded, Mullica Hill, winter 1966-1967 (AFN). White-crowned Sparrow numbers on CBCs are somewhat erratic. **Winter Maximum:** 125, Elsinboro, winter 1991-1992. **CBC Statewide Stats:** Average: 161; Maximum: 298 in 1995; Minimum: 37 in 1979. **CBC Maximum:** 93, NW Gloucester, 1981.

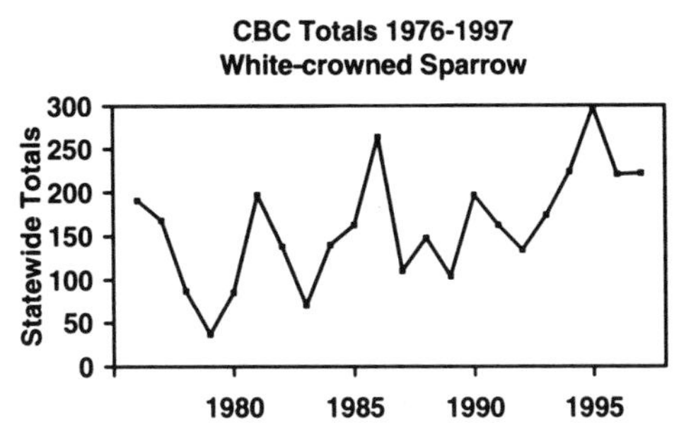

Spring: Compared to fall, the spring passage of White-crowned Sparrows is insignificant, and many observers fail to note it at all. Movement begins in late April and runs throughout May, with a noticeable peak in the middle of the month. A rare coastal fallout may occasionally produce numbers far in excess of the normal few (see maxima). **Maxima:** 100+, Sandy Hook, 19 May 1984; 12, Mickleton, 13 May 1978; 12, Sandy Hook, 20 May 1997.

Subspecies: The regular transient and winter visitor to New Jersey is the dark-lored *Z. l. leucophrys*. Several reports of pale-lored birds showing the characters of *Z. l. gambelli*, from the mid-1970s to the mid-1990s, led the NJBRC to add this subspecies to the Review List in 1996. ■

Golden-crowned Sparrow

Zonotrichia atricapilla

Range: Breeds in Alaska and western Canada. Winters from southern Alaska and southern British Columbia south to California into Mexico.

NJ Status: Accidental. NJBRC Review List.

Occurrence: There have been ten state reports of Golden-crowned Sparrows, and seven have been accepted by NJBRC. The seven records appear to involve five individuals, with one bird present three consecutive years. The seven accepted records are:

*Cape May Point**	*7 October 1962*	
Boonton	*9 January-12 April 1976*	*phs-NJA/RNJB 2:5; Reeves and Reeves 1976, at a feeder*
Boonton	*18 October 1976-1 April 1977*	*ph-NJA/RNJB 3:92; Kane 1977a, at a feeder*
Boonton	*winter 1977-February1978*	*Reeves 1978, at a feeder*
Frelinghuysen Twp.	*1 January-23 April 1983*	*ph-RNJB 9:81, at a feeder*
Mantua Township	*19 November 1996*	
Erma	*1 January- 28 February 1998*	*ph-RNJB 24:53*

Dark-eyed Junco

Junco hyemalis

Range: In eastern North America breeds from Manitoba east to Newfoundland, south to the Great Lakes and northwestern New Jersey and along the Appalachians to northern Georgia. Winters throughout southern Canada and almost all of the United States.

NJ Status: Rare and very local summer resident, common spring and fall migrant, common winter resident.

Breeding

Habitat: Nests at high elevations in northern hardwood forest.

Stone (1908) suggested that Dark-eyed Juncos might be found nesting in extreme northwestern New Jersey, noting their occurrence across the Delaware River in Pike County, Pennsylvania. However, neither Griscom (1923) nor Cruickshank

Dark-eyed Junco

continued

Statewide Summary	
Status	# of Blocks
Possible	2
Probable	8
Confirmed	5
Total	15

(1942) made any mention of them as active or potential breeding birds. There were a few highly probable records involving young birds capable of flight – e.g., Tillman's Ravine in 1949 and Ramapo Mountain in 1953 (Fables 1955), but the first confirmed New Jersey breeding record was a nest with eggs discovered on Bearfort Mountain in Passaic County in June 1972 (AFN). By the mid-1980s, Boyle (1986) considered them to be very rare and local breeding birds in the northwestern corner of the state.

Atlas observers found Dark-eyed Juncos in only 15 blocks, and despite five years of surveys they were Confirmed in only five blocks. All of the occupied blocks were in the Kittatinny Mountains and the Highlands of Sussex, Warren, and Passaic counties. Dark-eyed Juncos are birds of high elevation and most appropriate habitat has already been colonized. It is extremely unlikely that they will expand their breeding range beyond the Kittatinny Ridge and Highlands in New Jersey.

Possible
Probable
Confirmed

Fall: The first southbound Dark-eyed Juncos normally arrive in mid- to late September, although there are a number of reports as early as the first week of September. Peak numbers occur over a long period, from mid-October to early December.

continued on page 598

Physiographic Distribution — Dark-eyed Junco	Number of blocks in province	Number of blocks species found breeding in province	Number of blocks species found in state	Percent of province species occupies	Percent of all records for this species found in province	Percent of state area in province
Kittatinny Mountains	19	7	15	36.8	46.7	2.2
Kittatinny Valley	45	5	15	11.1	33.3	5.3
Highlands	109	3	15	2.8	20.0	12.8

continued from page 597

Maxima: 20,000+, Sandy Hook, 23 October 1989; 1,000s, Higbee Beach, 30 October 1988.

Winter: Dark-eyed Juncos are one of the most common species at feeders and weedy fields in winter, and are one of the most numerous passerines reported on CBCs. **CBC Statewide Stats:** Average: 13,937; Maximum: 18,995 in 1997; Minimum: 8,462 in 1979. **CBC Maximum:** 2,361, NW Gloucester, 1984.

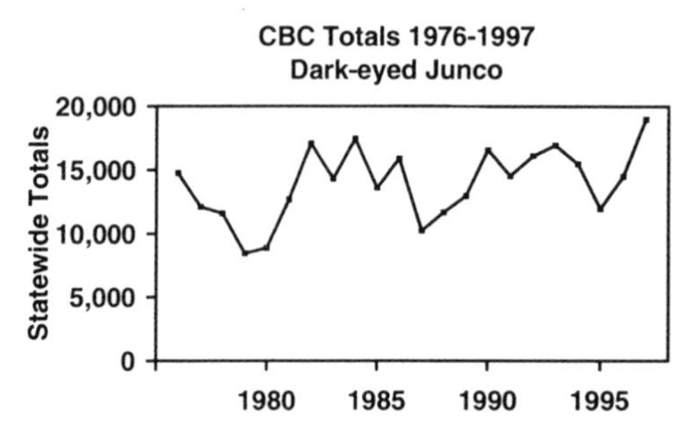

Spring: Juncos are typically moving northward from late February through early May, with the peak period of passage between late March and mid-April. **Maximum:** 100+, Bernardsville, 18 April 1996.

Subspecies: Breeding birds and migrants are "Slate-colored" Juncos, of the widespread subspecies *J. h. hyemalis*. A specimen of *J. h. cismontanus*, a western race of the "Slate-colored" Junco complex, was reportedly found dead at Mantoloking, 8 October 1952 (Fables 1955). A specimen of *J. h. montanus*, part of the north-western-breeding "Oregon" Junco complex, was obtained at Orange, 23 February 1958 (Bull 1964). "Oregon" Juncos are reported in New Jersey nearly every year between November and April. These western subspecies were added to the Review List in 1996. ■

Lapland Longspur

Calcarius lapponicus

Range: In North America breeds on the Arctic tundra from Alaska across northern Canada south; in the East, to northern Quebec and Labrador. Winters across southern Canada and the northern United States south along the Atlantic coast to North Carolina and occasionally farther.

NJ Status: Rare to uncommon fall migrant and winter resident.

Fall: Most records of Lapland Longspurs are from October through December, but there are occasional reports of birds as early as late September – e.g., one at Cape May Point, 21 September 1982. Most reports are from the coast, although certain inland areas regularly attract the species. **Maxima:** 30, Island Beach SP, 21 October 1977; 20, North Arlington, 19 November 1979.

Winter: The overwhelming majority of winter reports of Lapland Longspurs are of individuals or very small groups intermixed with Horned Larks or Snow Buntings. A few are seen on CBCs. **Maxima:** 40, Brigantine Island, winter 1974-1975; 20+, North Arlington, 21 December 1980. **CBC Statewide Stats:** Average: 5; Maximum: 26 in 1982; Minimum: 0 in four years. **CBC Maximum:** 21, Lower Hudson, 1982.

Spring: Passage of the few returning Lapland Longspurs, as well as the departure of most wintering birds, takes place mainly from March to mid-April. Despite the largest one-day maximum in New Jersey – 75, Newark Meadows, 6 April 1935 (Bull 1964) – the spring movement is normally even lighter than fall. There have been a very few records into May, including one remarkably late bird on 11 June 1993 at the South Cape May Meadows. **Maxima:** 7, Brigantine Island, 4 March 1980; 7, Lumberton, 5 March 1978. ■

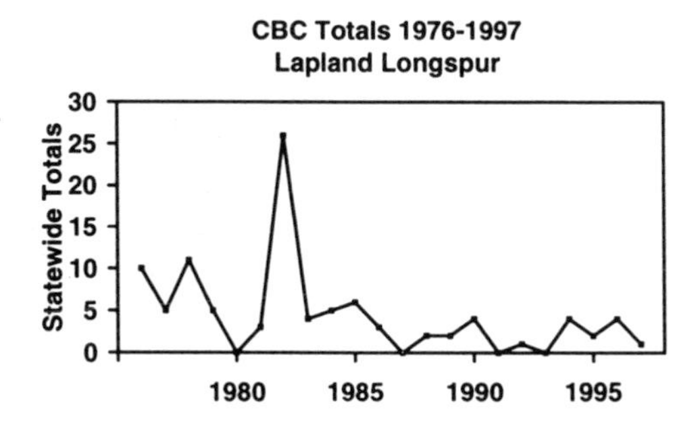

Smith's Longspur
Calcarius pictus

Range: Breeds locally from central Alaska to northern Ontario. Winters from southeastern Kansas and Arkansas south to Texas.

NJ Status: Accidental. NJBRC Review List.

Occurrence: There have been two state reports of Smith's Longspurs, and both have been accepted by the NJBRC: The two accepted records are:

South Cape May Meadows	*19-22 April 1991*	
Island Beach	*18-24 October 1995*	*ph-RNJB 22:1*

Chestnut-collared Longspur
Calcarius ornatus

Range: Breeds in the northern Great Plains. Winters from southern Arizona east to central Kansas, south to Texas and into central Mexico.

NJ Status: Accidental. NJBRC Review List.

Occurrence: There have been three state reports of Chestnut-collared Longspurs, and two have been accepted by the NJBRC. The two accepted records are:

Cape May Point	*18 June 1980*	*ph-RNJB 6:74, a male*
Sandy Hook	*14 January-mid-February 1984*	*ph-RNJB 10:25, a male*

Snow Bunting

Plectrophenax nivalis

Range: In North America, breeds on the Arctic tundra from Alaska to Labrador. Winters across southern Canada and the northern third of the United States.

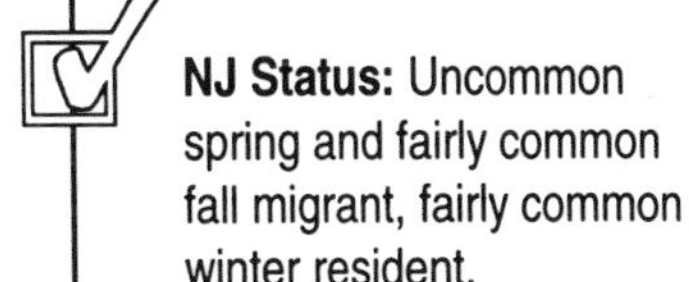

NJ Status: Uncommon spring and fairly common fall migrant, fairly common winter resident.

Fall: Snow Buntings usually appear in New Jersey before the end of October, with peak flights occurring from mid-November to early December. They are as likely to occur along the coast as they are inland. Overall, numbers at all seasons appear to have declined since the 1970s. **Maxima:** 1,000, Spruce Run Res., 15 November 1977; 500+, Tuckerton, November 1977.

Winter: The number of wintering Snow Buntings varies considerably from year to year. Even in winter the nomadic nature of this species makes it difficult to distinguish winter residents from those birds in passage. This is reflected in the variability in their CBC totals. **Maxima:** 500, Dutch Neck, winter 1974-1975; 320, Island Beach SP, 19 December 1987. **CBC Statewide Stats:** Average: 429; Maximum: 1,599 in 1977; Minimum: 35 in 1992. **CBC Maximum:** 452, Princeton, 1977.

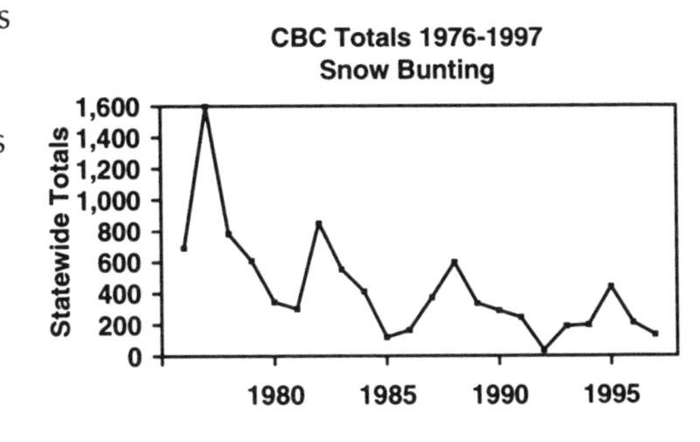

Spring: A rise in the numbers of Snow Buntings between mid-February and mid-March supports Cruickshank's (1942) contention that there is a light return flight at this season. All birds, however, have normally departed the state by the end of March. **Maxima:** 500+, Stewartsville, 10 March 1982; 300+, Bayonne, 16 February 1984. ■

Northern Cardinal

Cardinalis cardinalis

Range: Resident from eastern South Dakota east to Nova Scotia, south to Texas and Florida.

NJ Status: Common and nearly ubiquitous resident.

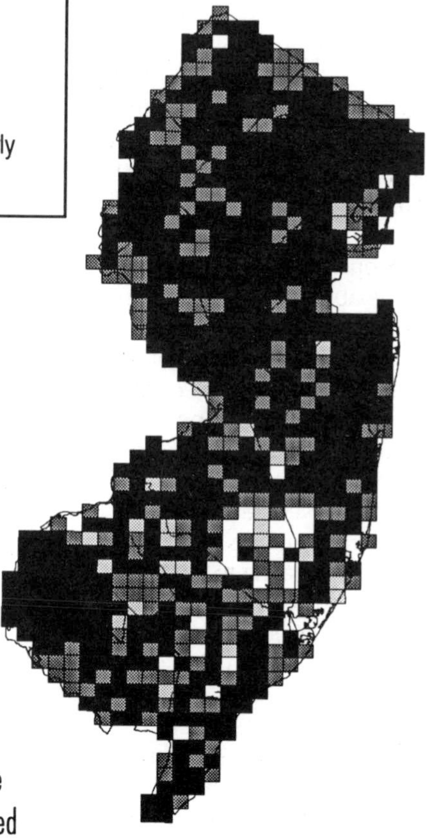

Breeding

Habitat: Nests in a wide variety of semi-open, brushy habitats.

Northern Cardinal's colonization of the northeastern United States is well documented. In the 1800s, Northern Cardinals were commonly captured and kept as

Statewide Summary	
Status	# of Blocks
Possible	25
Probable	188
Confirmed	596
Total	809

Physiographic Distribution Northern Cardinal	Number of blocks in province	Number of blocks species found breeding in province	Number of blocks species found in state	Percent of province species occupies	Percent of all records for this species found in province	Percent of state area in province
Kittatinny Mountains	19	18	809	94.7	2.2	2.2
Kittatinny Valley	45	45	809	100.0	5.6	5.3
Highlands	109	109	809	100.0	13.5	12.8
Piedmont	167	164	809	98.2	20.3	19.6
Inner Coastal Plain	128	126	809	98.4	15.6	15.0
Outer Coastal Plain	204	190	809	93.1	23.5	23.9
Pine Barrens	180	157	809	87.2	19.4	21.1

cage birds (Forbush 1929). Many of the caged birds in the United States escaped, or were released, and some of them formed the earliest breeding records for the Northeast (Forbush 1929). They have always been resident in southern New Jersey, but it is likely the release of caged birds helped give them a foothold in northern New Jersey.

Stone (1908) found cardinals to be absent from the northern counties of the state, and by 1923 Griscom noted that they were very local in the north. Writing in 1937, Stone described them as being at the northern limit of their range in southern New Jersey. Most modern observers would have difficulty relating to Cruickshank's (1942) description that this species was "accidental" in parts of Warren, Sussex, Passaic, and Morris counties. Fables (1955) described their increase as "marked" during the 1940s and 1950s. Bull (1964) considered their spread back into northern New Jersey in the 1950s as "positively phenomenal," stating that "few, if any, species have made such gains." It has been suggested that their dramatic range increase during the later half of the 20th century may have been linked to the widespread use of bird feeders increasing winter survival (Veit and Petersen 1993).

Boyle's (1986) description that Northern Cardinals "would be hard to miss in a day's birding anywhere in New Jersey" approximates the distribution found by Atlas observers. They were found in 95% of the blocks in the state, absent only from some sections of the Pine Barrens. Northern Cardinal's ability to nest in urban and suburban settings makes this species one of the most familiar birds in the state. The Atlas data probably represents this species' all-time largest range in the state.

Fall: Northern Cardinals are nonmigratory, permanent residents. There is no published information on the occurrence of fall migration of Northern Cardinal in New Jersey.

Winter: Statewide CBC totals of Northern Cardinals are fairly consistent each year. **CBC Statewide Stats:** Average: 4,180; Maximum: 5,304 in 1996; Minimum: 2,807 in 1979. **CBC Maximum:** 517, Cape May, 1996.

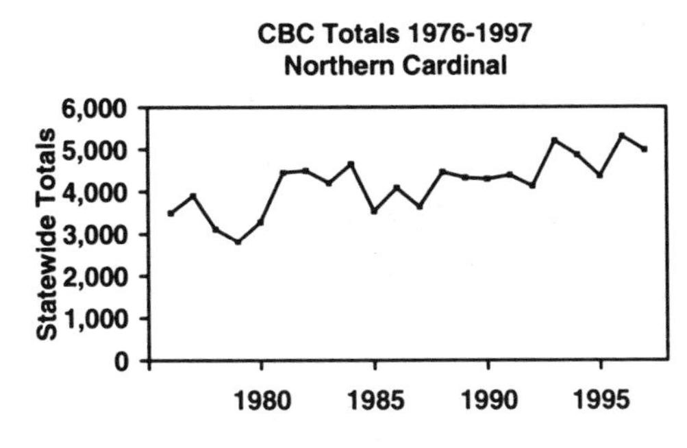

Spring: Northern Cardinals are nonmigratory, permanent residents. There is no published information on the occurrence of spring migration of Northern Cardinals in New Jersey. ■

Rose-breasted Grosbeak

Pheucticus ludovicianus

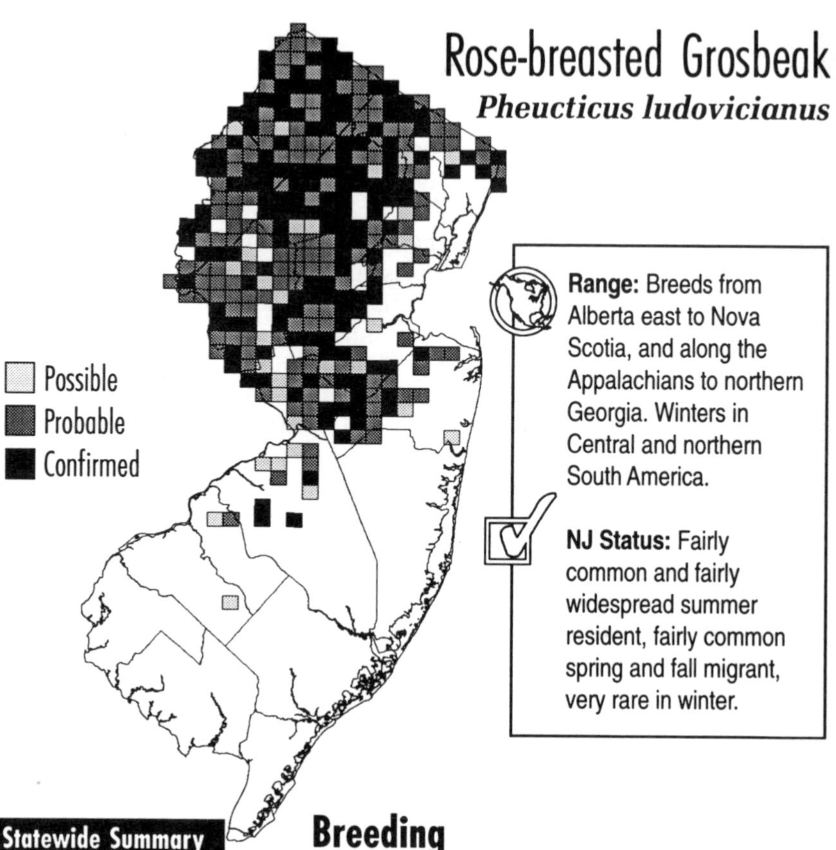

Range: Breeds from Alberta east to Nova Scotia, and along the Appalachians to northern Georgia. Winters in Central and northern South America.

NJ Status: Fairly common and fairly widespread summer resident, fairly common spring and fall migrant, very rare in winter.

Statewide Summary	
Status	# of Blocks
Possible	29
Probable	153
Confirmed	160
Total	342

Breeding

Habitat: Nests in open deciduous woodlands, favoring second growth, edges, and openings.

Stone (1908) noted that Rose-breasted Grosbeaks were common breeding birds in the northern half of the state, nesting southward in

Physiographic Distribution Rose-breasted Grosbeak	Number of blocks in province	Number of blocks species found breeding in province	Number of blocks species found in state	Percent of province species occupies	Percent of all records for this species found in province	Percent of state area in province
Kittatinny Mountains	19	19	342	100.0	5.6	2.2
Kittatinny Valley	45	43	342	95.6	12.6	5.3
Highlands	109	104	342	95.4	30.4	12.8
Piedmont	167	117	342	70.1	34.2	19.6
Inner Coastal Plain	128	44	342	34.4	12.9	15.0
Outer Coastal Plain	204	13	342	6.4	3.8	23.9
Pine Barrens	180	2	342	1.1	0.6	21.1

Rose-breasted Grosbeak

continued

diminishing numbers to Burlington County. Fables (1955) listed no breeding records south of Beverly in Burlington County and knew of no breeding records in the Pine Barrens.

Atlas surveys found that the range of Rose-breasted Grosbeaks had changed little since Stone's time, and they remain most commonly encountered in northern and central New Jersey. They were found in 96% of the blocks north of the Piedmont. Even though they were nearly absent from the urbanized, northeastern Piedmont, they were found in 70% of the blocks in that province. On the Coastal Plain, Rose-breasted Grosbeaks barely penetrate the Pine Barrens, their southward distribution ending at scattered locations in western Burlington County.

Fall: The first southbound Rose-breasted Grosbeaks arrive in late August. Peak flights occur from mid- to late September, with most having moved on by mid-October. **Maxima:** 1,000, Higbee Beach, 23 September 1983; 100+, Higbee Beach, 24 September 1989; 100+, Higbee Beach, 12 September 1992.

Winter: Rose-breasted Grosbeaks were reported on four CBCs between 1976 and 1997 (i.e., 1979, 1980, 1981, and 1986). There are also a few mid-winter reports, mainly of birds appearing at feeders.

Spring: Northbound Rose-breasted Grosbeaks arrive by late April, but peak numbers move through in early to mid-May. **Maxima:** 75, Princeton, 12 May 1988; 25+, Palmyra, 9 May 1997. ■

Black-headed Grosbeak

Pheucticus melanocephalus

Range: Breeds in southwestern Canada and the western states south into Mexico and east to Kansas, Nebraska and New Mexico. Winters primarily in Mexico.

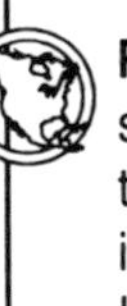

NJ Status: Very rare. NJBRC Review List.

Occurrence: There have been 40 state reports of Black-headed Grosbeaks, and 23 have been accepted by the NJBRC. Records extend from October to April. The first state record was of two birds, one at Rancocas Woods, 10 January to late-February 1954, at a feeder, and a second bird at the same location on 6 February 1954#. There are 10 photo records, mostly of birds at feeders. One of these feeder birds wintered in two consecutive years (1975-1976 and 1976-1977) at Bernardsville (ph-RBPF). This species was reported annually in the 1970s, less often in other decades. ■

Blue Grosbeak

Guiraca caerulea

Breeding

Habitat: Breeds in semi-open, brushy areas such as overgrown fields, hedgerows, landfills, and woodland edges.

Range: In eastern North America breeds from southern North Dakota east to central New Jersey, south to Texas and northern Florida. Winters in the Bahamas, Cuba, and Central America.

NJ Status: Uncommon and somewhat local summer resident, scarce spring and uncommon fall migrant, reported on one CBC.

Stone (1937) relayed a description of Blue Grosbeak's nest found by Audubon near Camden in 1829, but knew of very few other records for New Jersey. The first modern nesting record came from Cumberland County, near Bridgeton, in July 1952 (Fables 1955). By the mid-1960s Blue Grosbeaks had increased and were considered rare breeders in southern New Jersey (Bull 1964). From that point their range expanded and by 1981 they were established north to Monmouth, Somerset, and Mercer counties. Boyle (1986) found them uncommon, but increasing, summer residents south of the Raritan River. Blue Grosbeaks increased their range in other eastern states at the same time their range was increasing in New Jersey (Ingold 1993).

Atlas data indicated that most of the Blue Grosbeak's range in New Jersey is still south of the Raritan River, with 97% of their range south of the Piedmont. Fifty percent of their statewide range is within the Outer Coastal Plain, where they continue to increase.

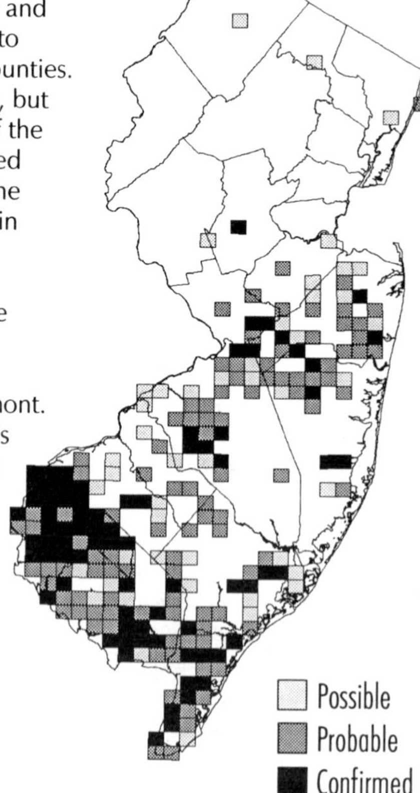

Statewide Summary	
Status	# of Blocks
Possible	47
Probable	103
Confirmed	78
Total	228

Blue Grosbeak

continued

They occurred in 33% of the Pine Barrens blocks, even though they are largely absent from the heart of the Pine Barrens. A Confirmation in central Somerset County, a Probable location in Bergen County, and scattered locations of Possible breeding birds in the northern counties suggest that a northward expansion may be continuing.

Fall: Central New Jersey is at the northern edge of Blue Grosbeak's breeding range. Consequently, migrants are few, although some birds remain into September. They are rare after mid-October, but lingering birds have been recorded into November. **Maxima:** 15, Higbee Beach, 11 September 1988; 7, Higbee Beach, 3 October 1990.

Winter: A Blue Grosbeak was photographed on the Cumberland CBC in 1992. There are no other winter reports.

Spring: Blue Grosbeaks return to their breeding grounds in late April, with only a few encountered elsewhere in migration. ■

Physiographic Distribution

Blue Grosbeak	Number of blocks in province	Number of blocks species found breeding in province	Number of blocks species found in state	Percent of province species occupies	Percent of all records for this species found in province	Percent of state area in province
Kittatinny Valley	45	2	228	4.4	0.9	5.3
Highlands	109	1	228	0.9	0.4	12.8
Piedmont	167	4	228	2.4	1.8	19.6
Inner Coastal Plain	128	56	228	43.8	24.6	15.0
Outer Coastal Plain	204	106	228	52.0	46.5	23.9
Pine Barrens	180	59	228	32.8	25.9	21.1

Indigo Bunting

Passerina cyanea

Range: In the east breeds from southern Saskatchewan east to New Brunswick, south to central Texas and northern Florida. Winters from southern Florida and Texas south to northern South America.

NJ Status: Fairly common and very widespread resident, common spring and fall migrant.

Breeding

Habitat: Nests in woodland edge habitats such as hedgerows, overgrown fields, powerline cuts, and forest clearings.

continued on page 608

continued from page 607

Indigo Bunting

Physiographic Distribution Indigo Bunting	Number of blocks in province	Number of blocks species found breeding in province	Number of blocks species found in state	Percent of province species occupies	Percent of all records for this species found in province	Percent of state area in province
Kittatinny Mountains	19	18	616	94.7	2.9	2.2
Kittatinny Valley	45	44	616	97.8	7.1	5.3
Highlands	109	107	616	98.2	17.4	12.8
Piedmont	167	128	616	76.6	20.8	19.6
Inner Coastal Plain	128	98	616	76.6	15.9	15.0
Outer Coastal Plain	204	132	616	64.7	21.4	23.9
Pine Barrens	180	89	616	49.4	14.4	21.1

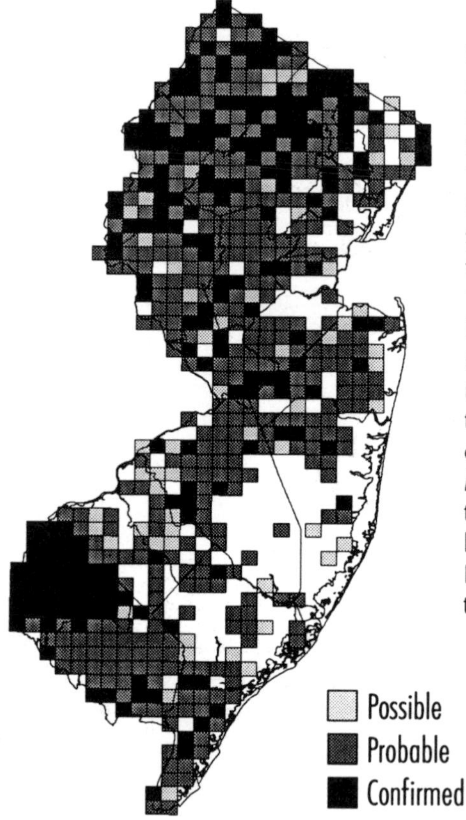

Indigo Buntings have widened their distribution in New Jersey since at least the mid-1950s. This matches an increase in their range and density throughout North America (Payne 1992). Stone (1908) described Indigo Buntings as common breeding birds, yet found them absent from most of the Cape May Peninsula (Stone 1937). Fables (1955) determined that Indigo Buntings were distributed mainly from Monmouth County northward, finding them scarce in the Pine Barrens, the southwestern corner of the state, and on the Cape May Peninsula. Leck (1984) noted that although they could be found breeding south to Cape May County, Indigo Buntings nested primarily in the northern half of the state.

Statewide Summary	
Status	# of Blocks
Possible	57
Probable	356
Confirmed	203
Total	616

Indigo Bunting

continued

From the Piedmont north, Indigo Bunting's distribution was close to historic range estimates. They were widespread throughout the provinces from the Piedmont northward, and were located in 87% of the blocks in those four physiographic provinces. Indigo Buntings were more broadly distributed in southern New Jersey than earlier in the 20th century. They were found in 65% of the blocks on the Outer Coastal Plain, and in nearly all the blocks in Salem, Cumberland, and Cape May counties. Elsewhere on the Outer Coastal Plain, they were absent from most of the barrier island and Atlantic coast saltmarsh blocks. They also occupied 77% of the blocks on the Inner Coastal Plain. Although absent from large, contiguous sections of the Pine Barrens, Indigo Buntings were nonetheless located in 49% of the blocks in that province.

Fall: Indigo Buntings begin migration by August and numbers peak in September. By mid-October only stragglers remain. The local population is so high that it is often difficult to distinguish migrants from local residents. **Maxima:** 150, Higbee Beach, 30 September 1996 (Sibley 1997); 60, Higbee Beach, 1 October 1994.

Winter: Indigo Buntings were reported on two CBCs between 1976 and 1997 (i.e., 1979 and 1990). Both were well documented (AB). There is one mid-winter record from Verona of a bird present nearly all of January 1957 (Bull 1964).

Spring: The first northbound Indigo Buntings normally reach New Jersey in late April or early May. Occasionally, however, a southerly weather system can produce a small fallout much earlier in April. **Maxima:** 30, Cape May Point, 20 May 1996 (Sibley 1997); 20, Higbee Beach, 28 April 1994. ■

Painted Bunting

Passerina ciris

Range: Breeds in the southern states from New Mexico east to the Carolinas and south to Florida. Winters south to Central America.

NJ Status: Very rare. NJBRC Review List.

Occurrence: There have been 24 state reports of Painted Buntings, and 14 have been accepted by the NJBRC

continued on page 610

continued from page 609

Painting Bunting

(four in fall, five in winter, five in spring). Seven birds were photographed, and three banded (all at Island Beach). The 14 accepted records are:

Cape May Point#	*4-5 May 1958*	*adult male*
Island Beach	*29 September 1961*	*ph-RBPF, banded, immature*
*Haddonfield**	*11-15 January 1963*	*ph-lost*
Island Beach	*8 September 1968*	*ph-RBPF, banded*
*Ogdensburg**	*18-26 November 1972*	*at a feeder*
Lebanon	*1 December 1976-1 February 1977*	*adult male at a feeder*
Island Beach	*12 May 1980*	*banded, female*
South Cape May Meadows	*12 June 1989*	
Brick Township	*14 December 1993-mid-January 1994*	*ph-RNJB 20:63, male at a feeder*
Colt's Neck	*29 January-28 February 1994*	*ph-RBPF, at a feeder*
Higbee Beach	*20-30 November 1994*	*ph-RBPF*
Higbee Beach	*13-15 May 1995*	
Medford	*mid-January-25 February 1996*	*ph-RNJB 22:49*
Higbee Beach	*15-17 May 1997*	

Dickcissel

Spiza americana

Range: Breeds mainly in the eastern Great Plains, occasionally farther east. Winters mainly in South America.

NJ Status: Rare and very local summer resident, rare spring and scarce fall migrant, very rare winter resident.

Breeding

Habitat: Nests in fields and meadows, often in planted fields; also at airports and landfills.

Historically, Dickcissels were very rare and irregular breeding birds in New Jersey. During the first half of the 19th century, they nested locally but regularly on the Coastal Plain, but

Dickcissel

continued

their numbers diminished after 1860. Early in the 20th century they were considered extirpated, and the last nest was confirmed near Plainfield in 1904 (Stone 1908). A pair attempted to nest near Evesboro, Burlington County, in June of 1939, but the field was mowed and the birds disappeared (Fables 1955). Leck (1984) noted breeding records in 1973 near Atlantic City, and Kane (1975a) reported Dickcissels breeding in 1974 at the Hackensack Meadowlands. There have been few nesting attempts in the 20th century, and Dickcissels habit of nesting in planted fields often leads to the same fate suffered by the pair in Burlington County in 1939. A small colony of five males and three females near Woodstown, Salem County in 1989 were seen mating and nest building, but were unable to fledge young before mowing disrupted their nesting attempts.

One indication of Dickcissels rarity as breeding birds is that during the five years of Atlas surveys, they were only found in six blocks, and they were only found in four of the five years. It is important to note that the

continued on page 612

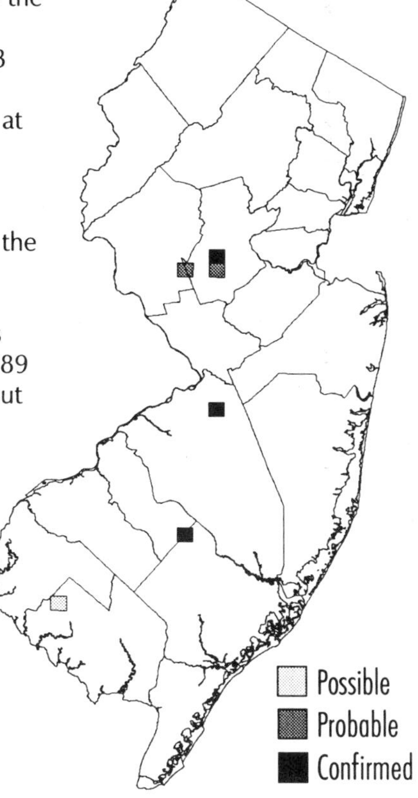

Statewide Summary	
Status	# of Blocks
Possible	1
Probable	2
Confirmed	3
Total	6

Physiographic Distribution

Dickcissel	Number of blocks in province	Number of blocks species found breeding in province	Number of blocks species found in state	Percent of province species occupies	Percent of all records for this species found in province	Percent of state area in province
Piedmont	167	3	6	1.8	50.0	19.6
Inner Coastal Plain	128	1	6	0.8	16.7	15.0
Outer Coastal Plain	204	1	6	0.5	16.7	23.9
Pine Barrens	180	1	6	0.6	16.7	21.1

continued from page 611

nesting attempt in 1989 in Salem County would have met the Atlas criteria for Confirmation, but no young were fledged. Interestingly, during 1997 and 1998, a small colony at Bright View Farm, Burlington County, produced fledglings for the first time in decades as a result of careful management and delayed mowing (L. Larson, pers. obs.).

Conservation Note: Conservation of grasslands is one of the greatest challenges facing Threatened and Endangered Species managers. Many grassland nesting birds occur in extremely low numbers, and they frequently change breeding locations from year to year. This nomadic breeding behavior makes tracking populations extremely difficult and makes habitat management necessary on a fairly wide scale. Given the rate of farmland loss in New Jersey, the only significant remaining breeding habitats for grassland birds in the state are airports, pasturelands, fallow fields, alfalfa fields, and some landfills. The ephemeral nature of these habitats (with the exception of airports) makes grassland bird breeding success a kind of avian roulette – with mowing, succession, and crop rotation controlling the outcome of nesting attempts. The Dickcissel's fate in New Jersey is further complicated by major pesticide poisoning on the Venezuelan wintering grounds – a fact that could ultimately offset grassland habitat management in North America.

Fall: Most Dickcissels recorded in fall are flying overhead along the coast giving their short "raspberry"-like call. They are usually seen flying overhead, rather than on the ground. Migrants are encountered between late August and early November, and maximum numbers occur in mid-October. **Maxima:** 15+, Higbee Beach, 16 October 1986; 15, Cape May Point, 26 October 1996.

Winter: Dickcissels are recorded with some regularity on CBCs, which is surprising as the great majority of the population winters in South America. In many years, individuals probably survive the winter. **CBC Statewide Stats:** Average: 1; Maximum: 6 in 1997; Minimum: 0 in nine years. **CBC Maximum:** 3, Cape May, 1997.

Spring: Although typically rare in spring, abnormally high numbers of Dickcissels were recorded at Cape May in 1996, when 13 individuals were seen between 10 May and 2 June (Sibley 1997). ■

Bobolink

Dolichonyx oryzivorus

Possible

Probable

Confirmed

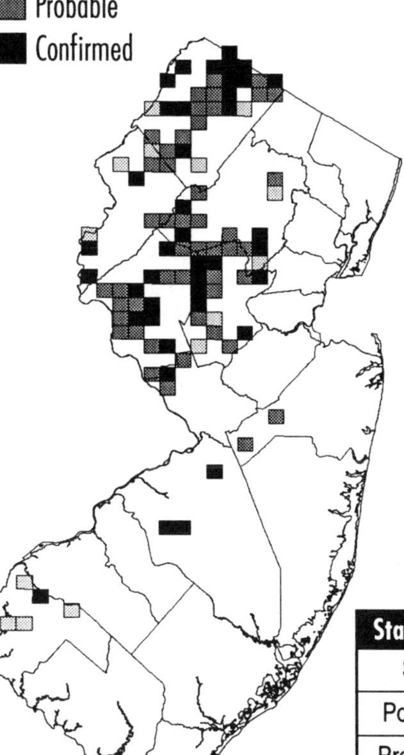

Range: Breeds from British Columbia east to Nova Scotia, south to Colorado and western New Jersey. Winters mainly in South America.

NJ Status: Uncommon and local summer resident, common spring and fall migrant, reported on two CBCs. Threatened Species in New Jersey.

Breeding

Habitat: Nests in extensive open hay fields, pastures, and meadows.

Bobolinks probably reached a period of peak abundance in the East following the clearing of the eastern forests in

continued on page 614

Statewide Summary	
Status	# of Blocks
Possible	14
Probable	47
Confirmed	40
Total	101

Physiographic Distribution **Bobolink**	Number of blocks in province	Number of blocks species found breeding in province	Number of blocks species found in state	Percent of province species occupies	Percent of all records for this species found in province	Percent of state area in province
Kittatinny Mountains	19	4	101	21.1	4.0	2.2
Kittatinny Valley	45	26	101	57.8	25.7	5.3
Highlands	109	24	101	22.0	23.8	12.8
Piedmont	167	37	101	22.2	36.6	19.6
Inner Coastal Plain	128	7	101	5.5	6.9	15.0
Outer Coastal Plain	204	3	101	1.5	3.0	23.9

continued from page 613

the 18th and 19th centuries. Since the mid-1800s, however, they have been on a severe and continuous decline in New Jersey and throughout much of the eastern United States. In the late 1800s a myriad of factors combined to reduce the Bobolink population. Shooting of migrants, trapping males for the cage-bird trade, and conversion of farmlands and meadows to urban areas curtailed the nesting of Bobolinks in the northeastern and southern portions of the state (Stone 1908, Griscom 1923, Cruickshank 1942). Even at the turn of the 20th century Stone lamented that the future of Bobolinks in New Jersey was uncertain: "What a pity that such a splendid bird as this can not be protected and perpetuated" (1908). More recently, the practice of early mowing of hay fields has destroyed nests and nestlings (Martin and Gavin 1995).

Atlas data indicated Bobolinks were more broadly distributed than many had suspected in New Jersey. They were found in only 12% of the blocks statewide, but they occupied 27% of the blocks from the Piedmont northward. They were most concentrated in a series of nearly contiguous blocks in the northwestern section of the state. Because their habitat requirements are well known, it should be possible to at least maintain, if not increase, the population of Bobolinks.

Conservation Note: Bobolinks rely on older hay fields for breeding. Of greatest concern to the future of the species in the state is the continuing loss of habitat to development. Management of these areas, in partnership with farmers, could greatly increase their breeding success. Perhaps with careful stewardship of the remaining Bobolink habitat in New Jersey, Stone's 1908 plea for conservation will be realized.

Fall: Bobolinks begin fall migration early, and a few may be noted as early as late June. The major movements occur from mid-August to mid-September. Passage is normally completed in the north by September, but continues in small numbers through mid-October along the southern coast. Coastal flights can be impressively large. **Maxima:** 15,000, Cape May Point, 3 September 1996; 6,000, West Cape May, 10, September 1994.

Winter: Bobolinks occasionally linger into December, and were reported on two CBCs between 1976 and 1997 (i.e., 1979 and 1982).

Spring: The earliest Bobolinks arrive in late April or early May, with maximum numbers present in mid- to late May. Migration is usually of single-sex groups, with the males arriving on territory about a week prior to the females (Martin and Gavin 1995). **Maxima:** 500, Princeton, 11 May 1982; 300, Dutch Neck, 19 May 1984. ■

Red-winged Blackbird

Agelaius phoeniceus

Range: Breeds from east-central Alaska to Newfoundland south throughout the United States. Winters throughout much of the United States

NJ Status: Common and nearly ubiquitous summer resident, common spring and fall migrant, fairly common winter resident.

Statewide Summary	
Status	# of Blocks
Possible	23
Probable	153
Confirmed	633
Total	809

Breeding

Habitat: Nests in a variety of fresh and saltwater wetland habitats, and some upland habitats, including pastures and fields.

continued on page 616

Physiographic Distribution **Red-winged Blackbird**	Number of blocks in province	Number of blocks species found breeding in province	Number of blocks species found in state	Percent of province species occupies	Percent of all records for this species found in province	Percent of state area in province
Kittatinny Mountains	19	19	809	100.0	2.3	2.2
Kittatinny Valley	45	44	809	97.8	5.4	5.3
Highlands	109	108	809	99.1	13.3	12.8
Piedmont	167	162	809	97.0	20.0	19.6
Inner Coastal Plain	128	126	809	98.4	15.6	15.0
Outer Coastal Plain	204	193	809	94.6	23.9	23.9
Pine Barrens	180	157	809	87.2	19.4	21.1

continued from page 615

Red-winged Blackbird

Red-winged Blackbird

Red-winged Blackbirds have been common and widely distributed breeding birds in New Jersey throughout the 20th century (Stone 1908, Boyle 1986). In New Jersey they are still regarded as an agricultural pest, and blackbirds may be shot if they are harming crops. Despite this, they are a candidate for being the most abundant species in North America (Yasukawa and Searcy 1995). Although they are often associated with cattail marshes, Red-winged Blackbirds nest in a variety of wetland habitats, and even take advantage of upland situations such as pastures and weedy fields. This gives them a much wider distribution than species confined to wetlands.

During the Atlas surveys Red-winged Blackbirds were one of the most widely distributed breeding birds in the state, occurring in 95% of blocks. There were few gaps in their distribution, and they were absent only from a few areas of the Pine Barrens and areas with similar habitat in sections of Cumberland and Cape May counties.

Fall: By mid- to late summer Red-winged Blackbirds begin to form large flocks which may concentrate at inland or coastal

Red-winged Blackbird

continued

marshes for roosting. The peak of their southward movements occurs later, usually in October or November. **Maximum:** 500,000, Woodstown, 26 November 1989.

Winter: Red-winged Blackbirds may be locally common where winter roosts form, but they are normally uncommon inland to northward. Spectacular roosts of mixed blackbirds have occurred along the marshes of the Delaware River near Salem and Trenton. CBC totals generally run to the tens of thousands, but CBC totals are highly variable. **Maximum:** 750,000, Salem County marshes, 3 January 1993.

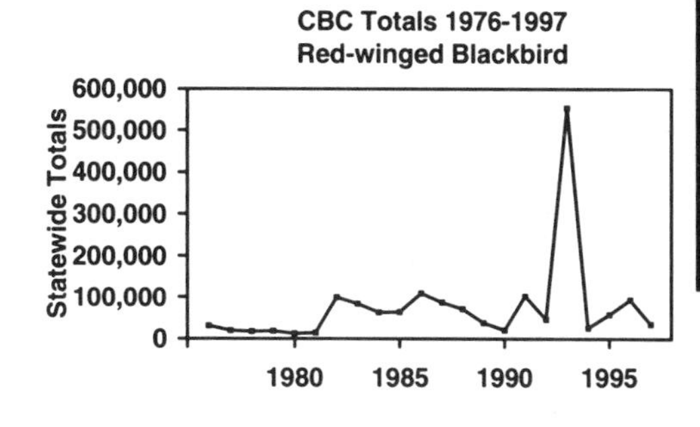

CBC Statewide Stats: Average: 77,577; Maximum: 553,381 in 1993; Minimum: 11,779 in 1980. **CBC Maximum:** 502,342, Trenton Marsh, 1993.

Spring: The first Red-winged Blackbirds move north into northern New Jersey by mid- to late February, and highest numbers occur in late March or early April. **Maximum:** 30,000+, Kenvil, 1 April 1983. ■

Eastern Meadowlark

Sturnella magna

Breeding

Habitat: Grassy or weedy fields, open meadows, or drier, upper zones of salt marshes.

As is the case with all grassland species, Eastern Meadowlarks have declined markedly during the 20th century. In 1908, Stone described them as an "abundant resident ... one of the

continued on page 618

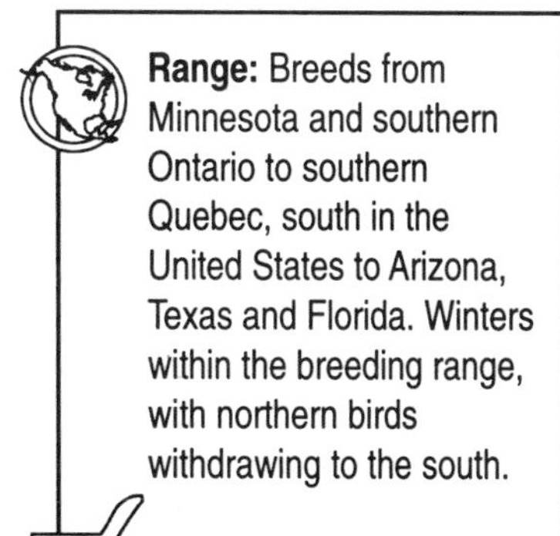

Range: Breeds from Minnesota and southern Ontario to southern Quebec, south in the United States to Arizona, Texas and Florida. Winters within the breeding range, with northern birds withdrawing to the south.

NJ Status: Uncommon and somewhat local summer resident, fairly common spring and common fall migrant, uncommon winter resident.

continued from page 617

Eastern Meadowlark

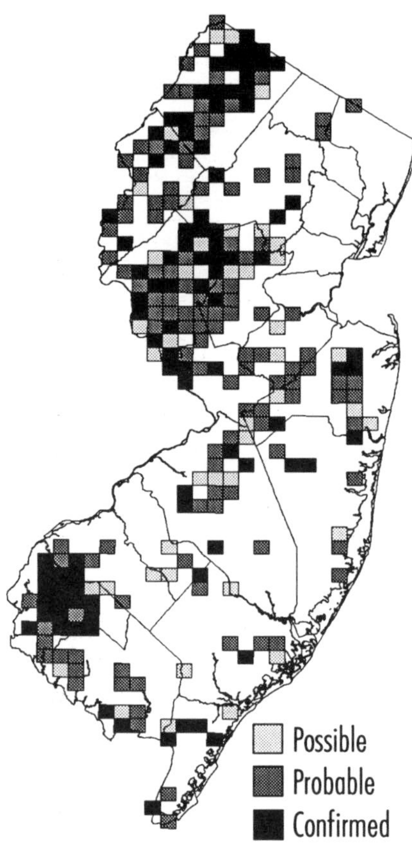

Statewide Summary	
Status	# of Blocks
Possible	42
Probable	120
Confirmed	94
Total	256

most characteristic birds of the open field." By the mid-1950s however, Fables (1955) noted a decrease in their numbers. Bull (1964) attributed this drop to the decline of agriculture and the urbanization of open areas. By 1986, Boyle considered Eastern Meadowlarks to be fairly common, but declining, breeding birds. Results from Breeding Bird Survey data indicated Eastern Meadowlarks are declining over much of their range, with the most severe declines noted in the urbanized Northeast, including New Jersey (Lanyon 1995).

The Atlas surveys showed that Eastern Meadowlarks were broadly distributed in the state. They were most densely distributed in western New Jersey and had a more patchy distribution in the eastern sections of the state. They occurred in each physiographic province, but only occurred in 30% of the blocks statewide. The Kittatinny Valley had the highest density of occupied blocks, but otherwise Eastern Meadowlarks occupied only 13-42% of the remaining physiographic regions. The only naturally occurring habitat they regularly use in the state is the upland edges of certain salt marshes. Outside of those areas, they rely primarily on man-made habitats such as farmland or airports for nesting. Consequently, many of the blocks occupied by Eastern Meadowlarks were concentrated in the farmlands of the Kittatinny Valley, Hunterdon County, and Salem County.

Conservation Note:

Farmland is subject to both human development and natural succession, making much of Eastern Meadowlarks breeding habitat ephemeral. Like many other grassland species, they often appear in areas for a year

Physiographic Distribution **Eastern Meadowlark**	Number of blocks in province	Number of blocks species found breeding in province	Number of blocks species found in state	Percent of province species occupies	Percent of all records for this species found in province	Percent of state area in province
Kittatinny Mountains	19	8	256	42.1	3.1	2.2
Kittatinny Valley	45	37	256	82.2	14.5	5.3
Highlands	109	31	256	28.4	12.1	12.8
Piedmont	167	59	256	35.3	23.0	19.6
Inner Coastal Plain	128	40	256	31.3	15.6	15.0
Outer Coastal Plain	204	58	256	28.4	22.7	23.9
Pine Barrens	180	23	256	12.8	9.0	21.1

or two when suitable habitat presents itself, only to disappear when the habitat changes. Eastern Meadowlarks seem less sensitive to subtle habitat changes than some other grassland species, such as Bobolinks. Many fields that support meadowlarks fail to have Bobolinks. However, the continuing loss of New Jersey farmland and concomitant increase in rural development probably presages an uncertain future for this species in the state.

Fall: Movements of Eastern Meadowlarks away from the inland areas in the north begins in August, but peak numbers are not reached until mid- to late October. **Maxima:** 600, Cape May Point, 26 October 1996; 350, Cape May Point, 23 October 1992.

Winter: Although regular in the southern part of the state, Eastern Meadowlarks are becoming increasingly rare in the north. Decreases attributable to the loss of agricultural land have occurred in the south as well – e.g., Cape May CBC had 1,100 in 1957. CBC numbers are variable, with the lowest numbers in the harshest winters. **CBC Statewide Stats:** Average: 515; Maximum: 1,099 in 1977; Minimum: 259 in 1986. **CBC Maximum:** 301, Cape May, 1984.

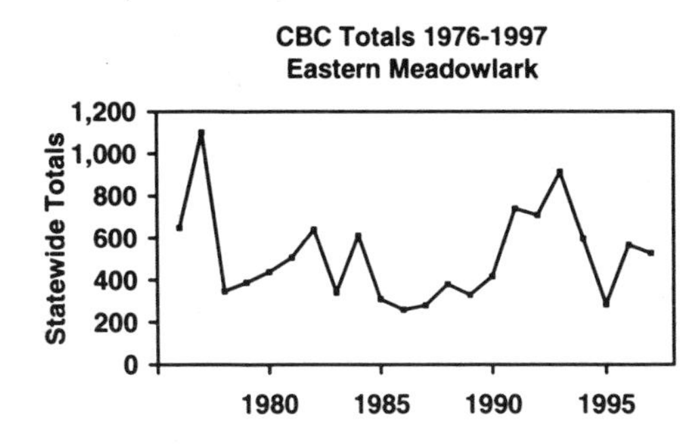

Spring: Northward movement of Eastern Meadowlarks normally begins in early March and quickly reaches a peak from mid- to late March. **Maxima:** 60, Hillsborough, 16 March 1992; 30+, Lumberton, 16 March 1991. ■

Western Meadowlark

Western Meadowlark

Sturnella neglecta

Range: Breeds from British Columbia across southern Canada to Ontario south to California, Mexico, Arizona, Texas and east to Illinois and western Ohio. Winters south of the northern range to Tennessee and Alabama.

NJ Status: Accidental. NJBRC Review List.

Occurrence: There have been eleven state reports of Western Meadowlarks, and eight have been accepted by the NJBRC. The eight accepted records are:

South Plainfield#	*28 April 1940*	
Columbus#	*June-August 1951*	
Hopewell#	*1-10 May 1953*	
Troy Meadows#	*2-9 May 1953*	
Bound Brook#	*10 April 1956*	*song only*
*Blawenburg**	*4-22 July 1961*	
Moorestown	*22 June-3 July 1965*	
Manalapan	*27 May 1997*	*a bird recorded singing*

Yellow-headed Blackbird

Yellow-headed Blackbird

Xanthocephalus xanthocephalus

Historic Changes: Yellow-headed Blackbirds have become more common in the eastern United States as migrants (Twedt and Crawford 1995). By the mid-1950s there were only three state records of Yellow-headed Blackbirds in New Jersey (Fables 1955). During the years from 1976 to 1980, 12 were banded in the state (Foy 1981).

Range: Breeds in the western United States and southwestern Canada east to Ontario and Illinois. Winters largely in the southwestern United States and Mexico.

NJ Status: Rare migrant and winter resident.

Yellow-headed Blackbird

continued

Fall: A few Yellow-headed Blackbirds have been seen as early as July, but the majority of fall sightings have taken place in August and September. Most reports have been near the coast, but the species has also been noted statewide. **Maxima:** 2, several times.

Winter: Yellow-headed Blackbirds are most reliably found in winter among the vast blackbird flocks in Salem County. Birds have occurred elsewhere in the state as well, often at feeders. There are now in excess of 75 winter records for the state, and they were reported on eleven CBCs between 1976 and 1997. **Maximum:** 4, Salem Nuclear Plant, December 1990-January 1991.

Spring: Formerly almost unknown in spring, Yellow-headed Blackbirds are now annual, although generally with fewer reports than during fall or winter. Birds are most likely in southern New Jersey in March and April, with stragglers noted occasionally into June. **Maximum:** 4, Elsinboro, 29 March 1992. ■

Rusty Blackbird

Euphagus carolinus

Range: Breeds from Alaska to Labrador south, in the East, to northwestern Massachusetts. Winters in the eastern half of the United States north along the coast to Massachusetts.

NJ Status: Fairly common spring and fall migrant, uncommon winter resident.

Fall: The earliest Rusty Blackbirds are expected in October, and peak numbers occur from mid-October through mid-November. While they are locally fairly common throughout New Jersey, they are much less concentrated than other blackbird species. They are also less likely to be found in large mixed flocks than other blackbird species, and they are frequently associated with wet, swampy thickets. **Maxima:** 600, Great Swamp, 7 November 1983; 400, Bernardsville, 19 October 1977.

Winter: Numbers of Rusty Blackbirds vary considerably from year to year depending on the severity of the winter, and CBC totals are similarly erratic. **CBC Statewide**

continued on page 622

continued from page 621

Rusty Blackbird

Stats: Average: 352; Maximum: 841 in 1979; Minimum: 88 in 1997. **CBC Maximum:** 372, Sussex, 1976.

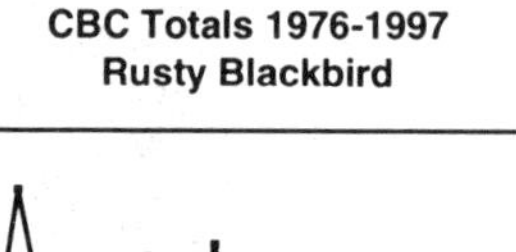

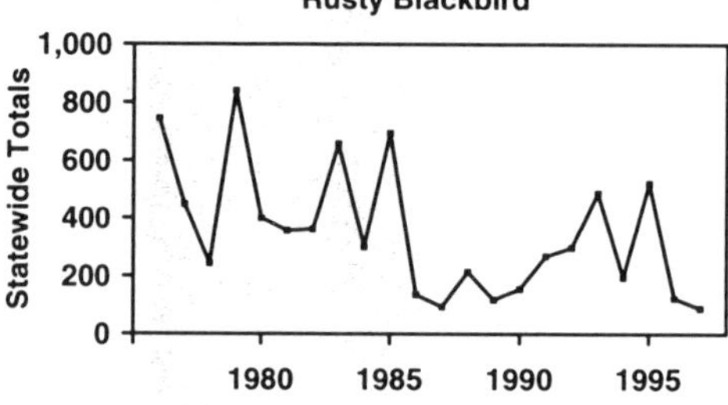

Spring: The first spring movements of Rusty Blackbirds sometimes begin by the end of February, but northward migration reaches its peak from mid-March to mid-April. Birds are noted, in considerably diminished numbers, into early May, and rarely later. **Maxima:** 250+, Great Swamp, 19 March 1983; 100s, Trenton Marsh, mid-April, 1990. ■

Brewer's Blackbird

Euphagus cyanocephalus

Range: Breeds in the western United States and Canada east to southern Ontario. Winters in the western and southern United States east to northern Florida and, sporadically, farther north along the Atlantic coast to Delaware.

NJ Status: Very rare. NJBRC Review List.

Occurrence: There have been 25 to 30 state reports of Brewer's Blackbirds, although there have been none reported since the species was added to the NJBRC Review List in 1996. Four records have been accepted by the NJBRC (all in fall) during a partial review of the historic records, although the completed review will likely include more accepted records. All remaining reports occurred from late October through April. The four accepted records are:

	East Brunswick	*5-23 November 1978*	*ph-NJA/RNJB 5:5; Wander 1979*
8	*Cape May*	*17 November 1973*	
1-3	*Cape May*	*14 November-8 December 1984*	
3-4	*Cape May*	*29 October-4 November 1988*	

Common Grackle

Quiscalus quiscula

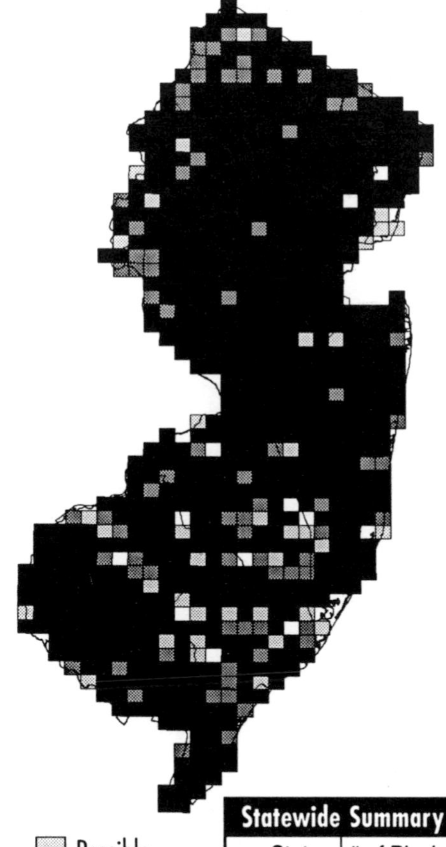

Range: Breeds from northeast British Columbia across southern Canada to Newfoundland and south through Texas and Florida. In winter, northern birds withdraw south.

NJ Status: Common and nearly ubiquitous summer resident, common spring and fall migrant, uncommon to common winter resident.

Breeding

Habitat: Nest in trees near open areas.

Common Grackles have long been broadly distributed breeding birds in New Jersey

continued on page 624

Possible
Probable
Confirmed

Statewide Summary	
Status	# of Blocks
Possible	37
Probable	78
Confirmed	717
Total	832

Physiographic Distribution Common Grackle	Number of blocks in province	Number of blocks species found breeding in province	Number of blocks species found in state	Percent of province species occupies	Percent of all records for this species found in province	Percent of state area in province
Kittatinny Mountains	19	19	832	100.0	2.3	2.2
Kittatinny Valley	45	45	832	100.0	5.4	5.3
Highlands	109	109	832	100.0	13.1	12.8
Piedmont	167	163	832	97.6	19.6	19.6
Inner Coastal Plain	128	126	832	98.4	15.1	15.0
Outer Coastal Plain	204	196	832	96.1	23.6	23.9
Pine Barrens	180	174	832	96.7	20.9	21.1

continued from page 623

Common Grackle

(Stone 1908, Boyle 1986). Their affinity for nesting in small patches of habitat such as backyards and parks, have provided seemingly limitless nesting opportunities. Less commonly, birds will also nest near natural openings in more extensive forest cover, and occasionally in wetlands.

Common Grackles were located in 98% of the blocks in the state, and were the second most broadly distributed nesting species in the state. They were absent from only 20 blocks statewide, and most of those were in the Pine Barrens and Outer Coastal Plain. Common Grackles are considered an agricultural pest species in New Jersey, and may be killed without limit if the birds are deemed harmful to a crop. Despite the open season, the species remains one of our commonest breeding birds.

Fall: Flocking of local Common Grackles, and perhaps some migratory movement, begins in July. Peak southbound flights, however, do not occur until October and November. **Maxima:** 350,000, Mt. Olive, 16 November 1988; 40,000, Woodstown, 5 November 1987.

Winter: Common Grackles can be numerous at certain large blackbird roosts along the Delaware River, but are otherwise found in smaller numbers. Grackles are usually quite uncommon in northwestern New Jersey, but even there, winter roosts may develop in extensive wetlands. The spectacle at the blackbird roosts is staggering. CBC totals usually number in the tens of thousands, but tend to be variable. **Maxima:** 3,000,000, Delaware River marshes, 29 December 1992; 500,000, Trenton, 30 December 1978. **CBC Statewide Stats:** Average: 50,952; Maximum: 152,942 in 1985; Minimum: 2,627 in 1978. **CBC Maximum:** 83,694, Salem, 1985.

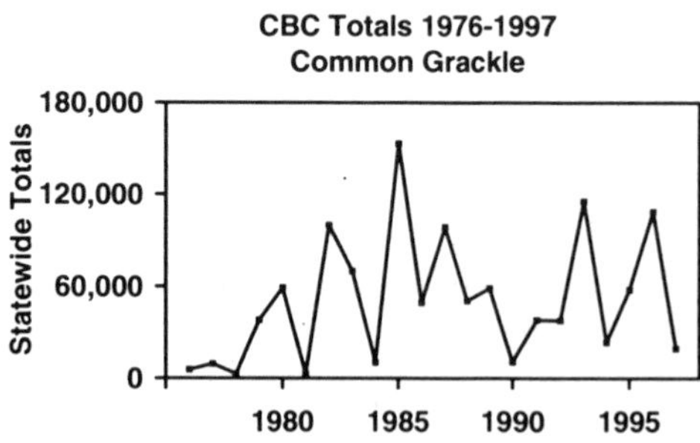

Spring: The first flights of Common Grackles normally take place by mid-February, with peak numbers occurring in March. Flocks are generally smaller in spring than in fall. **Maximum:** 30,000+, Kenvil, 1 April 1983.

Common Grackle

continued

Subspecies: The Common Grackles that breed in New Jersey are apparently all *Q. q. stonei*, the "Purple" Grackle, which breeds east of the Appalachians (Peer and Bollinger 1997). "Bronzed" Grackles, *Q. q. versicolor*, which breed to the north and west of New Jersey, can be found in migration and during winter (Fables 1955). Bronzed Grackles have been found at Cape May from November to April (Sibley 1997). In years with heavy snow to the north and west, they may occur in large numbers and even outnumber the Purple Grackles – e.g., 2,000 of 3,000 grackles, Cape May, 13 February 1994 (Sibley 1997). ■

Boat-tailed Grackle

Quiscalus major

Range: Breeds along the immediate Atlantic and Gulf coasts from Long Island to eastern Texas; also throughout peninsular Florida. Winters mainly within breeding range, but some birds at the northern extreme withdraw southward in winter.

NJ Status: Fairly common but local resident, uncommon spring and fall migrant, uncommon winter resident.

Breeding

Habitat: Breeding colonies are usually in small trees or shrubs adjacent to salt marsh. Boat-tailed Grackles are rarely found far from tidal waters.

The breeding range of Boat-tailed Grackles expanded northward from North Carolina during the late 19th century (Post et al. 1996). Prior to the 1950s there were only four records of the species in New Jersey (Fables 1955). The first nesting record for New Jersey occurred in 1952, when 15 pairs were found in three colonies at Gandy's Beach in Cumberland County (Fables 1955). By 1982 the species had expanded its range to include the Delaware Bay shore into Salem and Cape May counties, as well as along the entire Atlantic coast to Sandy Hook.

Boat-tailed Grackles have been very successful in their colonization of coastal New Jersey. Atlas surveys found Boat-tailed Grackles in only 10% of the blocks in the state, but located them in nearly all suitable habitat. There is a gap in their coastal distribution in Monmouth County, where no suitable habitat remains. There was also a similar gap in the distribution of both Saltmarsh Sharp-tailed and Seaside Sparrow, and a smaller but similarly placed gap in

continued on page 626

continued from page 625

Boat-tailed Grackle

the distribution of both Willet and Marsh Wren as well. The current northern outpost in the state is South Amboy at the head of Raritan Bay.

Fall: Though most Boat-tailed Grackles are resident (Post et al. 1996), Sibley (1997) documented flocks of up to 70 birds passing Cape May Point, mostly from mid-September to mid-November.

Winter: Boat-tailed Grackles can be seen in winter along the coast from Monmouth to Salem counties, but there is also some withdrawal from New Jersey in the colder months. **CBC Statewide Stats:** Average: 1,698; Maximum: 4,001 in 1996; Minimum: 141 in 1976. **CBC Maximum:** 2,870, Cape May, 1991.

Spring: The return flight of Boat-tailed Grackles is particularly noticeable along the coast, and large groups return in March and April. ■

Possible
Probable
Confirmed

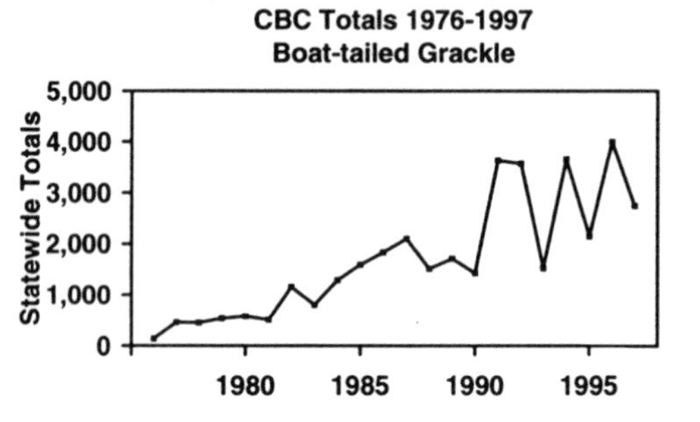

Statewide Summary	
Status	# of Blocks
Possible	11
Probable	23
Confirmed	50
Total	84

Physiographic Distribution Boat-tailed Grackle	Number of blocks in province	Number of blocks species found breeding in province	Number of blocks species found in state	Percent of province species occupies	Percent of all records for this species found in province	Percent of state area in province
Piedmont	167	1	84	0.6	1.2	19.6
Inner Coastal Plain	128	4	84	3.1	4.8	15.0
Outer Coastal Plain	204	76	84	37.3	90.5	23.9
Pine Barrens	180	3	84	1.7	3.6	21.1

Brown-headed Cowbird

Molothrus ater

Range: Breeds across southern Canada south throughout the contiguous United States (except southern Florida) to northern Mexico. Northern birds move to southern portions of the breeding range in winter.

NJ Status: Common and nearly ubiquitous summer resident, common spring and fall migrant, uncommon to common winter resident.

continued on page 628

Statewide Summary	
Status	# of Blocks
Possible	93
Probable	331
Confirmed	345
Total	769

Physiographic Distribution

Brown-headed Cowbird	Number of blocks in province	Number of blocks species found breeding in province	Number of blocks species found in state	Percent of province species occupies	Percent of all records for this species found in province	Percent of state area in province
Kittatinny Mountains	19	19	769	100.0	2.5	2.2
Kittatinny Valley	45	45	769	100.0	5.9	5.3
Highlands	109	109	769	100.0	14.2	12.8
Piedmont	167	152	769	91.0	19.8	19.6
Inner Coastal Plain	128	120	769	93.8	15.6	15.0
Outer Coastal Plain	204	170	769	83.3	22.1	23.9
Pine Barrens	180	154	769	85.6	20.0	21.1

continued from page 629

Breeding

Habitat: Brown-headed Cowbirds are brood parasites. Habitats of host species vary from open country to forest, but parasitism occurs most frequently at forest edges.

Fragmentation of the eastern forest following European colonization in the 1700-1800s enabled Brown-headed Cowbirds, a short-grass plains species, to spread east to the Atlantic Coast (Lowther 1993). They have been common in the East at least since the late 1700s, but there is a widespread belief that a number of nesting songbirds are significantly compromised by Brown-headed Cowbird's relatively sudden range expansion. It is estimated that about 50 species were hosts to Brown-headed Cowbirds before European settlement, although approximately 200 host species are now known (Terborgh 1989). In New Jersey, Brown-headed Cowbirds were recorded as common birds throughout the 1900s (Stone 1908, Leck 1984), but Fables (1955) pointed out they were least common in the northwestern hills.

Brown-headed Cowbirds have remained broadly distributed and common breeding birds in the state, and they were found in 90% of the Atlas blocks statewide. Contrary to Fables (1955) report that they were uncommon in the northwest, Atlas volunteers found them in 90-100% of the blocks from the Piedmont northward. During the Atlas, at least 28 host species were parasitised by Brown-headed Cowbirds. The most common host species were Song Sparrow (18 reports), Scarlet Tanager (11 reports), Common Yellowthroat (10 reports), Yellow Warbler (9 reports), and Red-eyed Vireo (8 reports). Several of these species are known to be heavily parasitised, but Scarlet Tanager is not normally regarded as a common cowbird host (Lowther 1993).

Fall: Southbound movements of Brown-headed Cowbirds may begin before August, and peak numbers are noted from late October to mid-November. They are frequently found in flocks of mixed blackbird species.
Maxima: 10,000, Sharptown, 24 October 1997; 7,500, Woodstown, 5 November 1987.

Winter: Unlike other blackbird species, CBC totals of Brown-headed Cowbirds generally number under 10,000. The listed statewide maximum (see

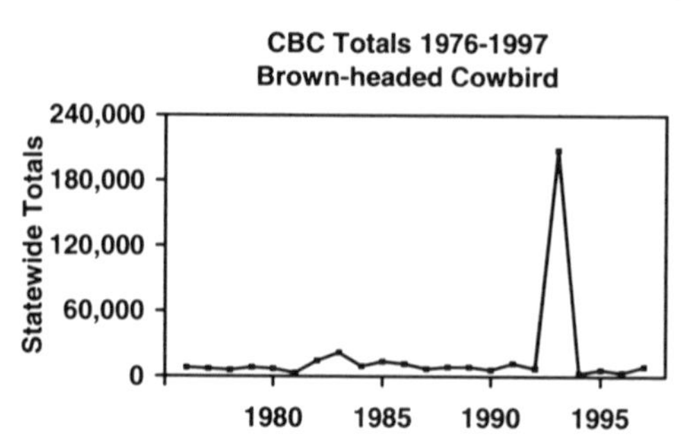

Brown-headed Cowbird

continued

below) was exceptional. They can be common at large blackbird roosts, but tend to be especially uncommon northward. **Maximum:** 120,000, Salem, 29 December 1979. **CBC Statewide Stats:** Average: 17,726; Maximum: 208,086 in 1993; Minimum: 2,844 in 1994. **CBC Maximum:** 200,026, Trenton Marsh, 1993.

Spring: Brown-headed Cowbirds normally arrive in northern New Jersey in early March, with a peak in late March to early April. **Maxima:** 800, Harmony, 1 April 1977; 400, Cape May Point, 8 April 1994 (Sibley 1997). ■

Orchard Oriole

Icterus spurius

Range: Breeds from southeastern Saskatchewan to southern New England, south to Texas and northern Florida. Winters from Mexico to northern South America.

NJ Status: Fairly common and widespread summer resident, uncommon spring and fall migrant.

Breeding

Habitat: Nests in orchards, parks, cemeteries, shade trees or tree rows in farmland, field edges, and stream sides.

During the 20th century, Orchard Oriole numbers have periodically fluctuated, at least in the northern part of the state. Stone (1908) noted that they were common breeding birds, but were more abundant in the southern part of the state than in the north. Fables (1955) suggested that they were declining in Essex, Union, and Morris counties in the north, and that they were essentially absent from the heart of the Pine Barrens. Bull (1964) also suggested that Orchard Orioles had declined in northern New Jersey, but were still found locally in lowland areas. By the mid-1980s, they had apparently increased as breeding birds throughout the state. Leck (1984) stated that "in recent years populations have been high," and Boyle (1986) described them as fairly common, but irregularly distributed.

Atlas data showed Orchard Orioles to be broadly distributed breeding birds that were found in all physiographic provinces. The three physiographic provinces where they occurred most frequently were the Inner Coastal

continued on page 630

continued from page 629

Orchard Oriole

Physiographic Distribution Orchard Oriole	Number of blocks in province	Number of blocks species found breeding in province	Number of blocks species found in state	Percent of province species occupies	Percent of all records for this species found in province	Percent of state area in province
Kittatinny Mountains	19	9	454	47.4	2.0	2.2
Kittatinny Valley	45	26	454	57.8	5.7	5.3
Highlands	109	52	454	47.7	11.5	12.8
Piedmont	167	87	454	52.1	19.2	19.6
Inner Coastal Plain	128	85	454	66.4	18.7	15.0
Outer Coastal Plain	204	121	454	59.3	26.7	23.9
Pine Barrens	180	74	454	41.1	16.3	21.1

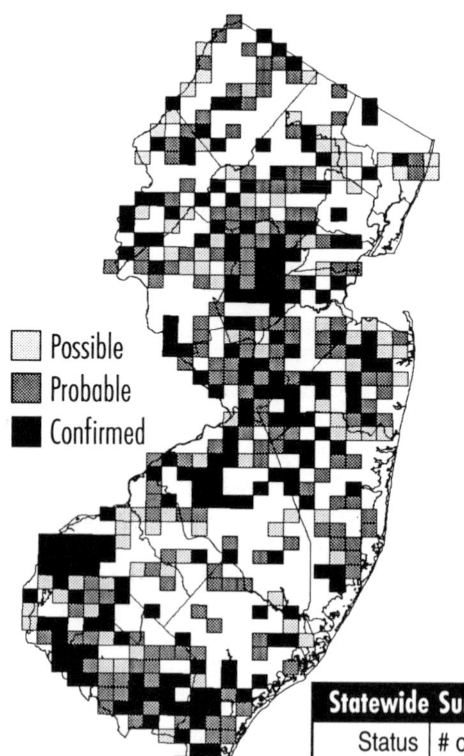

Statewide Summary	
Status	# of Blocks
Possible	87
Probable	166
Confirmed	201
Total	454

Plain, the Outer Coastal Plain, and the Kittatinny Valley. They were scarcest at higher elevations, in highly urbanized settings, throughout large areas of the Pine Barrens, and along the barrier islands. Orchard Orioles are increasing in other parts of their range in the Northeast (Scharf and Kren 1996). They are probably more broadly distributed in northern New Jersey than they were prior to the mid-1960s, and Atlas data indicated they are more widespread within the Pine Barrens than Fables (1955) suggested.

Fall: Orchard Orioles begin to depart from New Jersey extremely early in the fall, and migrants are often reported at coastal watches by mid-July. Most are gone from the state by the end of August, although there are a few reports into September.

Orchard Oriole

continued

Maxima: 22, Cape May Point, 12 August 1986; 6, Mercer County Park, 24 August 1991.

Spring: Orchard Orioles typically reach New Jersey in late April or early May, with passage completed by late May. At this season the species is normally seen in ones and twos. The all-time maximum of 150, Higbee Beach, 8 May 1984 is extraordinary. All other one-day maxima are of fewer than 20 birds. ■

Baltimore Oriole

Icterus galbula

Range: Breeds from southern Alberta east to Nova Scotia south to northeastern Texas and western South Carolina. Winters mainly from Mexico to northern South America.

NJ Status: Fairly common and very widespread summer resident, common spring and fall migrant, very rare winter resident.

Breeding

Habitat: Often nests near human habitation in widely-spaced trees, in cemeteries, parks, and pond and stream edges.

In the early 1900s, Baltimore Orioles were mostly absent from the Pine Barrens and the southern counties, but were common and widespread breeding birds elsewhere in the state (Stone 1908). Fables (1955) reported only two breeding records in the Pine Barrens, one in 1938 and the other in 1952. He also noted that Baltimore Orioles bred in the southwestern counties (presumably Salem to Burlington counties). The assessment that their breeding range was mainly confined to areas north and west of the Pine Barrens continued into the mid-1980s, when Boyle described Baltimore Orioles as a "common summer resident...in the north."

Atlas data indicated that Baltimore Orioles were found in 94% of the blocks from the Piedmont northward, where they have long been common and broadly distributed breeding birds. The Inner Coastal Plain was apparently conducive to Baltimore Orioles, since the species was recorded in 92% of the blocks in the province. They have dramatically expanded their range in southern New Jersey. While still absent from some sections of the Pine Barrens, they were nonetheless found in 72% of the blocks in that province. They were also

continued on page 632

continued from page 631

Baltimore Oriole

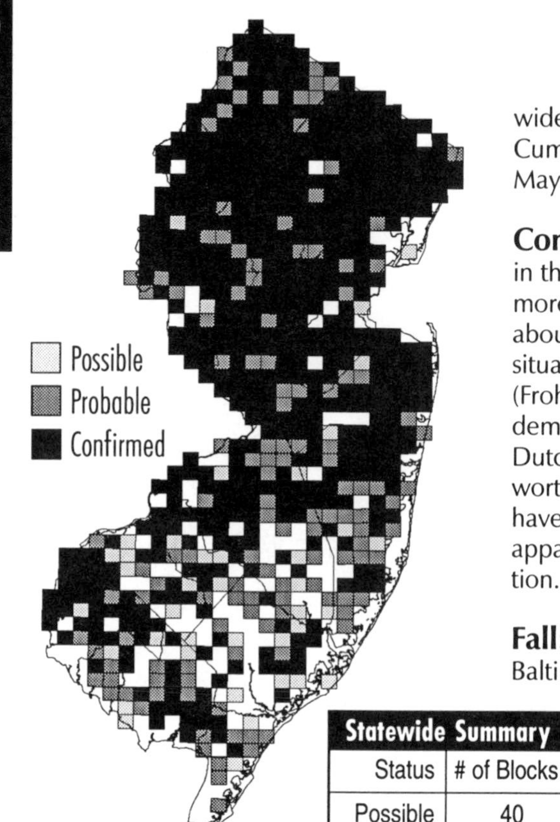

Statewide Summary	
Status	# of Blocks
Possible	40
Probable	130
Confirmed	516
Total	686

widely distributed in Salem, Cumberland and northern Cape May counties.

Conservation Note: A study in the late 1940s of 500 Baltimore Oriole nest sites found that about 60% of the nests were situated in American Elm trees (Frohling 1950). Given the demise of American Elms from Dutch Elm Disease, it is noteworthy that Baltimore Orioles have managed to adapt with no apparent harm to their population.

Fall: The southbound flight of Baltimore Orioles begins by mid-August, and peaks from late August to early September. By October, only stragglers remain in the northern interior while southern coastal observation points record a small number of migrants into Novem-

Physiographic Distribution

Baltimore Oriole	Number of blocks in province	Number of blocks species found breeding in province	Number of blocks species found in state	Percent of province species occupies	Percent of all records for this species found in province	Percent of state area in province
Kittatinny Mountains	19	19	686	100.0	2.8	2.2
Kittatinny Valley	45	44	686	97.8	6.4	5.3
Highlands	109	108	686	99.1	15.7	12.8
Piedmont	167	150	686	89.8	21.9	19.6
Inner Coastal Plain	128	115	686	89.8	16.8	15.0
Outer Coastal Plain	204	120	686	58.8	17.5	23.9
Pine Barrens	180	130	686	72.2	19.0	21.1

ber. **Maxima:** 1,000s, Cape May Point, 1 September 1988; 700+, Cape May, 29 August 1982.

Winter: In most winters several Baltimore Orioles remain, both north and south, through the Christmas Count season. CBC totals usually number fewer than ten. Those that survive to spring are often found at feeding stations where fruit is offered. **Maximum:** 4, Jake's Landing, 29 December 1996. **CBC Statewide Stats:** Average: 4; Maximum: 12 in 1995; Minimum: 0 in 1991. **CBC Maximum:** 6, NW Gloucester, 1981.

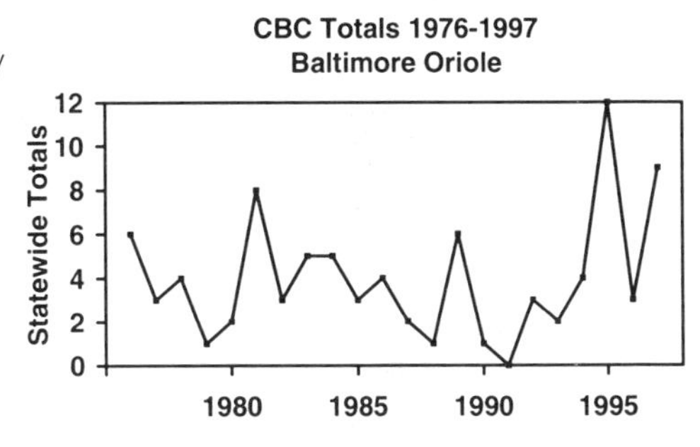

Spring: The first Baltimore Orioles arrive in late April with the bulk of the passage from early to mid-May. **Maxima:** 150, Higbee Beach, 8 May 1984; 50, Princeton, 12 May 1988. ■

Baltimore Oriole

Brambling

Fringilla montifringilla

Range: Breeds across northern Europe and Asia. Winters in Europe, northern Africa, and the Near East west to Japan.

NJ Status: Accidental. NJBRC Review List.

Occurrence: There have been two state reports of Bramblings, and both have been accepted by the NJBRC. The two accepted records are:

Stanton#	*15-17 December 1958*	*spec. Princeton Univ., adult male*
Branchville	*20-22 April 1965*	

Pine Grosbeak

Pinicola enucleator

Range: Breeds across North America from Alaska to Labrador, south through the western mountains, and in the East, south to western Maine. Winters largely in the breeding range, but sporadically irrupts south.

NJ Status: Very rare migrant and winter resident.

Historic Changes: In the 20th century, major irruptions of Pine Grosbeaks (100+ birds) into New Jersey have occurred during the winters of 1903-1904, 1929-1930, 1951-1952, 1954-1955, 1961-1962, 1968-1969, 1977-1978 and 1981-1982.

Fall: During invasion years, Pine Grosbeaks are usually first noted by mid-November, often when individuals or small flocks migrate past ridge-top hawk lookouts. **Maximum:** 60, Raccoon Ridge, 13 November 1977.

Winter: Normally very rare, large numbers of Pine Grosbeaks will occasionally invade the state and may become uncommon or even locally common. Most reports come from northern New Jersey during

Pine Grosbeak

continued

December and January. Pine Grosbeaks rarely reach the coast or southern part of the state; there are only four reports south and west of the Mullica River. During invasion years they can be reported in fair numbers on CBCs (e.g., 40 on the Ramsey count and 83 statewide in 1982). **Maximum:** 60, Newfoundland, winter 1981-82.

Spring: Pine Grosbeaks normally depart New Jersey by mid-March, but some birds have lingered into May (e.g., 12, Harbourton, 13 May 1978). ■

Purple Finch

Carpodacus purpureus

Range: In eastern North America, breeds from Manitoba east to Newfoundland, south to the Great Lakes, and southeast to West Virginia. Winters from the Great Lakes and Newfoundland south to Texas and northern Florida.

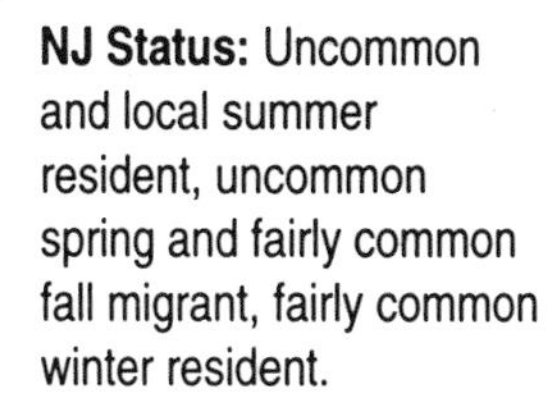

NJ Status: Uncommon and local summer resident, uncommon spring and fairly common fall migrant, fairly common winter resident.

Breeding

Habitat: Generally nests in conifers, often in planted stands of spruce, pine, or tamarack; often recorded in hemlock or occasionally hemlock-mixed hardwood forest, usually at high elevation.

The first nesting record of Purple Finches in New Jersey was a recently fledged male that was collected at West Orange on 23 July 1898 (Bull 1970). The next confirmation was 43 years later, 8 June 1941 at High Point, when a pair was seen nest-building (Cruickshank 1942). The breeding distribution described by Fables (1955) included Bergen, Sussex, and Warren counties. Bull (1964) was reluctant to consider additional breeding records due to possible confusion with House Finches. Kane and Marx (1972) documented nesting in Sussex County in Norway Spruce groves in 1971. Boyle (1986) considered them uncommon and local breeding birds in the northwestern part of the state. Breeding Bird Survey data indicated a 50% decline in the breeding population in the United States from 1966-1994, and that decline has been linked to the introduction and spread of House Finches in eastern North America (Wootton 1996).

continued on page 636

continued from page 635

Purple Finch

Atlas observers found that Purple Finches were restricted to the northern portion of the state. They were found in 84% of the blocks in the Kittatinny Mountains, but they became more local in the other provinces, dropping to 20-24% of the blocks in the Kittatinny Valley and Highlands. The list of counties with breeding Purple Finches has increased since 1955 to include Bergen, Passaic, Sussex, Warren, Morris, and possibly Hunterdon counties.

Map Interpretation: There are a number of Possible locations for Purple Finches in the southern Highlands that may represent either pioneering birds, or nonbreeders. Birds in that area should be watched carefully for Confirmation of breeding. Confusion with House Finches remains a possibility, just as it did when House Finches were first introduced in the 1940s.

Possible
Probable
Confirmed

Statewide Summary	
Status	# of Blocks
Possible	20
Probable	29
Confirmed	7
Total	56

Fall: The first migrant Purple Finches often arrive in early September, and numbers peak anytime from mid-October through November. Numbers of transients and passage dates are quite variable from year to year. These movements are probably the result of changes in food supply (Wootton 1996). The passage of immatures occurs prior to the passage of adults. **Maxima:** 500+, Bearfort Mt., 15 October 1983; 400, West Cape May, 19 October 1993.

Winter: Purple Finch numbers are erratic in winter, which is reflected by their CBC totals. They are generally more common in northern New Jersey than in southern New Jersey. A large fall flight does not always indicate a high winter count. **CBC Statewide Stats:** Average: 541; Maximum: 2,172 in 1983; Minimum: 54 in 1995. **CBC Maximum:** 633, Walnut Valley, 1983.

Spring: The northward migration of Purple Finches occurs between late March and mid-May. Migrants are usually less numerous than in autumn, although occasionally large flights have been noted – e.g., 936 banded, Boonton, 15 March-6 May 1939 (Bull 1964). **Other maxima:** 50+, Jockey Hollow, 8 May 1975; 36, Upper Saddle River, 18 April 1997. ■

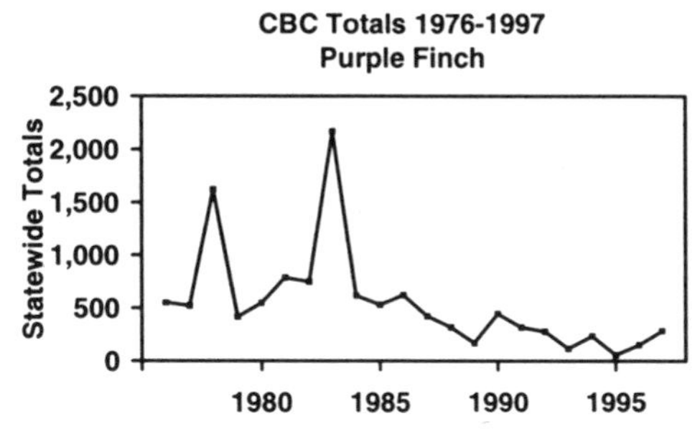

Physiographic Distribution

Purple Finch	Number of blocks in province	Number of blocks species found breeding in province	Number of blocks species found in state	Percent of province species occupies	Percent of all records for this species found in province	Percent of state area in province
Kittatinny Mountains	19	16	56	84.2	28.6	2.2
Kittatinny Valley	45	9	56	20.0	16.1	5.3
Highlands	109	26	56	23.9	46.4	12.8
Piedmont	167	5	56	3.0	8.9	19.6

House Finch

Carpodacus mexicanus

Breeding

Habitat: Breeds in a wide variety of human-made or human-influenced situations from ornamental evergreens to dwellings.

The explosion of House Finches in eastern North America began during the early 1940s on western Long

continued on page 638

Range: Introduced into eastern North America, now breeds throughout almost all of the United States and southernmost Canada. Winters in the breeding range.

NJ Status: Common and nearly ubiquitous resident.

continued from page 637

House Finch

Island, New York, when a number of illegally kept cage-birds from the California population were released into the wild (Bull 1964). As Bull (1964) properly noted, "Little did anyone realize what had happened or what was about to take place."

Many of the earliest reports of their spread were dismissed by birders as sightings of released or escaped cage-birds; so the pattern and timing of their early history in the east is poorly documented. New Jersey's first report of a House Finch was from Ridgewood in 1949, and by 1959 there had been reports from seven counties, both north and south. The first definite breeding record was at Oakhurst in the summer of 1963 (AFN). During the 1960s

Possible
Probable
Confirmed

Statewide Summary	
Status	# of Blocks
Possible	25
Probable	193
Confirmed	590
Total	808

Physiographic Distribution

House Finch	Number of blocks in province	Number of blocks species found breeding in province	Number of blocks species found in state	Percent of province species occupies	Percent of all records for this species found in province	Percent of state area in province
Kittatinny Mountains	19	19	808	100.0	2.4	2.2
Kittatinny Valley	45	45	808	100.0	5.6	5.3
Highlands	109	108	808	99.1	13.4	12.8
Piedmont	167	167	808	100.0	20.7	19.6
Inner Coastal Plain	128	128	808	100.0	15.8	15.0
Outer Coastal Plain	204	189	808	92.6	23.4	23.9
Pine Barrens	180	152	808	84.4	18.8	21.1

House Finch

continued

there was an enormous population surge, and by 1973 birds were noted on every CBC in the state.

House Finches have become one of New Jersey's most widely distributed breeding birds. The only obvious gap in their distribution is in the heart of the Pine Barrens; otherwise their range is nearly contiguous throughout the state. Along with European Starlings, House Finches are a striking reminder of the speed with which an introduced species can populate a new region.

Fall: There are some migratory movements of House Finches noted in New Jersey, particularly at Cape May in October and November – e.g., 2,300, Higbee Beach, 23 October 1993 (Sibley 1997). This behavior has apparently recently developed in this species since their introduction into the East; western birds from the presumed parent populations exhibit little migratory tendency (Hill 1993).

Winter: House Finches are most evident in winter when they become ravenous visitors to feeding stations around the state. CBC totals rose sharply in the early 1980s and have continued an upward trend. **CBC Statewide Stats:** Average: 13,188; Maximum: 21,982 in 1994; Minimum: 3,513 in 1976. **CBC Maximum:** 3,280, Cape May, 1995.

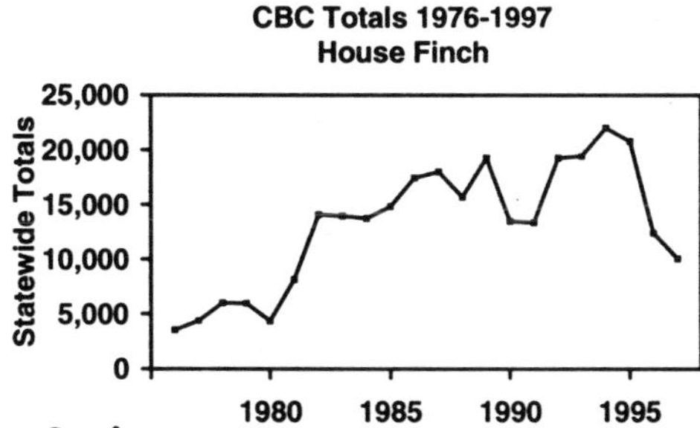

Spring: Even though migration of House Finches has been noted in fall in New Jersey, there is little evidence of a return flight in spring. ■

Red Crossbill

Loxia curvirostra

Breeding

Habitat: Nests in coniferous forests.

Red Crossbills are extremely rare breeding birds in New Jersey, but in the vastness of the

continued on page 640

Range: In eastern North America, breeds from Manitoba east to Newfoundland, south to Wisconsin, and south along the Appalachians to North Carolina. Winters mainly within the breeding range.

NJ Status: Rare and very local summer resident, rare and unpredictable migrant and winter visitor.

continued from page 639

Physiographic Distribution Red Crossbill	Number of blocks in province	Number of blocks species found breeding in province	Number of blocks species found in state	Percent of province species occupies	Percent of all records for this species found in province	Percent of state area in province
Pine Barrens	180	1	1	0.6	100.0	21.1

Pine Barrens, they may nest more often than is suspected. One nest has been found in the state: Tom's River, June 1941 (Fables 1955), with young birds noted at that site from 1935 to 1943. Two other historic reports of confirmed nesting are: adults with fledglings at Harrisville, 24 July 1956 (Kunkle et al. 1959), and an adult male and two juveniles collected at Quaker Bridge on 28 June 1963 (Murray 1972).

During the five years of Atlas surveys there was only one report of breeding Red Crossbills: Atsion, 7 July 1996, a juvenile. The observers reported the rarity, and the birds were again seen on 11 July 1996. Due to the extreme rarity of the species, as well as the young bird's mobility, the record was classed Possible rather than Confirmed.

Historic Changes: Red Crossbills are irruptive, and occur in New Jersey in vastly different numbers from year to year. A number of major flights (>500 birds) reached the New York City area in the late 19th and early 20th centuries. No further irruptions occurred until 1952-1953, a nearly 50 year interval (Bull 1964). Subsequent major flights have occurred into New Jersey in 1969-1970, 1973-1974 and 1975-1976.

Possible
Probable
Confirmed

Statewide Summary	
Status	# of Blocks
Possible	1
Probable	0
Confirmed	0
Total	1

Red Crossbill

continued

Fall: During both moderate or major flight-years Red Crossbills may first be noted as early as October, but sizeable flocks arrive in November. Occasionally Red Crossbills invade the state by the hundreds. Normally, however, they occur in lower numbers, or sometimes, none are recorded in the state during fall. **Maxima:** 200+, Cape May Point, 23 November 1975; 70, Sunrise Mt., 31 October 1988.

Winter: Some Red Crossbill incursions dissipate after the fall rush, and only a few birds may linger throughout the winter. In other years good numbers are recorded throughout the winter. CBC totals show substantial variation. Between 1976 and 1997, there were ten years with no Red Crossbills recorded, but in 1976 there were 682 tallied statewide. **Maxima:** 400, Deal, 3 January 1976; 130, West Milford, 29 February 1988.

Spring: In those years when an incursion of Red Crossbills continues throughout the winter months, birds will occasionally linger into spring, sometimes even into May. **Maxima:** 45+, Vernon, 19 May 1990; 25, Trenton, 21 May 1988;

Subspecies: There are reports that two subspecies of Red Crossbill have occurred in New Jersey – *L. c. minor* and *L. c. sitkensis* (Bull 1964). The former is the subspecies that has bred in the Pine Barrens and is assumed to be the most common representative in irruption years, although this is undocumented. *L. c. sitkensis* was collected once: Morristown, 3 February 1888 (Fables 1955). ■

White-winged Crossbill

Loxia leucoptera

Range: Breeds from Alaska to Labrador, irregularly south to northern New England. Winters within the breeding range south unpredictably to the northern third of the United States.

NJ Status: Very rare migrant and winter visitor.

Historic Changes: White-winged Crossbills are very infrequent and erratic visitors to New Jersey. Infrequently, however, major irruptions involving hundreds of individuals reach the state, and at those times White-winged Crossbills may appear to be locally common. Major invasions (> 500 birds) of the 20th

continued on page 642

continued from page 641

White-winged Crossbill

century have occurred in 1899-1900, 1952-1953, 1963-1964, and 1981-1982.

Fall: White-winged Crossbills may arrive as early as late October, but often they arrive even later in the season. Most records have been from northern and inland portions of the state; White-winged Crossbills are much rarer along the coast. **Maxima:** 75, Raccoon Ridge, 12 November 1981; 20, Allamuchy Mt., 15 November 1981.

Winter: There is often no hint of a White-winged Crossbill invasion during fall, and sometimes they appear in New Jersey as late as January or February. However, during the 1981-1982 incursion, birds arrived steadily from early November into February, with peak abundance reached from late January to early February (Kane 1982a). They have been recorded on six CBCs from 1976 to 1997. During major invasions they are reported in fair numbers on CBCs (e.g., 30 on the Assunpink count and 34 statewide in 1982). **Maxima:** 600+, Clinton Res., 1 February 1982; 215, Clinton Road, 13 December 1997.

Spring: White-winged Crossbills often depart New Jersey in March, although there have been a few reports into May, and sometimes even later. The only reference to breeding birds in New Jersey was when a small flock of young White-winged Crossbills was noted in Pitch Pines at Pine Lake Park, Ocean County on 4 July 1936 (Fables 1955). **Maxima:** 30, Vernon, 19 May 1990; 20-30, Clinton Road, 8 April 1988. ■

Common Redpoll

Carduelis flammea

Range: Breeds from Alaska to Newfoundland. Winters mainly in Canada, although irregular irruptions can extend the wintering range to the northern half of the United States.

NJ Status: Rare to uncommon migrant and winter resident.

Historic Changes:

Since 1975 there have been four major flights of Common Redpolls (>1,000 birds): 1977-1978, 1986-1987, 1993-1994, and 1997-1998. Although these were major invasions, they do not measure up to the incursions of 1946-1947, when huge flocks were found at Pine Brook; 1952-1953 when one flock of 2,000

Common Redpoll

continued

was reported from Newfoundland; and 1959-1960 when over 2,800 birds were banded in Bergen County.

Fall: During moderate or large flight-years, the earliest Common Redpolls are noted in November. Common Redpolls are irruptive migrants that may be common one year and entirely absent the next. They have occurred statewide, but are much more likely in the northern portion of the state, even in invasion years. **Maxima:** 120, Yard's Creek Res., 26 November 1993; 20, Alpine, 22 November 1981.

Winter: Some invasions of Common Redpolls begin in late winter, from January to March. They may become most conspicuous after a snowfall, when they inundate feeding stations. CBC totals are highly variable. Maxima: 500, Old Mine Road, 24 January 1998; 400, Layton, 30 January 1978. **CBC Statewide Stats:** Average: 47; Maximum: 335 in 1994; Minimum: 0 in seven years. **CBC Maximum:** 147, Boonton, 1994.

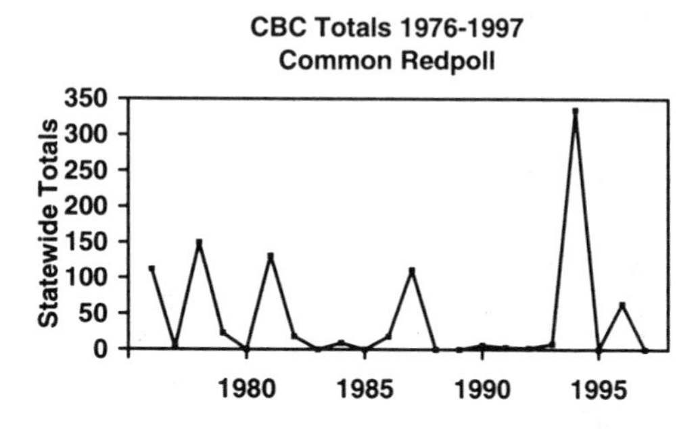

Spring: Normally Common Redpolls depart by the end of March, but rarely some may remain into April (e.g., 100+, Bordentown and 80, Culver's Lake following the unseasonable blizzard of 6 April 1982). **Maximum:** 200+, Plainfield, early March 1978. ■

Hoary Redpoll

Carduelis hornemanni

Occurrence: There have been 21 state reports of Hoary Redpolls, and three have been accepted by the NJBRC. All three were identified as *C. h. exilipes*. Many of the reports occurred during flight years and were probably correct. However, given the difficulty of separating Common and

continued on page 644

Range: In North America breeds from Alaska to Baffin Island. Winters mainly in Canada, rarely farther south.

NJ Status: Accidental. NJBRC Review List.

continued from page 643

Hoary Redpoll

Hoary Redpolls in the field, it is unlikely that reports will be accepted without a detailed description and an accompanying photograph. The three accepted records are:

West Englewood	*1 April 1960*	*Gill 1961, spec. UMMZ #155143*
Plainfield	*11-16 February 1978*	*phs-NJA/RNJB 4:23, 4:41;Koellhoffer and Dowdell 1978*
Rockaway	*18 January-26 March 1994*	*ph-RNJB 20:33*

Pine Siskin

Carduelis pinus

Range: In eastern North America breeds from Manitoba east to Newfoundland, south to northern New Hampshire, and sporadically farther south. Winters within the breeding range, and erratically south to most of the United States

NJ Status: Rare and very local summer resident, rare to common migrant and winter resident.

Statewide Summary	
Status	# of Blocks
Possible	1
Probable	1
Confirmed	1
Total	3

Breeding

Habitat: Nests in conifers.

Pine Siskins are very rare breeding birds in New Jersey. There are records of five nests in northern New Jersey prior to the Atlas. They are: West Orange (two nests built, at least one young raised), May-July 1972 (Kane

Pine Siskin

continued

Physiographic Distribution Pine Siskin	Number of blocks in province	Number of blocks species found breeding in province	Number of blocks species found in state	Percent of province species occupies	Percent of all records for this species found in province	Percent of state area in province
Highlands	110	3	3	2.7	100.0	12.9

1975b); Wyckoff (nest with eggs), 23 April-2 May 1978 (Buckman 1978) ; Lopatcong (nest built but abandoned), late April 1982; Dumont (nest built but abandoned), early May 1982; Budd Lake (adult feeding three fledglings, 35 birds banded in breeding condition), May 1988. It is likely that the report of six birds at Marlton in June-July 1981 also represented a breeding record. One bird was seen to feed another, and upon capture, two birds were found to be young of the year. On 8 July 1986 at the same location, another young bird was captured. All nesting attempts occurred after large fall or winter incursions. Following invasion years there have been many additional reports of birds lingering into June and July, and almost certainly there have been more nesting attempts than have been reported.

Atlas volunteers found three records of Pine Siskins during five years of surveys. The single Confirmed nesting attempt at Green Pond, 18 July 1995, was a nest built but later abandoned. No successful nesting attempts were reported during the Atlas period.

Fall: Southbound movements of Pine Siskins are variable from year to year, and periodically incursions may occur statewide. Siskins occasionally appear as early as September, but October more often brings the vanguard of birds. Their numbers peak from late October through November. Recent major irruptions (>1,000 birds) occurred in 1977-1978, 1981-1982, 1986-1987, and 1987-1988. The largest fall invasion on record was probably the coastal flight of 1973, when 4,000-5,000 birds were noted in Cape May on 29 October and 10 November 1973 (AB). **Other maxima:** 1,000s, Cape May, 24 November 1987; 500+, Raccoon Ridge, 28 October 1981.

Winter: Fall invasions of Pine Siskins sometimes lead to high winter counts as well. However, it is just as likely that migrants will move farther south, leaving New Jersey with only modest winter numbers. Infrequently a large influx of birds will arrive in January or February. CBC totals are, not surprisingly, variable.

continued on page 646

continued from page 645

Pine Siskin

Maximum: 400, Tourne Park, 8 February 1982. **CBC Statewide Stats:** Average: 533; Maximum: 4,642 in 1978; Minimum: 17 in 1993. **CBC Maximum:** 588, Pinelands, 1982.

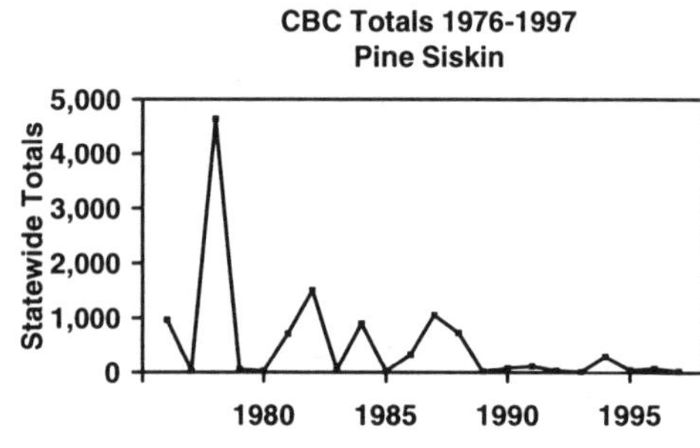

Spring: Pine Siskins are normally very rare spring migrants. Even when a large invasion has taken place, the return flight in March and April is never as conspicuous as that of fall. Following a flight year numbers of Pine Siskins sometimes remain in New Jersey through mid-May, or even later. **Maxima:** 20, Ogdensburg, 28 April, 1976; 12, Goshen, 28 April 1987. ■

American Goldfinch

Carduelis tristis

Possible
Probable
Confirmed

Statewide Summary	
Status	# of Blocks
Possible	79
Probable	435
Confirmed	217
Total	731

Range: In eastern North America breeds from Manitoba east to Newfoundland, and south to Oklahoma and Georgia. Winters throughout the United States.

NJ Status: Common and nearly ubiquitous summer resident, common spring and fall migrant, common winter resident.

American Goldfinch

continued

Breeding

Habitat: Most commonly nests in shrub thickets and hedgerows surrounding overgrown fields and pastures.

American Goldfinches have been considered a common and broadly distributed breeding bird in New Jersey throughout the 20th century (Stone 1908, Boyle 1986), and are New Jersey's State Bird. They are among the latest breeding songbirds in the state, sometimes waiting until August or even later to initiate nests – e.g., female feeding young in nest, Thompson Grove Park, 22 September 1984.

The Atlas surveys found American Goldfinch in 86% of the blocks statewide. From the Piedmont northward, they were recorded in 95% of the blocks, and they were found in 80% of the blocks south of that province. They were absent from some parts of the Pine Barrens and from most of the barrier islands. American Goldfinches were only Confirmed in 30% of the blocks in which they were present, probably the result of the lateness of their nesting season.

Fall: The southbound passage of American Goldfinches begins by early September, and peak flights can occur anytime between late September and late November. Although the magnitude of the autumn flight is variable from year-to-year, they are generally common migrants, especially along the coast. **Maxima:** 2,000+, Turkey Point, 26 November 1989; 1,000+, Higbee Beach, 29 November 1989.

Winter: The number of wintering American Goldfinches is subject to wide fluctuation from year-to-year, possibly the result of the abundance of their favored seeds (Bull 1964).
continued on page 648

Physiographic Distribution

American Goldfinch	Number of blocks in province	Number of blocks species found breeding in province	Number of blocks species found in state	Percent of province species occupies	Percent of all records for this species found in province	Percent of state area in province
Kittatinny Mountains	19	19	731	100.0	2.6	2.2
Kittatinny Valley	45	42	731	93.3	5.7	5.3
Highlands	109	104	731	95.4	14.2	12.8
Piedmont	167	157	731	94.0	21.5	19.6
Inner Coastal Plain	128	116	731	90.6	15.9	15.0
Outer Coastal Plain	204	147	731	72.1	20.1	23.9
Pine Barrens	180	146	731	81.1	20.0	21.1

continued from page 647

American Goldfinch

CBC Statewide Stats: Average: 3,401; Maximum: 5,341 in 1982; Minimum: 2,182 in 1980. **CBC Maximum:** 951, Barnegat, 1982.

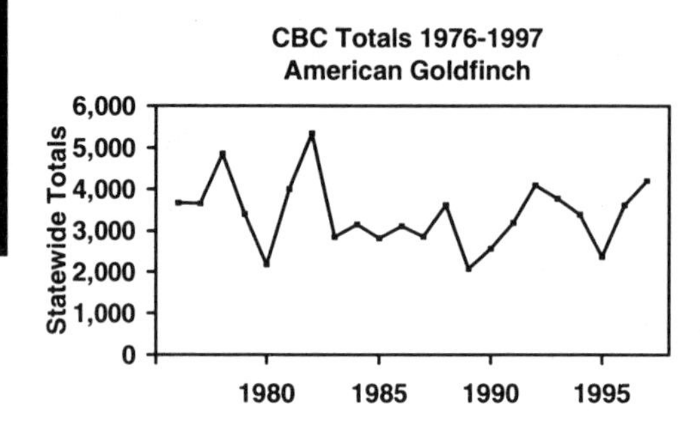

Spring: American Goldfinches occur in passage from late March through May. The largest numbers occur in April although the magnitude of the spring flight is much smaller than that of fall. **Maximum:** 75, Sandy Hook, 4 May 1997. ■

Evening Grosbeak

Coccothraustes vespertinus

Range: In eastern North America breeds from Manitoba east to Newfoundland, south to Wisconsin and New Hampshire, occasionally farther south. Winters within the breeding range, irregularly farther south.

NJ Status: Irregularly rare to common migrant and winter resident.

Historic Changes: Prior to the mid-1800s Evening Grosbeaks were a bird of the Northwest. In the second half of the 19th century, a gradual southern and eastern expansion began, punctuated by the great easterly invasion of 1889-1890 that brought the first records of the birds to many northeastern states. Eight birds found at Summit on 6 March 1890 constituted New Jersey's first state record (Stone 1908). The next came in 1910-1911, which were followed by eight invasions in the next 23 years (Stone 1937). By the early 1940s Cruickshank (1942) expected records annually, and by the late 1940s Evening Grosbeaks were regularly recorded in New Jersey (Bull 1964).

There are two breeding records for Evening Grosbeaks in New Jersey following a massive fall flight in 1961. The New Jersey breeding records are: Smoke Rise, July 1961, an adult feeding young (Bull 1964); and Branchville, July 1961, a male feeding young (Bull 1964). It is probably no coincidence that most extralimital

Evening Grosbeak

continued

breeding records in the northeast are associated with the presence of feeding stations (Bull 1974, Veit and Petersen 1993).

Fall: The timing of migration as well as the numbers of Evening Grosbeaks in New Jersey in fall is irregular. In some years, especially those years with massive flights, birds may be noted by mid-September. The height of migration is normally mid-October to early November, but this is variable. Since the mid-1980s, observers have reported declines in both the numbers and frequency of Evening Grosbeaks during migration. **Maxima:** 700+, Franklin Lakes, 17 October 1975; 600, Sunrise Mt., 26 September 1975.

Winter: In winter, Evening Grosbeaks are most often reported in northwestern New Jersey or in the Pine Barrens. The largest flight on record was in mid-January 1950, when an estimated 3,000 birds were in Bergen County alone, and more than 600 were at feeders in just five northwestern New Jersey communities. CBC totals are expectedly erratic. **CBC Statewide Stats:** Average: 607; Maximum: 2,284 in 1978; Minimum: 0 in 1993 and 1995. **CBC Maximum:** 587, Lakehurst, 1978.

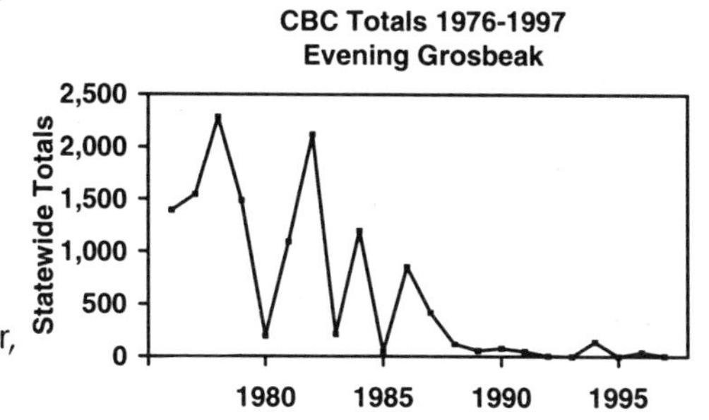

Spring: The return passage of Evening Grosbeaks is less conspicuous than fall migration, and often it is not detected at all. In those years when a substantial spring flight occurs, numbers reach their height between mid-April and early May. The heaviest spring flight on record was in 1969 (e.g., hundreds over Island Beach on 4 May 1969) (AFN). Most depart the state by mid-May, although there are several later records. **Maxima:** 50, Bearfort Mt., 15 April 1977; 50, Knowlton, 3 May 1980. ■

House Sparrow

Passer domesticus

Range: Introduced. Breeds from central and southern Canada south throughout the United States. Winters within the breeding range.

NJ Status: Common and nearly ubiquitous resident.

Breeding

Habitat: From city to farmland, House Sparrows nest on, in, or near human-made structures.

House Sparrows colonized New Jersey as a result of deliberate releases in

continued on page 650

continued from page 649

House Sparrow

Brooklyn, New York, in the early 1850s; Manhattan, New York, in the early 1860s; and Philadelphia, Pennsylvania, in 1869 (Stone 1908). The first New Jersey record was from Chatham in 1868. Just forty years later, Stone (1908) termed this species an "abundant resident, except in [the] most remote spots." House Sparrows, like European Starlings, are detrimental to several native bird populations because they compete with these species for limited cavities for nesting.

Atlas data indicated that House Sparrows were common and broadly distributed. Where forest is extensive and humans are scarce, such as in parts of the Pine Barrens or the wilder areas of northern New Jersey, House

Possible
Probable
Confirmed

Statewide Summary	
Status	# of Blocks
Possible	32
Probable	76
Confirmed	663
Total	771

Physiographic Distribution

House Sparrow	Number of blocks in province	Number of blocks species found breeding in province	Number of blocks species found in state	Percent of province species occupies	Percent of all records for this species found in province	Percent of state area in province
Kittatinny Mountains	19	12	771	63.2	1.6	2.2
Kittatinny Valley	45	45	771	100.0	5.8	5.3
Highlands	109	106	771	97.2	13.7	12.8
Piedmont	167	164	771	98.2	21.3	19.6
Inner Coastal Plain	128	127	771	99.2	16.5	15.0
Outer Coastal Plain	204	186	771	91.2	24.1	23.9
Pine Barrens	180	131	771	72.8	17.0	21.1

House Sparrow

continued

Sparrows are scarce or absent. The Pine Barrens and Kittatinny Mountains had the lowest rate of occupation for this species, 73% and 63% respectively, but all other provinces had over 90% of the blocks occupied by House Sparrows. The long breeding season, conspicuous nest building, and multiple broods gave Atlas volunteers ample opportunities to Confirm this species.

Fall: While generally considered nonmigratory in North America (Lowther and Cink 1992), some fall movement of House Sparrows has been noted at Cape May in September and October (Sibley 1997).

Winter: It is possible there has been a drop in the wintering numbers of House Sparrows. Post-nesting roosts of thousands of birds could be found in the early part of the 20th century (Stone 1937), although nothing approaching this magnitude exists today. CBC numbers are quite consistent. **CBC Statewide Stats:** Average: 12,604; Maximum: 20,382 in 1982; Minimum: 8,829 in 1979. **CBC Maximum:** 7,541, Lower Hudson, 1984.

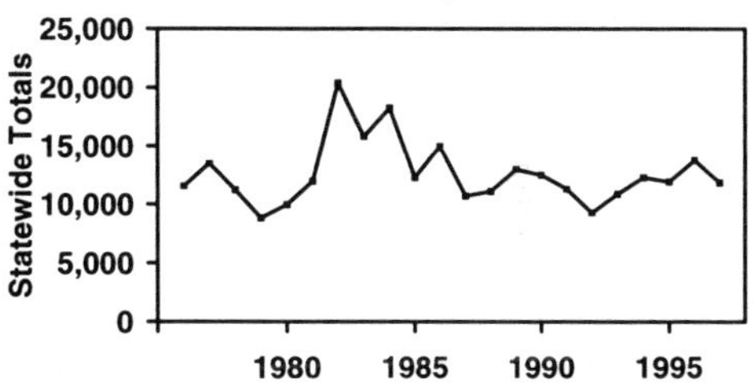

Spring: House Sparrows are primarily nonmigratory, permanent residents. There is no published information on the occurrence of spring migration of House Sparrows in New Jersey. ■

Appendix A

Atlas Block Summary

Topographic Map Name	Topographic Map Number	Block Location	Possible	Probable	Confirmed	Total Breeding	Observers
Milford	1	CE	6	45	44	95	Fred Tetlow
	1	SW	15	43	37	95	Fred Tetlow
	1	SE	8	40	50	98	Jim Zamos
Port Jervis South	2	NW	8	43	50	101	Deuane Hoffman
	2	CW	7	43	53	103	Deuane Hoffman
	2	CE	6	45	55	106	Deuane Hoffman
	2	SW	17	32	43	92	Sharon Wander, Wade Wander
	2	SE	11	39	82	132	Scott Angus, John Carey
Unionville	3	CW	9	19	102	130	Scott Angus, Dennis Miranda
	3	SW	4	39	78	121	Scott Angus, Jerry Liguori, Don Traylor, Donna Traylor
	3	SE	21	37	87	145	Scott Angus, Jerry Liguori
Lake Maskenozha	5	SE	13	43	45	101	Ed Fingerhood, Fred Tetlow, Chris Walters
Culvers Gap	6	NW	11	38	56	105	Fred Tetlow
	6	NE	7	42	46	95	Fred Tetlow
	6	CW	11	45	44	100	Fred Tetlow
	6	CE	10	22	71	103	Fred Tetlow
	6	SW	12	31	57	100	Fred Tetlow
	6	SE	14	31	53	98	Fred Tetlow
Branchville	7	NW	13	36	59	108	Fred Tetlow
	7	NE	4	29	47	80	John Carey
	7	CW	7	40	49	96	Fred Tetlow
	7	CE	6	31	42	79	Donald Traylor, Donna Traylor, Jim Zamos
	7	SW	12	34	48	94	Fred Tetlow
	7	SE	9	38	36	83	Donald Traylor, Donna Traylor, Jim Zamos
Hamburg	8	NW	24	34	83	141	Scott Angus, Jerry Liguori
	8	NE	17	31	85	133	Scott Angus, John Faber, Dennis Miranda
	8	CW	16	32	84	132	Scott Angus, Jerry Liguori
	8	CE	19	39	42	100	John Faber, Dennis Miranda
	8	SW	8	38	66	112	Scott Angus
	8	SE	23	41	35	99	John Faber, Dennis Miranda
Waywayanda	9	NW	20	46	43	109	Dennis Miranda
	9	NE	24	35	39	98	Dennis Miranda
	9	CW	22	55	23	100	Dennis Miranda
	9	CE	25	42	38	105	John Faber, Dennis Miranda

Topographic Map Name	Topographic Map Number	Block Location	Possible	Probable	Confirmed	Total Breeding	Observers
	9	SW	21	46	26	93	John Faber, Dennis Miranda
	9	SE	26	44	31	101	John Faber, Dennis Miranda
Greenwood Lake	10	CW	11	27	40	78	Ken Witkowski
	10	SW	15	30	54	99	Pete Bacinski, Deuane Hoffman, Linda Mack
	10	SE	11	26	57	94	Pete Bacinski, Judy Cinquina, John Holinka
Sloatsburg	11	SW	6	31	37	74	Pete Bacinski, Judy Cinquina, Kathy Hartman
Bushkill	12	SE	27	16	62	105	Alan Boyd
	13	NW	23	27	43	93	Chris Walters, Ed Fingerhood, Fred Tetlow
Flatbrookville	13	NE	16	25	40	81	Brian Hardiman, Tiffany Black Hardiman
	13	CW	27	28	54	109	Brian Hardiman, Tiffany Black Hardiman
	13	CE	10	42	36	88	Thomas Halliwell, Sharon Wander, Wade Wander
	13	SW	4	33	47	84	Roger Johnson
	13	SE	21	42	34	97	Sharon Wander, Wade Wander
	14	NW	3	30	44	77	Jim Bangma, Niroo Patel
Newton West	14	NE	2	30	51	83	Jim Bangma, Niroo Patel
	14	CW	13	41	38	92	Sharon Wander, Wade Wander
	14	CE	20	24	45	89	Blais Brancheau
	14	SW	7	35	52	94	Sharon Wander, Wade Wander
	14	SE	9	25	60	94	Marjorie Barrett
	15	NW	3	29	50	82	Jim Bangma, Niroo Patel
Newton East	15	NE	5	38	43	86	James Zamos
	15	CW	5	32	60	97	James Zamos
	15	CE	4	29	54	87	James Zamos
	15	SW	11	32	48	91	Tom Halliwell
	15	SE	8	34	44	86	Scott Angus, Tom Halliwell
	16	NW	13	29	49	91	John Carey, Tom Halliwell
Franklin	16	NE	12	28	54	94	Dennis Miranda, Ken Witkowski
	16	CW	13	25	56	94	Joe Burgiel
	16	CE	10	32	46	88	Ken Witkowski
	16	SW	7	39	47	93	Bill Boyle, Karen Thompson
	16	SE	4	44	51	99	Elizabeth Radis, Rick Radis, Tim Vogel
	17	NW	10	30	57	97	Pete Bacinski Deuane Hoffman, Linda Mack, Ken Witkowski
Newfoundland	17	NE	13	36	55	104	Pete Bacinski, Bill Boyle, Dan Lane, Linda Mack
	17	CW	10	30	62	102	Pete Bacinski, Linda Mack, Dave Oster
	17	CE	4	29	62	95	Pete Bacinski, Linda Mack, Linn Pierson, Dale Rosselet
	17	SW	5	39	71	115	Rick Radis
	17	SE	8	31	52	91	Pete Bacinski, Bill Boyle, Dan Lane, Linda Mack, Rick Radis
	18	NW	5	24	52	81	Pete Bacinski, John Holinka, Dan Lane, Linda Mack
Wanaque	18	NE	9	25	70	104	John Holinka, Dan Lane
	18	CW	11	34	46	91	Elizabeth Bush, Pete Bacinski, Dan Lane, Ken Witkowski Hardiman
	18	CE	6	31	57	94	Elaine Barrett, John Holinka
	18	SW	12	29	51	92	Dan Lane, Glenn Mahler, Eileen Mahler, Ken Witkowski Hardiman

Topographic Map Name	Topographic Map Number	Block Location	Possible	Probable	Confirmed	Total Breeding	Observers
	18	SE	7	29	52	88	Pete Bacinski, Elaine Barrett, Joe Broschart, Milt Levy
	19	NW	9	26	41	76	Scott Vincent, Ken Witkowski
Ramsey	19	NE	13	27	38	78	Judith Collis, John Kolodziej, Mary Ellen Shaw, Patricia Shaw
	19	CW	20	18	40	78	Jim Bangma, John Brotherton, Rob Unrath, Scott Vincent, J. Worall, Fyke Nature Club
	19	CE	7	14	57	78	Irene Franz, Mike Franz, Charles Mayhood, Rob Unrath
	19	SW	10	21	34	65	Ryan Bakelaar, John Kolodziej, Ken Prytherch, Pat Shaw
	19	SE	15	16	34	65	Charles Mayhood, Robert Hoek, Stiles Thomas, J. & C. Gaitskill
	20	CW	6	16	37	59	Judy Cinquina, Kathy Hartman, Rosemarie Widmer
Park Ridge	20	CE	8	12	26	46	Jean Burton, Betty Butler, Gerri Byrne, Linda Peskac, Max Ugarte, Nilda Ugarte
	20	SW	3	8	53	64	Robert Hoek, Charles Mayhood, Stiles Thomas
	20	SE	5	10	32	47	Jean Burton, Betty Butler, Linda Peskac
	21	SW	11	18	34	63	Betty Butler, Rich Kane, Linda Peskac, Ron Warner
Nyack	23	NW	18	27	51	96	Dennis Briede
Portland	23	NE	17	17	55	89	Alan Boyd
	23	CW	16	13	62	91	Dennis Briede
	23	CE	9	36	32	77	Dennis Briede
	23	SE	11	34	37	82	Thomas Halliwell
	24	NW	16	34	41	91	Thomas Halliwell
Blairstown	24	NE	11	34	47	92	Thomas Halliwell
	24	CW	11	34	36	81	Thomas Halliwell
	24	CE	14	19	52	85	Alan Boyd
	24	SW	9	31	41	81	Thomas Halliwell
	24	SE	10	25	51	86	Alan Boyd, Charlene Kelly
	25	NW	10	33	55	98	Marjorie Barrett
Tranquility	25	NE	10	39	48	97	Thomas Halliwell
	25	CW	14	29	40	83	Dale Stevens
	25	CE	1	32	59	92	Thomas Halliwell
	25	SW	6	32	47	85	Thomas Halliwell, Kevin McCarthy
	25	SE	7	34	48	89	Thomas Halliwell
	26	NW	11	22	52	85	Marjorie Barrett
Stanhope	26	NE	12	36	42	90	Emily Anderson, Mike Anderson, Thomas Halliwell
	26	CW	3	32	53	88	Thomas Halliwell
	26	CE	6	22	52	80	Sheryl Nowell
	26	SW	11	21	62	94	Thomas Halliwell
	26	SE	9	36	49	94	Irving Black, Thomas Halliwell
	27	NW	5	28	76	109	Jim Dowdell, Vince Elia, Rick Radis, Clay Sutton, Tim Vogel
Dover	27	NE	10	18	101	129	Rick Radis, John Reed, Tim Vogel
	27	CW	16	18	61	95	Jim Grundy, Clifford Miles, Jon Van De Venter

Topographic Map Name	Topographic Map Number	Block Location	Possible	Probable	Confirmed	Total Breeding	Observers
	27	CE	12	12	76	100	Bob Flatt, Tim Halliwell, Carol Knapp, John Knapp, John Reed, Janet Sedicino, Jon Van De Venter
	27	SW	7	35	49	91	Rick Radis, Tim Vogel
	27	SE	7	26	57	90	Rick Radis
	28	NW	16	21	47	84	Eileen Mahler, Glenn Mahler, Rick Radis
Boonton	28	NE	4	30	65	99	Rick Radis, Tim Vogel
	28	CW	2	26	54	82	Rick Radis, Tim Vogel
	28	CE	19	19	41	79	Eileen Mahler, Glenn Mahler
	28	SW	13	23	72	108	Carol Knapp, John Knapp, Rick Radis, Tim Vogel
	28	SE	12	27	53	92	Carol Knapp, John Knapp, Clifford Miles
	29	NW	10	18	53	81	Carol Knapp, John Knapp
Pompton Plains	29	NE	11	19	37	67	Joseph Broschart, Benita Fishbein, Carol Knapp, John Knapp, Marie Kuhnen
	29	CW	11	18	47	76	Carol Knapp, John Knapp, Eileen Mahler, Glenn Mahler, Scott Vincent
	29	CE	13	16	38	67	Joseph Broschart
	29	SW	0	18	48	66	Robert Leonard
	29	SE	7	19	49	75	Joseph Broschart, Jennifer Hanson, Wally Koenig, Robert Leonard
	30	NW	13	10	49	72	Bill Elrick, Dale Rosselet, Gordon Schultze, Rob Unrath
Paterson	30	NE	5	5	21	31	Bill Elrick, Gordon Schultze
	30	CW	10	16	45	71	Joseph Broschart, Dennis Schvejda
	30	CE	9	6	22	37	Hugh Carola
	30	SW	10	11	27	48	Ralph Mitrano, Jr., Dennis Schvejda
	30	SE	8	6	42	56	Pete Both, Hugh Carola, Robert Guthrie, Bill Prather, Ken Samra
	31	NW	13	8	31	52	Jim Bangma, J. Burton, Betty Butler, Heather Gamper, Linda Peskac
Hackensack	31	NE	6	14	42	62	Christopher Byrne, Geraldine Byrne, G. Narry Byrne
	31	CW	7	16	35	58	Jim Bangma
	31	CE	0	4	32	36	Rich Kane, Max Ugarte, Nilda Ugarte
	31	SW	7	4	33	44	George H. Byrne, Geraldine Byrne, Jim Hayes
	31	SE	2	7	23	32	Judith Collis, John Kolodziej
	32	NW	8	10	35	53	Jim Hayes
Yonkers	32	NE	16	16	40	72	Sandy Bonardi, Lois Gebhardt, Hollyce Kirkland, Nancy Slowik, Janet VanGelder
	32	CW	6	22	44	72	Muriel Danon, Brian Moscatello, Janet Sedicino
	32	CE	7	12	53	72	Sandy Bonardi, H. Davis, Hollyce Kirkland, Linda Rozowicz, Nancy Slowik, Janet VanGelder
	32	SW	9	14	21	44	Maria Brough, Ruth Comfort, Dick Engsberg
	32	SE	17	14	37	68	Sandy Bonardi, Bill Shadel, Nancy Slowik
Bangor	33	SE	10	22	46	78	Richard Dunlap
	34	NW	13	22	36	71	Bov Machover, David Mandell, Starr Saphir
Belvedere	34	NE	31	18	53	102	Alan Gregory
	34	CW	29	18	50	97	Arlene Koch, Bernie Morris, Pauline Morris

Topographic Map Name	Topographic Map Number	Block Location	Possible	Probable	Confirmed	Total Breeding	Observers
	34	CE	16	22	32	70	Bob Machover
	34	SW	18	21	42	81	Arlene Koch, Bernie Morris, Pauline Morris
	34	SE	23	28	26	77	Joshua W. C. Cutler
	35	NW	22	11	51	84	Alan Gregory, Monica Gregory
Washington	35	NE	12	35	30	77	Deuane Hoffman
	35	CW	7	38	48	93	Ed LeGrand, Deuane Hoffman Shaw
	35	CE	13	25	39	77	Deuane Hoffman, Bob Machover, Starr Saphir
	35	SW	13	16	39	68	Virginia Cole, Bob Machover
	35	SE	13	46	31	90	Don Freiday
	36	NW	20	24	39	83	Alan Boyd
Hackettstown	36	NE	16	20	57	93	Alan Boyd
	36	CW	19	18	48	85	Alan Boyd
	36	CE	9	28	41	78	David Harrison, Charlene Kelly Club
	36	SW	13	29	38	80	David Christ, Edmund LeGrand
	36	SE	11	34	40	85	David Harrison, Regina Harrison
	37	NW	9	20	48	77	Alan Boyd, George Nixon, Valerie Nixon
Chester	37	NE	15	29	43	87	David Harrison
	37	CW	15	31	48	94	Joe Burgiel, David Harrison
	37	CE	18	30	52	100	Joe Burgiel, David Harrison, Regina Harrison
	37	SW	17	27	52	96	Joe Burgiel, David Harrison, Lee Pierson, Steven Sobocinski
	37	SE	16	32	41	89	Kevin J. McCarthy, Steven Sobocinski
	38	NW	12	18	54	84	Emily Anderson, Mike Anderson, Robin Anderson, Carol Knapp, John Knapp
Mendham	38	NE	11	14	56	81	Carol Knapp, John Knapp
	38	CW	14	24	43	81	Emily Anderson, Mike Anderson, Robin Anderson, David Harrison
	38	CE	19	17	48	84	Emily Anderson, Mike Anderson, Robin Anderson
	38	SW	16	26	44	86	Mike Newlon, Steven Sobocinski
	38	SE	11	13	49	73	Eileen Mahler, Glenn Mahler
	39	NW	17	18	44	79	David Harrison, Roger Johnson, Rich Kane, Tim Vogel
Morristown	39	NE	6	22	47	75	Roger Johnson
	39	CW	5	15	49	69	Georgia Eisenhart, Sharon Fullogar
	39	CE	8	21	41	70	Roger Johnson
	39	SW	2	33	36	71	Alfred Howard, Allan Keith
	39	SE	14	13	38	65	Georgia Eisenhart, Eileen Mahler, Glen Mahler, Sharon Fullogar
	40	NW	15	17	50	82	David Hall, Roger Johnson
Caldwell	40	NE	17	20	41	78	David Hall
	40	CW	10	18	29	57	Roger Johnson
	40	CE	8	15	36	59	David Hall, Dave Oster
	40	SW	5	18	53	76	Richard Ryan
	40	SE	9	23	49	81	Feliz Gallagher, M. Grosso, David Hall, Jonathan Klizas, M. Kuhnen, Ann Manger, Barbara Murray, John Murray, Susan Stevenson, Phil Stevenson
	41	NW	4	14	32	50	Benita Fishbein, Marie Kuhnen, Theodore Proctor

Topographic Map Name	Topographic Map Number	Block Location	Possible	Probable	Confirmed	Total Breeding	Observers
Orange	41	NE	10	12	33	55	Robert Dickison, David Hall, Patrick Hamill, Marie Kuhnen, Theodore Proctor
	41	CW	5	19	33	57	Benita Fishbein, Marie Kuhnen, Jonathan Klizas, Theodore Proctor, Rosemarie Walsh
	41	CE	11	7	19	37	Ralph Mitrano, Jr., Bruce Zatkow
	41	SW	5	4	10	19	Pete Bacinski
	41	SE	12	14	30	56	Brian Moscatello, Janet Sedicino
	42	NW	2	18	21	41	Jim Bangma
Weehawken	42	NE	5	11	25	41	Jim Bangma
	42	CW	4	15	23	42	Theodore Proctor, Bruce Zatkow
	42	CE	6	5	34	45	Jim Hayes
	42	SW	8	14	31	53	Anne Galli, Barbara Jugan, Bill Richardson, Edward Saamans, Don Smith
	42	SE	13	4	22	39	John Holinka
	43	NW	0	8	38	46	Linn Pierson,
Central Park	43	CW	0	2	22	24	Linn Pierson
Easton	44	NE	20	27	64	111	Richard Dunlap
	44	CE	13	4	23	40	Joyce Matthews
	44	SE	13	21	40	74	Christopher Aquila, Don Freiday, Dave Womer
	45	NW	7	14	47	68	Jane Bullis, Jim Mershon
Bloomsbury	45	NE	10	24	42	76	Ann Brown, Sharon Fullagar, Deuane Hoffman
	45	CW	13	13	68	94	Richard Dunlap
	45	CE	9	21	45	75	Sharon Fullagar, Deuane Hoffman
	45	SW	6	58	23	87	David Womer
	45	SE	18	34	26	78	Rich Talian
	46	NW	10	30	32	72	Bob Machover
High Bridge	46	NE	11	30	18	59	Laurie Gneiding, Betty Jones, Kenn Jones
	46	CW	14	20	39	73	Bernard Morris, Pauline Morris
	46	CE	14	23	54	91	Edmund LeGrand
	46	SW	17	24	33	74	Bernard Morris, Pauline Morris
	46	SE	5	31	46	82	David Harrison, Regina Harrison
	47	NW	6	28	38	72	Barbara Wilczek, Bill Wilczek
Califon	47	NE	25	28	30	83	David Fantina, Tom Sabel
	47	CW	7	38	27	72	Ed Patten
	47	CE	10	33	31	74	John DeMarrais
	47	SW	22	25	27	74	Donna Gaffigan, Laurie Gneiding
	47	SE	10	39	35	84	John DeMarrais
	48	NW	7	36	43	86	David Harrison, Lee Pierson
Gladstone	48	NE	9	36	42	87	Lee Pierson, Steven Sobocinski
	48	CW	9	29	57	95	Lee Pierson
	48	CE	6	34	46	86	Lee Pierson
	48	SW	8	30	40	78	Lee Pierson
	48	SE	1	37	44	82	Linda Fields, Lee Pierson, Alan Schreck
	49	NW	13	23	44	80	Rich Kane, Mike Newlon, Arthur Panzer
Bernardsville	49	NE	8	17	77	102	Mike Anderson, Rich Kane, Sefton Vergiano
	49	CW	7	20	46	73	Joyce Payeur, Rich Kane
	49	CE	10	24	59	93	Eileen Mahler, Glenn Mahler De Venter
	49	SW	11	26	35	72	David Harrison, Steven Sobocinski
	49	SE	10	32	43	85	Dave Harrison, Steven Sobocinski

Topographic Map Name	Topographic Map Number	Block Location	Possible	Probable	Confirmed	Total Breeding	Observers
	50	NW	13	19	57	89	Mike Newlon
Chatham	50	NE	9	21	35	65	Mike Newlon
	50	CW	12	32	39	83	Mike Newlon
	50	CE	7	9	58	74	Dick Burk, Chris Gulliksen, Hollace Hoffman, Andy Lamy, Rosemary Knapp, Dana Knowlton, Nancy Lilly, Walt Lilly, Ginny Seabrook, John Seabrook
	50	SW	15	20	48	83	Mike Newlon De Venter
	50	SE	6	12	39	57	Chris Gulliksen, Hollace Hoffman, Dana Knowlton, Leo Weiss
	51	NW	6	16	25	47	Jonathan Klizas, Dick Ryan
Roselle	51	NE	14	17	42	73	Edward Samanns, Phil Stevenson, Sue Stevenson
	51	CW	7	24	44	75	Henry Burk, Nancy Eichman, Rosemary Knapp, Ginny Seabrook, John Seabrook, Jim Springer
	51	CE	14	13	33	60	Else Greenstone, Wayne Greenstone, David Harrison
	51	SW	5	13	17	35	Vi Debbie, Johnathan Klizas
	51	SE	8	8	28	44	Else Greenstone, Wayne Greenstone
	52	NW	5	5	10	20	Pete Bacinski
Elizabeth	52	NE	2	10	14	26	Pete Bacinski, Edward Samanns
	52	CW	7	19	36	62	David Harrison, Ginny Seabrook, John Seabrook, Junius Williams
	52	CE	6	7	20	33	Pete Bacinski
	52	SW	8	19	23	50	Scott Barnes, Hank Burk, Fred Virazzi
	52	SE	7	8	17	32	John Holinka
	53	NW	12	5	24	41	John Holinka
Jersey City	53	NE	10	0	11	21	John Holinka
	53	CW	15	4	22	41	John Holinka
	53	CE	12	3	22	37	John Holinka
	53	SW	7	6	19	32	John Holinka
	55	NW	3	60	8	71	Dave Womer
Riegelsville	55	NE	12	9	56	77	Bob Machover, Starr Saphir
	55	CE	6	58	13	77	David Womer
	56	NW	3	58	13	74	David Womer
Frenchtown	56	NE	5	46	30	81	Don Freiday
	56	CW	5	60	13	78	David Womer
	56	CE	6	56	9	71	Don Freiday, David Womer
	56	SE	5	14	51	70	Tom Koelhoffer
	57	NW	10	36	25	71	Peter Kwiatek
Pittstown	57	NE	17	14	43	74	Donna Gaffigan, Robert Jordan
	57	CW	9	20	33	62	John DeMarrais
	57	CE	8	28	24	60	Peter Kwiatek
	57	SW	4	27	37	68	John DeMarrais
	57	SE	4	26	20	50	Peter Kwiatek
	58	NW	27	7	26	60	Donna Gaffigan
Flemington	58	NE	16	16	45	77	Robert Wargo
	58	CW	6	48	31	85	Don Freiday
	58	CE	5	26	28	59	Edward Patten

Topographic Map Name	Topographic Map Number	Block Location	Possible	Probable	Confirmed	Total Breeding	Observers
	58	SW	11	12	28	51	Bruce Doerr
	58	SE	4	26	34	64	Bruce Doerr, Karen Wolzanski, Dave Womer
	59	NW	6	33	37	76	Ed Patten, Lee Pierson
Raritan	59	NE	4	36	29	69	Lisa MacCollum, Lee Pierson
	59	CW	7	24	39	70	Ed Patten
	59	CE	8	22	33	63	Lee Pierson
	59	SW	2	23	44	69	Lisa MacCollum, Ed Patten
	59	SE	8	19	35	62	Lisa MacCollum, Lee Pierson
	60	NW	12	18	44	74	Dave Fantina
Bound Brook	60	NE	6	26	42	74	Dave Fantina, George Roussey
	60	CW	9	14	42	65	George Roussey
	60	CE	10	15	46	71	George Roussey
	60	SW	7	22	40	69	George Roussey
	60	SE	4	13	46	63	George Roussey
	61	NW	6	14	33	53	Chris Gulliksen, Dana Knowlton
Plainfield	61	NE	4	10	35	49	Chris Gulliksen, Dana Knowlton, Nancy Lilly, Walter Lilly
	61	CW	5	13	52	70	Nancy Lilly, Walter Lilly
	61	CE	0	15	45	60	Nancy Lilly, Walter Lilly
	61	SW	4	15	52	71	Joan Labun, Nancy Lilly, Walter Lilly, Michael Rothkopf
	61	SE	8	16	15	39	David Harrison, Ronald Midkiff
	62	NW	6	20	35	61	Bob Harsett, Ginny Seabrook, John Seabrook
Perth Amboy	62	NE	9	17	31	57	Jim Springer
	62	CW	8	12	23	43	Jim Springer
	62	CE	8	15	30	53	David Harrison, Ronald Midkiff, George Roussey
	62	SW	11	9	32	52	Thomas Gillen, David Harrison, Jack Harrison, Elizabeth Kelley, Christopher Stitt
	62	SE	7	19	23	49	David Gillen, Thomas Gillen, David Harrison, Jack Harrison, Sara Ann Joselson
	63	NW	9	14	30	53	David Harrison, Theodore Proctor, Jim Springer
Arthur Kill	66	NE	10	11	51	72	Christopher Aquila, Steve Byland
	66	CE	50	14	15	79	Bruce McNaught, Nancy Wottrich
	66	SE	30	22	21	73	Bruce McNaught, Nancy Wottrich
	67	NW	9	36	24	69	Ed Patten
Stockton	67	NE	4	28	34	66	Ed Patten
	67	CW	9	34	32	75	Pam Thier, John Mitchell
	67	CE	6	37	33	76	Ed Patten
	67	SW	12	21	51	84	Beverly Jones, Robert Jones
	67	SE	9	22	44	75	Beverly Jones, Robert Jones
	68	NW	25	16	19	60	Bruce Doerr
Hopewell	68	NE	23	26	25	74	Marian van Buren
	68	CW	13	30	28	71	Don Freiday
	68	CE	9	38	41	88	Brian Dendler, David Dendler, Don Freiday
	68	SW	8	33	42	83	Cathy Freiday, Don Freiday
	68	SE	7	15	61	83	Hannah Suthers
	69	NW	15	22	36	73	Christopher Aquila, David Dendler, Bob Sanders, Dave Womer

Topographic Map Name	Topographic Map Number	Block Location	Possible	Probable	Confirmed	Total Breeding	Observers
Rocky Hill	69	NE	5	25	33	63	Laurie Larson, Arlene Oley, Fred Ward
	69	CW	8	20	47	75	Fred Ward
	69	CE	7	18	36	61	Fred Ward
	69	SW	8	3	53	64	Ursula Gerhart-Brooks
	69	SE	7	26	32	65	Fred Ward, Kimberly Young
	70	NW	16	31	19	66	Joe Zurovchak
Monmouth Junction	70	NE	15	31	28	74	Joe Zurovchak
	70	CW	3	15	48	66	Arlene Oley
	70	CE	7	26	19	52	Eileen Hayes, Brad Merritt
	70	SW	4	22	35	61	Brad Merritt, Karen Thompson
	70	SE	7	14	46	67	Chris Williams, Paula Williams
	71	NW	4	16	22	42	Chris Williams, Paula Williams
New Brunswick	71	NE	15	9	37	61	Joan Labun
	71	CW	13	16	29	58	Linda DeLay
	71	CE	14	9	21	44	Derek Lovitch
	71	SW	5	28	42	75	Chris Williams, Paula Williams
	71	SE	2	24	41	67	Kathryn Hackett-Fields, Kathi Ricca, Joseph Sapia
	72	NW	5	13	36	54	David Gillen, Thomas Gillen
South Amboy	72	NE	4	14	42	60	Chris Aquila, Rich Brown, Rich Kane, Laurie Larson, Jim Williams, Jim Wilson
	72	CW	8	4	37	49	Derek Lovitch
	72	CE	1	18	48	67	Rich Kane
	72	SW	20	19	22	61	Peter Adams
	72	SE	8	24	30	62	Laurie Larson, Jim Williams
	73	CW	9	18	34	61	Bob Dieterich, Rich Kane
Keyport	73	CE	14	27	44	85	Maryellen Boyle, Thomas Boyle
	73	SW	16	20	33	69	Thomas Boyle, Steven Budnicki, Bob Dieterich, Robert Olthoff
	73	SE	11	15	43	69	Nerses Kazanjian
	74	NE	12	10	31	53	Susan Phelon
Sandy Hook	74	CW	2	14	31	47	Rich Kane
	74	CE	13	8	27	48	Susan Phelon
	74	SW	3	24	35	62	Robert Olthoff, Don Sutherland
	74	SE	9	30	42	81	Scott Barnes, Susan Draxler, Elizabeth Warnke
	76	NW	9	17	45	71	Beverly Jones, Robert Jones
Lambertville	76	NE	6	39	31	76	Martin Rapp
	76	CE	8	28	31	67	Jim Williams
	77	NW	13	19	35	67	Fred Ward, Steve Schnur
Pennington	77	NE	17	12	40	69	Jean Bickal
	77	CW	10	22	49	81	Jim Williams
	77	CE	4	25	30	59	Philip Moylan, Deborah Wedeking, Paul Wedeking
	77	SW	9	13	48	70	Jim Williams
	77	SE	14	12	33	59	Jean Bickal
	78	NW	9	29	49	87	Laurie Larson, Hannah Suthers
Princeton	78	NE	8	12	42	62	Karen Thompson
	78	CW	2	16	55	73	Libbie Johnson
	78	CE	2	18	53	73	Laurie Larson
	78	SW	7	31	31	69	Steve Gates, Laurie Larson
	78	SE	2	24	45	71	Louis Beck, Eileen Katz

Topographic Map Name	Topographic Map Number	Block Location	Possible	Probable	Confirmed	Total Breeding	Observers
	79	NW	20	18	31	69	Henry Schaefer
Hightstown	79	NE	4	24	39	67	Chris Williams, Paula Williams
	79	CW	5	23	38	66	JIM Williams
	79	CE	7	25	31	63	Arlene Oley, Jim Williams
	79	SW	6	23	16	45	Richard Brown
	79	SE	15	18	25	58	Richard Brown, Laurie Larson
	80	NW	14	11	26	51	Joan Labun
Jamesburg	80	NE	16	21	22	59	Peter Adams
	80	CW	30	12	17	59	Peter Adams
	80	CE	4	30	26	60	Jim Williams
	80	SW	4	26	32	62	Laurie Larson
	80	SE	1	33	26	60	Laurie Larson
	81	NW	12	34	20	66	Christopher Aquila
Freehold	81	NE	32	7	22	61	Chris Schmidt
	81	CW	4	26	30	60	Jim Williams
	81	CE	2	27	22	51	Jim Williams
	81	SW	7	17	37	61	Pete Bacinski, Scott Barnes, Rich Ditch, Cynthia Wood, Michael Wood
	81	SE	14	15	23	52	David Donnelly, Cynthia Wood, Michael Wood
	82	NW	9	21	43	73	Bob Dieterich, Robert Olthoff
Marlboro	82	NE	6	15	42	63	Fred Armstrong, Janice Casper, Michael Casper, Bob Dieterich, Joyce O'Keefe
	82	CW	10	14	35	59	Robert Olthoff, Don Sutherland
	82	CE	15	9	49	73	Tom Bailey, Ronald Berry, Andrew Spears
	82	SW	8	27	39	74	Robert Olthoff, Don Sutherland, Cynthia Wood, Michael Wood
	82	SE	11	17	45	73	Robert Olthoff, Don Sutherland, Michael Wood
	83	NW	6	15	40	61	Don Sutherland, Jane Sutherland
Long Branch	83	NE	11	21	33	65	Linda Mack
	83	CW	6	13	54	73	Tom Bailey, Nerses Kazanjian
	83	CE	3	6	34	43	Don Sutherland, Jane Sutherland
	83	SW	10	23	38	71	Robert Olthoff, Susan Phelon, Don Sutherland, Jane Sutherland, Mike Wood
	83	SE	11	12	36	59	Robert Bowman, Bruce Murray, Leslie Murray, Barbara Shields, Larry Shields
	86	NE	14	2	21	37	Jean Bickal
Trenton West	87	NW	1	28	27	56	Jean Bickal, Laurie Larson
Trenton East	87	NE	16	22	30	68	Mark Witmer
	87	CW	19	16	28	63	Robert Mercer
	87	CE	10	23	21	54	Lou Beck Eileen Katz, Jane Snyder, Mark Witmer
	87	SW	22	13	14	49	Robert Mercer
	87	SE	14	13	26	53	Jean Bickal
	88	NW	7	13	38	58	Rich Kane, Laurie Larson
Allentown	88	NE	14	10	53	77	Richard Brown
	88	CW	4	18	46	68	Rich Kane
	88	CE	13	21	24	58	Richard Brown
	88	SW	9	21	34	64	Jean Bickal
	88	SE	9	23	29	61	Laurie Larson
	89	NW	15	14	53	82	Tom Bailey

Topographic Map Name	Topographic Map Number	Block Location	Possible	Probable	Confirmed	Total Breeding	Observers
Roosevelt	89	NE	7	31	32	70	Laurie Larson
	89	CW	13	11	61	85	Tom Bailey
	89	CE	15	27	18	60	Rich Brown
	89	SW	3	24	39	66	Laurie Larson
	89	SE	9	24	30	63	Richard Brown
	90	NW	24	14	29	67	Richard Brown, Rich Ditch
Adelphia	90	NE	11	13	22	46	Richard Brown
	90	CW	9	27	27	63	Richard Brown
	90	CE	18	14	17	49	William McElroy
	90	SW	9	19	46	74	Leo Aus, Richard Brown
	90	SE	8	9	52	69	Richard Brown
	91	NW	3	28	40	71	Phil Misseldine, Robert Olthoff, Don Sutherland
Farmingdale	91	NE	6	29	43	78	Robert Olthoff, Don Sutherland, Mike Wood
	91	CW	10	16	54	80	Stephanie Belvedere, Robert Olthoff, Jay Estelle, Rose Estelle
	91	CE	8	21	54	83	Robert Olthoff
	91	SW	2	26	33	61	Robert Olthoff
	91	SE	11	18	65	94	James Herder
	92	NW	5	24	32	61	Don Sutherland, Jane Sutherland
Asbury Park	92	NE	4	15	23	42	Barbara Shields, Larry Shields, Don Sutherland
	92	CW	10	20	37	67	Fred Armstrong, Joyce O'Keefe
	92	CE	5	18	26	49	Don Sutherland
	92	SW	21	25	51	97	George Wenzelburger
	92	SE	7	18	25	50	Phil Misseldine, Robert Olthoff, Don Sutherland
	93	SE	13	9	44	66	Tom Bailey
Frankford	94	CW	3	2	46	51	Craig Malone, Ron Melcer
Beverly	94	SW	17	32	30	79	Frank Windfelder
	94	SE	15	9	48	72	Linda Kemple
	95	NW	10	23	14	47	Laurie Larson, Jerry Liguori
Bristol	95	NE	0	10	29	39	Laurie Larson, Jerry Liguori
	95	CW	21	20	16	57	Elio Bartoli
	95	CE	10	17	28	55	Elio Bartoli, Jerry Liguori
	95	SW	28	15	23	66	Karl Anderson
	95	SE	3	16	27	46	Jerry Liguori
	96	NW	8	25	29	62	Ward Dasey
Columbus	96	NE	6	29	27	62	Ward Dasey
	96	CW	14	24	22	60	Frank Rush, Peggy Rush
	96	CE	8	34	33	75	Tom Bailey, Ed Bruder, Robert Confer, Ward Dasey, Laurie Larson
	96	SW	7	25	35	67	Edgar Bruder, Jerry Liguori, Bill Seng
	96	SE	15	23	37	75	Michael Hodanish
	97	NW	35	14	14	63	Jerry Liguori, Bill Seng
New Egypt	97	NE	14	21	19	54	Jerry Liguori, Bill Seng
	97	CW	29	13	24	66	Jerry Liguori, Bill Seng
	97	CE	19	30	27	76	Jerry Liguori, Bill Seng, Brian Vernachio, Nikki Vernachio
	97	SW	4	35	53	92	Philip Warren
	97	SE	20	20	16	56	Jerry Liguori, Bill Seng
	98	NW	3	26	40	69	Janice Casper, Michael Casper

Topographic Map Name	Topographic Map Number	Block Location	Possible	Probable	Confirmed	Total Breeding	Observers
Cassville	98	NE	5	27	44	76	Janice Casper, Michael Casper
	98	CW	8	22	53	83	Mike Carr, Gary Gentile, Karen Gentile, Jerry Liguori, Robert Olthoff, Bob Simansky, Don Sutherland, Jane Sutherland
	98	CE	15	31	38	84	Mike Carr, Jerry Liguori, Robert Olthoff, Bob Simansky
	98	SW	33	16	11	60	Jerry Liguori
	98	SE	4	22	46	72	Robert Olthoff, Dan Williams, Melinda Williams
	99	NW	11	13	53	77	Robert Olthoff
Lakehurst	99	NE	10	23	37	70	Stephanie Belvedere, Michael Casper, Robert Olthoff
	99	CW	6	24	42	72	Jerry Liguori, Don Sutherland, Jane Sutherland
	99	CE	10	23	35	68	Don Sutherland, Jane Sutherland
	99	SW	9	18	46	73	Robert Olthoff, Dan Williams, Melinda Williams
	99	SE	8	22	37	67	R. C. Conn, Robert Olthoff, Don Sutherland, Alex Tongas, G. N. Vriens
	100	NW	12	20	36	68	Stephanie Belvedere, Rich Brown, Daniel Lane, Bob Olthoff
Lakewood	100	NE	17	20	40	77	Ward Halligan, Robert Olthoff, Don Sutherland, Alex Tongas
	100	CW	9	23	27	59	Daniel Lane, Jerry Liguori, Robert Olthoff, Don Sutherland
	100	CE	19	17	37	73	Janice Casper, Michael Casper, Jerry Liguori, Robert Olthoff, Don Sutherland, Alex Tongas
	100	SW	9	23	30	62	Daniel Lane, Lillian Levine, Robert Olthoff, Don Sutherland
	100	SE	3	20	35	58	Robert Olthoff, Don Sutherland, Alex Tongas
	101	NW	6	21	9	36	Phil Misseldine, Don Sutherland, Alex Tongas
Point Pleasant	101	NE	5	15	18	38	Robert Olthoff, Don Sutherland
	101	CW	10	11	32	53	Vince Elia, Dan Lane, Don Sutherland
	101	SW	10	28	23	61	Phil Misseldine, Robert Olthoff, Don Sutherland, Alex Tongas
	103	NW	4	11	23	38	Ward Dasey
	103	NE	5	15	57	77	Tom Bailey, Steve Tischner
Philadelphia	103	CW	7	9	11	27	Jerry Liguori, Bill Seng
Camden	103	CE	13	17	29	59	Sharon Gurak, Steve Tischner
	103	SW	3	8	45	56	Jean Gutsmuth
	103	SE	28	24	31	83	Gail Cannon
	104	NW	8	6	13	27	Sandy Amos
	104	NE	18	16	19	53	John LaVia
	104	CW	16	15	9	40	Jerry Liguori, Bill Seng
Moorestown	104	CE	12	25	19	56	Ward Dasey, Jerry Liguori, Bill Seng
	104	SW	16	15	32	63	Megan Edwards
	104	SE	4	10	38	52	Byron Campbell, Claire Campbell
	105	NW	13	31	29	73	Don Birchall, Ward Dasey, Diane Merkh
	105	NE	19	25	30	74	Ward Dasey, Frank Rush, Peggy Rush
	105	CW	4	25	50	79	Ward Dasey
Mt. Holly	105	CE	5	24	41	70	Ward Dasey, Keith Faust
	105	SW	7	12	50	69	Tom Wilson

Topographic Map Name	Topographic Map Number	Block Location	Possible	Probable	Confirmed	Total Breeding	Observers
	105	SE	3	28	67	98	Ken Tischner
	106	NW	7	51	23	81	Bob Confer, Janet Confer, Len Little
	106	NE	11	56	30	97	Bob Confer, Janet Confer, Len Little
	106	CW	19	19	24	62	Donald Jones
Pemberton	106	CE	14	39	29	82	Donald Jones
	106	SW	1	14	84	99	Ken Tischner
	106	SE	8	37	30	75	Ward Dasey, Donald Jones, Jerry Liguori, Diane Merkh, Bill Seng
	107	NW	11	18	51	80	Joey Little, Len Little
	107	NE	9	8	70	87	Joey Little, Len Little
	107	CW	7	25	55	87	Len Little, Bill Murphy, Naomi Murphy
Browns Mills	107	CE	7	16	52	75	Len Little
	107	SW	4	32	33	69	Len Little
	107	SE	6	30	37	73	Len Little
	108	NW	6	14	61	81	Joey Little, Len Little
	108	NE	8	21	38	67	Daniel Lane, Jerry Liguori, Robert Olthoff, Don Sutherland
	108	CW	3	10	71	84	Len Little
Whiting	108	CE	10	17	41	68	Tom Boyle, Dan Lane, Jerry Liguori, Robert Olthoff, Donald Sutherland
	108	SW	7	16	41	64	Jerry Liguori, Bob Olthoff, Don Sutherland, Jane Sutherland
	108	SE	9	24	29	62	Daniel Lane, Jerry Liguori, Robert Olthoff, Don Sutherland
	109	NW	10	40	25	75	Jerry Liguori, Bob Olthoff, Don Sutherland
	109	NE	7	23	25	55	Jerry Liguori, Robert Olthoff, Don Sutherland, Alex Tongas
	109	CW	10	13	32	55	Lois Morris, Robert Olthoff, Don Sutherland, Albert Weber
Keswick Grove	109	CE	7	16	34	57	Robert Olthoff, Ray Steelman, Don Sutherland,
	109	SW	6	24	28	58	Jerry Liguori, Bill Seng, Don Sutherland, Jane Sutherland
	109	SE	15	29	28	72	Tom Boyle, Maryellen Boyle, Jerry Liguori
	110	NW	7	21	34	62	George Carty, Virginia Carty, Christopher Claus, Lynn Hunt, Robert Olthoff, Betty Shemella, Ted Shemella, Cynthia Smith, Don Sutherland, Jane Sutherland, Brian Vernachio
	110	NE	17	21	37	75	Barbara Brozyna, Nicole Dieckmann, Don Sutherland, Fred Lesser, Brian Vernachio
	110	CW	6	22	30	58	Lynn Hunt, Robert Olthoff, Jackie Parker, Keith Parker, Betty Shemella, Ted Shemella, Don Sutherland, Brian Vernachio
Toms River	110	CE	2	21	24	47	Robert Olthoff, Kathy Pascale, Don Sutherland
	110	SW	13	26	43	82	Tom Boyle, Maryellen Boyle, Nancy Eriksen, Don Sutherland, Jane Sutherland
	110	SE	12	22	34	68	Jerry Liguori, Robert Olthoff, Bill Seng, Don Sutherland
	111	NW	12	24	41	77	Barbara Brozyna, Nicole Dieckmann, Fred Lesser, Alex Tongas, Brian Vernachio

Topographic Map Name	Topographic Map Number	Block Location	Possible	Probable	Confirmed	Total Breeding	Observers
	111	CW	13	22	20	55	Vince Elia, Robert Olthoff, Jackie Parker, Keith Parker, Don Sutherland
	111	SW	6	16	14	36	Phil Misseldine, Alex Tongas
Seaside Park	112	SW	13	18	33	64	Sheryl Forte
	112	SE	13	21	55	89	Sheryl Forte
	113	CW	14	37	9	60	Nick Pulcinella
	113	CE	24	9	8	41	Nick Pulcinella
Marcus Hook	113	SW	7	20	59	86	Sheryl Forte
	113	SE	19	26	10	55	Sandy Sherman
	114	NW	14	20	11	45	John Miller, Joan Walsh
	114	NE	6	17	12	35	Joan Walsh
Bridgeport	114	CW	13	19	22	54	Eva Cassel, Robert Cassel
	114	CE	21	23	15	59	Edward Manners
	114	SW	33	4	5	42	Patricia Brundage
	114	SE	23	38	13	74	Edward Manners
Woodbury	115	NW	20	6	50	76	Mary Blasko
	115	NE	9	10	36	55	Sandra Keller
	115	CW	16	9	37	62	Mary Blasko
	115	CE	28	1	10	39	Lynn Varnum
	115	SW	10	12	32	54	Mike Hannisian, Mike DeLozier, Susan DeLozier
	115	SE	10	24	19	53	James Merritt
Runnemede	116	NW	21	10	17	48	Sandra Amos
	116	NE	9	20	42	71	Claire Campbell
	116	CW	15	15	27	57	Sandra Amos
	116	CE	32	0	3	35	Michael R. O'Brien
	116	SW	26	16	24	66	Megan Edwards
	116	SE	39	0	7	46	Michael R. O'Brien
Clementon	117	NW	1	34	36	71	Philip Warren
	117	NE	8	23	23	54	Ward Dasey, Diane Merkh
	117	CW	24	17	30	71	Douglas Kibbe, Karenne Snow
	117	CE	12	18	36	66	Tom Wilson
	117	SW	13	16	14	43	Karenne Snow
	117	SE	5	14	53	72	Tom Wilson
Medford Lakes	118	NW	0	7	28	35	Doris Boyd, Howard Boyd, Ken Tischner, August Sexauer
	118	NE	0	8	21	29	Doris Boyd, Howard Boyd, Joseph DeCanio
	118	CW	5	30	12	47	August Sexauer
	118	CE	17	20	12	49	Paul Kerlinger
	118	SW	17	33	35	85	Ward Dasey
	118	SE	8	29	8	45	Paul Kerlinger
Indian Mills	119	NW	13	34	8	55	Don Jones
	119	NE	13	22	8	43	Don Jones
	119	CW	14	6	8	28	Jerry Liguori, Bill Seng
	119	CE	22	9	30	61	Jerry Liguori, Bill Seng
	119	SW	13	28	29	70	Ward Dasey, Jerry Liguori, Diane Merkh, Bill Seng
	119	SE	8	31	33	72	Edgar Bruder, Douglas Kibbe
Chatsworth	120	NW	22	21	10	53	Doris McGovern
	120	NE	5	10	17	32	Jerry Liguori
	120	CW	7	13	20	40	Jerry Liguori

Topographic Map Name	Topographic Map Number	Block Location	Possible	Probable	Confirmed	Total Breeding	Observers
	120	CE	2	5	22	29	Jerry Liguori
	120	SW	27	31	13	71	Jerry Liguori, Frank Windfelder
	120	SE	19	7	9	35	Ed Bruder
Woodmansie	121	NW	15	16	14	45	Tom Boyle, Nerses Kazanjian, Susan Phelon, Bill Seng, Bob Simansky, Don Sutherland
	121	NE	8	20	15	43	Brian Vernachio
	121	CW	9	24	24	57	Tom Boyle, Steven Kerr, Bob Olthoff, Bill Seng, Don Sutherland, Dave Sutton
	121	CE	8	31	29	68	Tom Boyle, Mike Carle, Steven Kerr, Jerry Liguori, Robert Olthoff, Bill Seng, Don Sutherland, Dave Sutton Womer
	121	SW	12	31	16	59	Tom Boyle, Jerry Liguori, Bob Olthoff, Bill Seng
	121	SE	15	22	29	66	Tom Boyle, Mike Carle, Jerry Liguori, Robert Olthoff, Bill Seng, Don Sutherland
Brookville	122	NW	12	26	26	64	Nicole Dieckmann, Robert Olthoff, Brian Vernachio
	122	NE	22	28	27	77	Tom Boyle, Nicole Dieckmann, Robert Olthoff, Susan Phelon, Don Sutherland, Brian Vernachio
	122	CW	31	17	36	84	Jackie Parker, Keith Parker
	122	CE	22	20	17	59	Jackie Parker, Keith Parker, Bill Seng
	122	SW	15	37	36	88	Al Majewski, Bill Seng
	123	NW	4	10	12	26	Phil Misseldine, Alex Tongas
Forked River	123	CW	9	19	16	44	Phil Misseldine, Alex Tongas
	123	SW	10	17	26	53	Fred Lesser, Phil Misseldine, Robert Olthoff, Ray Steelman, Don Sutherland, Alex Tongas
	124	SE	6	10	36	52	Doug Kibbe, Sheryl Forte
	125	NW	7	12	43	62	Sheryl Forte
	125	NE	10	15	58	83	Sheryl Forte
Barnegat Light	125	CW	12	9	52	73	Sheryl Forte
	125	CE	10	23	37	70	Sheryl Forte
	125	SW	22	10	41	73	Doug Kibbe, Sheryl Forte
Wilmington South	125	SE	9	16	48	73	Doug Kibbe, Sheryl Forte
Penns Grove	126	NW	7	19	42	68	Sheryl Forte
	126	NE	9	19	44	72	Sheryl Forte
	126	CW	13	16	48	77	Scott Edwards, Sheryl Forte
	126	CE	13	17	39	69	Joe Usewicz, Sheryl Forte
	126	SW	11	16	42	69	Sheryl Forte, Flora Woessner
	126	SE	11	25	38	74	Sheryl Forte, Flora Woessner, Louise Zemaitis
Woodstown	127	NW	13	22	23	58	Scott Stepanski
	127	NE	13	10	32	55	Scott Stepanski
	127	CW	14	5	2	21	Mike DeLozier, Susan Preiksat
	127	CE	12	6	1	19	Joan Walsh
	127	SW	11	19	29	59	Louise Zemaitis
	127	SE	16	26	28	70	Louise Zemaitis
Pitman West	128	NE	14	15	14	43	Joan Walsh
	128	NW	18	12	23	53	Joe Usewicz
	128	CW	13	27	33	73	Sandra Sherman
	128	CE	11	31	31	73	Sandra Sherman
	128	SW	0	33	7	40	Judith Siverson

Topographic Map Name	Topographic Map Number	Block Location	Possible	Probable	Confirmed	Total Breeding	Observers
	128	SE	0	32	6	38	Judith Siverson
Pitman East	129	NW	29	11	19	59	Megan Edwards
	129	NE	26	10	16	52	Megan Edwards
	129	CW	24	21	29	74	Chris Walters
	129	CE	23	23	24	70	Chris Walters
	129	SW	17	27	34	78	Erica Brendel
	129	SE	12	21	35	68	Ed Fingerhood
Williamstown	130	NW	2	29	54	85	Ken Tischner
	130	NE	0	18	45	63	Ken Tischner
	130	CW	19	11	16	46	Claire Campbell, Karenne Snow
	130	CE	6	34	43	83	Jerry Liguori, Bill Seng, Ken Tischner
	130	SW	10	25	16	51	Vince Elia
	130	SE	4	36	13	53	Jerry Liguori, Bill Seng
Hammonton	131	NW	13	33	40	86	Ward Dasey
	131	NE	4	21	15	40	Ward Dasey, Diane Merkh
	131	CW	12	19	12	43	Bill Seng
	131	CE	6	22	8	36	Tom Baily, Ward Dasey
	131	SW	5	25	26	56	Ward Dasey, Diane Merkh
	131	SE	15	22	33	70	Sandra Sherman
Atsion	132	NW	11	20	25	56	Ward Dasey, Jerry Liguori, Diane Merkh, Bill Seng
	132	NE	5	33	31	69	Ed Bruder
	132	CW	8	23	13	44	Jerry Liguori
	132	CE	20	7	7	34	Matthew Pettigrew
	132	SW	11	32	27	70	Jerry Liguori
	132	SE	21	13	7	41	Douglas Kibbe, Matthew Pettigrew
Jenkins	133	NW	7	13	22	42	Alan Brady, Sally Brady, Don Jones
	133	NE	9	14	32	55	Jerry Liguori
	133	CW	3	30	16	49	Jerry Liguori, Bill Seng
	133	CE	1	13	1	15	Jerry Liguori, Bill Seng
	133	SW	3	31	5	39	Jerry Liguori, Bill Seng
	133	SE	2	29	5	36	Jerry Liguori, Bill Seng
Oswego Lake	134	NW	9	10	8	27	Jerry Liguori, Bill Seng
	134	NE	14	17	30	61	Mike Casper, Lynn Hunt, Jerry Liguori, Robert Olthoff, Bill Seng, Don Sutherland, Joselson
	134	CW	16	16	36	68	Mike Casper, Lynn Hunt, Robert Olthoff, Don Sutherland
	134	CE	21	13	31	65	Dave Sibley, Joan Walsh, Louise Zemaitis
	134	SW	20	26	18	64	Mike Casper, Joan Ferrante, Lynn Hunt, Jerry Liguori, Robert Olthoff, Bill Seng, Don Sutherland
	134	SE	12	17	32	61	Joan Walsh, Louise Zemaitis
West Creek	135	NW	11	37	30	78	Robert Olthoff, Bill Seng
	135	NE	6	4	12	22	Jerry Liguori, Bill Seng
	135	CW	13	38	36	87	Fred Lesser, Al Majewski, Robert Olthoff, Don Sutherland
	135	CE	4	6	13	23	Jerry Liguori, Bill Seng
	135	SW	16	11	17	44	Vince Elia, Bill Seng
	135	SE	6	5	9	20	Jerry Liguori, Bill Seng

Topographic Map Name	Topographic Map Number	Block Location	Possible	Probable	Confirmed	Total Breeding	Observers
Ship Bottom	137	NE	6	19	47	72	Rob Blye, Sheryl Forte, Doug Kibbe
	137	CE	8	13	40	61	Sheryl Forte, Christine Githens
	137	SE	18	5	18	41	Sheryl Forte, Doug Kibbe
	138	NW	12	13	49	74	Rob Blye, Sheryl Forte, Doug Kibbe
	138	NE	14	16	53	83	Sheryl Forte, Doug Kibbe
	138	CW	5	10	36	51	Sheryl Forte
Delaware City	138	CE	10	20	43	73	Sheryl Forte, Matthew Pettigrew
	138	SW	5	19	42	66	Sheryl Forte
	138	SE	11	22	36	69	Sheryl Forte
Salem	139	NW	9	15	45	69	Sheryl Forte Buren
	139	NE	7	19	42	68	Sheryl Forte, Rich Kane, Paul Kerlinger, Louise Zemaitis
	139	CW	15	24	43	82	Sheryl Forte, Matthew Pettigrew
	139	CE	15	28	35	78	Sheryl Forte, Rich Kane, Paul Kerlinger, Francis Ponti, Louise Zemaitis
	139	SW	4	25	41	70	Scott Edwards, Sheryl Forte
	139	SE	3	15	44	62	Sheryl Forte
Alloway	140	NW	15	14	43	72	Sheryl Forte, Jerry Haag, Louise Zemaitis
	140	NE	7	16	39	62	Jack Mahun, Sheryl Forte
	140	CW	5	18	37	60	Sheryl Forte, Louise Zemaitis
	140	CE	6	20	41	67	Sheryl Forte
	140	SW	8	15	33	56	Sheryl Forte, Paul Taylor
	140	SE	4	31	37	72	Sheryl Forte, Joe Merlino, Paul Taylor
Elmer	141	NW	16	21	11	48	Suzanne McCarthy
	141	NE	13	21	4	38	Suzanne McCarthy
	141	CW	2	10	49	61	Jean Gutsmuth
	141	CE	23	4	16	43	Gary Anderson, Jr.
	141	SW	36	1	11	48	Alan Eastwick, Jean Gutsmuth, Chip Krilowicz
	141	SE	17	13	36	66	Alan Eastwick
Newfield	142	NW	7	20	18	45	Karenne Snow, Scott Stepanski
	142	NE	7	18	24	49	Claire Campbell, Karenne Snow, Scott Stepanski
	142	CW	11	19	11	41	Claire Campbell, Karenne Snow, Scott Stepanski
	142	CE	12	16	8	36	Claire Campbell, Karenne Snow, Scott Stepanski
	142	SW	7	10	33	50	Claire Campbell, Linda Dunne, Pete Dunne, Karenne Snow
	142	SE	7	19	13	39	Claire Campbell, Vince Elia, Karenne Snow, Scott Stepanski
Buena	143	NW	10	25	19	54	Betsy Searight, John Searight
	143	NE	5	22	22	49	Margaret Atack, Jerry Liguori, Betsy Searight, John Searight, Bill Seng
	143	CW	6	24	18	48	Betsy Searight, John Searight
	143	CE	12	22	26	60	Mike Shapiro, Roseanne Shapiro
	143	SW	24	14	18	56	Dan Brill, Betsy Searight, John Searight
	143	SE	17	22	20	59	Mike Shapiro, Roseanne Shapiro
Newtonville	144	NW	4	29	15	48	Jerry Liguori, Bill Seng
	144	NE	5	17	16	38	Vince Elia, Mike Scheffler
	144	CW	13	15	23	51	John Rokita
	144	CE	1	20	22	43	John Peterson, Kathy Peterson
	144	SW	15	33	13	61	Joe Usewicz

Topographic Map Name	Topographic Map Number	Block Location	Possible	Probable	Confirmed	Total Breeding	Observers
	144	SE	15	19	15	49	Heather Green, Bill Seng, Amy Spano
Egg Harbor City	145	NW	10	30	23	63	Jerry Liguori, Bill Seng
	145	NE	22	23	21	66	Ward Dasey, Bill Seng
	145	CW	6	21	49	76	Jack Connor, Jesse Connor, Betsy Searight, John Searight
	145	CE	17	20	25	62	Jack Connor, Jesse Connor
	145	SW	31	12	13	56	Paul Castelli, Jerry Liguori
	145	SE	14	9	43	66	Jack Connor, Jesse Connor
Green Bank	146	NW	13	27	12	52	Ward Dasey, Vince Elia
	146	NE	14	23	17	54	Vince Elia, Jerry Liguori, Bill Seng
	146	CW	9	19	41	69	Jerry Liguori, Bill Seng, Joan Walsh, Louise Zemaitis
	146	CE	22	19	20	61	Jerry Liguori, Bill Seng, Joan Walsh, Louise Zemaitis
	146	SW	11	16	44	71	Jack Connor, Jesse Connor
	146	SE	12	5	4	21	Paul Castelli, Bill Seng
New Gretna	147	NW	24	20	30	74	Lynn Hunt, Robert Olthoff, Don Sutherland, V. Eugene Vivian
	147	NE	10	6	19	35	Dave Sibley, Joan Walsh, Louise Zemaitis
	147	CW	14	15	30	59	Lynn Hunt, Robert Olthoff, Jackie Parker, Keith Parker, Don Sutherland
	147	CE	17	4	13	34	Jerry Liguori, Bill Seng
	147	SW	19	6	12	37	Lynn Hunt, Robert Olthoff, Jackie Parker, Keith Parker, Don Sutherland
	147	SE	0	1	16	17	Sue Bennett
Tuckerton	148	NW	16	4	13	33	Jerry Liguori, Bill Seng
	149	NE	6	9	13	28	Ward Dasey
	150	NW	8	36	22	66	Jay Darling, Pete Dunne, Bert Peterson, Eric Peterson
	150	NE	7	45	32	84	Clay Sutton
	150	CE	5	36	32	73	Clay Sutton
Beach Haven	150	SE	4	33	37	74	Clay Sutton, Pat Sutton
Taylors Bridge	151	NW	7	41	25	73	Vince Elia, Byron Swift
Canton	151	NE	20	19	24	63	Vince Elia, Byron Swift
	151	CW	15	35	22	72	Vince Elia, Byron Swift
	151	CE	11	31	16	58	Vince Elia, Byron Swift
	151	SW	20	31	16	67	Anita Guris, Paul Guris, Byron Swift
	151	SE	23	28	13	64	Anita Guris, Paul Guris
	152	NW	22	11	15	48	Meagan Edwards
Shiloh	152	NE	7	22	22	51	Vince Elia
	152	CW	4	23	24	51	Vince Elia
	152	CE	9	19	17	45	Vince Elia
	152	SW	21	21	20	62	Anita Guris, Paul Guris
	152	SE	8	30	15	53	Vince Elia
	153	NW	4	45	17	66	Clay Sutton, Pat Sutton
Bridgeton	153	NE	7	22	21	50	Vince Elia, Stephen Field
	153	CW	8	42	27	77	Clay Sutton, Pat Sutton
	153	CE	6	19	23	48	Vince Elia
	153	SW	6	38	23	67	Clay Sutton, Pat Sutton

Topographic Map Name	Topographic Map Number	Block Location	Possible	Probable	Confirmed	Total Breeding	Observers
	153	SE	7	23	22	52	Vince Elia
Millville	154	NW	10	27	27	64	Vince Elia, Stephen Field
	154	NE	10	20	31	61	Vince Elia, Stephen Field
	154	CW	18	38	14	70	Steven Kerr
	154	CE	6	27	30	63	Vince Elia, Judith Siverson
	154	SW	14	39	14	67	Steven Kerr
	154	SE	8	20	24	52	Vince Elia
Five Points	155	NW	9	16	20	45	Buster Raff
	155	NE	12	31	20	63	Buster Raff
	155	CW	9	35	9	53	Ted Nichols, Joan Walsh
	155	CE	8	30	18	56	Buster Raff
	155	SW	20	20	33	73	Ted Nichols
	155	SE	7	24	12	43	Jerry Liguori, Bill Seng
Dorothy	156	NW	13	34	12	59	Joe Usewicz
	156	NE	11	22	23	56	Heather Green, Bill Seng, Amy Spano
	156	CW	4	16	26	46	Margaret Atack, Matthew Klewin
	156	CE	9	18	30	57	Andy Krivenko, Bill Seng
	156	SW	1	25	40	66	Margaret Atack Matthew Klewin
	156	SE	14	11	16	41	John Lapolla
Mays Landing	157	NW	16	38	20	74	Jerry Liguori, Joe Mangino
	157	NE	16	13	42	71	Jack Connor, Jesse Connor, Michael R. O'Brien, Betsy Searight, John Searight
	157	CW	15	13	54	82	Jerry Liguori, Joe Mangino
	157	CE	8	13	15	36	Joan Janowitz
	157	SW	23	9	25	57	Bob Blumberg, Bill Seng
	157	SE	10	11	28	49	Ed Bristow, Patricia Bristow
Pleasantville	158	NW	1	5	15	21	Bill Seng
	158	NE	26	27	28	81	Bill Seng, David Sibley, Joan Walsh
	159	CW	22	14	15	51	Joan Janowitz
	158	CE	29	30	25	84	Jerry Liguori, Bill Seng
	158	SW	11	8	36	55	Jerry Liguori, Bill Seng
	158	SE	6	8	38	52	Betsy Searight, John Searight
Oceanville	159	NW	18	6	10	34	Bill Seng
	159	CW	0	18	4	22	Sue Bennett
	161	NW	22	29	5	56	Anita Guris, Paul Guris
	161	NE	20	38	19	77	Anita Guris, Paul Guris
	161	CE	17	11	11	39	Anita Guris, Paul Guris
	162	NW	7	47	19	73	Clay Sutton
Brigantine Inlet	162	NE	2	51	17	70	Clay Sutton
Ben Davis Point	162	CW	6	49	20	75	Clay Sutton, Pat Sutton
	162	CE	2	61	31	94	Clay Sutton, Pat Sutton
	162	SW	7	32	28	67	Clay Sutton, Pat Sutton
Cedarville	162	SE	2	18	70	90	Pete Dunne
	163	NW	9	39	36	84	Mike Fritz
	163	NE	2	61	26	89	Clay Sutton, Pat Sutton
	163	CW	10	35	38	83	Mike Fritz, Clay Sutton
Dividing Creek	163	CE	1	18	60	79	Mike Fritz
	163	SW	8	66	39	113	Clay Sutton, Pat Sutton
	163	SE	1	31	65	97	Pete Dunne

Topographic Map Name	Topographic Map Number	Block Location	Possible	Probable	Confirmed	Total Breeding	Observers
	164	NW	7	52	33	92	Jim Dowdell, Vince Elia, Clay Sutton
	164	NE	3	32	25	60	Vince Elia
	164	CW	11	22	34	67	Vince Elia
Port Elizabeth	164	CE	5	18	21	44	Vince Elia
	164	SW	0	26	68	94	Pete Dunne
	164	SE	9	25	36	70	Vince Elia, Bill Glaser, Mitch Smith, Louise Zemaitis
	165	NW	6	25	30	61	Vince Elia
	165	NE	6	24	32	62	Vince Elia
	165	CW	8	28	38	74	Vince Elia
Tuckahoe	165	CE	16	31	29	76	Paul Kosten, Karen Williams
	165	SW	6	20	34	60	Vince Elia
	165	SE	13	44	13	70	Paul Kosten, Karen Williams, Louise Zemaitis
	166	NW	8	31	16	55	Jerry Liguori, Bill Seng
	166	NE	7	47	16	70	Eric Stiles
	166	CW	7	17	10	34	Dave Jenkins
Marmora	166	CE	20	14	31	65	Michael O'Brien, Mitch Smith, Louise Zemaitis
	166	SW	12	31	12	55	Dave Jenkins
	166	SE	22	17	35	74	Michael O'Brien, Mitch Smith, Louise Zemaitis
	167	NW	30	4	50	84	Lee Ellenberg, Joanne Stiefbold
	167	NE	6	12	40	58	Carolyn LaMountain
Ocean City	167	CW	42	21	11	74	John Williamson
	167	CE	6	7	26	39	Carolyn LaMountain
	167	SW	2	8	33	43	Jeannine Fuscillo
	168	NW	10	10	27	47	Carolyn LaMountain
	169	NE	0	7	20	27	Pete Dunne, Linda Dunne
Atlantic City	169	CE	1	12	0	13	Clay Sutton, Pat Sutton
	170	NW	2	32	56	90	Linda Dunne, Pete Dunne
	170	NE	8	34	36	78	Vince Elia, Clay Sutton
	171	NW	12	23	24	59	Alma Vogels, Earle Vogels
Fortescue	171	NE	9	29	41	79	Vince Elia
Port Norris	171	CW	17	17	17	51	Linda Dunne, Pete Dunne
	171	CE	11	33	15	59	Bill Glaser
Heislerville	172	NW	11	19	51	81	Dave Sibley, Joan Walsh, Louise Zemaitis
	172	NE	21	29	34	84	Paul Kosten, Karen Williams
	172	CW	4	14	30	48	Bill Glaser, Eileen Katz
	172	CE	13	36	41	90	Jeanne Fritz, Michael Fritz
	172	SW	5	48	45	98	Clay Sutton, Pat Sutton
Woodbine	172	SE	10	16	35	61	Chris Bennett, Karen Bennett
	173	NW	13	33	45	91	Jeanne Fritz, Michael Fritz
	173	NE	20	14	30	64	Bette McCarron, Jack McCarron
	173	CW	10	35	35	80	Michael Fritz
	173	CE	5	4	26	35	Jeanne Fritz, Michael Fritz
	173	SW	8	10	26	44	Alma Vogels, Earl Vogels
Sea Isle City	174	NE	18	20	17	55	Bill Glaser
	174	CE	11	25	38	74	Jim Dowdell
	174	SE	12	32	45	89	Jim Dowdell
	175	NW	2	33	56	91	Richard Crossley
	175	NE	9	19	21	49	Chris Bennett, Karen Bennett

Topographic Map Name	Topographic Map Number	Block Location	Possible	Probable	Confirmed	Total Breeding	Observers
	175	CW	9	24	44	77	Jim Dowdell
Rio Grande	175	CE	3	10	29	42	Dave Githens, Mitch Smith, Louise Zemaitis
	175	SW	4	30	53	87	Richard Crossley, Joan Walsh
	175	SE	2	10	36	48	Dave Githens, Mitch Smith, Louise Zemaitis
Stone Harbor	176	NW	7	15	31	53	Alma Vogels, Earle Vogels, Dave Ward
	176	CW	7	15	25	47	Alma Vogels, Earle Vogels, Dave Ward
Avalon	177	NW	3	12	42	57	Vince Elia
	177	NE	14	21	35	70	Keith Seager
	177	CW	5	14	61	80	Thomas Parsons, Karl Lukens
	177	CE	1	16	34	51	Bill Glaser, Dave Sibley, Joan Walsh
Cape May	178	NW	9	10	24	43	Dave Sibley, Joan Walsh

Appendix B

GAZETEER

Absecon .... Atlantic Co.
Allaire SP .... Monmouth Co.
Allamuchy Mountain SP Morris / Sussex / Warren Co.
Allentown .... Monmouth Co.
Alpha Grasslands .... Warren Co.
Alpine Lookout .... Bergen Co.
Amwell .... Hunterdon Co.
Andover .... Sussex Co.
Assunpink WMA .... Monmouth / Mercer Co.
Atlantic City .... Atlantic Co.
Atsion .... Burlington Co.
Avalon .... Cape May Co.
Avon .... Monmouth Co.
Barnegat Inlet .... Ocean Co.
Batsto .... Burlington Co.
Bay Head .... Ocean Co.
Bayonne .... Hudson Co.
Beach Haven Inlet .... Ocean Co.
Beach Haven .... Ocean Co.
Bear Swamp .... Cumberland Co.
Bearfort Mountain .... Passaic Co.
Bearfort Mountain .... Passaic Co.
Belleplain State Forest .... Cape May Co.
Belmar .... Monmouth Co.
Bernardsville .... Somerset Co.
Beverly .... Burlington Co.
Billingsport .... Gloucester Co.
Black River NWR .... Morris Co.
Blackwell Mills .... Somerset Co.
Blairstown .... Warren Co.
Blawenburg .... Somerset Co.
Boonton Reservior .... Morris Co.
Boonton .... Morris Co.
Bordentown .... Burlington Co.
Bound Brook .... Middlesex Co.
Branchville .... Sussex Co.
Brick Township .... Ocean Co.
Bridgeton .... Cumberland Co.
Brielle .... Monmouth Co.
Brigantine Island .... Atlantic Co.
Brigantine NWR .... Atlantic Co.
Bright View Farm .... Burlington Co.
Budd Lake .... Morris Co.
Bull's Island .... Hunterdon Co.
Camden .... Camden Co.
Canistear Reservoir .... Sussex Co.
Cape Island .... Cape May Co.
Cape May Court House .... Cape May Co.
Cape May Point SP .... Cape May Co.
Cape May Point .... Cape May Co.
Cape May .... Cape May Co.
Caven Cove, Jersey City .... Hudson Co.
Celery Farm, Allendale .... Bergen Co.
Centennial Lake-Braddock's Mill .... Burlington Co.
Chatham .... Morris Co.
Chatsworth .... Burlington Co.
Cheesequake SP .... Middlesex Co.
Cherry Hill .... Camden Co.
Cherry Ridge .... Sussex-Passaic Co.
Chester .... Morris Co.
Chimney Rock .... Union Co.
Cinnaminson .... Burlington Co.
Clarkesville .... Burlington Co.
Clinton Reservoir .... Passaic Co.
Clinton Rd., West Milford Twp. .... Passaic Co.
Cold Spring Inlet .... Cape May Co.
Columbus Sod Farm .... Burlington Co.
Columbus .... Burlington Co.
Commonwealth Reservoir .... Essex Co.
Compromise Rd., Mannington Twp. .... Salem Co.
Conasconk Point .... Monmouth Co.
Corbin City WMA .... Atlantic Co.
Corson's Inlet .... Cape May Co.
Croton .... Hunterdon Co.
Culvers Gap .... Sussex Co.
Culvers Lake .... Sussex Co.
Deal .... Monmouth Co.
Delaware Water Gap .... Warren Co.
Dennisville .... Cape May Co.
Denville .... Morris Co.
Dividing Creek .... Cumberland Co.
Duck Pond .... Sussex Co.
Dumont .... Bergen Co.
Dutch Neck .... Mercer Co.
Eagle Rock Reservation .... Essex Co.
East Brunswick .... Middlesex Co.

East Orange ..... Essex Co.
East Point ..... Cumberland Co.
East Rutherford ..... Bergen Co.
Eatontown ..... Monmouth Co.
Edgewater ..... Bergen Co.
Elizabeth ..... Union Co.
Elmer Lake ..... Salem Co.
Elmer ..... Salem Co.
Elsinboro ..... Salem Co.
Englewood ..... Bergen Co.
Erma ..... Cape May Co.
Evesboro ..... Burlington Co.
Fair Haven ..... Monmouth Co.
Fairton ..... Cumberland Co.
Fairview Farm ..... Somerset Co.
Featherbed La., Mannington Twp. ..... Salem Co.
Fishing Creek Marsh ..... Cape May Co.
Five Mile Beach, Wildwood ..... Cape May Co.
Flanders ..... Morris Co.
Flemington Jct ..... Hunterdon Co.
Flemington ..... Hunterdon Co.
Floodgates ..... Gloucester Co.
Florence ..... Burlington Co.
Fort Lee ..... Bergen Co.
Fortescue ..... Cumberland Co.
Fostertown Rd., Lumberton Twp. ..... Burlington Co.
Franklin Lakes ..... Bergen Co.
Freehold ..... Monmouth Co.
Frelinghuysen Twp ..... Warren Co.
Gandy's Beach ..... Cumberland Co.
Garret Mountain ..... Passaic Co.
Gibbsboro ..... Camden Co.
Goshen Landing ..... Cape May Co.
Goshen ..... Cape May Co.
Grassy Sound ..... Cape May Co.
Great Meadows ..... Warren Co.
Great Swamp NWR ..... Morris Co.
Green Pond Mountain ..... Morris Co.
Green Pond ..... Morris Co.
Greenbrook Sanctuary ..... Bergen Co.
Greenwood Lake ..... Passaic Co.
Grovers Mill ..... Mercer Co.
Hackensack Meadows ..... Bergen Co.
Hackensack ..... Bergen Co.
Haddonfield ..... Camden Co.
Hainesport ..... Burlington Co.
Haledon Reservoir ..... Bergen Co.
Halsey ..... Sussex Co.
Hamilton Square ..... Mercer Co.
Hancock's Bridge ..... Salem Co.
Harbourton ..... Mercer Co.
Hardwick ..... Warren Co.
Harmony ..... Warren Co.
Harvey Cedars ..... Ocean Co.
Hawthorne ..... Bergen Co.
Hay Neck ..... Cumberland Co.
Hazlet ..... Monmouth Co.
Heislerville ..... Cumberland Co.
Hereford Inlet ..... Cape May Co.
Hidden Valley Ranch, Cape Island ..... Cape May Co.
Higbee Beach ..... Cape May Co.
High Point State Park ..... Sussex Co.
Hillsborough ..... Somerset Co.
HMEC ..... Bergen Co.
Hoboken ..... Hudson Co.
Holgate ..... Ocean Co.
Holmdel ..... Monmouth Co.
Hopatcong ..... Sussex Co.
Hopewell ..... Mercer Co.
Island Beach SP ..... Ocean Co.
Island Beach ..... Ocean Co.
Jake's Landing ..... Cape May Co.
Jarvis Sound ..... Cape May Co.
Jersey City ..... Hudson Co.
Jockey Hollow ..... Morris Co.
Johnson Park ..... Middlesex Co.
Keansburg ..... Monmouth Co.
Kearny Marsh ..... Hudson Co.
Kenvil ..... Morris Co.
Kingwood ..... Hunterdon Co
Knowlton ..... Warren Co.
Kuser Bog ..... Sussex Co.
Lafayette ..... Sussex Co.
Lake Como ..... Monmouth Co.
Lake Girard ..... Sussex Co.
Lake Mohawk ..... Sussex Co.
Lake Musconetcong ..... Morris Co./Sussex Co.
Lake Parsippany ..... Morris Co.
Lake Watchung ..... Somerset Co.
Lakehurst ..... Ocean Co.
Lambertville ..... Hunterdon Co.
Lavallette ..... Ocean Co.
Lebanon ..... Hunterdon Co.
Lebanon State Forest ..... Hunterdon Co.
Leonardo ..... Monmouth Co.
Liberty SP, Jersey City ..... Hudson Co.
Lincoln Park ..... Morris Co.
Linden ..... Union Co.
Lindenwold ..... Camden Co.
Linwood ..... Atlantic Co.
Little Beach Island ..... Ocean Co.
Little Egg Inlet ..... Atlantic / Ocean Co.
Long Beach Island ..... Ocean Co.
Long Branch ..... Monmouth Co.
Longport ..... Atlantic Co.
Loveladies ..... Ocean Co.
Lumberton ..... Burlington Co.
Lummis Mill Pond ..... Cumberland Co.

Lyndhurst	Bergen Co.
Lyons	Somerset Co.
Madison	Morris Co.
Malaga Lake	Atlantic Co.
Manahawkin	Ocean Co.
Manalapan	Monmouth Co.
Manasquan Inlet	Ocean / Monmouth Co.
Mannington Marsh	Salem Co.
Mantoloking	Ocean Co.
Mantua Township	Gloucester Co.
Marlton	Burlington Co.
Marshalltown	Salem Co.
Mauricetown	Cumberland Co.
Medford	Burlington Co.
Mehrhoff Pond	Bergen Co.
Mendham	Morris Co.
Merrill Creek Reservoir	Warren Co.
Metuchen	Middlesex Co.
Mickleton	Gloucester Co.
Millington	Somerset Co.
Monmouth Beach	Monmouth Co.
Montclair	Essex Co.
Moore's Beach	Cumberland Co.
Moorestown	Burlington Co.
Morristown	Morris Co.
Mount Holly	Burlington Co.
Mt. Laurel	Camden Co.
Mt. Olive	Morris Co.
Mt. Pleasant	Warren Co.
Mt. Tabor	Morris Co.
Mt. Horeb	Somerset Co.
NAFEC	Atlantic Co.
Naval Weapons Station Earle	Monmouth Co.
New Brunswick	Middlesex Co.
New Lisbon	Burlington Co.
New Sharon	Monmouth Co.
Newark	Essex Co.
Newark Meadows	Essex Co.
Newfoundland	Passaic Co.
Newton	Sussex Co.
Norbury's Landing	Cape May Co.
North Arlington	Bergen Co.
North Cape May	Cape May Co.
North Wildwood	Cape May Co.
Northvale	Bergen Co.
Norwood Scout Camp	Bergen Co.
Nummy Island	Cape May Co.
Oakland	Bergen Co.
Ocean City	Cape May Co.
Ocean Drive	Cape May Co.
Oceanville	Atlantic Co.
Ogdensburg	Sussex Co.
Old Mine Road	Warren Co.
Old Tappan Reservoir	Bergen Co.
Oldman's Creek	Gloucester Co.
Ong's Hat	Burlington Co.
Oradell	Bergen Co.
Oradell Reservoir	Bergen Co.
Orange	Essex Co.
Overpeck Creek	Bergen Co.
Overpeck Park	Bergen Co.
Palisades	Bergen Co.
Palmyra	Burlington Co.
Paulinskill Lake	Sussex Co.
Paulinskill Marsh	Sussex Co.
Pedricktown	Salem / Gloucester Co.
Pennington	Mercer Co.
Pennsauken	Camden Co.
Pequannock Watershed	Sussex / Passaic Co.
Petty's Island	Camden Co.
Phillipsburg	Warren Co.
Picatinny Arsenal	Morris Co.
Pine Brook	Morris Co.
Pine Lake	Burlington Co.
Pine Valley	Camden Co.
Piscataway	Middlesex Co.
Plainfield	Union Co.
Plainsboro	Middlesex Co.
Pleasantville	Atlantic Co.
Point Breeze	Hunterdon Co.
Point Pleasant	Ocean Co.
Pond Creek Marsh	Cape May Co.
Princeton	Mercer Co.
Quaker Bridge	Burlington Co.
Raccoon Creek	Gloucester Co.
Raccoon Ridge	Warren Co.
Ramapo Mt	Bergen Co.
Ramsey	Bergen Co.
Rancocas Creek	Burlington Co.
Rancocas Nature Center	Burlington Co.
Rancocas Woods	Burlington Co.
Raritan Arsenal, Bonhamtown	Middlesex Co.
Rattlesnake Mt	Sussex Co.
Reed's Beach	Cape May Co.
Ridgewood	Bergen Co.
Rifle Camp Park	Passaic Co.
Ringwood	Passaic Co.
Rio Grande	Cape May Co.
Riverton	Burlington Co.
Rockaway	Morris Co.
Rosedale Park	Mercer Co.
Round Pond	Sussex Co.
Round Valley Reservoir	Hunterdon Co.
Roxbury Township	Morris Co.
Salem	Salem Co.
Salem Cove	Salem Co.
Salem Marsh	Salem Co.
Salem Nuclear Plant	Salem Co.

Sand Brook ... Hunterdon Co.
Sandy Hook ... Monmouth Co.
Sandyston Township ... Sussex Co.
Saw Mill Lake Campground ... Sussex Co.
Schooley's Mountain ... Morris Co.
Scott's Mt ... Warren Co.
Sea Girt ... Monmouth Co.
Sea Isle City ... Cape May Co.
Sea Bright ... Monmouth Co.
Sergeantsville ... Hunterdon Co.
Seaside Heights ... Ocean Co.
Seaside Park ... Ocean Co.
Seven Mile Beach, Avalon ... Cape May Co.
Shark River Inlet ... Monmouth Co.
Sharptown ... Salem Co.
Shellbay Landing ... Cape May Co.
Sherman-Hoffman Sanctuary ... Somerset Co.
Shrewsbury ... Monmouth Co.
Smoke Rise ... Morris Co.
Somerville ... Somerset Co.
Sommer's Beach ... Atlantic Co.
South Amboy ... Middlesex Co.
South Cape May Meadows ... Cape May Co.
South Plainfield ... Middlesex Co.
Sparta Mountain ... Sussex Co.
Spring Lake ... Monmouth Co.
Spruce Run Reservoir ... Hunterdon Co.
Stanton ... Hunterdon Co.
Stanton Station ... Hunterdon Co.
Stewartsville ... Warren Co.
Stokes State Forest ... Sussex Co.
Stone Harbor ... Cape May Co.
Sunfish Pond ... Warren Co.
Sunrise Mountain ... Sussex Co.
Supawna Meadows ... Salem Co.
Surf City ... Ocean Co.
Swartswood Lake ... Sussex Co.
Tarkiln Pond ... Cape May Co.
Taylor's Refuge ... Burlington Co.
Tenafly ... Bergen Co.
Tewkesbury Township ... Hunterdon Co.
Thompson Grove Park ... Monmouth Co.
Thompson Park ... Monmouth Co.
Thompson's Beach ... Cumberland Co.
Tillman's Ravine ... Sussex Co.
Tom's River ... Ocean Co.
Tourne Park ... Morris Co.
Trenton ... Mercer Co.
Trenton Marsh ... Mercer Co.
Troy Meadows ... Morris Co.
Tuckahoe ... Cape May Co.
Tuckahoe WMA ... Cape May Co.
Tuckerton ... Ocean Co.
Turkey Point ... Cumberland Co.
Turkey Swamp Park ... Monmouth Co.
Upper Montclair ... Essex Co.
Upper Saddle River ... Bergen Co.
Vernon Crossing Marsh ... Sussex Co.
Vernon ... Sussex Co.
Villas ... Cape May Co.
Vincentown ... Burlington Co.
Vineland ... Cumberland Co.
Voorhees ... Camden Co.
Wallkill NWR ... Sussex Co.
Wanaque Reservoir ... Passaic Co.
Watchung Reservation ... Union Co.
Wawayanda State Park ... Sussex / Passaic Co.
Weehawken ... Hudson Co.
Week's Landing ... Cape May Co.
Well's Mills ... Ocean Co.
West Cape May ... Cape May Co.
West Englewood ... Bergen Co.
West Milford ... Passaic Co.
West Orange ... Essex Co.
West Paterson ... Passaic Co.
Wharton State Forest ... Burlington / Atlantic / Camden Co.
Whitesbog ... Burlington Co.
Whitesville ... Ocean Co.
Whiting ... Ocean Co.
Whittingham WMA ... Sussex Co.
Wildwood ... Cape May Co.
Wildwood Crest ... Cape May Co.
Wolf Lake ... Sussex Co.
Woodbine ... Cape May Co.
Woodcliff Lake ... Bergen Co.
Woodstown ... Salem Co.
Wreck Pond ... Monmouth Co.
Wyckoff ... Bergen Co.
Yard's Creek Reservoir ... Warren Co.

Appendix C

Plant Names

Coniferous Trees

Atlantic white cedar .... *Chamaecyparis thyoides*
Red cedar .... *Juniperus virginiana*
spruce .... *Picea sp.*
Eastern hemlock .... *Tsuga canadensis*

Deciduous Trees

Sycamore .... *Platanus occidentalis*
American Elm .... *Ulmus americana*

Shrubs

laurel .... *Kalmia sp.*
rhododendron .... *Rhododendron sp.*

Herbs

cattail .... *Typha sp.*
Phragmites (reeds) .... *Phragmites australis*
Spartina .... *Spartina alternifolia*

Lichens

Usnea sp.

Bibliography

Reference List

Andrle, R. F. 1971. Range extension of the Golden-crowned Kinglet in New York. *Wilson Bulletin* 83:313-16.

Austin, J. E., and M. R. Miller. 1995. Northern Pintail (*Anas acuta*) . In *The birds of North America*, eds. A. Poole and F. Gill, No. 163. Philadelphia: Academy of Natural Sciences Washington, D.C.: The American Ornithologists Union.

Bacinski, P. 1980. North central Jersey Highlands: Breeding bird survey 1979. *Urner Field Observer* 17:26-33.

Baird, P. H. 1994. Black-legged Kittiwake (*Rissa tridactyla*). In *The birds of North America*, eds. A. Poole and F. Gill, No. 92. Philadelphia: Academy of Natural Sciences; Washington, D.C.: The American Ornithologists Union.

Barber, R. 1985. Little Stint at Brigantine National Wildlife Refuge, New Jersey. *Cassinia* 61:77-78.

Bardon, K., and P. Lehman. 1998. First documented record of Thayer's Gull in New Jersey. *Records of New Jersey Birds* 24:2-4.

Beason, R. C. 1995. Horned Lark (*Eremophila alpestris*). In *The birds of North America*, eds. A. Poole and F. Gill, No. 195. Philadelphia: Academy of Natural Sciences; Washington, D.C.: The American Ornithologists Union.

Bent. A. C. 1921. *Life histories of North American gulls and terns*. Washington, D. C.: United States National Museum Bulletin, no. 113.

—. 1923. *Life histories of North American wild fowl.* Washington, D. C.: United States National Museum Bulletin, no. 126.

—. 1926. *Life histories of North American marsh birds.* Washington, D. C.: United States National Museum Bulletin, no. 135.

—. 1950. *Life Histories of North American wagtails, shrikes, vireos, and their allies.* Washington, D. C.: United States National Museum Bulletin, no. 197.

—. 1953. *Life histories of North American wood warblers.* Washington, D. C.: United States National Museum Bulletin, no. 1203.

Benzinger, J. 1987. Northern Saw-whet Owls in north Jersey Highlands. *Records Of New Jersey Birds* 13:2.

—. 1994. Hemlock declines and breeding birds II: Effects of habitat change. *Records of New Jersey Birds* 20:34-51.

Benzinger, J., P. Bacinski, D. Miranda, and T. Bosakowski. 1988. Breeding birds of the Pequannock Watershed, 1986-87. *Records of New Jersey Birds* 14:22-27.

Benzinger, J., and S. Angus. 1992. Breeding birds of the northern New Jersey Highlands. *Records of New Jersey Birds* 18:22-41.

Black, I. H. 1972. Northern New Jersey Highlands breeding bird survey 1971, Part II. *Urner Field Observer* 14:22-28.

—. 1975. Summer season field notes 1975 (Region 2). *Records of New Jersey Birds* 1, no. 1:5.

—. 1977. Summer season field notes 1977 (Region 2). *Records of New Jersey Birds* 3:196.

Bosakowski, T. 1994. Landstat reveals negative effect of forest fragmentaion on Barred Owl distribution. *Records of New Jersey Birds* 20:66-70.

Bosakowski, T., R. Kane, and D. G. Smith. 1989. Status and management of Long-eared Owl in New Jersey. *Records of New Jersey Birds* 15:42-46.

Boyajian, N. 1973. Hudson-St. Lawrence region, August 1973. *American Birds* 27: 753.

Boyle, W. J. 1986. *A guide to bird finding in New Jersey*. Newark, N.J.: Rutgers University Press.

Brady, A. 1988. Possible presence of an Anarctic Skua in New Jersey waters. *Cassinia* 87:7-9.

—. 1991. Major offshore nocturnal migration of Blackpoll Warblers, herons, and shorebirds. *Cassinia* 64:28-29.

Brauning, D. W. 1992a. Ring-necked Pheasant (*Phasianus colchicus*). In *Atlas of breeding birds in Pennsylvania*, ed. D. W. Brauning, pp. 112-13. Pittsburgh: University of Pittsburgh Press.

—. 1992b. Spotted Sandpiper (*Actitis macularia*). In *Atlas of breeding birds in Pennsylvania*, ed. D. W. Brauning, pp. 136-37. Pittsburgh: University of Pittsburgh Press.

—. 1992c. Upland Sandpiper (*Bartramia longicauda*). In *Atlas of breeding birds in Pennsylvania*, ed. D. W. Brauning, pp. 138-39. Pittsburgh: University of Pittsburgh Press.

Briskie, J. V. 1994. Least Flycatcher (*Empidonax minimus*). In *The birds of North America*, eds. A. Poole and F. Gill, No. 99. Philadelphia: Academy of Natural Sciences; Washington, D.C.: The American Ornithologists Union.

Brooks, S. C. 1927. Northern Hawk Owl at New Brunswick. *Auk* 44:251-52.

Brown, C. R., and M. B. Brown. 1995. Cliff Swallow (*Hirundo pyrrhonota*). In *The birds of North America*, eds. A. Poole and F. Gill, No. 149. Philadelphia: Academy of Natural Sciences; Washington, D.C.: The American Ornithologists Union.

Buckman, J. 1978. Attempted Pine Siskin nesting in Wyckoff. *Records of New Jersey Birds (New Jersey Audubon Supplement)* 4, no. 4:24.

Bull, E. L., and J. E. Jackson. 1995. Pileated Woodpecker (*Dryocopus pileatus*). In *The birds of North America*, eds. A. Poole and F. Gill, No. 148. Philadelphia: Academy of Natural Sciences; Washington, D.C.: The American Ornithologists Union.

Bull, J. 1964. *Birds of the New York area.* New York: Harper and Row Publishers.

Bull, J. 1974. *Birds of New York State.* Ithaca, New York: Comstock Publishing Associates.

Burger, J. 1996. Laughing Gull (*Larus atricilla*). In *The birds of North America*, eds. A. Poole and F. Gill, No. 225. Philadelphia: Academy of Natural Sciences; Washington, D.C.: The American Ornithologists Union.

Burger, J., J. Jones, and M. Gochfeld. 1985. Caspian Tern nesting in New Jersey. *Records of New Jersey Birds* 10:74-76.

Burger, J., M. Gochfeld, and F. Lesser. 1993. Attempted nesting of Brown Pelican in New Jersey. *Records of New Jersey Birds* 18:78-79.

Butler, R. W. 1992. Great Blue Heron (*Ardea herodias*). In *The birds of North America*, eds. A. Poole, P. Stettenheim, and F. Gill, No. 25. Philadelphia: Academy of Natural Sciences; Washington, D.C.: The American Ornithologists Union.

Cabe, P. R. 1993. European Starling (*Sturnus vulgaris*). In *The birds of North America*, eds. A. Poole and F. Gill, No. 48. Philadelphia: Academy of Natural Sciences; Washington, D.C.: The American Ornithologists Union.

Cannings, R. J. 1993. Northern Saw-whet Owl (*Aegolius acadicus*). In *The birds of North America*, eds. A. Poole and F. Gill, No. 42. Philadelphia: Academy of Natural Sciences; Washington, D.C.: The American Ornithologists Union.

Cant, G. B. Wilson's Plover again nesting in New Jersey. *Proceedings Linnean Society* 52-53:130-31.

Carey, M. D., E. Burhans, and D. A. Nelson. 1994. Field Sparrow (*Spizella pusilla*). In *The birds of North America*, eds. A. Poole and F. Gill, No. 103. Philadelphia: Academy of Natural Sciences; Washington, D.C.: The American Ornithologists Union.

Chapman, F. M. 1939. *Handbook of birds of Eastern North America.* New York: D. Appleton-Century Co.

Choate, E. A. 1966. Field notes (Region 5). *New Jersey Nature News* 11: 187-90.

Cimprich, D. A., and F. R. Moore. 1995. Gray Catbird (*Dumetella carolinensis*). In *The birds of North America*, eds. A. Poole and F. Gill, No. 167. Philadelphia: Academy of Natural Sciences; Washington, D.C.: The American Ornithologists Union.

Collins, B. R., and K. H. Anderson. 1994. *Plant communities of New Jersey: A study of landscape diversity.* New Brunswick, N.J.: Rutgers University Press.

Colvin, B. A., and P. L. Hegdal. 1995. Barn Owl (*Tyto alba*). In *Living resources of the Delaware estuary*, eds. L. E. Dove and R. M. Nyman, pp. 401-8. The Delaware Estuary Program.

Confer, J. 1988. Downy Woodpecker (*Picoides pubescens*). In *The Atlas of breeding birds in New York State*, eds. R. F. Andrle and J. R. Carroll, pp. 232-33. Ithaca: Cornell University Press.

Confer, J. L. 1992. Golden-winged Warbler (*Vermivora chrysoptera*). In *The birds of North America*, eds. A. Poole, P. Stettenheim, and F. Gill, No. 20. Philadelphia: Academy of Natural Sciences; Washington, D.C.: The American Ornithologists Union.

Conn, R. 1996. Chimney Rock and early hawk watching in the Watchungs. *Records of New Jersey Birds* 21:66-67.

Conway, C. J. 1995. Virginia Rail (*Rallus limicola*). In *The birds of North America*, eds. A. Poole and F. Gill, No. 173. Philadelphia: Academy of Natural Sciences; Washington, D.C.: The American Ornithologists Union.

Crocoll, S. T. 1994. Red-shouldered Hawk (*Buteo lineatus*). In *The birds of North America*, eds. A. Poole and F. Gill, No. 107. Philadelphia: Academy of Natural Sciences; Washington, D.C.: The American Ornithologists Union.

Crossley, R. 1997. Black-chinned Hummingbird (*Archilochus alexandri*): First New Jersey record. *Records of New Jersey Birds* 23:53-54.

Cruickshank, A. D. 1942. *Birds around New York City*. New York: The American Museum of Natural History, No. 13.

Custer, T. W., and R. G. Osborn. 1978. Feeding habitat used by colonially-breeding herons, egrets, and ibises in North Carolina. *Auk* 95:733-43.

Dasey, W. 1993. Summer field notes 1992 (Region 4). *Records of New Jersey Birds* 18:86-88.

Davis, W. E., Jr. 1993. Black-crowned Night-Heron (*Nycticorax nycticorax*) . In *The birds of North America*, eds. A. Poole and F. Gill, No. 74. Philadelphia: Academy of Natural Sciences; Washington, D.C.: The American Ornithologists Union.

Davis, W. E., Jr., and A. Kushlan. 1994. Green Heron (*Butorides virescens*). In *The birds of North America*, eds. A. Poole and F. Gill, No. 129. Philadelphia: Academy of Natural Sciences; Washington, D.C.: The American Ornithologists Union.

Debenedictus, P. 1995. Red Crossbill, one through eight. *Birding* 27:495-501.

DeJong, M. J. 1996. Northern Rough-winged Swallow (*Stelgidopteryx serripennis*). In *The birds of North America*, eds. A. Poole and F. Gill, No. 234. Philadelphia: Academy of Natural Sciences; Washington, D.C.: The American Ornithologists Union.

Dowdell, J., and C. Sutton. 1993. Status and distribution of breeding Red-shouldered Hawks in southern New Jersey. *Records of New Jersey Birds* 19:6-9.

Duffy, K., and P. Kerlinger. 1992. Autumn owl migration at Cape May Point, New Jersey. *Wilson Bulletin* 104:312-20.

Dugger, B. D., K. M. Dugger, and L. H. Fredrickson. 1994. Hooded Merganser (*Lophodytes cucullatus*) . In *The birds of North America*, eds. A. Poole and F. Gill, No. 98. Philadelphia: Academy of Natural Sciences; Washington, D.C.: The American Ornithologists Union.

Dunn, J., and K. Garrett. 1997. *A field guide to warblers of North America*. Boston: Houghton Mifflin.

Dunne, E. H., and D. J. Agro. 1995. Black Tern (*Chlidonias niger*). In *The birds of North America*, eds. A. Poole and F. Gill, No. 147. Philadelphia: Academy of Natural Sciences; Washington, D.C.: The American Ornithologists Union.

Dunne, P. 1978. Wood Stork at Cape May Point. *Records of New Jersey Birds (New Jersey Audubon Supplement)* 4, no. 1:38.

—. 1984. Northern Harrier breeding survey in coastal New Jersey. *Records of New Jersey Birds* 10:2-5.

Dunne, P., and C. Sutton. 1986. Population trends in coastal raptor migrants over ten years of Cape May Point autumn counts. *Records of New Jersey Birds* 12:39-43.

Eaton, S. W. 1988. Acadian Flycatcher (*Empidonax virescens*). In *The atlas of breeding birds in New York State*, eds. R. F. Andrle and J. R. Carroll, pp. 250-51. Ithaca: Cornell University Press.

Eddleman, W. R., R. E. Flores, and M. L. Legare. 1994. Black Rail (*Laterallus jamaicensis*). In *The birds of North America*, eds. A. Poole and F. Gill, No. 123. Philadelphia: Academy of Natural Sciences; Washington, D.C.: The American Ornithologists Union.

Ehrlich, P. R., D. S. Dobkin, and D. Wheye. 1988. *The birders handbook: a field guide to the natural history of North American birds.* New York: Simon and Schuster.

Ellison, W. G. 1992. Blue-gray Gnatcatcher (*Polioptila caerulea*). In *The birds of North America*, eds. A. Poole, P. Stettenheim, and F. Gill, No. 23. Philadelphia: Academy of Natural Sciences; Washington, D.C.: The American Ornithologists Union.

Eynon, A. E. 1939. Western Grebe in New Jersey. *Auk* 56:180-81.

Fables, D., Jr. 1955. *Annotated list of New Jersey birds.* Urner Ornithological Club.

Fahey, P. L. 1979. Spotted Redshank at Brigantine. *Records of New Jersey Birds (New Jersey Audubon Supplement)* 5, no. 1:3.

Farrell, J. H. 1996. Eastern Towhee (*Pipilo erythrophtalmus*) . In *Atlas of the breeding birds of Maryland and the District of Columbia*, ed. S. R. Robbins, pp. 388-89. Pittsburgh: University of Pittsburgh Press.

Fletcher, A. J. 1996. Horned Lark (*Eremophila alpestris*). In *Atlas of the breeding birds of Maryland and the District of Columbia*, ed. S. R. Robbins, pp. 232-33. Pittsburgh: University of Pittsburgh Press.

Forbush, E. H. 1929. *Birds of Massachusetts and other New England states.* Norwood, MA: Norwood Press.

Foy, R. 1981. Yellow-headed Blackbird bandings in New Jersey . *Records of New Jersey Birds* 6:50.

Freiday, D. 1986. Ivory Gull at Liberty State Park. *Records of New Jersey Birds* 12:20.

Frier, J. 1982. Osprey (*Pandion haliaetus*). In *New Jersey's endangered and threatened plants and animals*, ed. W. J. Cromartie, pp. 196-98. Pomona, N. J.: Center for Environmental Research, Stockton State College.

Frohling, R. C. 1950. Studies on Baltimore Oriole nest locations in New Jersey. *Urner Ornithological Club Bulletin* 2:1-18.

Galli, J. 1982. Great Blue Heron (*Ardea herodias*). In *New Jersey's endangered and threatened plants and animals*, ed. W. J. Cromartie, pp. 184-86. Pomona, N. J.: Center for Environmental Research, Stockton State College.

Galli, J., and J. Penkala. 1978. White-faced Ibis in New Jersey. *Records of New Jersey Birds (New Jersey Audubon Supplement)* 4, no. 1:36.

Gehlbach, F. R. 1995. Eastern Screech-Owl (*Otus asio*). In *The birds of North America*, eds. A. Poole and F. Gill, No. 165. Philadelphia: Academy of Natural Sciences; Washington, D.C.: The American Ornithologists Union.

Gibbs, J. P., S. Melvin, and F. A. Reid. 1992. American Bittern (*Botaurus lentiginosus*). In *The birds of North America*, eds. A. Poole, P. Stettenheim, and F. Gill, No. 18. Philadelphia: Academy of Natural Sciences; Washington, D.C.: The American Ornithologists Union.

Gill, F. B. 1961. A Hoary Redpoll specimen for New Jersey. *Wilson Bulletin* 73:388-89.

Giraud, J. P. 1844. *The birds of Long Island.* New York: Wiley and Putnam.

Gochfeld, M., and J. Burger. 1994. Black Skimmer (*Rynchops niger*). In *The birds of North America*, eds. A. Poole and F. Gill, No. 108. Philadelphia: Academy of Natural Sciences; Washington, D.C.: The American Ornithologists Union.

Gochfeld, M., J. Burger, and F. Lesser. 1988. First Royal Tern nest in New Jersey. *Records of New Jersey Birds* 14:66.

Godfrey, W. E. 1986. *The birds of Canada*, rev. ed. Ottawa: National Museums of Canada.

Greenlaw, J. S. 1996. Eastern Towhee (*Pipilo erythrophthalmus*). In *The birds of North America*, eds. A. Poole and F. Gill, No. 262. Philadelphia: Academy of Natural Sciences; Washington, D.C.: The American Ornithologists Union.

Greenstone, E. 1996. Montclair Hawk Watch 1957-1995. *Records of New Jersey Birds* 22:33-34.

Griscom, L. 1923. *Birds of the New York City region.* New York: The American Museum of Natural History, No. 9.

Grubb, T. C., and V. V. Pravosudov. 1994. Tufted Titmouse (*Parus bicolor*). In *The birds of North America*, eds. A. Poole and F. Gill, No. 86. Philadelphia: Academy of Natural Sciences; Washington, D.C.: The American Ornithologists Union.

Haines, R. 1942. Studies of the Long-eared Owl. *Cassinia* 31:12-16.

Hamas, M. J. 1994. Belted Kingfisher (*Ceryle alcyon*). In *The birds of North America*, eds. A. Poole and F. Gill, No. 84. Philadelphia: Academy of Natural Sciences; Washington, D.C.: The American Ornithologists Union.

Hanisek, G. 1976. Summer field notes 1976 (Region 1). *Records of New Jersey Birds* 2, no. 11:5-6.

Hanisek, G. 1978. Summer field notes 1978 (Region 1). *Records of New Jersey Birds (New Jersey Audubon Supplement)* 4, no. 5:28-29.

Hanisek, G. 1979. Arctic Loon at Round Valley. *Records of New Jersey Birds (New Jersey Audubon Supplement)* 5, no. 1:4.

—. 1981a. Summer field notes 1980 (Region 1). *Records of New Jersey Birds* 6:66-67.

—. 1981b. First New Jersey Black Vulture nesting. *Records of New Jersey Birds* 7:34-35.

—. 1982. Summer field notes 1981 (Region 1). *Records of New Jersey Birds* 7:65-66.

—. 1986. Summer field notes 1985 (Region 1). *Records of New Jersey Birds* 11:68-69.

—. 1987. Spring field notes 1987 (Region 1). *Records of New Jersey Birds* 13:38-39.

—. 1991. Summer field notes 1990 (Region 1). *Records of New Jersey Birds* 16:62-64.

Harrison, D. 1994. Summer field notes 1993 (Region 1). *Records of New Jersey* Birds 19:80-82.

Harrison, P. 1983. *Seabirds: An identification guide.* Boston: Houghton Mifflin.

Hartman, F. E. 1992a. Blue-winged Teal (*Anas discors*). In *Atlas of breeding birds in Pennsylvania*, ed. D. W. Brauning, pp. 76-77. Pittsburgh: University of Pittsburgh Press.

—. 1992b. Green-winged Teal (*Anas crecca*). *In Atlas of breeding birds in Pennsylvania*, ed. D. W. Brauning, pp. 70-71. Pittsburgh: University of Pittsburgh Press.

Hatch, J. 1982. The cormorants of Boston Harbor and Massachusetts. *Bird Observer of Eastern Massachusetts* 10:65-73.

Hayes, J. 1984. American White Pelicans in New Jersey. *Records of New Jersey Birds* 10:46.

Hepp, G. R., and F. C. Bellrose. 1995. Wood Duck (*Aix sponsa*). In *The birds of North America*, eds. A. Poole and F. Gill, No. 169. Philadelphia: Academy of Natural Sciences; Washington, D.C.: The American Ornithologists Union.

Hill, G. E. 1993. House Finch (*Carpodacus mexicanus*). In *The birds of North America*, eds. A. Poole and F. Gill, No. 46. Philadelphia: Academy of Natural Sciences; Washington, D.C.: The American Ornithologists Union.

Hitchner, B. H. 1996. Brown Thrasher (*Toxostoma rufum*). In *Atlas of the breeding birds of Maryland and the District of Columbia*, ed. S. R. Robbins, pp. 298-99. Pittsburgh: University of Pittsburgh Press.

Ingold, J. L. 1993. Blue Grosbeak (*Guiraca caerulea*). In *The birds of North America*, eds. A. Poole and F. Gill, No. 79. Philadelphia: Academy of Natural Sciences; Washington, D.C.: The American Ornithologists Union.

Iversen, E., and R. Kane. 1975. Eskimo Curlew specimen for New Jersey. *Records of New Jersey Birds* 1, no. 7:7.

Jackson, G. L., and T. S. Baskett. 1964. Perch-cooing and other aspects of behavior of Mourning Doves. *Journal of Wildlife Management* 28:293-307.

Jehl, J. 1960. Bell's Vireo in New Jersey. *Wilson Bulletin* 72:404.

Johnson, K. 1995. Green-winged Teal (*Anas crecca*) . In *The birds of North America*, eds. A. Poole and F. Gill, No. 193. Philadelphia: Academy of Natural Sciences; Washington, D.C.: The American Ornithologists Union.

Jones, P. W., and T. M. Donovan. 1996. Hermit Thrush (*Catharus guttatus*). In *The birds of North America*, eds. A. Poole and F. Gill, No. 261. Philadelphia: Academy of Natural Sciences; Washington, D.C.: The American Ornithologists Union.

Kane, R. 1973. Nesting birds of the spruce plantings in the Pequannock Watershed. *New Jersey Nature News* 28:132-33.

—. 1974. Birds of the Hackensack Meadows, 1970-73. *New Jersey Nature News* 29:83-87.

—. 1975a. Comeback of the Dickcissel. *Records of New Jersey Birds* 1, no. 1:2-3.

—. 1975b. Notes from the field. *Urner Field Observer* 5:29-31.

—. 1976. The 1975 fall shorebird migration in the Hackensack Meadowlands. *Records of New Jersey Birds* 2, no. 2:7-14.

—. 1977a. Golden-crowned Sparrow returns. *Records of New Jersey Birds* 3:92.

—. 1977b. Bohemian Waxwing at Skylands Manor. *Records of New Jersey Birds* 3:94.

—. 1978. Birds of the Kearny Marsh. *Records of New Jersey Birds (New Jersey Audubon Supplement)* 4, no. 5:22-27.

—. 1982a. White-winged Crossbill invasion in New Jersey. *Records of New Jersey Birds* 8:22-23.

—. 1982b. Natural Bluebird nest sites in New Jersey. *Records of New Jersey* Birds 8:38-39.

—. 1983. Fall shorebird migration in the Hackensack Meadowlands, 1971-1980 . *Records of New Jersey Birds* 9:24-32.

—. 1985. Breeding birds of Troy Meadows. *Records of New Jersey Birds* 10:77-80.

—. 1996. Northern Shrike invasion, 1995. *Records of New Jersey Birds* 22:30-31.

Kane. R., and D. Githens. 1997. *Hackensack River migratory bird report*. Bernardsville, N. J.: New Jersey Audubon Society.

Kane, R., and D. Roche. 1975. New Jersey's first Franklin's Gull. *Records of New Jersey Birds* 1, no. 4:2.

Kane, R., P. A. Buckley, and J. Golub. 1989. Large-billed Tern in New Jersey: North America's first confirmed occurrence. *American Birds* 43:1275.

Kane. R., and P. Kerlinger. 1994. *Raritan Bay wildlife habitat report*. Bernardsville, N. J.: New Jersey Audubon Society.

Kane. R., P. Kerlinger, and R. Radis. 1991. Birds of the Arthur Kill tributaries. *Records of New Jersey Birds* 17:22-23.

Kane, R., W. J. Boyle, and A. R. Keith. 1984. Breeding birds of Great Swamp. *Records of New Jersey Birds* 11:29-33.

Kane, R., and W. Marx. 1972. Northern New Jersey Highland breeding bird survey 1971-72, Part I . *Urner Field Observer* 14:5-21.

Kaufman, K. 1994. Greenland White-fronted Geese: over-reported? *Birding* 26:380-82.

—. 1996. *Lives of North American birds.* Boston: Houghton Mifflin Co.

Kerlinger, P., and C. Sutton. 1989. Black Rail in New Jersey. *Records of New Jersey Birds* 15:22-26.

Kerlinger, P., and D. S. Wiedner. 1991. Vocal behavior and habitat use of Black Rails in south Jersey. *Records of New Jersey Birds* 16:58-62.

Knapton, R. W. 1994. Clay-colored Sparrow (*Spizella pallida*). In *The birds of North America*, eds. A. Poole and F. Gill, No. 120. Philadelphia: Academy of Natural Sciences; Washington, D.C.: The American Ornithologists Union.

Koellhoffer, T., and J. D. Dowdell. 1978. Hoary Redpoll in Plainfield? *Records of New Jersey Birds (New Jersey Audubon Supplement)* 4, no. 2:41.

Kokorsky, E., and G. Schultze. 1978. Say's Phoebe in New Jersey. *Records of New Jersey Birds (New Jersey Audubon Supplement)* 4, no. 1:37.

Komorowski, G. 1962. Field notes (Region 2). *New Jersey Nature News* 17:105-7.

Kricher, J. C. 1995. Black-and-white Warbler (*Mniotilta varia*). In *The birds of North America*, eds. A. Poole and F. Gill, No. 158. Philadelphia: Academy of Natural Sciences; Washington, D.C.: The American Ornithologists Union.

Kunkle, D. 1975. Second Summer Tanager nests in New Jersey. *Records of New Jersey Birds* 1, no. 7:2-3.

Kunkle, D. (Chairman), and The State List Committee (Urner Ornithological Club). 1959. *First supplement to the annotated list of New Jersey birds.*

Lanyon, W. E. 1995. Eastern Meadowlark (*Sturnella magna*). In *The birds of North America*, eds. A. Poole and F. Gill, No. 160. Philadelphia: Academy of Natural Sciences; Washington, D.C.: The American Ornithologists Union.

Larson, L. 1991. Summer field notes 1990 (Region 3). *Records of New Jersey Birds* 16:65-68.

—. 1997. New Jersey Records Committee official list of New Jersey birds. *Records of New Jersey Birds* 22:88-91.

Laughlin, S., and D. Kibbe. 1985. *The atlas of breeding birds of Vermont.* Hanover, N.H.: University Press of New England.

Leberman, R. C. 1992a. Common Moorhen (*Gallinula chloropus*). In *Atlas of breeding birds in Pennsylvania*, ed. D. W. Brauning, pp. 128-29. Pittsburgh: University of Pittsburgh Press.

—. 1992b. Wood Thrush (*Hylocichla mustelina*). In *Atlas of breeding birds in Pennsylvania*, ed. D. W. Brauning, pp. 272-73. Pittsburgh: University of Pittsburgh Press.

Leck, C. 1982. Declines in some forest birds over twenty years. *Records of New Jersey Birds* 14:7.

Leck, C. F. 1984. *The status and distribution of New Jersey's birds.* New Jersey: Rutgers University Press.

Lehman, P. 1997. First record of Calliope Hummingbird in New Jersey. *Records of New Jersey Birds* 23:54-57.

—. 1998a. A Eurasian Collared-Dove at Cape May: First sighting in New Jersey. *Records of New Jersey Birds* 24:5-6.

—. 1998b. Skuas off New Jersey. *Records of New Jersey Birds* 23:78-80.

Levine, E. 1988. Black-crowned Night-Heron (*Nycticorax nycticorax*). In *The atlas of breeding birds in New York State*, eds. R. F. Andrle and J. R. Carroll, pp. 50-51. Ithaca: Cornell University Press.

Lowther, P. E. 1993. Brown-headed Cowbird (*Molothrus ater*). In *The birds of North America*, eds. A. Poole and F. Gill, No. 47. Philadelphia: Academy of Natural Sciences; Washington, D.C.: The American Ornithologists Union.

Lowther, P. E., and C. L. Cink. 1992. House Sparrow (*Passer domesticus*). In *The birds of North America*, eds. A. Poole, Stettenheim P., and F. Gill, No. 12. Philadelphia: Academy of Natural Sciences; Washington, D.C.: The American Ornithologists Union.

MacWhirter, R. B., and K. L. Bildstein. 1996. Northern Harrier (*Circus cyaneus*). In *The birds of North America*, eds. A. Poole and F. Gill, No. 210. Philadelphia: Academy of Natural Sciences; Washington, D.C.: The American Ornithologists Union.

Marti, C. D. 1992. Barn Owl (*Tyto alba*). In *The birds of North America*, eds. A. Poole, P. Stettenheim, and F. Gill, No. 1. Philadelphia: Academy of Natural Sciences; Washington, D.C.: The American Ornithologists Union.

Martin, S. G., and T. A. Gavin. 1995. Bobolink (*Dolichonyx oryzivorus*). In *The birds of North America*, eds. A. Poole and F. Gill, No. 176. Philadelphia: Academy of Natural Sciences; Washington, D.C.: The American Ornithologists Union.

Master, T. L. 1992. Kentucky Warbler (*Oporornis formosus*) . In *Atlas of breeding birds in Pennsylvania*, ed. D. W. Brauning, pp. 346-47. Pittsburgh: University of Pittsburgh Press.

McCarty, J. P. 1996. Eastern Wood-Pewee (*Contopus virens*). In *The birds of North America*, eds. A. Poole and F. Gill, No. 245. Philadelphia: Academy of Natural Sciences; Washington, D.C.: The American Ornithologists Union.

McCaskie, G., and M. A. Patten. 1994. Status of the Fork-tailed Flycatcher (*Tyrannus savana*) in the United States and Canada. Western Birds 25:113-27.

Meanley, B. 1957. Notes on the courtship behavior of the King Rail. *Auk* 74:433-40.

Meanley, B., and D. K. Weatherbee. 1962. Ecological notes on mixed populations of King Rails and Clapper Rails in Delaware Bay marshes. *Auk* 79:453-57.

Meritt, J. K. 1974. Field notes (Region 4). *New Jersey Nature News* 24:186-87

Meritt, J. K. 1978. Townsend's Warbler in Burlington County. *Records of New Jersey Birds (New Jersey Audubon Supplement)* 4, no. 2:48.

—. 1987. Spring field notes 1987 (Region 4). *Records of New Jersey Birds* 13:44-47.

Miller, R. F. 1942. The Pied-billed Grebe: A breeding bird of the Philadelphia region. *Cassinia* 32:22-34.

Moldenhauer, R. R., and D. J. Regelski. 1996. Northern Parula (*Parula americana*). In *The birds of North America*, eds. A. Poole and F. Gill, No. 215. Philadelphia: Academy of Natural Sciences; Washington, D.C.: The American Ornithologists Union.

Moore, W. S. 1995. Northern Flicker (*Colaptes auratus*). In *The birds of North America*, eds. A. Poole and F. Gill, No. 166. Philadelphia: Academy of Natural Sciences; Washington, D.C.: The American Ornithologists Union.

Morse, D. H. 1994. Blackburnian Warbler (*Dendroica fusca*). In *The birds of North America*, eds. A. Poole and F. Gill, No. 102. Philadelphia: Academy of Natural Sciences; Washington, D.C.: The American Ornithologists Union.

Moskoff, W. 1995. Veery (*Catharus fuscescens*). In *The birds of North America*, eds. A. Poole and F. Gill, No. 142. Philadelphia: Academy of Natural Sciences; Washington, D.C.: The American Ornithologists Union.

Mulvihill, R. S. 1992a. Alder Flycatcher (*Empidonax alnorum*). In *Atlas of breeding birds in Pennsylvania*, ed. D. W. Brauning, pp. 202-3. Pittsburgh: University of Pittsburgh Press.

—. 1992b. Least Flycatcher (*Empidonax minimus*). In *Atlas of breeding birds in Pennsylvania*, ed. D. W. Brauning, pp. 206-7. Pittsburgh: University of Pittsburgh Press.

—. 1992c. Red-eyed Vireo (*Vireo olivaceus*). In *Atlas of breeding birds in Pennsylvania*, ed. D. W. Brauning, pp. 296-97. Pittsburgh: University of Pittsburgh Press.

—. 1992d. Common Raven (*Corvus corax*). In *Atlas of breeding birds in Pennsylvania*, ed. D. W. Brauning, pp. 236-37. Pittsburgh: University of Pittsburgh Press.

—. 1992e. Common Yellowthroat (*Geothlypis trichas*). In *Atlas of breeding birds in Pennsylvania*, ed. D. W. Brauning, pp. 350-51. Pittsburgh: University of Pittsburgh Press.

Murphy, M. T. 1996. Eastern Kingbird (*Tyrannus tyrannus*). In *The birds of North America*, eds. A. Poole and F. Gill, No. 253. Philadelphia: Academy of Natural Sciences; Washington, D.C.: The American Ornithologists Union.

Murray, B. G. 1972. Some rare specimens of New Jersey Birds. *Cassinia* 53:27-28.

Nisbet, I. 1970. Autumn migration of the Blackpoll Warbler: Evidence for long flight provided by regional survey. *Bird Banding* 41:207-40.

Nol, E., and R. C. Humphrey. 1994. American Oystercatcher (*Haematopus palliatus*). In *The birds of North America*, eds. A. Poole and F. Gill, No. 82. Philadelphia: Academy of Natural Sciences; Washington, D.C.: The American Ornithologists Union.

Parsons, K. C., A. D. Maccarone, and J. Brzorad. 1991. First breeding record of Double-crested Cormorant (Phalacrocorax auritus) in New Jersey. *Records of New Jersey Birds* 17:51-52.

Paxton, R. O. 1983. Hudson-Delaware region, Autumn 1982. *American Birds* 37:164.

Payne, R. B. 1992. Indigo Bunting (*Passerina cyanea*). In *The birds of North America*, eds. A. Poole, P. Stettenheim, and F. Gill, No. 4. Philadelphia: Academy of Natural Sciences; Washington, D.C.: The American Ornithologists Union.

Peer, B. D., and E. K. Bollinger. 1997. Common Grackle (*Quiscalus quiscula*). In *The birds of North America*, eds. A. Poole and F. Gill, No. 271. Philadelphia: Academy of Natural Sciences; Washington, D.C.: The American Ornithologists Union.

Peterjohn, B. G. 1989. *The birds of Ohio*. Bloomington, IN: Indiana University Press.

Peterson, J. M. C. 1988a. Common Raven (*Corvus corax*). In *The atlas of breeding birds in New York State*, eds. R. F. Andrle, and J. R. Carroll, pp. 286-87. Ithaca: Cornell University Press.

—. 1988b. Red-breasted Nuthatch (*Sitta canadensis*). In *The atlas of breeding birds in New York State*, eds. R. F. Andrle, and J. R. Carroll, pp. 294-95. Ithaca: Cornell University Press.

Phillips, J. C. 1926. *A natural history of the ducks*, Vols. III-IV. New York: Dover Publications.

Pierotti, R. J., and T. P. Good. 1994. Herring Gull (*Larus argentatus*). In *The birds of North America*, eds. A. Poole and F. Gill, No. 124. Philadelphia: Academy of Natural Sciences; Washington, D.C.: The American Ornithologists Union.

Post, P. W. 1979. An eruption of Tufted Titmice in the Northeast. *American Birds* 33:249-50.

Post, W., J. P. Poston, and G. T. Bancroft. 1996. Boat-tailed Grackle (*Quiscalus major*). In *The birds of North America*, eds. A. Poole and F. Gill, No. 207. Philadelphia: Academy of Natural Sciences; Washington, D.C.: The American Ornithologists Union.

Potter, J. K. 1923. Gray Kingbird (*Tyrannus dominicensis*) at Cape May, New Jersey. *Records of New Jersey Birds* 40:36.

Poulin, R. G., S. D. Grindal, and R. M. Brigham. 1996. Common Nighthawk (*Chordeiles minor*). In *The birds of North America*, eds. A. Poole and F. Gill, No. 213. Philadelphia: Academy of Natural Sciences; Washington, D.C.: The American Ornithologists Union.

Pravosudov, V. V., and T. C. Grubb. 1993. White-breasted Nuthatch (*Sitta carolinensis*). In *The birds of North America*, eds. A. Poole and F. Gill, No. 54. Philadelphia: Academy of Natural Sciences; Washington, D.C.: The American Ornithologists Union.

Preston, C. R., and R. D. Beane. 1993. Red-tailed Hawk (*Buteo jamaicensis*). In *The birds of North America*, eds. A. Poole and F. Gill, No. 52. Philadelphia: Academy of Natural Sciences; Washington, D.C.: The American Ornithologists Union.

Price, J., S. Droege, and A. Price. 1995. *The summer atlas of North American birds*. San Diego, CA: Academic Press, Harcourt Brace & Company.

Radis, R. 1990. Common Snipe nesting. *Records of New Jersey Birds* 16:3.

Reeves, C. 1978. The Reeves feeder in Boonton Township. *Records of New Jersey Birds (New Jersey Audubon Supplement)* 4, no. 2:42.

Reeves, C., and R. Reeves. 1976. Golden-crowned Sparrow in Boonton. *Records of New Jersey Birds* 2, no. 5:5-6.

Reid, W. 1992a. Common Merganser (*Mergus merganser*). In *Atlas of breeding birds in Pennsylvania*, ed. D. W. Brauning, pp. 84-85. Pittsburgh: University of Pittsburgh Press.

—. 1992b. Sora (*Porzana carolina*). In *Atlas of breeding birds in Pennsylvania*, ed. D. W. Brauning, pp. 126-27. Pittsburgh: University of Pittsburgh Press.

—. 1992c. Horned Lark (*Eremophila alpestris*). In *Atlas of breeding birds in Pennsylvania*, ed. D. W. Brauning, pp. 214-15. Pittsburgh: University of Pittsburgh Press.

—. 1992d. Henlow's Sparrow (*Ammodramus henslowii*). In *Atlas of breeding birds in Pennsylvania*, ed. D. W. Brauning, pp. 386-87. Pittsburgh: University of Pittsburgh Press.

Ricciardi, S. A. 1996. Ruby-throated Hummingbird (*Archilocus colubris*). In *Atlas of the breeding birds of Maryland and the District of Columbia*, ed. S. R. Robbins, pp. 198-99. Pittsburgh: University of Pittsburgh Press.

Richardson, M., and D. W. Brauning. 1995. Chestnut-sided Warbler (*Dendroica pensylvanica*). In *The birds of North America*, eds. A. Poole and F. Gill, No. 190. Philadelphia: Academy of Natural Sciences; Washington, D.C.: The American Ornithologists Union.

Robbins, C. S. 1996. Black-throated Green Warbler (*Dendroica virens*). In *Atlas of the breeding birds of Maryland and the District of Columbia*, ed. S. R. Robbins, pp. 334-35. Pittsburgh: University of Pittsburgh Press.

Robertson, R. J., B. J. Stutchbury, and R. R. Cohen. 1992. Tree Swallow (*Tachycineta bicolor*). In *The birds of North America*, eds. A. Poole, P. Stettenheim, and F. Gill, No. 11. Philadelphia: Academy of Natural Sciences; Washington, D.C.: The American Ornithologists Union.

Robinson, T. R., R. R. Sargent, and M. B. Sargent. 1996. Ruby-throated Hummingbird (*Archilochus colubris*). In *The birds of North America*, eds. A. Poole and F. Gill, No. 204. Philadelphia: Academy of Natural Sciences; Washington, D.C.: The American Ornithologists Union.

Rodewald, P. G., and R. D. James. 1996. Yellow-throated Vireo (*Vireo flavifrons*). In *The birds of North America*, eds. A. Poole and F. Gill, No. 247. Philadelphia: Academy of Natural Sciences; Washington, D.C.: The American Ornithologists Union.

Rosenfield, R. N., and J. Bielefeldt. 1993. Cooper's Hawk (*Accipiter cooperii*). In *The birds of North America*, eds. A. Poole and F. Gill, No. 75. Philadelphia: Academy of Natural Sciences; Washington, D.C.: The American Ornithologists Union.

Roth, R. R., M. S. Johnson, and T. J. Underwood. 1996. Wood Thrush (*Hylocichla mustelina*). In *The birds of North America*, eds. A. Poole and F. Gill, No. 246. Philadelphia: Academy of Natural Sciences; Washington, D.C.: The American Ornithologists Union.

Rowlett, R. A. 1980. Observations of marine birds and mammals in the northern Chesapeake bight. *USFWS Biological Services Program* FWS-OBS-80/04.

Santner, S. 1992a. Long-eared Owl (*Asio otus*). In *Atlas of breeding birds in Pennsylvania*, ed. D. W. Brauning, pp. 162-63. Pittsburgh: University of Pittsburgh Press.

—. 1992b. Red-breasted Nutcatch (*Sitta canadensis*). In *Atlas of breeding birds in Pennsylvania*, ed. D. W. Brauning, pp. 244-45. Pittsburgh: University of Pittsburgh Press.

Scharf, W. C., and J. Kren. 1996. Orchard Oriole (*Icterus spurius*). In *The birds of North America*, eds. A. Poole and F. Gill, No. 255. Philadelphia: Academy of Natural Sciences; Washington, D.C.: The American Ornithologists Union.

Schutsky, R. M. 1992a. Cattle Egret (*Bubulcus ibis*). In *Atlas of breeding birds in Pennsylvania*, ed. D. W. Brauning, pp. 56-57. Pittsburgh: University of Pittsburgh Press.

—. 1992b. Black-crowned Night-Heron (*Nycticorax nycticorax*). In *Atlas of breeding birds in Pennsylvania*, ed. D. W. Brauning, pp. 60-61. Pittsburgh: University of Pittsburgh Press.

—. 1992c. House Wren (*Troglodytes aedon*). In *Atlas of breeding birds in Pennsylvania*, ed. D. W. Brauning, pp. 252-53. Pittsburgh: University of Pittsburgh Press.

Scott, W. E. D. 1879. Notes on birds observed at Long Beach, New Jersey. *Bulletin of the Nuttall Ornithological Club* : pp. 222-28.

Serrao, J. 1985. Decline of forest songbirds. *Records of New Jersey Birds* 5:9.

Sharrock, J. T. R. 1976. *The atlas of breeding birds in Britain and Ireland.* Berkamstead: Poyser Publishing.

Sherry, T. W., and R. T. Holmes. 1997. American Redstart (*Setophaga ruticilla*). In *The birds of North America*, eds. A. Poole and F. Gill, No. 277. Philadelphia: Academy of Natural Sciences; Washington, D.C.: The American Ornithologists Union.

Shriner, C. A. 1896. *The birds of New Jersey.* New Jersey: Fish and Game Commission.

Shuford, W. D. 1993. *The Marin County breeding bird atlas.* Bolinas, CA: Bushtit Books.

Sibley, D. 1994. Identification of chickadees in New Jersey: A tool for the Breeding Bird Atlas. *Records of New Jersey Birds* 20:13-15.

—. 1997. *The birds of Cape May.* Cape May Point: New Jersey Audubon Society's Cape May Bird Observatory.

Sibley, S. C. 1988a. Common Moorhen (*Gallinula chloropus*). In *The atlas of breeding birds in New York State*, eds. R. F. Andrle and J. R. Carroll, pp. 144-45. Ithaca: Cornell University Press.

—. 1988b. Kentucky Warbler (*Oporornis formosus*). In *The atlas of breeding birds in New York State*, eds. R. F. Andrle and J. R. Carroll, pp. 412-13. Ithaca: Cornell University Press.

Smith, S. M. 1993. Black-capped Chickadee (*Poecile atricapillus*). In *The birds of North America*, eds. A. Poole, P. Stettenheim, and F. Gill, No. 39. Philadelphia: Academy of Natural Sciences; Washington, D.C.: The American Ornithologists Union.

Solem, J. K. 1996. Wood Thrush (*Hylocichla mustelina*). In *Atlas of the breeding birds of Maryland and the District of Columbia*, ed. S. R. Robbins, pp. 290-91. Pittsburgh: University of Pittsburgh Press.

Speiser, R., and T. Bosakowski. 1984. Status and future management of Goshawk nesting in New Jersey. *Records of New Jersey Birds* 10:29-33.

Stone, W. 1908. *The birds of New Jersey their nests and eggs. Report of the New Jersey State Museum.* Trenton: The John L. Murphy Publishing.

Stone, W. T. 1937. *Bird studies at Old Cape May*, Vol. I & II. Philadelphia: The Delaware Valley Ornithological Club at The Academy of Natural Sciences of Philadelphia.

Sutton, C., and P. Sutton. 1986. Breeding birds of Bear Swamp, Cumberland County, 1981-85 . *Records of New Jersey Birds* 12:21-24.

Sutton, P. 1996. Road mortality of Northern Saw-whet Owls in southern New Jersey, winter 1995-96. *Records of New Jersey Birds* 22:31-32.

Telfair, R. C. II. 1994. Cattle Egret (*Bubulcus ibis*). In *The birds of North America*, eds. A. Poole and F. Gill, No. 113. Philadelphia: Academy of Natural Sciences; Washington, D.C.: The American Ornithologists Union.

Terborgh, J. 1989. *Where have all the birds gone?* Princeton, N.J.: Princeton University Press.

The Committee on Classification and Nomenclature of the American Ornithologists Union. 1998. *Check-list of North American birds.* Lawrence, KS: Allen Press, Inc.

Todd, F. S. 1994. *10,001 titilating tidbits of avian trivia.* California: Ibis Publishing.

Turnbull, W. P. 1869. *The birds of East Pennsylvania and New Jersey.* Philadelphia: Henry Grambo and Co.

Twedt, D. J. 1995. Clay-colored Sparrow (*Spizella pallida*). In *The birds of North America*, eds. A. Poole and F. Gill, No. 192. Philadelphia: Academy of Natural Sciences; Washington, D.C.: The American Ornithologists Union.

Van Horn, M. A., and T. Donovan. 1994. Ovenbird (*Seiurus aurocapillus*) . In *The birds of North America*, eds. A. Poole and F. Gill, No. 88. Philadelphia: Academy of Natural Sciences; Washington, D.C.: The American Ornithologists Union.

Veit, R. R., and W. R. Petersen. 1993. *Birds of Massachusetts.* Lincoln, MA: Massachusetts Audubon Society.

Vickery, P. D. 1996. Grasshopper Sparrow (*Ammodramus savannarum*). In *The birds of North America*, eds. A. Poole and F. Gill, No. 239. Philadelphia: Academy of Natural Sciences; Washington, D.C.: The American Ornithologists Union.

Wander, W. 1979. Brewer's Blackbird: New Jersey's first confirmed record. *Records of New Jersey Birds (New Jersey Audubon Supplement)* 5, no. 1:5.

—. 1981. Breeding birds of southern New Jersey cedar swamps. *Records of New Jersey Birds* 6:51-65.

—. 1982. Breeding status of grassland birds in New Jersey. *Records of New Jersey Birds* 8:2-4.

—. 1986. *New Jersey Turnpike 1985-1990 widening technical study*, Volume II: Biological Resources, p. 91.

Wander, W., and S. A. Brady. 1977. First inland Great Cormorant for New Jersey. *Records of New Jersey Birds* 3: 74, 91.

—. 1980. Summer Tanager and Red-headed Woodpecker in the pinelands. *Records of New Jersey Birds* 6:34-37.

Warburton, M. 1968. Lark Bunting in New Jersey. *Wilson Bulletin* 80:495.

Watts, B. D. 1995. Yellow-crowned Night-Heron (*Nyctanassa violacea*). In *The birds of North America*, eds. A. Poole and F. Gill, No. 161. Philadelphia: Academy of Natural Sciences; Washington, D.C.: The American Ornithologists Union.

Welton, M. 1983. Status of Cliff Swallows in New Jersey. *Records of New Jersey Birds* 9:4-5.

Wheelright, N. T., and J. D. Rising. 1993. Savannah Sparrow (*Passerculus sandwichensis*). In *The birds of North America*, eds. A. Poole and F. Gill, No. 45. Philadelphia: Academy of Natural Sciences; Washington, D.C.: The American Ornithologists Union.

Wilson, A. 1808-1814. *American Ornithology*, Vols. I-IX. Philadelphia: Bradford and Inskeep.

Wolfarth, F. P. 1969. Field notes (Region 1). New Jersey Nature News *24: 123-25.*

Wolfarth, F. P. 1973. Field notes (Region 1). New Jersey Nature News *28: 156-59.*

Wolfarth, F. P. 1975a. Spring season field notes 1975 (Region 1). *Records of New Jersey Birds* 1, no. 4:6-7.

—. 1975b. Summer season field notes 1975 (Region 1). *Records of New Jersey Birds* 1, no. 7:4.

Woolfenden, G. 1957. Specimens of three birds uncommon in New Jersey. *Wilson Bulletin* 69:181-82.

Wootton, J. T. 1996. Purple Finch (*Carpodacus purpureus*). In *The birds of North America*, eds. A. Poole and F. Gill, No. 208. Philadelphia: Academy of Natural Sciences; Washington, D.C.: The American Ornithologists Union.

Wunz, G. A., and D. W. Brauning. 1992. Wild Turkey (*Meleagris gallopavo*). In *Atlas of breeding birds in Pennsylvania*, ed. D. W. Brauning, pp. 116-17. Pittsburgh: University of Pittsburgh Press.

Yasukawa, K., and W. A. Searcy. 1995. Red-winged Blackbird (*Agelaius phoeniceus*). In *The birds of North America*, eds. A. Poole and F. Gill, No. 184. Philadelphia: Academy of Natural Sciences; Washington, D.C.: The American Ornithologists Union.

SPECIES INDEX

Common Name

Species Index

Latin Name